THE
REAL GUIDE
TO
GRAD SCHOOL

THE REAL GUIDE TO GRAD SCHOOL

WHAT YOU BETTER KNOW BEFORE YOU CHOOSE
HUMANITIES & SOCIAL SCIENCES

Robert E. Clark
John Palattella, *editors*

Linguafranca
BOOKS

an imprint of
Linguafranca
THE REVIEW OF ACADEMIC LIFE

Published by Lingua Franca Books
22 West 38th Street
New York, NY 10018

Library of Congress Catalog Card Number: 97-74388

ISBN: 0-9630238-0-2

Designed by Point Five Design
Printed in the United States of America

ACKNOWLEDGEMENTS

Hundreds of scholars and students have generously given us good advice and lent us their expertise. We are particularly grateful to the following:

Margaret Anderson
Stanley Aronowitz
Bradley Ault
Fran Bartowski
Ann Birmingham
Ward Briggs
Peter Brooks
Diane Carson
Julie Clarke
David Colander
Thomas Di Piero
Mona Domosh
Clare Eby
Herbert Gans
Roberto González-
  Echevarría
Mark Engelke
Shoshana Felman
Phyllis Franklin
David Givens

William S. Green
John Gunnell
Judith Hallett
Lee Hansen
Heather Hendershot
Michael Holquist
Robert Ibarra
Brian Joseph
Grant Kester
William Kornblum
Dale Kunkel
Brian Leiter
Timothy Leonard
Patricia McWade
Frederick Newmeyer
Molly Nolan
Eileen O'Neil
Steve Nichols
Lara Pellegrinelli

D.N. Rodowick
Mark Rose
Matthew Santirocco
Edward Sideman
Jack Shuster
Tobin Siebers
Mark Slobin
Eric Smoodin
Siobhan Somerville
Joseph Strauss
Thomas Streeter
Peter Syverson
Allen Swinkels
Mark Taylor
Leo Treitler
Jim Uleman
Immanuel Wallerstein
Patrick Williams
Dennis Wrong

CONTRIBUTORS

Esther Allen

John Armstrong

Edward Batchelder

Leslie Camhi

Marc Caplan

Leonard Cassuto

Barry Cohen

Jonathan Cohen

Drew Digby

Liza Featherstone

Paul Freedman

Frederick Frommer

Veronica Fuechtner

David Glenn

Judy Goldman

John Hamilton

Annie Levine

Terese Lyons

Gage McWeeney

Elizabeth Merman

Rachael Preisser

Sean Redmond

Tamar Rothenberg

Barbara Schulman

Denise Sutton

Gloria Sutton

Renée White

TABLE OF

CONTENTS

TABLE OF
CONTENTS

INTRODUCTION

Maybe it's a passion, an instinct, or a quirk of character. Maybe you like to wrestle with complex problems. Maybe you cannot rest until you track down the missing pieces of an intellectual puzzle. Maybe when you helped run a laboratory experiment, you felt you had found your calling. Perhaps specialized prose, or abstract theory, or multivariate analysis no longer intimidate you. Or maybe at this point you simply know that you are not interested in going to business, law, or medical school, and you like what you've seen of the life your professors lead. There are hundreds of good reasons to go to graduate school—but let's get real.

No matter what your motivations, to decide to get a Ph.D. in the humanities or social sciences in the late 1990s takes guts. Your favorite undergraduate professors may have already warned you about the relentless pace of the work, the often petty disputes between different factions within a discipline, and the capriciousness of the academic job market. But you've probably already made the decision to pursue your passion about a subject no matter what the challenges.

Having a passionate commitment is one thing, but knowing how to choose among hundreds of graduate departments is something else. Of course, you can ask your favorite professors about particular

1

departments in a field, but even the most helpful and well-connected professors often can't maintain a grasp on the whole of most disciplines: they often contain too many subfields. So how else can you learn about what's out there? Those guide books available are either "how to's" about a single facet of graduate school (admissions, financial aid, the dissertation, the job search), or compendia of departmental addresses, phone numbers, and degrees offered—valuable information, but useless when it comes to deciding which department is best-suited to your interests and goals. And most of these guides provide *no* analysis of a discipline and never stick their necks out by identifying particular departments and scholars.

Let's say you are an aspiring geographer who is interested in global politics, comfortable with digital technology, and interested in the spatial organization of large cities. Knowing what the usual guides tell you won't help determine how friendly a given department is to the latest theories of world political systems, nor will it help you grasp the issues raised by the popularity of computer mapping, and no guidebooks inform you of how scholars interested in the city are viewing urban geography today. *The Real Guide* will not only brief you on the debates between traditional geographers and Marxist theorists, but it will also tell you about the latest work by computer-mapping whizzes and feminist geographers, as well as the ways that theorists of geography are now making connections between local and global issues that affect city life. And we'll tell you how the job market in the field has shaken out in recent years.

Your first scholarly task as a prospective graduate student is to meld the advice you'll get elsewhere with the analysis and guidance that *The Real Guide* offers. Because there are so many ways of researching graduate school—reviewing scholarly journals, quizzing professors, or surfing the Internet—a word about our approach is in order.

We began by looking at departments that are standard-bearers. Such departments, often at older and richer institutions, are the ones that students and professors mention as past models of excellence. Yet today departments are much less likely to be patterned after a few elite models. While the professorial star-system and institutional name-brands are still important, their importance varies greatly from discipline to discipline. Accordingly, we discuss the workings of the prestige system on a discipline-by-discipline basis. And though a degree from an Ivy League institution or one of the great public universities is often, though not always, still valuable on the job market, to apply only to them is a grave mistake. We made a point of quizzing professors and graduate students about which lower-profile departments might be the best places to go to study particular topics or to employ particular research methods. So don't be surprised when this guide points to places you may never have heard of, and to areas of research new to you.

Of course, because departments and disciplines are not static, you'll have to confirm that some of the information we provide (like which professors are teaching where) is still current and complete. Nonetheless, if you read our overviews carefully, along with the introduction to them, "The Disciplines Now," you'll have a much better grasp of the big picture of the disciplines than all but a few students. You'll come away with a realistic—and often hard-nosed—assessment of how the field is changing, one you can weigh along with what you learn from professors and students.

DAY BY DAY

There are many incalculables in graduate school: how economic and social forces outside the academy are impinging upon a discipline; how disciplines jockey for funding within universities; and how the fickle nature of intellectual trends, only now taking shape, will affect your studies over the next few years. There is little advice that applies to every student in every discipline. To introduce you to the graduate student experience nonetheless, we gather here observations culled from interviews with hundreds of professors and students around the country about the special—and peculiar—qualities of graduate school.

NARROW BUT DEEP

Unlike your undergraduate years, it's the department, not the university, that will be your home ground in graduate school. Even if you had wanted to study only one subject as an undergraduate, most undergraduate programs have a distribution requirement that didn't let you do so. Graduate departments turn this requirement upside down. Many will discourage you from taking classes *outside* the department. Though a squad of registration police will not swoop down should you choose to take a few such courses, most programs will keep you so busy filling gaps in your knowledge within your home discipline that you will have little time to go a-roving.

The large claim that a program makes on your time contradicts the buzz that you've probably already heard about how all fields are growing more interdisciplinary. As you might expect, fields known for having interdisciplinary origins, like sociology, anthropology, comparative literature, and women's studies, have fairly open borders, but even students in those disciplines are often surprised by how restricted their studies will be and by how much there is to learn about even the smallest of subspecialties. Some professors regret this state of affairs, claiming it can stifle originality and curiosity. Yet they can do little about the situation since graduate school is in fact a training ground of intellectual specialization.

Particular graduate departments have more than a casual stake in cultivating their reputation in a subspecialty—new historicism in English, rational choice theory in economics and political science, or visual culture studies in art history, for instance. A department's visibility to the rest of the profession is often a result of having been the originator of a method or having on staff many of a field's major players. And though professors do not usually want their students to promote their views simply by parroting them, they nonetheless want to inculcate in that next generation of scholars the ideas about their specialties they developed or that they inherited from their teachers.

Because subspecialties are often so complex that they cannot be mastered in six or seven years, the most common scenario for graduate students is to test their wings in a well-established subspecialty before moving on to broader areas, often only after they are safely tenured six or seven years after finishing a Ph.D. Of course, this shouldn't deter you from checking with current graduate students to get as much information as you can about the possibilities for doing interdisciplinary projects. After all, no one can say when the crossing of disciplinary borders by a young scholar will shake up the discipline. The academy rewards these innovators mightily, but as the histories of the disciplines in this volume will show, academic fields are slow to accept more than one or two innovators at a time. For the openness of disciplines to specific new areas of research, see the disciplinary chapters themselves.

LITTLE FIEFDOMS

If departments tend to become fiefdoms known for a subspecialty, they'll also be the little realm in which you spend most of your time.

And you'll be spending it with a fairly small cohort of students and professors. Most of your classmates will come from your department, not from all over the university as they did in the undergraduate classroom. This may seem claustrophobic, especially if you are accustomed to a large and varied group in your classes, but the flip side of belonging to a small group is the collegiality and ongoing dialogue you'll establish with like-minded people. After all, departments assume that you are studying with those who will be your future peers in the profession.

Students rarely criticize programs for being too small. They point out instead that small programs usually fund students better, allow for closer working relations with faculty, and have a realistic sense of how many students they can place in jobs. There are, of course, excellent large departments at both state and private institutions, and in highly variegated fields, like English or American history, departments need to have a certain number of faculty simply to cover perennial favorites like the English Renaissance, or the period from the Civil War to the Progressive era. Each disciplinary chapter suggests the role that size tends to play in that particular discipline, but in nearly every discipline the size of programs affects everything from the required curriculum to the resources available to help you work on a research topic.

Regardless of a program's size, most students are surprised by the length of time for which they will be closely identified with it. You will encounter senior professors who will talk as if they just finished their stint in graduate school. And when you meet junior professors, or graduate students from another department, the first questions they will ask you will be: Where do you go to school, and whom are you working with? Of course, this kind of networking greases the wheels in any occupation, but in the academy it is a testament to how particular places and teachers leave a very deep mark. Deciding where to attend graduate school will be a step toward molding your professional identity.

STAKING YOUR CLAIM

From the moment they arrive at graduate school, many students are numbed by the pressure to walk, talk, and think like a professional specialist. Many students miss the intellectual freedom that they enjoyed in college to ponder and explore ideas in more freewheeling fashion. In graduate school, professors will just assume you are reading all the latest books and journals and are well versed in a field's

5

core works, regardless of your new standing. And outside the seminar room, there are other pressures to professionalize early. Graduate students, besides doing much of the introductory teaching at universities, now organize their own conferences, edit their own journals, and compete to publish—the same kind of work that professors do, if not on the same level of proficiency.

There is quite a bit of tension over the subject of professionalization. It is not uncommon now for graduate students in English, comparative literature, art history, and many other fields to have several articles and a book under contract with a publisher in order to compete for a tenure-track job. Graduate students feel the need to bolster their credentials and imitate successful professors in a market where full-time jobs are in very short supply. Senior professors, especially those who were first hired in the days when a nearly-completed dissertation was suitable evidence of scholarly promise, do not always like to dwell on the facts of today's tougher market. But tough markets have existed for more than a decade, and every entering class now has a few students who come to graduate school having already mapped out their careers, and who seem to have started preparing their scholarly resumes in prep school.

The pressure to professionalize can be intimidating to students less sure of themselves—or more open-minded. But remember two things: All graduate students actually have large gaps in their knowledge—some are just more practiced than others at using jargon and strategic name-dropping to paper them over. If you think you mastered the art of bluff and bull as an undergraduate, wait until you hit graduate school. Even so, in every graduate program you'll find students who are simply obsessed by their studies and not intrigued by the games of professional networking, status-seeking, or prestige. Although it may take some doing, you can find a congenial group of peers, and you can balance the time you spend on professional goals with labors of love.

In most programs, there are semiofficial ways to resist the pressure to act as though you were a professional expert too soon. Lecture series arranged by the department or university bring in scholars from outside who have fresh insights and approaches different from those you find around you. Money for students to run informal discussion or writing groups is often in the departmental budget. And even if you wanted to shut yourself away from the non-academic world, you can't, because graduate students often need to supplement their incomes with jobs outside the university.

Professors from very different disciplines agree that the university and the corporation of the future will want to hire flexible generalists who can teach a variety of subjects and skills. For the moment, however, departments have more than enough on their hands training students to become research specialists in a single discipline. If students can cultivate a second career or set of skills, they'll have to do so on their own, with the knowledge that some professors will think that having outside interests betrays a lack of do-or-die commitment to becoming a professor. The trick is to maintain concentrated attention to your academic work as well as the sanity-saving attitude that there is a world beyond the seminar room and the library stacks.

The most flexible and transferable academic skill is teaching, since public speaking, organizing complex information, and leading group discussions are useful in almost any realm, inside and outside the university. Many graduate students say that teaching is also the most satisfying part of graduate school.

Teaching your own classes will give you the chance to broaden your own knowledge, express your own point of view, and pass on your excitement about the same questions that brought you to graduate school in the first place. Apart from self-interested motivations, of course, teaching is also a hands-on service to your students. Learning how to get students from different backgrounds and majors involved in the classroom will force you to clarify your own ideas so that everyone can understand them. And to keep your students energized—or at least awake—you'll have to find a way to present material that will prompt good discussion. Teaching can thereby return you to the heart of a subject, which can put the more specialized research you are doing as a graduate student into perspective. At many schools you'll have the chance at some point to teach courses that touch on your own area of specialization, or at least your principle field. Usually this requires you to read books that you would not otherwise read and, as in introductory courses, to find a way to make your topic clear and attractive to a wide audience.

As we've noted, few students enter graduate school knowing enough about every aspect of their discipline to teach a class about it. At times you might be desperately reading about the subject you are preparing to teach up until the moment you walk into the classroom.

If nothing else, such cramming will help you develop your ability to think on your feet, and you'll have the chance to feel like a genuine professor. More often, though, you'll have the satisfaction of being an expert and authority about the topics that mean the most to you, but without sounding too lofty, since students have a blessed way of bringing discussion back to the nitty-gritty. Even so, who doesn't enjoy knowing the most about a subject of anyone in the room, and actually having others write down what one says?

Believe it or not, many students go into graduate school not knowing what kind of teaching they'll be doing. Ask faculty and students about the role that teaching plays in their program, since that varies widely from institution to institution. Although many departments tell prospective students that classroom teaching is important to them, investigate carefully how often faculty might visit your classroom to give you guidance, or whether the program offers, or even requires, courses in pedagogy.

STANDING YOUR GROUND

Even though as a teacher and colleague-in-training you'll find companionable peers in graduate school, it's likely that you will have a trickier relationship to your classmates than you had in your undergraduate days. Standing out is harder. Competition in graduate school is generally more fierce, partly because graduate school brings together the brightest students within a single academic discipline. But there is also a change in classroom dynamics. While undergraduate classes concentrate on conveying information, graduate school concentrates on conveying critical methodologies and techniques. When thrown this material, often without a context that illuminates its origins and purposes, graduate students are anxious to sound sophisticated and critical, not overawed. One common way to do so is for students to tear into shreds whatever is put before them, whether it be an article by a leading scholar of the discipline or the work of a fellow classmate. Finally, graduate students jockey much more than undergraduates to be the favorites of a particular professor—with good reason. Teaching and research assignments, fellowships, and job recommendations depend in part on such relationships. With such high stakes, and with the attention in many fields to self-scrutiny and identity politics, the gloves are off in many a graduate classroom.

Though the sparring can get rough, it does have its usefulness for professors-in-training. Every teacher has to learn how to deal with the occasional hostile student, and at conferences and in journals, the exchanges will not always be polite. For every professor or student who is an intellectual bully, you'll find many who go out of their way to make the classroom an open, fair, and judicious forum. If intense debates at the graduate level can be daunting and take some adjustment, at their best they ask of students and faculty a high level of preparation, argumentation, and evidence.

WORLD ENOUGH AND TIME

You'll be spending fewer hours in the classroom in any case. Graduate students only often take two or three courses a semester, each of which might meet only once or twice a week. And exams are infrequent, which means that you'll often have the freedom to read until four in the morning if you like. The trade-off for this greater freedom, however, is that you will have few built-in forces to keep you on schedule, and will have to rely on yourself to develop focus and discipline.

Although such autonomy might sound like heaven, graduate students quickly learn that it can turn into a time-consuming black hole. Because so much research has already been done on so many subjects, "background" reading can seem endless. And once you are teaching your own classes, you'll find that your own students can absorb virtually all of the time that you choose to give them. It will often be hard to know when you are "done" with work. Add to this dilemma the fact that many students are so obsessed with their subject that it seems like play to study it, and the reasons why graduate students often work every day and round the clock are clear.

There are many unsurprising tactics you can use to manage your work and keep it separate from play—breaking tasks into small pieces, scheduling your reading and writing as if they were just like any other type of job, and taking regular breaks, social and otherwise. But in the end it seems to go with the territory that graduate students are wholly wrapped up in their studies.

For many students, however, the biggest shock of graduate school is their adjustment to a strange status of privileged poverty. A lucky few land full fellowships that cover the rent, the cost of their books, and an occasional meal out. But many students in graduate school have their first experience of running out of grocery money and wearing their clothes until they disintegrate. And a confusing aspect of this status is that while money is very tight, students also enjoy some privileges of the rich—controlling their own time and pondering arcane if not eccentric questions. The expected payoff—the transition upon graduation to professional work and a living wage—is now chancy, making the economic status of graduate students even more troubling.

The association of the academy with low income may be as old as the middle ages, when professor-clerics, sworn to poverty, founded the first universities, or perhaps it is a legacy of the Puritan association of scholarship with asceticism and humility in the United States. But there is no doubt that the tradition of scholarly poverty runs deep, and so might the feelings you experience when some of your friends from college who went into law or business start to build their savings, prepare to buy houses, and start families while you are still writing your dissertation and preparing to move to anywhere that the job market takes you. Sustaining your intellectual drive while scraping to pay the rent will take heartiness. No one, of course, can predict how you'll do financially, but it is safe to say that the rewards for hard work and accomplishment are as precarious in the academy as in any other tight job market—with the added factors that training takes longer, and you might very well work harder for more uncertain rewards than less talented peers who went into business. And most professors admit that the job market has systemic, not just incidental, inequalities. You can count on your education taking longer and costing more than it appears at the outset. (See the Finances chapter for details.) Try to follow through on any chances you have in school to cultivate marketable nonacademic skills, though, as noted, to do so requires inventiveness and stealing time from your other work.

YEAR BY YEAR

The disciplines and particular departments within them have quite varied requirements for coursework, exams, and the dissertation, so see individual chapters for the most common patterns of organization within individual disciplines. Even so, the process of graduate school has a few predictable phases.

FIRST YEAR

Students settle into the department and begin to form working relationships with faculty and peers. Many institutions have courses designed to bring nonmajors up to speed about theoretical approaches in the discipline and to fill in the gaps in their knowledge about major figures or key texts in the discipline.

A graduate seminar, composed of ten or twelve students, is often run by letting one student per week, in round-robin fashion, present his or her own written work or a response to an assigned reading. Students also write a final paper for the course. When not taking seminars, graduate students in some institutions attend many of the same upper-level lecture classes as undergrads. Most programs cap the first year by requiring that you pass language-proficiency exams, some form of an M.A. exam or essay, or a required course in pedagogy. In some programs the first year is a weeding-out period. Many students are admitted but only a few can continue to the second year and receive ongoing funding for the rest of their graduate study.

SECOND YEAR

This year marks the transition from being a student of research to preparing to produce research. Coursework continues and, gaps or not, most students think about a subspecialty at this time—in the humanities, a focus on periods, genre, and theoretical approaches. In the social sciences students also focus their interests, but often do so by helping faculty design or conduct experimental research. Naturally enough, picking a subspecialty is inseparable from finding congenial professors and classmates. Common sense advice is to work with a mixture of junior and senior faculty. That way you'll be likely to stay abreast of the cutting-edge research of young scholars, but also have the perspective of senior scholars who have seen trends come and go. Senior faculty also tend to have more power over the distribution of funds in a department and might have extensive professional connections to colleagues around the United States. Often students begin to teach their own classes at this time; check with particular departments.

THIRD YEAR

Before this point you worked with one professor at a time on your courses. But now you have to put together the committees that will examine you for your oral comprehensive exams and direct your dissertation. Which five to seven professors comprise a group that will work well together? You'll want to avoid assembling merely a group of cronies, because the mix of ideas should be spicy, with surprises. But you'll also need to find professors who share a common language and interests. This can be a problem for students in all fields, especially for those in interdisciplinary fields like anthropology or sociology.

After much agonizing, orals are in the end brief. Some departments administer a written exam before oral exams, the latter sometimes lasting for two or three successive days, but at most places the actual oral exam will be over in a morning or afternoon, and you'll wonder why you worried about it for a year or more. Orals generate tremendous anxiety because no matter how well students prepare, every discipline is vast, and committee members with very different interests might not work well together. One way to cut the tension is to remember that orals were intended to be an official chance to let students perform a deep and intense review of their discipline, to read things they would not otherwise, and to focus their research. Despite the lore you'll hear about students fainting, having heart attacks, or falling into catatonic bouts during oral exams, at some institutions exams are pro forma, and nearly everyone passes them. At others they are used as an important assessment of your scholarly promise.

FOURTH YEAR AND BEYOND

Some schools trumpet the speed with which they take students through the program, but the average length of time to finish a Ph.D. in the humanities and social sciences, according to the National Research Council, is eight years, with ten years not uncommon. The dissertation, the task that preoccupies most students after their fourth year, takes up more time than any other part of graduate school. Students spend years trying to come up with the perfect project because the dissertation is a bizarre document: It is supposed to summarize existing research, is often the source of the writing samples you'll submit when on the job market, and some professors will tell you to make it serve as a practice-run for your first published book. The dissertation is traditionally expected to convey a distinctive personal voice, yet it is a single voice cobbled together from your own thoughts, the voices of past scholars, and the input of your committee. And book-length essays of all kinds simply take a long time to write.

You've probably noticed that *funding* tends to last five years at a maximum, but research and writing the dissertation commonly takes two or three years on its own. Another reason that finishing a dissertation takes so long is that students tend to support themselves during the end of their studies with teaching jobs. They need to feel connected to their profession, and also require a schedule flexible enough to allow long research and writing stints. But untenured teaching is very poorly paid, so simple survival takes much time and energy. That is one among the many reasons why it is crucial that you think long and hard about the funding offered by particular departments, and the likelihood of sharing expenses with a partner or getting financial help from your family.

Despite the complaints of the author of Ecclesiastes over two millennia ago about "the weariness of the making of many books," and despite the publication avalanche of the last forty years, if we take into account the number of living college graduates around the world, it is still an elite few who finish graduate school. (Roughly only one of six who begin Ph.D. programs in the humanities and social sciences finish them.) And it is an even a smaller number who produce a book-length work of scholarship, a dissertation, that other educated readers can understand and admire. In recent years there have been calls to eliminate the dissertation, to scale down the number of graduate departments, and to make graduate education a shorter and sweeter experience. But even if none of those changes materialize (and the reform manifestos are thin on the logistics of how they might), at the end of your studies you'll have worked with some of the smartest and best-informed authorities now alive, made some lifelong friends, mastered an immense amount of information, and enjoyed for years the chance to follow your thoughts wherever they lead.

PART ONE: THE BASICS

CHAPTER 1

THE RISE OF THE RESEARCH SCHOLAR

What is graduate school, exactly? You may have had a taste of graduate coursework in an advanced undergraduate course, and had a sprinkling of grad students as classmates. The truth is, though, that even when grad students and undergrads sometimes cross paths, their worlds are quite distinct.

Earning a bachelor's degree means mastering a body of general knowledge by taking courses in several disciplines—majoring in one but remaining a generalist. Graduate students have to develop specialized expertise within a discipline; they not only learn more about a subject, but about the methods and theories of doing research in a field. One studies not just archaeology, but the social significance of clay tobacco pipes in 1850s Manhattan and the dating techniques necessary for identifying them. Not just American literature, but attitudes toward history as they are reflected in the fiction of Willa Cather, and the historiography necessary for explaining them. One of the standard accolades for a graduate research project—a compliment with a trace of fatigue—is to proclaim it "exhaustive."

To acquire specialized training, graduate students, unlike undergrads, spend most of their time with peers and professors within their own department. The department is not just home base but a little universe unto itself. Most graduate students do two or three years of coursework within their departments before they even begin to start writing their dissertations. Depending on how long it takes them to clear that hurdle, the total time graduate students spend earning a Ph.D. will be from five to twelve years. And the relationship between students and their home department is not just long lasting; it tends to follow them far beyond the walls of their home institution. When graduate students go to academic conferences, submit articles to journals, and finally enter the job market, the rest of the profession tends to identify them not only as individual scholars but also as representatives of their graduate departments. Although it may seem a bit daunting, choosing a department is a serious and long-term decision.

None of this is to say that graduate students don't cultivate interests beyond their narrow grooves. Under the banner of interdisciplinarity or cultural studies, many graduate students are stepping outside the limits of their disciplines to make use of the latest research in others. But even as they venture far afield, graduate students are expected to eventually become experts about a carefully defined subject or question.

Developing that kind of authority is essential because graduate students are, by and large, professors-in-training. They learn not only how to teach undergraduates but also how to produce some of the knowledge that undergraduates will study. This aspect of the graduate school experience is often called apprenticeship—a reference to the medieval custom of having the master of a craft train and certify novices—because a graduate student often learns how the nuts and bolts of a discipline fit together, and how to handle the tools of the discipline, by working closely with a faculty mentor.

> Graduate students learn not only how to teach undergraduates but also how to produce some of what undergrads study.

Academic apprenticeship and specialization were formalized at the end of the nineteenth century, along with the peculiarly intimate and sometimes confusing connections between departments and disciplines. Understanding the changes that took place at that time will shed light on what professors will expect you to be doing, even if few of them will ever say so directly.

THE EMERGENCE OF GRADUATE EDUCATION

Graduate students sometimes perceive themselves as the newest initiates to the ancient tradition of their discipline. Don't be taken in; graduate school is actually rather new. Though the university has been around since the middle ages, graduate school didn't take its modern shape until the 1880s. At that time, research universities such as Johns Hopkins, Clark, and Chicago were founded, and old liberal arts colleges like Harvard and Yale transformed themselves into research institutions fitted with the modern essentials: departments, disciplines, "majors," junior and senior faculty, research libraries, laboratories, scholarly journals, university presses, disciplinary associations, and graduate students.

Prestigious schools of today that boast of their venerable reputations and tough admissions requirements forget their fairly recent past as sleepy, modest places. Strange to say, these new institutions are quite a contrast to the colleges from which they sprang. The typical antebellum college scorned vocational concerns, such as training future lawyers and doctors, as well as the newest research in the humanities. Most of these colleges prepared students for the ministry, or, if they were like Princeton and Yale, they groomed wealthy students for entry into polite society. The antebellum college was something like a club devoted to transmitting the values of a mercantile culture, a group that viewed national leadership as the birthright of the white gentlemanly class and had little or no interest in theoretical research undertaken for its own rewards. The rituals of social class—formal dances, elaborately planned pranks, and sporting events—took precedence over classroom instruction. Colleges did award postgraduate degrees in the form of the Master's, but they simply conferred the degree as a matter of course to students who remained in residence three years after completing their bachelor's degree and paid an extra fee. These graduate students did not have to follow a prescribed course of study in their three years. The only requirement was that they manage to stay out of jail.

The two most common features of a present-day research university—the tightly defined major within a discipline, and the research library—did not exist at most antebellum colleges. Students didn't "major" in a discipline because the modern disciplines did not yet act as the organizational units around which the curriculum was structured. Students didn't lug around day-packs bulging with books because textbooks were scarce; a single textbook often included the material for a student's entire course of study. And students rarely read books in libraries because the libraries that housed books were often quite small. The first president of the University of North Carolina kept the university library in a tiny upper bedroom of his house for twenty years.

The instruction that did take place in the old colleges stymied the imagination. The Yale Report of 1828 offers a fair sample of the coursework. Undertaken to quell the outcries of a handful of faculty for a practical curriculum that included modern languages, the report spelled out a mind-numbing regimen. Study of the Classics—rhetoric, math, logic, and snippets of Greek and Latin literature—was said to instill "the most effective discipline of the mental faculties. Every faculty of the mind is employed." Classroom instruction consisted largely of recitations—litanies of names, dates, and parts of speech— absorbed by rote memorization. Though it may seem dubious today, educators believed that this punishing routine, besides acting as a curb to headstrong students, transformed mushy young minds into supple intellects.

The first large-scale challenge to the educational philosophy of antebellum colleges was the 1862 Morrill Act, which mandated that the states use revenues from the sale of federal lands to endow colleges. The act enabled the establishment of public universities in states where previously there were none, in Illinois and Maryland for example, and it underwrote the diversification and specialization of undergraduate curricula at existing state colleges and universities. Morrill funds provided both upstart colleges and older institutions with the cash and clout to teach what the act's sponsor, Vermont Congressman Justin Morrill, described as "such branches of learning as are related to agriculture and the mechanic arts." Though it is no surprise that schools given their charter under Morrill were belittled as "cow colleges," from these schools developed the great research universities of the Midwest, which eventually were on a par with or superior to the old Eastern liberal-arts schools. What's more, the Morrill Act was the first important step in making U.S. universities attractive to students from around the world—and it proved that government largesse could spur intellectual progress.

When Johns Hopkins University opened its doors a decade and a half after the implementation of the Morrill Act, it ushered in changes that made the act seem like small potatoes. Named after the Baltimore grocer-king who bankrolled it, Johns Hopkins was founded in 1876, and its first president was Daniel Coit Gilman. The cornerstone of Gilman's design for Hopkins was the German academic ideal of *Lehrfreiheit*—the belief that professors should possess the freedom to teach and conduct research without outside interference. As Gilman explained to a Hopkins trustee in 1875, the university's educational agenda would be "the devotion of the candidate to some particular line of study and the certainty of his eminence in that specialty; the power to pursue independent and original investigation, and to inspire the young with enthusiasm for study and research." In fact, Gilman prized the research mission so highly that he wanted Hopkins to open its doors to graduate students only, but the Hopkins trustees disagreed, and convinced Gilman to incorporate an undergraduate college into the university.

> The cornerstone of Johns Hopkins was *Lehrfreiheit*— the belief that professors are free to conduct research without outside interference.

Gilman's secular ideas about the research mission and graduate education spread like gospel truths. Clark and Chicago, established in 1889 and 1892 respectively, modeled themselves on Hopkins. In 1891 Henry Wade Rogers, the president of Northwestern University, challenged his university with questions that referred explicitly to a Hopkins-like research mission. "Are we keeping in the foremost ranks of modern discovery? Are we taking up the new branches of knowledge as they come successively into existence? Are we continually harmonizing the knowledge which we have inherited from previous generations with the knowledge which this generation has acquired, or are we simply guarding ancient truths?"

And Charles Eliot, the president of Harvard, even admitted that progressive as he was, "the graduate school of Harvard University, started feebly in 1870 and 1871, did not thrive until the example of Johns Hopkins forced our faculty to put their strength into the development of our instruction for graduates." Indeed, when Harvard celebrated its 250th anniversary, in 1884, it redesigned the university shield by moving *Christo et Ecclesiae* ("for Christ and Church"), the center of the old shield, to a lesser place beneath *Veritas* ("truth"), the new principal motto. The new shield represented the impact of the reforms that Eliot had instituted at Harvard to raise it to the level of Hopkins. The quest for the pursuit of disinterested truth had bumped the goal of religious and moral instruction from the center to the periphery of the university.

There are different ways of explaining the changes that occurred at Harvard and elsewhere. Some historians trumpet a new Enlightenment in which reformers like Eliot toppled the mostly wealthy, mostly Protestant elite. Others tell a story of gradual accommodation in which a scientific research mission and informal social goals have struggled to coexist in the modern university ever since the founding of modern graduate schools at the end of the mid-nineteenth century, the balance tipping one way or the other at different times. Yet whoever tells the story, all tend to agree that higher education was changed utterly by the crystallization of the specialized research mission at Hopkins.

The Hopkins model still holds sway. University professors are more specialized today than at any time in the past, and graduate students are specialists in training. Understandably, some might object to putting too much stress on the idea of specialization in the humanities and social sciences. After all, specializing in them is not the same thing as specializing in engineering, medicine, or law, which all involve professional skills that depend on studying different objects—electrical as opposed to chemical engineering, the physiology of the skeleton as opposed to anesthesiology, the law applied to shipping as opposed to entertainment. Moreover, medical schools and law schools, unlike the humanities and social sciences, train people to practice their professions outside academia and have a licensing system. No license is required to create or forward a new interpretation of Shakespeare, as much as some professors might like one to be. And finally, though they do specialize, graduate students in the humanities and social sciences continue to broaden their knowledge of their own disciplines. You may do research on the rise of social movements in the United States in the 1960s, but you have to know enough about U.S. history to teach the Colonial period to undergraduates, both as a T.A. and, later, as an assistant professor.

> University professors are more specialized today than ever, and graduate students, as apprentices, are specialists in training.

The distinctive kind of specialization in the humanities nevertheless works something like specialization in the licensed professions. In *The Academic Revolution*, a landmark history of university expansion in the United States, Christopher Jenks and David Riesman identify two principles as definitive of academic specialization. Professors reserve the exclusive right, first, to evaluate the validity of each other's work, and second, to exert absolute control over the training of new practitioners.

In this sense, specialization in the humanities is perhaps more "pure" than it is in law. Practicing lawyers may ignore, or even feel contemptuous of, the articles published in academic law journals, but humanities academics have to keep up to date with the publications in their field. Today good advice is not just "publish or perish," but "do your best to publish in the right places." In fact, as far as professional evaluation goes, there is no better example than academic journal publication and the peer-review process that guides much of it. Writers who are published in academic journals are rarely paid more than a nominal fee for their labors and rarely expect to have a general readership. Instead, their reward lies in the prestige that comes from publishing an article that has survived the peer-review process, as well as in gaining the opportunity to share their research with their colleagues.

> In a sense, specialization in the humanities and social sciences is perhaps more pure than it is in law.

Here's how peer review works. An academic submits an essay, unsolicited, to a journal. An editor forwards the submission to several anonymous readers, the most expert professors the editors can find, who will read the essay often not knowing who wrote it. These readers are called "referees"—professors who judge whether or not the author is playing within the boundaries of a particular body of knowledge within a discipline. They then report back to the editor, suggesting the essay either be rejected, reconsidered after its author undertakes revisions, or published as is. At some journals, a board of editors also reviews a piece to see if they are willing to associate their journal and their reputations with its publication. After weighing these suggestions, the editor makes a choice.

Peer review is an example of specialization because it involves like-minded scholars judging their work according to accepted professional standards. Graduate students learn about these standards through the apprentice model mentioned earlier, the academy's version of on-the-job training. As an apprentice scholar today, a graduate student takes whatever she learns as a research or teaching assistant, and what she gleans from working with her favorite professors and dissertation advisor, and finds a way to to make that knowledge her own. The goal of apprenticeship is not replicating the work of one's mentors but learning the skills that will enable one to undertake research on one's own and to teach a specific body of knowledge.

When a graduate student in English specializes in Shakespeare, for instance, professors teach her the methods of analysis (theories of dramatic poetry and methods of literary criticism) and various fields of reference (Elizabethan society and texts) necessary for undertaking research that advances the state of knowledge in Shakespeare studies. When the aspiring Shakespeare scholar earns a Ph.D., the degree alerts other professors that she can transmit the specialized culture of the research university—from the essential bibliographic tools to the study of Tudor manuscripts—as well as conduct seminars on the various fields of Renaissance literature. And if our newly minted Ph.D. lands a tenure-track job at a research university and assiduously plies the trade—writing some influential articles, publishing well-received books, and gaining tenure—in ten years time she will be training the next generation of apprentice Shakespeareans.

APPRENTICESHIP UNDER FIRE

Over the last decade, and especially in the humanities, apprenticeship has come under fire. This is due less to flaws in the apprenticeship tradition than to the volatile economic conditions of higher education. The dismal academic job market especially threatens to make apprenticeship obsolete. Following the latest debates about apprenticeship might be the last thing you'll want to do while also trying to research graduate programs, file applications, write personal statements, take the GRE, investigate financial aid possibilities, and, if you are a senior in college, stay on top of coursework. Nonetheless, a few hard truths about the economic and intellectual conditions of graduate school are important to consider before you apply to departments. To make a smart choice about any school, you'll need to talk as much as possible to faculty, and especially students, about how its training really works.

According to Cary Nelson, a professor of English at the University of Illinois at Urbana, one of the abuses of apprenticeship that graduate students must endure is the possibility of a prospectless future. Says Nelson, "The problem with graduate study now—in a long-term environment where jobs for new Ph.D.'s are the exception rather than the rule—is that apprenticeship has turned into exploitation. Without a viable job market, Ph.D. programs have only one economic rationale—they are a source of cheap instructional labor for universities." Since 1989, full-time openings have dropped 50 percent in English and 37 percent in political science, yet the number of Ph.D.'s awarded in these fields keeps rising. Apprentices are being trained for full-time jobs that don't exist, Nelson reasons, so the paltry salaries they earn as teaching and research assistants are exploitative.

> Apprenticeship has come under fire because graduate students in many disciplines face a prospectless future.

Though Nelson thinks the situation is dire, he does not think it irreparable. For one, he thinks graduate programs should scale back admissions to make the supply of new Ph.D.'s more in line with demand. Nelson has also suggested that professional associations should discourage departments from creating new Ph.D. programs, lest the glut of new Ph.D.'s be exacerbated.

Some graduate students have taken the situation into their own hands by unionizing. Consider the bitter graduate student grade strike that occurred at Yale from December 1995 to January 1996. The strike was orchestrated by the Graduate Employees and Students Organization (GESO), which wanted to pressure the Yale administration into recognizing it as a union with the right to engage in collective bargaining. Graduate students working as teaching assistants refused to submit final grades, and though the strike wore on for six weeks, causing havoc for administrators and undergraduates, the Yale administration did not agree to GESO demands.

Invoking the apprentice model, Yale administrators insisted that graduate students cannot organize because they are students, not workers, who have been admitted, not hired, and who receive stipends, not wages. GESO, for its part, claimed that it wanted to unionize graduate students as a way of winning basic benefits like adequate health insurance and some measure of job security while they devote a decade or so to intellectual pursuits that might very well not pan out into academic careers. Graduate students may be apprentices, but apprenticeship no longer does them economic justice. As apprentices, graduate students carry out the basic functions of the university—at many schools doing the majority of teaching—and GESO wanted them to be compensated accordingly.

Graduate students at the University of Iowa advanced a similar set of concerns during their successful drive to unionize. (Iowa graduate students voted to unionize on April 16, 1996, certifying as their collective bargaining agent the United Electrical, Radio and Machine Workers of America.) The students began their efforts to unionize over three years ago because they were no longer willing to tolerate extremely low wages and substandard benefits. Graduate students at Iowa teach more than 40 percent of undergraduate classes, yet they pursue their degrees and carry out the basic work of the university with the understanding that, at best, only one in three will end up with a tenure-track job. The union, which has 1,250 members, has improved the lot of graduate students, successfully bargaining with the university administration to raise the base salary of graduate teaching and research assistants 19 percent.

Yale and Iowa are not isolated cases. There are recognized graduate student unions based on similar platforms at thirteen state universities: UC-Berkeley, Florida, South Florida, Kansas, Iowa, UMass-Amherst, UMass-Lowell, Michigan, Rutgers, SUNY, Oregon, Wisconsin-Milwaukee, and Wisconsin-Madison, home of the first graduate student union, founded in 1971. And there are recognition drives under way at Illinois-Urbana, UC-San Diego, and UCLA, among others.

What remains to be seen is whether the current strains in the apprenticeship system signal a sea-change in the whole process of training new research specialists, or simply a minor shift. For the next few years, while you are in graduate school, you can expect the emphasis on research, specialization, and close relationships with mentors to stay at a premium. But no one really knows whether scholarly training will remain a mostly autonomous enterprise, or if the current reorganization of the disciplines and the changes in the missions of scholarship that we describe in the rest of this book will alter the structure and mission of graduate school more fundamentally.

FURTHER READING

Julie A. Reuben,
The Making of the Modern University: Intellectual Transformation and the Marginalization of Morality
(Chicago)

Cary Nelson, ed.,
Will Teach for Food
(Minnesota)

Michael Tomasky,
"Waltzing with Sweeney:
Is the Academic Left Ready
to Join the AFL-CIO?,"
Lingua Franca, February 1997

Chris Lehmann,
"Popular Front Redux?,"
The Baffler no. 9

Emily Eakin,
"Walking the Line:
A Report from the
Yale Grade Strike,"
Lingua Franca,
January/February 1996

Christopher Jenks
and David Riesman,
The Academic Revolution
(Chicago)

CHAPTER 2

ADMISSIONS

Consultants are cashing in on the boom in the anxiety market. For a few bucks you can buy a reading from a crystal-ball reader, but small fortunes are made by the peddlers of guides to everything from tightening your abs to discovering your inner child, from piano tuning to sex. Always looking for new fields for worry, consultants have recently invaded college admissions. On the low end, a modest fee will pay for consultants to suggest courses and hobbies that supposedly give high school students an admissions edge. For teens with more anxious parents or more money to burn, there are consultants who'll run a college applicant's life and claim to know all the strings to pull—for upwards of $2,500. The problem is that no consultant can really tell a student what school is right for them. The interviewing, phone-calling, and the other investigation a student must do cannot be done by proxy; no second party can give students the gut feeling that a school is the right environment for them and that it suits their particular goals.

Educational consultants have not tackled the graduate school application process—yet. But if they do, their prognostications and plots would not be worth their fees. According to the college admissions officers and student counselors we interviewed, the views of a university that one can get from the outside are often mirages. And the professors who actually admit students into graduate programs are not likely to reveal their secrets to consultants; they tend to get prickly about outside interference in admissions deliberations.

All that said, there probably is a paying market for graduate school consultants—not because they would be helpful, but because the admissions process is capricious, arbitrary, and anxiety-producing. The graduate admissions process has an *Alice in Wonderland* logic, and because some departments are trimming enrollments in response to reduced funding and the downturn in the academic job market, admission is now much more competitive. Washington University in St. Louis, for instance, recently announced that it is cutting the number of graduate students admitted so that it can afford to guarantee funding for them all. Faculty think it's hard to justify large doctoral programs given the downturn in the academic job market. Explaining the decision to accept fewer students in his department, Richard J. Smith, chair of the anthropology department at Washington University in St. Louis, says, "Students used to graduate and then find tenure track-jobs in anthropology. Now, as in engineering and many other fields, it is more common that they go into postdoctoral jobs. The job market is unpredictable years down the line. Students who enter now cannot count on the same outcomes."

Without pretending to banish fear and uncertainty, or to take the place of legwork by an applicant—the only reasonable way to make such a personal choice—this chapter explains the nuts and bolts of the graduate admissions process and gives realistic advice about improving your chances of getting in.

THE APPLICATION PROCESS

First of all, graduate admissions is a different game from undergraduate admissions. Undergraduate applicants apply to an entire college or university, and their qualifications are evaluated by a cadre of admissions officers whom students will never see in the classroom. What's more, undergraduate applicants—judged as an amalgam of demographic characteristics, extracurricular activities, and geographical pockets—remain a faceless lot to all but a few admissions officers. And they are completely anonymous to college professors, who have little say in undergraduate admissions decisions.

But professors in graduate programs have everything to say about who sits in their seminar rooms because applicants are their potential colleagues. Though you mail your application to the university's graduate dean, when you apply to graduate school you are in fact applying to a single department, and your qualifications are evaluated by a departmental committee made up of the faculty who will educate you. Graduate faculty admit those candidates whom they are eager to work with in the classroom and on research projects. The graduate dean, largely on the recommendation of a department's faculty, gives the final OK to an applicant.

> Though you mail your application to the graduate dean, you are actually evaluated by a single department.

The importance of this arrangement should not be underestimated, for it affects everything from when graduate admissions committees meet to how they evaluate an applicant's credentials. While the admissions staff of an undergraduate college toils all year long, a department's graduate admissions committee executes its task in a short burst of energy. It meets for several weeks in late winter or early spring, just as semester workloads are starting to pile up, and often during or after faculty have worked on a grueling debate about hiring a new professor. In a given week, an assistant professor might find herself having to slog through a stack of essays about Toni Morrison's *Sula*, sip cocktails with a job candidate, and assess fifty graduate applications. Under such a workload, faculty often resort to old-boy and -gal networks or to the relative prestige of an applicant's undergraduate institution to quickly come to a decision and to keep proceedings as short and sweet as possible.

Many professors can tell a story about admissions committee meetings that began with friendly chat over coffee but quickly flared up into shouting matches. Faculty get heated up for a variety of reasons. One professor wants to accept those students who seem talented enough to complete their degrees. Another professor is on the lookout for recruits for her special interest or point of view. Yet another wants to keep the whole incoming class small enough to give some kind of financial support to as many of the students as possible.

At the same time, the committees at some universities don't even make much of a fuss over the initial application. They rely instead on some form of the Ph.D. qualifying exam given to students after they've been in graduate school for a year or two to weed some of them out. In this instance, many students are admitted through a wide gate into graduate school, often without financial support, and only a select few are given funding and allowed to write a dissertation after M.A. exams and essays. Talk to current students in a program about when the weeding out is done, and how; departments are not always forthcoming with that information.

THE GRE

When pared to essentials, a graduate school application consists of four testaments to an applicant's qualifications: an undergraduate transcript, GRE test scores, letters of recommendation, and the personal statement. In the humanities, an application often has a fifth component, a writing sample. Though no component in and of itself is a fail-safe measure of your qualifications, no measure has been singled out more often for criticism than the GRE. Universities do not uniformly require the GRE, and some programs waive the test for applicants who have been out of school for more than five years. Nonetheless, nearly 390,000 people had to take the GRE General Test in 1994-95, compared to 272,000 ten years earlier.

As with the SAT tests administered by the Educational Testing Service (ETS), the GRE is designed to measure aptitude, or an individual's capacity for learning. In conjunction with other criteria, the GRE is used to predict how well people, according to their levels of aptitude, will perform the tasks necessary for academic achievement. Like its forerunners, the Stanford-Binet IQ scale and the Army Alpha and Beta tests, the GRE facilitates the ranking and organization of diverse social groups according to the measurement of perceived aptitude as a single numerical quantity.

Henry Chauncey, founder of ETS, wanted tests to guide people to their place in society.

Henry Chauncey, founder of the ETS empire, wanted ETS to become for education what the standard gauge was for the railroad. Chauncey claimed that standardized intelligence tests could help guide people to their proper places in society. "To many the prospect of measuring in quantitative terms what have previously been considered intangible qualities is frightening, if not downright objectionable," admitted Chauncey in 1950 in the first ETS *Annual Report*. But he saw more gains than losses if the tests were used properly. "Life may have less mystery but it will also have less disillusionment and disappointment. Hope will not be a lost source of strength, but it will be kept within reasonable bounds."

FACULTY AND THE GRE

Some faculty are skeptical about the GRE's reliability as a measure of an applicant's qualifications. According to David Bordwell, a professor of film at the University of Wisconsin at Madison, the GRE is not all that useful because it cannot predict whether an applicant has the imagination and grit necessary for doing well in graduate school. Several years ago, Bordwell's department conducted a study of its admissions procedures and concluded that the admissions committee's judgment of an applicant's writing ability was a much more valid predictor of an applicant's promise than the GRE. (The study correlated admissions credentials of students—GRE scores, letters of recommendation, writing samples—with the actual academic achievements of the same students as shown by publications and jobs.) This conclusion confirms the findings of an extensive 1985 study of the graduate admissions process that was funded by the GRE Board itself. The study found that the GRE most frequently functions as a *secondary* measure of evaluation, invoked "only to compensate for otherwise less than satisfactory [primary] credentials."

> Rampant grade inflation has forced some departments to use the GRE as a primary measure of qualifications.

Other faculty admit that the GRE, despite its flaws, is carrying more weight in graduate admissions decisions. Frederick J. Newmeyer, a professor of linguistics at the University of Washington at Seattle, is irked that rampant undergraduate grade inflation has forced his department to use the GRE as a primary measure of the intellectual qualifications of applicants. "The most common single undergraduate grade given out at my institution is a 4.0," says Newmeyer. "Students have come to expect that—less than a 3.0 often provokes a complaint." Indeed, according to a 1996 *Seattle Times* report, almost 63 percent of all undergraduate grades at Washington—Seattle fall in the highest grade range, 3.1 to 4.0, compared to 48 percent twenty years ago. Newmeyer and other faculty admit that the GRE is not an unimpeachable measure of intellectual ability, but at least it provides a stable scale of evaluation when grades alone can't be trusted.

Despite the problems associated with the GRE in admissions decisions, and even though ETS, in the explanatory literature it mails to graduate departments, expressly advises against using the GRE to rank students, there is one all-important area for students in which the GRE is relied upon heavily: the selection of fellowship and scholarship recipients. According to faculty, graduate school deans rank fellowship candidates by their GRE scores because there is no other easy and painless way. Logistically, it's impossible for a dean to pore over the applications of all the people that departments nominate for scholarships. Only an überdean could be familiar enough with the arcana of each department's many subspecialties to appreciate very fine distinctions between nominees. Such an omniscient dean would have to know that an applicant's keen interest in the physiology of fasting among thirteenth-century French nuns meshes perfectly with the research of the history department's quiet but widely admired scholar, and also that an applicant in sociology's insights into mathematical theory are just the thing to reinvigorate that department's fortunes. But, alas, deans are administrators forced to work under deadlines too, and so the aspiring medievalist, who scored a 700 verbal and 680 analytic, is passed over for a student fascinated by peasant life in early modern Europe with a competent personal statement, a 760 verbal, and an almost perfect score on the analytic section.

> Only a Super Dean could know every department's subspecialties and make fine distinctions between candidates.

Considering that test points can make or break one's chances for a fellowship, it's worth considering enrolling in a test-prep class or, if you can't afford a class, preparing well ahead of the test on your own. ETS states flatly in its *General Test Descriptive Booklet* that the effect of test preparation on test performance is negligible since "GRE General Test questions are designed to measure skills and knowledge acquired over a long period of time." But this statement does not deter ETS itself from outlining test-taking strategies and including a small sample of practice questions in the *Booklet*. Nor does it prevent ETS from publishing the series *Practicing to Take the GRE General Test*. This series, along with those thriving cram-mills familiar to any American student, Kaplan Education Centers and The Princeton Review, are a testament to what ETS denies. The test-prep companies are doing very well.

Preparation works for several reasons. First, practice reduces the anxiety of test taking. Second, the GRE is less a measure of intelligence than of "testwiseness," or the mastery of skills required by multiple-choice testing, and those skills are easily teachable. Understanding the structure of multiple-choice questions is more important than fully understanding their content. Multiple-choice questions do not demand a formulated answer; instead, they ask you to select the correct answer from those already formulated. If you don't immediately know the answer, it's easier and quicker to approximate an answer by evaluating the alternatives instead of trying to work out the problem.

GRE CAT

But due to changes in GRE administration and format, such back-of-the-envelope strategies may soon be retired, along with the No. 2 pencil. The first change occurred in 1993, when ETS introduced a computerized GRE test (GRE CAT)—the usual GRE test but administered, taken, and scored on a computer. Test takers no longer filled in the dots on a multiple-choice answer sheet. Questions appeared one by one on a computer screen, and test-takers used point and click with a mouse to choose an answer. In 1996, more than one-quarter of GRE takers (over 100,000 people) sat for the GRE CAT. If all goes according to ETS's plan, in a decade all GRE-takers will be taking GRE CAT.

And they will take an expanded GRE. ETS recently announced plans to change the format of the General Test, perhaps as soon as the 1997–98 school year. The current three-section format will be replaced by a five-section one. The new test will feature revisions of those old standbys—the verbal, analytic, and quantitative sections—along with new sections on mathematical reasoning and writing. ETS will offer the new and improved General Test in two convenient formats: One features Verbal, Analytical, Writing, and Quantitative Reasoning; the other contains Verbal, Analytical, Writing, and Mathematical Reasoning. A graduate department must choose which package is pertinent for applicants to it and advise applicants accordingly.

ETS claims that the new five-section format, which provides graduate admissions committees with a broader range of measures, is more sensitive to the task of predicting an applicant's ability to succeed in graduate school. Moreover, some sections in the new format dispense with what has long been the most controversial feature of the test, the multiple-choice question. On the mathematical reasoning test, for instance, test takers will use the mouse to shade in graphs or plot points on a matrix to

> In a decade, all GRE-takers will be taking a computerized version of the test.

answer questions; instead of just filling in the dots and "picking the right answer" they'll be *supplying* an answer.

What's more, ETS hopes that the GRE CAT will quash the coaching racket. Unlike the paper test, the GRE CAT does not show an entire section of the test at once. GRE CAT is a "tailored test" that proceeds through a section question by question. If you answer a question right, the test bumps you ahead to harder questions; if you answer a question wrong, you are bumped back to a lower level of difficulty. Tailored testing renders useless the most basic coaching strategy: to answer easy questions first, then return to the difficult questions and hazard a guess.

LETTERS OF RECOMMENDATION

How should you pick professors to write letters of recommendation? They should be in the field of study of the department to which you apply, as distinguished and senior as possible, and quite familar with your academic accomplishments and your college career. (Though when picking writers, remember that a lukewarm paragraph from an academic star may not help as much as an enthusiatic and detailed letter from a known rising scholar.) Your recommendations should also be well rounded; you don't want all of your recommenders to write the same kind of letter. Of course, one recommender should praise your intellectual talents and scholarly promise; she should know you as a thinker and writer. But it's also important that another recommender discuss the life you've cultivated outside of the classroom, in order to convey a sense of your personality and seriousness to an admissions committee.

> A lukewarm paragraph from a big name is less help than a detailed letter from a rising star.

If possible, pick professors who have contacts with the graduate departments to which you are applying. It's easier for a member of a graduate admissions committee to judge the sincerity of a letter written by someone familiar—a former student or colleague, or a graduate school classmate—than someone anonymous. In other words, let your recommenders network for you.

OF MYSELF I SING—SORT OF

Along with your undergraduate grades and letters of recommendation, the personal statement is a primary measure of evaluation, something faculty use to pluck stellar applications from the pile. Yet the personal statement is unique among primary measures. Grades speak to your college academic achievements, albeit in a quantified manner. In the personal statement, you have the floor.

Personal statements that read like the garden variety "what I did on my summer vacation" essay will not send faculty into a swoon. Nor will tabloid-style disclosures or self-congratulatory puff pieces. Also, faculty warn against rhapsodizing about a subject. Ethereal remarks about your love of learning, or a mushy reminiscence about falling in love with literature while reading Chaucer on Hadrian's Wall, are not likely to impress. Faculty take for granted that you love learning. "Why else apply to graduate school?" says Thomas Di Piero, a professor of comparative literature and former director of graduate studies of the visual culture studies program at the University of Rochester.

> A history professor says, "A prospective student called me up the other day and was interviewing me. I was impressed."

So what works? Di Piero's advice is widely echoed. "What we want to know is why someone wants to study in our department. A memorable personal statement should communicate that the applicant knows what kind of work they want to do and the professional commitments necessary to do it." The strongest essays persuade faculty that an applicant's intellectual interests mesh with those of the scholars already teaching at a department; they show that you have done your homework about what is going on right now in a department. (This means looking for recent publications by faculty to be sure you are up to date on their interests.) You can't write a boilerplate statement about your ambitions that is just nipped and tucked to suit each particular department. Ultimately, the ideal way to apprise a department of your qualifications is to explain what kind of work you want to do, and why a department's resources—its faculty, its reputation, the university's libraries—are exactly what you need to do it. Says Ed Ayers, a professor of American history at the University of Virginia who recently served on the admissions committee, "A student called me up the other day and was interviewing *me*. I was impressed." Far from being taken aback, professors in many departments are more than willing, and even prefer, that you have several conversations with members of the department. A winning essay develops from the beginnings of professional relationships; there is no coaching or consultant's tips that can substitute for that.

The personal statement is also the only chance you have to explain mitigating circumstances that should be weighed in your application. This is a difficult issue: Without engaging in special pleading, you need to explain why an occurrence—a death in the family or a serious illness— perhaps prolonged the time you spent in college, or why you might have come to a discipline like classics, and learning Greek, late in your academic career. It's best not to dwell on the issue; keep your explanation short, clear, and unapologetic. If you think your case is an especially delicate one, ask one of your recommenders to address it.

> Personal statements must show that you've done your homework and know what is going on in a department right now.

Finally, make sure to show your personal statement to a professor before mailing your application. Not only is it valuable to have someone read the statement to make sure it is error free, but a professor—especially someone familiar with the department you are applying to—can provide valuable tips on your approach and style.

Even the sharpest powers of persuasion, however, are no guarantee that an application will make the final cut. Graduate programs, after all, are tailored to suit the needs of faculty more than the needs of students. Faculty teach in graduate programs in order to conduct research, and graduate students—by taking courses, acting as research assistants, teaching introductory courses, and choosing dissertation advisors—enable the system to operate. This can turn the application process into a crapshoot.

You're a bright, aspiring Kantian? Tough luck. For although your intellectual qualifications are impeccable and you got along swimmingly with graduate students during your campus visit, the philosophy department's Kantian prefers students from East Coast universities, not a Midwest college like yours. Compounding your misfortune is a coincidental glut of applications from aspiring Kantians this year, which makes competition fierce. Several junior faculty on the admissions committee are privately glowing over your application, but ultimately they must placate the resident Kantian, who is also a senior faculty member, and reject you. They'd like to argue in your defense, especially since the intellectual life you cultivated at a small college makes you all the more accomplished in their eyes, but as sometime Machiavellians they can't risk estranging their colleague, whom they need as an ally in their own battles on other committees and even for the applicants that are interested in their fields. In a word, although it is natural to think that the application process is impartial, fair, and all about you, it is in fact as much about the departments to which you apply. Acceptance decisions do not necessarily reflect your qualifications.

THE WRITING SAMPLE

The writing sample helps faculty determine if you are capable of doing the work they would expect you to do in graduate school. You need not submit a publishable piece of writing, but do choose a writing sample that demonstrates your intellectual enthusiasm and agility. If at all possible, the writing sample should address a topic or issue that you want to investigate further in a graduate program. And it should be something you wrote for an upper-level course. You won't make much of an impression on an admissions committee if you turn in a paper you wrote for Art History 101.

> Admissions decisions are about the departments— not just about you.

A writing sample marred by grammatical errors won't win a committee over, either. As unbelievable as it sounds, faculty who have served on graduate admissions committees report that applicants have submitted writing samples filled with everything from spelling errors to the marginal comments of college professors and the grade awarded. The presentation of the writing sample, not just the content, matters. Ask professors for help on editing and proofing.

ONCE YOU ARE ACCEPTED

Acceptance letters are mailed out mid-March, though it's not uncommon for some departments to drag their feet until the end of April or early May. Once you are accepted, make sure that the conditions of your acceptance are clear, and that they are spelled out *in writing*. What is your financial aid package; what, if any, are your teaching obligations; what, if any, are the time limits placed on funding? (Financial aid is discussed in detail in the next chapter.) Having the conditions of your acceptance in writing is crucial, for more than a few graduate students can tell a story about being promised something over the phone only to be given something less once they arrived at school.

If you did not already do so, visit a department before deciding to enroll. Only a visit can help you determine if a program is right for you—both academically and socially. What is the chemistry between faculty and graduate students? Among graduate students? What are the undergraduates like? (Chances are you will be teaching them.) What is the graduate student quality of life? Does the city, or university, have a good transportation system? What's the housing situation? How well-stocked is the library? How plentiful are off-campus employment opportunities? How much do graduate students network for each other?

Finally, it may not be a bad idea to negotiate with a department for a sweeter deal. If your first choice department offers you a package that is not as attractive as that offered by your second choice, call your first choice and see if it can improve its offer.

APPLICATION TIMETABLE

FEBRUARY	Register for GRE General Test
APRIL	Take GRE General Test
SUMMER	Obtain applications and brochures, research programs, register and prep for GRE Subject Tests
SEPTEMBER	Contact faculty and employers about letters of recommendation
OCTOBER	Take GRE Subject Tests, start working on statement of purpose, request undergraduate transcripts
NOVEMBER	Finish statement of purpose, polish writing sample (if required), visit campus, double-check on letters of recommendation
DECEMBER	Polish statement of purpose, collect letters of recommendation, assemble and mail applications
MID-MARCH TO APRIL	Respond to notification

CHAPTER 3

FINANCES

Unless you can afford to pick up the tab yourself, going to graduate school requires a tremendous amount of financial aid. Adding up tuition and living expenses, the annual cost of graduate school can be just under $10,000 for a state resident enrolled in a public university, to as much as $30,000 for someone studying in a private university. And given that graduate study itself is as time-consuming as working nine to five, it's virtually impossible for a student to attend graduate school full time while holding down a full-time job to pay the bills.

But there is help, and universities are the biggest source. According to the National Research Council, 1995 doctoral recipients in the humanities and the social sciences who received financial support got roughly half of it from universities. University aid takes several forms: tuition waivers, fellowships, and assistantships (which grant students a lump sum of money in exchange for labor such as teaching or conducting research). Students pooled slightly less than half of their support from federal and state loans, familial contributions, and part-time jobs. A much smaller amount of student aid (roughly 6 percent) came in the form of fellowships and scholarships from the National Science Foundation, National Endowment for the Humanities, and various nonfederal foundations.

Overall, nearly 60 percent of full-time doctoral students receive some kind of financial aid from one or more of the three sources mentioned above. Of course, just because the odds of receiving financial aid are good doesn't mean you'll be washing down filet mignon with Cordon Rouge every night of the week. A diet of rice and beans is more likely. To make sure you can afford even that, plus a roof over your head, and the books and hours of free time you'll need to nourish your mind, you should investigate the four main funding sources: fellowships, assistantships, grants, and loans. This chapter offers a start by surveying them for you.

But first we need to pause over a fundamental question: Are you truly willing to risk racking up thousands of dollars of debt, possibly compounding your undergraduate debt, to pay for a graduate education at a time when academic job prospects are not exactly rosy? And even if you do land a tenure-track job, you can't count on having the earning power of a doctor or lawyer to pay off debts quickly. (See Charts 1, 2, and 3.) While it's impossible to put a price on the value of an education, only a fool would be so idealistic as to lose sight of its real costs.

ELIGIBILITY

When you tick the "yes" box about financial aid on your graduate school application, you automatically become eligible for any fellowships and assistantships administered through the university. If you want to apply for federal and state loans, the university financial aid office is the place to begin your search.

Eligibility requirements for university-based aid vary widely from school to school. General eligibility requirements for most federally sponsored programs administered through a university financial aid office are more straightforward: U.S. citizenship or resident alien status (green card holder); at least half-time enrollment (as determined by the particular university you are attending); and satisfactory progress towards the degree (again, as determined by the particular university).

Caveat emptor: If you are wavering between pursuing an M.A. and Ph.D., some students suggest applying to a Ph.D. program to increase your chances of receiving funding. Doctoral students regularly receive much more university-based aid than master's students. In fact, departments often defer awarding aid to master's students until the second year, after seeing which students survived the first year rat race. If you find that you don't really want to continue in a program all the way through to the Ph.D., you can almost always exit the program after the second year with an M.A.

A BUDGET

The awarding of financial aid is often based on a student's calculated financial need. Financial need is the difference between the annual cost of school and a student's own funds—or, in the lingo of the financial aid office, his or her "expected personal contribution." Graduate programs are required to publish a "standard" personal budget for graduate students, and you can use this to begin estimating the annual cost. But the budget is only a place to begin. For one thing, you need to figure out whether the budget has been calculated on a nine-month school year or twelve-month calendar year. And even with this adjustment made, the figure may not be the most realistic. Talk to any graduate student and you'll quickly learn that it usually falls short. (University-generated budgets are, after all, part of the university's public relations materials.) In other words, be prepared either to tighten your belt several notches or to explain to the financial aid office why it should accept your own estimate of costs.

What should you consider as personal costs? It's easy to remember room and board, but don't forget the following: utilities, clothing, transportation, medical expenses, books, supplies, child care, credit card debt, pocket money. Again, talking to graduate students about expenses will allow you to make a realistic estimate of your own.

The calculation of expected personal contribution varies from university to university, but it is generally 35 percent of a student's reported assets and 50 percent of a student's summer earnings. The federal calculation is 35 percent of the student's reported assets and 50 percent of summer earnings above $1,750. If you are married, your spouse's financial information from tax returns must be included in your total annual earnings.

While these base calculations are standard, financial aid offices do have the liberty to modify them to accord with individual student needs. For instance, if medical bills soaked up all your assets and earnings last year, the financial aid office can factor those bills into its calculations of your financial need. You must be prepared to document the bills, or any other such cost, though, before the financial aid office will factor them into its calculations.

THE FOUR STREAMS OF AID

What follows is a breakdown of the four main funding streams. Since funding rules and interest rates change, make sure to contact the appropriate agency to obtain the most recent information.

FELLOWSHIPS

A fellowship is the Rolls-Royce of graduate financial aid. Fellowship money, which usually covers tuition and a lump sum for expenses, is awarded with no strings attached: You don't have to grade papers for it; you don't have to teach for it. It's just given to you because of your talent and promise. And because competition for fellowships is fierce, fellowship recipients are often seen as the golden boys and girls of a department, no mean factor when other goodies like plum teaching jobs or research projects are apportioned.

Most fellowships are granted by individual universities on the basis of merit, not need. Students either apply for them or are nominated for them by their graduate departments, with the final decision in either case made by a dean. Check with departments for details.

You can also apply for the following non-university-based fellowships and scholarships:

Jacob K. Javits Fellowships

These fellowships are open to students in the arts, humanities, and the social sciences who have not yet completed more than twenty semester hours of graduate study. In 1995, fifty-six fellowships ranging up to $14,000 were awarded. The program was suspended for 1996–97 academic year but has been reinstated for the 1997–98 academic year. The application deadline is February 1. To obtain an application, call (202) 260-3574.

Patricia Roberts Harris Graduate Study Fellowships

Administered by the university, these fellowships are designed to increase the participation of women and minorities who are underrepresented in academic and professional fields. Contact the university for information, deadlines, and an application.

Andrew W. Mellon Fellowships

These awards are for the first year of study only, and are for doctoral students who will ultimately pursue teaching. For 1998, the fellowship is $14,000 plus tuition and mandated fees. Any college senior who expects a degree before September 1998, or any graduate of the last five years, may apply, so long as he or she has not pursued graduate work leading to a Ph.D. Students who hold a master's degree are eligible, so long as the degree was earned in a terminal master's program. The deadline for application requests is December 8, and completed applications must be submitted by December 31, 1997. Many undergraduate campuses have faculty members who serve as Mellon advisors and provide informational brochures to interested students. In 1996, 902 applications were received and 85 fellowships were awarded. Call (609) 452-7007 to request an application. Information is available on the Web at: http://www.woodrow.org/mellon.

National Science Foundation Fellowships

Competition is open to graduate students in the social sciences (anthropology, sociology, economics) as well as the sciences. Applicants must be U.S. citizens and have completed no more than twenty semester hours of study. The application deadline is November 1. In 1996, 5,400 applications were received and 1,000 fellowships were awarded. Call (423) 241-4300 to request an application.

Ford Foundation Predoctoral Fellowships for Minorities

Ford fellowships are open to minority students beginning graduate studies in all fields. The three year fellowship includes a $14,000 stipend as well as a $6,000 grant applied to tuition and fees. In 1996, roughly 1,500 applications were received and 50 fellowships were awarded. The application deadline is November 4. Call (202) 334-2872 to request an application.

Free Fellowship Booklet

This booklet contains information on fellowship opportunities for U.S. citizens and foreign nationals in many fields of study, including the humanities and the social sciences. The booklet is available from the Publications Office of the National Science Foundation, 4201 Wilson Blvd., Arlington, VA 22230.

Disciplinary Associations

Check with the disciplinary associations to see if they offer fellowships or scholarships. You can find association phone numbers at the end of each disciplinary chapter.

ASSISTANTSHIPS

Assistantships are the most common kind of university-based aid awarded to graduate students. An assistantship is a bit like an undergraduate work-study program. Through the recommendation of a department, the university grants a graduate student a stipend and tuition waiver in exchange for services. You have to pay taxes on a stipend, but not on a tuition waiver.

Assistantship falls into two groups: teaching (TA's) and research (RA's). Students in the humanities tend to be TA's, and they do everything from grading and leading discussion groups for a faculty member to actually teaching their own introductory-level classes. When a humanities student is granted an RA, it usually involves helping a faculty member do research for a book. A TA in the social sciences usually grades papers and exams for an individual faculty member and only occasionally teaches, but then students in the social sciences are usually granted RA's, for which they do lab work under the supervision of a faculty advisor. Assistants work anywhere between five and twenty hours a week.

When you inquire about assistantships, ask departments about time limits, which are often tucked away in the fine print of financial aid agreements. Departments impose time limits on assistantships to deter students from working on their degrees beyond the time for which they have assistantship funding.

GRANTS

Grants are almost always awarded to universities, not individual graduate students, but this doesn't mean that graduate students shouldn't be familiar with them. Grant money awarded to a university trickles down to departments and faculty, and the latter use it to fund research, which almost always involves hiring graduate students as research assistants.

In effect, a grant is a cross between a fellowship and an assistantship. It is a sum of money awarded to a university or individual in exchange for a certain kind of work. Basically, an institution, much like a corporation or government agency, uses a grant to pay someone else to do its research. That person may use his or her findings in scholarly publications, but sometimes there are a few financial or other bureaucratic strings attached.

As you investigate departments, ask for a history of the grants they have received: A grant-rich department is one that can afford to treat its graduate students well. When it comes time to write a dissertation in certain fields and for certain topics, grant money can be available to you indirectly through a faculty sponsor, and occasionally in direct aid.

LOANS

Though there are many sources of financial aid, many graduate students still must take out loans to make ends meet. This can be expensive. According to an NRC report, in 1995 60 percent of responding social science Ph.D.'s reported graduating with cumulative debt (combined undergraduate and graduate school debt). Among debtors, nearly 15 percent were in the red $30,000 or more; 10 percent graduated owing $5,000 or less; the remaining 35 percent graduated owing between $5,000 and $30,000.

Humanities doctorates were not as deeply in debt. In 1995, though nearly 56 percent reported graduating with cumulative debt, the biggest group of debtors, 14 percent, owed $5,000 or less. Only 7 percent owed $30,000 or more. The remaining 35 percent owed between $5,000 and $30,000.

The borrowing and repayment schedules are key points for consideration before filling out a loan application. Each type of loan has different implications when it comes to the daunting process of managing your debt. (The different kinds of loans outlined below are described in more detail in the Financial Aid chapter of the U.S. Department of Education's *1997–98 Student Guide*.)

Direct Stafford Subsidized Loans

Direct Stafford subsidized loans are low-cost, government-guaranteed loans. If a university does not participate in the Direct Loan program, the funds are lent to the student by a bank, credit union, or other lender that participates in the program. The loan is "subsidized" in that the interest is paid by the federal government—not you—during the loan period and a six-month grace period. It is "direct" because the U.S. government lends you the funds. Eligibility is based on need, not merit. The maximum amount a graduate student can borrow is $8,500 annually to a maximum of $65,000, less any amount borrowed as an undergraduate. These loans are for one academic year and are disbursed in at least two payments. In 1995, 601,000 graduate students borrowed a total of $4,578,000,000 in Stafford subsidized loans, with an average of $7,617 per student.

The interest rate equals the 91-day Treasury Bill rate plus 3.1 percent, and cannot exceed 8.25 percent. Interest on the loan does not accumulate during school, and you are not required to make any payments until six months after you graduate or leave school. Repayment may take up to ten years but can be deferred longer under special circumstances. Minimum monthly payments, once they start, are $50. Applications are available at any university or lending institution involved in the program. You'll pay up to 4 percent of the loan in fees that are deducted proportionally from each disbursement of your loan.

Direct Stafford Unsubsidized Loans

Stafford unsubsidized loans are not based on financial need. As with the subsidized loan, the unsubsidized loan is "direct" because the U.S.

chart 1 **Examples of Monthly Student Loan Payments for Student Borrowers**

TOTAL AMOUNT BORROWED	AVERAGE MONTHLY PAYMENT
$5,000	$61
10,000	121
15,000	182
20,000	243
30,000	364
50,000	607
75,000	910
100,000	1,213

NOTE *Calculations assume a standard 10-year repayment and an 8 percent interest rate.*

chart 2 **Monthly Student Loan Payments for Doctoral Recipients in Different Fields**

FIELD OF STUDY	CUMULATIVE DEBT LEVEL	AVERAGE MONTHLY PAYMENT
PHYSICAL SCIENCES	$8,500	$103
ENGINEERING	9,300	113
LIFE SCIENCES	9,800	119
SOCIAL SCIENCES	14,500	176
HUMANITIES	10,000	121
EDUCATION	10,100	123
OTHER	12,000	146
TOTAL	10,500	127

NOTE *Calculations assume a standard 10-year repayment schedule and an 8 percent interest rate. Median debt levels were available for Ph.D. recipients, rather than average debt levels. As a result, a normal distribution is assumed for Ph.D. recipients.*

SOURCE *Summary Report 1993: Doctorate Recipients from United States Universities, Thurgood and Clarke, 1995.*

government lends you the funds. Graduate students may borrow up to $8,500 annually to a maximum of $65,500, less any amount borrowed as an undergraduate. The interest rate is based on the 52-week Treasury Bill rate plus 3.1 percent, and like the Stafford subsidized loan, cannot exceed 8.25 percent. Unlike the Stafford subsidized loan, the interest on an unsubsidized loan is not paid by the federal government, so interest on the loan accumulates to the borrower from the day the loan is disbursed. In 1995, 401,000 graduate students borrowed a total of $3,135,000,000 in Stafford unsubsidized loans, with an average of $7,818 per student.

Repayment begins six months after you graduate. During this grace period, you don't have to pay any principal, but interest is charged. You can either pay the interest or allow it to be capitalized. That is, the interest will be added to the principal amount of your loan and additional interest will be based on the higher amount. Clearly, if you choose to pay the interest as it accumulates, you'll repay less in the long run.

The minimum monthly payment and length of repayment varies according to the repayment plan you choose. In the Standard Repay-

chart 3 **Comparison of Monthly Student Loan Payments to Monthly Earnings**

DOCTORAL RECIPIENTS	MONTHLY LOAN REPAYMENT	STARTING SALARY	MONTHLY SALARY	LOAN PAYMENT AS A % OF MONTHLY SALARY
MATHEMATICS	$103	$39,500	$3,292	3%
COMPUTER SCIENCE	103	56,513	4,709	2
PHYSICS/ASTRONOMY	103	50,600	4,216	2
CHEMISTRY	103	50,933	4,244	2
ENGINEERING	113	55,200	4,600	2
LIFE SCIENCES	119	41,600	3,467	3
SOCIAL SCIENCES	176	42,600	3,550	5
HUMANITIES	121	32,800	2,733	4
EDUCATION	123	N/A	N/A	N/A
OTHER	146	N/A	N/A	N/A

NOTE *Calculations assume a standard 10-year repayment schedule and an 8 percent interest rate. Mathematics, computer science, and physics/astronomy are all classified under physical sciences. Starting salary information represents gross income and was obtained from the following sources: for humanities Ph.D. recipients:* Survey of Humanities Doctorates, *National Research Council; for physical sciences Ph.D. recipients: National Association of Colleges and Employers; and for engineering, life sciences, and scoial sciences Ph.D. recipients:* SRS 1991 Survey of Doctorate Recipients, *National Science Foundation.*

ment Plan, for instance, you must pay at least $50 for up to ten years. You'll pay up to 4 percent of the loan in fees that are deducted proportionally from each disbursement of your loan.

Perkins Loans

The Perkins loan is available to students with exceptional financial need. The university is the lender, and it makes the loan with government funds. Depending on when you apply, your level of need, and the funding level of the school, you can borrow up to $5,000 annually to a maximum of $30,000. The loan is disbursed in two equal installments each year. There are no fees.

The interest rate is 5 percent, and both the interest and the principal do not begin to accumulate until after you leave school. Repayment begins nine months after graduation, and may take up to ten years. Minimum monthly payment depends on the size of the debt and the length of repayment.

State Loans

State and regional funding, which comes in the form of both loans and grants, accounts for only 3 percent of all student aid disbursed each year. Some states are more generous that others. In addition, to qualify for state aid a student must be a resident of the state. Moreover, some funding is restricted to certain population groups (women, African Americans). The federal financial aid information brochure available at most financial aid offices includes a list of all state agencies that grant loans.

WHEN TO APPLY

You need not wait until you are accepted to a graduate program to apply for a loan. The necessary paperwork can be filed after January I of the year in which you are applying for aid; the deadline for filing is May I. (For the 1998–99 school year, file after January I but by May I, 1998.) The Free Application for Federal Student Assistance (FAFSA) is the standard form filed for federal loans, though other forms are sometimes also required. And remember, annual loans *are not* rolled over automatically: You must renew your application for federal aid each year.

The FAFSA requires financial information from the previous tax year. Make sure you have the following documents handy:
- U.S. Income Tax returns, W-2, and 1099 forms for the fiscal year that just ended
- Records of untaxed income
- Current bank statements and mortgage information
- Records of investments: stocks, bonds, mutual funds, CD's, and money-market accounts
- Social Security number

FURTHER READING

April Vahle Hamel, *The Graduate School Funding Handbook* (Pennsylvania)
Patricia McWade, *Financing Graduate School* (Peterson's)

FREE PUBLICATIONS

Foundation Grants for Individuals, National Commission for Cooperative Education, 360 Huntington Avenue, Suite 384CP, Boston, MA 02115

Graduating into Debt: The Burdens of Borrowing for Graduate & Professional Students, The Education Resources Institute, 330 Stuart Street, Suite 500, Boston, MA 02116-5237

WEB SITES

http://www.finaid.com
This site provides links to almost every web site concerning financial aid.

http://www.ed.gov/prog_info/SFA/StudentGuide
This is the site for the Department of Education's *Student Guide to Financial Aid*.

http://fdncenter.org
The site for The Foundation Center, an independent nonprofit information clearinghouse that disseminates information on foundations, corporate giving, and grants.

http://www.studentservices.com
This site provides information on over 180,000 scholarships, grants, and loans from the private sector.

http://www.fastweb.com
FastWeb is a searchable index of scholarships.

PHONE NUMBERS

Federal Student Aid Information Center
(800) 433-3243

RESOURCES

PART TWO: THE DISCIPLINES

CHAPTER 4

THE DISCIPLINES NOW

Many graduate students and professors have told us that they went into graduate school flying blind. No one had ever outlined for them more than a subfield of a discipline. Apart from what they learned in introductory undergraduate classes, no professor had talked with them about the history of a discipline, from its origins in the research university to its present dimensions. And their discussions with faculty about their graduate school plans rarely touched upon the deep intellectual currents that roil underneath debates today.

Graduate school's intense focus on the methods of a single discipline is one of the first qualities that separates graduate from undergraduate study. As we've explained in the introduction to the *The Real Guide*, in graduate school your intellectual world centers on a discipline, and your home in that world is a department. If college is like a cafeteria, graduate study is like culinary training—in a specific cuisine. This is so even for graduate students interested in interdisciplinary study or emerging fields. The Ph.D. they will be awarded and the jobs they will seek will stem from the traditional disciplines.

The Real Guide provides a glance at both practical and intellectual issues for the sake of helping you with your impending decision about the right discipline to study and where to study it. Based on interviews with hundreds of professors and graduate students, each of the twenty-three chapters in the following section tells you what is going on in a particular discipline right now, and names some of the departments at the heart of these developments. After highlighting the perennial debates of the discipline, we bring out the nuances that distinguish departments so that you can establish a basis for choosing those that are best for you.

Of course, the landscapes of disciplines alter rapidly as some scholars tackle old questions with new tools, while others conduct research that raises altogether new questions. Since their discipline emerged a half century ago, for instance, comparative literature scholars have cultivated an increasingly cosmopolitan and interdisciplinary perspective. In addition to asking students to master several European languages, the field has absorbed ideas and methods from philosophy, history, and linguistics to develop a perspective subtle enough for comparing the literatures of nations around the world. But a cosmopolitan approach means something very different to the field's current generation of postcolonial critics, who examine the impact of European colonialism on the national identity and culture of former Third World colonies, than it did to an earlier generation of émigré scholars, who studied the highwater marks of European literature and set up the time-honored standards of the field. In nearly every field there is a submerged battle about the mission of the discipline as well as a debate about the current meaning of its key principles. Each chapter brings these issues to the surface.

Nearly every discipline is in motion. Almost everyone has an opinion about how open a discipline is to new methods and how much it has been affected by new constituencies of students. To truly determine a discipline's porousness, talk to as many faculty and students in various stages of their careers as possible. We provide information to start that process. For those students intrigued by newer research areas it makes sense to read several chapters. If you are keen on cultural studies, for instance, it is interesting to see the different ways that departments of anthropology, comparative literature, English, and history are all searching now for the best ways to explore the broad territory of culture. And students in traditional fields might also be intrigued by different approaches to the same topics: Budding linguists might want to read the anthropology and sociology chapters as well as the linguistics chapter to compare the approaches taken to language and society.

The identity of a department itself can change very quickly too, as faculty come and go or shift the focus of their attention from one area of scholarship to another. In classics, philosophy, linguistics, and archaeology, most departments are so small, and graduate students so closely identified with their faculty mentors, that the departure of one or two key professors can make or break a department, leaving graduate students in the lurch. And even in larger disciplines like English, sociology, and political science, where a cluster of powerful departments used to hold sway, you have to be wary. The combination of a depressed academic job market, in which even top graduates from top schools can't net jobs, and the rise of interdisciplinary scholarship, which licenses scholars to look for ideas beyond the borders of their discipline, have chipped away at the authority of

If college is like a cafeteria, graduate school is like culinary training in a specific cuisine.

disciplinary powerhouses. We spotlight lower-profile institutions and name particular scholars. But no guide can cover so many fields and institutions comprehensively. Though suggestive, our lists are far from exhaustive, and you'll learn of many schools and scholars other than those we mention. *The Real Guide* highlights those that came up in hundreds of interviews.

With these facts of academic life in mind, we provide the scoop on core issues and cutting-edge topics, all to help you research departments and intelligently interview professors and graduate students. We even direct you to resources for learning the late-breaking news about faculty moves and departmental realignments—phone numbers of professional associations, titles of association-produced handbooks and overviews, and Web addresses with links to individual departments.

All twenty-three chapters in the following section adhere to the same format, with variations made to suit the special nature of each discipline. The first part features a short profile of a graduate student or two. While no one student is representative, these profiles are meant to bring the graduate experience to life—the breadth of a field and the myriad expectations and aspirations that students have about doing graduate-level study. These profiles are then rounded out by a more general sketch of a discipline's aims.

To choose among the offerings of graduate departments today, you have to understand the history of the discipline and how it has shaped the different intellectual and methodological paths that departments have taken. Following the student profiles is a historical overview of a discipline, an overview that highlights perennial questions as well as broad intellectual trends. How, for example, did art history come to be divided between object-oriented scholarship and theoretical work? Are all economists allergic to philosophical questions? Why is Spanish the Cinderella of the modern languages? What's the difference between a Ph.D. in religion and one in theology? Or between one in historical musicology and one in ethnomusicology? What do cultural anthropologists and physical anthropologists have in common? The overview makes no claim to being a complete intellectual history of a discipline—in so short a space it can only touch lightly on major issues. Its purpose is to orient you to a particular field, and equip you with important questions to ask. And we are certain to tell you about some research areas few students know much about.

The third and final part of the chapter is a map of the current state of graduate study for any given field. It describes the hurdles you will have to clear during the early years of graduate school, such as language exams and core curriculum requirements. If you want to pursue graduate study but are wavering between the M.A. and Ph.D., this section can help you make that decision. Whenever possible, we single out those departments with top-notch terminal master's programs, and we offer an honest appraisal of the value of the master's degree within and outside the academy. Note well, though, that we have concentrated on the doctorate, not the master's.

Many students may want to read several chapters to see how different disciplines cover broad areas like "culture."

For those with their sights set on the Ph.D., we point out particular problems with the national rankings in that field, and we identify departments according to their specialties—something no rankings have done. Which communication departments favor the study of the political economy of the media? Which favor media effects? Which geography departments will train you in Geographic Information Systems? If you're a linguist, where can you study dialectology, sociolinguistics, or cognitive science? For students of French, which departments specialize in Francophone studies? How truly interdisciplinary are departments in classics or English, though many claim to be so?

Lastly, we report on the current academic and nonacademic job prospects for recent Ph.D.'s. We do not forecast what your academic job prospects might be like when you earn your degree eight or ten years from now. Our aim is a more realistic one: providing you with a window on the academic profession by describing the state of the current job market.

In virtually every discipline, some of the most exciting work crosses disciplinary boundaries and falls under the rubric of one or more "studies": cultural studies, African-American studies, American studies, medieval studies, and others. But there are relatively few free-standing, Ph.D. degree-granting departments in those areas. Consequently, our chapters treat them as movements emanating from the traditional disciplines. As you talk to professors about graduate school, it's best to ask realistic questions about the opportunities a graduate student has to do such research. Is interdisciplinary work really a matter for your second book, not your dissertation? Does everyone praise the latest work at conferences but then hire quite traditional scholars? You'll have to judge the state of the newest work in conversations with as wide a range of people within a particular discipline as you can.

> Nearly every discipline is in motion as scholars tackle new questions; we chart the directions they are taking.

Another note: *U.S. News and World Report*, *Newsweek*, Princeton Review publications, and the National Research Council can provide you with numerical rankings of departments. But such rankings are so flawed, out of date, and based on arguable criteria that many top departments, from some at the University of California at Berkeley to some at Yale University, refuse to participate in the surveys on which the rankings are based. And less well-known schools are often off the radar screen too—not because their professors are less talented or their graduates less successful in the job market, but because they are overshadowed by large departments or ones doing the safest and least interesting scholarship. No guidebook can mention every important scholar or place to do graduate research. But if you read the historical overviews carefully, ask questions of faculty, and investigate the departments mentioned within subspecialties, you can avoid ending up at the wrong place, an expensive and serious mistake. You'll also be much better prepared than most students entering grad school. Instead of gambling on the accuracy of a someone's Top Ten list, these chapters will tell you all you need to make an informed choice.

CHAPTER 5

ART HISTORY

Before Joan Cummins started graduate school, she was teaching art history to high school students. Cummins enjoyed helping a bunch of skeptical adolescents learn to appreciate the stylistic nuances of twentieth-century European paintings, but the meaning of the paintings themselves was not fundamentally important to her. So she set out in search of art with some "heavy-duty philosophy behind it," and found it in India.

Now an eighth-year graduate student at Columbia University, Cummins specializes in the ritual use of sun god temples in India, a specialty somewhat renegade in an area that has always been more concerned with a work's formal qualities than its function. Like most of her classmates, Cummins has had to learn two languages, German and French, yet due to her research interests she's one of the very few to have tackled Sanskrit, too. Also, unlike many of her Columbia cohorts, Cummins is not a slave to contemporary theory, which includes things like psychoanalysis, poststructuralism, and French feminism. Because theory is European, she doesn't think it relevant to the study of India. This doesn't mean that Cummins and theory are not on speaking terms, though. A knowledge of theory, along with a knowledge of Western art, is an indispensable job credential.

Besides, though passionate about her specialty, Cummins enjoys teaching outside it. "Seeing new work sharpens my sense of what's distinctive about what I'm looking at."

After earning a B.A. in classical civilizations, Rebecca Furer enrolled in the terminal master's program at Tufts University, a training ground for future curators. It's unusual today for a classicist to be following this path, though at the beginning of the century it would certainly have been typical. But Furer is no more a musty-object fetishist than a Great Books elitist. She has always studied art within a historical context, and is deeply committed to bringing interdisciplinary scholarship into the museum, a leaning that her curatorial choices will reflect. In a recent course, Furer proposed an exhibit around an array of objects meant to address the roles of free men, free women, and slaves in ancient Greece, by looking at their everyday relationships toward work and recreation. "Museums can be so stagnant and stale, particularly in dealing with classical material," says Furer. "But there are so many ways of making it new."

WHY ART HISTORY?

Although their interests and intellectual orientations are unusual, Cummins and Furer are typical graduate students in that their careers are playing out the seismic shift that is disrupting the entire field of art history—the crumbling of traditional and deeply cherished boundaries. Art history is catching up with a series of intellectual revolutions that have swept through the rest of the humanities during the past twenty years. Multiculturalists are challenging the Western slant of canons, while feminists are disputing the viability of canons altogether. And although notions of universal standards of quality are being questioned throughout the humanities, they are an especially controversial issue in art history because connoisseurship—the project of establishing, in a technical, materially based way, a work's greatness—has long been the field's bedrock. Even more controversial are the art historians who are defying divisions between high and low culture, only to meet the stiff opposition of those who defend the field as a bastion of high culture. To this day, tea is served every afternoon at the Institute of Fine Arts at New York University.

The truth is that art history's rarefied reputation has made it particularly vulnerable to the budget slashing that is afflicting all of the humanities in this era of shrinking resources. To stretch their dollars, departments are demanding that new professors be versatile. Only a handful of colleges and universities, for instance, could afford to hire Cummins if all she could teach was Buddhist temple art, no matter how erudite her discourse.

Intellectual revolution and economic turmoil are reinforcing each other, making art historians both excited and anxious about the field's future. In thinking about graduate school, you need to consider what kind of career you want after you earn your degree. Do you want to be a curator, a professor, or both? What about being a museum educator? You also need to consider your intellectual, political, and aesthetic interests. When you look at Manet's *A Bar at the Folies-Bergère*, do you consider what it says about the role of women in nineteenth-century French culture? Perhaps you prefer to examine the painting techniques Manet used instead. Or maybe you're not drawn to Manet, or even painting, at all, but gravitate to forms of visual experience that have only just begun to be taken seriously, like digital media or the history of fashion.

HOW ART HISTORY HAS TAKEN SHAPE

Insiders have a tendency to refer melodramatically to art history's current upheavals as a "crisis," but this is hardly the first time the field has undergone a major paradigm shift. Over the course of art history's development, its practitioners and approaches have undergone several transformations.

In pre-nineteenth-century Europe, histories of art and artists were written primarily by practicing artists. But in the United States, art history began as a field for the well-to-do, a way for them to make sense of their family heirlooms and paintings purchased on European tours. Art history began evolving into a full-fledged academic discipline in the late nineteenth century at colleges like Vassar, Smith, and Bryn Mawr, universities such as Harvard, Yale, and Princeton, and lesser-known schools like Rockford Female Seminary, in Illinois.

Its very origins defined art history as an intensely object-oriented field. The original proposal for Princeton's art history program, written in 1881, even went so far as to lament that "a vast majority of accomplished and instructed men and woman are unable to tell whether their plates and cups are pottery or porcelain." One Harvard class in the history of techniques, "the egg-and-plaster course," required students to practice actual techniques—doing frescoes in the trecento manner, making silverpoint drawings, or painting a tempera panel.

Standards of connoisseurship, date attribution, classification, judgments about quality and authenticity, and knowledge about techniques and types of materials used were all central to the nascent discipline, and after World War I they were pursued in a manner that was so factually based that art history seemed to belong more to the sciences than the humanities. A major scholarly project might consist of cataloging the pertinent visual traits of all known Asian sarcophagi.

In the 1920s, the foremost art historians were all factually minded scholars.

John Coolidge, the director of Harvard's Fogg Museum from 1948–1968, observed that when he was an undergraduate at Harvard in the early 1930s, one of his professors, the prominent Chandler Post, had a memory of Western art that was "as comprehensive, accurate, and nondiscriminatory as the phone book." In the 1920s, the new departments at Columbia and NYU were staffed with such factually minded scholars, but not all of their work was as dry as Post's. Consider Bernhard Berenson, one of the foremost art historians of this period, who during his lifetime was an adviser and authenticator for major art collectors such as Boston art patron Isabella Gardner. Also, Berenson was an independent scholar who devised his own very influential method for determining a work's authenticity. He studied all the works that could be indisputably attributed to a particular artist, isolated their characteristics, then searched for those traits in works whose authenticity was uncertain. Both in the emphasis of his studies—the Italian Renaissance—and in his dedication to the science of authentication, Berenson was typical of art historians of his era.

Yet Berenson's work was by no means limited to technical considerations. He wrote extensively about the psychology of art, pioneering the notion that a viewer has a physical response to an artwork's aesthetic details, such as space or composition. In *The Florentine Painters of the Renaissance*, Berenson labeled this notion "tactile values." And despite being snubbed by powerful art historians—Roger Fry wrote to a colleague soon after the publication of *Florentine Painters* that he hoped Berenson would "[get] over his theories"—Berenson contributed greatly to the field's glamour. He had a legendary forty-room, eighteenth-century villa near Florence, which held his own renowned collection of Renaissance and Asian art, and where he hosted scholars and travelers from all over the world.

Art history became a more intellectually rigorous endeavor in the 1930s. After Hitler came to power in 1933, a host of German-Jewish scholars from all disciplines emigrated to the United States. Among them was Erwin Panofsky, who put the history into art history, essentially reinventing the discipline and establishing the United States as an art history superpower. NYU was particularly active in recruiting these émigrés.

Panofsky and his colleagues shared Chandler Post's preoccupation with collecting information about a work's age, materials, authorship, and condition, but they were just as engaged in creating historical narratives about artworks. Panofsky scorned mere connoisseurship, believing that physical detail, though important, did not tell the whole story, since art was always infused with the values of the culture that produced it. In this vein, Panofsky greatly strengthened the iconographic tradition pioneered by German art historian Aby Warburg. He looked at recurring visual themes and symbols in paintings, like Father Time, or at the neo-Platonic ideas expressed in Renaissance works. And Panofsky, even more than Berenson, became a cultural celebrity. Well-received books like *Studies in Iconology* (1939) and *Albrecht Dürer* (1943) demonstrated that in addition to being a brilliant thinker, Panofsky was a clear and lively writer accessible to specialists and nonspecialists alike.

> Erwin Panofsky scorned mere connoisseurship, believing that art was infused with the values of the culture that produced it.

Panofsky's methods were often resisted by die-hard connoisseurs, but, as a scholar of philosophy, literature, history, and religion, he laid the foundations for the interdisciplinarity central to the field today. Panofsky has sometimes been misremembered as a narrow formalist because of his dedication to physical detail, but he was not viewed that way in his time. More recently, critical theorists like Keith Moxey of Columbia and Michael Ann Holly of the University of Rochester have revived Panofsky's work, and acknowledged their own debt to him. And to this day, Panofsky's example survives in the work of popularizers who exist outside the field but play an important role in debates about art. Though neither are art historians, Marxist art critic John Berger, who hosted the famous BBC series *Ways of Seeing*, and the

Columbia philosophy professor emeritus and *The Nation* magazine art critic Arthur Danto, who has written extensively on postmodernism in painting, have contributed greatly to the field.

But Panofsky's pioneering work notwithstanding, art history remained an object-centered discipline and a world unto itself, one relatively unconcerned with art's relationship to the rest of society, until the 1960s. Then social art historians at last linked art history to social history, connecting developments in the art world to political and cultural changes. In *Absolute Bourgeois: Artists and Politics in France 1848–1851* (1973), Marxist art historian T.J. Clark asked questions about art's economic context and production, and its role in keeping the ruling classes in power. And Linda Nochlin of NYU's Institute of Fine Arts foregrounded feminism in the field with her widely influential 1971 essay "Why Are There No Great Women Artists?" Besides emphasizing social questions, Clark and Nochlin also brought nineteenth-century art, especially French, into vogue.

> Art history remained an object-centered discipline, and a world unto itself, until the 1960s.

The theory revolutions of the 1980s continued the push to bring art into a larger social context and conversation. Multiculturalists called into question art history's Eurocentrism, and its focus on white artists. Meanwhile feminism widened its lens further, to encompass not only women's exclusion from the artistic canon, but the patriarchy inherent in having any kind of canon at all. And while some feminists began to analyze men's demeaning ways of painting women, others explored the ways art might show a woman's sexuality as powerful—an issue central to feminist film studies as well.

As art historians began to see art as a dynamic part of a broader cultural landscape, they turned to other disciplines for new tools. When University of California at Santa Barbara professor Ann Bermingham remembers her graduate school days, twenty years ago, she offers a portrait of a cloistered field: "We had our own little world, totally isolated from the rest of the university. We even had our own library; there was this assumption that you'd never need to use the main library. No one would ever believe that now." Some art historians, having turned to semiotics and literary theory, now view works and cultures alike as "texts" laden with ideological meanings—the bourgeois values of the Second Republic, for instance. Says Stanford University professor Wanda M. Corn, "It is no longer possible to be see art as separate from its context, to be innocent about its relationship to ideology." This means overturning concepts previously taken for granted—the nature of genius, for instance, or the ability of canonical works to transcend their historical origins. Even history itself is subject to scrutiny; historiography (the study of the principles, theory, and history of writing history) is creeping into many art history courses. Says Corn of all these changes, "I don't know of a single department that isn't engaged in totally rethinking itself."

Some art historians are still producing monographs on single artists or detailed studies of particular techniques, while others are writing dissertations on the specifics of niche decorations from the tombs of Byzantine Egypt or the votive columns of the Acropolis in the archaic period. But the field has embraced a whole new range of subject matter and approaches. At Harvard in the early 1930s, John Coolidge proposed writing an undergraduate honors thesis on the aesthetic evolution of automobile design. The department flatly rejected his idea. But Coolidge's topic would seem perfectly reasonable now—at some programs, even passé. Top programs have recently awarded Ph.D.'s for dissertations like "Pretty Vacant: Neo-Expressionist Painting, Situationist Theory, and Punk Rock." Dolls, performance art, landscape gardening, and housing subdivisions are now also acceptable subject matter, and the field has embraced theoretical influences from Immanuel Kant to Julia Kristeva.

The latest development on the theory front is the arrival of "visual culture studies." Over the past decade, visual culture has become the focal point for scholars in film studies, art history, comparative literature, and English who are concerned less with interpreting the aesthetic characteristics of objects like paintings than with theorizing how viewers, in Western and non-Western cultures alike, come to understand what images mean. The approach is by and large an anthropological one, as W.J.T. Mitchell, a professor of English and art history at the University of Chicago and a prominent voice in the field, makes clear. "If there is any foundational postulate to visual culture, it is that vision is a mode of cultural expression and human communication as fundamental and widespread as language."

Still, not all theorists embrace visual culture studies. Some worry that it forces art to take a back seat to ideology—that art becomes an

> The latest development on the theory front is the arrival of "visual culture studies."

allegorical staging ground for all sorts of social struggles. Rosalind Krauss, a professor at Columbia and an editor of *October*, whose work is highly theoretical, recently told *ArtNews*, "Students in art history graduate programs don't know how to read a work of art.... They're getting visual studies instead, a lot of paranoid scenarios about what happens under patriarchy or under imperialism." While it's worth noting that similar complaints were launched back in the 1970s against the Marxist T.J. Clark, what's not at all clear is whether such fears were well founded. UC-Irvine professor James D. Herbert emphasizes that many of his colleagues in the field of modern European art were trained by Clark, and says he has never met art historians better able to read paintings as works of art.

As debates over the value of visual culture studies suggest, theory in art history is not something that one can easily take a stand for or against. And contrary to stories sometimes told in the field, the theory craze is not the result of a simple struggle between crusty traditionalists and trendy radicals. Radicals tangle with each other as much as they grouse about the Hilton Kramers of the world. High-profile theory can, for instance, sometimes be at odds with multiculturalist objectives. Far Eastern art at Columbia is increasingly marginalized and underfunded because the Asianists are not doing "cutting-edge work." In other words, they aren't applying Derrida to eighteenth-century Chinese brush painting. All in all, the theory craze is a hodgepodge of approaches, some brilliant and some silly, that dramatize the field's uncertain relationship to the sociopolitical and cultural landscape, a point of anxiety since the 1960s.

WHAT'S NEXT

Though intellectual and economic changes are now affecting art history, some things remain pretty constant. For one, it is overwhelmingly a discipline of white women. Nearly eight times as many whites as people of color earned doctorates in the field in 1995; twenty years ago, whites outnumbered people of color nine to one. And according to the National Research Council, nearly twice as many women as men received art history doctorates in 1995. Even twenty years ago, women Ph.D.'s outnumbered men by more than 10 percent, and this despite the sexism of some scholars. UC-Santa Barbara professor Ann Bermingham recalls that when she was a graduate student at Harvard in the mid-1970s, a time when there were no women faculty in Harvard's art history department, one professor told her, "we almost never give fellowships to women. They don't pan out; they just get married."

Art history is just as well known for the sophistication and variety of people who study it. Whether in the academy or the museum, the art historian still tends to be something of an aesthete and a cosmopolitan. True to this reputation, graduate students in art history have quite diverse intellectual backgrounds. As undergraduates they have majored in literature, history, politics, sociology, and philosophy, among other disciplines. Many, though not all graduate students, have done some undergraduate work in the field. Some are frustrated artists, others lifelong museum-goers.

As in other fields, when art history students talk about the differences between their graduate and undergraduate experiences, they overwhelmingly cite the stress of competing for funding over any particular intellectual challenge. The less you have to worry about money, students say, the better your intellectual experience will be. Stanford, UCLA, and Harvard rank high on the generosity scale. Caveat emptor at Columbia or Princeton; though both fund many students, they do not guarantee funding for all students who receive it, which can create a high stress level for students who must worry whether their work has been good enough for their funding to be renewed.

Another major difference is the prevalence of personality politics. Undergraduates do not have to curry favor with faculty the way graduate students do. Perhaps because the study of valuable art is never wholly detached from the networking game of the art market, politicking in academia can count as much as intellectual issues. One first-year graduate student was flatly told to pick her courses with an eye to meeting the stars. "My adviser said, 'You have to make political alliances.'" One reason she had to worry about faculty members liking her was the simple fact that they were the ones who controlled the purse strings.

Students also agree that there's not a lot of hand-holding in art history departments at the graduate level. Professors expect you to pick up on an idea and run with it, with minimal guidance on their part. Other students are equally astonished that theory is treated as a subject in its own right. Though students do increasingly encounter theory as undergraduates, theory itself is rarely the centerpiece of a college

> Whether in the academy or the museum, the art historian still tends to be something of an aesthete and a cosmopolitan.

course. Those who didn't dabble in theory at all as undergraduates may find the switch from memorizing slides or doing source studies to deciphering the theories of Gilles Deleuze a tough adjustment.

Most art history programs require doctoral students to demonstrate reading knowledge of one European language, typically German or French, plus whatever additional language is needed for a specialty, such as Sanskrit or Chinese. Typically, coursework takes two to three years. Everyone has to take at least one course in non-Western art as well as a methods course, which is generally where students first seriously engage the theoretical debates of the field. After coursework, students at some programs take oral exams, while students at other programs write a master's thesis, and then take exams. After clearing these hurdles, students then start dissertating.

Art history is caught up in long-standing battles about questions of methodology and ideology. As a graduate student who will have to decide what to study and how to go about studying it, you will invariably find yourself negotiating the battle lines. Students stress that it is crucial to take a position in these battles without being consumed by them. "You have to figure out how your ideas fit into the broader discussion," offers a Columbia student. "And you have to know your own voice so you don't just get assimilated into a particular camp."

You do have some choice, however, about the nature of the methodological battles you can fight, as they play out differently from one department to another according to their scholarly predilections. NYU's Institute of Fine Arts, for instance, is the leading object-oriented graduate program, though it also follows in the tradition of Panofsky's broader interests. While social context is not ignored at the Institute, most people go there for a Ph.D., as did NYU graduate Margaret Oppenheimer, "in order to know whatever is going to help us to best understand the object." Yale has also been staunchly object oriented, though the recent hiring of some critical theorists hints that changes are in the making. Some onlookers worry that the art history department there will go the way of the comparative literature program, losing the work entirely in a sea of meaningless jargon. John Finlay, who studied Chinese art history at Yale in the early 1990s and is now an assistant curator at the Brooklyn Museum, recalls a course he took that had guest lec-

> Art history is caught up in long-standing battles about questions of methodology and ideology.

turers every week. One week some folks from the comparative literature department spoke and, Finlay says with glee, "they were hilarious! They sat with their *backs* to the slides, didn't turn around and look at them once. They just opened their mouths and all this intertextuality poured out."

Students with an appetite for intertextuality should investigate the department at Rochester, a pioneer in the field of visual culture studies. UC-Irvine, whose art history Ph.D. program is relatively new, is an up-and-coming spot for visual studies, and soon will actually offer a Ph.D. in that specialty. UC-Santa Cruz is moving in this direction, too.

Students who want to pursue critical theory but are also committed to exploring a range of approaches should check out Stanford, Northwestern University, the University of Texas at Austin, and UC-Santa Barbara. Chicago's department is friendly to interdisciplinary studies, and has a study group on visual culture that has sparked exchange between the art history and English departments. With many of UC-Berkeley's leading scholars retiring, it's unclear if the program will continue its emphasis on the social history of art. Columbia is another place to study the social history of art, as well as cutting-edge semiotics, and is often the scene of pitched battles between social historians and structuralists. No department is especially strong in Marxist theory right now; in fact, Marxism most often appears as a straw man for object-oriented scholars and postmodern theorists alike to demolish.

> Feminist approaches to art history are ever varying.

Feminist approaches to art history are ever varying. The 1996 College Art Association conference featured plenty of gender studies papers, but they couldn't have been more different. Some focused on the rediscovery of under-appreciated female artists, like Jo Hopper or Gwen John, while another focused on the Weimar Republic's censorship of erotic art. The University of California departments are receptive to feminist work and have strong feminist scholars—like UC-Santa Barbara's Abigail Solomon-Godeau. Northwestern is also notable in this regard. Some say that East Coast departments still tend to be more suspicious of feminist scholarship because it is not thought to be theoretically rigorous. In the broader consideration of gender issues, no single department is known for a queer studies approach, so students have to go where the individual queer theorists are: Norman Bryson is at Harvard, Richard Meyer is at USC, and Michael Camille is at Chicago.

Programs that favor object-oriented scholarship—especially NYU, Yale, and the terminal master's program at Williams College—have good track records placing students in curatorial jobs (and they are often at odds with theoretically oriented programs). The mutual contempt between NYU and Columbia is perhaps representative, but some see the tension as regional, too. Schools on the West Coast tend to be less engaged with the museum approach. Quips James D. Herbert of UC-Irvine, "We're a lot closer to Disneyland than to the Met."

> The gulf between museum people and theory-oriented academics may be widening.

As John Finlay's bemused comment about intertextuality suggests, the gulf between the museum people and theory-oriented academics may be widening. Museums are certainly informed by social history, multiculturalism, and gender studies, and many exhibits now reflect that. And although Finlay himself is no attribution geek—his dissertation is on the role of painting in the mid-eighteenth-century Imperial Palace's hierarchy, particularly its audience and its display—he feels, and many others agree, that theory, by moving art history further away from actual works of art, has made scholarship less useful and scholars less relevant to museums. This divide between the academy and the museum might be a problem for some students soon to be Ph.D.'s, for a number of reasons—not the least being that quite a few universities are trying to cut costs by hiring someone to hold a double appointment as professor and museum curator.

At universities that have a museum, animosity between the museum and the art history department can be fierce. But there are a handful of departments where the relationship between the theorists and the museum folks is a relatively happy and dynamic one. Harvard's Norman Bryson sees no conflict between his department and the museum. "Students here work very closely with the objects in the collection" at the Fogg Museum, he stresses. Under the helpful eye of Fogg curators, some of whom are museologists with strong theoretical leanings, students frequently help design and develop exhibits. But this peace between theory and the museum at Harvard has not come easily. The social history wars of the 1960s and 1970s were bitter; in 1986 Harvard's fine arts department, which had always been housed in the museum, divorced itself from the Fogg by moving into a new building. If anything, the subsequent theoretical and multicultural revolutions at Harvard seem to have provided the department and the museum with more common ground.

Whether you are an aspiring curator or a theoretician passionate about deconstruction, you still have to specialize in historical periods and geographic regions. Be on the lookout for a department with not one but at least two scholars teaching in your area of interest, since art history professors tend to change institutions frequently and unexpectedly. Joan Cummins, the graduate student mentioned at the beginning of this chapter, found herself in the lurch when her advisor—the one Columbia scholar working on Indian art—left. Also, try whenever possible to work with faculty who are full professors. Rebecca Furer, also mentioned earlier, discovered that since both of the classicists at Tufts are adjuncts, they don't offer many courses, even between them.

Given the field's ferment, categorizations about particular areas of study are difficult to make. Here are a few, but make sure to talk to graduate students and professors alike to get the latest skinny. Columbia is strong in modern art (1880 to the present), as are Northwestern, UC-Berkeley, Harvard, NYU, and UT-Austin, though it's important to note that Harvard, NYU, and Columbia are weak in American art. Yale and Stanford are strong in American art generally. With the exception of historically black colleges, and especially Howard University, very few departments have more than one African Americanist, despite the enormous amount of lip service given to the "diaspora" at CAA conferences. For eighteenth-, nineteenth-, and early twentieth-century studies, Stanford, Yale, the University of Pennsylvania, UC-Santa Barbara, and Michigan are good. Yale is a leader in the Renaissance, while Chicago has excellent, cutting-edge medievalists. Yale is strong in Japanese and Chinese art, and UCLA is generally strong in Asian studies. For Mesoamerican studies, check out UT-Austin. UC-Santa Barbara offers courses in Chinese, Islamic, pre-Columbian, and Chicano art. And Harvard, Bryson boasts, is "the least Eurocentric" program anywhere, "wonderful" for students who want to work on Islamic, Asian, and African art.

> Aspirings curators and theoreticians still have to specialize in historical periods and geographic regions.

Those who want to study ancient art should decide whether to put the emphasis on the ancient or on the art. If they are also interested in the art of later periods, an art history program is a good choice. But for students who want to pursue Latin and Greek languages, history, and literature as well as art, a classical studies program might be best. (See the Classics chapter.) Some programs, like Yale, have ancient art programs within both classical studies and art history. Among art history programs, some of the best places for classicists are Yale, Harvard, Columbia, Princeton, and NYU's Institute of Fine Arts. Elsewhere, UCLA's Donald Preziosi, and Northwestern's Whitney Davis, are both at the forefront of contemporary critical theory, and both specialize in ancient art.

> Many scholars see the field's burgeoning multiculturalism as a continuation of its traditions.

Period vogues are less relevant these days, now that nearly any content is acceptable. But certainly modernists are more popular than ever, as is the twentieth century in general. Photography is one of the hippest new areas. Weimar Germany also seems to be enjoying a chic moment, and the nineteenth century is still very much in vogue. If art history had a What's Out list, it might include ancient and classical art, as well as Baroque—none of which are nearly as popular among young scholars as they once were. But these areas, too, are still very much alive.

It's important to note that many scholars see the field's burgeoning multiculturalism as a continuation of—rather than a break with—its traditions. The study of European art always involved the study of many cultures, since culturally Europe has never been a unified entity. And for classicists, even Greece has always encompassed a vast array of artistic styles and cultural values. The same might be said of interdisciplinarity, which, as Bryson points out, has always been essential in Asian and classical studies; and few Renaissance art historians have ever managed to completely ignore the historical and philosophical context of works.

If you turn to the National Research Council rankings for an accounting of departmental strengths, keep in mind that they are a source of both information and misinformation. The NRC's top five—Columbia, NYU, UC-Berkeley, Harvard, and Yale—do have a lot to offer, but not necessarily any more than many departments with a lower ranking, or no ranking at all. Says UC-Irvine's James Herbert, himself a Yale Ph.D., the NRC rankings are most sensitive to departmental resources. Highly ranked programs have money and libraries, yet, as Herbert emphasizes, art history isn't physics. "In a physics department it really matters if you have a linear accelerator in your yard. Art history is not so capital-intensive. What's most important in our field is faculty, who's teaching where." Although Columbia and NYU top the NRC list, Richard Shiff of UT-Austin mentioned them immediately when asked what programs he steers aspiring students away from. Why? "They'll get lost in the crowd." Students are often better served by smaller departments.

Remember, though, that while art history is not as capital-intensive as physics, resources are nothing to sneeze at. Even if you are not crazy about visual culture studies, you could learn a thing or two while playing around in Columbia's two-year-old Media Center for Art History, which uses computer-animated video to make art stills come alive. If you went to Harvard, you wouldn't read all 237,820 volumes in its art history library, but you'd certainly enjoy your guaranteed funding and your grant for overseas research.

Another reason the NRC rankings are particularly ill-suited to evaluating art history programs is that the NRC measures quality according to traditional ideas of scholarship, so departments that are challenging long-standing ideas about art and art history aren't likely to earn high marks. UC-Irvine and Rochester will never inch up the NRC scale, opines Herbert, "because they aren't art history programs in the traditional sense." The data is also skewed by professors' tendency to rank their own alma maters highly, as well as departments that used to be good. Princeton, for example, gets consistently high marks simply because it always has, even though, as Herbert points out, "the people who made it great simply aren't there anymore."

THE JOB MARKET

Undertake graduate study in art history only if you are going to love being a student. The consensus is that the academic job situation is bad, and not getting much better. If you go into art history with an academic job as the only acceptable outcome, you face a very daunting market. Stanford's Wanda Corn reports that a recent search for a film scholar with joint appointments in art history and comparative literature yielded over two hundred applications, and that junior faculty openings in art history routinely attract between eighty and ninety job seekers. And remember, not all applicants are freshly-minted Ph.D.'s: Many earned their degrees several years ago and are still searching for full-time work. Professors on hiring committees say they are staggered at the numbers, the high quality, and often the irrelevance, of job applications. People are so desperate they will apply for a position that isn't remotely in their area. Renaissance scholars are trying to convince search committees that they can teach Douglas Sirk films.

Job seekers with Ph.D.'s from even the most dazzling visual culture programs have an especially hard time finding teaching jobs in art history at colleges or research universities. For one, there are only a handful of jobs each year that are strictly interdisciplinary. Also, in the competition for art history jobs that are not interdisciplinary, visual culture Ph.D.'s tend to lose out to Ph.D.'s from more traditional departments. Despite the rise of theory in art history over the past several decades, many art history departments are still object-oriented, and thus hire young scholars who can teach survey courses. This preference places visual culture Ph.D.'s —with neither experience teaching survey courses nor strong undergraduate backgrounds in traditional art history—at a distinct disadvantage.

The best way to improve your chances of landing an academic job, whether you do visual culture studies or not, is to be as versatile as possible—within reason. Says UT-Austin's Richard Shiff, "When we have searches we are never impressed by overly specialized people. No matter how good they are." In the current environment, too, as Herbert points out (and others agree), "you will not get an academic job if you can't engage theory on some level." It is also more important than ever to be a good teacher; universities can't afford scholars who just churn out articles. Stanford is one place that prepares students particularly well for teaching; it offers teaching assistants extensive training and pedagogical support.

Pursue graduate study in art history only if you will love being a student.

The museum job market is only slightly better than the academic one. It used to be common for museum curators to have only an M.A. Today, however, to get a curatorial position without a Ph.D. you need a rare combination of luck and relevant experience. It does happen, though—John Finlay landed a curatorial job at the Brooklyn Museum through a well-connected advisor. Students who are currently planning to earn a master's degree to prepare for museum jobs are not totally pessimistic, though they fully realize they may have to return to school for their Ph.D.'s.

And even Ph.D.'s can have a tough time finding curatorial work. Consider the experience of Margaret Oppenheimer, a recent Ph.D.

from NYU's Institute of Fine Arts. Eleven years ago, after she got her B.A. with a double major in art history and literature, Oppenheimer was hired as an intern at the Cedar Rapids Museum of Art, and was soon promoted to assistant curator. Now, an M.A., a Ph.D., and years of museum work wiser, she is having trouble netting a full-time curatorial job. Though she doesn't for a minute regret acquiring such an education, she rightly sees her situation as a dramatic indication of a tight market.

A burgeoning field within museums is museum education. Curators prepare the exhibit while museum educators work to make it accessible to the public, often writing the label copy and even planning special programs for younger museum-goers. The consensus is that only an M.A. is needed for a museum education job, and the CAA job listings bear that out. Rebecca Furer's master's degree may well land her such a job. Grady Turner, a recent Columbia M.A., is a new hybrid, a "curator for education" at the New-York Historical Society. Interestingly, too, museum education people are far more powerful than they used to be; they are more involved in creating exhibits because museums are increasingly interested in reaching wider audiences.

> A burgeoning field within museum studies is museum education.

For academic jobs the M.A. is basically useless, unless you are planning to pursue graduate education in some other field. If you want to get a Ph.D. in American studies with an emphasis on art, for instance, it's not a bad idea to earn an M.A. in art history first. At places like Columbia, where students aren't encouraged to go into museum work, the master's program is basically a money maker for the university since candidates usually pay their own tuition. Funding for M.A. candidates is scarce, and faculty are equally scant. Many Ph.D. programs don't even offer a terminal master's degree.

Increasingly, both M.A.'s and Ph.D.'s are being creative about their career paths, given the eye-of-the-needle nature of both academic and museum jobs. Some M.A.'s go on to study library science and become art librarians. Oppenheimer free-lances. She has done exhibition catalogue research and writing for the Wichita Art Museum, written text for an art calendar, and contributed articles to art publications, including *Metropolitan Museum Journal* and *The Gazette des Beaux-Arts*. She does not recommend this regime as a way to make a living, however, as the work flow is quite sporadic; with a dismal job market, "there are people who will do the work for free, to get experience. I could get more if I'd lower my rates. But I've paid my dues." Oppenheimer has been resourceful enough to get additional work as a medical writer, which pays better and is far steadier.

Gallery and auction house jobs are another option for those with contemporary interests and a sales bent. So are editorial jobs, with publishers of art books, for instance. Some graduates have made documentary films or TV programs about art. The Internet is creating opportunities as well; some art historians are digitizing slide libraries and producing art history CD-ROMs.

RESOURCES

NRC TOP TEN
Columbia
NYU
UC-Berkeley
Harvard
Yale
Princeton
Johns Hopkins
Northwestern
Penn
Chicago

ASSOCIATIONS
College Art Association
(212) 691-1051

Association for Art History
(812) 855-5193

JOURNALS
Art Journal
Art History
ArtNews
Critical Inquiry
October

CONSTELLATIONS

OBJECT-ORIENTED
NYU
Williams College
Yale

VISUAL CULTURE STUDIES
Harvard
Rochester
UC-Irvine
UC-Santa Cruz

TRADITIONAL WITH INTERDISCIPLINARY LEANINGS
Harvard
Northwestern
Stanford
UC-Santa Barbara
UT-Austin

SOCIAL ART HISTORY
Columbia
UC-Berkeley

MODERN ART
Columbia
Harvard
NYU
Northwestern
UC-Berkeley
UT-Austin

AMERICAN ART
Stanford
Yale

EIGHTEENTH, NINETEENTH, AND EARLY TWENTIETH-CENTURY STUDIES
Michigan
Penn
Stanford
Yale

RENAISSANCE ART
Yale

MEDIEVAL ART
Chicago

ASIAN ART
Harvard
Yale
UCLA

ISLAMIC ART
Harvard

WEB ADDRESSES
World Wide Web Virtual Library: Art History
http://www.hart.bbk.ac.uk/VirtualLibrary.html

Art History Resources on the Web
http://witcombe.bcpw.sbc.edu/ARTHLinks.html

CHAPTER 6

CLASSICS

Scott Perry, a graduate student in ancient history at the University of North Carolina at Chapel Hill, studies what he calls "associational behavior in the Roman Empire," especially as it relates to Roman *collegia funeraticia*, or funeral clubs, organizations that lower-class Romans and freed slaves formed in order to buy tombs and pay the cost of funerals. Perry is interested, he says, "in those *collegia* categorized as 'professional' that nonetheless provide this (seemingly) 'religious' service." As he sees it, the long-standing tradition in classics scholarship of studying professional, religious, domestic, and social collegia separately does not accord with their actual functioning in the ancient world, and stems from seeing the ancients through twentieth-century eyes "colored, to a disturbing extent, by the development of trade unionism in the West over the past century."

Perry wants to determine what kinds of concerns brought working-class Romans together, an interest that makes him one of a growing number of classical historians who are turning away from the kings, queens, generals, and traitors to investigate the life of those Greeks and Romans who just worked for a living. "There's a whole hive of activity just under all the battles and consular elections. It's just common sense. People should be the historian's concern, and there are always a lot more people on the bottom than on the top." Perry hopes that his scholarship can contribute "a fuller picture of the lives of the poor and the friendless in the ancient world, people who were so afraid of dying and being forgotten that they insured their funerals in preparation. The way a culture approaches the end of life must surely inform the way its people live."

WHY CLASSICS?

The study of classics has long been seen as the pinnacle of a liberal education, at the heart of the humanities, since literature, history, philosophy, anthropology, theology, politics, mathematics, geography, biology, and law tend to begin the story of their development in the classical word. Winston Churchill believed that all students should be taught English, "and then," he said, "I would let the clever ones learn Latin as an honor and Greek as a treat." Churchill is not alone. Homer is back on the best-seller list, thanks to Robert Fagles's new translation. High school Latin enrollments are on the rise. And some classics departments are reorganizing toward classical studies—forging interdisciplinary links with departments of Near Eastern studies, history, philosophy, and English.

The centrality and flexibility of classics make it a natural hub for intellectual developments that affect all the academy. Many of the key intellectual movements of the nineteenth and twentieth centuries have strong roots in classical studies. Marx began his career with a doctoral dissertation on Democritus's influence on Epicurus, which helped him to evolve the theory of dialectical materialism. Freud not only drew on Sophocles for his identification of the Oedipal complex, but took inspiration from Aristotle's theory of catharsis. Ferdinand de Saussure, the father of semiotics, studied under Georg Curtius, whose work had laid the groundwork for the modern study of Greek etymology.

But if classics has often been a hub of the university and its intellectual developments, it is also a markedly diverse field. There is only one defining interest among classical scholars—Greco-Roman antiquity—but because classical antiquity is so vast and varied in both time and space, the specific interests of individual classicists can be quite remote from each other. While other disciplines are only now trumpeting their interdisciplinary excursions, classics has always included the study of literature, history, philosophy, art, and archaeology. The main fields of classics as it is defined today—literature, history, and archaeology—do not coexist within a single department in any other discipline. (Imagine a Spanish department expecting an archeological dig at La Mancha to revolutionize the study of *Don Quixote*.) And the subfields of classics each feel a pull toward extra-departmental companions: archaeology toward the social and laboratory sciences, literary studies towards contemporary critical methods. Classics is also an inherently international field, practiced in very different ways in the United States, France, and Italy.

One notable attempt to describe how classics developed, Rudolf Pfeiffer's *History of Classical Scholarship* (1968), takes two volumes and five hundred pages just to get up to 1850. Nonetheless, spotlighting the animating ideals of the founding of classical studies and the enormous changes of the last twenty-five years will provide you with a foundation for understanding what departments are doing today.

HOW CLASSICS HAS TAKEN SHAPE

In the third to first centuries B.C.E., Greek scholars at Alexandria were already analyzing Homer as we do, as an ancient classic, but it was not really until the Renaissance that the study of Greek and Roman literature began to take on the character it has today. The scholar-poets who led the Renaissance revival of literary scholarship, such as Petrarch (1304–1374) and Boccaccio (1313–1375), were fascinated by Rome as the symbol of a recoverable past that offered models and lessons for their own times. Later scholars like Erasmus (1469–1536) then took up ancient Greek, which had been all but forgotten except by Byzantine librarians and Arab philosophers and scientists. The most important task became the collection and copying of whatever literature had survived from antiquity. Although a few exceptional figures did more, the study of classical texts did not go much beyond raiding the literature for great ideas and stories, using classical texts as exercises in rhetoric and logic, and appreciating and imitating the style of the ancients.

The sun around which modern classics revolves is philology, the rigorous study of all aspects of a text, a practice that separates academic classical research from the everyday study of canonical texts for their own sake. The foundations of philology were laid in Germany in the eighteenth and nineteenth centuries by students and teachers such as Friedrich August Wolf, whose *Prolegomena to Homer* (1795) marked the first scientific analysis of the history of a text. Like an archaeologist, Wolf stripped away the layers of evidence and sifted out what we could know about the transmission, oral and written, of the *Iliad* and the *Odyssey*.

Following Wolf's lead, German scholars developed what they called "the science of antiquity," *Altertumswissenschaft*. The uncontested father of this new field was Ulrich von Wilamowitz-Moellendorff, whose *History of Classical Scholarship* (1921) boldly defined its mission as the study of "Greco-Roman civilization in its essence and in every facet of its existence." The breadth and depth of the research conducted by this generation of classicists is represented by such monumental publications as Theodor Mommsen's *Corpus Inscriptionum Latinarum* and the journal *Rheinisches Museum für Altertumswissenschaft*, the latter still active today. And other projects embarked upon during this period are still in progress. The comprehensive Latin dictionary, the *Thesaurus Linguae Latinae*, is completed only up to the letter "P"—and this after a century of work.

The effects of the ideal of *Altertumswissenschaft* on American education cannot be overestimated. For one thing, universities like Göttingen attracted many American students who then brought the science of antiquity back to these shores. Among them was the statesman and Harvard University Greek scholar Edward Everett—best known for speaking at Gettysburg right before Lincoln's famous address—and Basil Lanneau Gildersleeve, who received his Ph.D. from Göttingen in 1853. Of Gildersleeve's many contributions to American academic life, he is most often remembered as a founder of Johns Hopkins University, the first graduate research university in the United States based on the German model, and as the creator and first editor of the *American Journal of Philology* in 1880, still one of the field's most prestigious journals.

> Whatever one's philological subspecialty, the watchword is evidence.

Besides advances in the study of textual, historical, linguistic, and archaeological evidence, during this time classics was refined by its division into subfields: numismatics, the study of coins; epigraphy, the study of inscriptions; paleography, the interpretation of ancient (mostly medieval) manuscripts; and papyrology, the study of texts on papyrus.

But whatever the subspecialty in the German philological tradition, the watchword was—and continues to be—evidence. Old-school philologists conceive of what they do as an objective, forensic science rather than as interpretive work. A poem, viewed this way, is not an aesthetic object any more than is a pot shard—both are merely pieces of a puzzle to be fitted into their historical context. But because poems are poems as well as grist for the evidence mill, the study of classical literature and art has never fully toed a rigid philological line. The poet speaks to his contemporaries and for his times, but poems are also written to speak beyond the contexts in which they are created. At some point every kind of researcher must focus on interpretation. Rarely, however, are interpretive questions raised without a struggle.

> The philological tradition has always battled with the field's interpretive and hermeneutic impulses.

The philological tradition has always battled the interpretive-hermeneutic impulse. In 1872, for example, Wilamowitz-Moellendorff, then aged twenty-four, and a young professor of philology at the University of Basel named Friedrich Nietzsche, aged twenty-eight, clashed over *The Birth of Tragedy*. Wilamowitz-Moellendorff savaged Nietzsche's first book for what he asserted was a lack of scholarship and a zest for intuition—in short, too little philology, too much hermeneutics. Although history has made its judgment, at the time, the pamphlet in which Wilamowitz-Moellendorff launched his critique, *Zukunftsphilologie!*, sold out and even turned its author a profit while *The Birth of Tragedy* languished on the shelves. Disgusted with his colleagues, Nietzsche left his chair at Basel in 1879.

While different factions among classicists warred with one another in Europe, scholars such as Gildersleeve and William Watson Goodwin, a prominent professor of Greek at Harvard, had been establishing an alternative philological tradition in the United States, with its own theories of grammar, definition, and customs for the use of textual examples.

There were, however, always international exchanges about both the methods and the heritage of antiquity—one of the most notable took place after the influx of German immigrants fleeing Nazism, such as Werner Wilhelm Jaeger. Jaeger had held Nietzsche's chair at Basel, then succeeded Wilamowitz-Moellendorff at Berlin before he came to the United States in 1937, where he taught at the University of California at Berkeley, the University of Chicago, and Harvard. He is principally remembered now for *Paideia*, a three-volume history of the shaping of the Greek character and of Greek culture as a model for the European character.

Though *Paideia* was a manifesto for classical humanism as Europeans understood it, Jaeger's work was given wide dissemination in the United States in an English translation by Gilbert Highet, a Glasgow native who himself became the most popular classicist in the country— host of a national radio show, a literary editor of *Harper's* magazine and a Book-of-the-Month Club judge. Highet's popular and accessible journalism about classical literature and his charismatic teaching style at Columbia University had their peak of influence in the 1940s and 1950s. He was the last "celebrity" classicist, although classicists have not vanished from the public eye—consider Garry Wills, the political commentator and classics Ph.D.

But the back-and-forth between philology and hermeneutics continues. A few influential classicists still dismiss anything that smells of "theory" in the belief that it violates the evidentiary rigors of *Altertumswissenschaft*. An editorial statement in the *American Journal of Philology* in 1987 that seemed to spurn anything but the most orthodox application of philology raised an alarmist debate that culminated in a volume with the dour title *Classics: A Discipline and Profession in Crisis?* (1989). But these days much of the dust has settled, and most scholars agree that self-scrutiny within the field in the last decade has benefited all of its factions.

Even so, the field has lately been transformed by the same intellectual currents active elsewhere in the humanities and social sciences. Though classicists themselves joke that they are proverbially ten years behind the theoretical developments in other fields, Nietzsche's intellectual offspring, poststructuralists and otherwise, have made some headway. The journal *Arethusa*, for instance, edited by John Peradotto of SUNY Buffalo, has brought many contemporary theoretical debates into classics. (*Arethusa* is published by John Hopkins University Press, right alongside Gildersleeve's brainchild, the *American Journal of Philology*.) Gildersleeve's department at Johns Hopkins, after some hard times, now includes Marcel Détienne, author of *The Gardens of Adonis: Spices in Greek Mythology* (1977), who, along with Jean-Pierre Vernant and Pierre Vidal-Naquet, co-authors of *Myth and Tragedy in Ancient Greece* (1988), has done provocative research about Greek culture in the Lévi-Straussian, anthropological vein.

Although a few scholars go out of their way to resist such changes, "new" methodologies can claim to be nourishing a tradition of their own. In 1942, twenty years before Julia Kristeva's influential use of the term "intertextuality," Giorgio Pasquali identified an ancient poetics that he termed "*arte allusiva*," or "the art of allusion." Since then, classicists have come to understand how the Greeks and Romans often wove their poems in complex webs of citation and imitation. And while deconstructionists have alienated the term "text" from its traditional meaning, there is still the need for a theoretical framework useful for understanding the poetry of cultures that existed before the idea of a text did. There has been lively scholarship as well into the differences between the intertextualities of literate poets like Vergil (see Joseph Farrell, *Vergil's Georgics and the Traditions of Ancient Epic: The Art of Allusion in Literary History*) and of illiterate ones like Homer (See Cornell University professor Pietro Pucci's *Odysseus Polytropos: Intertextual Readings of the Odyssey and the Iliad*). Among those who introduced narratology into classics are K.W. Gransden (*Vergil's Iliad: An Essay on Epic Narrative*), J.K. Newman (who performed a Bahktinian reading in *Pindar's Art: Its Traditions and Aims*) and John Winkler (*Auctor and Actor: A Narratological Reading of Apuleius's "The Golden Ass"*). Such an approach has proliferated on more mainstream authors like Homer (John Peradotto, *Man in the Middle Voice: Name and Narration in the Odyssey*) and Ovid (A.M. Keith, *The Play of Fictions: Studies in Ovid's Metamorphoses Book 2*).

> Despite Freud's debts to classical literature, psychoanalytic theory was until recently peripheral to classics.

Despite the importance of classical literature to Freud, psychoanalytic theory has never been "in" in classics, although *When the Lamp is Shattered: Desire and Narrative in Catullus* by Duke University's Micaela Janan, who relies on Lacanian theory, has been well received. A number of recent books, for example *The Interpretation of Roman Poetry: Empiricism or Hermeneutics?* edited by Karl Galinsky of the University of Texas at Austin, and *History as Text: The Writing of Ancient History*, edited by Averil Cameron of Keble College, Oxford, gathers some of the better articles employing the latest approaches to Latin literature and Roman studies.

As in the disciplines of literature and history, the exploration of the margins of geography, society, and literature is becoming increasingly popular. In *Excursions in Epichoric History: Aiginetan Essays*, Thomas Figueira of Rutgers University rewrites an important period of Greek history from the viewpoint not of Athens but of the nearby island Aigina. In the wake of *Power and Persuasion in Late Antiquity* (1992), by Peter Brown of Princeton University, late antiquity has received a great deal of attention from scholars like Alan Cameron of Columbia and James O'Donnell of the University of Pennsylvania. The Greek novel, long a poor cousin of its poetic counterparts, is seeing a renaissance as well, thanks largely to the work of James Tatum of Dartmouth College. Interest in the novel goes hand in hand with interest in the Greek east, since novels like *Heliodorus'í Aithiopika* (Ethiopian Tales) are set in Africa and the Near East. The plot of *John of Damascus's Barlaam and Ioasaph* has roots in nothing less than the story of the Buddha. Conversely, the standard Asian depictions of Buddha were influenced by the sculpture of Greeks dwelling in Bactria (straddling modern Afghanistan, Uzbekistan, and Tadjikistan) after the conquests of Alexander the Great.

The past twenty-five years have also seen antiquity's previously ignored members—slaves, blacks, and women—receive serious scholarly attention. As early as 1970, Howard University professor Frank M. Snowden's much-praised *Blacks in Antiquity: Ethiopians in the Greco-Roman Experience* opened the door for scholarship on race in the ancient world. It has since been followed up by his *Before Color Prejudice: The Ancient View of Blacks*, and Lloyd A. Thompson's *Romans and Blacks*. And Keith Bradley of the University of Victoria has written several critical studies of ancient slavery, most recently *Slavery and Society at Rome*. The controversy most visible to those outside classics in the last ten years has been over Cornell government professor Martin Bernal's *Black Athena* (1987), which contends that the Egyptians and other Semitic peoples exerted a greater influence over Greece than has been generally believed—even that the Pharaoh Sesostris occupied the Greek mainland in the second millennium B.C.E. Bernal argues that the racism, overt and covert, of European scholars during the last two hundred years has worked to erase Semitic and African military and cultural achievements from the historical record.

Though the assertions in *Black Athena* potentially support the existing multicultural research of many classicists, Bernal's scholarship has been roundly criticized, most recently in *Black Athena Revisited*, a collection of academic essays edited by Mary Lefkowitz and Guy MacLean Rogers of Wellesley College. (Bernal's field is Chinese history, and the consensus is that he is not a reliable classical philologist.) Lefkowitz has taken it upon herself, in *Not Out of Africa* (1996), to correct blatant historical inaccuracies put forward by a number of Afrocentrist scholars in the wake of Bernal—for example, that Aristotle stole ideas from the Egyptian library of Alexandria, which Lefkowitz points out was not built until after he died.

As for the role of women in the ancient world, classicists have recently corrected exclusions and the occasional misogyny of the field. Wilamowitz-Moellendorff once wrote, "It is no small sign of the dignity of Attic history that only one woman is found in it." (The woman he meant was the goddess Athena.) In 1973, a special issue of *Arethusa* on women in antiquity eventually sold two thousand copies—over four times as many as were first printed—and Sarah Pomeroy's milestone book, *Goddesses, Whores, Wives, and Slaves* (1975), remains popular today. *Sowing the Body: Psychoanalysis and Ancient Representations of Women*, by Page du Bois of the University of California at San Diego, goes beyond psychoanalytic and Marxist theory to explore Greek constructions of female gender. Courses on women in antiquity are now common at many universities, and virtually all those professors who laid the groundwork for current research into women in antiquity are still teaching and writing: Sarah Pomeroy of CUNY Graduate Center (in women's history and ancient history), Marilyn A. Katz of Wesleyan University, Mary Lefkowitz of Wellesley, Amy Richlin of the University of Southern California, Helene Foley of Columbia, Judith Hallett of the University of Maryland at College Park, and Marilyn Skinner of the University of Arizona, the current editor of *Transactions of the American Philological Association*. One of the most useful recent overviews of scholarship on women and gender in antiquity was just published by Barbara McManus of the College of New Rochelle: *Classics & Feminism: Gendering the Classics*. *Feminist Theory and the Classics*, edited by Nancy Sorkin Rabinowitz of Hamilton College and Amy Richlin, is an excellent companion volume.

> The most serious resistance to issues of sexuality and gender originates not from within classics but from outside it.

The most serious resistance to discussions of sexuality and gender issues is not from inside classics but from the outside. U.S. scholars working on gender and sexuality are often apathetic about the distant past. Amy Richlin, professor of classics and gender studies at USC, notes that at the Berkshire Conference on Women's History, the largest gathering of U.S. feminist historians, "Over 80 percent of the panels were nineteenth century or later and had to do with the United States or England. People doing classics have a real problem with so much attention given to only the present and English-speaking countries." Nevertheless, Richlin, like others, finds connections between past and present, as evidenced by her recent article for a legal journal, "Roman Oratory, Pornography, and the Silencing of Anita Hill." What's more, as scholarship has taken an even broader approach to gender and sexuality since the 1970s, classicists have been ahead of theorists in other fields. Michel Foucault's three volume *The History of Sexuality* (1978–86) could not have been written without *Greek Homosexuality* (1978), a pioneering work by British classicist K.J. Dover.

> Classicists quickly computerized most of their canon and were among the first scholars to begin Web projects.

Women's activism has done much to battle a variety of scholarly and professional inequities. In 1973, when women made up almost 25 percent of all practicing classicists, they presented less than 7 percent of the papers at the American Philological Association (APA) annual meeting. The Women's Classical Caucus, founded in 1972, insisted that the APA program committee try reviewing all submissions anonymously. By 1975, the number of papers presented by women had almost tripled, and the experiment became practice. Anonymous refereeing is now the norm in journals as well, a practice which has benefited not only women but also scholars at non-elite institutions and graduate students. From the election of three female APA presidents in five years to the protocol established for interviewing freshly-minted Ph.D.'s for their first jobs, prejudices of every kind have been brought to light and procedures put in place to correct them.

Despite what you might expect, classicists were among the first in the humanities to get into computers. 1972 saw the creation of the *Thesaurus Linguae Graecae* (http://www.tlg.uci.edu/~tlg/), a computerized version of all Greek literature directed by Theodore Brunner at the University of California at Irvine. (All addresses given hereafter assume the preface http://.) The Packard Humanities Institute has a similar project for Latin. The Data Bank of Documentary Papyri is produced at Duke (odyssey.lib.duke.edu/papyrus/texts/DDBDP.html). Cornell houses the epigraphical equivalent (132.236.125.30/). Dee Clayman at CUNY Graduate Center directs The Database of Classical Bibliography (web.gc.cuny.edu/dept/CLASS/dcb.htm), a CD-ROM version of the standard annual bibliography, *L'Année Philologique*.

Professional classicists probably know the *Thesaurus Linguae Graecae* best, but *Perseus*, a multimedia reference of classical texts, maps, and photos, directed by Gregory Crane (now moving from Tufts University to the University of Notre Dame), has the broadest appeal. The Perseus Web site (www.perseus.tufts.edu) is used by 2,500 people each day, and was designed to lure non-classicists into classics before, during, and after college. Says Crane, "The technology allows you to break out of the possibilities of academic publishing. Instead of selling five hundred to one thousand copies of a book, you get to everyone on the Web. You have to pull back and ask, 'What are the issues I'm addressing?' 'Why should the non-specialist care about what I do?' Students need to be thinking about this in grad school."

Elite institutions have been slow to accept computers as an integral part of research, but James O'Donnell of Penn, currently the editor of the on-line version of *Bryn Mawr Classical Review,* is one of the most visible advocates for the use of computers in classics. Penn professor Joseph Farrell's Vergil Homepage (ccat.sas.upenn.edu/~joef/vergil/home.html) invites use and contributions from high school students as well as university scholars.

The best way to judge the overall tone and direction of classics is to browse through the journals. An obvious starting place is *Transactions of the American Philological Association (*TAPA*)*, the annual publication of the APA. Each volume of TAPA publishes a dozen or so articles as well as the presidential address from the previous year's annual APA meeting. Although TAPA tries to be broad, you can easily detect a bias towards Greek. In the 1991 volume, for example, fifteen out of nineteen articles were on Greek authors. Besides TAPA, some of the more prominent journals in the United States are *Classical Philology,* edited by Elizabeth Asmis of Chicago, and *American Journal of Philology,* edited by Philip Stadter of UNC-Chapel Hill. An interesting feature of *AJP* is its editorial column "Brief Mentions," a rarity for academic journals, which includes short book reviews, comments on recent academic trends, and biographical notes about authors.

In the wake of the soul-searching of the 1980s, many classicists have penned personal accounts of the state of the discipline.

Some of the best journals of broad interest from Britain are *Journal of Roman Studies, Journal of Hellenic Studies, Classical Journal,* and *Greece & Rome.* A number of other European journals are equally important: from France, *Revues des Études Anciennes (*REA*)*, *Revues des Études Grecques (*REG*)*, and *Revues des Études Latines (*REL*)*; Italy, *Rivista di Filologia e di Istruzione Classica,* and *Studi Italiani di Filologia*

Classica; Germany, *Rheinisches Museum für Philologie, Historia, Mnemosyne,* and *Zeitschrift für Papyrologie und Epigraphik,* to name a few. In archaeology, there is the *American Journal of Archeology, Jahrbuch des deutschen archaeologischen Instituts,* and *Journal of Roman Archeology.*

In the wake of the soul-searching of the late 1980s, a growing number of classicists have penned fairly personal accounts of the state of the discipline. In September 1995, the journal *Classical World* published an essay by John Heath of Santa Clara University, "Self-Promotion and the 'Crisis' in Classics," along with responses to it. Heath argues that the real crisis of the field is that funding flows overwhelmingly to the star scholars of classics and to elite research institutions at the expense of smaller, poorer teaching colleges. Issues of social class, sexuality, national identity, and alcoholism in the profession were explored in *Compromising Traditions: The Personal Voice in Classical Scholarship,* edited by Judith P. Hallett of Maryland–College Park and Thomas Van Nortwick of Oberlin College. And Bernard Knox's books, *Backing Into the Future* (1994) and *The Oldest Dead White European Males* (1993), take a long and informal view of what classical studies has meant for the general reader, often placing recent works, such as Derek Walcott's epic poem *Omeros* (1990), within the classical tradition. These writings offer insights into some issues you'll encounter if, like most classicists, you teach courses for non-classics majors.

WHAT'S NEXT

Si haec legere non potes: (If you can't read this. . . .) Just about all classics programs presuppose that entering graduate students have studied Latin and Greek for two years, though it is becoming increasingly rare for students to have this background. Two well-established programs offer crash courses in Latin and Greek to prepare students who came late to the languages. The Latin/Greek Institute at CUNY Graduate Center compresses four to six semesters of either language into ten intensive weeks over the summer. In addition to the basic programs, in 1998 they will offer seven-week upper-level programs for more advanced students who still need experience in reading. Penn offers a postbaccalaureate program at a more relaxed pace: For two semesters students take reading courses in Greek and Latin as well as auditing graduate or undergraduate courses according to their needs and interests. UCLA has recently begun a similar program.

If you want to hone your skills by earning an M.A. before applying to a Ph.D. program, some of the best programs that offer a terminal M.A. (meaning that you must go elsewhere to earn a Ph.D.) are: the University of Arizona, Boston College, Florida State University, the University of Florida, the University of Georgia, the University of Kansas, Kent State University, the University of Kentucky, Maryland-College Park, University of Nebraska, University of Oregon, San Francisco State University, Texas Technical University, Tulane University, the University of Vermont, Washington University in St. Louis, and Wayne State University.

All classics programs require translation exams not only in Greek and Latin, but also in French and German (sometimes Italian can be substituted). This is not just a formality: no classics dissertation can be done using only articles written in English. Much of the scholarship you'll need to consult was done in Europe and never translated. You are also expected to master subfields that your research touches upon, and this often requires flexible language skills. For instance, if you are working on a text, you may still have to work with artifacts such as epigraphs or papyri, and if monuments are your focus, you may need to conduct research on the relevant historical and literary sources. Even the most pious acolyte of theory has to concede that even Derrida, in *Dissemination* (1972, trans. 1981), relies not only on sources in the anthropology of ancient Greece, but artifacts pertaining to Roman law as well (texts, coins, inscriptions, excavations). Think of classics as multimedia.

> Much of the scholarship you'll need for your research was written in European languages and never translated.

If budding classicists have the time and resources, one option is to improve their modern and ancient language skills by studying in secondary schools or other institutions abroad. (The American Academy in Rome or Athens, the Universities of Heidelberg and Tübingen, and Oxford University are popular places for doing so.) Most students, however, pick up courses designed to give them a "reading knowledge" of modern languages wherever they can.

Siquidem haec legere potes: The National Research Council rankings produced a top ten that is a mix of Ivies and traditional state school powerhouses: Harvard, UC-Berkeley, University of Michigan, Princeton, Yale University, Brown University, Chicago, UT-Austin, UCLA, and Columbia. Of course, this comes as no particular surprise. Classics is a discipline with an elite image, so it makes some sense that the most visible departments are at universities with high general prestige. Keep in mind, however, that because a small number of top programs produce the scholars who land jobs at all kinds of institutions, many of the best teach at non-elite schools. The difference for students between a "top" and a "second tier" school may not be as extreme as the rankings make it seem.

More generally, the NRC data is not especially reliable. Even before the NRC report was published in 1995, the APA raised the concern that the NRC data was incorrect for 80 percent of the schools listed in the rankings, and that over a dozen schools weren't taken into consideration at all. A much better source of information is the APA *Guide to Graduate Programs in the Classics in the United States and Canada* (available from the APA for $15). For each of about seventy M.A. and Ph.D. granting institutions, the guide lists the admissions requirements (GRE score, undergraduate grades), number of students, number of degrees granted, amount and type of financial aid, and faculty and their interests, as well as curricular strengths and "special opportunities"—information that the departments have supplied at the APA's request. There is also a faculty index that shows where particular scholars teach.

> Look for programs with outstanding research facilities, which means a well-provided library and often a museum.

Harvard and Yale top the rankings because of their outstanding research facilities, which in classics means a well-provided library and often a museum. Good research libraries are essential because classical texts are either out of print or out of the price range of the average graduate student. Schools almost always cooperate to grant library privileges to all students within a region. Museums are another matter. If you are going into archaeology, or just think you will want hands-on experience with artifacts, look for a school with its own museum or collection—think not just of Harvard or Yale, but Michigan's Kelsey Museum, or schools located near a famous collection like New York's Metropolitan Museum of Art. (Museums and collections are listed in the APA *Guide* under "special opportunities.")

But beyond these general criteria, bear in mind that picking a graduate program in classics is a decidedly personal affair. Even though the same basic training in philology, the same essential texts, and the same training in the use of evidence are stressed in all departments, individual classicists take any of a number of approaches to study an extraordinary variety of topics. Rather than having different methodological or ideological foci, the difference between programs is rather in the number and quality of faculty and the particular mix of interests they bring to their scholarship. Most reading lists are the same, but if you're interested in Plato, look for a Platonist on the faculty. Any classicist can teach the *Symposium*, but you want someone who studies it.

> Any classicist can teach the *Symposium*, but you may want to study it with a specialist in Plato.

Traditional departments like Harvard's stress the constants in classical studies: philological skills and knowledge of the basic texts. Believing that the field ain't broke, they haven't tried to fix anything, and concentrate on the "vertical" breadth of literature, history, archaeology, philosophy—a veritable soup to nuts in the Greco-Roman sphere. More innovative departments like Chicago stress interdisciplinary study and offer more flexibility in reading lists and exams. Their breadth is "horizontal," placing the Greco-Roman sphere in the larger context of the Mediterranean or within a broad concept of the humanities. New York University's Matthew Santirocco advises: "Pick a small department you like over a large one you don't. It's like stock. You want to look for departments on the make."

All types of department give the same core training—nobody gets a Ph.D. in classics without reading Homer—but they tend to differ in the kind of research their students end up doing. Harvard's Charles Segal says that in his department, "we're very much concerned with a philological approach and have emphasized that students demonstrate a command of languages and philological techniques, a command of the technical aspects of study. Of course, students are free to pursue other areas too. We don't limit their interests. But we do demand that they develop a solid base in languages." So, while Harvard faculty have a great breadth of interests and are known for some very innovative work—Segal himself was one of the first to bring structuralist interpretation into classics—it is still a conservative program designed to train the student in such things as "prose composition, intensive exegesis, and historical linguistics," according to the department's self-description. Interdisciplinary study is possible, but not built into the program.

Many programs still resemble the traditional model of scholarship established at Johns Hopkins, and that Chicago and then Harvard eventually followed. Among top-ranked departments in that pattern are Yale, Bryn Mawr, and Cornell. As mentioned, there is a trend towards an interdisciplinary approach that takes the ancient Mediterranean as a single subject shared by many departments. At Chicago, for instance, the department of classics now cooperates with the art history, history, philosophy, New Testament, and early Christian literature departments; the Committees on the Ancient Mediterranean World, Archaeological Studies, Medieval Studies, and Social Thought; and the Oriental Institute and the Divinity School. Two eminent classicists at Chicago, Glenn Most and Martha Nussbaum, are not members of the classics department at all, but of the Committee on Social Thought and the Law School, respectively. Accordingly, the classics department at Chicago *requires* that students take two courses outside classics for the Ph.D.

Similar programs (in various stages of development) are Penn's Center for Ancient Studies, NYU's Center for Ancient Studies, and Columbia's degree in Classical Studies. In general, the presence of a "Center" means you are encouraged to take courses outside your department, while a "Graduate Group," "Program," or "Committee" is an entity that you might apply to in addition to a classics department if you have strong interdisciplinary interests.

One of the best ways to judge departments is to attend the joint meeting of the American Philological Association and the Archaeological Institute of America, held every December 27–31, where you'll find almost every classicist and classical archaeologist in the United States under one roof. (In 1997, the meeting is being held in Chicago.) Dozens of sessions cover an almost overwhelming variety of topics, making it easy to see what's going on (and what's not). The atmosphere is relaxed enough that you can introduce yourself to the professors who present papers and have your questions answered.

In archaeology, the two most prominent programs in the United States, UC-Berkeley and Michigan, stress that classical archaeology is, as the name implies, half classics and half archaeology. Michigan boasts one of the finest research museums in the United States, the Kelsey Museum, which houses the classical art and archaeology department and is closely associated with the classical studies department. Excavations at Karanis (Egypt) in the 1920s and 1930s formed the basis of the collection, and they now have excavations in Paestum, Leptiminus, and Coptos (Italy).

At UC-Berkeley, archaeology can be studied by two routes: through the department of classics and classical archaeology, or through the interdisciplinary Graduate Group in Ancient History and Mediterranean Archaeology, one of the oldest of such programs in the country. Crawford Greenewalt directs the excavation at Sardis in Greece (though it is actually sponsored by Harvard).

Bryn Mawr's program is smaller but also well-respected. Harvard, Princeton, and Penn have long traditions of archaeology that they are now trying to strengthen. Penn has a Graduate Group modeled after UC-Berkeley's and sponsors a dig at Gordion, though its director, Kenneth Sams, is actually at UNC-Chapel Hill—another good program.

All these programs are strong in classics but it is worth mentioning that some programs have an art historical focus which does not emphasize classical philology nearly as much as the programs already mentioned. At Columbia, for example, the department of art history and archaeology has a large faculty, with two classical archaeologists: Richard Brilliant and Natalie Kampen. NYU's Institute of Fine Arts has almost a dozen archeologists who specialize in the ancient Mediterranean and digs at Aphrodisias, Samothrace, and Abydos.

> In classics, the documentary historian works much like an archaeologist.

Unlike the classical archaeologist, the classical historian is really just a classicist who focuses on history rather than literature. The documentary historian—one who works with coins, papyri, and inscriptions—works much like an archaeologist. Because of the papyrus finds at Karanis, and the presence of Ludwig Koenen (who retired as this book went to press), Michigan is again one of the best places to study papyrology, as is Columbia, with its large collection and the U.S. czar of papyrology, Roger Bagnall. Stanford University and Duke have more recently entered the field, and Duke is home to the Duke Databank of Documentary Papyri. Epigraphy is less easily studied in the United States, but UNC-Chapel Hill has three epigraphers—George Houston, Jerzy Linderski, and William West—as does UC-Berkeley—Robert Knapp, Ronald Stroud, and Leslie Threatte. Numismatics is probably best studied not at any university but during the summer at the American Institute of Numismatics in New York City. But bear in mind Columbia professor Roger S. Bagnall's warning to students of papyrology,

"You've got to be trained in something else in addition if you're going to be employable in this country," advice that applies to students of epigraphy and numismatics, too.

For nondocumentary historians, the choices are greater. UC-Berkeley's Graduate Group in Ancient History and Mediterranean Archaeology is as strong in the latter as the former, with Roman historian Erich Gruen (author of *The Last Generation of the Roman Republic: Culture and National Identity in Republican Rome*) as the director of graduate studies. Penn has a similar program. With its interdisciplinary wealth, Chicago offers a great breadth and faculty who have recently published some fascinating scholarship, such as Christopher Faraone's research on Greek magic, *Magika Hiera: Ancient Greek Magic and Religion*. The programs at Harvard, UT-Austin, and Brown are also strong. At some schools, ancient history is shared between classics and history. Columbia's program, led by Roger S. Bagnall and William Harris, is one such program. This can mean that some of the department faculty have much less training in ancient languages than others, and correspondingly less interest in textual study, a matter to look into on a case-by-case basis.

Like history, philosophy is sometimes shared between departments, sometimes not. The classical philosopher, too, is mainly a classicist who specializes in philosophical (most often Greek) texts. You are best off looking for a strong department with someone prominent—Duke has Diskin Clay, and UC-Berkeley has John Ferrari and Anthony Long. NYU's Seth Benardete came from Chicago, where he was the student of Leo Strauss, and now carries on the Straussian tradition in his work on Plato.

Literature is by far the largest field of study for classicists. And any of the programs mentioned so far are strong primarily because they are strong in literature. Harvard boasts two of the top Hellenists in Charles Segal and Greg Nagy, as well as Latinists Richard Thomas and Richard Tarrant. UC-Berkeley has John Ferrari and a rising star in Shadi Bartsch. Brown, with Michael Putnam and David Konstan, is another excellent program.

Literary theory is still not central to the field of classics as a whole, but it may be coming into its own. USC's department makes a point of teaching theory—Roman literature (A.J. Boyle), feminist (Amy Richlin), and even psychoanalytic (Richard Caldwell). The University of Washington at Seattle classics department participates in a Ph.D. in theory and criticism, and their luminary is Stephen Hinds, who wrote *The Metamorphosis of Persephone: Ovid and the Self-Conscious Muse*. Cornell has not only Pietro Pucci but etymological innovator Frederick Ahl, author of *Metaformations: Soundplay and Wordplay in Ovid and Other Classical Poets*, who has taken Saussure's interest in anagrams to an extreme. It is often the younger faculty members, like Micaela Janan at Duke and Michaele Lowrie at NYU, who pursue contemporary perspectives. Besides *Arethusa*, most current literary criticism can be found in the journals *Helios* and *Materiali e discussioni per l'analisi dei testi classici*.

THE JOB MARKET

The job market in classics is not any worse than in other humanities and social science fields. Despite the scares of the last few years and thanks to the efforts of the APA, no classics departments have actually been abolished. Jobs are on the increase, just not fast enough to keep pace with the number of new and recent Ph.D.'s seeking them. The APA has a placement service to make it easier for employers and applicants to find each other, and according to their statistics, 130 jobs were advertised between July 1995 and June 1996, up from 105 in 1994–95. By February of 1997, there were already 109 jobs (two more than in February 1996), though the 536 candidates registered with the placement service translates into a ratio of one job for every five seekers.

Greek is much more popular than Latin, despite a greater need for Latin teachers at the undergraduate level. If you want to compete with fewer people for jobs, become a Latinist. But because the field is so small, overall hiring in classics is more sensitive to the random effects of retirements than to predictable market trends. Undergraduate enrollments in Latin and Greek are reportedly on the rise—but so are the number of part-time or nontenure-track positions.

The majority of Ph.D.'s will end up at nonresearch institutions, and even in secondary schools. Whether this is good or bad depends on your goals—if your dream is to teach Latin at an inner-city high school, there are healthy institutions, private and public, in New York City, Philadelphia, Boston, Detroit, St. Louis, and elsewhere to do so. If you have your hopes set on being on the faculty of Yale, it is no surprise that you are in for fierce competition.

RESOURCES

NRC TOP TEN
Harvard
UC-Berkeley
Michigan
Princeton
Yale
Brown
Chicago
UT-Austin
UCLA
Columbia

ASSOCIATIONS
American Philological
Association
(508) 793-2203

JOURNALS
*American Journal of
Philology*
Arethusa
Classical Philology
Helios
*Transactions of the
American Philological
Association*

FURTHER READING
*Guide to Graduate Programs
in the Classics in the United
States and Canada* (APA)

Phyllis Culham and
Lowell Edmunds, eds.,
*Classics: A Discipline and
Profession in Crisis?*
(University Press of
America)

CONSTELLATIONS

JOHN'S HOPKINS MODEL
Bryn Mawr
Cornell
Harvard
Yale

INTERDISCIPLINARY PROGRAMS
Chicago
Columbia
NYU
Penn

ARCHAEOLOGY
Bryn Mawr
Harvard
Michigan
Penn
UC-Berkeley
UNC-Chapel Hill

DOCUMENTARY HISTORY
Chicago
Columbia
Duke
Michigan
Penn
Stanford
UC-Berkeley
UNC-Chapel Hill

ANCIENT HISTORY
Brown
Harvard
UT-Austin

PHILOSOPHY
Duke
NYU
UC-Berkeley

LITERATURE
Brown
Cornell
Duke
Harvard
NYU
UC-Berkeley
USC
Washington-Seattle

M.A. PROGRAMS
Arizona
Boston College
Florida
Florida State
Kansas
Kent State
Kentucky
Maryland-College Park
Nebraska
Oregon
San Francisco State
Texas Tech
Tulane
Vermont
Washington University
    in St. Louis
Wayne State

WEB ADDRESSES
American Philological Association
http://www.scholar.cc.emory.edu/scripts/APA/APAa-MENU.html

Archeological Institute of America
http://www.csaws.brynmawr.edu/aia.html

Classics and Mediterranean Archeology
http://www.rome.classics.lsa.umich.edu/welcome.html

Electronic Resources for Classicists
http://www.tlg.uci.edu/~tlg/index/resources.html

CHAPTER 7

COMPARATIVE LITERATURE

Gabrielle Civil, in her fourth year at New York University's Ph.D. program, has the breadth of interest typical of comparative literature graduate students. As an undergraduate she completed a triple major in English, French, and comparative literature, and while doing literary and philosophical theory alongside a detailed study of poetry by Francophone Caribbeans and African American women, she was drawn to the differences between the intellectual and cultural roles that poets and poetry have assumed in the Caribbean and the United States.

When she decided to pursue this interest further, Civil, who is a poet herself, chose graduate study in a discipline that would welcome her interest in contemporary and noncanonical poetry. Comparative literature has always brought cutting-edge literature into university debates, and it also has a rich tradition of comparing the roles of literature in different cultures from a theoretical viewpoint. Civil expected that she would not have to justify her interests as often as she might have to do in a national literature department, such as English or French, which tend to put a single literature first. Also, instead of dealing only with the questions raised by applying interpretive techniques to particular texts, a comparative literature department would encourage the exploration of theoretical issues.

WHY COMPARATIVE LITERATURE?

While comparative literature can chart its origins in the United States to the period just prior to World War II, it wasn't until the late 1940s that a generation of comparativists set out to transform a provincial field into a cosmopolitan one. This new group of scholars was at pains to fight racial, ethnic, and national stereotypes by demonstrating that literature around the world shared forms, themes, and ideas. Differences among literary traditions, they argued, were a subject for investigation and speculation, not nationalist chest thumping. The postwar generation insisted that no national literature could be fully understood except in relationship to the other literatures that it incorporated and answered. And finally, because they insisted that professional literary critics should be as unrestrained by disciplinary borders as literature itself was by national borders, comparativists had no qualms about branching out into other realms of the university, such as philosophy, history, and fine arts departments.

But several movements are now redefining comparative literature's interdisciplinary aims. Postcolonial studies, for one, has expanded the body of literature being compared to include the non-European, and has made issues of migration, exile, travel, and hybridity as crucial as politics, power, interpretation, and language. On a different front, cultural studies is making a bid to be the new home for interdisciplinary and cross-cultural research. The chief difference between the traditional comparativist approach and the newer cultural studies approach is that the traditionalists tend to read both the texts they discuss and the theoretical texts impinging on their arguments in the original languages. Another distinction lies in the fact that cultural studies, on the whole, uses the term "text" more broadly than does comparative literature. Not only can the language vary, but so can the medium: Cultural studies refers to films, paintings, and even rituals and customs as "texts." These differences are the subject of one of the livelier debates in comparative literature, as the comparativists argue about whether to embrace cultural studies or to stick to their more language-and-text oriented approach.

The newness of cultural studies, though, like the newness of postcolonial studies, can present serious problems for students when they assemble committees for oral exams and the dissertation. Perhaps most importantly, neither enjoys the status of an established university department. (*Comparative Literature in the Age of Multiculturalism* [1995], edited by Charles Bernheimer of the University of Pennsylvania, collects a wide variety of points of view about both cultural studies and postcolonial studies from prominent comparativists.) But this problem aside, why these, and not other movements, are so important to the field of the moment, is hinted at by the history of the discipline.

HOW COMPARATIVE LITERATURE HAS TAKEN SHAPE

The scholarly generation that transformed comparative literature departments after World War II was composed mostly of European émigrés who fled the national rivalries and genocidal politics of the war years. Nearly every member of this cohort had seen fascists deploy literature, music, and film to stir hatreds and to glamorize dreams of conquest. The émigré generation coalesced around the determination to free literature from such propaganda and to show that works of art belonged to a cosmopolitan elite. If literature had been used to stoke imperialist ambitions, then they would use it to rebuild an educated international community. René Wellek and Erich Auerbach at Yale University, Leo Spitzer at Johns Hopkins University, and Wolfgang Kaiser at Harvard University, among others, set out to train a new U.S. generation of comparativists who would be less provincial and more attuned to the whole of high culture.

When the émigrés first arrived, the United States was only just developing its own class of professional literary and cultural interpreters. Wellek said of his move from the University of Prague to the Princeton University of the 1920s, "It was like being sent back to the latter nineteenth century." Shakespeare was studied by way of word-by-word comparison of different versions of *Hamlet*—with no reference to what the play might mean. Wellek was also surprised to find the Princeton faculty divided between Royalist Anglo-Catholics and, as he recalled, another faction "deeply committed to the values of the Old South." Faculty with the comparativist impulse—to be citizens of the world—did teach there, but they were a minority. Remarkably, Princeton was more up-to-date than many of the U.S. insti tutions Wellek visited—Smith College and the University of Iowa being just two of them.

So the motives for revamping U.S. departments were several. Not only was there the determination to make them more international, but there was also an emphasis on turning the departments from inward-looking coteries, detached from current events, into the lively forums for debate that the émigrés had experienced in their European education. The émigrés insisted that fledgling comparative literature departments follow the European custom of small seminar classes led each week by a different student in round-robin fashion. And they formed reading groups and led library drives to develop well-selected collections of foreign literature. Because graduate training in comparative literature was intense and ambitious, the departments of the 1950s also put a premium on keeping down overall enrollments and fostering close collaboration between students and senior faculty. That tradition remains a drawing card at the best comparative literature departments and humanities programs today.

European scholars, relocated in the U.S., set the standards for exploring the relationships between philosophy and literature.

Erich Auerbach's landmark *Mimesis* (1946) is emblematic of the encyclopedic learning and mastery of several national literary traditions that was the hallmark of the émigré generation's work. *Mimesis* examined the transmission of the concept of the literary imitation of reality in European literature from Homer to Joyce, and throughout the 1940s, 1950s, and the early 1960s, scholars referred to *Mimesis* more often than to any other work of literary criticism. During the same years, successive volumes of Wellek's *The History of Modern Criticism* ranged across the landscape of Continental philosophy, psychoanalysis, linguistics, history, and political theory. With the broad studies of literary concepts like *Mimesis* and the critical surveys of a wide variety of fields like Wellek's, the émigrés set the standards for U.S. scholarship about literary genres, themes, periods, and the relationship between philosophical movements and literary texts.

Led by Wellek, the Yale comparative literature department of the 1940s and 1950s established the major currents within the discipline, particularly on theoretical matters: What is literature? What are the social roles of literature? What can other disciplines best contribute to literary analysis? How can the study of literature enrich other disciplines? Are there general rules about the textual and cultural transmission of ideas? What happens to readers and to texts when we read? At Harvard a different, less influential tradition developed, which focused more often on literary history than on theoretical questions. The Harvard comparativists stressed the nature of genres and periods, the production and reception of texts by writers, editors, and publishers, and source studies.

> Comparativists are always open to giving a hearing to philosophical ideas on the margins.

A stress on theory or history represented more a division of labor than a dispute about either the most effective way to interpret literature or the most urgent needs of literary study. In fact, during this period the top departments made it a principle that graduate students train in *both* theory and history. No matter how intense their interests in philosophical/literary questions, students had to acquire a working familiarity with traditional "periods" and "genres." They had to know at least one national literature thoroughly enough to teach courses in its major historical periods, as well as cultivating expertise in at least one period or theme prominent in two national literatures, even as they were encouraged to keep current with new research in linguistics, philosophy, and even psychoanalysis,

The émigré generation embodied a combination of talent and ambition that many comparativists claim has not been seen before or since in American letters. Departments today do not expect students to match the skills of an Auerbach or a Wellek, nor even to study the same topics they did. But the drive toward high intellectual standards—and the refusal to remain trapped in the provincial—have never gone out of fashion. An equally important contribution of the émigré generation was the flexibility of the field and its openness to philosophical movements on the margins. Wellek's *Kant In England*, published in the late 1920s, for instance, could not have anticipated the field's eventual turn to Continental theories of structuralism, deconstruction, poststructuralism, and postmodernism in the 1960s. But when that happened, Wellek did not break stride. The studies of literary theory that he had started publishing in the 1930s and continued to shepherd into the 1980s evaluated the latest Continental theories of literature—though not always sympathetically—without missing a beat.

In the 1960s and 1970s, Roland Barthes, Jacques Derrida, and Jacques Lacan brought to literary criticism and cultural theory new ideas about meaning and interpretation, power and domination, the unconscious and ideology. Their ideas, loosely grouped together under the rubric of deconstruction, aimed to reveal the logical inconsistencies embedded in a text and to explain how a text disguises them. Soon, long-standing philosophical concepts of transcendent and organic meaning were under assault as deconstructionists wanted to force language to own up to its utter arbitrariness.

This, at least, was the approach to deconstruction taken by the comparative literature department at Yale, which at the time included Paul de Man, J. Hillis Miller, Geoffrey Hartman, and Harold Bloom. The work of the Yale School, as this group came to be known, and its Continental influences took the humanities by storm. Before long, it provided the intellectual muscle behind a boom in scholarly journals and even set off a brisk trade in crib books, from trade publications like *Derrida for Beginners* to hundreds of university press monographs which, like Cornell University professor Jonathan Culler's *On Deconstruction* (1982), offered a crash course in deconstruction for scholars in disciplines other than literature.

The truth was, though, that as it traveled from France to the United States, deconstruction was transmuted. In France it was one tool among many to use in broad philosophical inquiry about matters of ontology and epistemology; in America it became primarily a technique for reading. Scholars have used deconstruction as a kind of spotlight to shine on textual fragments, and its later critics liked to say it was no more than a variation on the "close reading" popularized by the New Critics during the 1950s.

As deconstruction prompted the rereading of canonical texts and the reappraisal of cherished humanist ideals, it roused the interest of literary scholars in other fields of contemporary philosophy. Phenomenology, hermeneutics, psychoanalysis, and other theories began to show up on graduate syllabi—even in first-year courses. During the heyday of deconstruction, feminists, African Americanists, film theorists, sociologists, and anthropologists all staked their claims on the origins of Theory. Not surprisingly, several of these disciplines insisted that *they* were the ones who imported Theory into U.S. universities, and gave it the status

> As deconstruction traveled from France to the United States, it was transmuted.

worthy of a capital T. But it's hard not to see comparative literature departments as ground zero for the carnival of theory. Not only can comparative literature departments point to their field's tradition of keeping pace with developments in philosophy, one which dates back at least to the émigrés, but no one can dispute the lead they took in creating conferences, seminars, and colloquia where all of the contenders for Theory Champion came together.

In the 1970s, comparative literature departments became ground zero for the carnival of theory.

In 1976, for instance, Murray Krieger, a comparativist at the University of California at Irvine, established an annual summer conference, the School for Criticism and Theory, which has come to be known casually as "Theory camp." The conference, originally hosted by UC-Irvine, has since moved to several prominent campuses in literature and comparative literature—Northwestern University in 1981, then to Dartmouth College in 1986—before settling at Cornell in 1996. These summer meetings have not only introduced new theory but have also charted the impact of theory throughout the humanities and become something like an intellectual boot camp, a place for scholars to cut their teeth on the latest tracts from the Continent. Though every year the scope of the conference broadens, the board of directors today features many of the scholars who became leading theorists during the halcyon days of deconstruction.

While the rise of the "theorist" apparently represented something of a paradigm shift in the discipline, comparative literature departments had in fact always been a home for theory. For deconstructionists to turn repeatedly to Nietzsche and Heidegger was not so different from the ways that the émigré generation turned to Kant and French philosophers of the Enlightenment. And deconstructionists also had their historical interests, frequently revisiting the linguistics of Saussure, the psychoanalytic theories of Freud and his commentators, and the political and linguistic theories of Rousseau. Perhaps more significantly, deconstruction was consistent with the long-standing comparativist impulse to go behind the curtain and demystify all apparently monolithic systems of meaning. Where the émigré generation had hoped to free literature from its role in propping up idealized national images, deconstructionists wanted to free philosophy and language from supporting idealized humanist beliefs—namely, that language is organic and that the self is coherent. For deconstructionists, philosophical texts were the starting point for investigation, not sources of authority about morals, society, or the self.

But the salad days of Theory were short. In the late 1980s and early 1990s, books about the "fall of deconstruction" and the critic's role in the "wake" of theory began to appear. One force behind the fall came in the form of the politically conservative writers of the culture wars who linked deconstruction with their nemesis, cultural relativism. Deconstruction, they claimed, was an attempt to make any text or cultural artifact the equal of any other, and therefore an attack on all stable notions of literary value. Allan Bloom, in his best-selling attack on academic feminism, area studies, and multiculturalism, *The Closing of the American Mind* (1987), repeatedly singled out comparative literature departments as an acid-bath of cultural relativism and the starting place for politically correct attacks on the Western canon. Dinesh D'Souza made similar charges in *Illiberal Education* (1991), even going so far as to claim that Wellek's landmark *Theory of Literature* claimed that Shakespeare's plays had no more inherent artistic worth than graffiti. (Wellek responded to D'Souza in print that he never made such a claim and had devoted much of his career to the canon of European literature.)

> Deconstruction was consistent with the traditional comparativist impulse to go behind the curtain.

Certainly, the deliberately abstruse terminology of theory was an easy target for anti-theory fulmination. Theorists, after all, had adopted the habit of incorporating seemingly unnecessary slashes, hyphens, and parentheses into words and phrases, and they loved to use obscure Greek rhetorical terms. But a deeper resistance to theory stemmed from the pragmatic focus of much university study in literature, which emphasizes explanation over hypothesis and tends to mine texts primarily for moral touchstones or stylistic models. Within this context, deconstruction was labeled a sterile, apolitical technique, mostly useful within a self-referential, unedifying intramural discussion, rather than recognized as a demystification of humanist clichés about authorship, the autonomy of texts, and the nature of the self.

For all the uproar they caused, deconstruction and literary theory lent comparative literature departments a decided élan. They became the place where other scholars expected to hear about the latest developments in Continental philosophy. And the theoretical turn was also proof that comparativists were unusually willing to take interpretive risks and to at least give a hearing to provocative ideas before they gained wide currency. As a technique and a way to write criticism in another key, deconstruction widened the already broad universe of objects of study open to comparativists. Stanley Fish, a professor of literature at Duke University, has argued that at the very least deconstruction became one more tool in the critic's repertoire and prompted an explosion of exciting scholarship.

During deconstruction's rise, in the late 1970s and early 1980s, the ideological dimensions of the comparativist's universe were challenged by postcolonial studies, and no one is more responsible for issuing that challenge than Columbia University comparative literature professor Edward Said. Building on Continental theory but using it in a decidedly political manner, Said's 1978 book *Orientalism* proposed that from Aeschylus onward the West has never permitted the East to represent itself. Said detailed the cultural misunderstandings resulting from Orientalism (Western representations of the East), and, true to the charter of comparative literature, he also argued that the cultures of the East and West could not be understood except in relationship to one another.

Despite Said's tendency to cast his arguments in bald terms (THE East, THE West), he succeeded in pushing the field further toward becoming a truly comparative universe. A new set of texts became required reading. The Egyptian feminist Nawa El-Sadawi joined Nagib Mahfouz and the Moroccan writer Abdelkebir Khatibi on course syllabi. The theories of the Martinique native and French-educated psychiatrist Frantz Fanon, who explored how images of the Other underpin race relations, acquired a weight that comparativists had formerly reserved only for the philosophical concepts of the European canon. And even *that* canon was shaken up. Due to Said's application of his work, Michel Foucault's examination of the intertwining of

> Resistance to theory stemmed in part from the pragmatism of U.S. education.

knowledge and power became at least as important as Derrida's pronouncements on deconstruction. All in all, the parochialism of comparative literature toward non-Western scholars was loudly challenged, and a generation of scholars from outside Europe joined comparative literature departments around the United States.

"They cannot represent themselves; they must be represented," states Said's ironically-cited epigraph for *Orientalism*. Starting in the mid-1970s, Said took it upon himself to represent Palestinian points of view to the media. With the authority borne of his journalism and scholarship, he became one of the most frequently and widely interviewed of all U.S. academics, a roving source of opinions about Palestine, the Intifada, and developments around the decolonizing world. From the banks of the Jordan to the banks of the Hudson, Said's roles in scholarly and in public life were tightly knit, and his ambition to make them so was his second contribution to comparative literature.

Edward Said preserved cosmopolitan ambitions even as he opposed imperialism.

Said dubbed his efforts as "adversarial internationalism," but by any name Said politicized the field even as he preserved the cosmopolitan ambitions of the émigré generation by opposing imperialism and cultural hegemony.

But a second wave of post-colonial scholars—Gayatri Spivak of Columbia, Aijaz Ahmad, who is based in New Delhi but is often in the United States, and Homi K. Bhabha of the University of Chicago—is much less accepting of the European canon than Said, as he has noted in his book *The World, The Text, and The Critic* (1983). Said goes on to chart the pain caused by having his own arguments turned against him, by being renounced for not adequately examining his own biases about the colonial experience, gender, and power. He even quipped that he has been "Gorbacheved by the revolution."

But regardless of how one evaluates Said's work, there's no questioning that thanks to his efforts one of the central issues in comparative literature is no longer whether or not to fold non-Western literatures and cultures into the comparativist mix, but how. Said has created freedom for comparativists to cross time periods, cultures, and critical discourses, and in so doing he has changed the nature of the discipline.

Today the field of comparative literature stretches beyond literary texts to all matters of popular culture, including medical treatises, films, travel memoirs, etiquette books, and cyberspace communities. One of the reasons for its expansion is the insurgence into the field of cultural studies, which favors an ideological analysis of cultural artifacts and makes all matter of culture, high and low, fodder for analysis.

The interest among comparativists in popular culture is actually stretches back into the field's early history. In the 1920s and 1930s, Walter Benjamin and Siegfried Kracauer wrote about street signs, dance halls, synchronized swimming, photography, and film, and their work was familiar to comparativists long before cultural studies emerged as an academic field in the United States in the 1980s. And comparative literature departments were among the first to embrace the academic study of film in the 1970s. Nor are cultural studies scholars bashful about adapting methods from sociologists, anthropologists, and art historians to understand the production and consumption of culture. Some proponents of cultural studies envision it as the spearhead of the new, interdisciplinary university, while for others it is merely the latest move in the constant systole and diastole of the past fifty years in literary study between attention to form and attention to context.

Paradoxically, the vast expansion of comparative literature's field of inquiry under the influence of cultural studies has led in certain quarters of the field to a renewed emphasis upon the "literary." Alongside wide-ranging analyses of popular culture, scholars are now asking themselves what specific qualities of literary texts and their transmission are *not* shared by other artifacts, such as historic documents. What distinguishes literature from other objects of study? Far from embracing a new formalism, however, scholars such as Harvard professor John Guillory have turned the question of literature and its transmission into a broad analysis of social value, drawing upon the work of French sociologist Pierre Bourdieu, who has emerged as a key theoretical figure for such investigations.

WHAT'S NEXT

Although today's comparativist is no longer likely to be an émigré cosmopolite, a knowledge of several modern and ancient languages is still a key defining feature of the comparative literature scholar. Ten years ago, programs at elite schools such as Princeton and Yale required students to do serious work in three national literatures. On top of that, students needed to acquire a reading knowledge not only of French and German, but of a pre-Renaissance language (Old French or medieval German) and an ancient language (Latin or Greek). Today many graduate programs, including those at New York University and Columbia, allow students to substitute a demonstrated expertise in a second discipline (art history or political science) or in a subject that stretches across several disciplines (gender, vision, or

East European political history) for mastery of a third national literature. Language requirements have become much more flexible too, and while some comparativists have lamented a perceived loss of rigor, others celebrate the partial demise of Eurocentrism. Hebrew, Chinese, and Arabic are now generally accepted as ancient languages, along with Latin and Greek; Spanish, Thai, or Croatian may stand in lieu of French and German. Still, students seeking acceptance at top-flight programs should have a strong background in languages, which includes at least fluency in a second language other than English.

> Be sure to consider the relative strengths of the national language programs and those "sister" disciplines in the arts.

How much theory are entering graduate students expected to know? Opinions vary, though most professors agree that it's more important for students to have a broad and sensitive understanding of one or two national literatures than to have entirely worked out a theoretical perspective by the first year of graduate school. And they should have a passing knowledge of a range of theoretical approaches, whether psychoanalytic, postcolonial, feminist, or phenomenological. Just as importantly, they should be adept at the conceptualization of literary problems and familiar with techniques of close interpretation.

Sometimes graduate students will overcompensate for a lack of theoretical expertise by latching on to a single vantage point—using, say, Lacanian film theory as a prism through which to view the whole of culture. But one of the many challenges of graduate school is to allow literature and theory to illuminate each other, rather than using theory to explain literature in a reductive manner.

In fact, as the field keeps reinventing itself, one of the greatest challenges facing graduate students is to grapple with the following difficulty: Students are simply responsible for a longer, more cosmopolitan history. They must struggle not only with Heidegger and Lacan but also with Argentine novelist Luisa Valenzuela. Those who study the epic may find themselves reading the medieval French classic *The Romance of the Rose* alongside the tenth-century Japanese proto-novel *The Pillow Book of Sei Shonagon*.

Where to do graduate study in comparative literature depends largely on your interests. It's risky, however, to choose a program based solely on the presence of one or two eminent scholars in your chosen specialty. Your interests are likely to change, professors can be difficult to work with, and celebrity academics move around quite a bit.

When considering a particular program, be sure to consider the relative strength of the university's national literature departments as well as any "sister" disciplines in which you have a serious interest, such as art history, philosophy, or law. Courses are often cross-listed and opportunities sometimes exist for working across disciplines and with professors from other departments. Be wary of small programs that discourage students from taking courses outside the department, and try to learn of any interdepartmental rivalries that could make collaborations difficult. Also investigate whether or not comparative literature faculty members have joint appointments and to what extent their obligations to another department reduce the time they can devote to the comparative literature department and its students. Finally, because the National Research Council rankings of comparative literature graduate programs are not sensitive to any of these local issues, they should be used only with the utmost caution.

For nearly two decades, Yale dominated the study of comparative literature in this country. Today, though its prestige has waned considerably, it still turns up on most people's lists of top graduate programs. Headed by Slavicist Michael Holquist and French scholar Peter Brooks, Yale is strong in literary theory, the legacy of deconstruction, and French literature. In recent years it has strengthened its attention to Judaic studies as well, under the guidance of Benjamin Harshav and Geoffrey Hartman, both of whom spend much time in the comparative literature department teaching poetics and deconstruction, respectively. And Yale is home of Lacanian theorist Shoshana Felman, among the first comparativists to link psychoanalysis with deconstruction. Yale is not a place to study film or popular culture, however, and collaborations with its English department have reportedly become more rare.

> Be wary of the pressure to work out a full-fledged theoretical position in your first years.

The legacy of deconstruction lives on in several other places. Cornell's program is strong in European studies and psychoanalysis; faculty there include French scholar Emily Apter (a recent hire), literary theorist Jonathan Culler, cultural critic Richard Klein, intellectual historian Dominick LaCapra, and Biddy

Martin, who gives strength to the program in gay and lesbian studies. Cornell's beautiful surroundings and tradition of equal funding for all graduate students encourages a highly collegial atmosphere. The Humanities Center at Johns Hopkins is also noteworthy for its emphasis on literature, philosophy, and critical theory. Faculty there include literary theorists and scholars Stephen Nichols and Neil Hertz and art historian Michael Fried. Under the influence of scholar and former Yale School member J. Hillis Miller and theorist Andrzej Warminski, the department at UC-Irvine remains faithful to the Yale School's tradition of rhetorical reading. And at Emory University, Cathy Caruth is known for working in the vein of Continental theory, applying poststructuralism to the study of trauma.

Among traditional programs emphasizing literary-historical questions of period and genre, Princeton is known for intensive guidance of graduate students. Stanford University has a very good reputation as a small program with particular strengths in Renaissance and Modernist literature; it accepts few students and funds them well. Indiana University is a very large program with a traditional perspective and a strong emphasis on interdisciplinarity. The program at the University of California at Berkeley, headed by French scholar Timothy Hampton, also has an excellent reputation: it is large and fairly conservative, though it manages to offer a variety of perspectives by drawing upon the university's eminent roster of faculty in English, French, and rhetoric, including French scholar Leo Bersani, queer theorist Judith Butler, and film theorist Kaja Silverman.

In recent years, Harvard has developed an extraordinary faculty in the departments of African American studies (K. Anthony Appiah, Henry Louis Gates Jr., Cornel West), English (including Marjorie Garber and Barbara Johnson), and French (Susan Suleiman and Naomi Schor), but the comparative literature department itself remains relatively small and quiet. Comparative literature at Brown University is also small, but it is cross-fertilized by Brown's large English department and by the Department of Modern Culture and Media, where feminist film theorist Mary Ann Doane teaches.

Columbia's program in comparative literature cross-lists all courses and appointments. Students are required to have an M.A. in a national literature before continuing comparative studies on the doctoral level. As such, the program is dependent upon the various strengths and weaknesses of national literature and related departments, which boast an eminent mix of scholars. Columbia is particularly strong in postcolonial studies, literary theory, and European literature; faculty include Edward Said, David Damrosch, and Gayatri Spivak (in English), Michel Riffaterre (in French), Andreas Huyssen (in German), and Rosalind Krauss (in art history). There is a tremendous amount of competition for funding and attention at Columbia; students who prosper must be independent and hardy. The collection of scholars at the Graduate Center of the City University of New York has a strong feminist component, especially in Victorian and modernist literature, due to the presence of Mary Ann Caws, Rachel Brownstein, and Nancy K. Miller.

> To compete for jobs, comparative literature students must match the abilities of students in national literature programs.

Duke ranks very high on most people's lists of programs with a cultural studies orientation. The department there is called simply "Literature." Headed by French scholar and theorist Fredric Jameson, it is enriched by Duke's vibrant programs in English, French, and Spanish, with particular strengths in literary, feminist, and queer theory. Faculty includes Toril Moi in French, and Stanley Fish and Eve Kosofsky Sedgwick in English. Comparative literature at Penn is also known to have a broad base of support for cultural studies, with noteworthy faculty including Charles Bernheimer in French, and Houston Baker and Achille Mnembe in African-American Studies. Finally, under the direction of Jennifer Wicke, NYU has a vibrant if eclectic comparative literature department that is still negotiating the transition between a more traditional focus and a cultural studies orientation. Faculty and associates at NYU include Caribbean studies scholar Kamau Brathwaite, Manthia Diawara in Africana studies, French scholar Kristin Ross, cultural theorist Avital Ronell in German and Andrew Ross in American studies. Be aware, however, that at least for the moment, collaborations with the university's hidebound English department are rare.

THE JOB MARKET

To compete effectively in the academic job market, comparative literature students must match the skills of job candidates from national literature departments. They must have a firm grounding in a basic expertise, usually language teaching or expository writing. They must be able to teach broad-based courses in the humanities (such as "great books" courses in a core curriculum), seminars in their field of specialty (and a secondary specialty), as well as survey courses in a national literature. Above all, they must bring to the table a strong theoretical background and interdisciplinary interests that distinguish them from the pack of job seekers.

Impeccable credentials are essential because the job market in comparative literature is incredibly competitive, nearly cutthroat. The numbers alone explain why. In 1995, one hundred ninety-one Ph.D.'s were awarded in comparative literature, yet only twenty-eight full-time positions were advertised that year. In 1996, at least one hundred fifty Ph.D.'s were awarded but only thirty full-time positions were advertised.

RESOURCES

NRC RANKINGS
Yale
Duke
Columbia
Harvard
Princeton
Cornell
Johns Hopkins
UC-Irvine
Stanford
UC-Berkeley

ASSOCIATIONS
American Comparative
  Literature Association
(541) 346-0737
Modern Language
  Association
(212) 475-9500

JOURNALS
Camera Obscura PMLA
Critical Inquiry Representations
Diacritics Social Text

CONSTELLATIONS

THEORY
Brown
Columbia
Cornell
Duke
Emory
Johns Hopkins
UC-Irvine
Yale

FRENCH LITERATURE
Columbia
Penn
UC-Berkeley
Yale

FURTHER READING
Charles Bernheimer, ed., *Comparative Literature in the Age of Multiculturalism* (Johns Hopkins)

WEB ADDRESSES
Eclat! The Essential Comparative Literature and Theory Site
http://ccat.sas.upenn.edu/CompLit/Eclat/

LITERARY HISTORY
Indiana
Princeton
UC-Berkeley

MODERNIST LITERATURE
CUNY Graduate Center
Stanford

CULTURAL STUDIES
Duke
NYU
Penn

POSTCOLONIAL STUDIES
Chicago
Columbia

CHAPTER 8

ENGLISH

James McNelis recently completed his dissertation at the University of Washington at Seattle. It's a critical edition of *The Master of Game* (ca. 1406), the only surviving full-length hunting manual in Middle English and a crucial source for the author of *Sir Gawain and the Green Knight*. When researching his master's thesis on *Sir Gawain*, McNelis noticed that *The Master of Game* had not been edited since 1904, long before a series of revolutions in scholarly editing had taken place. Today it's unusual for a graduate student to be doing textual editing, though several decades ago it would have been more common. "I was lucky," says McNelis, whose edition of *The Master of Game* is under contract at a German press. "A ball that had been dropped rolled my way."

McNelis is no dusty medievalist. He entered the field after spending some time outside the academy working as a technical editor and writer for computer companies. In fact, publishing and editing have been central to his graduate school career. McNelis cut his teeth in publishing by working for the journal *Modern Language Quarterly*, which is edited at Washington-Seattle, and he is the founding editor and publisher of *Envoi*, an on-line medieval and Renaissance journal specializing in book reviews.

"I couldn't imagine life outside the academy," says Annalee Newitz, who entered graduate school at the University of California at Berkeley after spending her undergraduate years as a poet "madly in love with literature." These days Newitz is passionate about theory. "I was writing poems about decapitated birds, violated female bodies, and exploding houses. But poetry was too ambiguous. If I wanted to explain what was affecting me and my social world, I had to spell it out." Once in graduate school, Newitz fast became a self-described "theory head" as keen about philosophy as prime-time television. Having co-edited a recent anthology, *White Trash: Race and Class in America*, Newitz is now finishing her dissertation, an examination of how violence and terror represent class warfare, and how the popular media treat social issues.

McNelis and Newitz have more in common than may first appear. Each relies on the close reading of texts literary and otherwise, each scrutinizes the cultural context of texts, and each upholds the discipline's standards for critical analysis and interpretation. And both are grappling with current intellectual interests of their respective fields—violence, the body, ritual, and the relationship between popular and high culture.

WHY ENGLISH?

Studying English will give you the opportunity to read for pleasure scores of important and exciting books and even to tell people that you are "working" while doing so. But don't expect to spend your days as a graduate student curled up on a sofa, turning pages without a care in the world. The facts of professional life and the use of contemporary methods for studying literature are the source of anxiety as well as excitement for graduate students today. On the employment front, the academic job market in English is abysmal. It is not uncommon to hear horror stories about Ph.D.'s as talented as McNelis or Newitz spending upwards of eight years looking for full-time teaching jobs, all the while working several part-time teaching jobs as gypsy scholars to make ends meet.

Complicating the turmoil caused by a tight market is the fact that English professors have led some of the charges in the "culture" and "canon wars." Duke University's Stanley Fish has toured campuses across the United States, debating the essayist Dinesh D'Souza about the effects of politics, feminism, and multiculturalism on higher education in the United States. Cary Nelson, of the University of Illinois at Urbana, has edited several volumes that have criticized right-wing assaults on radical scholars and has attempted to prompt a civil debate about the purposes of the humanities. Meanwhile, a new professional organization, the Association of Literary Scholars and Critics, has emerged as a traditionalist answer to the explosion of theoretical methods that have emerged in the last thirty years.

That English professors have been outspoken of late simply reaffirms their long-standing place as often the largest and most visible university discipline. More than art history, philosophy, or even American history, English professors teach the bulk of what deans call "service courses"—the writing courses in which undergraduates sharpen their critical thinking and learn how to do college-level research. English departments also offer most of the survey courses in which undergraduates receive much of their general education and meet our culture's most valuable literary work, new and old. As English goes, so goes the perceived mission and mood of the university.

HOW ENGLISH HAS TAKEN SHAPE

Literary criticism as we know it is a recent invention, around for little more than a century. Debates about form and meaning, and arguments over style and structure, have always taken place among readers, but until quite recently the public forum for them was more often literary societies than college classrooms. In the mid-nineteenth century, while college students who were enrolled in classics courses parsed obscure Greek verbs and memorized snatches of Homer and Vergil, the members of literary societies gathered to read and discuss the British and American fiction of the day. Societies often housed libraries as large as those of the neighboring college or university, and their members could read more widely than today's students do in survey courses. During the latter half of the nineteenth century the novelist, critic, and editor William Dean Howells mastered the European literature of his day, much of it in the original languages, as a member of literary societies. At that time, a college degree, let alone graduate training in the study of literature, was by no means the norm among the literary tastemakers of the United States.

Literature departments only gradually got into the act of teaching modern literature and methods of literary criticism. As H.C.G.

Brandt, a professor of German literature at Hamilton College, exclaimed in 1883 at the first meeting of the Modern Language Society (the professional organization for literature and language professors), if teachers of modern languages do not realize "that their department is a science," then the idea will persist that "*anybody* can teach" French or German or English. The study of literature, Brandt emphasized, is a science that had to be approached as such.

Early literary scholars were philologists who investigated a work's linguistic and historical origins.

Literary scholars became scientists by becoming philologists, textual scholars who investigated a work's linguistic and historical origins. And instead of studying modern literature, they studied canonical poems and plays. Not everyone may care that Henry Wadsworth Longfellow's poem "Hiawatha" makes use of a little-known metrical scheme from Finnish epic poetry, but early literature professors enamored of philology applauded such erudition. Needless to say, not all writers made as inventive a use of their erudition as did the poet Longfellow. Francis March's 1879 textbook, *Method of Philological Study of the English Language*, was typical in format and approach. A line or two from Shakespeare or a classical author was followed by philologically-based questions about word etymology and linguistic structure. Student boredom with such drills is amply recorded in the memoirs of the day.

At the start of the twentieth century, a skirmish broke out between philologists and those literary critics who wanted to study the aesthetic dimensions of literature, which marked the first major shift toward literary study as we know it. Led by public university professors such as Fred Lewis Pattee of Pennsylvania State University, a popular critic and historian of mass-market fiction, the early literary critics had less "scientific" prestige than philologists, but also a more populist agenda. For example, Stuart Sherman, a teacher and journalist who taught high school before getting his Ph.D. from Harvard University in 1906, was a promising practical critic who berated philologists for using pedantic methods that robbed literature of pleasure and repelled all but specialized scholars. The philologists, Sherman complained, turned students into nothing but "zealous bibliographers and compilers of card indexes." Such remarks damaged Sherman's career at Harvard, then the summit of English departments and a bastion of philology, though Sherman eventually prospered at Illinois-Urbana.

Of course, many literary critics would be lost were it not for the guideposts provided by philologists and their cousins— bibliographers and historians of the text. What writer or student hasn't done at least some research into etymology? Nonetheless, despite the centrality of textual scholarship and its research methods, English departments eventually turned from philology to literary criticism in a movement that, as we'll see, has actually been more dialectical than it first seems.

The New Criticism is the most important of recent movements that put criticism in the forefront. The term "New Criticism" was coined by John Crowe Ransom, a member of a circle of scholars and poets at Vanderbilt University known as the Agrarians, a stridently anti-industrial and anti-urban group that idealized the values of the Old South. But along with the perspective of the Agrarians, several other important currents fed into New Criticism, many imported from Britain: The linguistics of I.A. Richards and the pronouncements of T.S. Eliot about literary canons were crucial, and even the attention of F.R. Leavis to the social context of fiction played a part, as did the eclectic philosophical and linguistic writings of William Empson.

The New Criticism is most recognized for making "close reading" the staple of literary interpretation. Cleanth Brooks's *The Well-Wrought Urn* (1947), a study of Romantic poetry and Keats, compactly and forcefully embodied the technique. For Brooks, a text was a self-sufficient literary artifact, a well-wrought urn that was a reservoir of myriad and ambiguous meanings, teased out by careful and prolonged attention to every word and rhythm of a text and the literary devices within it. Most New Critics applied the method to lyric poetry, particularly to that of the Elizabethans, John Donne and his contemporaries, and the British Romantics. In the 1950s, Mark Schorer of UC-Berkeley extended the method of close reading to prose fiction.

The New Criticism prospered partly due to the wildly popular literary anthologies Brooks edited with fellow English professor Robert Penn Warren, as well as to Brooks's charisma as a teacher and his effectiveness in passing on his ideas to his students, many of whom became prominent professors. One of Brooks's special talents was to convey a compelling nostalgia for unhampered private feeling, the pastoral, and pre-industrial society, an alternative realm to the

> The New Criticism is most recognized for making "close reading" the staple of literary interpretation.

frantic technological energies of the 1950s. "The tendency of science is necessarily to stabilize terms, to freeze them into strict denotations," he explained. "The poet's tendency is by contrast disruptive. The terms are continually modifying each other, and thus violating their dictionary meanings."

Although they cultivated nostalgia for imagined aristocratic worlds that stood apart from the everyday bustle of the 1950s (Brooks's first scholarly publication, a study of Southern dialect, was used by Vivian Leigh when she worked on the accent of Scarlett O'Hara for *Gone With the Wind*), Brooks and his fellow New Critics made literary study in the United States more democratic in the end. They provided professors, and especially those at the booming state universities, with the tools necessary for teaching the growing range of undergraduates represented in the postwar university, which now included World War II veterans as well as an increasing number of first-generation college students and first generation U.S. citizens.

Indeed, even University of Chicago professor Gerald Graff, himself the author of several books that take to task the political ideology underlying the New Criticism, has acknowledged his indebtedness to its pedagogical methods. "I remember the relief I experienced as a beginning assistant professor," Graff recalls, "when I realized that by concentrating on the text itself I could get a good discussion going about almost any literary work without having to know anything about its author, its circumstances of composition, or the history of its reception. Furthermore, as long as the teaching situation was reduced to a decontextualized encounter with a work, it made no difference that I did not know how much the students knew or what I could assume about their high school or other college work....Given the vast unknowns on both sides of the lectern, 'the work itself' was indeed our salvation."

Though the New Criticism dominated postwar literary study, it was not the only method available to literary critics. A rival for their attention was structuralism, a European import which also figured prominently in anthropology, comparative literature, and psychology departments. But because of its entrance into literary studies by way of University of Toronto professor Northrop Frye and his *Anatomy of Criticism* (1957), structuralism took a quite distinctive form in English departments.

Unlike the New Critics, Frye analyzed much more than a literary work's language and internal forms. He claimed that most literary expression could be categorized by universal allegorical patterns, themes, and genres. He proposed an example-laden theory that claimed that comedy, tragedy, romance, and irony underpin the narratives of all literary works, which in turn echoed certain organic processes like the change of seasons and quotidian rhythms. And Frye argued that symbols, along with their temporal and spatial patternings, are clues to the deep structures of the literary universe itself. All literary works are different, Frye proposed, yet they are all somehow spun from the same "great codes."

> Frye argued that symbols, along with temporal patterns, are clues to the deep structure of the literary universe itself.

More shocking to professors of English than Frye's synoptic views about the connections between particular literary works, however, were his methods and his breadth of reference. Frye did not base his case on textual scholarship of any kind—scrutinizing neither manuscripts nor single poems. Neither did he shoehorn his interests into a single period or field. Frye was confident enough about his conclusions to mention a dozen major literary works, from various times and nations, within a single paragraph of his criticism. Finally, Frye refused to subordinate literary criticism, and literature itself, to any other framework—ethical, historical, or formal. He proposed that while value judgments were an inevitable residue of criticism, the critic's chief task was descriptive, not prescriptive, and this alone was enough to justify critical analyses.

Frye's insistence on the literary critic's independence from the work of other disciplines, and his claims to objectively construct theories about deep literary structure, placed the critic, not the author, at the center of the critical enterprise. This position at the center was soon to be stressed by Frye's professor-descendants, who defined themselves as critics and theorists first and as scholars second. Even so, Frye conveyed his immense learning in a lucid, accessible manner. His courses on the Bible at Toronto regularly attracted over eight hundred students, and many of his books were popular successes. (One of his later works outsold every other nonfiction book in Canada—except Jane Fonda's workout guide.)

Another type of structuralism, distinct from Frye's efforts to understand the underlying structure of the literary universe, was also becoming prominent by the late 1960s. It combined the semiotics of the Swiss linguist Ferdinand de Saussure and the cultural anthropology of French anthropologist Claude Lévi-Strauss. Since its introduction, this Continental variety of structuralism has become so familiar and influential throughout the humanities that it has become a methodological given, now barely visible as a "movement" due to its broad acceptance. Of numerous guidebooks to it, the most useful for students of literature is Cornell University professor Jonathan Culler's *Structuralist Poetics* (1974), which appraises the limitations of structuralism as well as explaining its goals and charting its growth.

Structuralism's biggest impact was the way it dignified the role of literary theorist.

As complicated as the history of structuralism is, a few of its consequences for literary study are clear. For one thing, Continental-style structuralists insisted on the careful sifting of evidence in ways that were reminiscent of philologists laboring over sources and etymology. Some structuralists tirelessly unearthed, catalogued, and compared the hundred uses and associations of a word like "justice" within a text. Pointing out how poetry could enrich one's sensibility even in a modern industrial world, in the style of New Criticism at its most extreme, was no longer enough. Thanks to the influence of structuralism's emphasis on measurable evidence, the preachy tone of some of the New Criticism was for a time less pronounced in literary analysis.

But undoubtedly the biggest impact of structuralism on literary study was the increased dignity it gave to the role of the literary theoretician in the United States. The New Critics, of course, were literary theoreticians of a kind. Some, like I.A. Richards, were trained in linguistics, and many were sophisticated readers in Continental philosophy of language and hermeneutics. But even so, they were reluctant to call themselves theorists, in part because they associated theoretical enterprises with scientific thought, which they often vehemently rejected. Although even Frye relied heavily on interpretive theories, he culled them from literary sources, mostly the Bible and William Blake.

Critics after the structuralists, however, were not shy of calling themselves theoreticians or of looking to other disciplines for interpretive theories to apply to literature, including semiotics, cultural anthropology, philosophy, psychology, and even the laboratory sciences. With this change came another swing of the pendulum from context to text. Critics after structuralism were more likely again to see themselves as scientists rather than as lay preachers. In a sense, structuralists made literary texts into the proving ground of interpretive theories developed elsewhere.

In any case, today English departments are host to a carnival of theory. At your first Modern Language Association conference, as you divide your time between listening to talks, waiting for elevators, and wondering if professors ever wear anything besides tweed or black, it will dawn on you that there are probably more literary theories than there are spots on a leopard. If vertigo overwhelms you while pondering this fact—so much so that instead of retiring to your room, you repair to a couch bunkered by ferns and potted palms—keep one thing in mind: All the theories current in literature departments— psychoanalysis, African-Americanist, postcolonialism, Marxism, postmarxism, feminism, postfeminism, queer, new historicism, deconstruction, pragmatism, structuralism, postmodernism, poststructuralist, multicultural, multimedia, Foucauldian, Derridean, hermeneutic—are simply different theories of interpretation.

> In graduate school, you may very well read not only novels and poems, but newspapers, diaries, and court records.

What does this mean? In college you read novels, plays, and poems, and may have dabbled in deconstruction. In graduate school you may find yourself reading not only novels, plays, and poems, but newspapers, diaries, paintings, pornography, dime novels, and court records, all the while meeting a variety of methodological approaches to these objects of study. Moreover, you will find yourself being asked to interpret theories of interpretation. That is, you will learn not only how to interpret *Bleak House* through the lens of Michel Foucault's theories of power, but also how to interpret Foucault through some other theoretical lens, such as Marxism or psychoanalysis.

You will learn how to use various theories of interpretation and will also consider ways in which interpretations and theories can, in turn, serve different ideological agendas. During the culture wars, it's become commonplace for defenders of the Great Books to claim that the sky is falling because tenured radicals are using theory to politicize literature. Whether attacking African-American studies or postcolonial criticism, the defenders of the Great Books have complained that newer methods are preoccupied with the obvious point that language is linked to power, a reductive approach to literature. And their opponents counter that anything less than candid self-scrutiny by readers about what they value and why will perpetuate racism, sexism, class-inequality, and other abuses. They insist that attention to the politics of literature is part of helping to remedying these wrongs.

Much ink has been spilled over the question of whether or not literature can function as politics by other means, and this is not the place to take stock of that complex debate. In fact, the theory rage has more or less subsided, yet theory itself has hardly faded away. Remarks Duke's Stanley Fish, "The difference between today and fifteen years ago is that people then marched under the banner of theory. Now theory forms a set of vocabularies and models that you might or might not apply. It's another set of materials to call on, rather than something you religiously affirm or denounce."

By Fish's lights, literary theory today is not a position one takes but an essential resource in professional training. Whatever your political sympathies and critical proclivities, keep in mind that in the academy all theoretical tools tend to be used toward the same ends.

> Though the rage over theory has more or less subsided, theory itself has hardly faded away.

By learning how to use and interpret theories of interpretation you can choose to become a literary theorist. By learning how to be a literary theorist you can gain the credentials to become one of the custodians of a discourse within criticism. And by demonstrating that you have learned how to manipulate a discourse of criticism, you will be ready to perform part of the role of an English professor as a professional interpreter of literary objects.

Many object to Fish's perspective, but few can deny that he accurately charts the main pattern of professional training taken by the current luminaries in English. Although English professors still follow in the other traditions noted earlier in this history, and have many goals besides becoming professional interpreters, Fish's conception of professionalism does describe the dominant mode in the discipline now.

Instead of exhaustive accounts of all the theoretical movements that have developed over the past several decades, we offer a glimpse of those that have most stirred the waters. All in all, the movements born in the 1970s have remained highly theoretical, with important exceptions. Because feminist theorists and scholars of African-American literature have developed new canons of literature for general as well as academic readers, and because they have reinvigorated traditional textual scholarship as well as literary biography, we list them first.

FEMINIST

Since 1970, when Kate Millett published her groundbreaking book *Sexual Politics*, feminist criticism has concerned itself with the treatment of sexual difference in literary texts and in culture itself. In so doing, feminists have not created a single map of literature but what Catherine Stimpson of New York University calls "a portfolio of maps." Speaking generally there have been three "waves" of feminist scholarship, roughly in sync with and interacting with feminism outside the academy. The first wave, in the nineteenth and early twentieth century, centered on winning equal rights for women and was tied to political movements for universal suffrage, radical politics, sexual freedom, and religious reform. Scholarship of the 1970s, the second wave, drew on these traditions and tended to show how gender differences developed socially and historically, not just for women but for men too, and strove to recover the work of women writers and women's history. Feminist scholars collected forgotten work by women authors, critics, philosophers, scientists and others.

Once this work was widely disseminated in teaching anthologies and scholarly books in the 1980s, feminists launched a grand reevaluation of canons, tastes, and norms of gender, class, and race, as well as the normative assumptions of elite groups. During this time, Continental feminism and the penchant for linguistic and philosophical theory within it also established itself in the United States. A long-simmering debate intensified between feminists who thought that feminism meant primarily that women should have their fair share of existing privileges, and others who thought that feminism entailed a whole new conception of first principles and reevaluation of "privileges." Was feminism a lens through which to examine traditional values and research, or was it a whole new discipline in itself?

The third wave, still breaking, is harder to categorize. Feminist research sometimes initiated, sometimes made alliances, and sometimes collided with movements in cultural studies, postcolonialism, literary and film theory, and social science research. Defining the third wave is even more difficult, and possibly a limiting exercise, because feminists have been among the most interdisciplinary of scholars; the other chapters of this book trace their influence on virtually every discipline. Nonetheless, at the 1994 Modern Language Association convention, twenty-five leading feminist professors of literature, asked to take stock, turned as often to the vulnerability of feminism in literary studies in the current political climate as to charting feminism's evident successes throughout the academy. Right now, the prevailing mode is one of self-assessment. The projects of the first two waves continue, as do debates about what direction feminist scholarship will take. See the chapter on Women's Studies, which spells out some of the major debates going on today.

> Feminism in literary studies is a "portfolio of maps," not a political position reducible to labels.

Because it affects the very existence of feminist approaches to literature, the argument about whether to use the term "feminist literary criticism" or "gender studies" is worth noting. Both kinds of scholarship examine how gender and sexuality are represented in literary and cultural texts, yet "feminist" specifies an angle of analysis committed to the equality of the sexes, whereas "gender" does not necessarily imply such politics. (Indeed, part of the debate is over whether the term "gender" can be used in a neutral or apolitical fashion.) This difference implies that gender studies is feminist criticism minus the feminism, but this is not always the case, for many gender studies scholars also consider themselves feminists. One thing about the rubric "gender studies" is clear. Gender studies is often a euphemism for gay and lesbian criticism and feminism. With academic downsizing proceeding apace for vulnerable and new fields, "gender" is the term of choice when, for a variety of other reasons, "feminist" or "gay and lesbian" can be seen as red flags.

Remember, however, that feminism is a portfolio of maps, not a political position reducible to labels. *Feminisms in the Academy* by Domna C. Stanton and Abigail Stewart, both professors at the University of Michigan, *Feminisms* by Robyn R. Warhol of the University of Vermont and Diane Price Hearndl of the University of New Mexico at Las Cruces, and many other guides round up broad interdisciplinary approaches to feminism. If you are not already familiar with the journals listed at the end of the Women's Studies chapter, or have not visited the Web sites there, those suggestions will lead you to hundreds of books, myriad fields of study pertinent to English literature, and other resources.

AFRICAN-AMERICAN STUDIES

Despite the rich literary and critical tradition of African-American writing in the United States, African-American literary theory did not blossom until the early 1980s. Up to that time, when academics had discussed African-American writing, it was usually as an avenue into sociology or politics, not explicitly into literary theory. But due to the efforts of Yale's Robert Stepto, University of Pennsylvania professor Houston Baker, and Harvard University professor Henry Louis Gates Jr., literary theorists began to consider African-American literature as a tradition notable for its linguistic forms and aesthetic concerns. These scholars coined a critical language for discussing African-American writing by combining the pronouncements of earlier writers like W.E.B. Du Bois, Richard Wright, Langston Hughes, James Baldwin, and Ralph Ellison with some of the theoretical insights of deconstruction and poststructuralism. Their method is best embodied in Gates's adaptation of the practice of "signifyin(g)," which by synthesizing black vernacular with an academic term embodies the very syncretic, ironic aesthetic of the African-American tradition it described. As practical critics, these scholars have edited new scholarly editions of classic and rediscovered writers, created teaching anthologies of black literature, and been leaders in interdisciplinary classroom teaching that features every realm of black culture in the United States.

Feminist scholars of African-American literature, among them bell hooks of CUNY Graduate Center, Yale's Hazel Carby, and editor and writer Barbara Smith, have tried to explain how key elements of identity are revealed in literature. According to hooks, African-American theory must engage more explicitly with feminist practice and postmodernist ideas, all the while questioning the shortcomings of postmodern theory in understanding social class. Carby proposes that African-American feminism has been assimilated to a bourgeois humanism, neglecting writers like Jessie Fauset and Nella Larsen. Smith argues that African-American women's writing is essentially lesbian in outlook. These scholars all share an interest in uniting theoretical and practical insights into black culture, despite obvious differences in approach and subject matter.

NEW HISTORICISM

New historicists concentrate on the reciprocal relationship between literature and society. Clearly, this approach distinguishes them from the New Critics, who sometimes acted as though poems and novels existed in a vacuum, but it also separates them from old-style literary historians, who held that a literary work mirrors a world-view shared by most members of society. As Stephen Greenblatt, a Harvard scholar of Renaissance and Jacobean drama, explains in his famous essay "Towards a Poetics of Culture" (1987), a text can transmit a diverse, even contradictory, range of social beliefs (an idea that echoes deconstruction). For new historicists, a poem or a play is more a kaleidoscope than a mirror. And by extension, Greenblatt suggests that just as texts are neither autonomous nor consistent, so too are individuals shaped by an array of contradictory social beliefs and institutions. The self is a kaleidoscope of kaleidoscopes.

> For new historicists, a text can transmit a diverse, even contradictory, range of social beliefs.

Though in the early and mid-1980s new historicists worked almost exclusively on Elizabethan and Jacobean drama and poetry, scholars who researched other periods and genres soon got into the act. In *The Gold Standard and the Logic of Naturalism* (1987), for instance, Walter Benn Michaels of Johns Hopkins University uses a new historicist approach to explain how the novels of Frank Norris and others embody the contradictory attitudes toward the gold standard and paper money that rocked American society in the late nineteenth century. Like Greenblatt, Michaels rejects both a formalist approach and a crudely deterministic one in the way he interprets how literature both shapes and is shaped by social meanings.

One of the distinctions between new historicism, feminist, and African American scholarship is that though drawing on Marxism, cultural studies, and a raft of other methodologies with explicit ideological agendas, new historicists rarely take political positions about matters outside the academy. This is not to say that the movement ignores political questions, but that new historicist manifestos have concentrated on the academic role of the movement—its main thrust has concerned ways to interpret literature, to examine the politics of the past, and to assess various interpretative theories.

POSTCOLONIAL STUDIES

Postcolonial studies is the Caliban of literary study. Heavily indebted to the 1950s writings of Aimé Césaire and Frantz Fanon, and bolstered by Columbia University professor Edward Said's research on "orientalism," postcolonial studies examines how Western society affected colonial nations and was in turn affected by them, including the intellectual life as well as the cultural resources of colonies. But just as importantly today, postcolonial critics examine how former colonials wrote back, often in the language of the oppressor, to challenge and correct the Western imports foisted upon them. (See the chapter on Comparative Literature.)

Postcolonial studies is all over the map. It studies literatures written at different times in Latin America, the Caribbean, Australia, India, Africa, and North America. Writers as disparate as Salman Rushdie, Isak Dinesen, Wilson Harris, and Gabriel García Márquez are discussed, while canonical writers such as Jane Austen, W.B. Yeats, and Joseph Conrad now come in for reevaluation to the extent that their work concerns questions of colonial politics, nationality, and hybridity. Postcolonial critics examine how facets of European culture, such as university curricula, were taught and received in former colonies, while also studying forms of expression that English professors once ignored, like Australian Aboriginal oral culture.

WHAT'S NEXT

There are one hundred forty-nine Ph.D. programs in English in the United States. When you start to investigate departments, the most meaningful initial distinction is size. Many state universities have large Ph.D. programs in English, while most of the small ones are at private universities, usually wealthy ones. Big programs like UCLA or Illinois-Urbana have large faculties and offer many courses. Large size confers advantages other than just variety. When students come up with dissertation ideas, a large department will most likely have more than one professor qualified to advise them. Another plus is that if you enroll at a big department you'll have more student colleagues and more of an opportunity to avoid the incestuous relationships that plague small departments. The downside is that sometimes you'll have to fight harder to be recognized—and funded.

Small programs like Princeton University, Stanford University, and Rice University offer certain other benefits, the most important of which is better funding. Since smaller programs have fewer students to fund, they are almost always more generous than public universities. The drawback of a small department is, of course, the flipside of the benefits of a large one: fewer choices of faculty to work with and perhaps less diversity among your classmates. If you want to write about Dickens but you don't get along with the department's Dickensian, you can either bite the bullet and work with her anyway, or pick another dissertation topic.

Whether you like it or not, you should think about a department's prestige. One recent job-market candidate from a large state school advises prospective students, "You should not even think about throwing yourself into this profession if you can't go to one of the elite institutions." Another state university graduate even suggests "mortgaging your soul if you have to" in order to go to a high-profile school.

Name brands matter, then, but you should be wary of the national rankings that underwrite their value. The rankings provided by the National Research Council are based on self-reported and frequently inaccurate statistics. English is such a large field—both conceptually and in terms of the size of programs—that no poll can be sensitive to its nuances. And perhaps more than in most other disciplines, celebrity power counts in English, so that the presence of even one or two of the best scholars in a subfield in an otherwise low-profile department can mean the difference between getting an interview and being ignored in the job market when you finish your degree. The choice of a department is a highly personal matter, for which an intelligent decision requires at least a couple of visits to a department to get its feel.

With the weakening of the old walls between subjects, students have many new options for specialization. The period and genre boundaries have lost much force because departments have hired theorists, African Americanists, and postcolonialists, to say nothing of specialists in feminism, composition, and emerging fields like literature and science. "I recently helped evaluate an English department at another university," explains Patrick Brantlinger of Indiana University. "Three decades ago, two-thirds of its faculty specialized in traditional literary periods. Today, this department includes just one medievalist and two Renaissance scholars. Only about one-third of its faculty now concentrate in traditional areas. Half a dozen are in creative writing; another half-dozen in composition; another half-dozen in film studies; five or six do theory or cultural studies; four are linguists; three are African Americanists; and there is also a lone folklorist. I suspect that the stories are similar at many other universities."

Yet though the old divisions based on covering the whole history and generic fields of English literature are weakening, don't believe the hype that a brave new interdisciplinary age has dawned. The traditional organization of the field still affects how scholars define themselves and how the job market works. "I do not think that current trends are causing English departments automatically to evolve into cultural studies," offers Brantlinger. Departments still cater to periods and genres, and if you have a particular interest that falls in these categories, you should pursue it. Keep in mind, though, that attention to previously unrecognized literatures, the rise of composition studies, and the staying power of theory have changed the balance of power in departments. In light of this development, we offer the following breakdown of fields old and new (and notable faculty). The list is far from exhaustive and the order in which schools are mentioned is not an order of precedence. As in every discipline in this book, finding the program that is right for you is a matter of personal legwork; the institutions named are simply well-known starting places.

> The traditional organization of the field according to periods and genres still affects how scholars define themselves.

For medieval, consider Cornell, the University of Virginia, UC-Berkeley, Harvard, Yale (Lee Patterson), UCLA, Toronto, and Indiana. For Renaissance: Harvard (Stephen Greenblatt), Michigan, Penn, Virginia, Chicago, and Duke. For eighteenth-century British, UC-Berkeley (Catherine Gallagher), Chicago (J. Paul Hunter), Brown University (Nancy Armstrong), Stanford (John Bender), Penn (John Richetti), Harvard, and Virginia. For nineteenth-century British: Princeton, Virginia, Penn, Yale, UCLA, Michigan, Indiana (Susan Gubar), UC-Berkeley, Duke, the University of Southern California, Rice, and the University of Tulsa.

For colonial American, consider Harvard (Sacvan Bercovitch) and Columbia (Andrew Delbanco). And for nineteenth- and twentieth-century American, look to Penn (Nina Auerbach, Peter Conn), Chicago (Robert von Hallberg, Lauren Berlant), Duke, Stanford,

UC-Berkeley, UCLA, Princeton (Elaine Showalter), Columbia (Ann Douglas), the University of California at Davis, Rutgers University (Richard Poirier), Michigan, Brown (Robert Scholes), Washington-Seattle, the University of Pittsburgh (Paul Bove), and the University of California at Santa Barbara. For twentieth-century British: Princeton, Brown, and UC-Davis. For American literature in general: UC-Berkeley, Duke (Cathy Davidson), Johns Hopkins (Walter Benn Michaels), Yale, Stanford (Marjorie Perloff), Columbia, the University of Utah, Brandeis University, and Rutgers (Myra Jehlen). For African American: Harvard (Henry Louis Gates Jr.), Princeton (Arnold Rampersad), Virginia (Eric Lott), and the University of Maryland at College Park. For Native American, the University of Oklahoma and New Mexico-Las Cruces. For Asian-American, the University of Wisconsin at Madison.

For poetry: Cornell (Roger Gilbert), Princeton, and Stanford. For feminism: CUNY Graduate Center, Indiana, Rutgers, and Washington-Seattle. For postcolonial studies: Columbia (Edward Said) and Yale (Sara Sulieri Goodyear). For cultural studies, check out Illinois-Urbana (Cary Nelson), UC-Santa Barbara (Constance Penley), the University of Minnesota at Twin Cities, and Oklahoma. For textual and bibliographic studies: the University of South Carolina, Virginia, Indiana, and Penn State. For composition/rhetoric: Pittsburgh, Purdue University, Oklahoma, Miami University of Ohio, the University of Texas at Austin, and Penn State. For theory: Duke (Stanley Fish), Johns Hopkins, the University of California at Irvine (J. Hillis Miller, Brook Thomas), Cornell (Jonathan Culler, Cynthia Chase), and Rutgers.

Emory University, the University of Georgia, Penn State, UC-Santa Barbara, and Illinois-Urbana are up-and-coming departments, while Johns Hopkins is noted as a small department especially attentive to its students. Michigan and Indiana are large departments known for taking good care of their students. Departments well-known for placing students include UC-Berkeley, the University of Iowa, Stanford, Penn, and Princeton.

Though it's important to choose a department with an eye to specialization, there are dangers to specializing too early. It's one thing to enter graduate school planning to study Shakespeare, and it's another to enter with the goal of writing a Lacanian dissertation that analyzes the female characters of Shakespeare's *Henry VI* cycle. Given the fierce competition for jobs, it's easy to succumb to the lure of narrowing your expertise to fit the kinds of scholarship that seem to land students jobs. Try to resist. Early specialization inevitably shrinks the broad interests most students bring to the field to fit a confined area of mastery. Such narrow expertise is likely to fit neither the job market nor your genuine areas of interest, and faking enthusiasm grows taxing quickly.

Because being an apprentice literary scholar involves learning how to teach as well as how to do specialized research, nearly all Ph.D. programs in English include a teaching requirement, but the exact requirement varies widely. A few graduate students must teach for two semesters, most for four or more. Some students start teaching in their first year, some in their second year, while a small number might not teach at all. At Chicago, for instance, an otherwise commendable tradition of having senior faculty teach even introductory undergraduate courses means that graduate students are not guaranteed teaching slots at the university itself. At Yale, however, graduate students teach for many years as the leaders of their own writing classes and as discussion section leaders of larger literature courses. It's almost unheard of for a Yale student to graduate without several years of teaching experience, but it's also rare for Yale students to finish their Ph.D.'s in less than seven years. At Princeton, on the other hand, the English department funds its graduate students generously so that they need to do little teaching, but they are expected to move through the program at a brisk pace. Some Princeton students graduate in as little as five or six years, and with as little as a year's teaching experience. Teaching is often the most satisfying part of your grad school years; even so, many departments treat teaching as though it is a burden or a distraction from the real work of scholarship. Talk to several students about this issue, taking care to not put too much weight on any single personal testimonial.

The amount of preparation required of students before they start teaching varies, too. In some programs, before students start to teach they take a required course in pedagogy, where they grapple with different pedagogical philosophies, draft mock assignments and syllabi, and sometimes even go through dry runs of paper grading. Then, once students start to teach, they periodically confer with faculty mentors to discuss the problems and the triumphs they have experienced

> Nearly all Ph.D. programs in English include a teaching component.

in the classroom. Columbia, for instance, is somewhat unusual in having an elaborate teacher-preparation program for both composition and Great Books instructors. Other programs use a sink-or-swim approach: Graduate students are tossed into the classroom with a tremendous amount of responsibility and hardly any guidance.

Most apprentice English teachers begin by teaching composition courses, and occasionally have the opportunity to teach a literature course or two. Graduate students who teach literature courses are often discussion leaders who are assigned a group of students from within a large lecture course. The drawback to teaching literature is that a student must teach someone else's syllabus and do most of the grading for the course. But the advantage is that the subject matter of a literature course can overlap with your own area of research—and one of the best ways to learn book is to teach it.

Composition courses have always been stigmatized as the grunt work of English departments, which is why composition instructors are usually graduate students or adjuncts, not professors. (But increasingly, professors who teach composition or direct a program in comp have earned their Ph.D.'s from a composition/rhetoric program.) Though graduate students are paying their dues by teaching comp, there are invaluable benefits. A composition course is as much a lab for instructors as for those students who must face the horrifying fact that an essay can have more than five paragraphs. Because composition instructors usually design and teach their own courses, they have the freedom to test pedagogical methods and to cultivate a teaching style. Also, teaching composition provides you with the most transportable skill in academia. A demonstrated ability to teach writing will allow you to maintain a part-time membership in the profession even if you decide to earn your living elsewhere. And because improving their writing is a priority for many students, you'll find your efforts appreciated and have the satisfaction of imparting an essential skill.

THE JOB MARKET

Although the job market is tough throughout the humanities, no other discipline has sparked a popular trade book about the problem. Donald J. Snyder's *The Cliff Walk: A Job Lost and A Life Found* is an account of his experience as an English teacher at an elite university who becomes a rough-work carpenter when he is downsized from his job and unable to find another academic position in today's market. Since 1989, the number of advertised job openings for Ph.D.'s has dropped nearly 50 percent, and the job placement rate for new Ph.D.'s (including temporary positions without the possibility of tenure) is 45 percent. It is not unheard of for a single position at a small teaching college to attract upwards of 700 applicants. Many English Ph.D.'s are willing to work as freeway flyers, commuting between part-time teaching positions that do not pay a living wage even if an instructor accepts two or three of them at once. Even though this bad news is well known, however, the attractions of English are so strong that top grad schools report a rise in applications.

Perhaps because of its size and importance at most institutions, or possibly due to the prolixity of its professors, English is the field that has most often and most publicly questioned its purpose, mission, and hiring practices. From the ritual self-examining presidential addresses of the Modern Language Association annual convention to volumes by individual English professors, a variety of schemes are in the air to ameliorate a chronic oversupply of Ph.D.'s and to help new Ph.D.'s find nonacademic jobs. So far, however, those professors suggesting reforms usually concede that their ideas will do little to counteract the effects of several decades of too few jobs for too many candidates. Although the legend that the job market will rebound has been long-lived, what hard data is available does not bear that out. If you want to earn an English Ph.D., take seriously the faculty warnings you are likely to hear. You cannot expect a job to await you.

If this situation seems daunting, you might consider earning an M.A. to test the waters. The top English programs, however, will not provide financial support for students who intend to earn an M.A. only. And if you decide to enrolling in a Ph.D. program later, many programs will look askance at you for not enrolling in a Ph.D. program from the outset, since going straight for the Ph.D. is taken to signal an all-consuming and requisite commitment to becoming an English professor. As a credential for other employment, an M.A. is useful for public high school teaching, and might help you if you are looking for a job in publishing or at a not-for-profit institution, museum, or corporate education program. For academic teaching jobs an M.A. is helpful at secondary schools and community colleges, but increasingly Ph.D.'s who already have teaching experience compete for those positions.

RESOURCES

NRC TOP TEN
Yale
UC-Berkeley
Harvard
Virginia
Duke
Stanford
Cornell
Penn
Columbia
Chicago

ASSOCIATIONS
Modern Language Association
(212) 475-9500

JOURNALS
American Literature
Contemporary Literature
Critical Inquiry
Eighteenth Century Studies
ELH
Modern Fiction Studies
PMLA
Raritan
Representations
SAQ
Speculum

FURTHER READING
Gerald Graff, *Professing Literature* (Chicago)
Stephen Greenblatt and Giles Gunn, eds.,
Redrawing the Boundaries (MLA)

WEB ADDRESSES
Jack Lynch's Literary Resources Page
http://www.english.upenn.edu/~jlynch/Lit
Voice of the Shuttle
http://humanitas.ucsb.edu

CONSTELLATIONS

MEDIEVAL
Cornell
Duke
Harvard
Indiana
Toronto
UC-Berkeley
UCLA
Virginia
Yale

RENAISSANCE
Chicago
Duke
Harvard
Michigan
Penn
Virginia

EIGHTEENTH-CENTURY BRITISH
Chicago
Brown
Harvard
Stanford
Penn
UC-Berkeley
UC-Santa Barbara
Virginia

NINETEENTH-CENTURY BRITISH
Duke
Indiana
Michigan
Princeton
Penn
Rice
Tulsa
UC-Berkeley
UCLA
USC
Virginia
Yale

NINETEENTH- AND TWENTIETH-CENTURY AMERICAN

Brown
Chicago
Duke
Michigan
Pittsburgh
Princeton
Rutgers
Stanford
UC-Berkeley
UC-Davis
UCLA
UC-Santa Barbara
Washington-Seattle

TWENTIETH-CENTURY BRITISH

Brown
Princeton
UC-Davis

AMERICAN LITERATURE

Brandeis
Columbia
Duke
Johns Hopkins
Rutgers
Stanford
UC-Berkeley
Utah
Vanderbilt
Yale

AFRICAN-AMERICAN STUDIES

Harvard
Maryland-College
  Park
Princeton
Virginia

LATINO STUDIES

UCLA

ASIAN-AMERICAN STUDIES

Madison-Wisconsin

NATIVE AMERICAN STUDIES

New Mexico-Las
  Cruces
Oklahoma

POETRY

Cornell
Princeton
Stanford

THEORY

Duke
Florida-Gainesville
Johns Hopkins
Rutgers
UC-Irvine

FEMINISM

CUNY Graduate
  Center
Indiana
Rutgers
Washington-Seattle

POSTCOLONIAL STUDIES

Columbia
Yale

CULTURAL STUDIES

Illinois-Urbana
Minnesota-Twin
  Cities
Oklahoma
Rochester
UC-Santa Barbara

TEXTUAL AND BIBLIOGRAPHIC STUDIES

Indiana
Penn State
South Carolina
Virginia

COMPOSITION/RHETORIC

Miami of Ohio
Oklahoma
Penn State
Pittsburgh
Purdue
UT-Austin

CONSTELLATIONS

CHAPTER 9

FILM STUDIES

Alison Trope grew up in Los Angeles, where she came to love film and hate Hollywood. "I'm something of a modernist," confesses Trope, who as an undergraduate designed her own major on early twentieth-century Russian and German history and art. But, now a sixth-year graduate student at USC, Trope is writing a dissertation that bridges the gap between high and low culture: It's a history of film exhibition in museum spaces, the Museum of Modern Art, the American Museum of the Moving Image, and Planet Hollywood among them. "Cinema exhibition has long been a subject of film studies scholarship," notes Trope. "With museums the issues are fascinating. When film was first shown at MoMA in the 1930s, it was deemed low culture, but today MoMA is perceived as an elitist outpost of film, while Planet Hollywood is seen as trash." Trope is explaining this shift and its relationship to the rise of middlebrow taste.

"After I finished college," recalls Kelly Hankin, "I discovered a whole new realm of scholarship, lesbian film theory, and I immediately became excited about being an academic—as a means of furthering my personal growth." For Hankin, a fourth-year graduate student at the University of Rochester, the intellectual challenge of film studies is due in no small part to the field's overlap with her nonacademic interests. Hankin is a curator and programmer for the Rochester Lesbian and Gay Film Festival, and through academic research she has uncovered material to program, while through programming she has learned to appreciate the value—and limits—of research. "Though you do want to challenge an audience, you can't just expect an audience to like a film that academics have labeled as critical. In order to know what to program, you have to know something about your audience."

WHY FILM STUDIES?

When strangers strike up a conversation in a bus, bar, or supermarket, chances are they talk about the movies, not politics or Proust, because in the United States movies are the cultural vernacular, the demotic language of democratic culture. Of course, movies haven't necessarily assumed such status through popular appeal alone. The dream factories have long been economic powerhouses. In 1993, for instance, the total receipts for motion pictures alone were $48 billion. And in 1995, media conglomerates like Disney, Time Warner, and Turner Broadcasting further concentrated their power in the entertainment and communications industry with merger and acquisition deals valued at $93 billion, double the 1993 total.

No matter the cause, strangers do chat about film as much as they talk about the weather. And it is the film scholar's task to enrich that conversation—not only by surveying what people say about films but by discerning what films say to us about culture and society, whether it be in terms of economics, politics, entertainment, or art. Few film scholars expect their work to catapult them into a career as the next Pauline Kael. And for good reason: Film scholars tend to frown upon colleagues who manage to publish in mainstream venues like *Cineaste*, *Sight and Sound*, or the *Village Voice*. Nonetheless, though film studies tailors the study of mass culture to the interests of a select academic audience, film scholars take great pleasure in studying a subject that some academics still consider suspect.

Films have been made for over a century; film studies has existed for barely thirty-five years. Yet a remarkably diverse range of scholarship has appeared under the banner of film studies. To the uninitiated at least, the field may appear to be less a haven for intellectual diversity than a harbor for intellectual schizophrenia. Film studies scholars study television as well as film, *Star Trek* as well as *Stella Dallas*, porno magazines as well as *Psycho*, *Ricki Lake* as well as *Citizen Kane*, fascism as well as film stock. Besides having appointments in film studies departments, film scholars also teach in English, art history, comparative literature, communication, and media studies departments. Some university presses have even augmented their film studies offerings with media studies books about Disney, the Internet, and talk shows, among other things.

And the roiling mix of departments, institutional affiliations, and intellectual coteries is as diverse as the subjects being studied. Unlike a discipline such as linguistics, in which different scholars generally agree that a single figure, Noam Chomsky, is in large part responsible for the discipline's contemporary foundations, film studies is without an intellectual figurehead or a methodological consensus. Instead, departments and professors organize themselves around two unresolved controversies, the first long-standing and the second more recent: the place of mass culture in film studies, and the effect of digital media on film studies. Because film studies is such a mélange, the best way to survey the field and ponder graduate study in it is to become acquainted with the history of these two controversies, the kinds of trade-offs they involve, and the way they will complicate the pleasure you derive from sitting in the dark watching movies.

HOW FILM STUDIES HAS TAKEN SHAPE

Film departments were first established in five universities—USC in 1932, and UCLA, New York University, City College of New York, and Boston University by the end of the 1940s. By the end of the 1950s, a handful of English, art history, and speech and communication departments at such places as Indiana University, the University of Iowa, the University of Wisconsin at Madison, and the University of Texas at Austin offered individual courses in film history and criticism, often under the innocuous title "film appreciation." The nascent field finally acquired academic legitimacy in 1959 with the founding of a professional society, the Society of Cinematologists. The society has since scrubbed away the scientific veneer: It's now called the Society for Cinema Studies, or SCS. In 1969 SCS had one hundred members, in 1979 more than three hundred. Today it has swelled to over 1,300 members, roughly 400 of whom are graduate students.

Film studies coalesced around the culture of postwar American film buffs that flourished in film appreciation societies sponsored by the George Eastman House in Rochester, New York, and the Museum of Modern Art in New York City. These societies prized European art cinema—Italian neorealism and the French New Wave—and its critical stance of auteurism, which treated film as the aesthetic medium of a director's personal expression. By 1957 these societies were so active that MoMA sponsored a conference on motion picture education, which met for the next three years. And in 1959 many society members joined the fledgling Society of Cinematologists.

In 1963 in the *Journal of the Society of Cinematologists*, Robert Gessner, a founding member of the Society of Cinematologists, proposed a way for film study to take its place in academe's sacred halls. First, there was the question of language. "'Movies' and 'scholarship,'" wrote Gessner, "are words which sound strange when heard in juxtaposition. The two [have] not been considered marriageable in the traditional halls of academe." Gessner hoped, however, that "a wider acceptance of *cinema* [would] eventually signal admittance at a high-church ceremony." By the late 1960s, film studies scholars were accepted into the university because they had acted on Gessner's plan and developed curricula devoted to art cinema, not "movies."

"Scholarship" and "movies" used to sound strange in juxtaposition.

Explains David Bordwell, a professor of film at Wisconsin-Madison, they were able to prove that film studies is "a clearly humanistic endeavor with three basic concerns: theory (aesthetics), history (empirical research), and critical analysis (interpretation)." Film scholars outfitted themselves with the humanists' tools by culling critical and research methods from literary study, drama, history, and communication departments. Their archival research techniques were from historians, and their close reading techniques from the New Critics, literary critics who saw the text as a free-standing aesthetic object with a structure that should be explored in its own terms.

Film studies, then, took shape in a procrustean bed of high culture that chopped off film's existence as a medium of popular culture. The nascent field favored "films" like *Citizen Kane* or *Bicycle Thief*, not "movies" like *Picnic* or *West Side Story*. Nonetheless, the mere fact of film studies' existence was—and continues to be—scandalous to those academics who prefer Plato or Ezra Pound over what they call Hollywood trash. Some film scholars even speculate that many introductory film courses are scheduled at night because film is still regarded by academics as mere entertainment, something to kick back and watch after a hard day in the physics lab or the philosophy seminar.

> Intro film courses were scheduled at night because some academics still regarded film as mere entertainment.

But precisely because film studies has built a foundation on its reputation as a school for scandal, it has been keen to establish intellectual precedents in the academy. Over the years scholars from different areas of the humanities have migrated to film studies because it has been receptive to different critical theories, especially those considered too flashy or radical for other disciplines, such as sociology, philosophy, or even American history. So, since the 1960s, when it was cobbled together from interdisciplinary resources—drama, literary studies, communication—at many universities, film studies has been a vanguard discipline, home of perpetual intellectual ferment.

One crucial period of ferment was the mid-1970s, when film studies was transformed by a wave of Continental critical theory. At this time it became *de rigueur* for American and British film scholars dissatisfied with auteurism and aesthetics to do a stint of coursework at the Center for Critical Studies in Paris, where they tackled the work of Roland Barthes, Jean-Louis Baudry, and Christian Metz, among others. Observing film through the lens of semiotics and psychoanalysis, these scholars stressed the link between film's form and ideology, or film's reproduction of dominant social values. Film was seen as an expression of mass culture.

What's more, Continental theory was especially crucial to feminists, who made serious inroads into film studies by using theory to explain both the patriarchal perspective of classical Hollywood cinema and the ways that alternative cinema, both male- and female-authored, subverted that perspective. New publications like *Screen*, *New Left Review*, *Camera Obscura*, and the British Film Institute pamphlet series made semiotics, psychoanalysis, and feminist film theory widely available to faculty and students who couldn't make the trek to Paris. At conferences and in curricula, the theories of film as mass culture competed with the appreciation of film as high culture.

Since the 1970s, much of the controversy in film studies has stemmed from the differences between scholars who focus upon film and its institutions as their primary object of study and those who use film, or any other media, to raise theoretical questions about identity and mass culture. Scholars who take film and its institutions as their primary object of study advance the mission defined by SCS in its early stages. They use archival research and the close analysis of film texts to explore the aesthetic dimensions and industrial protocols of film production. They write histories of film conventions and institutions and analyze film style and narrative, changes in the technological apparatus, genre characteristics of national cinemas, and the economic organization of the film industry. Noted scholars in this tradition are David Bordwell and Noël Carroll of Wisconsin-Madison, who together edited *Post-Theory: Reconstructing Film Studies*; Kristin Thompson of Wisconsin-Madison and Janet Staiger of UT-Austin, who co-authored *The Classical Hollywood Cinema: Film Style and Modes of Production to 1960*; Lea Jacobs of Wisconsin-Madison, who wrote *The Wages of Sin: Censorship and the Fallen Woman Film, 1928-1942*; Charles Musser of Yale University, who edited *The Emergence of Cinema: The American Screen to 1907*; and Janet Wasko of the University of Oregon, who wrote *Hollywood in the Information Age*.

Film and media scholars who downplay film-based questions in favor of theoretical or sociological studies of institutions and audiences think their work is valuable exactly because it defies academic standards of canonization and taste. Reception scholarship—the outgrowth of theories of spectatorship, which appeared in the 1970s as alternatives to text-based aesthetic criticism—studies the metapsychology of viewing, considering a viewer's response to a film, and especially how a viewer experiences social ideology or personal pleasure. Following the lead of British critic Stephen Heath and French film theorist Christian Metz, feminist film scholars like Laura Mulvey of the British Film Institute, UCLA professor Janet Bergstrom, and University of California at Berkeley professor Kaja Silverman drew on semiotics and psychoanalysis to explain that a film is a system of signs encoded with social meanings, and that this signifying system defines a certain role or identity for the spectator.

> Theories of film as mass culture competed with the appreciation of film as high culture.

But some scholars, feminists no less, grew frustrated with theories of spectatorship because they skirted the nettlesome question of how audiences interpret what they watch. Feminists wanted to study not only how mass culture traffics in certain images of femininity, but also how women and men react to those images. Thus, newfangled reception scholars turned to ethnography to develop a more supple method for examining media's meanings and uses. In fact, over the past decade, reception scholars working in film, TV, and video have been the major architects of cultural studies, which has infused many of the other disciplines described by this guide, and which claims that cultural consumers are active makers of meaning, not dupes who passively and uncritically absorb mass culture. To clue yourself in on the scholarship that reception scholars produce, you might peruse *Textual Poachers: Television Fans and Participatory Culture* by Henry Jenkins of MIT; *The Future of an Illusion: Film, Feminism and Psychoanalysis* by Constance Penley of the University of California at Santa Barbara; *Make Room for TV: Television and the Family Ideal in Postwar America* by Lynn Spigel of USC; and *The Desire to Desire: The Woman's Film of the 1940s* by Mary Anne Doane of Brown University.

> Film scholars are leaders in cultural studies, an influence on most of the other disciplines in the humanities and social sciences.

Another reason that film studies is changing is that the film industry itself constantly develops according to technological innovations. Most recently, digital media has drastically altered image production and forged new links between the entertainment and communications industries. Faculty and students in film studies and in other disciplines are using hypertext, CD-ROMs, and the Web to do research, write papers, and conduct seminars. Syllabi are crammed with books and articles about the Web, virtual reality, and hackers. Unlike the theory revolution of the 1970s, which radiated from Paris to British and U.S. satellites, the digital revolution of the 1990s is diffuse. Faculty stress that semipermeable departmental boundaries and interdisciplinary curricula are vital for anyone who wants to study digital media or use it to produce research. According to Marsha Kinder, a professor of film at USC and author of *Blood Cinema* (a CD-ROM about Spanish films), understanding the hybrid nature of hypertext involves studying it from many disciplinary angles: print media, TV studies, computer science, architecture, and communication. Working with digital media can also take a film scholar far afield.

143

When producing the *Blood Cinema* CD-ROM, Kinder worked closely with a visual designer and an interface designer, and she notes that her collaboration with them was much more demanding and enlightening than what usually occurs between, say, the author of a book and the designer of the book's dust jacket.

The interdisciplinary nature of digital media, however, is defined as much by administrative timidity as by intellectual upheaval. Kinder warns that students keen on digital media need to keep in mind that the conservative fiscal policies of departments, deans, and publishers have hampered research and development. "Things are moving very slow on the money end," Kinder says, "because administrators and publishers are leery of making big investments in an undefined area that people are still trying to understand." In fact, Kinder formed her own company to produce *Blood Cinema* after the university press that published her book balked at the idea of publishing a companion CD-ROM. At many universities there is not an umbrella department for media study, nor a single program on digital media, let alone TV or video, and this sends faculty and students scrambling to different departments to study digital media like Tom Stoppard characters in search of a plot.

Interdisciplinarity is currently an institutional necessity for studying digital media because intellectual resources are dispersed throughout the university. This situation is likely to change, though. Professors like Kinder are busy establishing themselves as authorities on hypertext, virtual reality, and digital culture in order to establish the academic viability of the field and thereby increase their chances of convincing a dean to fund digital media programs.

> Because of funding problems, some departments can't invest in digital media.

In terms of assessing digital technology's impact on film studies, scholars are clumped into three groups: traditionalists, pragmatists, and trendsetters. Traditionalists are excited about digital media but nonplussed about their effects on the study of film. This small, tenacious group, led by Bordwell and Carroll, is convinced that there are formal problems and research issues unique to film, such as film exhibition and industry self-regulation, and that film scholars should remain committed to studying them. If anything, they argue, digital media will enhance the study of film-based problems: Scholars can upgrade their research and pedagogical methods with state-of-the-art tools, like CD-ROMs. If there are formal problems specific to digital media, they believe, some other program should study them, as has been the case at Wisconsin-Madison and NYU.

For pragmatists, "film studies" has become an elastic term, both a handy conceit for the study of visual and popular culture that includes a constellation of media (film, TV, video, virtual reality, hypertext, the Internet) and a necessary reminder of the discipline's historical roots in the study of film, the first technology of visual mass culture. For pragmatists like UC-Santa Barbara's Constance Penley, film studies should embrace scholars who focus on the cultures and social institutions that feed on visual technologies. Pragmatists study Star Trek fans, MUD users, pornography consumers, film-industry regulators, the FCC, gay fans of Hollywood musicals, and the censorship of children's media. Pragmatists envision film studies as a big tent.

> In terms of digital technology, there are traditionalists, pragmatists, and trendsetters.

There are digital enthusiasts, however, who are less sanguine about the ability of traditionalists to fend off the challenge of digital media. These trendsetters foresee the obsolescence of film's mechanical- and celluloid-based medium. After all, they stress, computer-generated moving images now appear alongside words, achieving an intertextuality greater than that of most films on celluloid. And increasingly, films in production are transferred to video and edited on an AVID computer, not in the cutting room. With more audacity than trepidation, trendsetters predict that film studies will go down one of two paths: either retreating as a university discipline into media or visual studies, or hardening into full-scale connoisseurship and joining ranks with art history. "Film studies programs risk becoming archaic if they don't change to adapt the new media," warns David Rodowick, a professor of film and visual culture at Rochester. "They will be overwhelmed by the telecommunications side of things. It's hard to imagine film studies standing alone; film will have to be understood as a part of a constellation of other media." To upstarts like Rodowick, traditionalists who champion truth in advertising (film studies is about *film*, as in *celluloid*, damn it!) are simply circling their wagons.

But those who hear the death knell of film studies in the whir of a hard drive are actually carrying on the kind of boundary-testing that has always been a film studies tradition. In fact, although they value

different kinds of intellectual ferment, the traditionalists, the pragmatists, and the trendsetters make their cases on much the same
grounds. Each group stakes out traditional humanities turf, claiming
that its own approach to film or media provides students with the
critical skills necessary for understanding the cultural vernacular, be
it crash-and-burn Hollywood cinema, television melodramas, or the
Net's trendy anarchy.

WHAT'S NEXT

As you consider your graduate school options, a crucial decision is
whether to enroll in a film studies department proper or to study film
or media as part of another humanities Ph.D. program. There are a
handful of American universities with graduate departments in film
studies, and they are generally regarded as the most prestigious because
they are the oldest film departments in the country and because most of
them focus exclusively on film. These departments are the UT-Austin
(radio, TV, film), Iowa (communication), Wisconsin-Madison (communication), NYU (cinema studies), Northwestern University (radio,
TV, and film), USC (critical studies), and UCLA (film and TV).

UT-Austin, Wisconsin-Madison, NYU, and UCLA attract students mainly interested in national cinemas (especially American
cinema), archival research, and the aesthetic tradition of scholarship.
Wisconsin-Madison, NYU, and UCLA are also known as media-spe-
cific programs: Instead of working on many media, students must
focus their coursework on the history and theory of one medium—
film, TV, or video. USC and Northwestern, though, attract students
who want to study television as well as film and who want to study
media through the lens of social or cultural history. Iowa is known for
pioneering work on film and media theory.

It's common knowledge among professors and graduate students
that the production side and the critical side of film programs rarely
share common interests, at least within graduate school. At NYU,
UCLA, and USC, there is a long-standing history of standoffs between
the M.F.A. students who do film production and the Ph.D. students
who write film history and theory. The scholars accuse the producers
of being anti-intellectual, while the producers accuse the scholars of
murdering creativity with analysis. At least as a Ph.D. student you have
the consolation of not having to worry about paying off the tens of

thousands of dollars in debt that an M.F.A. student can incur producing a thesis film, a debt often piled on top of thousands of dollars in outstanding student loans.

The majority of the academic venues for studying film and media studies are small, interdisciplinary programs. If you thumb through the SCS membership directory, you will notice that most of the members are not affiliated with a film studies department or program per se. They're part of mass communication; telecommunication; media ecology; media studies; twentieth-century studies; modern culture and media; drama; philosophy; English; American studies; cultural studies; visual and cultural studies; visual culture; art history; and rhetoric. Notable interdisciplinary programs are at UC-Berkeley, Brown University, the University of Illinois-Urbana, Duke University, Indiana, the University of Wisconsin at Milwaukee, the University of Pittsburgh, Rochester, and UC-Santa Barbara.

> At least Ph.D. students don't have to pay off the loans that film production students take out to make student films.

Since these programs are not media-bound, they afford you more latitude for defining your interests. The downside is that, even if you do outline an earth-shattering idea about ethnographic film and photography, you may be swamped by a double workload that prevents you from developing it. Film students in some comparative literature and English departments must often fulfill language and teaching requirements not germane to their work in film. And a film student in an English department may find herself teaching composition courses instead of introductory film courses. Because the requirements of these interdisciplinary programs vary widely, you should investigate interdepartmental programs on a case-by-case basis.

To make an informed decision about where to go, faculty and graduate students alike stress the importance of considering a department's or program's interdisciplinary affiliations with other humanities departments. What is a film studies department's policy on students taking courses offered by an English or comparative literature department, which historically have been home to the best scholarship on film and media outside film studies proper? How do the specialties of a film studies department predispose it to work in other departments? For instance, a film studies department like that at Wisconsin-Madison, which favors a cognitive approach to the study of film reception, is likely to establish alliances with behavioral science departments. But a department like that at UC-Santa Barbara, which studies film reception through the lens of social identification, is likely to forge bonds with sociology, anthropology, or literature departments.

If you're considering an interdisciplinary film or media program, carefully investigate how often faculty will be teaching courses in film or media, or what kinds of interdepartmental obligations might prevent them from advising dissertations. Many eager students have been sold by brochures that tout a program's luminaries only to learn after enrolling in the program that these figures hardly cast any light at all, since they only teach one course a year, and spend much time jet-setting around the academic lecture circuit. You need to research these nitty-gritty issues to avoid getting lost in bureaucratic black holes, getting caught on the borders of interdepartmental turf wars, or being abandoned in the aisles of the academic supermarket.

> Research the formal connections between departments to avoid being caught in a bureaucratic black hole.

Well-established programs at large schools have a decided advantage over small programs when it comes to resources. Small programs sometimes have trouble scraping together film-rental budgets for graduate students teaching introductory film courses, and so allocating funds for digital media on the scale of, say, USC, which is known for its rich resources, is very difficult for them to do. Also, departments like Wisconsin-Madison, UT-Austin, UCLA, and USC have huge print and paper archives, which are crucial if you want to do historical research.

Some smaller programs, however, do boast unrivaled advantages. Students at Rochester can intern and do research in the library and print and paper archives at the George Eastman House/International Museum of Photography, indispensable also because it curates programs that feature visiting filmmakers, retrospectives, and touring shows, as well as films culled from its massive archive. If you go to school in the vicinity of New York City, you can see a lot of films, and you can easily use the film and document archives at MoMA and the American Museum of the Moving Image, or the TV archives at the Museum of Television and Broadcasting. Students who attend small programs on the West Coast like UC-Santa Barbara or UC-Berkeley also have access to important research resources. In

Los Angeles, in addition to the USC and UCLA archives, there are the various studio archives, a new branch of the Museum of Television and Broadcasting, the American Film Institute archives and library, and the Motion Picture Academy of Arts and Sciences Library. The Pacific Film Archives, which houses paper documents, is in Berkeley. And students close to the Hollywood production hub can conduct field research on the Hollywood culture industry or the Pacific Rim digital technology industry.

THE JOB MARKET

Academic jobs in film studies are less specialized than those in other disciplines. Job listings in English, for instance, are usually narrowly defined in terms of a form (drama), period (Romantic), or nation (England), but in film studies, job listings are wide-ranging, defined in terms of media (film, TV, video, digital media) and methods (historian, theorist). It's uncommon, for instance, to find a listing for a specialist in American cinema. Moreover, job advertisements often call for more than one specialty: not just film history, but also TV, popular culture, video, or digital technology. In light of these factors, the consensus among faculty is for job-seeking graduate students to hit the bricks with a résumé that demonstrates their versatility. You must develop the depth that enables you to shine in your field of specialization, as well as the breadth necessary to teach different historical and theoretical approaches to a single medium, or even courses in different media.

Faculty advise students to have versatile skills before they enter the job market.

Versatility is crucial also because film studies departments do not have a monopoly on film and media studies appointments. Though there is a chance that you might land a job in a well-established program that boasts eminent film or media scholars, it's more likely that you will end up in an English or communication department, where teaching introductory courses on film history will probably be your bread and butter.

But faculty stress that no matter how versatile your knowledge or what kind of academic job you seek, it's essential that you go on the market having already demonstrated a commitment to the profession's standards. Most importantly, you should go on the market having completed your dissertation. Also, you should have attended conferences and presented papers at them in order to see how the field works, to stay abreast of issues, and to become acclimated to professional discourse. Faculty opinion is more mixed about graduate students needing to have published articles to gain a competitive edge on the job market. Some suggest that publications indicate a commitment to scholarly exchange, whereas others interpret resumes with long publication lists as a sign that a student has sacrificed intellectual development for hyperprofessionalization.

For those who want to work in film outside of the academy but still want to acquire a degree of expertise and education at the postgraduate level, earning an M.A. from an East or West Coast film studies department is your best bet for landing a job reading scripts for a production company or working in its business office. Some students have hitched an M.A. to a law degree and worked in the public policy area of communications or entertainment law.

But there is more to the nonacademic employment scene than working in Hollywood. People who hold M.A.'s have ended up as film programmers at art museums, or as curators in film archives. They

RESOURCES

ASSOCIATIONS
Society for Cinema Studies
(314) 984-7532

American Studies Association
(301) 405-1364

Modern Language Association
(212) 475-9500

JOURNALS
Camera Obscura
Cinema Journal
Jump Cut
October
The Quarterly Review of Film and Video
Screen
The Velvet Light Trap
Wide Angle

WEB ADDRESSES
Consoling Passions: Television, Video, and Feminism
http://www.pitt.edu/~cptv/cphome.html

American Film Institute
http://www.afionline.org/home.html

SCREEN-site
http://www.sa.ua.edu/TLF/contents.htm

have also worked for off-beat film distributors or media production companies. The problem is that these jobs are not advertised in academic circles; you'll learn about them only because you have kept an ear to the ground in nonacademic film and media communities.

Some caveats about going the M.A. route: Unlike most Ph.D. students, who are granted stipends or teaching assistantships, M.A. students almost always pay their own way. Moreover, a Ph.D. program is less likely to dote on M.A. students because it is not making a long-term investment in them, and the department does not profit from their labor. Unlike Ph.D. students, M.A. students don't teach introductory courses to undergraduate students. And M.A. students are often faced with less than desirable course offerings. It's not unheard of for them to find themselves lumped together with juniors and seniors in upper-level undergraduate courses, for which they earn graduate credit simply by writing longer papers or writing more frequently than undergraduates.

> For most film studies students, home will be an English or other department, teaching beginning film courses.

CONSTELLATIONS

FILM HISTORY
NYU
UCLA
USC
UT-Austin
Wisconsin-Madison

FILM THEORY
Duke
Iowa
Pittsburgh
Rochester
UC-Berkeley

POPULAR CULTURE
Chicago
Duke
UC-Santa Barbara
USC

TELEVISION
Northwestern
USC

DIGITAL TECHNOLOGY
Iowa
Rochester
USC
UT-Austin

CHAPTER 10

AMERICAN HISTORY

Kathleen A. Brosnan almost went straight from her undergraduate program at Knox College into a political science Ph.D. program. But now she's glad
she hesitated. Brosnan went to law school
instead, yet after six years of practicing law, she
came to realize that law "is no longer a profession, it's a business.
The law has lost its professional etiquette." As a lawyer, Bronsan
spent all of her spare time reading history books, and that, combined with her desire to teach in college, prompted her to apply to
the graduate history program at the University of Chicago, where
now she is putting the finishing touches on her dissertation,
"Uniting Mountain and Plain: Urbanization, Law, and Environmental Change in the Denver Region, 1859–1900." Bronsan homed
in on her project after reading William Cronon's *Nature's Metropolis:
Chicago and the Great West*. She realized that she could take another city
in the American West and push the edges of Cronon's pathbreaking
work, combining her legal and historical expertise.

The result is a project that follows the advice of many professors: It
touches many different historical subfields. Grounded in social history, Brosnan's research also covers territory in urban, western, environmental, legal, business, and geographic history, and her

dissertation committee has a diversity to match. It includes Kathleen Conzen, a social historian with interests in the history of the American West; William Novak, a legal/public policy historian; and Michael Conzen, a historical geographer.

WHY AMERICAN HISTORY?

If you were to judge by the newspapers, bookstores, or the History Channel, you might think that history was made up of interesting personalities, places, and events, all of which fall together into a clear story-line, and that historians do little more than write journalism, appear on television, and develop and update textbooks. But historians have always done much more. Those who were trained since the 1960s have been especially eager to combine the methods of history with those of anthropology, sociology, psychology, and, to a lesser extent, literary theory. This generation has, according to Eric Foner of Columbia University, "grappled with the most pressing issues and persistent themes of our national experience: definitions of liberty and equality, causes of social change, and the exercise of national power." At its best, Foner opines, "American history is not a collection of facts, and not a politically sanctioned listing of indisputable truths. Instead it is a mode of collective discovery about the nature of society."

HOW AMERICAN HISTORY HAS TAKEN SHAPE

The study of history can be traced to the ancient Greek and Hebrew practice of using history as a way to define collective identity. History's power to bolster ethnic, cultural, and national cohesiveness has been used—and sometimes abused—by peoples around the world ever since. And while the effectiveness of history as a unifying social force remains important, another mission, formalized in the late nineteenth century in the university, attempted to make historical investigation a "science" pursued "objectively."

That goal took hold in the United States when scholars here imitated what they believed was the historical approach developed by German historians, notably Leopold von Ranke and Hermann von Holst. (Von Holst eventually moved from the University of Freiburg to the University of Chicago.) Today historians of the profession recognize that these scholars, even though they did not follow the German ideals of "science" and "objectivity" as closely as they believed, nonetheless made history in the United States a much more professional field than it had been.

This emergent professionalism was an odd—if not exotic—mind-set to American historians. In the early nineteenth century, before the quest for a science of history, the field was more the province of wealthy amateurs than the home of academic research. Although this generation sometimes taught at universities, many had no academic affiliation and wrote for the educated general reader instead. Henry Adams's histories, for example, take special care to convey a strong narrative to a broad audience. Adams taught at Harvard University and participated in projects to make historical research more professional and academically rigorous, but he was skeptical of a scientific notion of history. George Bancroft arranged some of his histories like stage plays, with prologues, acts, and an epilogue. Despite the fact that such historians were often skilled at archival work and some had studied extensively at German universities, their literary style and sometimes magisterial self-regard bothered the new professionals, who were attempting greater detachment. Bancroft's ten volume *History of the United States* (1834–74), for instance, was dismissed by more than one professorial wag as "The Psychological Autobiography of George Bancroft, as Illustrated by Incidents and Characters in the Annals of the United States."

> The amateur generation wanted to inculcate the public with the origins and goals of democracy to foster civic virtue.

One of the goals of that first amateur generation was to draw upon the traditional use of history to inculcate the public with the origins and goals of democracy, in order to strengthen an enlightened electorate. As to the civic mission of early historians, Chicago professor Peter Novick adds a proviso, noting that the gentleman historians tended to think that what was good for their largely upper-middle-class, white, and male selves was also good for the country. Although it would be wrong to say that the amateur generation's goals—informing the electorate, boosting their own interests, and telling ripping good yarns—were ever fully replaced by a "scientific" history, their methods receded from the center of academic historical research after the turn of the century.

Another important trend within the profession took effect after World War II with the rise of "consensus scholarship." One of the central theses of the consensus scholars was that different sides in American political battles shared assumptions about American identity, the sanctity of private property, and the relationship of the individual to the state, especially when compared to the warring social factions of Europe. *The American Political Tradition and the Men Who Made It*, by Columbia's Richard Hofstadter, *The Liberal Tradition in America*, by Harvard's Louis Hartz, and *The Genius of American Politics*, by Daniel Boorstin, then of Chicago, were the defining works of the movement. In its most extreme form, consensus scholarship downplayed social injustices and political fault lines in favor of an imagined, mostly contented, American society that cohered around liberal values.

Columbia professor Alan Brinkley has pointed out, however, that this widely held view of consensus scholarship is too simple. "Consensus scholarship has been widely derided by the left as a Cold War effort to celebrate capitalism and delegitimize challenges to it. But the most important consensus historians were highly critical of certain American values and institutions, especially the universal commitment to economic self-aggrandizement through competitive capitalism." Louis Hartz, for example, felt that ideas about personal gain were so dominated by John Locke's philosophy that intellectual life in the United States was straitjacketed. "The psychic heritage of a nation 'born equal' was a colossal liberal absolutism, the death by atrophy of the philosophic impulse." Even though there were differing critical perspectives within consensus scholarship—particularly with regard to capitalism—the movement marked a moment, the last of its kind, in which prominent historians shared a common mission and a core of issues to debate.

> Consensus scholarship offered mid-century scholars a common mission and a core of issues to debate.

By the mid-1960s the center of consensus did not hold—not even in the methodologically conservative field of political history. "With society rent asunder by the civil rights movement, antiwar protests, and feminist demands, a new generation of historians had difficulty reconciling myths of national progress and consensus with the tensions around them," says Rutgers University social historian Alice Kessler-Harris. "They sought to explore the dynamic interaction of a multiracial and multiethnic population; to understand how interest groups and classes competed for power; and to develop a sense of how race, sex, and ethnicity served to mold and inhibit conceptions of common national purpose."

Brinkley further explains, "The real story of modern America was the decline of genuine democracy: the steady increase in the power of private, corporate institutions; the growing influence of those institutions over the workings of government; and hence the declining ability of individuals to control the circumstances of their work and their lives." As elections and the rest of the democratic process seemed less important to the working of government, books like Barry Karl's *The Uneasy State* or William Appleman Williams's *Contours of American History* appeared. A thorough reevaluation of the American past and methods for interpreting it was under way. Established subfields of American history—politics, biography, diplomacy, war—were reshaped in the 1960s, and new fields blossomed.

> The outlook of scholarship was altered by the methodological breakthroughs and social movements of the 1960s.

And at roughly the same time, the profession also took a quantitative turn. Statistical techniques borrowed from the social sciences allowed historians to make better use of birth records, the census, wills, and voter rolls to get a more complete view of the past. The older style of history might be represented by Kenneth Stampp's ringing denunciation of slavery, *That Peculiar Institution* (1956), a milestone text that nevertheless came to be seen as paying too much attention to the victimization of slaves rather than to the particularities of their "agency," which evidence collected in the new quantifying might invite. A new "from the ground up" style emerged among historians who had collected masses of different kinds of quantitative data about the lives of ordinary individuals; although social historians led the way in quantification, those at work on political and moral issues also performed bottom-up analysis. Eugene Genovese's *Roll, Jordan, Roll: The World the Slaves Made*, and Herbert Gutman's *The Black Family in Slavery and Freedom*, for example, pointed out that though slaves could rarely free themselves, they were far more resourceful than helpless victims would have been.

The hottest new or recharged subfields parallel to quantitative history were women's history, African-American history, social history, urban history, labor history, and ethnic and immigration history, along with smaller fields like gay and lesbian history and the history of cinema. Some of these areas, like urban history, were completely remade by the revivals of the 1960s. By including quantitative data and a sense of history from the bottom up, Harvard's Stephan

Thernstrom refocused attention from the political elite of a city to the lives of immigrants and the urban poor. Books like Thernstrom's *The Other Bostonians*, and Princeton University professor Christine Stansell's *City of Women: Sex and Class in New York, 1789–1860* broadened the range of urban history, while *Chants Democratic: New York City and the Rise of the American Working Class, 1788–1850*, by Princeton's Sean Wilentz, showed how many forces interacted to affect the lives of urban

> ## Women's history challenged basic assumptions about historiography itself.

working people. In fact, says Wilentz, "few historians today would argue that economic interest alone determined people's views of the world."

Approaches to even the most traditional subfields of history also grew more varied. Southern history followed up the seminal work that C. Vann Woodward had begun as early as the 1950s by challenging the tendency of consensus historians to focus on the urban middle class, giving shorter shrift to rural life and the rural poor. The new history of the West began to dramatically challenge pervasive myths about the frontier. By including an understanding of the environment, women's history, and Native American and Latino history, Western historians like Patricia Limerick of the University Colorado at Boulder and Richard White of the University of Washington at Seattle began to see the West as more than a place for soldiers and farmers to "conquer." The study of antebellum America was equally transformed by the study of gender, labor, citizenship, class, and race.

A new phase in the development of feminist scholarship intensified in the 1970s and 1980s. Women's history no longer just folded the story of women into American history, but challenged basic assumptions about historical methodology itself. Linda Kerber of the University of Iowa traces three phases of scholarship: Early women's history showed how gender differences developed socially and historically, not just for women but for men too; the second phase traced how historians generalized from the experience of the dominant racial and class groups, thus distorting the past; the third phase studied specific ways that women were excluded from political and economic power. Recent women's history has carried on all three phases of scholarship, with a slight tilt today toward the study of the social construction of gender.

Not only did the quantitative approach initiate whole new ways of exploring history, but it helped shift the pecking order of prestige in the discipline. Previously a small group of elite schools, notably the Ivy League, dominated the profession. But as large social science departments grew up at state universities, simultaneously with a general boom in enrollments at state schools, quantitative approaches were taken up by newer departments. Some departments doubled, tripled, and quadrupled in size. UCLA, the University of California at Berkeley, the University of Minnesota at Twin Cities, and the University of Wisconsin at Madison all grew to have more than fifty full-time faculty members.

The excitement created by new fields and methods in the 1970s gave way to a period of reassessment in the 1980s. According to Foner, "The very diversity of the 'new histories' and the portrait of America they have created seem to have fragmented historical scholarship and impeded the attempt to create a coherent new vision of the national experience." Many fields within American history began to question whether they were overspecialized or had pushed a thesis too far. In working-class history, for instance, the study of the political power of workers was probably overstated because historians were anxious to portray workers as more than the pawns of larger forces. Some social histories of ethnic groups eliminated any reference to the political, which led one group of historians to agree in the late 1980s and early 1990s to "bring the politics back in." The University of Michigan's Terrence McDonald carefully studied fiscal and political policy in late-nineteenth century San Francisco; UC-Berkeley's Robin Einhorn traced political economy in Chicago; Theda Skocpol of Harvard studied intersections and disjunctions between social policy and politics.

The field hardest hit by this reevaluation was quantitative history. During the 1970s and early 1980s, nearly every social, family, and urban historian made an argument that drew on quantitative data. The best of them made subtle connections between birthrates, wealth, and other data— *From Peasants to Farmers*, by Jon Gjerde of UC-Berkeley, which is about Norwegian immigration to the Midwest, and Chicago professor Kathleen Conzen's research into *Immigrant Milwaukee*, are prime examples. But in slavish deference to the quantitative trend, other historians simply threw in ill-sorted and unrevelatory data, sometimes overlooking the effect of market forces or religious or ethnic identity on the motivation

> The quantitative approach shifted prestige in the discipline away from Ivy League departments.

of individuals. An excellent quantitative study required expertise in statistics as well as history and needed a small army of data gatherers to make the findings representative, but by the late 1980s many historians came to realize that not all evidence could be quantified. Even the best quantitative history ignored ideas, beliefs, and irrational events, leaving readers with a two-dimensional portrait of the past.

A famous example of the problem with quantitative history was a study that led one of its authors to a Nobel Prize in economics. When Robert Fogel and Stanley Engerman published *Time on the Cross* in 1984, claiming that slaves were only moderately exploited, most historians didn't know how to respond. Historians who wanted to know how Fogel and Engerman reached their conclusions were left to grapple with a mathematical equation that few had the training to dispute or even comprehend. Winthrop Jordan of the University of Mississippi recalls that historians "tended to simply roll over and say, 'Gee whiz.'" Today, quantitative methods are used more selectively, though they are still crucial to the work of major historians like Eric Monkkonen of UCLA, a specialist in urban history.

> Even the best quantitative history gave short shrift to ideas, beliefs, and irrational events.

In the wake of quantification, the standards for excellence in the discipline shifted slightly. Today the best historical research contains a subtle and nuanced argument, an adequate documentary base, and often an account of unquantifiable phenomena. And this material is conveyed in a style clear enough for a wide audience, if not the general public, and accessible enough to historians outside narrow subfields. The fields with the most vitality frequently involve using new techniques to examine a well-established subject, such as incorporating the insights of queer and women's history to study manhood in the colonial era, or using legal history's understanding of contracts to study the lives of beggars and their place in the social hierarchy after the Civil War. There is also increasingly a return to narrative history, often synthesizing the results of work done within subfields, and including the insights of recent literary and philosophical theory.

Chicago's George Chauncey, for instance, combined the techniques of social history with the methodologies of cultural studies in his award-winning book *Gay New York: Gender, Urban Culture, and the Making of the Gay Male World, 1890–1940*. Like other social historians, Chauncey used oral histories, police and legal records, and demographic information, but he combined them with theories about the creation of gender to give a picture not just of gay life in New York City, but of the evolution of definitions of sexuality and manhood. In *Nature's Metropolis: Chicago and the Great West*, Wisconsin-Madison's William Cronon likewise drew on the theories of economic geographers, statistics from bankruptcy records, and an environmental historian's eye for changes in the landscape.

Looking back on each period of historiography in the twentieth century, it's easy to see how historians were influenced by the political, social, and economic trends of the moment. After the United States joined World War I in 1917, American historians jumped on the Allied bandwagon, highlighting the evils of everything German. During the Great Depression, historians rewrote the history of urban political machines without making much use of a vast published literature about political corruption. FDR's coalition, after all, rested on alliances with the previously despised machines. And the consensus historians for the most part downplayed domestic ideological discord in the 1950s while the country mobilized to compete with the perceived threat of the Soviet Union and communism. At the same time, a few historians have always been far ahead of the curve and made audacious arguments: Think of C. Vann Woodward or William Appleman Williams

WHAT'S NEXT

Admissions committees look for students who can combine solid analytical skills with the curiosity to look afresh at old issues or the promise to open new issues. Yet, almost paradoxically, admissions committees also seek students who already have a fairly clear focus on the epochs and questions that interest them. Moreover, several faculty members who have recently served on admissions committees stress that they want to know that an applicant is committed to American history as a career—in other words, is more than a history buff.

An undergraduate major in history is not a prerequisite for pursuing graduate study, so long as you have taken enough courses to know what the study of American history entails. Students with a wide variety of educational backgrounds and intellectual interests are welcome now because most American history is interdisciplinary. In addition, an increasing number of programs—Chicago, Princeton, and Stanford University, among top departments—are offering more funding to students who took time off from academia after completing their undergraduate degrees because they assume that older students are more committed, focused, and dedicated to a professional career than those fresh out of undergraduate school. As in other humanities fields, admissions committees in history weigh undergraduate grades as well as GRE scores, personal statements, and letters of recommendation. Some request a writing sample, while a handful require applicants to complete a short writing assignment.

Most graduate programs require students to do coursework in core subject areas and in varied methodologies, and to conduct research on original materials. At UCLA, coursework in subject areas is concentrated in a core historiography course, while at Brown University a student and advisor devise a course of study appropriate to the student's interests. Some programs, such as UCLA and Michigan, offer intense courses in methodologies of history, while others, such as Northwestern University, expect students to pick up methodology on their own. Most programs require research on original material for both the M.A. thesis and the dissertation. Chicago is rather demanding on this score: It requires doctoral students to complete two research papers, each of which is the equivalent of an M.A. thesis, before writing a Ph.D. proposal (though one of the research papers can cover the same subject as the dissertation).

The timing and type of the Ph.D. qualifying exams vary widely from program to program. At The University of North Carolina at Chapel Hill and at Colorado-Boulder, students take oral exams in the third or fourth year; at Stanford they have written exams as early as the end of the first year. In general, oral comprehensive exams usually cover two areas: works of historiography pertinent to a student's concentration in a large field (nineteenth-century urban history, for example); and a smaller field outside one's concentration (women's clubs in a particular time and place, for instance). But the shape of the exams varies enormously and should be checked with particular departments. Universities also vary widely in the weight they place on oral exams, also something to investigate case-by-case.

If a career as a college or university professor is your goal, it helps to base your choice of a graduate program on official rankings, such as those published by the National Research Council. Most professors in American history believe the NRC rankings are flawed, in part because they fail to distinguish between European and American history programs, but still, a degree from a program in the NRC top ten will open more doors than a degree from a lower-ranked one. A study prepared for a professional association of the chairs of history departments estimates that 80 percent of the historians with full-time academic appointments at major universities and colleges, including small private colleges and state universities, have degrees from universities ranked among the top twenty-five programs.

> Find the most generally respected program that also excels in several subfields that interest you.

The trick of picking the right graduate school is to find the most respected program that excels in the subfields that interest you. Doctoral programs can be grouped in several ways: the very top programs excellent in a broad range of fields, other top programs with a narrower range of strengths, very good programs with strengths in many areas but not enough to rank with the very top programs, and good schools with a handful of outstanding scholars. Any program with a widely acknowledged leader of a subfield, such as Iowa's Linda Kerber in women's history or Washington-Seattle's Richard White in history of the West, can give you an edge in the job market if that leader chairs your dissertation committee. At the same time, a degree from a powerhouse like Yale University or UC-Berkeley will move your job application to the top of the pile at a wide variety of institutions.

Some of the best programs are strong virtually across the board. UC-Berkeley, frequently ranked the top program in the country, is strong in social history, family history, labor history, political history, and intellectual history. Yale, the other program most frequently ranked number one, is strong in religious, colonial, intellectual, western, social, and diplomatic history. Michigan excels in women's, quantitative, urban, military, family, ethnic, and social history. Other schools with a broad range of strengths include Columbia, UCLA, Wisconsin-Madison, and the University of Pennsylvania. Stanford is highly respected for the training it gives graduate students in a wide range of fields, with Albert Camarillo in Chicano and Western history, Barton Bernstein in foreign policy and social history, Estelle Freedman in social and women's history, Karen Sawislak in social and urban history, and Jack Rakove in early political history and the American Revolution.

Other highly ranked programs have a narrower range of strengths: Chicago is a good choice for nineteenth-century (Kathleen Conzen and Neil Harris), African-American (Thomas Holt, Julie Saville), and gender and queer studies (George Chauncey). Princeton stands out in Southern (James McPherson, Nell I. Painter), social (Elizabeth Lunbeck), nineteenth-century (Christine Stansell), and African-American. For African-American history, also consider the University of Texas at Austin. Northwestern is a good choice for nineteenth-century and early twentieth-century (Josef Barton, Henry Binford, James Oakes, Robert Wiebe), and for social history. You might want to consider Harvard, but many professors note that the department is top-heavy with senior faculty, and few younger scholars are given tenure.

UNC-Chapel Hill, Duke University, and New York University are frequently mentioned as programs whose fortunes are improving. UNC-Chapel Hill is especially strong in the study of the South and religious history but has a large faculty with a broad range of specialties. Duke has important scholars, such as Nancy Hewitt in women's and gender history. NYU is home to several big names in urban history—Thomas Bender for one—whose influence is felt in a wide number of subfields, including urban, labor, and intellectual history. NYU is also home to Robin Kelley, a rising star in African-American and twentieth-century history.

Large state universities have for some time been able to hire top scholars.

The University of California campuses at Irvine, San Diego, and Davis all have solid programs with wide numbers of specialties but they've been hurt by political battles in the state over affirmative action and university funding. UC-Irvine was poised to become a leader in theory when it was thrown off balance by troubles over state funding. UC-San Diego—with Amy Bridges and Steven Erie—is very strong in urban history, while UC-Davis—with Alan Taylor, Ruth Rosen, and Karen Halttunen—ranks high in social and cultural history. The University of California at Santa Barbara boasts one of the very top programs in public history.

Other large state universities have benefited from the tight job market and have been able to hire some of the very best recent graduates. The University of Virginia is home to Edward L. Ayers in Southern history and Nelson Lichtenstein in labor and political history. Minnesota-Twin Cities has blossomed with Sara Evans, Elaine Tyler May, and David Noble in twentieth-century history, Russell

Menard in social science history, and David Roediger in labor and race. Patricia Limerick has put Colorado-Boulder on the map in the field of Western history, while Iowa's Linda Kerber has attracted attention for her work on women's history, though it is too early to determine what effect the prominence of these scholars has had on the job prospects of their programs' graduates.

> The academic job market is most competetive for historians who have focused only on a single field of scholarship.

At some schools, many historians will not have appointments in the history department. Some of the best religious historians, for instance, are located in religious studies departments or in divinity schools. For example, Chicago, with Martin Marty, Jerald Brauer, and Catherine Brekus; UNC-Chapel Hill, with Donald Mathews; Yale, with Harry Stout; and UC-Santa Barbara are all able to draw on expertise in religious history held by scholars outside the department. And some economic historians, such as Robert Fogel and David Galenson at Chicago, are located in economics departments. It's important to ask students how well the study of history crosses bureaucratic lines at these institutions, though be sure to rely on the accounts of more than one or two students.

It's also important to consider the size of a graduate program and how size affects funding. Almost all of the top schools accept between twenty-five and fifty new graduate students each year, and list between ninety and 460 "active" graduate students. The number of students tends to influence how intensely you'll have to compete with your cohorts for faculty attention. Some programs are huge: UCLA has 450 full-time graduate students, while UC-Berkeley, with about the same number of faculty members has only 210 students. Others admit only a handful of students each year and provide almost all of them with a living wage in the form of a stipend or teaching assistantship. Notable in this respect is Princeton, which admits about twenty, and Yale and Stanford, which admit about twenty-five.

To find out the size of programs, you can either call them or look them up in the American Historical Association's *Directory of History Departments and Organizations*, which lists fairly complete information about American history departments in the United States and Canada: the faculty, including their specializations; the number of graduate students; the number of undergraduates; the number and types of degrees granted; and the titles of recent and in-progress dissertations. Most libraries will have a copy of the *Directory*, as do most history departments, though the latter don't always make it available to undergraduates.

THE JOB MARKET

Each year, about 325 students earn Ph.D.'s in American history. The Organization of American Historians, a professional organization for history professors, divides the discipline into about forty subfields by folding some broad fields, like intellectual and cultural history, into a single category. The categories and subcategories are chronological (the Colonial Era or the Progressive Era), methodological (quantitative history or psychohistory), subject-based (diplomatic history or queer history), and regional (Western history or New England history).

As in most humanities and social science fields, in the last ten years the number of people earning Ph.D.'s in American history has steadily outpaced the number of available full-time academic positions. According to statistics compiled by the American Historical Association, the largest organization of history professors, in 1995 there were an estimated 125.9 applicants for every one of the 177 job openings in American and European history. About 70 percent of history Ph.D.'s reported to the AHA that they will seek academic employment, though one survey found that a little over 18 percent of history Ph.D.'s had regular college or university appointments two years later. Another survey by the AHA found that about 50 percent of history Ph.D.'s found definite employment when they graduated. But both major history professional associations have been trying to do more research into the not well-answered question of what happens to Ph.D.'s after they get their degree.

The job market is most competitive for Ph.D.'s who have focused on only a single field of scholarship, such as the Civil War, and the candidates with the best chances are those who have persuasive credentials in both a traditional time period and a thematic field of history, such as women's history. The area where the supply curve most outstrips the demand curve is twentieth-century U.S. history, where in 1993 165 Ph.D.'s competed for thirty-two job openings. (The numbers overstate the imbalance slightly, because some sixty-five jobs were in general categories that draw applications from all sorts of specialists.) Most leaders of the profession say they are disturbed that a growing number of colleges and universities are hiring Ph.D.'s part time on a per-course basis, paying too little for such instructors to earn a living even if they accepted two or three such jobs at once.

Generally, like many Ph.D.'s in other fields, American history doctorates experience downward mobility on the job market, landing a job an an institution less prestigious than their graduate university. Admittedly, in good times or bad, the competition for jobs at prestigious research universities is intense. As a result, during a stagnant market like that today, even small liberal arts schools without competitive admissions policies can have their pick of newly-minted graduates from top schools. But this situation is not purely bad news. Top graduates of research institutions find they prefer the often lower-stress world of liberal arts colleges over the supercharged atmosphere at some research universities.

> Today even small liberal arts colleges can have their pick of newly-minted Ph.D.'s.

A master's degree in history can be used as a specialist credential to teach in high schools or in community colleges. The main alternative jobtrack for history Ph.D.'s is the realm broadly defined as "public history," which is the profession's catchphrase for jobs in museums, libraries, historical societies, preservation groups, and corporations. A tiny but growing option is academic administrative work, which some historians have found provides the opportunity to teach an occasional class while pursuing a career with a different kind of upward mobility.

If you want more information about public history, a good place to start is the journal *The Public Historian*. There are strong programs in this subspecialty at Indiana University, Purdue University at Indianapolis, The College of William and Mary, and NYU. Some of the nonacademic jobs in public history range from positions at the nation's larger museums, such as the many branches of the Smithsonian Institution in Washington, D.C., to private companies associated with museums, historical societies, and archives. Among leading academic scholars in the field are Gary Nash of UCLA, John Bodnar of Indiana, Eric Foner of Columbia, and Richard White of Washington-Seattle. Scholars now prominent as public historians but not in academic positions include Pete Daniel of the Museum of American History (a branch of the Smithsonian), and Kevin Starr, State Librarian of California.

RESOURCES

NRC TOP TEN
Yale
UC-Berkeley
Princeton
Harvard
Columbia
UCLA
Stanford
Chicago
Johns Hopkins
Wisconsin-Madison

ASSOCIATIONS
American Historical
Association
(202) 544-2422

Organization of
American Historians
(812) 855-7311

JOURNALS
*The American
  Historical Review*
*The Journal of
  American History*
The Public Historian
Radical History Review
Reviews in American History

CONSTELLATIONS

STRONG ALL-AROUND PROGRAMS
Columbia
Michigan
Penn
Stanford
UC-Berkeley
UCLA
Wisconsin-Madison
Yale

NINETEENTH-CENTURY HISTORY
Chicago
Northwestern
Princeton

TWENTIETH-CENTURY HISTORY
Minnesota-Twin Cities
Northwestern

SOCIAL HISTORY
Northwestern
Princeton
UC-Davis

AFRICAN-AMERICAN HISTORY
Chicago
Minnesota-Twin Cities
Princeton

WOMEN'S AND GENDER HISTORY
Chicago
Duke
Iowa

URBAN HISTORY
NYU
UC-San Diego

SOUTHERN HISTORY
Princeton
UNC-Chapel Hill
Virginia

WESTERN HISTORY
Colorado-Boulder

PUBLIC HISTORY
UC-Santa Barbara

RELIGIOUS HISTORY
Chicago
UC-Santa Barbara
UNC-Chapel Hill
Yale

THEORY
UC-Irvine

BOOKS
Directory of History Departments and Organizations (AHA)
Eric Foner, editor, *The New American History*, 2nd ed. (AHA)

WEB ADDRESSES
American Historical Association
http://chnm.gmu.edu/chnm/aha//

CHAPTER 11

EUROPEAN HISTORY

Matthew Gerber, a fourth-year graduate student at the University of California at Berkeley, is writing a dissertation about illegitimacy in early modern France from 1715 to 1804, with a focus on how the transformation of the French political state changed the legal status of bastards. His B.A. in humanities prepared him well for exploring historical particulars, which is what he enjoys most about graduate study. Gerber is spending the fall of 1997 in Paris doing archival research at the Bibliothèque Nationale—scrutinizing notary records, civil suits, and over 30,000 uncataloged notes from the Old Regime to determine how bastards were treated as heirs in property disputes. No matter what he is examining, Gerber always begins by treating sources as if they were factual records, even though he has turned to the close reading techniques of literary studies to understand the finer points of eighteenth-century lawyers' briefs. "Historians have a reputation for being theoretical balloon busters," he says. "Any theory that doesn't explain the facts is not a theory but a religion."

Joel Seltzer likes "to conjure up people from the distant past. You can't do that in the same way with later figures because the sources are *too* rich." A graduate student at Yale University just beginning his dissertation research, Seltzer plans to spend a year or two in the Czech

Republic scouring archives for original texts by and about the great preachers of the fourteenth century. Two broad schools of thought about Christianity in this period are dominant. The first sees Christianity as an imposition made by the powerful on the pagan beliefs of the common people. The other, which sees the division between the elite and ordinary people much less sharply, stresses interaction between groups more than coercion and points out the continuance of pagan beliefs despite repression. The usual assumption is that "Christianization" was well-advanced by the fourteenth century, though how advanced it actually was in Eastern Europe is still debated. For instance, scholars have long ignored Czechoslovakia and Eastern Europe. By studying sermons, Court of Inquisition documents, and other Latin and Czech sources, Seltzer wants to see if other historians' views can account for Czech history in a later time period.

What these projects share is an engagement with primary documents from the period and places in question. Whether a project involves archival work in the traditional sense or looks at other sorts of texts, graduate study in history means working with the original records of a civilization. To do this usually requires skills underemphasized in college courses: knowledge of languages, how to decipher centuries-old handwriting, and the ability to sort through records that were probably not drawn up to answer the questions you are putting to them.

WHY EUROPEAN HISTORY?

The infinite variety of the past and its essential irrecoverability makes the study of European history both intriguing and in some sense frustrating. History is a non-parsimonious discipline—that is, it does not strive for a single, elegant explanation—nor does it serve to predict the future. Santayana's cliché about those who fail to learn from history being doomed to repeat it does not imply that the past offers a blueprint for the future. The past provides lessons and warnings but not a path, program, or menu.

History insists on difference and uniqueness. While the Roman imperial administration and the British civil service of the nineteenth century may have traits in common, they do not exemplify readily comparable situations that could lead to a generalization about governmental elites. Though Byzantium would exert a religious, cultural, and political influence on Russia, the one is not simply the origin or continuation of the other. Mark Twain said that history does not repeat itself—though it rhymes.

Because of its anti-reductionist nature, history has emerged as a central discipline in the reconsideration of how to approach human reality and experience. Over the past decade, it has gained increasing importance for other disciplines in the social sciences and humanities. Indeed, far from being regarded as a plodding and undertheorized field, history, especially that of Europe, has compelled the attention of social and political scientists tired of arid quantitative analysis. Today there is at least a glimmer of recognition among sociologists and political scientists that because historical circumstances are particular, they call into question the law-like generalizations typical of the social sciences. In the humanities, both the new historicism, which places ideologies in historical context, and postcolonial studies, which examines the confrontation of Europe with its colonial "other," have learned much from history's rigorous scrutiny of textual sources.

But whatever use—or opportunity for challenge—history provides other disciplines, the past remains a collection of mysteries that both defy and demand explanation: the meaning and origin of the Holocaust, the unexpected success of the Russian Revolution and the unforeseen collapse of the Soviet Union, the reason for Spain's sudden colonial expansion, or the enduring appeal of nationalism in the twentieth century and the waning of other mass ideologies. There are also an infinite number of minor but intriguing mysteries: why a Parisian printer's apprentices celebrated the murder of alley cats in the 1730s; why sailors destroyed the brothels of London in 1668; why medieval naturalists thought pearls were created by lightning hitting oysters at the bottom of the ocean. Such questions, large and small, mark the complexity of the past and its allure for students.

HOW EUROPEAN HISTORY HAS TAKEN SHAPE

History is the least theory-driven discipline and at the same time the most receptive to theories, none of which tends to dominate. The very disciplinary identity of history is ambiguous: History is classed among the humanities at Stanford University and Yale, yet at UCLA and UC–Berkeley it is housed in the social sciences. History is eclectic, absorbing entire methodologies but transforming them in the process.

Obviously there are fashions. If the 1970s were dominated by the statistical quantitative methods borrowed from the social sciences, the critical theories of literary study have been more prominent in the 1990s. Historical information is now perceived more as a text than as a collection of social science data. This is not a mere methodological fad, but an attempt to grapple with the central paradox of research: The mass of information about the past that historians handle doesn't directly or transparently transmit its significance. The historian, then, is something of a detective, someone who juggles an immense number of clues but who is unlikely to identify a single answer. Historical explanation is tentative and full of pitfalls and detours, yet because it relies so heavily on the interpretation of sources, it also requires exacting and meticulous skills—especially in languages and even in paleography. The field is highly empirical, though its conclusions are provisional.

> History is a non-parsimonious discipline. It does not strive for a single, elegant explanation.

With the usual caveats about broad generalizations, one can identify three stages of development in the field over the last forty years: first, a postwar period in which political history dominated, especially the study of conflicts between military and economic powers; second, a movement among social historians in the 1960s to study a wider spectrum of society; and third, a destabilized approach that emerged in the 1980s and, drawing on interpretive theory, questions the perceived coherence and progressive movement of the past.

The shift from political to social history was under way in Europe before World War II and was most pronounced from 1945 to the 1970s. During these decades the French journal *Annales* pioneered the study of the large, impersonal forces shaping human experience: demography, geography, nutrition, and consumption. From such a view, political history was only a small part of historical reality, the fundamental structure of which depends on the entire range of human activities. History, then, had to be approached from as many paths as possible, not just as the chronology of passing events. Thus a typical Annaliste thesis would emphasize the geology, climate, vegetation, and other fundamental "structures" before investigating families, alliances, and patterns of settlement.

The *Annales* school was thus characterized by a concern for *histoire totale*—a history that encompassed everything about a society (food, rituals, kinship, rites of passage), not just the deeds of its powerful or more articulate members. Like anthropology, this approach produced cross-sectional rather than chronological studies that focused less on change than on enduring forms of social organization and material culture. Fernand Braudel's *The Mediterranean*, a classic of this era, is a massive collection of facts about the region in the late sixteenth century, organized not around the supposed superficialities of political and military events, but around the underlying forces of states, societies, and the even more basic factors of environment. Braudel largely ignored religion, power politics, and high culture.

In addition to the impersonal underlying structures of the past, the *Annales* school also emphasized the history of thought. The study of collective mental outlooks—*mentalités*—would come to dominate and eventually supplant the social science approach of the 1950s and 1960s. In *Times of Feast, Times of Famine* (1967), for instance, Emmanuel Le Roy Ladurie focused on such topics as the history of climate or the underlying social patterns of rural southern France. Yet later, in books such as *Carnival in Romans* (1979), he undertook more intensely local studies of popular attitudes and behavior to demonstrate how such things as space, community, anger, privacy, the supernatural, comfort, and family were regarded.

The *Annales* school was concerned with *histoire totale*— a history that encompassed everything about a society.

The other extremely influential journal of the postwar decades is *Past & Present*. Founded in 1952, this British publication resembled *Annales* in its concern for the non-elite classes of society and in the way that it, too, posed a broad concept of historical study that would examine mental constructs, everyday life, and comparisons across national and cultural boundaries. Less entranced by quantification than *Annales*, *Past & Present* focused on state power and political movements. It was especially concerned with change and social transformation: the crisis of the seventeenth century, for example, or the trauma of modernization. It also initiated a movement away from the social history of material culture toward a cultural history of attitudes and representations. Unlike *Annales*, *Past & Present* has not suffered from an identity crisis, although recently it has displayed less confidence about its own centrality in identifying mainstream research.

Certain aspects of the *Annales* and *Past & Present* schools were wholeheartedly embraced in the United States, but relatively late. The comparative and multifaceted thrust of these schools did not catch on until the 1960s, while quantitative history and the history of social movements, labor, and revolution peaked in the 1970s. American scholars who worked hard to transmit *Annales* ideas include Immanuel Wallerstein of SUNY Binghamton, Natalie Zemon Davis of the Institute for Advanced Studies in Princeton, New Jersey, and Robert Darnton of Princeton University. Orest Ranum and Robert Forster translated a number of key *Annales* texts, though their own work was not exclusively in the *Annales* mode. The department at Johns Hopkins University struck up close relations with the Ecole des Hautes Etudes in Paris that it maintains to this day, while the Princeton department, led by Lawrence Stone, became well-known for promoting work in the *Past & Present* vein.

> By the 1980s, due to a shift towards cultural history, history itself seemed less rational and progressive.

A new development in social history was perceptible by 1980. Not only was a quantitative social-science methodology becoming less attractive, but a shift toward cultural history called into question the assumptions of political and social historians alike about the nature of history. Whereas historians had previously viewed history as a collection of objective information with an innate coherence, now they started to regard history as an interpretable text. Event, biography, and narrative all experienced a revival after being obscured by the impersonal materialism of social history in its heyday. History emerged as something more contingent, accidental, and also more difficult to decode or simplify. Above all, history seemed less rational and progressive.

After the waning of social history as a paradigm, it was no longer possible for historians to note a drive toward the increasingly rational organization of society to explain historical change. Nor could they use a trend toward socialism or equality, the favored explanations of oppositional historians, as a controlling metaphor for social change. Entities such as states, classes, nationalities, and families, unquestioned in the past, came in for examination as constructs as much of the imagination as of material conditions. And due to the influence of Michel Foucault, many historians now understood power to reside in the mobilization of knowledge— "regimes of truth"—as much as in state bureaucracies or economic control. Gender cuts across class and economic organization (the definition of "working class," for example), and feminist theory calls into question the meaning and experience of industrialism, the Enlightenment, and the twelfth-century Renaissance.

Scholarship on the modern European state serves as a good case study for examining the changes in historiography that have occurred since World War II. In the postwar decades, the emergence of effective centralized state power was *the* major fact of European history. Historians regarded the state as an expression of rationality that replaced the violence, unpredictability, and disorganization of the feudal era. Why Britain and France made successful transitions to modernity and democratic systems while Germany and Russia did not were central questions, as was pinpointing when modernity emerged in the guise of effective state power. Such scholars as Crane Brinton, who wrote *Anatomy of Revolution* (1938), R.R. Palmer, author of *The Age of the Democratic Revolution* (1959-1961), and William Langer, editor of the series "The Rise of Modern Europe" (1934-1985), were concerned with the development of state institutions and the course of politics and revolution. Even medieval historians, notably Joseph Strayer at Princeton, argued for the modernity of their era by tracing the origins of the modern state to the ability of kings to use feudalism to achieve centralization.

States and nations are now seen not as objective social facts but as identities often forged against the facts.

After 1965 or so, a period dominated by social-historical approaches ensued, but the state remained a chief object of scholarship. Even as historians downplayed the study of great state leaders and their diplomatic and military maneuvers, they still viewed the emergence of centralized institutional power and state-imposed organization on society as the great unifying features of modernity. Charles Tilly of Columbia University focused on the process of state-making, something no longer viewed as the catalyst of political change and ideology but as a movement affecting the entire organization of society. Eugen Weber's *Peasants into Frenchmen* (1976) posited a contrast between a disorganized pre-modern world of local customs, dialects, and primitive outlook and the unifying, rationalizing modernization imposed by the educational and military discipline of the nineteenth-century French state.

More recently, and largely due to the impact of Michel Foucault, historians have regarded the state not as an inevitable or rational project but as a series of artifices and ideas. Books such as Benedict Anderson's *Imagined Communities* (1983) or the essays collected by Eric Hobsbawm under the title *The Invention of Tradition* (1983) show how the state, the nation, origins, and ethnicity are not objective, given elements of society but projections of the imagination, identities often forged against the "facts."

The succession of historiographic trends noted above—attention to political power, the lived experience of ordinary people, or the origins of modernity—have been common themes in many areas of European history, but rarely in exactly the same order. Consider the different lenses through which historians have perceived the history of Christianity and the Church: A concern with political power and institutional identity gives way to a broader social treatment involving the lower classes, followed in turn by a less rationalistic, less teleological emphasis on diversity, intensity, and strangeness.

> Historians have shifted their focus from military and political leaders to the lives of ordinary people.

In the last major shift, historians came to make less of the boundaries between "elite" and "popular" religious cultures overall. Also, they viewed religious belief less as a symbolic expression of social concerns than as a medium of transcendence and transformation. Columbia professor Caroline Bynum's *Holy Feast, Holy Fast* (1987), a study of the extremes of fasting in the late Middle Ages, discusses female piety as a chapter in the history of medieval belief rather than as a psychological or social statement. Both Peter Brown of Princeton and William Christian, who resides in the Canary Islands, delineate religious experience from the inside but with a very specific time and place in mind: Brown for late Antiquity, Christian for early modern Spain.

Within the overall gravitation in the discipline toward fragmentation and a less teleological sort of history, certain fields have experienced declines, whereas the Renaissance, the history of ideas (as opposed to the history of popular culture or mentalities), and economic history seem to be gaining a new vitality. Other areas—medieval Germany, Anglo-Saxon England—have almost disappeared in the United States for reasons that no one can explain. Though long neglected, still other areas are visibly undergoing a resurgence—notably Eastern Europe apart from Russia.

Perhaps the most important insights in recent decades have developed through the widespread application of cultural anthropology to the study of the past, a development that has tended to encourage both a broader view of societies and an understanding of culture as a symbolic system. In nearly every department today, history is seen less as a series of events put in motion by military and political leaders and more as a process understandable by examining the lives and outlooks of ordinary people and the social forces shaping their everyday experiences.

WHAT'S NEXT

What distinguishes graduate from undergraduate study in European history is having to confront masses of historical information and to interpret it in an original fashion. Commendably, undergraduate history courses strive for coherence and narrative stability. A long chronological span and a concentration on major trends allows the student to become familiar with the sweep and drama of historical events, even in courses that tend to deemphasize political or military ups and downs. Undergraduate American history majors occasionally work with newspapers, census data, immigration records, or other primary documents, but it is only in graduate school that most European history students come face-to-face with untranslated sources—the complex and often puzzling machinery (the nuts and bolts, as it were) churning away under the smooth surface of the secondary material read in undergraduate courses. Moreover, students are expected to find an original research topic within this recalcitrant mass, not merely because no one has yet looked at that village or those documents, but because there is only a slender interpretation of their significance and implications available.

Thus, the defining moment of many a graduate student career in European history is neither the oral exam nor the dissertation defense but the first confrontation with European archives and libraries. The experience of working with the raw material of history is exciting but requires considerable advance preparation. Much first- and second-year coursework is designed to prepare the student to identify areas of potentially fruitful research, examine masses of ill-assorted information, and master sprawling and unautomated bibliographic searching tools. Instead of an enjoyable lecture on chivalry or the Crusades, one is suddenly faced with hundreds of charters from one medieval monastery during one century—written in Latin. And a graduate level course about these charters seems to be devoted to reading only one or two—line by line. It is fascinating to look at what historical actors were writing and thinking and to pore over documents no other historian has seen, but there is also an undeniable element of tedium in this research.

Equally challenging and bewildering is the sheer quantity of documentation that has survived. The bureaucracies of recent history are not the only institutions to have generated record-packed rooms. In the first half of the sixteenth century, for instance, the notaries of even the smallest northern Italian towns generated such a mountain of records about economic and social transactions that they cannot all be read in a lifetime—even if the historian reading them didn't have to decipher their difficult script and deal with the murky issue of when the repository storing the records is open, if at all. One either likes this kind of research for its direct contact with the remains of the past, or comes to prefer the History Book Club's more convenient, tidy packaging and moves on to a different career.

Though hardly a small field, European history has certain built-in hurdles on the recruitment of Ph.D. students and hence on the size of graduate programs. The most significant is the knowledge of one or more foreign languages required for the study of all but British history. Admissions decisions are therefore influenced by the understandable reluctance of professors to supervise basic language instruction. In medieval history the ability to read Latin is indispensable, as is Latin and Greek in ancient history. Students also have to present two modern European languages for medieval and ancient history. For modern European fields, fluency in the language of the country or areas being studied is expected and little credence will be given to promises on the part of the student to learn languages later. The application of anyone who wants to go to graduate school in German history with only a year or so of undergraduate German is likely to move to the bottom of the pile.

> The defining moment of many a graduate career is that first confrontation with European archives.

A major in history with an emphasis in European is the most common denominator among graduate students. Most undergraduate history departments offer rather unstructured, cafeteria-style majors that aim more at breadth than depth, so graduate programs do not expect entering students to have done research or extensive coursework in one geographical or chronological area (though if they have, it has some persuasive effect). Finally, there is the GRE subject test in history, which covers both European and American history, but these days few departments pay any mind to it.

Over the last decade there have been several major trends in the field of European history: a movement away from political narrative; less attention to the modern state as the central topic; more attention to feminist theory and the study of gender; and challenges to notions of progressive or coherent historical development. Unlike some other fields, however, older methods and approaches have not been discredited or replaced. There has been a proliferation and revamping of subfields rather than outright supersession of historiographic principles. The study of European power politics, international relations, and military history are by no means eclipsed, while despite a considerable amount of discussion of historiography and the linguistic turn, relatively few historians at major institutions have completely embraced theory at the expense of empiricism. Strong programs in the history of modern European politics, for instance, are led by scholars such as Paul Kennedy (Yale), Robert O. Paxton and Fritz Stern (Columbia), and Charles Maier and David Blackbourn (Harvard University). Methodological debates and sustained attention to the impact of theory are more in evidence at the University of Chicago, the University of Michigan, and Cornell University than elsewhere, but they do not dominate every area.

> Relatively few historians have completely embraced theory at the expense of empiricism.

The disciplinary picture is complicated by differences among national areas. French history has been profoundly affected by a disenchantment with grand narrative and a fascination with the history of taste, leisure, the senses, and representation. For the most part, German history has tended to remain absorbed by questions of political evolution, modernization, and the origins and impact of Nazism. Not surprisingly, in many subfields of European history the very different historiographic practices native to European countries themselves affect how those countries are studied in the United States.

To make matters still more complex, the balance of specialization in graduate school has tilted away from geographical area (say, Germany) toward methodology (gender theory, for instance). Yet when it comes to the job market, colleges often retain a rather fixed idea of positions: a modern German historian, a historian of ancient Rome. It is important to find a manner of self-identification that acknowledges your specialization yet aligns you with recognizable categories within the profession. Thus a medieval historian might work on Germany but with particular attention to relations with Slavs in Eastern European cities, informed by comparative cultural anthropological theory.

In choosing where to go, the overall reputation of a department has to be weighed against the relative generosity of its financial aid offer. And it's equally important to consider which faculty members you can work with. If you plan to study interwar diplomacy, it may not be wise to apply to an outstanding department whose twentieth-century historians are interested in postwar leisure and consumer culture. (Chances are you will not have outlined a dissertation topic by the beginning of your graduate career but will at least have an idea of what country, era, and methodology interests you and so can investigate such faculty specialties accordingly.) Talk to professors to determine whether their current interests match up with your own, and chat with graduate students to find out about the quality of their working relationships with faculty. Keep in mind that not all programs that look outstanding on paper prove so in practice. Some distinguished scholars may be unapproachable or on perpetual leave, juggling joint appointments. On the other hand, don't choose a department exclusively on the basis of its cuddly atmosphere or a nurturing advisor. The strongest departments encourage you to find your own voice, not to become a clone of a well-known scholar or an advocate of a party line.

> In French history, a fascination with the history of taste, leisure, the senses, and representation is ascendant.

A recent Harvard Ph.D. remarked that in retrospect the best reason for attending Harvard was the Widener Library, the largest university library in the country. Libraries and other research resources on and off campus often do not play a big role in students' decisions about where to apply, but they are often crucial in enhancing or making possible the research topics they will actually undertake later. The most important independent libraries for European history are the Morgan Library in New York City (medieval); the Newberry Library, Chicago (Renaissance); the Folger Library, Washington, D.C. (England); and the Huntington Library, Los Angeles (England). Some of these libraries offer postdoctoral fellowships or cooperate closely with departments

Relatedly, interdisciplinary institutes focused on world affairs and area studies—a region-by-region approach to studying the world beyond the borders of the United States—are especially important for contemporary history. Some examples: the Hoover Institute at Stanford; Harvard's Center for European Studies and its Russian Research Center; Yale's Center for International Area Studies, International Security Studies Program, and Program in Agrarian Studies; UCLA's Center for Medieval and Renaissance Studies; and UC-Berkeley's International Political Economy Program.

Interdisciplinary institutes focusing on world affairs and area studies are crucial to the study of contemporary history.

In its most recent report, the National Research Council ranked the top ten history departments as follows: Yale, UC-Berkeley, Princeton, Harvard, Columbia, UCLA, Stanford, Chicago, Johns Hopkins, and the University of Wisconsin at Madison. Besides the usual problems with rankings in general—rapid obsolescence, pseudo-precision, self-fulfilling expectations—the NRC rankings evaluate entire history departments, and thus are unauthoritative guides to departmental strengths in the many fields of European history. Moreover, creating a top-ten list excludes distinguished programs that are not inferior to the group just named (notably Michigan, Cornell, the University of Pennsylvania).

It's more useful to assess graduate programs according to their offerings in the field's three traditional subdivisions: chronology (ancient, medieval, early modern, modern, contemporary), area or country (France, Eastern Europe), and approach (social, intellectual, political history). In some specializations, such as Russia, graduate study will encompass many centuries, from medieval to post-Soviet, as candidates will eventually be teaching survey courses spanning the chronological range of Russian history. In Western European fields such as British or French history, there is greater specialization. Students of Tudor-Stuart England, for example, may do very little with other periods of British history. If you are working on nineteenth-century France, you might have early modern France as an examination field, but are also likely to cross geographical boundaries or identify topics with cross-cutting theoretical implications. Often scholars will be most knowledgeable about a particular geographical region, but the questions they ask will have implications beyond national boundaries. Thus, Thomas Laqueur at UC-Berkeley or Joan Scott of the Institute for Advanced Study in Princeton, New Jersey, are British and French historians, respectively, but they are widely known for their work in the history of sexuality, labor, and gender rather than as national specialists.

What follows is a breakdown of prominent programs (and faculty) according to methodological, chronological, and geographical criteria. Moves of faculty members from one institution to another are common at the senior level and can radically alter the chemistry of a department, so verify the information offered in this book at the time you apply.

There are certain differences among notable programs in terms of approach and emphasis. Yale, Harvard, and Columbia are especially strong in the political and military history of modern Europe. Cornell, Chicago, UC-Berkeley, Michigan, and Johns Hopkins emphasize theory to a greater extent. UCLA's history department has some of the leading scholars of social theory and the European peasantry. Wisconsin-Madison has a continuing distinction in intellectual history.

> Assess programs according to their offerings in the areas of chronology, country, and approach.

In ancient history, the leading institutions for classical Greece and Rome are UC-Berkeley and Penn, both of which have programs in ancient history that have an identity separate from the history department. UC-Berkeley has an interdisciplinary program in ancient history and Mediterranean archaeology. Penn has a similar arrangement, along with the most important university museum collection for classical archaeology. Other notable departments in ancient history are Yale (Donald Kagan, John Matthews), Harvard (Ernst Badian), and Michigan (Sarah Humphreys, Bruce Frier).

For late antiquity and Byzantium, check out Princeton (Peter Brown), Harvard (Angeliki Laiou, Michael McCormick), and Chicago (Walter Kaegi). In medieval, Columbia (Caroline Bynum, Robert Somerville, Martha Howell), Princeton (William Chester Jordan), and Harvard (Thomas Bisson) are outstanding. UC-

Berkeley, Yale, UCLA, and the University of Toronto have tradi-
tionally been strong in this area but are rebuilding or in transition.
The University of Notre Dame has always been strong and its
Medieval Institute is probably the most important of such interdis-
ciplinary centers. The University of California at Santa
Barbara, the University of Minnesota at Twin Cities, and **Not all programs**
Johns Hopkins also offer excellent medieval programs. **that look**

For many years early modern history was dominated by
Princeton, Johns Hopkins, and UC-Berkeley. Retire- **outstanding on**
ments and increasing complexity about what this term **paper prove so**
exactly covers have shaken things up, and much depends **in practice.**
on what national or theoretical areas you are looking for.
In the Renaissance, Princeton (Anthony Grafton) and Cornell (John
Najemy) are strong. For the Reformation, perennial standouts are
Harvard (Steven Ozment, Robert Scribner), Wisconsin-Madison
(Robert Kingdon), UC-Berkeley (Thomas Brady), the University of
Virginia (Erik Midelfort), and the University of Arizona (Heiko
Oberman). And for the seventeenth and eighteenth centuries, check
out Columbia (Simon Schama) and Princeton (Robert Darnton).

The strongest programs in British history have been Yale and
Princeton, though Yale has some vacancies to fill. Stanford is perhaps
the leading program at the moment. In medieval British, Minnesota-
Twin Cities (Barbara Hanawalt) and the University of North Carolina
at Chapel Hill (Judith Bennett) attract attention, while for Tudor-
Stuart England, Duke University (Cynthia Herrup), Harvard (Mark
Kishlansky), Princeton (Peter Lake), Brown University (Timothy
Harris), and George Washington University (Linda Levy Peck) are
strong. In modern history, Yale (Frank Turner, Linda Colley, Robin
Winks), Stanford (Peter Stansky), Johns Hopkins (Judith Walkowitz),
and UC-Berkeley (Thomas Laqueur) stand out.

In German history, Harvard (Charles Maier) and Yale (Henry
Turner) are well-known for modern German political history and
international relations. Stanford (James Sheehan) and UC-Berkeley
(Gerald Feldman) have important and successful programs. Michigan
(Geoffrey Eley) and Chicago (Michael Geyer) emphasize theoretical
and cultural approaches. Wisconsin-Madison has made important
appointments to replace retirees and so remains strong in both the
intellectual and political history of Germany. Brown, UNC-Chapel

Hill, the University of Texas at Austin, and Georgetown University also have impressive programs in this area.

Johns Hopkins (Richard Kagan), Minnesota-Twin Cities (Carla Rahn Phillips, William D. Phillips), and Yale (Carlos Eire) are notable in early modern Spanish history. Wisconsin-Madison has the leading American scholar of twentieth-century Spain (Stanley Payne). In Italian history, apart from Renaissance high culture, check out Northwestern University (Edward Muir) and Brown (Anthony Molho) for early modern, and Columbia (Victoria de Grazia) for modern.

Russian history has undergone considerable upheaval with the collapse of the Soviet Union. Columbia (Mark von Hagen, Richard Wortman) and Harvard, both with major research institutes for Russian studies, have traditionally been outstanding in modern and Soviet history. Richard Pipes has retired from Harvard, and his replacement will determine much of the future of its program in modern Russian history. Chicago (Sheila Fitzpatrick, Richard Hellie, Ronald Suny) and Michigan (William Rosenberg, Valerie Kivelson, Jane Burbank) are the strongest programs for Russian history, including the medieval and early modern periods. Stanford (Norman Naimark, Terence Emmons, Steven Zipperstein) has excellent coverage in all periods. Princeton has very distinguished scholars (Laura Engelstein, Stephen Kotkin), but its graduate program is not as vibrant as might be expected. UC-Berkeley has probably the most successful graduate program in modern Russian history thanks especially to Reginald Zelnik.

> Though experts about a particular region, scholars often ask questions that cross national boundaries.

In Eastern European history, Harvard (Roman Szporluk) and Yale (Ivo Banac) stand out, while Indiana University and the University of Illinois at Urbana are known for their impressive institutional and library resources. Harvard (Susan Pedersen) and Johns Hopkins (Judith Walkowitz) are leaders in women's history; Michigan and Penn are also important.

For the history of science (including medicine), there are separate departments at Wisconsin-Madison, Indiana, and Harvard. Stanford has five well-regarded historians of science. Vanderbilt University does not have a special program in this area but has three well-known figures in the history of European medicine and science. Princeton has recovered much of its former eminence.

THE JOB MARKET

Flourishing and intellectually exciting as it may be, the field of European history is afflicted by the general downturn in the academic job market along with some particular problems of its own. The academic job market has been difficult for so long (since the early 1970s) that the field has attained an uncomfortable equilibrium, one in which the graduates of major programs are likely to get decent jobs, but not easily, and often not at research institutions.

Historians are acutely sensitive to the pitfalls of making predictions about the future, because forecasting is inevitably an extrapolation from the past—a past littered with what now seem hilariously inaccurate pronouncements of futurologists. The predicted shortage of Ph.D.'s in the 1990s quite dramatically did not happen. But on the other hand, several anticipated disasters—the expected shake-out of small nonselective colleges, radical cuts to public universities, the end of tenure—have not taken place yet. Universities are faced with cost constraints such as the decline in government support, high fixed costs of instruction, and the impossibility of further major increases in tuition. At the same time, demand for college education does not seem to be declining, and demographics argue for modest future expansion. The supply of positions in the field of European history is affected by such global tendencies as downsizing and the hiring of part-time and temporary rather than tenure-track faculty. There is also justifiable anxiety about the future of liberal arts subjects such as history in an environment that focuses on job training and marketable skills. So far, however, European history has not suffered more than other academic fields.

This is a bit surprising because the days when history departments were more or less evenly divided between U.S. and European fields are certainly over, but so far there has not been a wholesale shift at the expense of the latter. Departments are wary of simply expanding geographical options in course offerings where consistent student demand is unproven. The changing definition of U.S. history as concerned with something other than white modern Americans has led to more attention being paid to Mexico and the Spanish borderlands,

> The days when history departments were evenly divided between U.S. and European fields are over.

Native Americans, and the African diaspora in the seventeenth and eighteenth centuries. These salutary developments have not taken place to the detriment of European history. At the moment, it is probably *more* difficult to find a job in a traditionally defined area of U.S. history than in European because the severity of the job crisis in U.S. history is more recent and the supply of recent Ph.D.'s is greater relative to the number of openings. But this is admittedly cold and invidious comfort.

Unlike the 1970s, when undergraduate enrollments in history declined disastrously, the discipline is a reasonably popular undergraduate major today. There is not the sort of student shift towards economics and other "hard" social sciences, perceived as more practical, that took place twenty-five years ago. This is partly because subjects such as economics and sociology have lost some prestige in the last decades.

A European history Ph.D. can pursue other avenues besides college teaching, but unfortunately there is no easy or natural alternate career path in place. Unlike U.S. history, where there is training in public history available, European history programs don't offer programs that might allow for a career in an archive, as an editor for a historical papers project, or other public-sector work. There is, though, the possibility of earning a Master's of Library Science and working as a librarian with special responsibilities for collection development or rare books in your research field. This is often the route taken by those holding positions in research university libraries, great private libraries such as the Morgan or Newberry, or other research centers such as the Institute for Advanced Study.

Although public and private high schools in the United States need history and social studies teachers with training beyond the master's level, too often, just as in many humanities fields, secondary school teaching is considered a consolation prize. This is especially unfortunate because teaching in those venues is as rewarding as it is at colleges and universities, and salaries are competitive if not higher once teachers gain seniority. Teaching secondary-school students is also an opportunity to guide students in their first serious encounter with the past.

> Teaching in secondary school is an opportunity to guide students through their first serious encounter with the past.

Government service and publishing (especially at university presses) are other possibilities. Former senator and presidential candidate George McGovern received a Ph.D. in history. The American Historical Association increasingly emphasizes careers other than university teaching and offers advice, discussions, and workshops at its annual convention on nonacademic jobs. Committees and panels are also at work to make the organization more attentive to community college and secondary school faculty needs.

Most students entering graduate school, however, desire jobs in four-year academic institutions. Many students successfully retool or find rewarding jobs outside academia, but however upbeat the advice manuals may be, the transition from the study of European history to other occupations is rarely easy.

RESOURCES

NRC TOP TEN
Yale
UC–Berkeley
Princeton
Harvard
Columbia
UCLA
Stanford
Chicago
Johns Hopkins
Wisconsin–Madison

ASSOCIATIONS
American Historical Association
(202) 544-2422

Organization of American Historians
(812) 855-7311

JOURNALS
American Historical Review
Annales
Comparative Studies in Society and History
Past & Present
Representations

FURTHER READING
Directory of History Departments and Organizations,
(American Historical Association)

Joyce Appleby, Lynn Hunt, Margaret Jacob, eds.,
Telling the Truth About History (Norton)

WEB ADDRESSES
European History Resources
http://www.mel.lib.mi.us/humanities/history/HIST-europe.html

CONSTELLATIONS

ANCIENT HISTORY
Harvard
Michigan
Penn
UC–Berkeley
Yale

LATE ANTIQUITY AND BYZANTIUM
Chicago
Harvard
Princeton

MEDIEVAL
Columbia
Harvard
Johns Hopkins
Minnesota–Twin Cities
Notre Dame
Princeton
Toronto
UC–Berkeley
UC–Santa Barbara
UCLA
Yale

EARLY MODERN
Johns Hopkins
Princeton
UC–Berkeley

RENAISSANCE
Cornell
Princeton

REFORMATION
Arizona
Harvard
UC–Berkeley
Virginia
Wisconsin–Madison

CONSTELLATIONS

SEVENTEENTH AND EIGHTEENTH CENTURIES
Columbia
Princeton

BRITISH HISTORY
Brown
Duke
George Washington
Harvard
Johns Hopkins
Minnesota–
  Twin Cities
Stanford
Princeton
UC–Berkeley
UNC–Chapel Hill
Yale

FRENCH HISTORY
Chicago
Columbia
Cornell
Johns Hopkins
NYU
Penn
Princeton
Stanford
UC–Berkeley

GERMAN HISTORY
Brown
Chicago
Georgetown
Harvard
Michigan
Stanford
UC–Berkeley
UNC–Chapel Hill
UT–Austin
Wisconsin–Madison
Yale

SPANISH HISTORY
Johns Hopkins
Minnesota–
  Twin Cities
Wisconsin–Madison
Yale

ITALIAN HISTORY
Brown
Columbia
Northwestern

RUSSIAN HISTORY
Chicago
Columbia
Harvard
Michigan
Princeton
Stanford
UC–Berkeley

EASTERN EUROPEAN HISTORY
Harvard
Illinois–Urbana
Indiana
Yale

WOMEN'S HISTORY
Harvard
Johns Hopkins
Michigan
Penn

HISTORY OF SCIENCE
Harvard
Indiana
Princeton
Stanford
Vanderbilt
Wisconsin–Madison

INTERDISCIPLINARY INSTITUTES
Center for
  International Area
  Studies (Yale)
Center for European
  Studies (Harvard)
Center for Medieval
  and Renaissance
  Studies (UCLA)
Hoover Institute
  (Stanford)
International Political
  Economy Program
  (UC–Berkeley)
International Security
  Studies Program
  (Yale)
Medieval Institute
  (Notre Dame)
Program in Agrarian
  Studies (Yale)
Russian Research
  Center (Harvard)

CHAPTER 12

FRENCH

After his junior year in Dickinson College's program in Toulouse, Scott Carpenter spent a semester in southern Spain. He remembers "falling in love with Gothic architecture on his first visits to Paris and Chartres" and finding constant connections among his literature, art history, and social science courses in France. He decided then to apply to graduate school in French, and after completing his M.A. through New York University's program in Paris, he is now continuing his Ph.D. coursework in New York and thinking seriously about specializing in the late Middle Ages.

And then there's the path taken by Mojdeh Bahar, who, with a B.A. in French and Chemistry, deferred her admission to medical school to get a master's degree in French language and civilization. Born in Iran, she grew up in the United States and often visited French-speaking relatives in Switzerland before spending her junior year in France. She'd enjoyed her work as an undergraduate classroom assistant, as well as researching Hélène Cixous and *écriture féminine* for her senior thesis. When graduation came around, she just wasn't yet ready to put teaching and studying French behind her. Three years later, she's finished her courses towards the Ph.D. in French literature and is too busy preparing her dissertation proposal to think about stopping now. No longer reluctant to work on material that "hits close to home," Bahar plans to focus on the nineteenth-century writer Arthur de Gobineau, largely forgotten today except for his disturbing theories of racial inequality, but remembered in her particular family for his *History of the Persians*, oriental tales, and diplomatic stints in Teheran. "It's a subject that marries purely literary questions with cultural and political history," says Bahar.

WHY FRENCH?

France and all manner of things French—old-world charm, sophistication, fine cuisine—have turned generations of traveling Americans into Francophiles. But being a Francophile and studying French are two very different things. Students of French may savor French fashion and food, but they're not likely to think of their favorite boulangeries, boutiques, and bistros as being anything more than brief distractions from their books. Yet sometimes, following the example of Roland Barthes, they may think of these institutions as sites rich with national mythologies and ripe for analysis. Or else, inspired by Pierre Nora's recent work on collective memory, they may wonder how these places interact with the rest of French culture.

Until recently, most French departments in the United States were first and foremost departments of French literature. The field seemed clearly defined but never confining, since the canon of great French literature encompassed major works of philosophy, aesthetics, and political theory, as well as novels, poems, essays, and plays. In a sense, French literature was interdisciplinary *avant la lettre,* and French studies all the more so. Since at least the 1960s, when French departments led the humanities in opening their discipline to anthropologists, psychoanalysts, historians, and linguists, this openness has been a key attraction for students in French. And yet the study of French language and literature remained firmly grounded in solid French traditions of linguistics, rhetoric, textuality, and literary history even as it was a field without borders: Students of French could travel the intellectual world without ever leaving home.

As literary study of all kinds has undergone a recent reshaping, French has broadened even further. Departments of comparative literature, gender studies, media, film, philosophy, English, and

African-American studies have welcomed professors of French whose principal concerns reach beyond national literary and linguistic boundaries. Despite the concerns of some scholars over losing their comfortable sense of grounding in a diverse intellectual milieu, French departments are, in turn, setting themselves new goals and making ever more determined efforts to open their departments to the rest of the globe.

Many native French speakers from the world over choose to study in the United States because they assume that distance can bring insight, that cross-cultural perspectives will make their work more interesting, and that American teaching styles and small seminars are more satisfying than the grand professorial manner common in European universities. But with distance comes difference as well as insight: The American context affects the teaching of French for both American and foreign students. As Harvard University professor Naomi Schor emphasizes, to speak and read a language and to understand a culture are quite separate matters. You can't study another culture without losing sight of your own. She writes, we "need to recognize that the ability to translate into the terms of one's own culture the products of another—which is one of our main cultural missions—requires a deep understanding of one's own culture and a higher competence in the target symbolic system than in the source." To master French in the United States, in other words, is to never cease to study *les choses américaines*.

HOW FRENCH HAS TAKEN SHAPE

As the traditional language of diplomacy and elite society, French has long been seen as an always negotiable coin of the international realm. The famous *hauteur* of the French and unmistakable influence of their civilization's achievements have given the French language a cachet that is hard to quantify. The fortunes of other national language and literature programs have been tied to the social, political, and economic well-being of their respective nations or to the visibility of immigrant populations in the United States. So students of German, Spanish, and Russian have become accustomed to the periodic need, especially at times of war and anti-immigrant fervor, to redefine and justify the value of their disciplines. French, however, had roots in American soil and a hold on the American imagination well before it took its place in the university curriculum.

Though it lacked a base in a highly visible immigrant community, French was a touchstone of political thought in the American colonies, the favored second language of the founders of the American republic, many of whom felt a special affinity for the political philosophies of Montesquieu, Rousseau, and even the Jansenists of Port-Royal. In fact, when Benjamin Franklin, whose success as ambassador to France after 1776 was due in part to his command of the language, founded a library in Quaker Philadelphia, he bequeathed to it an impressive collection of books representing reformist French thought. As the language of both international aristocracy and egalitarian philosophy, then, French seemed to transcend national particularity.

When French education was undergoing reform in hopes of competing with Germany at the end of the nineteenth century, U.S. universities were also reorganizing themselves on the German model. French language and literature were taught in U.S. departments of Romance philology or Romance languages along with Provençal, Italian, and, less frequently, Spanish. (One residuum is that at some universities today French and Italian are still administratively grouped together.) The American and European professors who taught French were as likely to have studied in Vienna and Berlin as at the Ecole des Chartes in Paris.

> As the language of both the aristocracy and egalitarian theory, French seemed to transcend national boundaries.

Modern Language Notes (MLN), founded by the Romance language department at Johns Hopkins University in 1886, set a standard for the field when it announced its purpose as "the development of the scientific spirit" based on the belief in "the disciplinary value of literary criticism." The focus of the first formally trained Romance philologists was almost exclusively the medieval period and the tracing of its sources. Up until World War I, departments emphasized the scrutiny of texts like *Le Pèlerinage de Charlemagne* and the training of a small cadre of highly specialized research scholars who concentrated on the relation of such texts to the Latin tradition.

But state universities established an equally important commitment to the training of teachers. By 1910, the University of Wisconsin at Madison could boast "an unusually large number of courses in *modern* French literature and language." Ivy League schools followed suit. Columbia University's large department, for example, was an early proponent of the study of modern literature. At the turn of the century, it offered courses on the history of literary criticism, nineteenth-century literary movements and genres, and even a teaching-methods practicum conducted entirely in French.

By the 1920s, two sometimes discrete, sometimes intertwined currents characterized the discipline. Old-school philology and scholarship—the study of texts and their linguistic sources—seemed to hold sway in the Ivy League and continued to be pursued at many public universities. At the same time, other public institutions—along with prestigious women's colleges like Bryn Mawr—were developing a new type of modern French studies. By 1925, Wisconsin-Madison had a residential French House for women—and where men were encouraged to take their meals—at which French only was spoken. Before long, courses in phonetics and conversation were the largest draw, and departments that ignored popular activities like speaking French and discussing contemporary French culture became a minority. With the new emphasis on the practice of the French language, positions were designed for young native-speaking instructors from France, and cross-cultural exchanges increased. In 1925 Columbia offered a course on Franco-American relations in the eighteenth century, and five years later added a course with a title that strained for an up-to-date ring: "*Modification de la sensibilité moderne: le cinéma, le théâtre, le roman, la radio.*"

Further changes in the field accompanied the arrival of philologist Leo Spitzer on these shores. Spitzer pioneered the teaching of modern, even popular, French literature when students returning from World War I came to his classes in Bonn and Marburg in search of contemporary relevance rather than dry erudition. Spitzer, mindful of his frustration as a student in Vienna in the early years of the century—when even the best professors taught philology and literary history as rigidly separate topics—soon established a reputation for bringing historical depth and skill in linguistics to the study of stylistics from Villon to Proust. Spitzer once described his progress from student to teacher as an almost knightly adventure: "I made my way through the maze of linguistics, with which I started, toward the

> In the 1920s, old-school philology held sway in the Ivy League while public institutions pioneered new types of French study.

enchanted garden of literary history—and…I discovered that there is as well a paradise in linguistics as a labyrinth in literary history."

Spitzer fled Hitler's Germany in 1933 and settled at Johns Hopkins in 1936. There he continued his adventures and, along with Erich Auerbach, the famous Yale University comparativist, became a central figure among a generation of émigré scholars who injected cosmopolitan perspectives and concerns into American departments of comparative and French literature. After World War II he addressed a perceived weakening of the humanities with an insistent linguistically based caution: "If it is true that there is no value to be derived from the study of language, we cannot pretend to preserve literary history, cultural history—or history."

> In the 1930s, émigré scholars injected cosmopolitan concerns into American departments.

In the 1950s, American scholars focused their attention upon the Theater of the Absurd, the existentialists, and *écrivains engagés* like Sartre, Camus, and Beauvoir as well as upon questions of language. At the same time, scholars also studied the work of less polemical writers, especially the thematic approaches to literature of Georges Poulet, Jean-Pierre Richard, and other members of the Geneva School, whose phenomenological readings attempted to grasp the consciousness and subjectivity of major writers from Rousseau to Proust.

By mid-decade, a younger European-born generation of scholars in the United States that included René Girard, Michael Riffaterre, and Paul de Man brought some of the tendencies of the Geneva School to the United States, albeit in very different ways. Two decades later these scholars—Girard at Johns Hopkins and then Stanford University, de Man at Yale, and Riffaterre at Columbia—were all leaders in the general shift toward literary theory experienced throughout the humanities. Girard's psychological-anthropological theories of mimetic desire were closely tied to readings of Proust and Stendhal. Riffaterre's early stylistics and later theories of literariness developed through close readings of poets like Hugo and Baudelaire and prose masters like Chateaubriand and Proust. And de Man was a linchpin of the group of scholars at Yale who embarked on deconstructive-rhetorical readings of Rousseau and the British romantic poets. The work of these and other scholars marked a return in French to linguistics-based theories, though not performed in the same key as was the old philological research. And as disparate as the theories of this second generation of émigrés were, they shared a tendency to think not only in terms of French literature per se, but also of world literature, or literature *tout court*. These tendencies, as well as a fascination with crucial figures of modernity like Mallarmé and Proust, had marked the work of their predecessors in the Geneva School.

In 1966 Serge Doubrovsky published *Pourquoi la nouvelle critique?* in Paris, an influential defense of Barthes, Goldmann, and other critics who foregrounded their interdisciplinary interests in what was a new *querelle des anciens et des modernes*. (Doubrovsky taught at Smith College, then at NYU.) For over a decade, the academic establishment in France had been challenged by the work of Barthes, Jacques Lacan, Louis Althusser, Michel Foucault and other thinkers now accepted as intellectual superstars. Labeled "structuralists" because of their shared reference to Saussure's structural linguistics and Lévi-Strauss's structural anthropology, their work never belonged to a single, unified movement, except perhaps for a shared disregard for rigid disciplinary boundaries, disdain for traditional literary history, and rejection of humanistic notions of subjectivity. Structuralism formally arrived in the United States in 1966 when *Yale French Studies* (*YFS*), always a bellwether for U.S. departments, published a double issue on the subject.

> A second generation of émigrés thought not only of French literature, but of literature *tout court*.

No sooner was structuralism labeled than the poststructuralist movement appeared. May '68, the legendary grass-roots student-worker revolt against government rigidity and the bourgeois status quo, led to extensive university reform in France. But the publication of Jacques Derrida's *De la grammatologie* and *L'écriture et la différence* in 1967 and of Julia Kristeva's *Séméiotikè* in 1969 appeared to some American scholars to mark another revolution. At the time, both Derrida and Kristeva were affiliated with the writers and theorists of the journal *Tel Quel*. Founded in 1960 by Philippe Sollers, *Tel Quel* proclaimed the desire to "transform the world" through attention to literature's revolutionary textual excesses. In the first issue, Sollers described his collaborators as contradictory personalities with eclectic goals, but all sharing a belief in the revolutionary power of the literature of rupture and modernity: Mallarmé, Lautréamont, Artaud, Bataille, and the Surrealists.

The dissemination of structuralist and poststructuralist literary theory wasn't limited to *Tel Quel*. A number of new journals began to appear here and abroad, with editorial boards that were international and goals that were for the most part interdisciplinary. Of those which remain notable, *Poétique*, a review of literary theory and analysis, appeared in Paris in 1970, proclaiming itself a "journal without borders." *SubStance* was founded at Wisconsin-Madison in collaboration with editors at the University of Michigan, and it became a review both eclectic and serious, ranging over semiotics, philosophy, psychoanalysis, and deconstruction along with both contemporary American writing and work by writers still little known in the United States like Bataille, Blanchot, Leiris, and Jabès. The same year, 1972, also brought the first issue of *Nineteenth-Century French Studies,* which highlighted interdisciplinary approaches to a traditional "period." *Stanford French Review* appeared in 1977, and gradually developed as an international and interdisciplinary journal. *Diacritics,* from Cornell University, quickly became must-reading far beyond French departments. Noting the growing interest in Lacan and Derrida, *YFS* focused issues on *French Freud* (1972), *Graphesis: Perspectives in Literature and Philosophy* (1975), and *Literature and Psychoanalysis* (1977).

An integral part of this theoretical groundswell was French feminism. Language-based and—as far as many politically active feminists in the U.S. were concerned—"essentialist" currents of feminism reached American campuses through the work of French writers Luce Irigaray and Hélène Cixous. A translation of Cixous's 1975 article theorizing *écriture féminine*, "Le rire de la méduse," was published the

> Feminist theory branched out to address the body, nationality, class, and race.

following year in *Signs* and fueled the growing interest among American feminist literary scholars in the specificity of women's writing while at the same time prompting more attention to feminism's connections to psychoanalytic and philosophical theory. By the 1980s, the influence of feminist theory was tangible in American French departments. The literary canon was slowly expanding, thanks largely to the collective work of feminist scholars committed to doing more than to "add a woman and stir," as Nancy K. Miller, now of CUNY Graduate Center, described earlier approaches to remedying exclusions. Discussions of sexual difference that draw on French-inflected or Franco-American feminist theory branched out to include questions of the body, nationality, class, and race. Taking this approach as a starting point, Gayatri C. Spivak, now a Columbia professor, posed what would become a key question in French and American feminism: "Who is the *other* woman?"

In 1987, the field was shaken by a discovery on an altogether different front. The late Paul de Man, the deconstruction avatar at Yale, was found to have written anti-Semitic articles for a collaborationist newspaper as a young man in German-occupied Belgium. The widely publicized storm that ensued generated a thick dossier of responses and counter-responses. While ideological foes of deconstruction on both right and left cited the theorist's life story as proof of the bankruptcy of his antihumanist theory, friends, colleagues, and former students of de Man carefully addressed the furor and its lessons using, among other approaches, the tools of deconstruction. Others, like Duke University's Alice Kaplan in her book *French Lessons*, traced the practical implications of de Man's silence.

> Themes of memory, guilt, witnessing, and testimony now preoccupy many of the foremost French scholars.

Themes of memory, guilt, witnessing, and testimony have since come to preoccupy many of the country's foremost French scholars—but only partially in response to the de Man affair. In the late 1980s a new interest in history in France had coincided with the rise of new historicism in English departments and a general dissatisfaction with the arid formalism of American literary studies. And even as American scholars were sorting out the various meanings of poststructuralism and postmodernism, a new French trend in political thought and philosophy, often labeled the New Humanism, was gaining attention in the United States. The publication of Pierre Nora's *Lieux de mémoire*—a monumental, multi-authored examination of the construction of the French cultural memory, now being translated as *Realms of Memory*—may be most suggestive of the historical paths French studies will soon follow.

Francophone studies, covering the French-language based literatures and cultures of Africa, the Caribbean, Canada, Southeast Asia, the Middle East, and the South Seas, has also finally come into its own. Only ten years ago the field was a second-class citizen in European-focused French departments. But today it is burgeoning, most visibly by the hiring of important poets and novelist-critics like Maryse Condé and Edouard Glissant. Hardly a sudden boom, the flourishing of Francophone studies builds on years of scholarship by devoted groups of scholars, fostered often in undergraduate institutions and outside elite graduate programs. Members of the African Literature Association in particular have long been known for their commitment to mentoring students interested in this area, and undergraduate programs in Francophone studies at Dartmouth College, the University of New Hampshire, and SUNY Purchase have played a prominent part in making Francophone studies more visible in the discipline.

WHAT'S NEXT

Labels skew the expectations of French departments. All large departments offer courses covering the major periods and genres of French literature and literary and critical theory. Some training in textual analysis, stylistics, and linguistics (historical, descriptive, and applied) is almost as common. Ph.D. candidates are usually asked to demonstrate a reading knowledge of one or two languages in addition to French and English. Princeton University, Yale, Columbia, and a few other departments also require some Latin of all students, but many now consider what was once the foundation of the discipline as an essential for medievalists and linguists but only an option for others. Students with particular interests in French civilization, Francophone studies, linguistics, medieval studies, film, and other specific areas will want to investigate neighboring departments for courses complementing those in French.

Most often, students with undergraduate degrees in French entering graduate school are generalists, perhaps leaning toward a period or field, but with only limited exposure to literary and critical theory. Even Naomi Schor, the well-known Harvard feminist and theorist, has written that following her professors' advice about programs, she "arrived at Yale with only the slenderest theoretical baggage," and without any knowledge of the new "isms" for which the department was already famous in the grad-school world. So don't be alarmed to hear University A labeled a bastion of formalism, University B an outpost of deconstruction, and University C a haven for arcane erudition. Even some professors and students at those schools find those categorizations mystifying.

You may have been advised to go to a department because it's either hot and trendy or rigorous and solid. The first thing to bear in mind is that for the strongest French departments, these categories have seldom been mutually exclusive. The second point to remember is that generalizations often depend on the reputations of a few highly visible professors, famous scholars who in fact have little contact with students. What's more, some big names in French have been known to play musical chairs, leaving one highly ranked department for another. Famous visiting professors, whose courses can be immensely stimulating, may be on campus only a few weeks out of the year, and renowned scholars listed in university catalogues may have retired from teaching.

> In French it is common for students to do an M.A. at one university before enrolling in a Ph.D. program elsewhere.

Although big names can put departments on the map, seek out a department, large or small, with a reputation for intangibles like mentoring and essentials like funding that does not dry up for students midway through the program. Talking to current graduate students is crucial for investigating these questions and the tenor of a department. Be on the lookout for tensions and rifts, but be careful not to conclude too much from only one or two personal testimonies. Several large state universities—like Wisconsin-Madison, Michigan, the University of Virginia, and Louisiana State University—are known for their long-standing commitments to French and can be rewarding, hospitable places for students to earn an M.A. From there, you can decide to stay on or transfer to another school for the Ph.D.

Many successful and satisfied Ph.D.'s have followed just that path. Stamos Metzidakis of Washington University in St. Louis, who got a bachelor's degree at Princeton, an M.A. at Michigan, and a Ph.D. at Columbia, says this itinerary gave him the best of all worlds: "As an undergraduate I was inspired by my teachers, who were all extremely impressive scholars. At Michigan, I was offered a teaching assistantship, which was very important, since I wanted to find out as soon as possible if I actually liked teaching." For Metzidakis, then, having to teach and take courses from the very start was an advantage: His interest in the day-to-day reality of teaching was confirmed, even as he developed close contacts with his professors and gained time to figure out how and where to pursue his Ph.D.

Others who have gone this route, sometimes squeezing in a year in France as a teaching assistant between the M.A. and Ph.D., report that the two-step process gave them time to improve their French, boost their qualifications, and prepare for a move that would have been much too daunting straight out of college. For decades, Middlebury

College's three-summer M.A. and year-long M.A. in Paris have been the first step of many American students toward doctoral work in a top program. A word of caution, though. Some M.A.'s—Stanford's, for example—are labeled "terminal" in the university bulletin and truly are: Stanford will not consider accepting even the most talented former terminal-M.A. student into the Ph.D. program. If there's a good chance you'll set your sights on a career in university research and teaching and will want to stay where you are, enroll in a full Ph.D. program from the start.

Don't be surprised if the college professors you consult about graduate school have only a vague notion of the National Research Council rankings of graduate departments in French. Some may tell you that the top departments are "always up there" but won't necessarily explain—or know—why. Because the Northeast corridor has been the traditional hub of French studies and conferences in the U.S.—during high season for lectures a student may choose between going to hear Derrida at NYU and Kristeva at Columbia—some professors continue to refer to Yale, Columbia, NYU, and Princeton as the "Big Four" and think of CUNY Graduate Center and Rutgers University as their neighbors.

But since the lecture circuit now covers the entire country, thanks in part to the reach of the French Cultural Services (with offices in Cambridge, Chicago, San Francisco, and other major cities), depart-

> **Departments once considered isolated may in fact be anything but.**

ments once considered isolated may in fact be anything but. So if a professor with a good sense of your strengths and interests suggests a lower-ranked program or even one altogether overlooked by the NRC, be prepared to investigate. Some of these schools may have high regional profiles, special strengths, good funding, and a respectable job-placement record. Take the possibilities of downsizing very seriously, though, and make sure that any very small program on your list will be around for the long haul.

If you're focusing on French literature, look closely at departmental requirements. Princeton, Cornell, Johns Hopkins, and Yale encourage students to specialize almost from the start, which can lead well-prepared students to the speedy completion of their degrees, but may distress those who are still uncertain about their interests. The opposite extreme, exemplified by Columbia's long list of required courses and exams, assuring exposure to all literary periods and several theoretical approaches, can appear overwhelming or frustrating to those eager to be on their way. But many of those who have gone through such programs see them as exceptional preparation for the demands of college teaching on junior professors, which are likely to be: Teach a bit of everything. The larger public and private departments tend to be closer to the Columbia model.

> Departments are turning more and more to specialists in language pedagogy to coordinate their language programs.

Princeton and Stanford have special strengths in literary history and are known for providing solid training in the canon and a diversity of methodologies. Usually described as theoretically oriented, Yale, Columbia, and the University of Pennsylvania also have professors interested in more traditional literary-historical questions: from biographical criticism to the analysis of canon formation, the history of publishing, and the study of drafts and manuscripts (currently practiced in France under the rubric *critique génétique*). Large departments like Wisconsin-Madison, Michigan, Rutgers, and LSU also have strong faculty with unusually wide-ranging specializations. Johns Hopkins, now quite small but boasting an exciting roster of visiting professors, is notable for its emphasis on the close reading of medieval and Renaissance texts in the light of modern theory. Emory University stresses theory and interdisciplinarity. The University of Chicago, where the important ARTFL data base for French literature was created, leans to traditional approaches, as does the University of North Carolina at Chapel Hill, home of *Romance Notes*.

If you're especially interested in language and linguistics, consider Cornell, the University of California at Berkeley, Indiana University, Duke, and LSU. For interdepartmental connections, also look into universities with strong linguistics departments like Penn or Stanford. Remember that good language teaching in beginning courses is the bread-and-butter of the profession and essential if an undergraduate department is to attract students to advanced work in literature and culture. Departments are turning more and more to specialists in language pedagogy to coordinate their programs. Large universities with schools of education like Pennsylvania State University, the University of Texas at Austin, Wisconsin-Madison, and the University of Illinois at Urbana stand out. Even if language teaching is not your primary interest, take full advantage of the training available, because when you go on the job market you may have an advantage if you are familiar with the work of Judith Frommer at Harvard, Alice Omaggio Hadley at Illinois-Urbana, Jeannette Bragger at Penn State, and Claire Kramsch, director of the Language Center at UC-Berkeley, all specialists in the field of second-language acquisition.

French departments often appear intertwined with nearby comparative literature programs. In a field where literary theory has been so central, it is hardly surprising that formal ties and shared professorships with comparative literature are well established at many places. Peter Brooks at Yale, Jonathan Culler at Cornell, Fredric Jameson at Duke, and Michael Riffaterre at Columbia leap to mind as important theorists working simultaneously in both fields. At Harvard, Susan Suleiman, Alice Jardine, Naomi Schor, and Barbara Johnson lend a notable feminist cast to the comp lit–French connections, as do Nancy K. Miller and Mary Ann Caws at CUNY Graduate Center. Charles Bernheimer teaches in both comparative literature and French at Penn, where there is also an impressive interdisciplinary center for cultural studies. Brown University is known for its interdepartmental links, not only between French studies and com-

> French departments often appear intertwined with comp lit programs.

parative literature, but also between French and the Center for Modern Culture and Media, and the Pembroke Center for Teaching and Research on Women.

The French department at the University of California at Irvine, where Derrida has frequently been a visiting professor, stresses critical theory and also offers an emphasis on feminist studies. At UCLA, comparativist Samuel Weber directs the Paris Program in Critical Theory, where students can gain degree credit for coursework. Cornell can be a special draw for a future French comparativist, since its faculty members bring together interests in literary theory, history, psychoanalysis, women's studies, and cultural studies in a small department known for generous funding of students. NYU students in French report that comparative literature courses can be especially stimulating but are not necessarily part of their program. At Columbia, on the other hand, many French professors offer courses labeled comparative literature–French, and all students in the various graduate literature departments are expected to take several courses on theory or methodology.

With undergraduate programs looking for faculty equipped to develop new nonliterary courses drawing upon history, sociology, political science, economics, and the visual arts, many graduate departments are encouraging students to seek out relevant preparation throughout the university. Students interested in French civilization or cultural studies have a growing number of possibilities to choose from. NYU, with its active Maison Française and Institute for French Studies, has long offered an M.A. in Language, Society, and Culture. Columbia and Penn have established a joint Paris-based M.A. program in cultural studies. A few large departments like Penn State and Illinois-Urbana, which houses *The French Review*, have offered French Civilization tracks for the Ph.D. for some time, but this approach has not been widely adopted.

> Students of French civilization or cultural studies have a growing number of choices about programs.

It may come as a surprise to learn that the otherwise quite traditional program at Princeton has long had a specialist in Haitian literature and has recently expanded its coverage in other Francophone areas. For some time, Yale professor Christopher Miller has been sponsoring an impressive number of dissertations on Caribbean and African literature. (Yale's French department has a joint program with African-American studies.) In light of Louisiana's own Francophone culture and heritage, it's no surprise that LSU has also been at the forefront of the field. It boasts a Center of French and Francophone Studies, courses on Québec, Africa, and the Caribbean, and has recently hired the Algerian novelist Assia Djebar. Two Caribbean writer-scholars have settled in New York City: Edouard Glissant at CUNY Graduate Center and Maryse Condé at Columbia. From Harvard (where connections with the Du Bois Center may be possible) to Northwestern University to Stanford, Francophone studies is thriving.

State universities also offer unexpected possibilities for interdepartmental Francophone work. At Indiana, famous for its strengths in language and linguistics, there is strong interest in Haitian creole. At Wisconsin-Madison, with the largest department of African languages and literatures in the country and joint appointments with French and comparative literature, students can minor in African literature or area studies. Work in Québecois studies goes on at Duke (with its Center for Canadian Studies), at Michigan, and at UCLA. Long-standing undergraduate programs in Francophone literatures at New Hampshire, SUNY Purchase, and Dartmouth are home to scholars in the field, and recently the

University of Southwestern Louisiana has added a Ph.D. program in Francophone studies. The University of New Mexico has just opened a Francophone Summer School for undergrads and graduate students. Northwestern University is home to Françoise Lionnet, a leading scholar of postcolonial literatures, and at Brown, Réda Bensmaïa is a specialist in Maghrebian literature. Quite apart from the options in the United States, an American student wishing to focus on Francophone studies shouldn't overlook the exceptional offerings at the University of Toronto or the possibility of short-term study in Québec at Laval University or the University of Montreal.

THE JOB MARKET

Until quite recently, French was far and away the most widely studied language other than English in the United States, but now it runs a distant second to Spanish. The Modern Language Association's most recent survey of undergraduate enrollments shows French decreasing by 25 percent between 1990 and 1995. This precipitous loss has prompted departmental downsizing and reconfiguration. Ph.D.'s now compete for part-time adjunct positions and limited-term openings of one year or less. Only 75 percent of 1994 Ph.D.'s were employed in postsecondary institutions in 1995, and only 41 percent were in tenure-track positions. On the other hand, some tenure-track jobs demand new faculty members to fill an ever wider array of quite specialized needs. In the October 1996 MLA Job List, more than half of the sixty-eight tenure track and shorter-term junior-level job listings called for two or more specific secondary fields—like cultural studies, women's studies, or film studies—in addition to a concentration in a traditional period, genre, or specialty in French. There seems to be a growing demand for Francophone literature and competence in teaching a second foreign language, but data are too sketchy to predict an enduring trend.

Despite this extremely uncertain job market, you should be wary of trying to shape your profile to fit a specific slot. Still, hiring committees are likely to seek job candidates with a combination of skills, so a few tips are in order. If your Italian or Spanish is good, make it better. Take advantage of opportunities to learn about technological and other practical developments in language teaching. Non-native

French speakers should spend at least one semester studying, doing research, or working in France or another Francophone country, and a year of such study is common. Many departments offer student exchange with French universities or the Ecole Normale Supérieure, as well as possibilities for teaching or doing administrative work in France.

French was far and away the most widely studied language other than English in the U.S., but now it runs a distant second to Spanish.

French Ph.D.'s who pursue careers other than college teaching should look for ways of integrating their language and intercultural skills with other strong interests. Perhaps not everyone will be as creative as the Columbia alumnus who has become a Grammy-winning music producer, but career-changes can be enterprising and imaginative in many ways. A professor with a background in art history moved into gallery management. A medievalist bibliophile, who took an airline job so he could regularly travel to France for free, opened bilingual bookstores in Canada and Paris. One former Ph.D. candidate decided the solitude of scholarship wasn't for her and started a real estate consulting service for French businesses needing to house employees in the United States. Another went into public relations in the perfume industry. Quite a few Ph.D.'s have gone on to law school. Others, after reading Lacan and Freud, have earned degrees in psychology or social work in order to become therapists.

Getting another degree after defending your dissertation will probably be the last thing on your mind, but don't overlook chances to add to your credentials. If you're interested in translation work, special training and certification by PEN, the writers' organization, or the American Translation Association may be helpful. CUNY Graduate Center also has a special certificate program, and SUNY Binghamton's undergraduate program has traditionally been strong in preparing future translators. Teaching in exclusive private high schools can be a satisfying route for many Ph.D.'s and ABD's (graduate students who have done everything but finish their dissertations). But the higher salaries, greater job security, and wider mission of public schools strongly appeal to others. One Ivy League Ph.D. who was eager to live with her husband after several years of commuting returned to school for state certification to teach Spanish and French. She describes her teaching in an urban high school for the humanities as the most satisfying work she has done.

RESOURCES

ASSOCIATIONS

Modern Language Association
(212) 475-9500

American Association
of Teachers of French
(217) 333-2842

JOURNALS

Diacritics
differences
Nineteenth Century French Studies
Stanford French Review
SubStance
Yale French Studies

NRC TOP TEN

Yale
Princeton
Duke
Columbia
Penn
Stanford
UC-Berkeley
Cornell
Michigan
UC-Irvine

FURTHER READING

Alice Kaplan, *French Lessons* (Chicago)

Jean-Philippe Mathy, *Extrême-Occident: French Intellectuals and America* (Chicago)

Nancy K. Miller, *Getting Personal: Feminist Occasions and Other Autobiographical Acts* (Routledge)

WEB ADDRESSES

American Association of Teachers of French
http://www.utsa.edu/aatf/aatf.html

University of California at Santa Barbara
http//humanitas.ucsb.edu/depts/French/deptpage.html

FRENCH LITERATURE
Chicago
Columbia
Cornell
Johns Hopkins
Princeton
UNC-Chapel Hill
Yale

LITERARY HISTORY
Columbia
Penn
Princeton
Stanford
Yale

THEORY
Columbia
Emory
Penn
UC-Irvine
UCLA
Yale

FRENCH AND COMPARATIVE LITERATURE
Brown
CUNY Graduate
  Center
Columbia
Cornell
Duke
Harvard
NYU
Penn
Yale

FRANCOPHONE AND HAITIAN
Columbia
CUNY Graduate
  Center
Harvard
Indiana
LSU
Princeton
Wisconsin-Madison
Yale

QUÉBECOIS STUDIES
Duke
Michigan
Toronto
UCLA

LANGUAGE AND LINGUISTICS
Cornell
Duke
Indiana
LSU
Penn
Stanford
UC-Berkeley

CONSTELLATIONS

CHAPTER 13

GERMAN

As an undergraduate, Ashley Passmore became interested in nineteenth- and twentieth-century German philosophy and considered pursuing a philosophy Ph.D. but opted for German instead. "It seemed to me that philosophy didn't take in some other disciplines I was interested in, such as film, sociology, or literature. I was looking for a truly interdisciplinary field." A second-year graduate student in the University of Chicago's Germanic Studies department, Passmore is currently working on Jewish and Jewish-German identity in the Bukowina, formerly home to Yiddish Zionism and today part of Romania. She believes that tracing connections between the history of the land of books—*Bücherland*, as the Bukowina was known—and acclaimed Bukowina poets Paul Celan and Rose Auslender will lead to crucial questions about language and identity formation. And "having the opportunity to work with history, literature, and a new wealth of psychoanalytic theory," Passmore says, "I feel that I will never be bored by German, let alone exhaust it."

The relations between historical events and literary movements also fascinate Sascha Lehnartz, a third-year graduate student at Columbia University. He is using discourse analysis in an attempt to find a common poetic principle of play in Walter Benjamin's and

Franz Kafka's writings, and in linking those writings to early twentieth-century social movements in Germany such as reform pedagogy, the youth movement, and psychoanalysis. Formerly a comparative literature student in Berlin, Lehnartz is often asked why he came from Germany to the United States in order to study German literature. "I think American departments are generally more open to experiments and on the cutting edge of theory—for good or for bad. I find this inspiring."

WHY GERMAN?

Students are often first attracted to studying things German because of family ties to that nation or due to a passion for travel, skiing or beer. But what keeps them hooked is the intellectual richness of the discipline: from Marx to Mozart, from Goethe to Grass, from Fichte to Freud, from Berlin Cabaret to the rubble of the Berlin Wall, *From Caligari to Hitler*. Graduate study in German today is at the intersection of literature, music, theories of interpretation, psychoanalysis, and much more.

As is true for the other national language disciplines in this volume, scholars of German now debate how far afield the discipline should stray from its traditional focus on literature. Despite its role as the key to an awe-inspiring body of past intellectual and artistic achievement, the study of German is in transition right now, redefining structures and boundaries. "Each generation reconstitutes for itself what Germany is," says Chicago professor Sander Gilman, referring to the generational and ideological shifts that the study of German language and culture have experienced in this century. The research work undertaken in German departments in the United States has depended on the political relations and cultural exchange between Germany and America, but it has also been influenced by a series of attempts to unify the study of German language, culture, and politics within a single discipline.

German language and culture held an important but seldom-acknowledged role in the United States before World War I. Though literary scholars seldom mention the fact, in late-nineteenth century America Goethe's *Hermann and Dorothea* was as popular as Mark Twain's *Huckleberry Finn*, especially in the Midwest. And according to the American Council on the Teaching of Foreign Languages, in 1915 nearly one out of three high school students learned German.

The prestige of German took a nosedive, however, when the United States entered World War I, and xenophobia towards all things German spread through the nation. The poet William Carlos Williams recalled that his father-in-law Paul Herman, a German immigrant and a staunch backer of U.S. involvement in the war, was nearly run out of his hometown of Rutherford, New Jersey, by neighbors who falsely accused him of supplying machine guns to a German Bund. What's more, the federal government abolished the teaching of German in public schools, while in the marketplace familiar words like "hamburger" and "sauerkraut" were replaced by "liberty sandwich" and "liberty cabbage."

HOW GERMAN HAS TAKEN SHAPE

That German is the least visible national language in the United States is due mostly to the effect of war and xenophobia on German language and literature departments. German scholars in the United States kept a low profile during the 1920s and 1930s. With the rank nativism of World War I still a vivid memory, they rarely entered the bitter public debate over whether or not the United States should enter World War II. Scholars already in the United States remained active researchers, to be sure, but it was the generation of refugee German scholars who fled Nazi Germany for America that truly set the tone for the discipline during and after the war.

One of the most prominent émigrés, Erich Heller of Northwestern University, wrote about German culture as well as literature, but almost always with hostility to modern, communist, or leftist writers, including even Bertolt Brecht. For Heller, the death of Thomas Mann marked the outskirts of acceptable literary topics. "This generation of scholars," observes University of Minnesota at Twin Cities professor Jack Zipes, "was mostly male and German, either Jewish or humanitarians, and they identified with the very best—Goethe, Schiller."

Under the sway of this sensibility, German departments remained reluctant to become embroiled in political disputes well into the 1950s, even after the National Defense Education Act ushered in a new cohort of students, quite a few of them World War II veterans eager to study postwar German politics and culture. But the fraught political relationship between the United States and East Germany put postwar literature and communist writers beyond the pale. German departments skirted political issues—even in West German literature—in favor of noncontroversial and pre-twentieth-century West German writers. Heller himself proved an especially hostile critic of the postwar movement Gruppe 47, which included Heinrich Böll and Günther Grass.

German departments became even more isolated in the early 1960s, when they could no longer rely on the support of the midwestern German immigrant population that had often provided the moral and financial support that launched departments in the 1880s. German-towns in Chicago, St. Louis, Milwaukee, and Columbus, which once had their own German-language newspapers and radio stations, were weakened by the aging of their leaders, who tended to preserve an uncritical gaze towards the *Heimat*, and by the assimilation of the younger generation to U.S. pop culture.

But by the mid-1960s, U.S. German departments had outgrown their dependence on developments in Germany. Many young scholars had been trained at American universities, and when they took the reins from the German refugee generation, they overhauled both the canon and the prevailing view of humanist writers. Reading lists were updated to include contemporary writers like Hermann Hesse, Günther Grass, and Paul Celan. And whereas the ideological sympathies of writers had previously been taboo, scholars now embraced spirits who railed against the status quo. Even nineteenth-century rebels like Heinrich Heine and Georg Buchner experienced a renaissance on both sides of the Atlantic.

> By the mid-1960s, U.S. German departments had outgrown their dependence on developments in Germany.

East German literature also finally entered the canon as a field of U.S. research, one first staked out by Patricia Herminghouse of the University of Rochester when she founded the *GDR Bulletin* in 1975. Interest in authors like Irmtraud Morgner and Christa Wolf was triggered by the desire to find a third path, neither capitalist nor socialist, from which capitalism could be criticized. Whether or not Wolf's "utopian space" is a genuine new path, and whether or not it excludes men, sparks debates within feminist scholarship to this day.

As German departments expanded the literary canon, they also branched out methodologically—especially into literary theory. *New*

German Critique, founded in 1973 by Anson Rabinbach of Cooper Union, David Bathrick of Cornell, and Jack Zipes of Minnesota-Twin Cities, was a leading theory venue for Germanists. In its nascent years, the journal featured translations and discussions of Frankfurt School theoreticians such as Theodor Adorno, Max Horkheimer, and Herbert Marcuse, and later published the work of Jürgen Habermas, the influential contemporary philosopher and Frankfurt School disciple. Contrary to the previous tradition of publishing some articles in German alone, it also made a splash by publishing articles in English only. "We got to the young people and we changed other journals," boasts Zipes.

> As scholars began to study urban life, social theory, and film, many departments adopted the rubric of German *studies*.

The Frankfurt School was especially attractive to Zipes's generation for its strict anti-capitalist stance and its fusion of Marxism and psychoanalysis. Adorno and Horkheimer's *The Dialectic of Enlightenment* and Marcuse's *One-Dimensional Man* also broke ground in the criticism of mass culture. Literary and cultural theory of the Frankfurt variety had a complex and sometimes jealous relationship to French literary theory, though there was some cross-fertilization. The wide dissemination of Frankfurt School theory roughly coincided with an interest in Berlin as a hub of cultural production, the *Urmutter* of cosmopolitan life. (Think Liza Minelli in *Cabaret*.) Depending on a scholar's perspective, 1920s Berlin was either the epitome of cosmopolitan sophistication or a decadent breeding ground for Nazi horrors. Franz Hessel and Walter Benjamin wrote about the *flâneur*—a predecessor of the slacker—wandering about and observing city life at his own pace and with ironic flare and style. (Benjamin's unique mixture of materialist philosophy and religious mysticism still makes him an object of fascination among theorists and artists alike.) Vienna attracted similar attention as a nodal point of modernity, where thinkers and writers like Sigmund Freud, Arthur Schnitzler, Ludwig Wittgenstein, Rainer Maria Rilke, and Hermann Bahr interacted.

As many German departments became home to scholars studying urban life, Continental literary theory, and film, they renamed themselves German *studies* departments. Indiana University pioneered the trend by housing faculty from different disciplines like history, film studies, and sociology under the roof of a German Studies Institute, which offered a degree program in German studies separate from the one in German languages and literature. Departments at Cornell University, Harvard University, Johns Hopkins University, and Washington University in St. Louis adopted the Indiana model by founding autonomous Western European studies centers alongside departments primarily dedicated to German language teaching and literature. These programs distinguished themselves in research by encouraging the study of German politics, history, and culture up to the present moment.

> German studies expanded the commonly taught canon to overcome geographic notions of national identity.

An alternative model was established at Stanford University, one more attuned to *Geistesgeschichte*, or intellectual history. Instead of creating a separate institute, Stanford coordinated the study of philosophy, art history, film, and other fields by folding those research areas into the department of German language and literature. Under the Stanford model, canonical and non-contemporary literature received a bit more attention than in schools organized on the Indiana model. In 1976 both approaches gained an official imprimatur with the founding of the German Studies Association (GSA), a multidisciplinary group of scholars who study the history, literature, culture, and politics of German-speaking countries. The GSA publishes the interdisciplinary journal *German Studies Review*.

After winning official standing, German studies departments reshaped themselves in numerous other ways. They incorporated German-language Austrian and Swiss literature into the commonly taught canon to overcome geographic and ethnic-based notions of national identity. And they spotlighted not only the exile literature of the 1930s and 1940s, but German-language literature that is not Europe-based—a trend that continues in current scholarship on contemporary migrant literature, such as that by Azade Seyhan of Bryn Mawr College and Leslie Adelson of Cornell.

German studies scholars also helped the discipline to face more directly the unspoken issue haunting the field. Scholars of previous generations had needed to take positions about the Third Reich, if only to distance themselves from it. German studies scholars tended to focus instead on the Holocaust as the central event of modern German history. While still taking some inspiration from research that stretched back to Frankfurt School studies of anti-Semitism and fascism, German studies expanded this work to include cultural memory and trauma, topics that were then picked up by French and English departments. Eric Santner's *Stranded Objects* and Sander Gilman's *Jewish Self-Hatred* were pathbreaking in the study of cultural memory.

Simultaneous with the development of German studies in the United States in the 1970s and early 1980s was the rise of feminism in German academia—but a strain of feminism different from the 1970s grass-roots variety most visible in the United States. And this new feminism would affect the study of things German on these shores. Although marked by occasional connections to grass-roots feminism, German feminism, represented by pragmatic books like Alice Schwarzer's *Der kleine Unterschied und seine großen Folgen*, focused for the most part on aesthetics, including linguistic and philosophical perspectives. In 1976, Silvia Bovenschen sparked what has become a continuous debate with her essay "Is There a Feminine Aesthetic?" Sigrid Weigel's and Inge Stephan's work employing the French feminist theory of Hélène Cixous, Luce Irigaray, and Julia Kristeva has also proven influential in German studies. In the late 1970s, German departments at Washington University in St. Louis, Cornell, the University of Massachusetts at Amherst, and the University of California at Santa Barbara began to offer graduate students a minor in feminist studies. Cornell professor Biddy Martin even argues that feminist scholarship was the pipeline into most German departments for poststructuralist theory, be it Lacanian, deconstructive, or semiotic.

The political and theoretical differences between poststructuralist and socio-historical feminism are still hot topics, especially at annual meetings of Women in German (WIG). Founded in 1976, WIG provides a network for all people interested in feminist approaches to German literature and culture. Open to both men and women, WIG has a membership of about 500 professors and students, and publishes the *Women in German Yearbook*. WIG's annual conference is unusual in two ways: No two sessions are scheduled for the same time slot so every attendee can participate in every session if they choose, and its location is always a hotel near a beautiful beach. (The 1998 meeting will take place near San Jose, California, at the Montetoyon resort.)

> W.I.G. provides a network for all those interested in feminist approaches to German language, literature, and culture.

The conference is an ideal opportunity for students interested in gender issues to mingle with scholars such as Anna Kuhn of the University of California at Davis, Sara Lennox of UMass-Amherst, and Leslie Adelson of Cornell.

The most crucial question for most German departments throughout the 1990s, however, has been what role cultural studies ought to play in departments still committed to literary study. While defining cultural studies too rigidly is strongly resisted even by cultural studies scholars themselves, one can at least identify some of its primary concerns. First, cultural studies tries to obliterate the wall between high culture and pop culture, attending to both Goethe's *Faust* and Randy Newman's *Faust*. Second, instead of assuming that consumers simply absorb pop culture, it analyzes how consumers interpret and appropriate popular culture for themselves in active and carefully defined ways. And third, unlike its German cousin, *interkulturelle Germanistik*, which spends much of its energy dividing culture into things truly German and things not, U.S. cultural studies does not police the borders but rather studies the adaptation of non-German mass culture to Germany (for instance the rise of German rap music or the techno movement's annual "Love Parade" in Berlin).

> Many departments still require students to read their way from *Peter Schlehmil* to Peter Handke.

The impact of cultural studies on German departments is hardly welcomed by everyone, and runs up against criticisms that are echoed in other disciplines. Some say cultural studies usurps the rightful place of German studies. Conspiracy theorists see a plot hatched by English departments to co-opt German in a chase after contemporary culture and the trendy. Others detect a shrewd tactic to increase student enrollments. And many scholars, traditionalists and cutting-edge theorists alike, are concerned that entering students might wander down paths in cultural studies and stray from the well-kept *Autobahn* of language skills and textual analysis. "I am concerned with this premature anti-disciplinarity. It leaves a lot of room for dilettantism," worries Andreas Huyssen of Columbia.

The effects of cultural studies on graduate curricula have been varied. Many departments have never abandoned a "coverage" model that emphasizes "periods," "genres," and "major authors," and one way or another they still require graduate students to read their way from the Romantic novel *Peter Schlemihl* to Peter Handke (some start with the medieval author Hartmann von Aue). A few departments have abolished required courses on authors or periods altogether. Yale, Indiana, and Duke University insist on elements of the "coverage" model, but they also feature interdisciplinary and courses on non-canonical topics.

On the whole, very few departments have not modified their curriculum recently, giving students more freedom than they had ten years ago to cross disciplines and to explore German studies as well as cultural studies. Most departments mix coverage and experiment in ways that must be investigated on a case-by-case basis: They give students some say in designing their own program but require a concentration on particular research questions, genres, and authors. The University of Wisconsin at Madison, for instance, has developed strong offerings in the study of film but incorporates them into a traditional curriculum. By way of explaining this new fluidity, Sander Gilman says, "it is important to move away from a scholarly training that originated in nineteenth-century German ideology. Linguistics and the history of language are not central for our undertaking."

> To hone their skills, many prospective graduate students work as language assistants at a German or Austrian *Gymnasium*.

WHAT'S NEXT

Unless you spent your junior or senior year in a German-speaking country or were a German major as an undergraduate, think twice about enrolling in a doctoral program right after college. While perfection is not expected, graduate students need language skills good enough for them to teach undergraduate German language courses and to do at least some of their writing in German. To sharpen their skills, many prospective graduate students work as language assistants at a German or Austrian *Gymnasium* before moving on to doctoral programs. Some departments, notably Stanford, teach all graduate courses in German, though this is rare.

For a good opportunity to improve your language skills and to do some research work abroad, investigate whether or not a department offers an exchange program with universities in Germany, Austria, or Switzerland. Washington University in St. Louis, Minnesota-Twin Cities, and Wisconsin-Madison all offer a vast array of direct exchange programs with a variety of universities in German-speaking countries. A good gauge of the international connections of a department more generally is to ask how many students receive grants from the Fulbright Foundation or the DAAD (German Academic Exchange Service) each year.

Most departments require students to demonstrate reading knowledge of two additional languages besides German and English by the time they graduate. (Only one additional language is required for the M.A.) This can be done by passing a translation exam or taking a special class. Many departments offer language courses in Dutch, Swedish, or Norwegian, and some departments, such as Minnesota-Twin Cities and the University of California at Berkeley, even offer courses in Scandinavian literature.

> Undergraduate instruction in German language and literature is what keeps graduate programs in German alive.

Investigate how closely any graduate program you are considering is tied to a healthy undergraduate German department. Says David E. Wellbery of Johns Hopkins, "Undergraduate instruction is what keeps German graduate programs alive." University deans and others with their hands on the purse strings of graduate funding look to the numbers of undergraduate majors when they dispense financial support to programs. The size of a program matters more now than it did in the past because the whole field is shrinking—enrollment in German classes fell about 28 percent between 1990 and 1995, according to the Modern Language Association.

Ideally, you shouldn't have to teach in your first year, but you should teach for at least two years before graduating in order be competitive in the academic job market. Graduate departments at small universities may allow you to teach German language and literature courses or "Business German" at different levels, while those at large state schools may let you do nothing but lead undergraduates in endless German 101 drills. A department should offer up-to-date pedagogy training, ideally in the form of one or two courses and additional workshops focusing on the use of video material, the language lab, and new teaching techniques. To ensure you'll be treated like a professor-in-training and not just cheap labor, check with graduate students about how much attention faculty pay to training new teachers.

If you look to rankings for help in sorting out departments, those produced by the National Research Council should be taken with a grain of salt since they can be out of date by the time of publication if faculty move to new institutions. The field changes much faster than the rankings. New York University, for instance, which was ranked twenty-sixth by the NRC, recently improved its reputation by hiring two leading lights in the field, Eva Geulen and Avital Ronell. On the other hand, Ivy League German departments such as Harvard continue to be ranked in the top ten, even though many scholars recommend going there mainly for the vast library collections and the exciting environment of a large elite university.

A better way to judge departments is to find out in detail how they have responded to the rise of German studies, which has replaced or at least broadened the study of canonical literature nearly everywhere. Some departments, like Chicago, have no required courses apart from one in language pedagogy and strongly encourage students to enroll in courses outside the German department and to take the initiative in designing their overall course of study. Columbia also no longer requires courses about particular writers or periods. Other departments, such as Washington University in St. Louis, require students to take overview courses during the first and second year before doing specialized coursework. You need to judge for yourself how much structure you need and how soon to specialize.

Columbia, Cornell, Johns Hopkins, Stanford, UC-Berkeley, and Chicago are frequently singled out by students and scholars for the breadth of the research interests of faculty and for providing students with a solid grounding in two or three fields of specialization. The Germanic studies program at Chicago, with Sander Gilman and Eric Santner, is attractive to students interested in film studies, psychoanalytic theory, Jewish studies, and constructions of the outsider in German culture. UC-Berkeley is also strong in hermeneutics, the analysis of nationalism (Hinrich C. Seeba), and theoretical work on foreign language pedagogy (Claire Kramsch). Cornell boasts a vast array of resources—from its library collections to exchange programs—as well as a renowned faculty, including Peter Uve Hohendahl (intellectual history, literary and social theory), David Bathrick (GDR culture), Leslie Adelson (contemporary German literature, migrant discourse), and Biddy Martin (feminism and gender studies).

Teaching for at least two years is important in order to be competitive in the job market.

The programs mentioned above are excellent for the study of twentieth-century culture, especially modernism and the Weimar

Republic. But Columbia, Stanford, and Johns Hopkins also emphasize the study of the Enlightenment, classical Weimar, and romanticism, along with aesthetic theory and philosophy from the eighteenth to the early twentieth centuries. At Johns Hopkins, Continental philosophers from many historical periods are read in conjunction with literature; systems theory, hermeneutics, and semiotics (David E. Wellbery, Werner Hamacher) thrive there as well. Columbia and Stanford, which feature a broad theoretical range, embrace a mixture of discourse analysis, critical theory, and a historically grounded cultural studies approach. Stanford's German studies program is open to topics both canonical and contemporary, including popular culture. Students are given considerable freedom in planning their programs. "Germanists have participated most in tackling borders of the discipline," says Stanford's Russell Berman.

As noted above, many departments do attempt to cover periods, genres, and major authors from the medieval period to the present. Of departments especially committed to that project, Washington University in St. Louis, Minnesota-Twin Cities, and Wisconsin-Madison are recommended by many scholars and students in the field. All require a set of overview courses: mandatory Middle High German, German linguistics, and a bibliography seminar. Minnesota-Twin Cities also offers an introductory basic seminar that acquaints incoming students with critical theory from Kant to poststructuralism.

An incredible array of specialties lies beyond core training in periods, genres, and major authors.

Beyond this core training are further specialties within those departments. Washington University in St. Louis, Minnesota-Twin Cities, and Wisconsin-Madison offer a wide range of possibilities in major authors—from Hildegard von Bingen to Heinrich Böll. Wisconsin-Madison, with Klaus Berghahn and Jost Hermand, is particularly interesting for film and both Weimar periods—eighteenth and twentieth century. Minnesota-Twin Cities, with Jack Zipes and Jochen Schulte-Sasse, is a good place to specialize in women's literature, feminism, Austrian literature, and German-Jewish culture. Washington University in St. Louis, with Paul Michael Lützeler and Lynne Tatlock, is recommended for nineteenth-century women's literature, twentieth-century studies, and early modern and contemporary literature; it features yearly seminars with major scholars, critics, and writers from German-speaking countries such as Jurek Becker, Peter Schneider, and Uwe Timm.

You may wish to consider a few other programs that retain the coverage model such as Yale, the University of California at Irvine, and Ohio State University—the last is particularly strong in seventeenth- and eighteenth-century literature and woman writers. The resourceful department at the University of Virginia is usually recommended for students interested in hermeneutics, drama, and genre theory. Boasting top visiting scholars, a lecture series, and a theory colloquium, Princeton University's very active department is especially attractive for students interested in poetics, Walter Benjamin, and the Frankfurt School. The University of Washington at Seattle offers a joint doctoral degree program in Germanics and critical theory. Northwestern offers a program in German literature and critical thought, which concentrates on the German philosophy and aesthetics of the eighteenth, nineteenth, and to a lesser extent, the twentieth century; they are not only strong in the study of philosophical aesthetics but also literature and the history of science. The small UC-Santa Barbara program has developed into a think tank for discourse analysis (Wolf Kittler), deconstruction, and psychoanalysis. If you are more interested in the historical and socio-political context of German culture, Duke and Indiana are excellent choices.

> Academic downsizing has hit German departments especially hard.

If a department edits a scholarly journal, you might have the opportunity to get involved in the nitty-gritty of publishing. (*Modern Language Notes* is edited at Johns Hopkins, *Monatshefte* at Wisconsin-Madison.) You can also get involved in graduate-student journals—*Focus on Literature* at the University of Cincinnati or *New German Review* at UCLA—or graduate-student conferences. Conferences at Yale, the University of Virginia, and the Midwestern Graduate Seminar in German Studies at Chicago's Goethe Institute (sponsored by Chicago and Northwestern) draw graduate students from around the nation.

Academic downsizing has hit German departments especially hard. A few graduate German programs have closed, most recently the German program at SUNY Albany, which shuttered in the fall of 1996. Others have been merged into modern language departments with Spanish and French—at Queens College and City College of

New York, a bureaucratic move that is sometimes a prelude to reduction in size and funding. Then there's Bennington College, which offered a daunting justification for language downsizing. While most closings were explained as cost-cutting measures, Bennington administrators claimed that foreign language training was merely "skill transfer" and therefore not a proper subject for college instruction. Bennington sends language students to nearby high schools to fill the gap.

> Departments cannot survive by training graduate students to devote themselves solely to research and publication.

According to Lynne Tatlock, a professor at Washington University in St. Louis and incoming president of the American Association of Teachers of German (AATG), graduate departments cannot survive these times by devoting themselves solely to research and publication. "Some departments have just been sitting on their behinds for years," says Tatlock. She advocates establishing networks of exchange between professors of German and high school teachers, and between the German university programs within a region of the United States, as well as joining forces with organizations such as the Goethe Institute, the official German cultural agency.

With 7,300 members, the AATG is the largest professional organization in the field, and has always served two constituencies, university professors and secondary school teachers. The AATG publishes two journals, one for each group: *The German Quarterly*, founded in 1928, is a literary-critical journal for professors; *Die Unterrichtspraxis*, published since 1968, centers on pedagogy for high school teachers. But facing the recent downturn in enrollments, the two groups may have found common ground. Student-centered teaching approaches, new media like the Internet, and new classroom material such as German soap operas are now part of language classes in high school and college alike, while business German and literature in translation courses are drawing a new clientele of undergraduates. The AATG has also responded to the enrollment crisis with a series of Forums on the Future of German in American

Education, recommending further opening of the field toward the rest of the academy and revision of the graduate curriculum allowing "various exit points (new types of M.A. degrees)" to facilitate non academic career choices.

The M.A. is still widely treated as a preparatory step towards the Ph.D. Most programs grant an M.A. to students who successfully complete one to two years of coursework and either pass an oral exam or write a thesis. If you decide to look for work after earning an M.A., jobs translating technical manuals for German import-export companies or working the Berlitz and other private language-teaching circuit are possible, but academic teaching other than in high school or community colleges is unlikely.

THE JOB MARKET

As departmental cutbacks suggest, the academic job market in German is tight. In 1995, ninety-three Ph.D.'s were awarded in German. The December 1996 Modern Language Association (MLA) job list, the Bible of the overeducated unemployed, advertised only twenty German positions. According to the MLA, one-fifth of the eighty-five Ph.D.'s granted in German in 1993–94 are currently unemployed, while nearly another one fifth work outside academia. Many go into publishing or leave the academy behind for the computer business. Of the remaining three-fifths who actually landed a job within academia, only half have tenure-track jobs.

If you are concerned about your job prospects, you should pick a graduate program that provides ample teaching opportunities, offers a wide range of possibility for interdisciplinary work, and introduces you to literary and aesthetic theory. As a professor, chances are you will wear many hats. Even after landing a great job, you are bound to teach introductory language courses as well as a graduate seminar on Mann or Adorno. You might well increase your chances in the market considerably if you can also teach a second national language, especially if you are in the running for jobs at smaller institutions.

RESOURCES

NRC TOP TEN
UC–Berkeley
Princeton
Cornell
Harvard
Yale
Stanford
Washington
  University
  in St. Louis
Virginia
Johns Hopkins
Wisconsin–Madison

ASSOCIATIONS
Modern Language
  Association
(212) 475-9500

German Studies
  Association
(602) 965-4839

Women in German
(219) 481-6836

Germanistic Society
  of America
(718) 932-7337

American Association
  of Teachers
  of German
(609) 795-5553

JOURNALS
Germanic Review
German Studies Review
Journal of English and
  Germanic Philology
The German Quarterly
ML Quarterly
Monatshefte
New German Critique
Die Unterrichtspraxis

CONSTELLATIONS

INTERDISCIPLINARY APPROACHES
Chicago
Columbia
Cornell
Johns Hopkins
Stanford
UC–Berkeley

TWENTIETH-CENTURY CULTURE
Chicago
Columbia
Cornell
Johns Hopkins
Stanford
UC–Berkeley

MAJOR AUTHORS
Minnesota–Twin Cities
Ohio State
Princeton
UC–Irvine
Virginia
Washington University
  in St. Louis
Wisconsin–Madison
Yale

EXCHANGE PROGRAMS
Minnesota–Twin Cities
Washington University
  in St. Louis
Wisconsin–Madison

FURTHER READING
Robert Bledsoe, Bernd Estabrook, and J.
  Courtney Federle, eds.,
Rethinking Germanistik. Canon and Culture (Peter Lang)

Walter F. Lohnes and Valters Nollendorfs, eds.,
German Studies in the United States: Assesment and Outlook
(Wisconsin)

John A. McCarthy and Katrin Schneider, eds.,
The Future of Germanistik in the USA: Changing our Prospects
(Vanderbilt)

WEB ADDRESSES
Departure point for links to all German departments,
  major institutions, and organizations
http://www.stolaf.edu/stolaf/depts/german/aatg/index.html

Internet resources for Germanists provided by
  Wisconsin–Madison
http://polyglot.lss.wisc.edu/german/links.html

The official WIG website
http://macro.micro.umn.edu/wig.html

CHAPTER 14

SPANISH

Jorge Coronado was studying French in Paris when he found himself reading every Latin American novel he could get his hands on. "Paris is very important for Latin American writers," he explains, "and writers like Cortázar and Borges were very much in the air in Paris." Raised in a Puerto Rican neighborhood in Chicago by Peruvian parents, Coronado was initially drawn to French literature and pursued a comparative literature major at Williams College. But after his Parisian immersion in Latin American literature during his junior year abroad, he headed for Argentina, where he taught English and studied at the University of Buenos Aires for two years before heading back north to do graduate work in Spanish at Columbia University, where he is researching the relationship between the European and Latin American literary avant-garde in the early-twentieth century. Did he choose the right field? "Absolutely," says Coronado, now in his third year of graduate school. "I see a lot of comparison going on now in Spanish, which hasn't happened before. The scope of the work being done right now is very exciting."

Graziana Mignona took an even more aleatory route to graduate study in Spanish. Mignona grew up in the southern Italian town of Taranto, in the shadow of a fifteenth-century fortress built by the crown of Castilla y Aragon during the three-hundred-year Spanish domination of the region. As a teenager, she devoured the Spanish books in her father's library, especially the poetry of Federico García Lorca, and when she entered the University of Venice in 1987, she opted to major in Spanish and English. In 1989, a European Community scholarship enabled her to study in Barcelona for two years, where she wrote an undergraduate thesis on the filiation between three medieval Castilian manuscripts and an earlier manuscript in Catalán. Now a fourth-year graduate student at the University of California at Santa Barbara, Mignona is writing a dissertation comparing Spanish filmmaker Pedro Almódovar and Argentine novelist Manuel Puig. "As a teacher of Spanish in the United States, I think I'm enriched by my position as a foreigner to the language; my perspective is different from a native speaker of Spanish or an anglophone."

WHY SPANISH?

Spanish is the Cinderella of modern languages. After a long history of neglect and scorn, it has since 1970 become the most popular language studied in the United States. According to a 1995 Modern Language Association survey, undergraduate enrollments in Spanish have increased by 13 percent since 1990; Spanish now boasts more than 600,000 students, almost three times as many as its closest rival, French. In fact, more students are now studying Spanish than all other languages combined. (Spaniards now constitute no more than 10 percent of the 400 million people who speak Spanish worldwide.)

Accompanying this boom in enrollment is a tremendous explosion in the curriculum—and considerable debate as to what it should include. In 1995, the journal *Hispania* published a survey of required reading lists in Spanish graduate programs. Only four books appear on more than 75 percent of the lists: one Spanish novel, *Tiempo de silencio*, by Luis Martín Santos, and three Latin American novels, Carlos Fuentes's *The Death of Artemio Cruz*, Juan Rulfo's *Pedro Páramo*, and, of course, President Clinton's favorite, Gabriel García Márquez's *One Hundred Years of Solitude*. What this means, the study concludes, is that "among the leading fifty-eight Ph.D.-granting Spanish faculties in this country, there is...very little consensus on what should be required reading—the fundamental basis of common discourse—in the field."

Even the overarching nature of the canon is up for debate. While novels, poems, plays, or short stories were once accepted as central, now scholars are working on comic strips, advertisements, telenovelas, and political speeches. And even where works traditionally considered literary are the focus, the spectrum of methodologies to choose from is far wider than ever before. José Martí is viewed through the lens of gender theory; magic realism, via the narrative theory of Bahktin. Other critics are looking at writers and literary and cultural phenomena from the Spanish-speaking world in a global context.

What this means for you, the prospective graduate student in Spanish, is that your options are far more wide ranging than you might have imagined. Do you want to focus on Peninsular or Latin American literature? The Brazilian literary revival or "El Boom"? Chicano or Latino studies? Language instruction or literary criticism? How Spanish has become such a varied field is best explained by a look at its past.

HOW SPANISH HAS TAKEN SHAPE

In the early nineteenth century, knowledge of Spanish was considered an eccentricity in cultured circles in the United States. When William H. Prescott, the great blind historian of the Spanish Conquest, needed an assistant to read documents from Spanish archives to him, he could find no one in 1830s Boston who knew the language. Prescott did eventually hire an assistant—an aptly named Mr. English, who read Spanish documents aloud to Prescott without having the faintest idea of what he was saying.

By the late nineteenth century, Prescott's histories had gained some illustrious company: George Ticknor's history of Spanish literature, Washington Irving's *The Alhambra*, and Longfellow's translations from Spanish. And in 1904 in New York, the Hispanic Society of America was founded to promote the study of these books and all things Spanish. But despite these considerable efforts, and even as the number of people studying the language had begun to grow by the turn of the century, Spanish simply couldn't compare with French (considered the language of culture par excellence), and German (viewed as an indispensable tool for philosophic and scientific study). Then as now, students in beginning Spanish classes were for the most part drawn to it as an "easy" language for use as a practical tool in business and daily life. Even today, as Spanish rises from the ash bin to become the belle of the ball, the issue of cultural prestige still smolders.

Harvard University had established a Smith Professorship of French and Spanish (held by Ticknor and Longfellow in succession) as early as 1816, but the first systematic program for training teachers of Spanish was offered in North America by the University of Toronto in 1887 under the direction of W.H. Fraser. Fraser's background was typical of Spanish professors of his day: His training was in French and German, and one year of study in Europe was deemed sufficient to qualify him to head the newly formed department of Italian and Spanish. Although there were a few notable Hispanics, such as Federico de Onís at Columbia and Aurelio M. Espinosa at Stanford University, Spanish was for the most part taught by Anglo-American and British professors whose actual ability to speak the language was often dubious. This arrangement was the norm well into the 1930s, even as programs in Spanish were established at universities across the United States.

> Spanish was often taught in the last century by professors whose ability to actually speak the language was dubious.

The American Association of Teachers of Spanish and Portuguese was founded in 1915, when anti-German sentiments stemming from World War I were running high. Increased trade with Latin America compounded the appeal of Spanish and sent more students flocking to Spanish classes. Nevertheless, the early issues of *Hispania*, the Association's journal, struck an extremely defensive tone. "We are handling the language of a nation," complained a 1919 article, "whose unfortunate colonial experiences and luckless military conflicts [with the United States] tend to create feelings of repugnance, if not of scorn." The article proposed an all-out publicity campaign that, by increasing the "prestige-value" of Spanish, would demonstrate that "Spanish is worthy, as French is worthy."

At that time, the only aspect of Hispanic culture deemed fit for graduate study was Peninsular literature of the Golden Age and the medieval period that preceded it. Spain was, after all, undeniably part of Europe, and the United States had always kept an eye on Europe as a source of high culture. Centuries of European scholarship had accumulated around works like the *Poema de mio Cid* and authors like Gonzalo de Berceo, Cervantes, Quevedo, Lope de Vega, and Góngora, thereby eliminating doubts as to its prestige value. The prevailing scholarly method, loosely organized under the rubric of philology, was to study a text's use of language, variations in editions, and pieces of an author's biography for clues about the meaning of the work—but without attempting to construct a unified literary interpretation of the work or to link the meaning of a work's language to real-world politics or to present-day philosophical and theoretical issues.

The peninsular orientation grew even stronger in the 1930s, when the Spanish Civil War sent a flood of Spanish professors into exile at North American universities. In the mid-1950s, aside from one two-semester course on Latin American literature, the education of graduate students in Spanish at Harvard was focused entirely on Spain and primarily on literature written before 1681, the year of Calderón's death. It wasn't until the 1960s that the field exploded beyond the Golden Age into the ever-evolving and increasingly noncanonical universe that is Spanish today.

> With a communist Spanish-speaking country a few miles off the U.S. coast, federal money poured into research in Spanish.

The first rumbling of that explosion came after the 1959 Cuban Revolution. With a Spanish-speaking communist country a few miles off the U.S. coastline, private foundations and the federal government went on a spending spree to establish programs in Latin American studies, and Spanish departments benefited from the lavish funding. Then, over the course of the 1960s, El Boom—the elevation of writers like García Márquez, Asturias, Borges, Vargas Llosa, and Fuentes to world-class status in the international literary marketplace—brought prestige to the study of Latin American literature. Fostered by pivotal figures such as the late Emir Rodríguez Monegal, who came to Yale University in 1968 and was a close friend of many of the Boom writers, Latin American literature made increasingly significant inroads in U.S. universities. By the mid-1970s, "Spanish America had come to dominate literary scholarship in Spanish, and everything else followed along, even Cervantes," says Barnard College professor Alfred MacAdam.

The current landscape of Spanish studies in the United States was set over the course of the 1970s when political upheavals in Chile, Argentina, Nicaragua, Guatemala, and El Salvador brought Latin American students and professors into Spanish graduate programs in the U.S. Today, about 40 percent of graduate students in Spanish departments are from outside the United States, primarily from Latin America and Spain, and many students who are United States citizens or permanent residents are native speakers of Spanish. In fact, University of California at Berkeley professor Francine Masiello reports that because Spanish is the native language of a significant majority of the students in her graduate courses, it doesn't really make sense to think of Spanish as a "foreign" language.

Another enduring legacy of the 1970s is the seeming reluctance of Spanish departments to get tangled up in literary theory. With the possible exception of Marxist theory—which during the 1970s did drive programs at the University of Pittsburgh, the University of Wisconsin at Madison, and the University of California at San Diego— literary theory has never been the engine of Spanish.

One reason for theory's absence is that the theory craze has not centered on Spanish writers. Nor has there been a Spanish-speaking literary theorist with the impact of, say, Derrida, Foucault, or Kristeva. As Jean Franco, an emeritus professor of Spanish at Columbia, notes, however, the exclusion of Spanish from theory is largely a matter of "non-recognition," of failing to see the theoretical implications of Spanish literature. After all, Michel Foucault's *The Order of Things* begins with a discussion of a text by Borges, yet few would call Borges himself a theoretician. Quite simply, "people don't see where the theory is in Spanish, because they're thinking of the French model," says Franco.

> Since Spanish is the first language of many U.S. graduate students, it doesn't make sense to think of Spanish as a "foreign" language.

Furthermore, Julio Ortega, chair of Brown University's Spanish department, says that "when poststructuralist theory was very much in fashion, declaring the death of the text and the author, Latin American literature was very much alive." And not only El Boom's highly visible writers—from Mario Vargas Llosa to Octavio Paz—but the texts themselves may have made theory seem superfluous: Many Boom texts, like Julio Cortázar's *Hopscotch* or Borges's stories, contain reflections on the nature of the literary that are so explicit that there's no need for a critical methodology to extract them.

Still, many people in the field seem to have no compunction about expressing their antagonism toward theoretical ideas, Spanish or otherwise. "A student who doesn't know me inquires about my 'theoretical framework.' I reply that I don't have any, but that I do stipulate that no one is allowed to use the word 'totalize' in my presence," quipped Gustavo Perez-Firmat of Duke University in the *Latin American Literary Review* in 1992. And whether or not they use the word "totalize," Latin Americanists who rely heavily on theories imported from Europe and the United States risk being reproached as imperialists.

Many "Boom" texts require no special "method" to extract theoretical musings about literature and language.

What are the consequences of this perceived resistance to theory? "When I arrived at Yale as a graduate student in 1972, the heyday of deconstruction, the Spanish department did no theory," says Georgetown University professor Enrico Mario Santí, who suggests that an antitheoretical stance has cost the discipline much-needed prestige. "The institutional trend favors other fields in literature which are more theoretical. As a result, Spanish hasn't caught the attention of administrators, who are looking only for stars" in the theory galaxy. Paradoxically, even as Spanish was enjoying skyrocketing enrollments, its lack of theory stars allowed for the impression that it was not on the cutting edge.

In recent years, however, as cultural studies has stormed through all areas of literary study, Spanish may finally have come into its own. A slippery term that seems to mean something different to everyone who uses it, "cultural studies" in Spanish most often refers to the study of a wide variety of texts (both literary and nonliterary) and their political and social contexts, with special attention paid to their pro- duction and reception. Understood in this way, cultural studies turns out to be something Latin Americanists have been doing all along. In fact, the widespread influence of Marxism among Latin Americanists, who have always tended to interpret texts with attention to their larger cultural significance, is partially responsible for the emergence of cul- tural studies in the field. What's more, literature has long been highly politicized in Latin America, and so it's not unusual to see an influ- ential writer serve as a diplomat (like Paz, Fuentes, and many others) or run for president (like Vargas Llosa).

If the role of cultural studies is as not as volatile an issue for scholars of Spanish as it is in other national language departments, it still generates tension. As in the study of French or German, scholarship on novels, poetry, and drama has hardly died away, yet ideas about what constitutes an appropriate object for study are rapidly changing. Explains Harvard professor Doris Sommer, "Five years ago, my graduate students wouldn't have thought of doing a dissertation on salsa lyrics, but now I'm working with people doing salsa, telenovelas, everything."

Cultural studies has bolstered an emphasis on multidisciplinary and cross-cultural work. Everywhere you look in Spanish nowadays, a wall is falling, a connection is being made. The burgeoning areas of interest include: Caribbean studies, which can involve several languages besides Spanish and English, with French, Dutch, and Haitian Creole among them; gender and feminist studies; comparative studies of literature and film; and nineteenth-century Latin American literature, especially literature as an instrument of nation-forming. Also, there is nineteenth- and twentieth-century Peninsular literature, in which Spain is studied in contrast to, or as a model for, the rest of Europe; the colonial period, which involves both Spain and Latin America and often shades into anthropology and history; and the study of U.S. Latino culture, one of the most visible fields in Spanish—one that may well be growing into an altogether separate field of its own, called Latino studies.

> As cultural studies has stormed through all areas of literary study, Spanish may finally have come into its own.

Given all the walls falling, is it possible to be too interdisciplinary? The question meets with a resounding "yes" from faculty members who have recently served on committees hiring new junior faculty. Graduate students who traipse down too many paths without first establishing a solid expertise in language and literature may find their job applications dropping to the bottom of the pile. Faculty may worry that the student, although eager, is spread too thin. But then, this may be no fault of the student: Academic employment ads often seem to solicit applications from jacks-of-all-trades, and balancing between having substantial grounding in one or more areas as well as a toolbox of diverse skills may be an all but impossible task. When you're considering a graduate school, talk to both students and faculty about how the program balances the competing standards for flexibility and depth.

Careerism and intensified preprofessionalism are as controversial in Spanish as elsewhere, despite the current buyer's market for jobs. Faculty at UC-Berkeley, for example, are finding that while five years ago they urged graduate students to publish papers and attend conferences, today they are urging a new generation of students to ignore the premature pressure to sell themselves professionally while taking the time to develop intellectually.

WHAT'S NEXT

One result of the field's recent changes is a marked diversity among various graduate programs—a diversity that makes it more important than ever for prospective students to choose the school that will best suit their particular interests. If you are looking to the National Research Council rankings for guidance, however, keep in mind that its measure of perceived quality is skewed. Yale, for instance, widely considered among the top Spanish departments in the country, especially in Latin American literature, is absent from the NRC list. María Rosa Menocal, chair of the Yale Spanish department, explains, "The person who was designated to fill out and file the forms didn't do it, but in a way it was just as well because the rankings the NRC did publish were so problematic that we were perfectly happy not to be included." Others see the rankings as at least two decades out of date. Jean Franco, who recently retired from Columbia, which tops the NRC list, agrees with many observers and notes that "the NRC rankings clearly have a Peninsular slant"—which makes them especially unrepresentative of a discipline that is now dominated by the study of Latin American literature and culture.

> Today students are studying everything from salsa lyrics and comic strips to telenovelas and political speeches.

How, then, to choose? Students scouting out Spanish graduate programs are more and more regularly advised to look not only at the Spanish department but at the resources of the university as a whole. "Go where there is real intellectual excitement," urges Harvard's Doris Sommer, "to a place where not only the Spanish department is strong, but where there are other things going on." Departments like film and media studies, area studies, art history, political science, history, English, and ethnic studies, for example, all have much to offer students of Spanish. Universities that are singled out as encouraging such cross-fertilization include Harvard, Duke, New York University, Brown, Stanford, and the University of California at Santa Cruz.

Another frequently offered piece of advice is to choose one of the larger departments. "Most Ivy League Spanish departments are very small," cautions Jean Franco. But Wisconsin-Madison, UC-

Berkeley, Pittsburgh, and the University of Maryland all have large Spanish departments; the largest of all is at the University of Texas at Austin, which also boasts one of the nation's best Latin American libraries. Many students change their minds about what they want to study as their graduate education progresses, and a large faculty will offer a wider variety of options.

Rather than being all things to all people, most Spanish programs are trying to be tops in specific areas. UC–Berkeley, Stanford, NYU (with Sylvia Molloy), and Wisconsin–Madison are well known for gender and feminist studies; Harvard, the University of Virginia, and the University of Pennsylvania have strong reputations for the Golden Age. Yale (with Rolena Adorno), Duke (with Walter Mignolo), Brown (with Stephanie Merrim), and Pittsburgh are centers for colonial studies, and Duke has additional strengths in postcolonial theory. Departments that stand out in the growing field of nineteenth- and twentieth-century Peninsular studies are Columbia, Wisconsin–Madison, Stanford, and the University of Kentucky, which is also one of the larger departments. For contemporary Latin American literature, Yale is considered very strong (with Josefina Ludmer and Roberto González-Echevarría), as are Stanford, UC–Berkeley, NYU, Penn, and Brown (with Julio Ortega), which has a particularly illustrious permanent visiting professor, Carlos Fuentes.

> Rather than being all things to everyone, most Spanish departments now try to be tops in subspecialties.

Chicano and Latino studies are fields riven by intense struggles over nomenclature. Chicano studies deals with Mexican–Americans, even in the period prior to 1848 when the inhabitants of the western portion of North America were non-hyphenated Mexicans. Although "Latino" in theory designates anyone of Latin American origin living in the United States, in practice it applies only to non-Chicanos. The search for a truly global term has led to such peculiar descriptions as "the literature of the Spanish-American diaspora," a phrase intended to designate only Chicano and Latino literature but which, when taken at face value, refers to anything written by anyone of Hispanic ancestry in the Western Hemisphere. And there is the puzzle of how to define the experience of the Spanish-speaking students who are racially Japanese and have emigrated to California from Argentina and are taking classes in Chicano studies at the University of California at Irvine.

According to María Herrera-Sobek, who is about to assume the nation's first endowed chair in Chicano studies at UC-Santa Barbara, "Chicano literature became part of Spanish departments in the late 1970s and the 1980s, but is now moving into English departments." Indeed, Stanford students interested in pursuing Chicano studies have the option of doing so within either the Spanish or the English department, a situation that is not uncommon at other universities. Meanwhile, a growing number of separate departments or interdepartmental Ph.D. programs are being founded in Chicano studies at UC-Berkeley and UC-Santa Barbara, or, as at Rutgers University, in "Puerto Rican and Hispanic Caribbean Studies." And there is an intercollegiate department of Chicano and Latino Studies at the Claremont Colleges in California.

The UC system is particularly strong in Latino studies, no matter what the department may be called. Check out UCLA, UC-Berkeley (with Julio Ramos), and UC-Irvine, which offers a Ph.D. in U.S. Latino studies and is currently designing an ethnic studies Ph.D. Elsewhere, Vanderbilt University, Duke, the University of Texas at Houston, and the University of New Mexico are known as good places to do U.S. Latino work.

Portuguese may be resurgent because some of the best theoretical research is coming out of Brazil.

Though Portuguese has long been mentioned in tandem with Spanish—for instance, the American Association of Teachers of Spanish and Portuguese—it has usually been little more than a Spanish department sideline. But NYU professor Sylvia Molloy believes the time is ripe for a revival, particularly with regard to Brazil, which is producing some of the most interesting theoretical work in Latin America right now. The theoretician Roberto Schwarz, who lives in São Paulo, has stirred up attention in the United States for his sociology of Brazilian literature, and the novelist, poet, and critic Sylviano Santiago of Rio de Janiero is raising eyebrows with his theory of the hybridity of Latin American literature. Brown is one of the few universities that has a separate Portuguese department. Spanish departments with strengths in Portuguese include UC-Berkeley, Georgetown, UT-Austin, Wisconsin-Madison, the University of Georgia, UCLA (where the focus is primarily on Brazil), and UC-Santa Barbara (where the focus is primarily on Portugal).

Then, of course, there is the possibility of studying abroad. Though he says some of his best former students are now teaching in Latin America, Julio Ortega of Brown warns that it's difficult for the holders of Latin American Ph.D.'s to land a job in the United States. "For jobs, the first choice would be people who have done the dissertation here."

But not getting a Ph.D. in Latin America or Spain doesn't mean you shouldn't study there at all. Spending a year or two in Latin America or Spain before graduate school will give students whose first language is not Spanish a definite edge in getting accepted to the best programs, and, given the current predominance of native speakers in graduate programs, it will also help them maintain that edge once they're in. And time spent doing on-site research during graduate school can only enhance the credibility of any budding Latin Americanist or Peninsularist, whatever their native language. Brown and UC-Berkeley are known for having strong connections with universities in Latin America.

THE JOB MARKET

If you are thinking about graduate study in the field, you will be very encouraged to know that, according to the MLA, fully 90 percent of 1994 Ph.D.'s in Spanish were employed in postsecondary institutions in 1995, 61 percent of them in tenure-track positions. This rate of employment looks particularly good when contrasted with the current gloomy outlook for Ph.D.'s in other languages. In French, for example, only 75 percent of 1994 Ph.D.'s were employed in postsecondary institutions in 1995, and only 41 percent were in tenure-track positions. A matter to investigate, then, is how much a department supports its students when they go on the job market. Is there a placement committee? Is help readily available in the form of CV revising, mock interviews, phone calls to colleagues? Most importantly, where have recent graduates been hired?

The picture for Spanish Ph.D.'s is not entirely rosy, though. There is considerable unease on the part of the 40 percent of graduate students in Spanish who are not Hispanic that they may not fare as well on the job market as their Hispanic colleagues. These fears meet with a wide variety of responses. "The nature of identity politics within the discipline is such that if your background is not related to the area you want to study, you're going to have problems," Barnard professor Alfred MacAdam says flatly. But Sylvia Molloy, chair of Spanish at NYU, begs to differ, "Except perhaps in areas like Chicano and Latino studies, there is no handicap at all for non-Hispanic students." Jean Franco agrees with Molloy. "I think that good non-Latino students can get jobs without any prejudice." Several other professors couldn't comment on the issue because they hadn't worked with enough Anglo graduate students to form an opinion.

Dismissing the notion that anyone who pursues Chicano or Latino studies will be unemployable if not of Hispanic extraction, Herrera-Sobek cites the case of a British and decidedly non-Hispanic student of hers at UC-Irvine who was able to get a job in Chicano studies. Still, job listings that include phrases such as "Demonstrated involvement in the Mexican-American community is desirable" would seem to indicate that applicants with the requisite ethnic background will have an advantage.

For their part, graduate students whose first language is Spanish often feel they are at a disadvantage due to the difficulty they may have writing or teaching in English. Ads for jobs in Spanish often specify that the applicant must be fluent in Spanish and English, since junior faculty are often called upon to staff Intro to Western Civ or the ever-popular literature in translation courses. Moreover, writing well in English is a prerequisite for making it into the discipline's top ranks.

> The job market in Spanish looks especially good when compared to the gloomy outlook in other languages.

These issues notwithstanding, it's likely you'll read job listings that request a specialization in pedagogy and applied linguistics, which is the largest and fastest growing area in Spanish. The numbers alone tell the story. While Spanish has three times the undergraduate enrollment of its closest competitor, French, there are, on average, only about 30 percent more students in Spanish graduate programs than in French ones. Obviously, a lot of qualified people out there are spending a lot of time teaching basic Spanish to undergraduates. And there's a need for still more. Close to a third of the job listings in Spanish in the October 1996 MLA job list are specifically addressed to specialists in applied linguistics, pedagogy, or Hispanic linguistics.

While many Spanish graduate programs—such as Georgetown, UT-Austin, and Temple University—offer two separate tracks, one in literature and the other in applied linguistics, linguistics and education departments also grant Ph.D.'s in applied linguistics, often through joint course offerings with a Spanish department. Given this diversity of options, it's best to investigate on a case-by-case basis how departments teach linguistics. The strongest programs in applied linguistics, no matter how they might be housed, are offered at Ohio State University, the University of Illinois at Urbana, the University of Minnesota at Twin Cities, Cornell University, and the University of Arizona at Tucson.

RESOURCES

ASSOCIATIONS
Modern Language Association
(212) 475-9500
American Association of Teachers
  of Spanish and Portuguese
(970) 351-1090

JOURNALS
Hispania
Hispanic Review
Latin American Literary Review
Revista Hispánica Moderna
Revista Iberoamericana

Critical Inquiry
MLQ
New Literary History
Representations
Signs

NRC TOP TEN
Columbia
Duke
Brown
Princeton
Virginia
Penn
Wisconsin-Madison
Cornell
UC-Berkeley
Harvard

WEB ADDRESSES
University of Toronto Spanish and Portuguese Department site with
  excellent links to Internet resources in Spanish and Portuguese
http://www.chass.utoronto.ca:8080/spanish_portuguese/resources.html
Chicano/LatinoNet
gopher://latino.sscnet.ucla.edu/11/
LatinoWeb
gopher://latinoweb.com/favision

If you're not planning to study applied linguistics, don't make the mistake of assuming that basic language teaching is the exclusive province of those who do. Anyone going into Spanish should keep in mind that there's a good chance they'll be spending a great deal of time teaching introductory language courses. At both elite and lower-profile institutions, there is heavy demand for language instructors. Be sure to ask students and faculty about how much you will teach, if at all, and at what point in your studies you'll be likely to do it.

CONSTELLATIONS

CROSS-FERTILIZATION
Brown
Duke
Harvard
NYU
Stanford
UC-Santa Cruz

LARGE DEPARTMENTS
Kentucky
Maryland
Pittsburgh
UC-Berkeley
UT-Austin
Wisconsin-Madison

THE PENINSULAR GOLDEN AGE
Harvard
Penn
Virginia

NINETEENTH- AND TWENTIETH-CENTURY PENINSULAR
Columbia
Kentucky
Stanford
Wisconsin-Madison

CONTEMPORARY LATIN AMERICAN LITERATURE
Brown
NYU
Penn
Stanford
UC-Berkeley
Yale

GENDER AND FEMINIST STUDIES
NYU
Stanford
UC-Berkeley
Wisconsin-Madison

LATINO STUDIES
Duke
New Mexico
Rutgers
UC-Berkeley
UC-Irvine
UCLA
UT-Houston
Vanderbilt

CHICANO STUDIES
UC-Berkeley
UC-Santa Barbara

LANGUAGE AND LINGUISTICS
Arizona-Tucson
Cornell
Georgetown
Illinois-Urbana
Minnesota-Twin Cities
Ohio State
Temple
UT-Austin

CHAPTER 15

MUSICOLOGY

Lara Pellegrinelli spent much of her childhood with her parents in their Chrysler Imperial, listening to
their many eight-track tapes of Frank Sinatra. "I
hated it," she says, "I wanted to hear Michael
Jackson." It wasn't until she was in college that
she began to reconsider the Sinatra phenomenon. "He was
appearing at a theater right across from my dorm, and I was fascinated by all the publicity. I couldn't stop singing 'I Got You Under
My Skin,' and eventually I became interested in the whole African-
American background to Sinatra's singing style." A third-year graduate student at Harvard University, Pellegrinelli is researching a
dissertation on vocal jazz. "I ended up in ethnomusicology because
traditional musicology, though rich in methods of archival research,
excluded a lot of what really interested me, like ethnography and
African-American studies," Pellegrinelli says. "That led me to look
for something different."

Doctoral candidate Michaela Harkins got into musicology "because
I always wanted to teach, to share my love for the subject." Trained as
a violinist, Harkins grew up "thinking that there had to be a division
between performance and the study of musicology. Unfortunately, a
lot of people still feel that musicologists are failed performers, and

that performers are just music jocks—skilled but empty-headed."
Harkins took a year off after college to concentrate on her playing, and
ended up enrolling in the graduate program at the University of
Rochester's Eastman School of Music, where, she says, "that division is
blurred. I've come to see that you can continue performing at a high
level and still work on the academic side. They're complementary."
While Harkins is now researching the relationship between music, art,
and culture in 1920s Berlin, she's also rehearsing the Brahms A major
violin sonata for performance at a university concert.

WHY MUSICOLOGY?

"Without music," declared Friedrich Nietzsche, "life would be a mistake." Perhaps you've seen this aphorism blazoned on a greeting card
and considered sending it to your friend who's a classically trained
violinist. Or maybe to your head-banger buddy who loves Metallica.
Or that Fulbright Scholar you know studying polyrhythmic drumming
in West Africa. Or maybe even your grandmother, who loves that Tony
Bennett is singing again. "Music," after all, is a rather all-inclusive term.

For anyone interested in the serious study of music—something
quite different from the playing, composing, or appreciation of it—the
question is: What, exactly, did Nietzsche mean by "music"? Certainly
not heavy metal, nor Senegalese percussion, nor the mellifluous
singing of a lounge singer on a career rebound. No, Nietzsche was
referring to the established canon of Western art music of his time,
and even those contemporary compositions deferential to that canon
wouldn't be music to his ears. Yet all of these genres and more qualify
as valid objects of study in doctoral programs today.

Since the 1950s, the vast terrain that once encompassed all of
music studies (except for learning how to play it) has been subdivided
into three more manageable disciplines: historical musicology, ethnomusicology, and music theory. If your idea of music overlaps with
Nietzsche's view of the traditional classical canon, then historical
musicology is your natural home. Still the dominant force in graduate
music studies, historical musicology generally focuses on charting the
development of European art music up to the early twentieth century,
tending to favor Renaissance and Baroque over Classical and
Romantic composers. If, like your friend with the Fulbright, you're
drawn to world music and dream of fieldwork in foreign countries,

then ethnomusicology is the place for you. An ethnomusicologist studies the folk and popular musics of non-Western and Western cultures, particularly a music's place within the society that produced it. If you're intellectually excited by the close analysis of serial music, you should consider music theory, which is inclined toward scrutinizing individual works of European and American art music from the Classical period to the present.

Thus, if you're interested in pursuing graduate work in music, you might start by asking what sort of music you want to work with, and how. Would you prefer spending a summer in a dusty Eastern European library, producing an authoritative transcription of a recently discovered manuscript? Are you interested in using a computer to analyze the structure of a Bach organ fugue, or does your mind drift naturally to the problems of feminist theory and the history of opera performance? Or to the problems of set theory and twentieth-century composition?

To answer these questions, you will need to think hard about your academic interests, your background and strengths, and your career goals. Without music, life might well be a mistake, but not thinking carefully about how you want to study music in graduate school can have its own uncomfortable consequences.

HOW MUSICOLOGY HAS TAKEN SHAPE

Strangely enough, while music is one of the oldest of intellectual preoccupations, it is one of the youngest of university disciplines. Thinking about the structure of music dates back at least to the pre-Socratic philosopher Pythagoras, who deciphered the mathematical nature of musical intervals—legendarily, while listening to the striking of hammers of precisely pitched weights. But two centuries later, Aristotle argued that instrumental virtuosity—"those fantastic marvels of execution which are now the fashion"—was beneath the interest of the truly educated individual, being a mere physical skill on a par with, say, juggling.

And even some early twentieth-century scholars scoffed at the idea of musicology as a serious discipline. "Nonsense" is what Harvard president Charles W. Eliot reportedly thought musicology meant. "The word doesn't exist. You might as well speak of grandmotherology!" Liking something, apparently, was no good reason for studying it—and we might note in passing the smooth connection Eliot makes among music, the lack of intellectual worth, and the feminine. Contemporary feminist musicologists have a good deal to say about this.

Given this sort of intellectual resistance, it's not surprising that musicology didn't take root in American universities until the mid-twentieth century, and that it was in large part transplanted by the European émigrés who started arriving in America in the 1930s. Even to them it was a relatively young discipline; academic musicology didn't really blossom in Europe until the late nineteenth century when Guido Adler codified it as a discipline, *Musikwissenschaft*. In a taxonomic frenzy, Adler divided and subdivided the discipline into branches and sub-branches until absolutely everything in music was accounted for. Under "historical musicology," for instance, he lumped bibliography, biography, and the study of notational systems.

As a fledgling academic discipline in the United States, musicology shied away from subjective questions of taste and judgment, the slippery issue of how music actually affected audiences. The postwar boom in musicology programs in America—touched off by the spark of European intellectuals meeting the combustible material of young Americans raised on the LP—established itself as almost exclusively concerned with the accumulation of historically verifiable data and the close structural analysis of individual works. For instance, scholarly editions of works by Renaissance composers—often dated and organized through the examination of such details as manuscript watermarks—tended to take precedence over any consideration of music as an aesthetic or social event.

> As a fledgling discipline, musicology shied away from subjective questions of taste.

Because musicology was primarily extra-musical, it acquired a reputation for pedantry. Over breakfast, Arturo Toscanini once described a musicologist as someone who "neither scrambles eggs, as my cook has done, nor eats them, as we are about to do. He simply talks about them." And while performers and musicologists have snubbed each other at least since Aristotle, Toscanini did have a point. Musicologists had viewed themselves as historical researchers more than musicians and therefore weren't particularly interested in what musicians could do with their work. Nonetheless, talking about eggs—or specifically, about when the eggs were laid, by which chicken, and in which farmer's henhouse—has produced valuable results. Alfred Dürr and Georg von Dadelsen, for instance, discovered that Bach wrote the bulk of his cantatas within his first few years as Cantor in Leipzig, and not over his entire tenure as had been previously assumed. Due to such painstaking bibliographic work, the cherished image of Bach as a lifelong and devoted composer of Lutheran church music and as the conservative grandfather of German music has come in for reevaluation.

As a recent survey of musicology programs notes, the core of your record collection has been handed to you by musicologists.

More importantly, the production of all those monstrously weighty authoritative editions of the works of long-dead composers has provided a vast supply of orchestral resources for conductors like Toscanini. As Eugene Helm notes in *The Canon and the Curricula*, a recent survey of musicology programs, "The core of your record collection has been handed to you by musicologists." Now, *that's* a legacy.

Along with other humanities disciplines throughout the university, since the mid-1960s musicology's historical, factual approach has increasingly been forced to question its methodological roots in disinterested analysis. At the same time, ethnomusicologists and music theorists have begun to assert the primacy of their own methodologies in their own academic journals, and the discipline has fractured into the three fields already mentioned.

In practice, the three disciplines can't always be neatly separated, especially as the boundaries between them have blurred over the last decade. Theorists are now working on The Beatles and Steve Reich; musicologists are tackling Madonna and heavy metal; and ethnomusicologists, having retreated from foreign shores, are studying polka and jazz. The walls between specialties are breaking down, and the raging inferno of interdisciplinary study is sweeping through even the most ivory of academic research towers. Many departments are even encouraging contact between performing musicians and students working on their Ph.D.'s.

While the general consensus is that the best work being done today draws on all three specialties, the organization of musicology departments preserves the distinctions between them. For instance, a doctoral degree in each of the three specialties is offered by only seven departments: Harvard, the University of Michigan at Ann Arbor, CUNY Graduate Center, Kent State University, the University of Pittsburgh, the University of Texas at Austin, and the University of Washington at Seattle. Twenty-two offer doctorates in two of the three, and twenty offer doctoral degrees in only one, though nearly every department has professors with a serious interest in nondegree areas. Practically speaking, this means that if you are keen on undertaking a theory-based analysis of that gamelan music you've been performing, you may have trouble doing it in a department without the right balance of professors in the three disciplines. It's best, then, to examine the three specialties separately.

HISTORICAL MUSICOLOGY

In one of the earliest salvos in the war over musicology's soul, the University of California at Berkeley musicologist Joseph Kerman published an article in 1965 entitled "A Profile for American Musicology." Conservatively enough, Kerman laid out an objective, Adlerian list of the steps through which musicologists progress in dealing with music, but then he insisted that the topmost rung of this methodological ladder should involve an "insight into individual works of art." Music, Kerman argued, "cannot be understood in isolation, only in a context. The infinitely laborious and infinitely diverting ascent of the musicologist should provide this context."

For scholars in other disciplines, this statement may have been self-evident, and in fact Kerman was drawing on his reading of literary criticism, which, along with art history, shares many of the same scholarly orientations as musicology: an interest in close readings of individual texts, along with a more general concern with period, style, and the evolution of form. Nonetheless, the article struck a nerve among musicologists who warned that Kerman had mistaken subjectivity for scholarly judgment.

Kerman caused even more of a stir with his 1985 book *Contemplating Music*. Building on his earlier paper, Kerman all but dismissed what he termed "positivism" in musicology: the excessive preoccupation with historical minutiae at the expense of broader understanding. Kerman thought musicologists were stricken by "a widespread phobia as regards historical interpretation," and claimed that "there is something wrong with a discipline that spends...so much more of its time establishing texts than thinking about the texts thus established."

As an antidote to this interpretational phobia, Kerman offered the idea of criticism understood not as journalistic reviewing but rather "the study of the meaning and value of art works." Musicologists, Kerman presumed, enter the profession because they love music, and over the long run this personal investment has to be taken into consideration. Kerman's idea of criticism draws on a wide variety of methodologies. It certainly relies on positivistic musicology and music analysis, but it also tries to link a work to the social context in which it was generated, and to take into consideration the evolution of its meaning in later periods. As an example of criticism proper, Kerman cited his own book on the Latin sacred music of William Byrd, which ranged from an analysis of Byrd's contrapuntal imitation to an investigation of the ideological context of the songs' texts.

The difference between "new" and "old" musicology is viewed as either a radical rupture or an inevitable progression.

Kerman's compatriot in the drive to reform and revitalize musicology was his contemporary, CUNY Graduate Center professor Leo Treitler. Treitler's position, while allied, differed with regard to "positivistic" musicology. Treitler rejected the idea that musicology could even be considered positivistic since that term, drawn from science, refers to an epistemological approach based on gathering empirical facts and deducing from them incontrovertible natural laws. The preparation of a musical edition, Treitler argued, involves a range of interpretive decisions. Chopin, for example, was known to dispatch three different versions of the same composition on the same day—one to his British publisher, one to his French, and one to his German—leaving a musicologist with the tricky problem of determining which version, exactly, might be considered "authoritative." For Treitler, then, the very idea of a "finished" work is eaten away by the much more fluid concept of interpretation.

Despite their differences, Kerman and Treitler laid the foundation for the newest developments within the discipline, which are referred to, neatly enough, as the "New Musicology." Depending on whom you speak with, the difference between "new" and "old" musicology is either the result of a radical rupture with all traditional approaches or merely the inevitable progression of a field of inquiry that moves forward, step by step, until suddenly everyone discovers they're not in Kansas anymore. Insisting on the immensity of the rupture are both conservatives like Pieter van den Toorn of the University of California at Santa Barbara, whose *Music, Politics, and the Academy* is one of the few blasts launched from the right, and radicals like feminist musicologist Susan McClary of UCLA, whose *Feminine Endings* applies gender studies to composers from Monteverdi to Madonna. The vast majority of musicologists are somewhere in between; they welcome new approaches but recognize the worth of older approaches too.

For an incoming graduate student, the difference between the old and the new musicology could spell trouble, since you might well find yourself caught between warring faculty members. Fortunately, the consensus among musicologists is that few professors, even those at the extremes, are as ideologically contentious as their writings pretend. Virtually everyone can name the young Turks of new musicology: McClary; Robert Walser, of UCLA, who's written a book on heavy metal; and Gary Tomlinson, of the University of Pennsylvania, who's written on the connection between music and Renaissance magic. But few seem willing or able to cite the names of any unrepentant old guard. Even van den Toorn maintains a surprisingly civil discourse and seems more concerned with defending the validity of traditional theorists than with trashing new musicologists.

The conflict, for the most part, is one of methodology. The new musicologists are admired for their audacity and vigor in exploring new territory but at the same time are chided for having forgotten to bring along the traditional maps of the discipline. In *Feminine Endings*,

> Few musicology professors are as ideologically contentious as their writings pretend.

for instance, McClary analyzes Bizet's *Carmen* with an eye toward showing how the opera's main female character is consistently characterized by "chromatic excesses," causing the listener actually to desire her death, which promises the final resolution of these "unbearable tensions" into the major triad at the opera's end. It's not hard to see how someone who has devoted his life to establishing an authoritative edition of Pergolesi might be taken aback by McClary's leap from musicological analysis to feminist criticism. Where's the reliance on source studies? Where's the examination of the inner structure of the music? Where's the footnoting of established musicological work of earlier eras?

For others, though the new musicology diverges from source studies, it's still in keeping with historical musicology. As one graduate student says, historical musicology has always had to work in one way or another with the social context in which the music was produced. And as Allan Atlas, professor of musicology at CUNY Graduate

Center, points out, "Interpretive, critical approaches were part of nineteenth-century musicology, and the 'old musicology' was a reaction to that subjectivity. New musicology is related to 'pre-old musicology'—it's come full circle, but with a new array of sophisticated tools." Scrap the sensationalist story of young versus old musicology, and what you see is a discipline undergoing a healthy growth spurt.

For those who are interested in archival research but want to bend it to more radical ends, old and new musicology meet in work being done to rescue female musicians from the margins of history. The 1993 anthology *Rediscovering the Muses: Women's Musical Traditions*, edited by Kimberly Marshall, ranges from an examination of the performance practices of Australian aboriginal women, and gender ideology in Central Java, to the music of seventeenth-century nuns and women in the court of Margaret of Scotland. Such scholarship is responsible for the appearance of several CDs of the medieval mystic Hildegaard von Bingham (packaged for both classical and New Age markets), for pulling Clara Schumann out from under her husband's shadow, and for the performances of works by the American virtuoso pianist and composer Amy Beach. Thus, the musicologist still delivers the contents of our record—and CD—collections.

> Old and new musicology meet in the archival work being done to rescue female musicians from the margins of history.

ETHNOMUSICOLOGY

In his 1964 classic, *The Anthropology of Music*, the late Indiana University professor Alan Merriam defined ethnomusicology as "the study of music in culture." For Merriam, ethnomusicology is less a fixed thing set down in, say, the transcriptions of African musics than a relationship, an interplay between two dynamic and changing forces. And in fact, there has been long-standing and very dynamic dialogue between two camps within ethnomusicology—between those who focus on "culture" and those who focus on "music."

The culture camp, arrayed behind Merriam, has approached ethnomusicology primarily as an anthropological discipline: Music figures as but one facet of the culture under examination. The music camp, following the musicologist Mantle Hood, places music far more centrally. In *The Ethnomusicologist* (1971), Hood described the field as "directed toward an understanding of music studied in terms of itself and also toward an understanding of music in society." This may seem to be merely a more verbose rephrasing of Merriam, but the words "in terms of itself" actually point to a quite different approach. Where Merriam's books on the Basongye of Zaire have been criticized for relegating music to the margins, Hood's book on Javanese gamelan undertakes a close analysis of the modal systems of that particular music. Significantly, it was Hood who, while at UCLA, encouraged students to actually perform the non-Western musics they studied. (This requirement has since been adopted by other universities. Virtually every school now stresses the importance of performing the music being studied and either hosts visiting musicians or develops ties with performers already living in the area.)

> Virtually every department now stresses the importance of the performance.

And as much as ethnomusicology is a product of the interplay between the culture and music camps, it is a product of the interplay among various academic disciplines ranging from linguistics to cultural anthropology to music theory. The field traces its roots back to the Belgian musicologist François-Joseph Fétis, who in the mid-nineteenth century was one of the first to include a long section on non-European musics in his multivolume history of music. More crucially, Fétis rejected the Enlightenment doctrine of progress in the arts. Music doesn't evolve and improve, Fétis argued; it merely changes, and it changes in response to changes in the conditions and cultures of the people who produce it. Fétis approached music as an anthropological event and insisted it can be understood only in relation to the social context in which it was produced.

Although ethnomusicology had existed as a subset of musicology programs since the teens, it wasn't until the mid-1950s, when Hood founded the UCLA program, that it began to exist as a distinct academic field. And in 1954, a few members of the American Musicological Society, disgruntled they could not present papers on ethnomusicological topics at the AMS conference, founded the Society for Ethnomusicology, an event that lent further credibility to the fledgling field.

Since then, ethnomusicology has revamped itself. Consider the changes at the journal *Ethnomusicology*. In the 1950s and 1960s, the journal published notices of ethnomusicologists returning from afar with backpacks full of reel-to-reel tapes and featured articles like

"Selecting a Tape Recorder," or "The Rhythmic Orientation of Two Drums in Japanese Noh Drama." But recent issues have featured essays such as "Rhythm, Rhyme, and Rhetoric in the Music of Public Enemy" and have run reviews of Klezmer music. Due in part to the influence of younger ethnomusicologists who are studying the music of their own specific sociocultural or ethnic backgrounds, the major division that has marked ethnomusicology from the very beginning— the conceptual wall between the culture of the researcher and the culture being researched, between "us" and "them"—seems on the brink of collapse.

But this development doesn't mean that fieldwork or an interest in the musics of distant cultures is on the wane. The ongoing commercialization of world music has made undergraduate ethnomusicology courses popular, and professors are expected to be able to teach several different cultural musics.

MUSIC THEORY

It is not too surprising that the field of music theory has recently come under similar fire. This isn't too surprising. While context is the holy grail of new musicological round tables, the text itself is the hallowed object of music theory. The music theorist favors a pure analytical encounter with the structure of music—and, for the most part, with music as written rather than performed.

Theorists occupy an odd position. On the one hand, the very insistence that there *are* structures to be uncovered puts them somewhat to the right of Attila the Hun in the eyes of many of their contemporaries in other fields. As the current president of the Society for Music Theory said about Heinrich Schenker, the twentieth-century theorist whose ideas underlie much of current music theory, "He wasn't a post-modernist ahead of his time; he wasn't even a modernist; he was an early Romantic behind his time." On the other hand, as the biggest proponents of new music, theorists are on the cutting edge: A major branch of contemporary music theory is concerned with creating analytical systems equal to the task of uncovering the structures beneath twentieth-century, posttonal music.

Schenker's work forms as good a starting point for a discussion of music theory as any. Born in 1867 but writing his most important work early in this century, Schenker invented a complex system for

discovering and charting what he conceived to be the organic structure beneath every classical composition. Schenkerian analysis first
distills a given piece down to a single underlying structure (or *Ursatz*).
This *Ursatz* is then found to be replicated again and again throughout
the composition at different levels, from its simplest occurrence in
the background, through a more complex middle ground, to its
manifold occurrences in the foreground, which is what we actually
hear when we listen to music. Schenker did for a piece of music what
Adler did for the whole field of musicology: set up a system for
accounting for everything. Every note has its place, a place dictated
by a single, unifying theme. "*Semper idem, sed non eodem modo,*" was
Schenker's inscription for his major work, *Free Composition*. "Always
the same, but never in the same way."

Critics charge quite the opposite: Schenkerian analysis produces
the same results in the same way, regardless of the music. As evidence,
they point to the fact that Schenker manages to reduce Beethoven's
Ninth Symphony and a late song by Schubert to the same
Ursatz. Defenders respond that Schenkerian analysis is about
the interplay between back-, middle-, and foreground, the
ways in which Beethoven and Schubert arrive at such different places from the same point of departure.

More damning in this day and age is Schenker's assumption that there is an organic unity to the work, a unity
inherent to the composition itself and not its reception.
Much of the last forty years of philosophical art criticism has
sought to prove that the coherence of any artwork is a fiction,
one we've been taught to project onto it, and many have set out to
reveal the incoherence and ruptures within a piece rather than its
underlying unity. Music theory has not been immune to this trend in
art criticism. Indeed, two of the newest developments in the field are
an increased attention to music philosophy (to the language and
assumptions that theory makes about music) and to musical cognition
(the study of how music is perceived).

For theorists themselves, however, the primary problem with
Schenker's system is that it works for the repertory from Bach to
Brahms but not for much else. To theorize about twentieth-century
(or posttonal) music, theorists have turned to set theory. In set
theory, also called posttonal analysis, the composition is broken

> Schenker did for a
> piece of music
> what Adler did for
> the whole field of
> musicology: set up
> a system to account
> for everything.

down into smaller components as a means of revealing its fundamental structure; it's roughly like parsing a sentence grammatically. These segments, or sets, are then analyzed in their relation to each other. As you might expect, the really interpretive challenge is in the initial segmenting—twelve-tone compositions certainly lend themselves to being broken into sets of twelve tones each, but each of these sets can also break into smaller sets of four trichords, for instance. Unlike Schenkerian analysis, however, set theory is not hierarchical. There's no back-, middle-, or foreground in set theory, merely a succession of sets in which certain ones dominate.

Composition and theory (Schenkerian and posttonal alike) have co-existed in music departments for most of this century. When Arnold Schoenberg arrived in the United States during World War II, the leading theory outpost, Princeton University, was home to the composers Roger Sessions and Milton Babbitt. As a result, university positions in music theory were traditionally held by composers, and even today many doctoral programs combine theory and composition. It was only in the early 1960s—as the discipline began to separate itself from historical musicology by launching the first theory journal, *Journal of Music Theory*—that universities began to grant degrees specifically in music theory, rather than in composition or musicology.

The result has been a professionalization of the usual theory position. Where undergraduate music theory courses had been traditionally taught by professors with backgrounds in composition, they are increasingly being handled by those holding doctorates in theory. The field went through a long period of expansion by replacing retiring composers with theorists, and this hiring pattern, in the polite words of one theory professor, had "a negative effect on composers."

WHAT'S NEXT

Relying on rankings such as those produced by the National Research Council to help you evaluate programs is dicey at best. The most recent NRC rankings have been widely criticized by faculty and students for lumping historical musicology, ethnomusicology, and music theory into one category, and for being based on faulty information. Some universities, for instance, listed only their full-time, tenured faculty with the NRC, while others included their adjunct and part-time instructors—which scudges the representation of a department's overall quality. Indiana, for instance, counted only a single full-time faculty member in musicology, while the University of Illinois at Urbana tallied up its entire performance faculty, adjuncts included.

HISTORICAL MUSICOLOGY

In historical musicology, core coursework is designed to provide both the requisite skills for graduate work and an understanding of the broad outlines of the field. Given the variety of backgrounds of incoming students, many programs choose to send them through a battery of tests to discover their relative strengths and weaknesses and then tailor a core program to specific needs. Nonetheless, nearly everyone has to take a mix of methodology courses (usually focusing heavily on bibliography), theory and analysis courses, and survey courses on the history of Western classical music. Some schools add a mandatory ethnomusicology course, or courses that trace the history of some aspect of musicology itself (notation, music theory, or aesthetics). Programs associated with conservatories ask students to stay abreast of current performances of music, and nearly all programs require two or more non-English languages, of which one is almost always German, the other often French or Italian. Traditionally, languages were required for admission, but they now have become part of degree requirements. It's advised you get them over with early, however, to avoid having your research on, say, Adorno, hampered by your spotty knowledge of German.

As far as the new/old musicology split goes, it would be convenient if the generation gap could be mapped out according to different universities, but this isn't possible, so it's best to consider where specific professors are located. The University of California system is generally regarded as both high quality and fairly progressive (witness UCLA having both McClary and Walser, and UC-Berkeley having Kerman and Richard Taruskin). Other institutions with new musicology faculty include Penn (with Tomlinson), Princeton (with Carolyn Abbate), and CUNY Graduate Center (with Leo Treitler), while Yale University, Cornell University, Illinois-Urbana, and Michigan are sometimes cited as falling more toward the conservative center.

More important for many graduate students, though, is the divide between scholarship and musical performance. "A large number of students come to grad school with a lot of performing," says Cornell professor Rebecca Harris-Warrick, "and they don't want to give that up." In general, a school where musicology is a division of a larger conservatory (USC, Catholic University, the University of Iowa, Northwestern University, Illinois-Urbana, Indiana, the University of Kentucky, the University of Louisville, Michigan State University, Michigan, Kent State, Ohio State University, North Texas University, Washington-Seattle, the University of Wisconsin at Madison), or even a larger music department (the University of Kansas, the University of Maryland at College Park) is going to stress performance, giving you both the time and access to teachers to continue your own practicing. The downside is that, particularly at some of the larger conservatories, the musicology program may be slighted administratively. The intellectual demands of coursework may be lowered to allow performers to spend the necessary hours in the practice room. Depending on your own interests, this may be a trade-off you're more than willing to make. And in between the two extremes of scholarship and performance are CUNY Graduate Center and Eastman School of Music, which pride themselves on mixing practicing musicians into the musicology classes and on keeping the musicologists actively practicing.

> A large number of students come to graduate school with a lot of performing, and they don't want to give that up.

On the opposite side of the spectrum, some schools (Yale, New York University) make a sharp distinction between conservatory and scholastic programs. While they may theoretically allow you time to practice, serious study of an instrument may depend on you finding the right teacher or just finding the time on your own.

Depending on your interests, you may want to investigate not only a musicology department, but also opportunities for drawing on the resources of related departments. Old musicology tends to ally itself with history, while new musicology is more likely to find its intellectual partners in literary and visual studies. Consider also what resources exist in terms of ethnomusicology and theory. The good news is that, with around forty historical musicology programs to choose from, nearly every possible combination of variables exists.

ETHNOMUSICOLOGY

Core coursework in ethnomusicology resembles that of historical musicology, but tailored to problems specific to the field. The course on methodology will cover not only traditional bibliographical research, but also the more exotic problems of sound recording and filming in the field, as well as the ethics of studying living peoples' musics. Music analysis courses will also include sections on the transcription, notation, and tuning systems of different musics. And, not surprising for a field reconsidering its orientation, many programs require a course giving a historical overview of the field itself. Most schools require at least a reading knowledge of two languages other than English. A few insist on German, but most leave the choice up to the student.

With only nineteen universities offering doctorates in what is still a fairly new field, the most highly respected programs tend to be the oldest. UCLA is considered the mother of all ethnomusicology programs, having been founded by Mantle Hood. It also remains one of the largest in the country, offering some twenty professors with research interests exclusive to the field. In fact, it's the only ethnomusicology program in the country that has its own departmental identity, rather than being a branch of an expanded historical musicology department. Of equal prominence are Washington-Seattle, where, although part of an immense music department, at least five professors have ethnomusicological specializations; and Wesleyan University, where over half of the sixteen professors in the music department list an ethnomusicology specialization, and no doctorate in any other musicological field is offered.

The program at Indiana, though on the same campus as the School of Music, is actually associated with the Folklore Institute. Students split their coursework between the two and can take advantage of one of the largest archives of traditional music recordings. The program is also associated with the teachings of Alan Merriam, who, as mentioned above, quite literally wrote the book on academic ethnomusicology.

MUSIC THEORY

Basic coursework generally focuses on a thorough grounding in both Schenkerian analysis and posttonal analysis, and a comprehensive overview of the history of music theory, which can stretch at some universities into several semesters.

There are thirty-two doctorate programs in theory in the United States, with four (Brandeis University, Rutgers University, Kent State, Pittsburgh) offering a theory/composition degree. As any serious program will cover Schenkerian and set theory equally well, the differences among schools are mostly a matter of which professor's work happens to interest you more. Yale and CUNY Graduate Center have been cited as being a bit stronger in Schenkerian theory, while Eastman and Harvard are set-theory powerhouses. A more crucial difference between schools concerns the other departments which can feasibly be drawn into the theoretical mix: The music programs at Princeton and Columbia call on other humanities departments to focus on issues in the aesthetics and the philosophy of music, and may have a higher dose of contemporary critical theory; UCLA, Washington-Seattle, Florida, Ohio State, and Cornell link themselves up more with psychology departments to work on issues like music cognition.

THE JOB MARKET

Despite great optimism in the late 1980s that many academic positions in musicology would open up during the current decade, nothing of the sort has taken place. According to a 1992 study of the job market commissioned by the American Musicological Society, professors hired during the boom days of the 1960s are not being replaced as they retire, due to budget constraints and hiring freezes. This has led, according to the study, to "a crisis...[which] has persisted for over ten years and shows no sign of abating."

> Professors hired during the boom days of the 1960s are not being replaced as they retire, due to budget constraints and hiring freezes.

The study was not without good news, at least for recent graduates. Hires at the junior level accounted for around 67 percent of the total number of positions filled, and somewhat over half of these were tenure-track. The study also noted that positions generally regarded as less desirable (with heavy undergraduate rather than graduate teaching; in the Midwest or Canada rather than on the either coast; and at smaller, less prestigious universities) had a much lower application rate. An announcement of a tenure-track position at a private New

England university might attract over a hundred applications, but a similar position offered at a southwestern community college might attract fewer than forty.

A similar study done for the Society for Music Theory focused on the number of positions open each year over the last decade. It found that after a slight upward blip in the late 1980s, the number of positions advertised has subsided to around forty to fifty per year. And while this study didn't calibrate the number of doctorates applying for those positions, the fact that there are thirty-two U.S. universities offering Ph.D.'s in theory, that each university tends to produce more than two graduates a year, and that these new Ph.D.'s compete with unemployed Ph.D.'s or faculty looking to change jobs, indicates that the numbers aren't encouraging.

> According to the AMS, the key to being hired in musicology is diversity and flexibility.

And while no specific study has been done for ethnomusicology, the anecdotal evidence seems to bear out similar results: While every year one or more top-tier university hires an ethnomusicologist (recent examples including Duke and Washington University in St. Louis) and world music courses are increasingly popular at the undergraduate level, there are often only one or two ethnomusicology slots at larger universities, and many smaller universities have yet to hire even their first full-fledged ethnomusicologist.

The key to being hired in musicology, the AMS study concludes, is diversity and flexibility. Nearly 70 percent of the institutions responding to the questionnaire admitted to asking recent hires to teach subjects outside of musicology, usually performance or music theory. (This is not an isolated problem for musicologists. One professor told of an applicant for an ethnomusicology job being asked if he could deliver his job interview talk on Beethoven.) Given the constant need for undergraduate music appreciation instructors and the popularity of world music, one would do well to combine a dissertation on Mozart with some serious side work in Schenkerian analysis. Leading the school's African drumming ensemble wouldn't hurt either.

The possibilities for M.A. recipients are different, since most schools agree that an M.A. doesn't open many academic doors (other than the one to a doctorate program, of course). Given the few doors open even to qualified Ph.D. recipients, however, the AMS is now increasingly recommending the M.A. to students who aren't sure that they want to pursue teaching as a career. Anecdotal evidence suggests that most M.A. recipients gravitate toward administrative positions in the arts: Musicologists tend to work for orchestras or do archival work; ethnomusicologists often end up in the public sector working on documentaries or promoting festivals.

> The consensus among faculty is that life outside academe but still within music is quite possible.

For those who prefer life in the big city where they've been studying, however, the consensus is that life outside academe but still within music is quite possible. If you love to teach, there are always high schools and private lessons. If close involvement with professional musicians interests you, there are frequently administrative positions to be filled in arts organizations. Given the burgeoning amount of sheer historical information that needs to be processed and made available, archival positions— whether in libraries or doing research—seem to be popular, at least as a first step out of the university.

And then there's always writing. Though program notes for symphonic performances and recordings used to be, in the words of an older Cornell professor, "beneath contempt," they now tend to be written by highly trained musicologists. After all, someone has to write the liner notes for all those CD's university musicologists are responsible for putting in our collections. If it's any consolation, Nietzsche wrote plenty about music, and he didn't last long in the university system, either.

RESOURCES

NRC TOP TEN
Harvard
Chicago
UC–Berkeley
CUNY Graduate
  Center
Yale
Princeton
Penn
Eastman
Michigan
Illinois–Urbana

ASSOCIATIONS
American
  Musicological Society
(215) 898-8698

Society for
  Ethnomusicology
(812) 855-6672

Society for Music
  Theory
(617) 627-3564

College Music Society
(406) 721-9616

JOURNALS
Ethnomusicology
Journal of the American
  Musicology Society
Journal of Music Theory
Journal of Musicology
Music Theory Spectrum
Pacific Review of
  Ethnomusicology
Repercussions
Theoria
World of Music

CONSTELLATIONS

HISTORICAL MUSICOLOGY
Brooklyn College
Catholic University
CUNY Graduate Center
Cornell
Eastman
Illinois–Urbana
Indiana
Iowa
Kansas
Kent State
Kentucky
Louisville
Maryland–College Park
Michigan
Michigan State
NYU
North Texas
Northwestern
Ohio State
Penn
Princeton
UC–Berkeley
UCLA
USC
Washington–Seattle
Wisconsin–Madison
Yale

ETHNOMUSICOLOGY
Indiana
UCLA
Washington–Seattle
Wesleyan

MUSIC THEORY
Brandeis
CUNY Graduate Center
Columbia
Cornell
Florida
Kent State
Ohio State
Pittsburgh
Princeton
Rutgers
UCLA
Washington–Seattle
Yale

DEPARTMENTS OFFERING DEGREES IN ALL THREE FIELDS
CUNY Graduate Center
Harvard
Kent State
Michigan
Pittsburgh
UT–Austin
Washington–Seattle

FURTHER READING
Pieter van den Toorn, *Music Politics and the Academy* (California)

WEB ADDRESSES
American Musicological Society
http://musdra.ucdavis.edu/documents/ams/ams.html

Society for Ethnomusicology
http://www.indiana.edu/~ethmusic

Society for Music Theory
http://boethius.music.ucsb.edu/smt-list/smthome.html

CHAPTER 16

PHILOSOPHY

Jennifer Lackey's long-standing passion for intellectual puzzles led her to embrace her field early: As a college freshman, she found her first philosophy class so gratifying that she immediately declared her major in the subject. Although she took courses in a variety of its subfields, she found herself drawn to epistemology and the philosophy of mind. After college, she entered the Ph.D. program at the University of Chicago, but she decided to leave the program with an M.A. after one year for a department better suited to her interest in epistemic agency—the study of our active role in the process of acquiring knowledge. In 1995, Lackey joined the Ph.D. program at Brown University. Now finishing up her coursework, Lackey is beginning to brainstorm about her dissertation. Her hunch is that she'll address the internalist/externalist debate over epistemic justification, but she hopes at least part of her discussion will involve the consequences of different epistemological views on such subjects as mental causation and consciousness.

Joe Ramsey started graduate study at the University of California at San Diego in 1990 after doing undergraduate work in mathematics and philosophy at Indiana University of Pennsylvania and spending several years in China as an exchange student. Ramsey entered UC-San Diego wanting to think seriously about what he calls the problem of logical cognition: how to reconcile the claim that our thinking is logical with the belief that mental representations are best understood as complicated physical states of a dynamic system—the brain. The difficulty, as Ramsey sees it, is that logical and semantic properties such as truth, falsity, and constituent structure do not seem to apply straightforwardly to the brain states or processes underlying our thinking. Yet these properties seem necessary to describe what happens when we think. At first Ramsey hoped to work on these issues through the study of cognitive science, but several leading Kant scholars then at UC-San Diego persuaded him to approach the question through a Kantian framework. He took their advice and began to explore Kant, and after a brief hiatus taken for health reasons, he sharpened his focus on the problem of logical cognition and began to work on meshing his knowledge of Kant with the study of cognitive science.

WHY PHILOSOPHY?

There may never come a day when a graduate student in philosophy can talk to a nonphilosopher without having to suffer a look of amused incredulity. "You're a philosophy student? What are you going to do with that? Teach?"

Even for people who devote their professional lives to philosophy, it's difficult to describe the field. Still, they don't shy away from trying. Ask Columbia professor Sidney Morgenbesser, the recognized wag of the profession, and you'll probably get his famous three-sentence, three-shrug reply: "You make a few distinctions. You clarify a few concepts. It's a living." Put the question to Oxford University professor John Campbell, and he'll say, "Philosophy is thinking in slow motion. It breaks down, describes, and assesses moves we ordinarily make at great speed." Among the moves philosophers break down are such disparate topics as knowledge, language, confirmation, truth, justice, rationality, perception, normativity, possibility, interpretation, minds, societies, and actions. In each case, the goal of inquiry is a modest one: to understand the relevant moves as fully and accurately as possible.

Unlike most fields of study, philosophy is defined more by its methods than by its domain. For the majority of philosophers, philosophy is the field that explores the many ideas that make up the foundations of other fields: Thus, we have philosophy of history, philosophy of mathematics, philosophy of linguistics, philosophy of religion, philosophy of science, philosophy of geography, philosophy of logic, and political philosophy, to name but a few. Alongside inquiry into other fields, about a third of all philosophers in the United States study the history of philosophy itself, attempting to understand the ideas and arguments of other philosophers in history. Some would say that all philosophers are united in the centrality that each gives to rational argument as a means of arriving at truth, though this would seem to exclude at least some forms of post-modern philosophy.

The variety of work being done today by philosophers of all types is staggering. On a typical afternoon in a graduate lounge at a reasonably large philosophy department, it is not uncommon to find people working on mathematical proofs, translating passages of German or grappling with medieval commentaries on Plato, some poring over physics and political science journals, and still others disputing the ethics of physician-assisted suicide.

How did all of this work come to exist under one roof? Partly by the example set by ancient philosophers. Aristotle wrote works on biology, logic, rhetoric, politics, ethics, physics, metaphysics, language, and aesthetics. Thinkers since Aristotle have made arguments to reach conclusions in every area of rational inquiry. And where there have been arguments, there have been opportunities to examine presuppositions, critically evaluate inferences, and offer explanations—in short, philosophy.

HOW PHILOSOPHY HAS TAKEN SHAPE

By the late nineteenth and early twentieth centuries, there were already several philosophical movements indigenous to the United States. One of the most influential was Absolute Idealism, associated with Harvard University professor Josiah Royce, which held sway among American philosophers until at least the First World War. The basis of Absolute Idealism was, of course, idealism—the claim that knowers and the ideas they know do exist, but mind-independent objects in the world do not. Royce argued against the later point. The only explanation for how an individual mind thinks, he claimed, is the existence of something called an Absolute Mind, an entity containing all the ideas humans will ever think. Royce proposed as well that only an Absolute Mind could explain error. Our ideas are erroneous, Royce claimed, only insofar as they diverge from the ideas of an Absolute Mind.

Another important American philosophical movement was pragmatism, which also blossomed at Harvard, but sprang from earthier soil than Royce's notion of the Absolute Mind. Identified primarily with Charles Sanders Peirce, pragmatism starts with the so-called "pragmatic maxim," according to which a concept's meaning is understood in terms of its consequences for human experience broadly conceived. In the hands of Peirce's successor, Harvard psychology and philosophy professor William James, the pragmatic maxim was modified slightly to emphasize the consequences of accepting or rejecting concepts for any one individual. This emphasis on the individual led James to stress the importance of "concrete truths"—beliefs shown to be useful in individual experience. So truth—and James always stressed the lowercase nature of truth—did not devolve in Hegelian fashion from an Absolute Mind. Truth was instead a function of the relative fit between an individual's idea and his or her experience.

> James was insistent about the contingent and lower-case quality of all truths.

This conception of truth was taken up by philosopher and educator John Dewey, who used it to criticize how the philosophical tradition had defined human experience and its place in nature. Dewey preferred an "empirical naturalism," according to which human consciousness is not set over against nature but is a part of it. Other naturalists followed Dewey in denying anything above and beyond nature, and like him they came to understand nature quite broadly, as including not only the objects studied by natural science, but also human consciousness and values. Besides Dewey, other American naturalists included George Santayana, F.J.E. Woodbridge, Roy Wood Sellars, Morris R. Cohen, and Alfred North Whitehead.

Despite both the richness of empirical naturalism in American philosophy and the transmutation of James's and Dewey's work in the writings of Harvard philosopher Hilary Putnam and University of Virginia philosopher Richard Rorty, who has quite a following among literary theorists, the pragmatic tradition has not been widely studied or discussed by many philosophers until very recently.

Almost invariably, contemporary discussions of philosophy in the United States begin with the rise of logical empiricism (or logical positivism) in the 1920s and 1930s. Logical empiricism took root in the United States when many of its leading figures fled Western Europe for these shores to escape Nazism. Hans Reichenbach settled at UCLA in 1933, and Rudolph Carnap at Chicago in 1935.

The swagger of logical empiricists intimidated aging pragmatists and other naturalist philosophers.

Along with Reichenbach and Carnap, thinkers such as Moritz Schlick, Otto Neurath, A.J. Ayer, and Carl Hempel took it upon themselves to save philosophy from what they considered the nonsense of Hegel, Heidegger, and James. For logical empiricists, the main problem with philosophical nonsense—besides being just nonsense—was that it lacked scientific integrity. To remedy this defect, logical empiricists offered a "meaningfulness" criterion to distinguish sensical from nonsensical philosophical statements. Their hope was to reject as meaningless all statements that were neither analytic (necessary truths of logic or mathematics) nor synthetic (non-necessary truths known through experience of the world).

Logical empiricism was astoundingly successful in displacing its competitors in the American academy because at that time institutional philosophy was receptive to change. For one thing, in the face of increasingly rapid technological advances in the sciences, philosophers began to wonder what their discipline could accomplish. In addition, logical empiricism not only offered philosophers invaluable tools for the clarification of concepts in general scientific enterprise, but also lent credibility to their field by associating itself so closely with empirical science. Moreover, logical empiricists were strident in their dismissal of "meaningless" views, and their swagger often intimidated aging pragmatists and other American philosophers. In fact, pragmatists sometimes lost arguments more because they did not share a common vocabulary with their empiricist critics than because of some inherent weaknesses in their positions. In any case, from the mid-1940s to the late 1950s, logical empiricism was the lodestar of the American philosophical landscape.

No sooner had logical empiricism gained prominence as a movement, however, than it was riven by internal squabbles about some of its key commitments. First, there was the worry that the "meaningfulness" criterion was itself meaningless, since there seemed to be no clear method for verifying its own truth. Second, there was heated controversy about what should be counted as an acceptable means of verification. Antagonism over these issues plagued logical empiricism until the late 1950s and early 1960s, when the movement finally collapsed under the crippling attacks of such thinkers as Harvard's Willard V.O. Quine, who argued against the concept of scientific confirmation presumed by logical empiricism, and Princeton University's Thomas Kuhn, who claimed that the conception of science deployed by logical empiricists was at odds with the actual practice of science.

> Ordinary language philosophers thought they had found a method to reveal the nature of virtue or the good.

During the heyday of logical empiricism, a different philosophical tradition had grown and flourished in the United States and especially Great Britain. This "ordinary language" movement took language to be the appropriate starting point for philosophical inquiry. Whereas logical empiricists considered expressions of ordinary language at best misleading representations of underlying logical form, ordinary language philosophers claimed not only that ordinary language was adequate for philosophical purposes, but that careful attention to the use of ordinary language could reveal the nature of philosophically important concepts such as virtue or the good. Gilbert Ryle, J.L. Austin, and John Wisdom, among others, hoped that the analysis of inferences in ordinary language could either solve long-standing philosophical problems or else reveal them as mere pseudo-problems.

Philosophers began to challenge ordinary language philosophy in the 1950s, and the most serious defeats came at the hands of H. Paul Grice. Grice observed that many of the inferences we draw from a statement are based not on the concepts expressed by words in the statement, but by the more general pragmatic expectations we bring to all conversations. This observation was devastating to ordinary language philosophy because it suggested that the inferences in actual linguistic usage, taken by ordinary language philosophy to be revelatory of the structure of our concepts, typically reflected factors other than the nature of our concepts. If Grice was right, then contrary to the most central hopes of ordinary language philosophy, attention to ordinary language could not clarify the understanding of philosophical concepts.

Though neither logical empiricism nor ordinary language philosophy now dominates philosophy, both continue to shape inquiry into the philosophy of language, ethics, knowledge, and the mind. More generally, not only did both movements cause some to comment that the twentieth century marks a "linguistic turn" in philosophy, but they set a very high—and salutary—standard for logical clarity and argumentative rigor in philosophy. And philosophers such as Quine, Donald Davidson, and P.F. Strawson have been able to combine the best aspects of both movements to great success, applying techniques of logical analysis to actual linguistic constructions. This has been especially important in connection with the rise of generative linguistics and the cross-fertilization between research in that subject and the philosophy of language.

The subfields of philosophy are united more by their methodology and the sorts of questions they pose than by the subjects they explore or their institutional origin. For instance, philosophers interested in such disparate topics as morality, mathematics, and aesthetics have all wondered about the metaphysical and epistemological basis of their inquiry. Especially during this century, metaphysics and epistemology have become deeply intertwined with questions about language and mind.

Since every program will require that you study logic and assumes that you worked on it as an undergraduate, we don't draw attention to subspecialties within it as we do for the following areas of inquiry.

PHILOSOPHY OF MIND AND PHILOSOPHY OF LANGUAGE

Philosophy of language has occupied a central place in philosophy's core since the turn of the century. Key questions include the nature of language, reference, and meaning; interpretation; formal semantics; and the relationship between thought and language. Increasingly, some philosophy of language is closely related to some parts of linguistics. Other work in this field has merged with concerns in the philosophy of mind.

Philosophers of mind investigate numerous subjects: consciousness, the nature of mind, the basis of belief and desire, and the individuation of mental states. Philosophers writing from a feminist perspective, such as Louise Anthony of UNC—Chapel Hill, contribute to this field. And much contemporary work in philosophy of mind is informed by the burgeoning field of cognitive science, which is a melding of cognitive psychology, linguistics, computer science, and neurophysiology. (For a discussion of cognitive science, see the Linguistics chapter.) Don't worry if you are unfamiliar with these fields: Most graduate students who do cognitive science pick up what they need to know in graduate school.

An important starting point for discussion in philosophy of mind has been the status of the mental in the material world. At mid-century, Carnap and Ryle put forward two claims that countered Descartes's account of mind/body dualism: First, only material objects exist, and second, the term "mind" does not name any material object. Both Carnap and Ryle held that mental and psychological terms such as "belief" or "pain" are just shorthand for talk about observable bodily behavior. This view, subsequently termed "logical behaviorism," was roundly criticized in 1957 by Noam Chomsky for the insufficiency of its account of mental terms. Chomsky pointed out that although there are sometimes no observable behaviors associated with mental terms, such terms are meaningful nonetheless. Chomsky's attacks made behaviorism a very unpopular view, but most philosophers have nevertheless retained its materialist position that physical stuff is the only kind of stuff in the world, minds included.

> An important issue in philosophy of mind has been the status of the mental in the material world.

But if the materialist position is true, philosophers asked, one might wonder about the relation between minds and brains. From the 1950s to the 1970s, philosophers such as H. Feigl, J.J.C. Smart, and David Armstrong probed this relation with the proposition of "identity theories," according to which minds are just brains, and mental states and processes are just brain states and processes. Another materialist answer, defended in different ways by Donald Davidson of the University of California at Berkeley and Jerry Fodor of Rutgers University, is that while the mind is the brain, kinds of mental states and processes can't be straightforwardly reduced to kinds of brain states and processes. In 1975, Fodor argued for a conception of mind based on the needs of scientific research. He claimed that cognitive psychology presupposes that the mind has a "language of thought"—a system of representation which, like a spoken language, possesses both syntactic and semantic properties. Thinking, then, is just the interaction between and transformation of the syntactic properties of our mental representations. Yet because these representations have semantic properties as well, our thoughts are thoughts about something—about drinking a beer after a seminar on epistemology, for instance.

One point of extensive contemporary debate is how, exactly, these semantic properties are fixed. What makes my thought a thought about a beer, rather than a soda? Hilary Putnam of Harvard and Tyler Burge of UCLA argued in the late 1970s that the meanings of our thoughts must be determined by properties outside our bodies. Theories of meaning which attempt to account for these external factors have recently been offered by Fodor, Ruth Millikan of the University of Connecticut, Ned Block of New York University, and Gilbert Harman and David Lewis, both of Princeton.

Another important area of research in philosophy of mind involves consciousness. Questions here include NYU philosopher Thomas Nagel's famous "what is it like to be a bat?" as well as questions about what makes a system conscious and whether theories like functionalism inevitably fail to account for consciousness. Consciousness has been a fairly hot topic in the last five years, during which time there have been numerous special volumes and conferences devoted to the subject, but it's unclear whether this level of interest will continue.

EPISTEMOLOGY AND PHILOSOPHY OF SCIENCE

Epistemology is the theory of knowledge. Issues in this field include the source, presuppositions, nature, extent, and reliability of knowledge; the roles of reason and sense experience in knowledge; and the relations between such concepts as truth, belief, opinion, fact, error, and certainty.

Part of the reason for the downfall of logical empiricism in the 1950s was the weakness of its epistemology, which we might call classical foundationalism. According to classical foundationalism, we have a system of true beliefs about the world, and we use them to build up a structure of knowledge in a step-by-step, truth-preserving way. This sort of view is unpopular among contemporary epistemologists, who, with a variety of arguments, attach much greater importance to the fallibility of the processes by which we justify our beliefs. University of Arizona at Tucson professor Keith Lehrer, for example, argues that we are justified in accepting a proposition only if it is of a piece with our background beliefs. Lehrer's colleague Alvin I. Goldman takes a different approach and argues that justification comes only when our beliefs are formed by reliable belief-forming mechanisms. And Alvin Plantinga of the University of Notre Dame argues that justification depends on the proper functioning of our cognitive processes and that divine design is the best reason for trusting those processes. It should be clear that unlike classical foundationalism, all three of these views of justification take the possibility of false beliefs quite seriously.

Philosophy of science is a central concern of logical empiricists, and some of its questions about scientific methodology—especially those concerning the confirmation and falsification of scientific hypotheses—often converge around questions in epistemology. On the other hand, questions about the nature of scientific laws and explanations, and the reality of unobservable entities postulated by scientific theory, are more closely linked to metaphysics. Recently feminist philosophers have brought their analyses to both the bedrock assumptions of science and to the professional culture of the scientific enterprise. This work has developed from the rediscovery of the theoretical and practical contributions of women to science but goes beyond it to explore the role that gender sometimes plays in theoretical conceptions of scientific problems. In addition to these philosophical issues about science as a whole, questions germane to specific sciences are treated in subjects like philosophy of psychology, philosophy of biology, and philosophy of physics. Many philosophers of science are quite knowledgeable about some area of scientific inquiry and have at least some graduate level training in these fields as well as in philosophy.

METAPHYSICS

The term "metaphysics" probably originated as a title given to the work in the Aristotelian corpus following the Physics. (Aristotle himself did not coin this term.) What is now called metaphysics is in part what Aristotle took himself to be doing in that book: examining the notion of being at the highest level of generality. Central issues in contemporary metaphysics include ontology (what exists?), causation (what is it? what does it connect?), truth (does it have a nature? if so, what?), necessity (what is it? how should it be analyzed?), and identity (how does a thing remain what it is over time? are there essential properties that make it what it is?). Metaphysics remains one of the most important disciplines in philosophy's core and is taught by a specialist in almost every major department.

MORAL, POLITICAL, AND LEGAL PHILOSOPHY

General questions about ethics and morality have fascinated philosophers for millennia. Many philosophers have attempted to explain what qualities make an action good or a life virtuous. In this century, however, philosophical ethicists have focused on more abstruse philosophical questions about morality. The most vigorous recent debates in moral philosophy have been in metaethics, which investigates the metaphysical and epistemological status of ethical notions like values, and whether there are objective values and how we can know anything about them.

> A key metaethical problem is whether or not moral properties such as goodness really exist in the world.

An important metaethical problem dating from the early twentieth century is whether or not moral properties such as goodness really exist in the world. This came under renewed scrutiny by J.L. Mackie and Gilbert Harman in 1977. Mackie denied the existence of moral properties. He went on to conclude that no moral judgments are true because moral judgments relied on moral properties. For his part, Harman denied that the contents of our moral beliefs can be squared with objective moral facts. If Harman's view is correct, then bona fide moral belief provides no support for the reality of moral properties. In response to these claims, moral realists including Peter Railton, Nicholas Sturgeon, and David Brink argued that we must appeal to moral facts to explain the truth or falsity of our moral beliefs.

An intermediate position of sorts was advocated by David P. Gauthier and Thomas Scanlon. Known as constructivists, they argued that the truth or falsity of moral judgments is given not by the relation between moral judgments and stance-independent moral facts, but by whether such judgments are endorsed by norms that rational agents would accept under certain hypothetical circumstances. Today the most prominent anti-realist in ethics is Allan Gibbard of the University of Michigan. His position, norm-expressivism, holds that moral judgments merely express our endorsement of moral norms. Again, this account attempts to explain how our moral judgments can be true without requiring the reality of moral properties.

Aside from these questions about the reality of moral properties and what is required for the truth of moral judgments, ethical inquiry today includes active debates on a number of fronts: the nature of value, the relation between one's own interests and the interests of others, the structure of practical reason, the relation between moral belief and moral motivation, and the necessity of free will for moral responsibility. Issues in these areas are often described as problems of "normative ethics," rather than metaethics, since they concern what is good and bad, what people ought to do, and what should be pursued in life. In some cases, though, normative ethics and metaethics are tightly knit. The metaethical question of what moral facts there are would seem to depend on the question of which normative theory, if any, is true. Philosophers bringing feminist approaches to such questions have been particularly active, drawing on political and legal philosophy and social theory, among them Susan Okin of Stanford University's political science department, Alison Jaggar of Colorado, and Anita Allen of Georgetown Law Center.

Ever since the publication of John Rawls's *A Theory of Justice* in 1971, the notion of distributive justice and the proper justification of liberal political principles have both been major topics in social and political philosophy. Today, under the subject of "deliberative democracy," there are also debates on the justification of the state and the norms of good political decision making. Related debates at the intersection of legal and moral philosophy include the relation between morality and the law, the justification of international law, and the nature, limits, and justification of rights (especially property and free speech rights). Other active areas of research in legal philosophy include the purpose of punishment and the nature of legal reasoning and interpretation.

The applied fields of medical and business ethics, which are usually distinguished from more theoretical fields such as metaethics and normative ethics, are currently experiencing rapid growth. This growth stems partly from the need of undergraduate and professional students outside philosophy to learn about ethics for their own purposes. Also, this research has attracted attention (and funding) from nonacademic sources.

Since the 1970s, a body of work by philosophers about race and social and political identity has developed which does not fall neatly into the ordinary categories of philosophy, though in their broadest conception political and moral philosophy are the most likely home for such work. Rutgers, Syracuse University, and Michigan State University are leading institutions in this field, but also consider Harvard, home to Anthony Appiah, who has appointments in both the Philosophy and African-American Studies program, and whose writings have added depth to the study of racial identity. At Rutgers, Howard McGary and Jorge Garcia are leaders in this field, and the former's *On Philosophy and Slavery*, coauthored with William Lawson of Michigan State, has been well received. To these scholars add Bernard Boxill of the University of North Carolina at Chapel Hill, author of *Blacks and Social Justice*, and Laurance Thomas and Linda Alcoff of Syracuse University. Leonard Harris of Michigan State takes a wide view of the term philosophy, including philosophers and nonphilosophers alike in *Philosophy Born of Struggle*

> The applied fields of medical and business ethics are currently experiencing rapid growth.

HISTORY OF PHILOSOPHY

During the reign of logical empiricism, serious study of historical figures in philosophy went out of fashion. The joke among "scientific" philosophers was that some philosophers are interested in the history of philosophy, others in philosophy. But as empiricism fell, interest in philosophy's history reemerged. In the 1960s and early 1970s, for example, Princeton's Gregory Vlastos and Harvard's G.E.L. Owen revitalized American study of the pre-Socratics, Plato, and Aristotle by publishing new editions of their work. Although study of the ancient Greeks had never fallen out of fashion in Great Britain and continental Europe, Vlastos and Owen made it possible for a new generation of scholars of ancient philosophy to gain prominence in American universities.

Aristotle is the most studied ancient philosopher, and scholarship continues to pour forth on almost every part of his vast corpus.

The literature on Plato is also immense, but some parts of his dialogues—notably those concerning his theory of Forms and his remarks on the historical Socrates—have attracted more attention than others. These days, however, Aristotle and Plato share the limelight with Hellenistic philosophers such as the Epicureans, Stoics, and Skeptics.

In recent decades, medieval philosophy has received much less attention than ancient and modern philosophy. For the most part, Augustine, Maimonides, Aquinas, and other medieval thinkers are of interest only to contemporary Catholic and Jewish philosophers and those sympathetic with medieval conceptions of the divine. Contemporary academic philosophy in the United States has been largely indifferent to medieval thinkers except insofar as they have related to the study of modern philosophers.

Among modern philosophers, Descartes, Hobbes, Spinoza, Locke, Hume, and Kant are studied quite widely today. The attention given modern philosophy stems partly from the thematic similarities between contemporary and modern epistemology, metaphysics, ethics, and political philosophy. Also, since most of the texts in modern philosophy were written in modern European languages, a relatively large number of scholars have been able to read the original texts with authority.

For some time historians of philosophy, as well as professors in other disciplines, have done exciting work in reintroducing the neglected work of women philosophers. In *The Death of Nature*, Carolyn Merchant of UC-Berkeley discusses the ideas of both female and male metaphysicians of the sixteenth through the early nineteenth century. Erica Harth of Brandeis University has brought a new perspective to a turning point in philosophy with her book *Cartesian Women*. In MIT professor Ruth Perry's study of the seventeenth-century philosopher Mary Astell, discussion branches out from this single figure to create an intellectual portrait of the age; Perry effectively connects the philosophy and the politics of that day. Londa Schiebinger, a professor of history at Pennsylvania State University, is author of *The Mind Has No Sex*, which charts the contribution of women philosophers to the history of science in the early modern period. The women philosophers of the *salons* are the subject of scholarship by John Conely of Fordham University. The most complete overview of this area is Cleveland State University professor Mary Ellen Waithe's four volume *A History of Women Philosophers*.

CONTINENTAL PHILOSOPHY

Despite its name, Continental philosophy is not any more European than is analytic philosophy. Both originated largely in late nineteenth and early twentieth century Europe, and both are currently studied by philosophers all over the world. A better way to distinguish the two traditions is in terms of themes and projects: Philosophers in the Continental tradition are distinguished by both style—less analytical and argumentative than the Anglo-American tradition—and by themes and concerns, including, for example, a sense of the historically situated nature of philosophical inquiry, an emphasis on the connection between philosophy and pressing sociocultural issues, and an interest (often literary in character) in understanding the meaning of human existence. Analytic philosophers have traditionally viewed Continental philosophy as deliberately obscure and insufficiently attentive to argumentative detail, while Continental philosophers claim that analytic philosophy's obsession with details and distinctions precludes understanding matters of human significance.

> Philosophers in the Continental tradition are distinguished both by style and by themes and concerns.

Until recently Continental and analytic philosophers for the most part haven't addressed each other; hence, the split has played only a minor role in the everyday life of working philosophers and students. And while Continental philosophy isn't studied nearly as widely as analytic philosophy in the United States, there are many departments strong in the study of Continental figures such as Hegel, Marx, Nietzsche, Husserl, Heidegger, Sartre, Levinas, Derrida, Foucault, Kristeva, and Habermas.

WHAT'S NEXT

Most Ph.D. students in philosophy have completed substantial undergraduate coursework in the field, although programs do admit students with undergraduate majors in other fields. For some specialties—philosophy of mathematics, philosophy of linguistics, ancient philosophy—an undergraduate major in the relevant field of inquiry is a distinct advantage. But regardless of their research interests, applicants to graduate programs in philosophy are typically advised to have some grounding in philosophical logic, the history of philosophy (both ancient and modern), value theory (aesthetics or ethics), metaphysics/epistemology, and language/mind.

Competition for admission to philosophy programs is tough. According to the American Philosophical Association, three out of ten Ph.D. programs admit less than 10 percent of their applicants. At the best programs, admission rates are often 5 percent or lower. Given these figures, students keen on doing graduate work in philosophy but with less than stellar credentials—whether insufficient preparation in philosophy or a bachelor's degree from a low-profile department or one outside the analytic mainstream—should seriously consider completing a terminal M.A. in philosophy to improve their standing before applying to Ph.D. programs. While most terminal M.A. programs admit students with the understanding that they will complete only the M.A. at that institution, it's worth checking to see if it is possible to continue toward a Ph.D. at that institution if you might want to do so. If you're thinking about this option, though, bear in mind that students working toward a terminal master's take a back seat to Ph.D. students. Among the best terminal M.A. programs are those at Tufts University, Arizona State University, the University of Wisconsin at Milwaukee, Northern Illinois University, Colgate University, the University of Houston, Texas A&M University, the University of Missouri at St. Louis, and Virginia Polytechnic Institute.

> Philosophy is a field notorious for faculty moving from institution to institution.

There are several key issues to consider when you investigate a Ph.D. program: its strength in your subfield, its overall strength in the discipline, the job placement record of its recent Ph.D.'s, and the graduate student quality of life. To get some information about these issues, talk directly with current faculty and Ph.D. students in the program, keeping in mind that students are often much more reliable sources than the director of graduate studies or any other professor responsible for recruitment, who naturally are anxious to present their program in the best light possible.

It's crucial to study with professors who can also be your mentors, but given the annoying tendency of individual professors to move, change interests, retire, or die, finding someone to work with is no cakewalk. It's safer to look for a department with at least three faculty members in your area who could serve as potential advisors. Because philosophers disagree so much, it probably won't be possible to find an advisor who shares all of your philosophical views, but you should at least try to find someone whose general approach to philosophical questions is compatible with your own. Students attracted to a department by a specific faculty member should find out whether or not that person either is willing to take on new student advisees, is attending to her current students' work (an especially important issue when dealing with star faculty), or is planning to leave the department or retire.

Regardless of who ends up being your advisor, the requirements for the Ph.D. are pretty uniform between departments. Students take courses for approximately three years, and then spend a little less than a year jumping through whatever pre-dissertation hoops their departments require—usually a topical or preliminary exam of some kind. Most departments require coursework in a variety of subdisciplines (logic, ethics, ancient, modern, epistemology/metaphysics, mind/language, science), and many, though increasingly fewer, require reading proficiency in a foreign language. Students often take classes in other departments as needed. Although most programs claim their students finish in five years, most students take six or seven, depending on how much teaching they do and the level of funding they get while writing their dissertations.

Departments are becoming more specialized, which makes it harder to find a program strong in all the traditional areas.

Departments at private universities (Chicago, Princeton) generally provide more fellowship support, while state universities (UC-Berkeley, Arizona-Tucson) tend to fund their students with more teaching assistantships. Fellowship support is a plus in that it frees up time for research and writing, but teaching has its benefits, too—most notably, valuable qualifications for the job market, particularly if you expect to teach at a small liberal arts college.

The rankings of philosophy departments provided by University of Texas at Austin professor Brian Leiter in *The Philosophical Gourmet Report* are more accurate than those published by the National Research Council. The NRC rankings, though published in 1995, were based on surveys conducted in 1992–1993, so they are woefully out of date. As Leiter emphasizes, philosophy is a field notorious for faculty moving from institution to institution. Because it is produced annually and therefore is sensitive to faculty moves, *The Philosophical Gourmet Report* has become the standard guide to philosophy departments.

Although the *Gourmet Report* is a more complete listing of faculty affiliations and research interests than is available in most disciplines, any such guide to a small field, especially one in which all Ph.D.'s are masters of argumentation, provokes criticism. Professor Jaako Hintikaa of Boston University, for example, has written to the official journal *Proceedings and Addresses of the American Philosophical Association* that there is an "abundance of mistakes" in the *Gourmet Report*. As with any guide to a discipline, you'll have to check the descriptions of departments and the affiliations of scholars carefully. But there is no more complete starting point at present than the *Gourmet Report*. If you would like to see the American Philosophical Association's statement on all such rankings, it can be found on the Web at apaOnline.

According to Leiter, the ten strongest programs in analytic philosophy are Princeton, NYU, Rutgers, the University of Pittsburgh, Michigan, Harvard, UC-Berkeley, UCLA, UC-San Diego, Cornell University, Indiana University, Stanford, Arizona-Tucson, and UNC-Chapel Hill. Interestingly, the strongest philosophy departments are not always located at what have been traditionally regarded as the most prestigious universities. Indiana, Rutgers, and Pittsburgh, for example, are in a league above Yale University, the University of Pennsylvania, and Columbia University.

Departments are becoming more specialized, which makes it harder to find a program strong in all the traditional areas of philosophy. You should choose a department strong in your subfield, then, even if its overall reputation is weaker. Epistemologists, for instance, should go to Arizona-Tucson rather than Pittsburgh, and logicians should go to Indiana instead of Rutgers. See *The Philosophical Gourmet Report*, on which the following list of subfields is based, for the current status of subfields and the best departments (and faculty) in them.

Students interested in metaphysics should look at Princeton (Johnston, Kripke, Lewis), NYU (Field, Fine, Nagel, Schiffer, Unger, Sorensen), Brown (Kim, Sosa, Van Cleve), the University of Notre Dame (Plantinga, Van Inwagen), and Cornell (Boyd, Shoemaker). In epistemology, strong programs include Arizona

(Goldman, Lehrer, Pollock), Notre Dame (Plantinga), UC-San Diego (Paul Churchland, Kitcher), Rutgers (Foley, Klein, Stich), and Washington-Seattle (BonJour, Talbott).

For philosophy of mind, Rutgers (Fodor, Loar, McGinn, Stich, McLaughlin, Loewer), NYU (Block, Boghossian, Field, Nagel, Schiffer), Princeton (Kripke, Lewis, Harman, Johnston), Pittsburgh (Haugeland, McDowell), UC-Berkeley (Searle), UCLA (Burge), UC-San Diego (Patricia Churchland, Paul Churchland, Adrian Cussins), and Stanford (Dretske, Perry) are worth considering. Programs with strengths in philosophy of language include Princeton (Kripke, Lewis, Soames), NYU (Boghossian, Field, Fine, Schiffer) Pittsburgh (Brandom, McDowell), UCLA (Burge, Kaplan), UC-Berkeley (Searle), and Rutgers (Lepore, Loar, Neale).

In ethics, notable programs are Michigan (Anderson, Darwall, Gibbard, Railton, Regan, Velleman), Harvard (Korsgaard, Nozick, Scanlon, Sen), Princeton (Broadie, Cooper, Frankfurt, Harman, Johnston), Pittsburgh (Gauthier, McDowell), Cornell (Boyd, Irwin, Miller, Shue, Sturgeon), UNC-Chapel Hill (Blackburn, Boxill, Hill, Postema, McCord, Anthony), Arizona (Julia Annas, David Schmidtz, Holly Smith), and NYU (Dworkin, Kamm, Murphy, Nagel, Svavarsdottir, Unger).

Students who want to specialize in ancient philosophy should check out Princeton (Broadie, Cooper, Nehamas), Cornell (Fine, Irwin), UT-Austin (Hankinson, Mourelatos, White, Woodruff), Arizona (Julia Annas), and Washington-Seattle (Cohen, Keat, Roberts). Those who want to do modern philosophy should investigate Princeton (Frankfurt, Wilson), Michigan (Curley, Loeb), UC-Berkeley (Broughton, Stroud), Yale (Robert Adams, Della Rocca).

In the philosophy of science, check out Pittsburgh, which has a separate program in the history and philosophy of science, UC-San Diego (with Paul Churchland, Glymour, Philip Kitcher, Mitchell), Princeton (Lewis, Van Frassen), Michigan (Railton, Sklar), Chicago (Garber, Malament, Stein, Wimsatt), the University of Wisconsin at Madison (Elliot Sober, Daniel Hausman, Ellery Ells, Malcolm Foster), the University of Minnesota at Twin Cities (Beatty, Giere, Hellman, Waters), Rice (Longino).

> There is a gap between the instruction demanded of new hires and the philosophy taught in graduate school.

Departments for work in Continental philosophy are Penn State (Anderson, Colapietro, Conway, Duval, Foti, Golumbic, Harvey, Lingis, Russon, Sallis, Schoenbohm, Scott, Stuhr), Northwestern University (Hill, Lafont, Levin, McCarthy, McCumber), SUNY Stony Brook (Allison, Baynes, Casey, Ihde, Rawlinson, Silverman, Welton), Boston College, Boston University, Tulane University, the New School for Social Research, Emory University, Fordham, Vanderbilt University, Villanova University, the University of Memphis, Duquesne University, DePaul University, and the University of Loyola at Chicago.

In addition, there are many analytic programs whose faculty devote some attention to Continental philosophy. They are Chicago, Georgetown University, Indiana, UC-San Diego, Yale, Notre Dame, UT-Austin, and Wisconsin-Madison. Keep in mind, though, that students who are interested exclusively in Continental philosophy are likely to find the graduate programs at places like Penn State, Northwestern, and SUNY Stony Brook more congenial than the programs at places like UC-San Diego and UT-Austin. Students whose primary interests lie in Continental philosophy, and especially in postmodernism, should also seriously consider applying to programs in English and comparative literature at Yale, Duke, Cornell, and Johns Hopkins.

THE JOB MARKET

In an extraordinary understatement, a recent letter from the American Philosophical Association to prospective graduate students about current market conditions explains that "there are at present substantially more candidates seeking academic positions than there are positions available." The downturn in the market is exacerbated by the fact that there is a widening gap between the kinds of philosophy instruction now demanded of new hires—applied ethics, philosophy of feminism, African-American philosophy, non-Western philosophy—and the philosophy that is taught in the best graduate departments—naturalized theories of content, metaethics, philosophy of physics.

As a result, many recent philosophy Ph.D.'s, including those trained by the leading philosophers at the finest programs, have been unable to land tenure-track jobs teaching philosophy at the college level. It is becoming more and more common for newly-minted Ph.D.'s to move around the country taking post-doctoral fellowships, or one- and two-year jobs with heavy teaching loads, before securing a tenure-track position. Some studies predict that this situation will improve considerably in the next decade as many philosophers retire, but such predictions have been circulating since the mid-1980s, and the truth of the matter is that over the past five to ten years at least, many departments have left unfilled positions vacated by retiring faculty.

One rare piece of good news is that there has been an increase in the number of jobs advertised in every issue of the 1996–97 *Jobs for Philosophers* compared to the 1995–96 issue. The downside is that there have also been more job applicants this year than last. Those who grow frustrated with the academic market can take comfort in the fact that philosophers, because of their strong critical skills, are competitive candidates for nonacademic jobs in fields such as law, government, computer systems analysis, and business.

RESOURCES

NRC TOP TEN
Princeton
Pittsburgh
Harvard
UC-Berkeley
Pittsburgh (Program in History and
    Philosophy of Science)
UCLA
Stanford
Michigan
Cornell
MIT

ASSOCIATIONS
American Philosophical Association
(302) 831-1112

American Philosophical Society
(215) 440-3400

FURTHER READING
Brian Leiter, *The Philosophical Gourmet Report*. Updated
annually and available at no charge on the Web:
http://www.dla.utexas.edu/depts/philosophy/faculty/leiter/main.html

1995 Guide to Graduate Programs
(American Philosophical Association)

WEB ADDRESSES
Peter Suber's Guide to Philosophy on the Internet.
The most comprehensive collection of its kind
http://www.earlham.edu/suber/philinks.htm

Episteme Links
http://www.arroweb./com/philo

CONSTELLATIONS

OVERALL STRENGTH
Arizona-Tucson
Cornell
Harvard
Indiana
Michigan
NYU
Pittsburgh
Princeton
Rutgers
Stanford
UC-Berkeley
UCLA
UC-San Diego
UNC-Chapel Hill

METAPHYSICS
Brown
Cornell
NYU
Notre Dame
Princeton

EPISTEMOLOGY
Arizona-Tucson
Notre Dame
Rutgers
UC-San Diego
Washington-Seattle

PHILOSOPHY OF MIND
NYU
Princeton
Pittsburgh
Rutgers
Stanford
UC-Berkeley
UCLA
UC-San Diego

PHILOSOPHY OF LANGUAGE

NYU
Pittsburgh
Princeton
Rutgers
UC-Berkeley
UCLA

ETHICS

Arizona-Tucson
Cornell
Harvard
Michigan
NYU
Pittsburgh
Princeton
UNC-Chapel Hill

ANCIENT PHILOSOPHY

Arizona-Tucson
Cornell
Princeton
UT-Austin
Washington-Seattle

MODERN PHILOSOPHY

Michigan
Princeton
UC-Berkeley
Yale

PHILOSOPHY OF SCIENCE

Chicago
Michigan
Minnesota-
 Twin Cities
Pittsburgh
Princeton
UC-San Diego
Wisconsin-Madison

COGNITIVE SCIENCE

Arizona
Rutgers
UC-San Diego

CONTINENTAL

Boston College
Boston University
DePaul
Duquesne
Emory
Fordham
Loyola at Chicago
Memphis
New School
Northwestern
Penn State
SUNY Stony Brook
Tulane
Vanderbilt
Villanova

ANALYTIC PROGRAMS STRONG IN CONTINENTAL

Chicago
Georgetown
Indiana
Notre Dame
UC-San Diego
UT-Austin
Wisconsin-Madison
Yale

TERMINAL M.A.

Arizona State
Colgate
Houston
Missouri-St. Louis
Northern Illinois
Texas A&M
Tufts
Virginia Tech
Wisconsin-Milwaukee

CONSTELLATIONS

CHAPTER 17

RELIGION

"You can go to a university and study the practice of art. You can go to a university and study the practice of science. But if you go to a university and try to study the practice of religion, people are confused," says Kimerer La Mothe, a recent Harvard University Ph.D. in religion. While a student, La Mothe encountered many of the misconceptions that surround the field: Some assumed she was preparing for the ministry; others were certain that she was studying ancient texts. Rarely did anyone think that she was working out a position in the most controversial interdisciplinary debates of today.

Anyone harboring such doubts would do well to read La Mothe's dissertation, "The Religious Impulses of Modern American Dance: A Theological Consideration." La Mothe completed her thesis while she also maintained a busy career as a dancer and choreographer. Her dissertation weaves together Dutch phenomenology, the performance-studies theory of Emmanuel Levinas, early twentieth-century American theological debates, and the performances of Martha Graham. Although she concedes that more traditional topics are common in religion departments, La Mothe is confident that her own career prospects are strong and that her intellectual interests are in tune with the discipline:

"I came out of graduate school with a deep background in theology, art, dance, and postmodern and feminist theory. I'm very hopeful that the field is being cracked open and enriched. Almost everyone I know is doing some kind of interdisciplinary work."

"It's all because I saw *Schindler's List*," says Elsie Stern, a University of Chicago Ph.D. who just started teaching at Fordham University, by way of explaining how she came to write a dissertation about the synagogue as a site of Biblical instruction. "I was reading a lot of Midrash at the time and was struck by how the movie's postHolocaust obsession with testimony diverges from the classical Rabbinical tradition's approach to catastrophe, which is more moralistic and concerned with discerning God's response." Stern soon started researching the differences between professional and popular approaches to Biblical exegesis, specifically between that of Talmudic scholars and that of synagogue goers in Palestine in the sixth and seventh centuries. "The Bible isn't necessarily something that's stuck between two covers," offers Stern, whose research draws as much on her own faith commitments as her interest in theories of textual interpretation, which she became acquainted with as an undergraduate literature major and further cultivated at Chicago. "I always keep in my mind the image of a sixth-century woman going to the synagogue. She knows the Pentateuch in its entirety but is unfamiliar with the Prophets, because she only knows about the Bible through what she hears. To understand that woman's theology you have to understand its social context."

WHY RELIGION?

As theoretical debates in religion have become more open as well as more rigorous, the academic study of religion has also gained in stature. For nearly a century, religion departments were slighted stepchildren at most prestigious U.S. schools. But in the wake of recent challenges to scholarly notions of objectivity and neutrality, both theologians and scholars outside religion—anthropologists, literary theorists, historians, and psychologists among them—are taking part in an exciting exchange. "The joke going around here is that the religious studies program is in danger of absorbing the rest of the university," confides an instructor at DePaul University.

With its new stature has come a wider understanding of the nature of religious studies. Colleagues in other fields have finally learned that religion departments are not training grounds for the clergy. Today one can study power dynamics in nineteenth-century Shaker rituals or apply poststructuralist literary theory to the Dead Sea Scrolls. "A lot of things are up for grabs," says Dean Richard Rosengarten of Chicago. What's more, students who pursue Ph.D.'s in religion have a wide variety of relationships to their subject. Some are driven by faith, others are insistently secular. As religion professors say, you don't have to be a zebra to study zoology.

For nearly a century, religion departments were slighted stepchildren at the most prestigious U.S. schools.

That said, few scholars of religion are unmoved by the ethical and existential questions raised by their studies. Atheists and believers alike report initially being drawn to religious studies because the field touches on aspects of the human condition that other academic fields rarely face, even fields like literature and philosophy, which traditionally claim to examine the deepest questions. Some also say that academic religious studies offers a level of collegiality and ethical seriousness that other fields do not.

And religion isn't the focus of only academic attention, either. "There's obviously a very strong interest in religion in our culture right now," says Barbara DeConcini of the American Academy of Religion (AAR), the largest organization for religious studies professors. Everywhere you turn—from Bill Moyers's earnest PBS excursions through world religions to the furious debates surrounding the Christian Coalition—you can find arenas in which academic religionists are called upon to lead public debate.

Because so much ground is shifting, the choice of a graduate program that meets your particular interests is more difficult and important than ever. Should you opt for one of the field's giant programs, with its ample resources, large faculty, and reputation for stability? Or would you prefer a smaller, more intimate program, strong in a specialty, that may not offer many subfields? Would you flourish in a program tightly bound to a particular faith tradition (Catholic, Jewish, evangelical)? Or, at the other extreme, what about a public program with no seminary at all? A review of the field's history will shed light on the institutional options that await you.

HOW RELIGION HAS TAKEN SHAPE

From the founding of Harvard College in 1636 to the mid-nineteenth century, seminaries and theology were the nucleus of most private colleges in the United States. But in the decades after the Civil War, the academy's uneasy marriage of Protestant faith and Enlightenment principles began to unravel. In the course of a generation, almost all large U.S. universities embraced the German practice of favoring the needs of the academic research professor and the pursuit of *Wissenschaft* in a scientific spirit. This meant that academic publication and research, rather than the moral and religious instruction of the young, became the watchwords of the university mission. The evangelical piety of the schools' founding generations, although still respected sentimentally, no longer underwrote the curriculum. Academic theology, which made religious practice central to study and was once "the queen of the curriculum," quickly came to be regarded as an intellectual backwater, not a science at all.

This transition was marked by contradictions that endure to this day. For one, it was the liberal wing of the Protestant establishment—and not uncompromising atheists—who dislodged theology from the center of the academy. Many of the reforming advocates of the "scientific" German model were also devout, but they did not think that the new approach would be at war with religious doctrine. What's more, while graduate schools were reorganizing on the German model, a substantial number of U.S. dissertations were about topics that would fit quite well in today's religion programs. But by the 1890s, such topics came to be pursued within programs of philosophy or philology, not religion. An 1894 Harvard thesis, for instance, explored "The Yezidis, or Devil Worshippers: Their Sacred Book and Traditions." A Chicago religion professor was exaggerating only slightly when he pointed to the key turn-of-the century project as "the rewriting of Christian theology under the guiding principle of Evolution."

During the first half of the twentieth century, religion departments also varied widely in relation to particular faiths. Some were launched by secular social scientists and comparativists, while others were established by religious scholars alarmed by the rapid secularization of the academy. Programs developed eclectic strategies for handling the question of nonsectarianism. The University of Iowa's School of Religion, founded in 1924, was directed and also funded by a consortium of Jewish, Catholic, and Protestant leaders. But when Princeton University launched its department of religion in 1935, the school insisted that it have *no* link to the practice of faith, because, it argued, the mingling of practice and objective study might breed "a suspicion that has in the end driven the study of religion from an independent place in the curriculum." Nonetheless, the vast majority of doctoral work in religion centered on Christian texts and Christian theological questions.

In the early 1950s there were two defining movements within religion departments. With fascism, Stalinism, and the prospect of nuclear ruin all casting shadows over liberal philosophies and progressive teleologies, many thinkers became interested in the attempts of Paul Tillich and Reinhold Niebuhr to salvage liberalism by turning to the insights of neo-orthodox Christian theology. (Both scholars taught at Union Theological Seminary in New York City as well as at other institutions.) And the roughly fifteen schools offering Ph.D.'s in religion experienced a revival of academic theology. At roughly the same time, even social scientists who were teaching in religion departments backed away from statistics-based and functionalist accounts of religion in favor of ethical and political questions. To answer these questions, some turned to "phenomenology," a descriptive exploration "of expressions of the sacred" as they occurred in diverse religious practices. Phenomenology crystallized around the work of Mircea Eliade, the hugely influential Romanian-born scholar who taught at Chicago for many years, beginning in the late 1950s.

> Some say religion departments offer a level of collegiality and ethical seriousness that other disciplines do not.

During the 1960s, the number of graduate and undergraduate programs in religion increased dramatically. Most of the new programs offered a range of Eliadesque courses in comparative religion, which tended to stress the universality and commonality of humanity's religious impulses and to downplay both the study of religious conflict and the shrinking congregations of the old-line sects. Questions about a religion's local impact were left to sociologists who concentrated on religion's role in maintaining cultural cohesion, a project that prompted the political theorist Michael Harrington to comment, "There is an enormous irony in the fact that God is in his heaven in the social sciences—even as he seems to be vanishing from the altars."

Despite Eliade's attention to the sacred, the discipline of religion ended up consolidating itself in the 1960s on secular ground. There were several reasons for this. For one, the 1963 Supreme Court decision *Abingdon Township School District* v. *Schempp* banned expressive devotional studies in public schools, though it explicitly left the door open for the study of religion. This allowed state-funded religion departments to establish themselves on solid constitutional footing and further tipped the field away from the humanities and toward the social sciences. The balance was thrown even more toward the social sciences in 1964, when the fifty-five-year-old National Association of Bible Instructors voted to change its name to the American Academy of Religion (AAR). From this point on, religious studies was a professionalized field—several steps removed from divinity programs that had preparing the clergy as their mission.

Tillich's and Ricoeur's attempts to salvage liberalism countered the apocalyptic visions of the 1950s.

Claude Welch, a past president of the AAR, published *Graduate Education in Religion* in the 1970s, the first (and, so far, the only) thorough survey of the field. Although his data were heavily slanted toward the East coast—interviews on the West coast "were not carried through because of the campus disruptions"— many of Welch's insights were startlingly prescient. He projected that the annual number of new Ph.D.'s in religion would rise from 225 in 1970 to 475 in 1990, which turned out to be almost exactly correct. More importantly, he saw that the field was about to enter a period of conceptual uncertainty: Research would shift from the concerns of particular denominations to "regional, ethnic, and political patterns." Welch hypothesized that as religious studies interacted more fruitfully with other fields, it would gain stature but lose coherence, as some scholars' interests spiraled into areas that have "at best an oblique relation to religious studies." Academic theology might tend to drift "through the philosophy of religion into philosophical investigations that no longer have any concern with theological or religious questions."

If Welch had concerns about how religious studies might fare as it broadened its reach, he couldn't have anticipated how, over the last quarter century, religious studies has cast light into the research programs of other disciplines. In the 1970s, the late theologian and philosopher Paul Ricoeur was a central figure in the postmodernist turn throughout the humanities. Ronald Grimes, of Wilfrid Laurier University in Ontario, and other theorists of ritual have influenced the discipline of anthropology. Women's studies programs draw on the work of Emory University's Rebecca Chopp and other feminist theologians. Political philosophers pay close attention to the work of Jean Bethke Elshtain of Chicago's divinity school. Secular ethicists in philosophy departments follow the work of Princeton's Robert Wuthnow.

Not everyone is sanguine about this turn of events. Skeptics have come to view interdisciplinarity as a symptom of a disciplinary identity crisis. One scholar confirms Welch's forecast, "After the early 1970s, the age of the giants was over. The result has been a real loss in coherence." Such a lament cannot be dismissed as the grumblings of the old guard, for the loss of a distinctive and unified mission has led some departments to fear for their lives. In 1993, for instance, cost-conscious deans at the University of Pennsylvania proposed eliminating the school's eight-year-old religious studies program. They thought the program lacked an identifiable core, and planned to disband the department and relocate its professors to their seemingly rightful places in history, anthropology, and sociology. The program was spared thanks to a spirited campaign by alumni and the AAR, but elsewhere the anxiety remains. "When I taught at Vassar," says Columbia University's Mary McGee, "there was a constant fear, every time a new dean came in, that they'd dissolve us. Sometimes people had no clue. They were sure that we were training people for the ministry."

Welch worried about the drift of religious studies into fields of philosophy that no longer had any relationship to religious questions.

Conversations with religious studies skeptics who worry that the field has never quite gotten its act together always seem to return to the issue of the field's Christian legacy. Some say that the Protestant divinity schools, which were the field's first home, are a burden to escape. This complaint takes two forms. First, many scholars contend that the field has failed to become truly pluralistic. Simply grafting scholars of Buddhism or Islam onto existing departments won't do the trick, since the divinity school model is intellectually Christian-biased. Thus Jacob Neusner of The University of South Florida at Tampa, one of the founders of contemporary Judaic studies, argues that his field has been heavily shaped not by the traditional focus of scholarly Judaism as it applies to ethics and questions of everyday religious practice, but by a focus on "faith and matters of propositional belief" that is built into the Protestant tradition of many departments.

The second complaint, raised by a small number of social scientists in the field, is that the seminary tradition has the field overly preoccupied by private experience. Religious studies may have become admirably pluralistic, but most of its practitioners still fail the test of authentic academic study. They cling to fuzzy and unfalsifiable notions, such as a universal experience of "the sacred," yet fail to recognize how their own faith commitments might bias their work. According to these scholars, religious studies must banish theology to the divinity schools and concentrate on verifiable science. The most extreme version of this complaint is raised by the forty-member fringe group in the North American Association for the Study of Religion (NAASR), founded in 1985 by the University of Toronto's Donald Wiebe, who is known for a vehement positivist stance unusual in the discipline.

Alongside attempts to remove the sacred from the center of the discipline is a less-remarked-upon shift: the supplanting of the text by ritual. According to many younger scholars—particularly those in the social sciences—religious studies too often ties itself in knots analyzing sacred writings. It is time, they argue, to pay serious attention to religion's other dimensions—to ritual, praxis, and "performance." As a scholar of Hindu women's rituals insists, "Women aren't in the texts; women didn't write the texts; for most people, religion is not texts."

The tension between text and ritual is nothing new, of course. As Mary Gerhart of Hobart and William Smith Colleges recently quipped, "The death of Stephen (c. 36 B.C.E.) as recorded in Acts could be attributed to a dispute on the primacy of ritual over doctrine." The new subfield of "ritual studies" merely marks the latest revival of interest in how text and various types of religious praxis work together. Indeed, in some ways "ritual studies" is exactly what the field's late nineteenth-century pioneers—Max Müller, E.B. Tylor, and J.G. Frazer, who adduced wildly ambitious theories of religion and civilization from studies of animistic rituals—had intended it to be. But bolstered by cultural and methodological pluralism, ritual studies also offers scholars the opportunity to address questions that they believe their predecessors botched: It does not lose sight of the particularity of religious practices people perform in certain places, and it is reluctant to extrapolate general theories from these local rituals.

> The study of ritual, not just the study of texts, may move to the center of the discipline.

For the new generation of ritual theorists such as Catherine Bell of Santa Clara University, Michael B. Aune of the Graduate Theological Union at the University of California at Berkeley, and Volney

Gay of Vanderbilt University, even the sophisticated work of Eliade and his generation was not particular enough. They prefer the mode of "thick description" championed by cultural anthropologist Clifford Geertz of the Institute for Advanced Studies in Princeton, New Jersey, which allows one to get at the viscera of religious experience without strictly confining oneself to textual sources or facile functionalist frameworks. When they examine, say, Murrinh-patha funeral practices or hymn singing among midwestern Presbyterians, they begin with exhaustive explorations of the ritual's social, historical, and liturgical contexts. Only then do they venture with extreme caution to propose psychological or sociological explanations.

The new generation of ritual theorists prefer the mode of "thick description" championed in symbolic anthropology.

The *Journal of Ritual Studies*, founded in 1987 at the University of Pittsburgh, has become increasingly influential, and a recent anthology, *Religious and Social Ritual: Interdisciplinary Explorations*, with articles covering topics from the investiture ceremony for a Javanese sultan to a study of a patient's hospitalization for surgery as a "rite of passage," suggests why religionists describe ritual studies as one of the field's most heartening innovations, even though it is still in its infancy. Of the 217 dissertations categorized by the Council on Graduate Studies in Religion in 1992, only eight were placed under the heading "Ritual, Cult, Worship." "The acceptability of this stuff still varies by program," says Edmund Gilday, a historian of Buddhist ritual teaching at Grinnell College. "In the academy as a whole, there's still very little attention paid to performance. To this day, these themes are rarely addressed in the *Journal of the American Academy of Religion.*"

What is perhaps most remarkable about the turn toward ritual studies is that it's not the exclusive purview of social scientists of religion. Some theologians are renouncing excessive attention to words alone. Since 1980, the "postliberal" school of academic theology has placed ritual and praxis at the center of its projects. Especially prominent at Duke University, Stanford University, and Yale University, postliberal scholars, like some cultural anthropologists, insist that religion cannot be understood by studying only texts. A religion is not like a philosophical system; it is more like a culture, like a language. Yale's George Lindbeck writes, "Religion cannot be pictured as primarily a matter of deliberate choosing to believe or follow explicitly known propositions or directives. Rather, to become religious, no less than to become culturally or linguistically competent, is to interiorize a set of skills by practice and training. One learns how to feel, act, and think in conformity with a religious tradition that is, in its inner structure, far richer and more subtle than can be explicitly articulated."

> Some argue that to understand religion is not like understanding a philosophical system, but like studying a culture.

Liberation theology, the powerful combination of theology, religious practice, political thought, and textual study exemplified by radical Latin American Catholicism, is also attracting increasing attention. In the last ten years, a few activists and academics have attempted to transplant the methods and insights of liberation theology to religious communities in the United States. While there are no institutions with a highly visible cohort of liberation theologists, the movement has had an effect on theological thinking across the discipline. Roberto Goizueta, a professor at Loyola University in Chicago, spent much of the 1980s working in "base communities" in El Salvador. Today his studies center on a Latino parish in Chicago. When he describes this work to colleagues, many assume that he is researching the congregation as a social scientist would. But Goizueta is at pains to insist the contrary. "I do this work as a theologian. Through my participation in this community's worship I try to begin to articulate: What are the theological insights evident in this lived life?" Goizueta studies, for example, how distinctly Catholic rituals, which were in the past downplayed by parishes in order to gain acceptance within a largely Protestant society, are now returning as the church and community becomes more Latino.

WHAT'S NEXT

Religion programs lie across a continuum: At one end are public universities, where the constitutional prohibition against teaching religion tends to mean that no theology is offered at all. A few paradigmatic public university schools without theology are the University of California at Santa Barbara, Indiana University, and the University of Virginia. At the other end are institutions with a strong connection to a particular faith—Catholic, Jewish, evangelical, and others. Strong programs on this model, closely tied to faith traditions, are at Marquette

University, Jewish Theological Seminary, and Baylor University. In these programs, Ph.D. students are often a minority among a larger group of students who are preparing for divinity degrees.

The close connections at most schools between Ph.D. programs and divinity schools cannot be overemphasized because it makes the graduate study of religion very different from undergraduate study. Says William S. Green of the University of Rochester, "About half of graduate faculty have no contact with undergraduates." So you'll have to talk to lots of students and faculty to make sure that the elements of religion that interested you as an undergraduate will still be important once you enter a particular graduate school.

But most of the best-regarded programs fall between the extremes of no-theology and connection to a faith commitment, though structural variations are many. Chicago, for example, makes a point of unifying all religion students under one roof; Ph.D. students are enrolled in the divinity school itself. "If you're going to teach religion, you need to know how you stand on the major religious questions," says Dean of Students Richard Rosengarten. "You need to have wrestled with theology. Likewise, divinity students need a full exposure to debates within religious studies. They need to be aware of all the intellectual tools and conflicts."

Faculty and administrators both report that in the current job climate, they would prefer to admit students who clearly know what they're getting into. Consequently, Ph.D. programs are increasingly interested in students who have already earned either an M.A., a Master of Theological Studies, or a Master of Divinity degree. If you plan to earn such a degree just to test the waters of grad school, take into account that an M.A. is not a useful credential for university teaching. It is, however, respected by religious organizations and counseling programs geared to the members of faith communities.

Given today's job market, faculty are anxious to admit only those students who have already earned a master's.

But with or without a master's, your first year will typically involve some form of required core coursework that centers on the study of religious texts. At Princeton there is one, but only one, core course required for everyone, and UC-Santa Barbara requires two. At departments like Duke, the core touches on Christianity, Islam, and Judaism. Other institutions, such as Chicago, are much more concerned with educating the majority of their students in a particular canon and insist on more required courses. There are pros and cons to both impulses. A recent Harvard graduate says: "If theology is going to respond to critical theory effectively, it needs to be well-grounded in its own classics. The Chicago system is smart; no course at Harvard explicitly leads you through that." Most programs also offer a course in methodology, although the degree of openness to contemporary social, literary, and linguistic theory varies greatly from department to department. Again, talk to current students and faculty about that issue.

> Talk to a lot of faculty and students to make sure that what interested you about religion in college will still be part of grad school.

Although pursuing religious studies now does not necessarily entail poring over fragments of crumbling scrolls, most departments still require students to pass at least one foreign language exam in order to use the scholarship of the past. French, German, and Hebrew are common requirements, but of course in fields that concern non-Western regions other languages come into play. Elizabeth Castelli of Barnard College says it is common for students to soar into graduate religion programs on the enthusiasms of their latter years in college only to suddenly go into a tailspin when they realize, "Oh, my God—I have to learn Sanskrit to get my degree." Foreseeing these hurdles well in advance is wise. After languages are mastered, oral qualifying exams are generally taken in the fifth or sixth semester before preparing to write your dissertation, as in most other disciplines.

During your second year, you'll have begun to narrow your concentration, at which point you'll need to assemble a dissertation committee. As religion programs establish fuller ties with various interdisciplinary programs, this process can sometimes be a knotty one. The Princeton catalog, for example, urges Ph.D. candidates in religion to consider hooking up with "programs in East Asian Studies, Late Antiquity, Latin American Studies, Near Eastern Studies, and Political Philosophy, as well as recently established centers like that directed to the study of American Religions or that directed to Human Values."

As this advice suggests, religion programs are not always the best places to undertake the study of religions other than Judaism and Christianity. Taking an interdisciplinary approach within a language, area studies, or international affairs program may be a better option. William S. Green says that if you are interested in Islam, you might do best to study it in a Near Eastern Studies program rather than a religion department. (NYU has the best Near East Studies program in the United States.) Faculty and students report that the strongest programs in Buddhism are at Virginia, Michigan, and Columbia. The Graduate Theological Union, a consortium of denominational schools and independent research centers associated with UC-Berkeley, and UC-Santa Barbara are the best places to study Native American religions.

A variety of universities and independent seminaries offer doctorates in theology, or Th.D.'s, in addition to Ph.D.'s. These degrees are often preferred by those preparing for the ministry, and they generally have fewer required courses and less stringent language requirements than the Ph.D. (An important exception to this is Th.D. programs associated with Catholic institutions, which may be very rigorous indeed.) If one wishes to find academic employment with a Th.D. outside of a divinity school, the going will be hard. Though there is a lingering perception that Th.D. students tend to do research in the more conservative fields of religious studies, such as Judeo-Christian liturgical studies, it's best to investigate programs on a case-by-case basis. The Association of Theological Schools in the U.S. and Canada can provide information on the accreditation status of departments, which, along with conversations with faculty, will give you an idea of the purposes of particular programs. The largest U.S. Th.D. programs are at the Graduate Theological Union at UC-Berkeley, the General Theological Seminary in New York City, Emory, Boston University School of Theology, and Harvard. The largest programs in Canada are the University of St. Michael's and Wycliffe College, both in Toronto.

> Research into the Bible still makes up the lion's share of what is studied. Be sure just how open departments are to new research.

Those who look to the National Research Council rankings of Ph.D. programs in religion should do so with extreme caution. As the NRC prepared to conduct its first-ever evaluation of doctoral programs in religion in 1995, the NAASR (together with the Council on Graduate Studies in Religion) convinced the NRC to adopt highly controversial criteria. Only programs that generate a threshold number of Ph.D.'s, as opposed to theology or biblical studies degrees, were included. When the dust settled, fully thirty-three of the seventy-one U.S. religion programs had been excluded. (At least two prominent programs, Yale and the Graduate Theological Union, were left out because of paperwork problems, not due to the criteria.) Any and all rankings are incomplete and explain neither the missions nor the traditions of particular programs—nor the research interests of faculty there.

Top-ranked programs rarely identify themselves exclusively with only one research specialty or method: Departments tend to contain a diverse group of scholars and methodologies. There are a few places, however, associated with the movements described above. If ritual studies interests you, ask careful questions of a prospective school—even in large programs it may be difficult to find a mentor with serious experience in the study of performance. Ritual studies seems best established at Harvard, UC-Santa Barbara, and the Graduate Theological Union at UC-Berkeley. If you are most intrigued by the intersection of religion and U.S. history and culture, Princeton and Indiana are top choices. Virginia, Chicago, and Vanderbilt are strong in the study of ethics.

Teaching assistantships are easy to come by in some programs (at Brown University and Princeton, they're guaranteed), but difficult to secure at others. Because teaching experience is increasingly important for first-time job seekers, more and more new Ph.D.'s are accepting one-year appointments for the sake of gaining experience (and of course because long-term jobs are scarce). "In many senses, these one-year appointments are very helpful. But I wake up some mornings and ask: Am I being exploited or am I being empowered?" says a recent Ph.D. from a prominent research university.

As scholars throughout the humanities and social sciences are expected to cover more and more ground in the leaner universities of the 1990s, religion scholars must cultivate the breadth and flexibility necessary to teach undergraduate courses. "I was once the one historian of religion in a six-person department," recalls Mary Gerhart, "My graduate specialty was medieval Hinduism, but there was a sense that I ought to be able to teach everything."

In most fields, graduate programs tend to set the research agenda. But as a recent survey of religious studies put it, "Graduate programs are said to be 'out of sync' with the major developments in the field in the past three decades, most of which have emerged and been nurtured in undergraduate programs." One scholar is quick to agree: too many graduate programs, she argues, haven't come to terms with newer subfields and with the interests of students in growing undergraduate programs. Undergrads are fascinated by Buddhism, Hinduism, and Native American religions, and religion departments were among the first in the humanities to undertake serious multicultural study. There is one good result of this problem, however. Unlike the usual situation in other disciplines, new grad students may have the chance to do exciting teaching in introductory courses.

Some scholars, however, warn that undertaking graduate education in religion is even more of a gamble than it is in other humanities fields. Mark Taylor, who has taught in the undergraduate program at Williams College for many years, offered this assessment in the AAR's *Journal* in 1994: "There is no other field in which graduate education is more inadequate than in the study of religion. Graduate programs simply have not kept up with developments in other disciplines and are not preparing students in ways that enable them to become creative and productive teachers and scholars. Painful though it is to admit, departments are often getting what they deserve when the budgetary ax falls."

> Religion programs may not necessarily be the best place to study religions other than Judaism and Christianity.

The small size of the field and the concentration of institutions producing its new faculty also contribute to religion's vulnerability. Of the seventy-one North American Ph.D. programs in religion, just six schools—Chicago, Harvard, Yale, Vanderbilt, Princeton, and Duke—generate nearly a quarter of all Ph.D.'s. This lopsided profile, argues Rochester professor William S. Green, leaves the graduate study of religion especially susceptible to clubbiness and academic fads. But a recent Chicago Ph.D. points out that for fledgling alumni on the job market, clubbiness has virtues too: "Chicago and Harvard churn out so many people—they've infiltrated the whole academy. Chicago has a very energetic network throughout the country."

THE JOB MARKET

Religionists know as well as anyone how excruciating the academic job market can be. When candidates interview at table after table in the airplane-hangar-like auditorium of the AAR's annual convention in November, they may recall Theology 101 debates about the meaning and purpose of suffering. As of 1993, the last year for which statistics are available, at the 34 religion departments that belong to the Council of Graduate Studies, only 36 percent of Ph.D.'s were finding full-time tenure-track academic jobs within one year. One scholar who bounced around for eight years before finding a tenure-track position says, "Now that it's all over, people say to me, 'You had such courage.' But while it was happening, people wouldn't quite make eye contact with me."

Many say that religious studies within Asian studies is booming, as universities are continuing to expand these programs with suitable religion Ph.D.'s. Judaic and Islamic studies programs are also growing. But if Christianity is your topic, and especially if you want to use traditional methods, expect an extremely tight market. At recent AAR meetings, the ratio of applicants to available positions in "Biblical and Related Studies" has approached ten to one.

Again, remember that undergraduate programs go shopping for candidates who can teach broadly. In Asian studies especially, young scholars are sometimes startled to realize how many disparate religious traditions they are expected to have mastered. One recent job announcement reads: "The successful applicant should be able to teach introductory courses in all, and undergraduate courses in two or more, of South Asian, East Asian, and Japanese religions including methodologies in the History of Religions."

RESOURCES

NRC TOP TEN
Chicago
Harvard
Princeton
Duke
Emory
Virginia
Vanderbilt
Princeton
  Theological
  Seminary
UC-Santa
  Barbara
Jewish
  Theological
  Seminary

ASSOCIATIONS
American Academy of Religion
(404) 727-7920

North American Association
  for the Study of Religion
(408) 459-2696

JOURNALS
Method and Theory in the Study of Religion

WEB SITES
Epoche—UC-Santa Barbara's Graduate Student Journal for the Study of Religion
http://www.ucsbuxa.ucsb.edu/rgstd/resource/epoche.html

Religious Studies Resources on the Internet
http://www.mcgill.ca/religion/subject/html

"The most marketable people will be generalists in the best sense of the word," says a dean. "Religion is an inherently interdisciplinary field—potentially someone with a religion Ph.D. is able to do a number of things in academia: sociology, history, cultural studies. Many religion Ph.D.'s really have mastered several disciplines. The question is: Will academia recognize this?"

The world outside of the academy offers different kinds of opportunities. Religion Ph.D.'s find work in publishing, research, and, of course, working for religious institutions. As AAR executive director DeConcini says, "If you're a philosophy Ph.D., you can't hang a sign on your shingle and say you want to be a philosopher. But in religion, there are hundreds of churches and other faith-based organizations looking for committed people with expertise." Business and government agencies, too, are increasingly turning to academic experts to help ameliorate their acute, and sometimes hazardous, ignorance of the range of religious experience. The Justice Department, for example, has acknowledged that its agencies might have been able to avoid the 1993 Waco siege if they'd bothered to consult with more scholars of new religions.

CONSTELLATIONS

RITUAL STUDIES
Graduate Theological Union at UC-Berkeley
Harvard
UC-Santa Barbara

RELIGION AND U.S. HISTORY
Chicago
Indiana
Princeton

ETHICS
Chicago
Vanderbilt
Virginia

ISLAMIC STUDIES
NYU

BUDDHISM
Michigan
Stanford

NATIVE AMERICAN RELIGIONS
Graduate Theological Union at UC-Berkeley
UC-Santa Barbara

TH.D. PROGRAMS
Boston University School of Theology
Emory
General Theological Seminary in New York City
Graduate Theological Union at UC-Berkeley
Harvard
University of St. Michael's (Canada)
Wycliffe College (Canada)

CHAPTER 18

WOMEN'S STUDIES

Many students enter women's studies programs to develop skills that will enable them to improve women's lives. Consider the ambitions of Insook Kwon, who in 1995 entered the Ph.D. program in women's studies at Clark University after earning an undergraduate degree in South Korea and an M.A. at Rutgers University. While living in South Korea, Kwon was incarcerated for helping women textile workers unionize. She was the first woman to win a suit against the South Korean government for the sexual torture she endured in prison. With the money awarded her by the court, she founded the Labor Human Rights Center in Seoul, South Korea. After completing her Ph.D., Kwon plans to return to South Korea and augment her academic research on Korean women with hands-on work in the women's movement.

Other women's studies students focus on literature and the arts, many of them studying the cultural construction of gender in a range of "texts"—literary, legal, scientific, or mass media. Patti Duncan, a doctoral student at Emory University, is at work on a dissertation that examines how Asian-American women writers—Theresa Hak Kyung Cha, Mary Paik Lee, and Anchee Min, among others—use silences to complicate the simplistic histories of Asian-

American culture often taught in the United States. Duncan's thesis integrates Asian-American studies, history, literature, philosophy, postcolonial theory, and feminist theory. Like many women's studies students, she will seek a university teaching job after completing her Ph.D., but she also plans to remain politically active by working with Asian-Pacific communities, immigrants' rights groups, and lesbian, gay, and bisexual organizations.

WHY WOMEN'S STUDIES?

Outside observers do not always know what to make of a field that supports the work of students like Kwon and Duncan who aspire to be both scholars and activists. The National Women's Studies Association, founded in 1977, states in its constitution that women's studies refuses to accept sterile divisions between the academy and society, and that the field is designed to help women bring an end to all manner of discrimination.

The sheer variety of scholarship and activism taking place within women's studies makes the field difficult to categorize. As a doctoral-level academic research discipline, women's studies is the youngest in this book. The first undergraduate for-credit classes in the discipline were offered at San Diego State University in 1969. Now, nearly thirty years later, there are women's studies programs at more than 900 colleges and universities and 110 graduate programs in the country—from master's programs, to minors and concentrations embedded within traditional disciplines, to freestanding interdisciplinary Ph.D. programs at Clark and Emory (both of which were established in the early 1990s), to several Ph.D. programs currently in the works. Even so, the first Ph.D.'s in the field weren't awarded until 1995.

What's more, while other fields, like English, once had a well-defined mission and curriculum, women's studies has never had a single, prevailing mandate and is still debating whether it should. Women's studies scholars are always reassessing their topics, methods, and practices, and so the field is one of the most self-conscious and pluralistic of academic disciplines. From the outset, women of color, lesbians, and low-income women have roundly criticized the discipline for making pronouncements about women's lives based on the experiences of Euro-American, heterosexual, economically secure women. As a result of these and other challenges, the field is always undergoing self-scrutiny. Greater attention is placed on recognizing the *interdependence* of gender, race, class, and sexuality than on acquiring a traditional body of knowledge.

While as a research field women's studies is almost brand-new, feminist theory is not. In the field's M.A. and joint Ph.D. programs, feminist theory is thriving and highly visible. It is not, however, the sole focus of the discipline. In nearly every other discipline, graduate students learn to apply theoretical and methodological techniques to the general knowledge they acquired as undergraduates. In women's studies, however, students don't just apply theory to questions they have already studied as intellectual issues but are also encouraged to view their past activist projects through the lens of theory. More than other disciplines, undergraduate women's studies programs tend to have close ties to activism—to counseling centers and projects on labor, education, sexuality, and community welfare—both inside and outside the university community. Graduate women's studies programs build on such ties, and for some students it is an adjustment to study—as an academic research issue—activist work in which they have been deeply involved. Yet it is precisely the dynamic relationship between the theoretical and the practical that defines this discipline.

HOW WOMEN'S STUDIES HAS TAKEN SHAPE

Women's studies emerged in part from a general push toward academic inclusion supported by the adult education and equal opportunity movements of the 1950s and early 1960s. The American Council for Education, for instance, established its Commission on Educational Opportunities for Women in 1953. These efforts to increase women's educational opportunities and broaden knowledge about women's lives, history, and capacities all prepared the ground for the revolutionary changes of the 1970s—the critical decade for the growth of women's studies.

In fact, women's studies in the United States was one of many offshoots of the protest movements of the 1960s—civil rights, the New Left, student activism more generally, black power, and, of course, the feminist movement. Because the lines between these movements were often blurry, it is no surprise that some of the early feminist manifestos came from female members of Students for a Democratic Society (SDS), who argued that to be effective in SDS's larger revolutionary struggle, they must first fight for their own liberation. Female SDS members set up one of the first women's studies courses at the New Orleans Free School in 1966. The Free University of Seattle, founded by students at the University of Washington, established one of the earliest courses in women's history in 1965. The general push in the 1960s to establish free schools and to provide nontraditional students with educational opportunities was a key precedent for women's studies and helped to link the discipline with political activism.

> Women's studies in the United States was one of many offshoots of the protest movements of the 1960s.

Meanwhile, many women academics were coming under the influence of a new women's liberation movement. These scholars found that they shared experiences of marginalization in their respective fields: either as women or as researchers into women's issues, regardless of their discipline. Sociologist Alice Rossi, professor emeritus at the University of Massachusetts at Amherst, for example, received her Ph.D. in 1957 but could not find an academic position until 1969. That year, Rossi and several female colleagues who faced similar problems founded the Women's Caucus of the American Sociological Association. Other women activists took up academic careers to advance feminist goals. Sara Evans, now a prominent historian of U.S. women at the University of Minnesota at Twin Cities, is an example. As an undergraduate, she studied with one of the few professors then specializing in women's history. After activist work in the Chicago women's liberation movement, she began graduate school in 1969 to help put women's history on the map as an academic research subject.

By 1969 several fledgling women's studies programs had received administrative approval, one of the first being at San Francisco State University. The discipline slowly began to take root, though not at the most elite and high-profile institutions (the University of Pennsylvania and Rutgers University being two of the notable exceptions). By 1977, when the National Women's Studies Association was founded, there were 276 formal programs. This figure did not include every college or university that offered a few women's studies courses—a much higher number. By 1980 there were 332 well-established programs. Ten years later, the 1990 *NWSA Directory of*

Women's Studies Programs, Women's Centers and Women's Research Centers listed 621 programs, with 102 of them offering graduate work in women's studies (minors, concentrations, degrees). Beverly Guy-Sheftall's 1992 Ford Foundation report on the status of the discipline puts the count at more than 900 undergraduate programs.

During the 1970s, women's studies scholars put much of their energy into establishing their field's academic legitimacy—winning administrative support within universities, locating hard-to-find materials about women's lives for their courses, and conducting original research. As with many maverick projects, a great deal of progress was made on shoestring budgets, thanks largely to the enthusiasm, devotion, and hard work of the discipline's founding scholars.

Once a critical mass of feminist scholars and programs had established itself in the academy, by the early 1980s, women's studies emerged as a discipline of tremendous pluralism but also one in which two broad aims of scholarship could be identified. One objective is to transform our understanding of what knowledge is and how it is produced and reinforced. Although they've approached these subjects from different vantage points, philosopher Sandra Harding of the University of California at Santa Cruz, and sociologist Patricia Hill-Collins of the University of Cincinnati, for example, both point to alternative forms of being and knowing, emphasizing the role of subjectivity, emotions, and experience in the generation of knowledge.

> Initially, women's studies scholars put much of their energy into establishing their field's academic legitimacy.

Other feminist scholars, often with more direct ties to political reform and activism, focus much of their work on challenging conventional methods of research. They explore the issues surrounding quantitative approaches, question the hierarchical power relationships between researcher and researched, and propose techniques for incorporating process, conflict, and contradiction into their methods. In *Translated Woman: Crossing the Border with Esperanza's Story* (1993), for example, University of Michigan anthropologist Ruth Behar includes an economic and political analysis of her relationship with her subject, a poor Mexican market woman. In *Compelled to Crime: The Gender Entrapment of Battered Black Women* (1995), sociologist Beth Richie, a longtime activist against domestic violence in African-American communities, offers her analysis of incarcerated women who have been battered or sexually abused as an alternative to simpler cause-and-effect approaches to understanding crime.

Whether a project is anchored in scholarship or activism, women's studies tends to view it on multiple levels—examining its founding assumptions, its place in the research programs of the university and general society, and its possible social ramifications. Does the research incorporate individual experience? Is it too closely confined to the researcher's perspective or too abstracted from lived experience? How well has the researcher used the resources of other social science and humanities disciplines? Does the project transcend the concerns of a single group of women? Should it? Does the research promise to aid social progress? Whose interests are served by the research? Are the results quantifiable? Do they contribute to theoretical debates? Can they be persuasive in policy debates inside and outside the academy?

At the moment, a major issue in the field is whether or not women's studies can, or should, adopt a more international perspective. Feminist movements in non-Western countries have been dismissed in the U.S. as not really feminist—sometimes because scholars are not always aware of local and worldwide issues concerning statehood, class, racial subordination, and colonialism. The work of scholars Chandra T. Mohanty, Marnia Lazreg, Cynthia Enloe, and Partha Chatterjee, among others, calls for an international awareness that does not presume "feminism" is defined by a Euro-American, middle-class perspective.

> Women's studies asks whether scholarly research can, or should, be useful to policy debates outside the academy.

Another topic of debate is the recent shift from the study of women to the study of gender. Advocates of gender studies claim that the dearth of scholarship on masculinity in women's studies is detrimental to the field because gender cannot be understood by examining femininity alone. Critics consider gender analysis a backlash against feminism, a ploy to remove women's lives as legitimate subjects for research. The rhetoric of gender, they maintain, is increasingly used in a neutral fashion that avoids questions of power, privilege, and women's subordination. To study gender, they fear, would be to strip women's studies of politics. "This conversation goes on at most women's studies departments and has for a long time," says Ruth Perry, of the women's studies department at the Massachusetts Institute of Technology, who writes often about the history of the discipline. "It is not really between two deeply divided factions, but about the best strategies for the field, especially for researchers working on gender in new ways."

The place of postmodern theory within women's studies is another vexed issue. In many disciplines, especially in the humanities, the postmodern rejection of "grand" or hegemonic theory was part of a general challenge to intellectual orthodoxy—as when deconstruction proposed that there was no such thing as "the author." In women's studies, the question is how to combine the field's criticisms of patriarchy with postmodern challenges to humanist ideals. Is the attempt to understand the nature of inequality undermined by postmodern arguments? Should the attempt to produce generalizable forms of knowledge be abandoned? Are concepts such as patriarchy useful when they mean different things to different women in different circumstances?

Women's studies scholars have already begun to address these questions. Jane Flax of UC-Berkeley has detailed the ways in which women's studies and postmodernism share common ground in books such as *Disputed Subjects: Essays on Psychoanalysis, Politics, and Philosophy* (1993). Both feminists and postmodernists, Flax claims, criticize the universalist assumptions of theorists like Marx and Freud. (Feminists argue against their gender blindness; postmodernists argue against their rationalism and essentialism. Some scholars argue against both.) Feminism and postmodernism emphasize cultural construction, the notion that gender roles and other social relations are not natural and static but historically and culturally contingent. Both challenge notions of fixed identity, chart the manipulative tendencies of the mass media, and study information technology. And both grapple with the relations between theory and analytic thought, on the one hand, and the benefits and risks of applying social, cultural, and political research conclusions outside the academy, on the other.

> Some scholars fear that the study of gender will strip women's studies of politics.

Yet feminism itself is not immune to criticism from postmodernists. Postmodern theorists can claim that feminist theory is outmoded because women's studies is based on the premise of a universal subject, "woman." Postmodernism, then, can be inimical to the women's studies mission of sociopolitical change. *Feminism/Postmodernism*, a 1989 collection edited by historian Linda J. Nicholson, of SUNY

Albany, and *Feminists Theorize the Political*, a 1992 anthology edited by philosopher Judith Butler of UC–Berkeley and historian Joan Scott of the Institute for Advanced Study in Princeton, New Jersey, offer various perspectives on the implications of postmodernism for feminism.

Can postmodern theory provide useful insights into how to pursue liberating projects sustained by analyses of male power, privilege, and oppression? If conceptualizing, analyzing, and theorizing inequality in universal terms is no longer possible, how are feminists to know where to channel political activity and what form their politics must take?

> Because Ph.D. programs are relatively young and small, money tends to be tight.

As in all other fields, the intellectual debates in women's studies are linked in complex ways to the available sources of institutional support. Because Ph.D. programs in women's studies are relatively young and small, money tends to be tight, and new students may feel the pinch even at a secure and growing department. In the early days of the field, the Ford, Carnegie, Rockefeller, Rockefeller Brothers, Mellon, Helena Rubenstein, Russell Sage, Exxon, and Lilly Foundations contributed generously to the field. This start-up money was part of an effort in the 1970s to counter the discriminations of the past, to kick off research, and to provide initial support for scholars doing work in what would come to be called identity politics.

Many of these philanthropic sources have continued to play a role in the growth and legitimization of women's studies. Undoubtedly, the single most active private funder of women's studies–related projects has been the Ford Foundation. From 1972 to 1986, Ford funneled more than $70 million into women's studies, and the foundation has continued to lead other donors in both the number and the total annual amount of awards. By the early 1990s, analysts had identified four distinct types of women's studies funding at Ford: individual research fellowships, research grants to campus-based and independent centers, grants for related activities such as publishing and national organizations, and awards to programs and centers that support minority women's studies. More recently, women's studies projects in developing nations, as well as U.S.-based research on Third World women, have received funding from other major foundations, including the Carnegie Corporation and the John D. and Catherine T. MacArthur Foundation.

The effects of this funding history cannot be overestimated. Foundations were generous with money in order to "get the word out." And the Fund for the Improvement of Postsecondary Education, the National Institute of Education, and the Women's Educational Equity Act (all operated under the Department of Education) supported research about women throughout the 1970s, as did the National Endowment for the Humanities and the National Science Foundation.

But many successful programs that depended on federal support were left high and dry during and after the Reagan–Bush era. A 1985 study concluded that during the period 1980–1984, while federal moneys allocated to all types of research rose almost eighty percent, funding for research on women either declined or disappeared entirely from the eight federal programs and departments primarily involved in generating the funds. The loss of these critical funds has not been offset by subsequent increases in support from private foundations. Today, the vast majority of women's studies programs receive *no* outside moneys, and only four percent of programs reporting in a 1985 Ford Foundation report relied on grants for more than one quarter of their budget.

The dispersal of existing funds has by no means been predictable, and new students should carefully investigate the flow of funds to particular departments. In general, programs with an international component, such as close connections to an area studies or an international affairs program elsewhere in the university, have managed to do well, even in the academic funding crunch. Nevertheless, partly because so much work is done collaboratively and in a close community, the financial hardships in women's studies— like the windfalls—tend to be shared by the whole program.

On balance there is plenty of good news, not the least of which is the steady growth in the number of undergraduate programs in the field. Some state governments have also supported feminist research. In 1986, for instance, New Jersey's Department of Higher Education funded a $1.2 million gender–integration project. The most far-reaching effort of its kind at that time, it sought to integrate issues of "women and gender, race/ethnicity, class, and sexuality" into the curricula of all two- and four-year public and private colleges in the state. Another positive trend has been the increase in the number of universities that have initiated large-scale curriculum–integration efforts of their own.

> Many successful programs were left high and dry during, and after, the Reagan–Bush era.

The University of Maryland—home to the National Women's Studies Association—allocated more than $400,000 for a "major faculty development effort to incorporate diversity into the curriculum."

Bolstering this financial support are the more than eighty Centers for Research on Women, at such institutions as Brown University, Stanford University, Wellesley College, Barnard College, Smith College, Radcliffe College, Pennsylvania, Rutgers, SUNY Buffalo, Vassar College, and many others. There are also a number of highly respected refereed journals that have been instrumental in defining the intellectual agenda of women's studies, including *Signs: The Journal of Women in Culture and Society, Feminist Review, Feminist Issues, Feminist Studies, Women's Studies International Forum,* and *Gender & Society.* Among university presses, Yale, Chicago, Rutgers, Oxford, Princeton, and Indiana have devoted entire series to the field, as has trade publisher Routledge—many of whose titles have been successful with academic and nonacademic readers alike.

WHAT'S NEXT

As noted above, Emory and Clark have the only two freestanding Ph.D. programs in women's studies in the United States. The University of Washington at Seattle has proposed a Ph.D. program that is pending, while the University of Iowa has approved a Ph.D. program but has yet to come up with the funding needed to launch it. In the interim, Iowa students can enroll in another Ph.D. program within the university and complete a concentration in women's studies.

The Emory program has nine core faculty, all of whom have joint appointments in women's studies and another department. (Altogether, fifty faculty are associated with the program in some way.) Emory regards itself as a training ground for future scholars, and, accordingly, most of its students hope to take up academic careers—although the uncertainty about job prospects in today's academic climate means that many of them will continue to be involved in projects outside the university. In May 1995, Emory awarded its first two Ph.D.'s in women's studies; four more were awarded in the spring of 1997. Currently, there are thirty-four full-time Ph.D. students at Emory, most in their mid-twenties to early thirties. There are also almost one hundred students in the certificate program, which offers graduate students in traditional disciplines official recognition for focused research and course work in women's studies. Emory accepts six Ph.D. students annually, and they all receive full funding for four years. According to students there, the guaranteed funding situation and the university-wide emphasis on teacher training are among Emory's greatest assets.

At Clark, the thirty interdisciplinary women's studies faculty are all based in traditional disciplines, although efforts to implement joint appointments are under way. One of Clark's distinguishing features is that the women's studies Ph.D. candidates form an unusually diverse group: Almost half are from the developing world; several are U.S. women of color; many have activist backgrounds; and more than one third are of "nontraditional" age (between thirty-five and sixty). Clark's first Ph.D. students entered in 1992, and as of 1997 there were fifteen full-timers. The program awarded its first Ph.D. in May 1997 to a student who had already landed a tenure-track job at California State University at Long Beach. The Clark program accepts two to four students annually, all with tuition waivers, but offers stipends to only one or two incoming students. For those who get them, stipends are renewable for up to three years, after which the students must fend for themselves. Some have earned money by teaching at Clark while others have found intermittent teaching jobs at area colleges. Although at least half of Clark students plan to teach at the university level upon graduation, the majority seek to combine teaching with policy work or community activism.

Master's programs in women's studies are thriving, especially if they have an international or social science focus.

The Clark and Emory programs are broadly comparable in terms of their faculties' connections to traditional disciplines. The academic focus within each program is slightly different, however. The program at Clark has a development and geography emphasis and a strength in the social sciences, while Emory has especially close ties to literature, anthropology, and theology/religion. There are two required core seminars for all students at Emory and three at Clark, but otherwise both programs encourage students to design their own curriculum. Also, both aim to promote a comparative and global perspective on the experiences of women in different societies, classes, and races. The Emory program offers more graduate courses in women's studies per semester than Clark, while Clark students have a greater voice than their Emory counterparts in shaping women's studies admissions choices, curriculum, policy, and programs, all of which are debated in student-faculty committees.

Prospective students may want to look into joint Ph.D. programs: women's studies combined with another discipline. Some of these programs are better funded and provide access to more university-wide resources than the full women's studies Ph.D. programs. Harvard offers a Ph.D. in religion, gender, and culture; and the University of Wisconsin at Madison offers an M.A. and Ph.D. in women's history. Since 1994 Michigan has offered joint programs both in women's studies and psychology and in women's studies and English, and they guarantee five years of funding for all students enrolled in these joint programs. Michigan's joint programs are so well regarded that the university is increasing the number of students admitted annually, and there are plans to implement a new component in women's studies and history by the 1998–99 academic year. There is also a movement afoot in Michigan's law school to establish a women's studies and law degree, which would be one of few such programs in a professional school in the United States.

A number of schools now offer full master's degree programs in women's studies, while many more offer certificates or concentrations within traditional disciplines. Ohio State University's M.A. program accepts about fifteen students a year and provides all of them with either teaching or research assistantships. Students in that two-year program can choose to take comprehensive exams or to write a master's thesis as their final project. At San Diego State University, the two-year-old program funds about half of the eight or so students accepted each year and offers about three graduate women's studies courses a year, with another five advanced undergraduate courses available to graduate students.

> Joint Ph.D. programs are often better funded and provide access to more university-wide resources.

Georgia State University admits eight to ten students annually to its master's program but gives only one of them a fellowship. Many students there pursue degrees part-time in order to continue their careers or to earn a living while they study. Georgia State offers about six graduate level courses annually. The Rutgers master's program, one of the few one-year programs, offers the largest number of women's studies courses at the master's level in the United States—thirty-two per year—but does not offer stipends or fellowships. The University of Arizona at Tucson funds the majority of its students through teaching or research assistantships and offers twenty-two courses per year. Arizona also offers specializations in women's studies through its anthropology, literature, history, and sociology Ph.D. programs.

THE JOB MARKET

Despite the many programs, centers for research, and university presses, students still must consider where they can put their talents to work. Where do women's studies students find jobs? In their book, *Women's Studies Graduates: The First Generation* (1995), Barbara F. Luebke and Mary Ellen Reilly, both of the University of Rhode Island, surveyed eighty-nine people who had majored in women's studies as under-graduates. They found no simple post-graduate employment pattern. Women's studies graduates are taking jobs in aviation and union orga-nizing, in health, social, and human services, in education and library services, in law and government. Many of these former students went on to law school, medical school, or other professional training. Most said that an interdisciplinary background in women's studies had been excellent preparation for their pursuit of professional degrees.

As a group, graduates of women's studies master's programs also tend to pursue a wide range of careers. These programs do not nec-essarily assume that students will go on to complete a Ph.D. and so accept students with diverse goals. To date, for example, graduates of the M.A. program at Ohio State have gone on to law school, to a variety of Ph.D. programs, and to government, art, editing, or social service positions. One Ohio State graduate now runs a black studies program at another university. The University of Alabama has one of the oldest women's studies M.A. programs in the country. Now twenty years old, it has been very successful in placing alumni in jobs in that region. About one third of Alabama's M.A. graduates teach in universities, while others have pursued administrative careers or jobs in editing and publishing. Some direct and staff women's cen-ters, and many recent grads have gone on to law school.

It is only at the doctoral level that these career trends change: Doctoral programs in most disciplines regard it as their central mis-sion to produce the next generation of professors. Women's studies Ph.D. programs are poised to follow in this tradition—a number of students now enrolled in such programs show the promise of long, productive academic careers, as well as a commitment to pedagogical innovation and grass-roots activism.

RESOURCES

NRC TOP TEN
Not Available

ASSOCIATIONS
National Women's
  Studies Association
(301) 403-0525

JOURNALS
Feminist Issues
Feminist Review
Feminist Studies
Gender & Society
Signs: The Journal of Women in
  Culture and Society
Women's Studies International Forum

FURTHER READING

Karen Kidd and Ande Spencer, *Guide to Graduate Work in Women's Studies*
(National Women's Studies Association)

Barbara F. Luebke and Mary Ellen Reilly, *Women's Studies Graduates,*
The First Generation (Teacher's College Press)

Laura Nichols and Linda Martin, *NWSA Directory of Women's Studies*
Programs, Women's Centers, and Women's Research Centers (National Women's
Studies Association)

Catherine Stimpson and Nina Cobb, *Women's Studies in the United States*
(Ford Foundation)

PH.D. PROGRAMS
Clark
Emory
Iowa (pending)
Washington–Seattle
  (pending)

JOINT PH.D. PROGRAMS
Harvard
Michigan
Wisconsin–Madison

M.A. PROGRAMS
Alabama
Arizona–Tucson
Georgia State
Ohio State
Rutgers
San Diego State

CONSTELLATIONS

WEB ADDRESSES
Canadian Women's Studies Online,
maintained by the University of Toronto
http://www.utoronto.ca/womens/cdnwomen.htm

National Women's Studies Association
http://www.feminist.com/nwsa.htm

Sources for Women's Studies, Feminist
Information on the Internet
gopher://una.hh.lib.umich.edu:70/00/interdirsstacks/women%3ahunt

Women's Studies on the Internet
http://www.oise.on.ca/webstuff/departments/women-net.html

Women's Studies Calls for Papers,
Bibliographies, Course Syllabi
http://www.inform.umd.edu:8080/EdRes/topic/WomensStudies

CHAPTER 19

ANTHROPOLOGY

Rebecca Ackerman recently traveled to Kenya and Belgium where, using a special mathematics and a 3-D digitizer camera, she studied early human remains. The special math she employed will help to chart the degree of similarity among particular australopithecine specimens as well as their divergence from other primates and humans. The digitizer is more accurate than hundreds of caliper measurements, and it is also more versatile because it can overlay the reconstructed facial features of different individuals for comparison. Ackerman's research will probably lead to new empirical findings, but it will also raise theoretical questions. How useful is the category "australopithecus"? Do the old classifications now need revision because modern tools for dating and measurement are so much more accurate? And of course, what might her study of the remains tell us about the individual specimens themselves, the australopithecine species, and human evolution?

Ackerman is working on this project for her dissertation in physical anthropology at Washington University in St. Louis. But she developed a wide range of expertise earlier as an M.A. student at the University of Arizona at Tucson. There with anthropologists from the Arizona State Museum, Ackerman worked on Native

American burial sites. She also worked in the lab of the city's medical examiner analyzing remains of the recently deceased. During three M.A. years, she picked up basic technical training in radiography, hair and fiber analysis, and the making and interpreting of casts. Meanwhile she taught introductory courses in physical anthropology and human evolution. Her path from M.A. to Ph.D. is not uncommon among physical anthropologists today.

Tejaswini Gantis came to New York University's Ph.D. program in cultural anthropology after earning a B.A. at Northwestern University in political science and an M.A. in anthropology at the University of Pennsylvania. As an undergraduate, she felt that political science put too much stress on rational choice and game-theory modeling, and took too little account of culture or cultural difference—subjects that particularly fascinated her as a first-generation U.S. citizen whose parents were born in India. When she began graduate school, the most popular topics in South Asian studies were the environment and economic development. At first, she gravitated in that direction, thinking her love of Indian popular culture was too personal and nonacademic to pursue. But when she read academic journal articles about Indian film, she became convinced that she knew the subject at least as well as any academic writer. So, when her favorite professors left Penn she transferred to NYU, where the ethnography of media is taken as seriously as development studies had been at Penn. Her dissertation now concerns the role of the Bombay film industry in Indian modernization and nation-building.

Gantis's research challenges traditional anthropological depictions of India as a rural nation centered around caste. She points out that this "traditional" view is in fact the progeny of the elite filmmakers of Bombay who have defined the Indian culture for the outside world. In addition, she poses her work against that of film studies scholars who look only at the films themselves without heeding the contexts of cultural production and reception.

WHY ANTHROPOLOGY?

Anthropologists like to say that their field cannot be easily defined. After all, the discipline straddles the social sciences, humanities, and biological sciences; observed from the outside, it can look a bit like Dr.

Dolittle's pushme-pullyou, fighting itself ferociously to move in both directions at once. Anthropologists might explain that although the field moves in many different directions, it works. Besides, "Anthropology is what anthropologists do," they'll say, and what anthropologists do is to combine attention to detail with a flexibility of method unparalleled among the sciences, human or otherwise.

No matter how much anthropologists differ over definitions of their discipline, they'll all agree that they share an interest in exploring and describing how things have worked in different human societies, often distant from our own in time and space, so as to better understand past and present human social and biological life. They focus on details of social interaction, language, and physiology in ways that other social scientists do not. Like sociologists, anthropologists examine human behavior, but anthropologists—until very recently—concentrated mainly on studying nonliterate peoples and performed extensive archaeological research, while sociologists more often study modern urban societies.

Today, anthropologists study the behavior of just about anyone, anywhere: musicians in the Republic of Congo, stock traders in China, immigrants in Germany, factory workers in Japan, doctors in San Francisco. Since so many famous studies are conducted in far-flung places, anthropologists can find themselves mistaken for missionaries, tourists, or Crocodile Dundees with tenure. But the work anthropologists do is firmly grounded in scientific methods of data collection, observation, and analysis. Many anthropologists consider themselves scientists, but not all of them share the same definition of science or use the same tools. Physical anthropologists (also called biological anthropologists) and archaeologists use laboratories and sophisticated technologies to examine human remains, primate behavior and physiology, and artifacts. Linguistic anthropologists rely on interviews, tapes, and transcripts to do written analysis of spoken language. Cultural anthropologists can use any of those tools but often replace them with tools of their own—like ethnographic studies, which leads some anthropologists to travel to remote villages, and others to study the culture of mall shoppers, skyscraper workers, criminals or police squads. Method in cultural anthropology is rarely taught as a hard-and-fast procedure. Instead, it is often

Many anthropologists consider themselves scientists, but not all of them share the same definition of science.

worked out in the field. For this reason cultural anthropologists often stake out their own distinctive but carefully defined positions in regard to scientific procedures—positions so varied that cultural anthropology is funded by both the National Science Foundation and the National Endowment for the Humanities.

HOW ANTHROPOLOGY HAS TAKEN SHAPE

Around 1900 Columbia University professor Franz Boas and his colleagues described their discipline as a "complete science of humankind." They then proceeded to shape anthropology in the U.S. as a discipline that works in four areas: the biological history of human beings, the linguistics of peoples without written languages, prehistoric archaeology, and the ethnology of peoples without written historic records. These areas evolved into the four fields which now make up the discipline: physical (or biological) anthropology, linguistic anthropology, archaeology, and cultural (or social) anthropology.

The Boas school formalized the important and enduring anthropological principle of cultural relativism—the belief that people everywhere prefer their own culture not because it is inherently better or more evolved than any other, but because it is theirs. Cultural relativism provided a basis from which to challenge the racist assumptions of many early anthropologists and of turn-of-the-century social-Darwinists. Boas argued that racial classifications were meaningless, that culture was not innate, and that there were no processes of cultural evolution parallel to those of biological evolution. Applying these insights, Boasian anthropology concentrated on the cultural consequences of immigration, migration, and exile—not to find normative ideals of culture but to explain the contingency of cultural values. Much has occurred in anthropology since Boas first laid down some of its ground rules, however. There are other schools that have evolved from the work of other widely influential scholars—Leslie A. White of the University of Chicago and the sociologist Talcott Parsons of Harvard University, for example. But for our purposes, it's best to single out recent developments in the discipline by discussing the four fields that Boas established, since those categories still hold. We will, however, also discuss more recent divisions and collaborations in the discipline.

For the purposes of applying to schools, you'll have to pick one of the four fields. This can be a hard decision since anthropology programs accept students from a wide variety of undergraduate backgrounds. Some of them might not know whether cultural anthropology or linguistic anthropology will be their final home. Even so, your application must demonstrate that you have a clear idea of how the faculty and resources at a given department will match your research interests. And you cannot assume that faculty from subspecialties will work together. Although at times the four fields have cross-fertilized one another, bear in mind that anthropology's divisions are wide and deep. A number of excellent programs do not even offer training in all four fields, and anthropologists are no more likely to be in touch with all aspects of their field than are professors in other academic disciplines. For example, the cultural anthropology professors and students at a given institution might share little more than a mailing address with the physical anthropology crowd. In fact, they may rarely even talk to one another.

> Boas's cultural relativism challenged the racist assumptions of many early anthropologists.

Of course, no one can predict when the next interdisciplinary movement might unite large sections of the discipline, and interdisciplinary scholars do cross more and more boundaries. But, at the moment, anthropology remains divided, and Boas's divisions best reflect the field's current shape.

PHYSICAL ANTHROPOLOGY

Much of physical anthropology concerns the search for the physiological origins of humankind. Although there is lively debate within the field about particular theories, physical anthropologists assume that their research moves forward by informed invention and revision, not revolution. While specific conclusions are fair game for challenge, many scholars in this area assume their research programs are not likely to be fundamentally shaken.

The crucial debate at the moment is about theories of the origins of "recent" (about 200,000 years ago) human history. On the one hand, there is the "out of Africa" or "replacement" theory, which holds that modern humans evolved in Africa and then displaced other populations around the world. On the other hand, there is the "multiregional" or "continuity" theory, which holds that populations in Africa, Asia, and Europe interbred and evolved into modern *homo sapiens*. Not only does this debate have implications for ethnic and national claims to be the "first" humans, but it is a flash point for controversy regarding the decisiveness of scientific protocols.

> Washburn and DeVore sparked interest in whether or not human traits were "hard-wired" inheritances from earlier primates.

Physical anthropology is also influenced by recent technological advances in molecular genetics, particularly advances in analyzing DNA. One active research field is forensics; another is the history of population movements. Since only a small portion of molecular research, even with primates, can actually be done on site, pursuing this subfield requires that a department be connected to a good network of labs and research facilities. The strongest departments in this area are associated with medical schools and biochemistry departments. Primatology—the study of primate genetics, anatomy, and social behavior—is another active branch of physical anthropology. Two Harvard anthropologists, the physical anthropologist Sherwood L. Washburn and his colleague in cultural anthropology, Irven DeVore, were early leaders in newer methods of primatology. Starting in the 1950s, they studied the social behavior of primates in search of clues to human evolution. Their theory that early humans could be understood by analogy to primates sparked debate about whether or not traits such as altruism, aggression, or nurturing were "hard-wired" inheritances from earlier primates.

These questions have been investigated by field biologists as well as by anthropologists, notably Richard Wrangham of Harvard, whose new book *Demonic Males* argues that male violence for its own sake can be observed among chimpanzees. The biologist Frans de Waal has studied Bonobo monkeys—genetically as close to humans as chimpanzees—and noted their apparently harmonious matriarchal culture. By paying sexuality as much attention as other researchers have violence, de Waal proposes that sexual relations promote social cohesion at least as well as hierarchies of dominance do.

LINGUISTIC ANTHROPOLOGY

Although linguistic anthropology came to prominence before the 1920s, when Boas's students Edward Sapir and Benjamin Whorf studied Native American languages, the field did not take its current orientation until the 1960s and 1970s. At that time its focus shifted from language structure to patterns of language use. Working under the rubric "the ethnology of speaking," Dell Hymes (now emeritus at the University of Virginia, but at the University of Pennsylvania for many years) proposed that utterances are directed social acts, and thus that language is a collective institution best studied with close attention to social context—especially the relationships between language and gender, class, and environment. And, as postcolonial societies struggled with the coexistence of native and imposed tongues, sociolinguists studied variations among social classes. Attention to the social surroundings of language expanded to include history, economics, and politics.

Although an important field, linguistic anthropology is a small part of the discipline and overlaps somewhat with sociolinguistics. Sociolinguists study the social dimensions of spoken language, just as linguistic anthropologists do. But the former tend to take a quantitative approach to language variation and class, and they generally avoid making arguments about whole cultures. Linguistic anthropologists, on the other hand, tend to conduct studies comparing speakers from different groups. They take a less statistics-bound approach and are willing to propose broad theories of culture that do not isolate language from other social and political structures.

The most distinctive methodology of linguistic anthropologists, however, is that they research language use according to the ethnographic model of participant observation. They may live among their subjects for months or years, recording casual as well as formal conversations. From this pool of ethnographic data, a linguistic anthropologist might try to discover how a pronunciation was learned, whether speakers are aware of differences in pronunciation, how speakers interpret mispronunciations by others, or how speakers react to accusations that their pronunciation is inadequate. They set out to construct and analyze as complete a cultural portrait of language as possible from close observation of those on the inside, in addition to applying theoretical and empirical techniques.

> What's most distinctive about linguistic anthropologists is their use of participant observation.

ARCHAEOLOGY

Every archaeology department in the U.S., except those at Boston University and the University of Michigan, is administered from within an anthropology department, a custom that harks back to the way the discipline was organized at its founding.

Archaeology is the subject of the next chapter, and there we discuss several subfields within archaeology: anthropological archaeology, classical archaeology, cultural resources management, and others. Here it is appropriate to spotlight one ethical issue among anthropological archaeologists in order to suggest the kinds of questions that arise from working with present-day cultures.

Just as anthropologists perennially debate who should study whom and how, museums have found themselves at the center of controversies over the possession of artifacts and human remains taken from Native American lands. The Native American Graves Protection and Repatriation Act, passed by Congress in 1990, declared that museums, if asked, must return to Native Americans anything taken from their communities' graves. Though many feared that museum collections would be decimated as a result of the bill, this has not happened. Some archaeologists report that their relations with Native American communities have actually improved since the bill's passage because many tribes have asked museums to hold on to their collections and keep them well preserved.

> Why has archaeology stressed hunting, by men, rather than gathering, by women?

The Museum of the American Indian, in New York City, a branch of the Smithsonian Institution, has created projects to aid Native American communities in starting or improving their own museums. (In addition, the staff of the museum includes a large Native American contingent.)

But archaeologists are not only concerned with who finds, controls, and studies artifacts; they must also confront the need to revise common assumptions about how to interpret the surviving record of cultures. Why has archaeology often stressed hunting, by men, rather than gathering, by women? Can archaeologists investigate symbolism and ideology in the same manner in which they investigate subsistence and migration? Kent Redford and other scholars who work in developing interdisciplinary fields such as ecological studies, for instance, question whether indigenous peoples live in harmony with their environment or whether they are instead at the mercy of their surroundings and struggling to survive in any way they can. For the last twenty years, James Deetz (of UC-Berkeley) and others have combined the methods of anthropology, history, and archaeology to study these types of issues. Their interdisciplinary research includes texts like inventories, journals, and public documents.

CULTURAL ANTHROPOLOGY

Most cultural anthropologists agree that if their field once shared a language or method, it has been pushed aside by wave after wave of competing theories and approaches. But changes in the discipline notwithstanding, nearly all cultural anthropologists agree upon one thing: the continued importance of fieldwork. Culture is studied in any number of disciplines, but only anthropologists write ethnographies based on fieldwork. Living within and participating in a culture, for anthropologists, is generally acknowledged as the fundamental method of approach. While the ethnographic model has been severely criticized for being neither scientific nor objective, no one is prepared to relinquish it. Consequently, it's the rare cultural anthropologist who does not begin a career by writing an ethnographic, fieldwork–based dissertation.

Before turning to the founding of cultural anthropology, a few more words about the variety and sprawl of the field need mention. In the 1950s, Alfred Kroeber and C. Kluckhohn's *Culture* demonstrated that the term "culture" was one of the most flexible words in the English language. Logically enough, this has led to opportunities as well as turf wars within the discipline and beyond it. Sociologists, historians, literary scholars, and others all write about culture, but cultural anthropologists insist that they alone understand culture with the intimacy and particularity of the participant-observer. The premium placed on fieldwork does not, however, unify or simplify cultural anthropology. So many different kinds of participant-observer study have been done that fieldwork cannot be identified with a single model or method. And at the same time, cultural anthropology is not wholly separable from the other three anthropological fields: What cultural anthropologists do involves—and affects—the work being done by anthropologists in physical, linguistic, and archaeological studies.

Something of this breadth was present even at the field's inception. The birth of modern cultural anthropology in the 1920s and 1930s is often called the "classic" period. Once ensconced at

Columbia, Franz Boas sent an army of graduate students out to record particular aspects of threatened Native American civilizations. Their method was to select a rich practice, idea, or symbol within a community—beadwork, tool types, social structure, myths—and to study that aspect of the culture exhaustively, then pool their individual insights into a broader perspective.

Other Boas students took the cultural anthropological enterprise in a different direction. Part of the founding mission of anthropology was to conduct research as if one were a detached scientific observer. But an equally venerable tradition was established by anthropologists who acted as advocates for the communities they studied. Margaret Mead and Ruth Benedict, both students of Boas, connected their personal experiences as observers of particular communities to larger social questions. For instance, in her famous *Coming of Age in Samoa* (1928), Mead found some of the sexual and family customs that she observed in Samoa enviable, less bound by patriarchy and hierarchy than the cultures of the industrial world.

> Because participant-observer studies vary so widely, fieldwork cannot be pinned down to a single model.

However, both she and Benedict challenged the notion that studying the particulars of cultures led to universal patterns or "rules" and insisted instead that the search for scientifically valid cultural "laws" was misplaced. Cultures, they believed, were more like irreducible "individual personalities writ large."

In the period between the 1920s and the 1950s, anthropology was also deeply marked by two movements that were influential throughout the social sciences and the humanities: functionalism and structuralism. Both movements resist summary. In fact, in most affected disciplines, from sociology to geography, at least one book-length work is devoted to charting the rise and fall of each movement. Functionalism, most closely identified in anthropology with the British social research of R. Radcliffe-Brown and Bronislaw Malinoski, drew on the sociology of Emile Durkheim, and accordingly tended to downplay the roles of conflict and revolution in society. Instead, functionalists favored the analysis of forces they believed were the self-equilibrating mechanisms of a "social organism." Structuralism, as employed by Claude Lévi-Strauss, incorporated the analytic techniques of linguists Ferdinand de Saussure and Roman Jakobson. Structuralists tended to begin their studies by identifying a binary opposition, like nature/culture, which was then used as a springboard for elaborate analyses of language, cognition, ceremony and ritual, and social organization. As different as functionalism and structuralism were, both assumed that cultures could be analyzed as self-enclosed and self-correcting systems; both were preoccupied with charting systems and investigating rationalizable structures; and both sought to keep their observations disinterested.

> Structuralism and functionalism both treated cultures as self-enclosed, self-correcting systems.

During the 1960s, a materialist, sometimes Marxist, anthropological school put down roots at a number of American universities—Columbia, Michigan, the Graduate Center of the City University of New York, Yale University, the University of California at Berkeley, and the New School for Social Research—and maintained itself for at least the next generation. Materialist anthropologists began to study how global economic conflicts and modernization affected preindustrial societies. Some turned to the relationship between the impoverished societies that anthropology traditionally studied and their interactions with dominant cultures; for example, the workings of the Bureau of Indian Affairs. Others developed political and economic theories; the most explicitly Marxist of these were called "cultural materialism."

The other major division in cultural anthropology of the 1960s and 1970s was the symbolic school, most closely associated with the best-known living anthropologist, Clifford Geertz of the University of Chicago and the Institute for Advanced Study in Princeton, New Jersey. It was only in the early 1970s that literature departments began to engage seriously with the revolutionary theory that had inspired anthropologists since Boas—that all interpretations were relative, not absolute, truths. Geertz's variation on this theme was that scientific interpretations were sometimes just as flexible as literary ones. Facts, even in ethnography, were inseparable from interpretations. The most famous Geertzian phrase, as fundamentally important as it is fuzzy, is "thick description." Thick description refers to a dense layering of observations—made over a period of time and by various observers—that collectively clarify a carefully defined cultural phenomenon. Geertz's 1973 essay "Deep Play:

Notes on the Balinese Cockfight," was a tour de force of thick description. In it he imaginatively conveyed the perspectives of all the human participants in the sport. Later, however, Geertz was taken to task for failing to mention the oppressive political situation in Indonesia at the time and also for failing to consult the Balinese themselves about their views of cockfighting.

Symbolic anthropologists in the Geertzian mode collected facts and interpretations to construct or uncover "webs of significance"— the meaning- and power-making patterns that people spin, and in which they are inevitably tangled. While Geertz established a beach-head at the Institute for Advanced Study, Marshall Sahlins carried on the symbolic tradition at Chicago. Harvard was also a center for symbolic anthropology from the 1960s through the early 1980s, as was Virginia, home to Victor W. Turner, Roy Wagner, David J. Sapir, and Christopher Crocker.

But as early as the 1970s, the field of cultural anthropology could no longer be charted according to a stark materialist/symbolic dichotomy. The 1970s were ushered in by the publication of a collection called *Reinventing Anthropology*, edited by Dell Hymes. The contributors to this volume attacked both materialist and symbolic paradigms, arguing that they inadequately addressed issues of gender, identity, objectivity, and the past and present missions of the discipline. Articles examined anthropology's collusion with imperialism, provided an anthropological reading of the student movements of the 1960s, and mapped the agenda for a "critical anthropology" that spoke truth to power. A key article in the collection was by cultural anthropologist Laura Nader, who argued that fieldwork about small apparently isolated communities ignored the connections of such communities to modern urban cultures. In the years since the Hymes collection was published, not only have these oversights become hot topics in the discipline, but they have inspired research into postcolonialism and the study of science and its effects—research which draws on both material and symbolic analysis.

> "Thick description" refers to a dense layering of observations that clarifies a cultural phenomenon.

The long-standing debate about what groups anthropologists study and why also intensified in the 1970s. Feminists pointed out the strangely peripheral and homogenous depictions of women in most ethnographic accounts. Rayna Rapp of the New School, for example, questioned Marxist categories of sex and labor that cast women in passive roles. In the landmark volume *Woman, Culture, and Society*, Sherry Ortner of Columbia and the late Michelle Rosaldo analyzed how gender differences have underpinned long-standing anthropological concepts, like nature and culture, or public and private. A variety of feminists agreed about the social problems caused by female subordination, whether they approached the topic from a material or a symbolic angle. Anthropologists of color, particularly those native to regions that had been studied, noted what outsiders had misunderstood about their culture and the consequences of those mistakes for the discipline as well as for the groups studied.

> Feminists pointed out the peripheral and homogeneous depictions of women in most ethnographies.

Following these challenges, cultural anthropology also began to readdress the postmodern fascination with the role of interpretation in ethnography. Drawing heavily on literary criticism and French poststructuralist theory, anthropologists George Marcus of Rice University and Michael Fisher of MIT's Science and Technology Program, and the literary scholar James Clifford of the University of California at Santa Cruz's History of Consciousness program, stressed that ethnography is a kind of storytelling. In *Writing Culture: The Poetics and Politics of Ethnography* (1986), Clifford proposed that ethnography is an act of writing enmeshed in the conventions of narrative and of authorial point of view as much as in empirical observation, concluding that its truths are both incomplete and partial.

Consider, for instance, the ongoing battle between Chicago's Marshall Sahlins and Princeton's Gananath Obeyesekere over the death of Captain Cook. According to Sahlins, Cook was killed in 1779 by distraught Hawaiians who mistook him for the god Lono, whose sudden appearance on their shores did not accord with their mythical system. Not so, says Obeyesekere, who claims that Cook was killed in battle after being enlisted by the Hawaiians to fight alongside them against neighboring groups. According to Obeyesekere, Sahlins's account falls into a Western colonialist genre in which natives, blinded by superstitions, treat Europeans as gods. But according to Sahlins, Obeyesekere is the one who has misunderstood the Hawaiians by discounting the value of their local myths and, instead, assuming they acted like rational eighteenth-century Europeans. Oddly enough, given their disagreement, Sahlins and Obeyesekere share an anthropological charter: to explain how an observer's perspective shapes the conclusions drawn about other cultures.

The postmodern turn in cultural anthropology of the 1980s also influenced physical anthropology and archaeology. For one, researchers began to recognize that what they were finding was in part determined by what they expected to find and by the stories they wanted to tell. In 1983, Sherwood Washburn looked back on his work on primate behavior in the 1950s and 1960s and concluded that he had not been objective, but had instead tried to make the story he told about evolution consistent. Washburn's reflection was emblematic of a more generalized questioning of the confidence that had driven the positivist research of previous decades. During the same period Marxist and feminist perspectives brought questions about gender and labor to bear on archaeological sites. Today, archaeologists are even more attuned than before to clues about labor patterns (indicated by bone stress as well as by manufacturing techniques for projectile points and pottery), social hierarchies (where the archeological record adds evidence of the relations between men and women), and the control of material resources (hearth areas associated with women, butchering areas associated with men). Joan M. Gero and Margaret W. Conkey's collection of essays, *Engendering Archaeology: Women and Prehistory* (1991), is a useful introduction to new research in these fields.

SPECIAL PROGRAMS AND SUBFIELDS

Applied anthropology—which the American Anthropology Association classes as a fifth field—refers to any work related to anthropology done by anthropologists outside of the academy. Examples include public administration, medical anthropology (especially in the fields of nursing and public health), anthropology and education, criminology, transportation science, urban planning, development assistance in foreign countries, and advocacy for threatened groups.

Applied anthropology is a growing field, partly because there is such a variety of possible jobs for graduates, but also because an M.A., not a Ph.D., is often the highest academic credential needed to find a job. For information on the kind of work going on in applied anthropology, look at the journals *Human Organization* and

Practicing Anthropology, especially the Winter 1993 issue of the latter, which rounds up a selection of student comments about the work they have done after graduating from applied programs.

A few other attractive subfields in anthropology tend to have more fluid identities than the four-field structure in the discussion above suggests. Such fields are often taught in "programs" rather than full-fledged "departments." Medical anthropology, for instance, is cited by professors and students as an ideal field in which to combine biological and cultural research interests. Often associated with medical schools, it is well-funded and respected by physical and cultural anthropologists alike. Employment possibilities are broad and can be found in institutions from cognitive science departments to health maintenance organizations.

Visual anthropology describes a number of practices, from the study of visual culture to the ethnographic use of film or video. Though the term "ethnographic film" may suggest drowsy *National Geographic* TV specials, films in this field today can offer rich accounts and critiques of an enormous range of subjects, from political life in the former Zaire to Indonesian puppet theater traditions. Indigenous media—the use of film or video by aboriginal or native artists and activists—offers visual anthropologists the opportunity to work as observers or collaborators.

There are also interdisciplinary programs that blend anthropology and technology. The charter of Science and Technology Studies (STS) is to study science as a culture in action by drawing upon methods from history, anthropology, and sociology. STS does not require a background in science—at MIT, for instance, students come from literature, law, and museum backgrounds.

For those whose interest in anthropology is determined more by a subject than by a method, interdisciplinary programs can be rewarding. But bear in mind that the job market does not always keep pace with hot research areas. For any subfield, it's a worthwhile exercise to scan the job listings from the American Anthropological Association to see how departments currently define their hiring needs.

WHAT'S NEXT

Because anthropology is anchored in specific methods of data collection and analysis, graduate training becomes specialized very quickly.

Graduate school applications will at a minimum require you to indicate which of the four fields you plan to study, and many programs,
though not all, will ask you to define your interests very specifically. As
a rule of thumb, particularly if you are in a field with a lot of breadth
(such as cultural anthropology), it is best to choose the program with
the largest number of people doing the same kind of work that you are
interested in. If you think there is a possibility that you would change
fields later, it would probably be safest to join a big department.

The subdivisions of the discipline can be lumped into the four
main fields, plus applied anthropology: cultural anthropology, with
50 percent of the AAA membership; archaeology, 25 percent; physical, 13 percent; applied, 10 percent; linguistics, 2 percent. Note
that the fields of archaeology, physical or biological anthropology,
and linguistic anthropology are represented in the AAA by one sub-
division each, while twenty-seven of the divisions below have some
relation to cultural anthropology.

There are a seemingly infinite number of smaller divisions
beneath the four main fields—Chicago professor George Stocking
calls them "adjectival anthropologies." The AAA divides them into
thirty-one special associations of anthropologists with the labels cultural, humanistic, linguistic, medical, psychological, work, urban,
visual, ethnological, archaeological, political and legal, biological,
education, general, museum, nutritional, culture and agriculture,
environmental, practice of anthropology, consciousness, North
American, European, Africanist, Latin American, Central States;
black, feminist, Latina and Latino, senior, community college, and
student anthropologists. The AAA's annual *Guide to Departments* is full
of statistics about the most recent crop of Ph.D.'s. In 1995, ninety-
three academic departments awarded 464 Ph.D.'s in anthropology.
The AAA's portrait of the model 1994–95 Ph.D. is "Christine," who
is white, female, and forty years old, did fieldwork for social anthropology in North America, and took 8.4 years to complete her
degree. But this is only a hypothetical composite. Check with the
actual departments you are considering for the demographics of new
students to get a picture of the actual cohort you will join.

For those planning a career in academia, the usual procedure
these days is to get right onto the Ph.D. track, picking up a master's
along the way. Getting an M.A. at one place and a Ph.D. at another

used to be more common, but it lengthens the time spent in graduate school and has fallen out of favor in anthropology. If you change your mind about academia after acquiring a master's, having an M.A. can lead to professional careers in such fields as museum curating, consumer research, and cultural resource management.

Two important factors in choosing a program are faculty engagement with graduate students, and resources. The first can best be gauged by talking with students. As for resources, the older, larger departments and the universities based in major cities have a definite advantage: Chicago is a mecca for social science; Harvard's libraries are unparalleled; and NYU has developed a program that draws heavily on New York City's wide range of resources such as museums and research institutes. Nonetheless, smaller programs may offer opportunities for travel or exchange. Consider them on a case-by-case basis. Princeton University, Johns Hopkins University, and Rice are good examples of small but excellent programs with substantial resources.

There is consensus that few departments are now associated with any particular approach or method, particularly in the flexible field of cultural anthropology. Faculty are scattered and in motion, and few of the prominent anthropologists today have the discipline-shaping role of Boas, Geertz, Sahlins, or Wolf. Today, any one person's work seems unlikely to shake the intellectual foundations of the entire discipline. There are instead small pockets of influence. Rice and the University of California at Santa Cruz emphasize postmodern anthropology, Princeton is still strongly associated with symbolic anthropology, and Cornell University houses the best Southeast Asia program in the country. But there is no way to assess the current situation at a particular department without talking to the faculty about their areas of specialization and their identity as a department—and making sure you are current with what they have written recently. Points of view and positions can change quickly.

The National Research Council rankings provide a very rough idea of the visibility of departments to the rest of the field, but few professors think that the rankings are a realistic assessment of the state of the field today. Small programs tend to be overlooked, and the particular strengths of programs are ignored completely. In

> An M.A. can lead to professional careers in museum curating and cultural resource management.

terms of archaeology, for instance, the rankings don't take into account a program's affiliation with a museum. (See the Archaeology chapter.) Departments are judged sweepingly, as single entities, even though almost none operates as such. Most professors agree that the rankings document little more than outdated notions of prestige.

Core requirements also vary from department to department. The AAA *Guide* lists each department's specific requirements. Though it's rare for students to be required to take courses in all four major fields, some large departments do require students to take core courses in three. (However, some of the best departments don't even offer courses in all four fields.) Since many graduate students enroll in anthropology programs with no prior experience in the discipline, an overview course is usually required in the first year, along with a course in theory or history. Harvard may be the only program in the country that still requires a course in kinship. Most programs have a language requirement, but rigor in language training varies as does the number of languages required. Cultural anthropologists are expected to do fieldwork, as are many linguists. Archaeologists and physical anthropologists do field, lab, or museum work. Most programs expect students to teach, often by leading one of the discussion sections of a larger course at a big institution, and sometimes by conducting a class about an area of the world in which they specialize. But opportunities to teach also vary from department to department.

> Most professors think that rankings document little more than outdated notions of prestige.

In making up a short list of schools, we've identified the specialties that particular programs held in the past. But be advised that these are impossible to keep current: a few hirings or a few professorial departures can change the emphasis of a department dramatically.

PHYSICAL ANTHROPOLOGY

Don't limit your research into physical anthropology just to programs that list that specialty within an anthropology department. Much significant physical anthropology takes place outside of anthropology departments, often in psychology or zoology. Among anthropology departments, the University of California at Davis and Harvard are strong in primate studies, and NYU is strong in primate genetics. NYU is part of the New York Consortium, along with Columbia and CUNY Graduate Center. Consortium students take classes from all three schools, participate in joint seminars, and have a broad array of labs, zoos, and museums in which to do research. Duke University is strong in primate behavioral ecology and, along with SUNY Stony Brook, in primate anatomy, but at both schools the physical anthropology programs are separate from the umbrella anthropology departments. (Both Duke and SUNY Stony Brook are also connected to good medical schools, if medical anthropology intrigues you.)

Osteology, the study of skeletons and related physiology, is always work in progress since each significant find leads to debates and revisions of the story of human origins. (One professor reported perennial arguments over whose fossils are oldest.) UC-Davis, SUNY Stony Brook, Duke, the New York Consortium, and Northwestern regularly receive funding from the National Science Foundation for work in osteology. It is harder to get good training in fossil work, a branch of osteology: Ideally you want to work on an active dig, but not all programs have digs currently underway. Pennsylvania State University and the biology department at UC-Berkeley usually do.

> Osteology is always work in progress: each major find leads to revisions of the story of human origins.

Many departments offer no graduate training in physical anthropology. At some places, specialities that were once unified under anthropology have split off: Physical anthropology at UC-Berkeley, for instance, has relocated to the biology department. The most common areas for graduate student research—molecular genetics, primate behavior, fossil studies, osteology, and comparative anatomy—can be pursued in biology, psychology, paleontology, or biochemistry departments, which are often housed in medical schools or in independent research centers.

Smaller anthropology departments may be dominated by their subspecialties. If you go to Duke, for instance, you have to do primates; at Harvard, you have more options, but if you decide you want to do molecular genetics you might not be in the best place. Of course, the advantage of enrolling in an anthropology department is that you are more likely to get training in general anthropology. Penn State is cited by many as the strongest program in human anthropological genetics, with a concentration of people doing distinct but related work on bones, primatology, fossil studies, and laboratory genetics.

Given that many physical anthropology projects are conducted in teams where the collaboration between student and professor is especially close, professors stress that it's crucial to talk to other students to make sure that you would be able to apprentice with senior professors effectively. Look to the journals for people working in your area of interest, find out where they teach, and talk to the up-and-coming generation as well as to the old hands.

LINGUISTIC ANTHROPOLOGY

Though the field of linguistic anthropology is vast, the number of departments where it can be studied is minuscule. Since there aren't very many linguistic anthropologists (even the best places have only two or three), it's hard to find a concentration of experts. According to David Givens of the AAA, of the ninety-four programs offering Ph.D.'s in anthropology, only 20 percent provide training in linguistic anthropology. UCLA is a notable exception. It has a whole team of linguistic anthropologists engaged in microethnographic analyses (the study of language and context in small groups), but studying in that department also means you will find less focus on general anthropology than is typical elsewhere.

One way that students may be trained in anthropology and linguistics is to attend a school where anthropology has connections with other departments: Chicago, Arizona-Tucson, and the University of Texas at Austin have programs for relevant interdisciplinary graduate work in linguistics. In general, look at the offerings in cultural anthropology that emphasize the study of the use of language and also at related programs—in sociology, for example. You should also consider finding a strong area studies program related to your linguistic specialty. If, for instance, you're fascinated by African languages, you'll find your choices narrowed since they're taught only at certain schools. Graduate students in linguistic anthropology are not likely to be happy in a department where the linguist feels shut off from everyone else. And, such a situation would be ironic given that the charter of the subfield is to study the context and the community, not just the language. As one professor advised, students should find out whom the linguistic anthropologists talk to—outside of their departments.

ARCHAEOLOGY

A good archaeology program of any kind needs a well-equipped, up-to-date lab and a good museum. In practice, that means that the top twenty anthropology departments in the NRC rankings, which tend also to be the largest and best-funded departments, are the place to start your search. The AAA publishes a guide to programs, but it lists only archaeology programs within anthropology departments, not those within classics or art history departments. Classics or art history departments might be an attractive option not just for students already in those disciplines, but for anthropologists who want to study cultures in the Mediterranean or the anthropology of, say, medieval cultures.

A glance at the 1995 *Annual Review of Anthropology* shows that anthropological archaeology is broadening its sights. The debate over the earliest appearances of *homo sapiens* continues. But it is joined by newer topics, including political economy in early Mesopotamian states, frontier studies that focus on regions of social exchange with Mexico and Canada, and the archaeology of slavery in North America. Another central issue for archaeologists is gender in the prehistoric past. One archaeologist asserted that in gender studies, archaeology lags behind cultural anthropology by about twenty years: a claim borne out by the fact that archaeology's first large symposium on gender did not occur until the 1988 AAA annual meeting.

Departmental specialties in archaeology are more often topical or regional than theoretical: Vanderbilt University works on Mesopotamia; Penn on Mayan cultures, Europe, and the Near East. Institutions in the Southwest are likely to have strong Native American programs. Arizona-Tucson is one of the few places where ethnoarchaeology, or the archaeology of living populations, is being practiced seriously. It is also the home of "garbology," the archaeology of the material culture of garbage. Various kinds of work are being pursued in different programs, and so the advice about linguistic anthropology also applies to archaeology: Figure out what you want to do, and try to find the best people doing similar work. (See the Archaeology chapter.)

CULTURAL ANTHROPOLOGY

Keeping current with the constantly shifting faculty makeup of particular departments is especially important for students of cultural anthropology. The above history of the discipline traces the past identities of departments—Columbia as the home of Boas; Princeton, Virginia, and

Chicago as centers for symbolic anthropology; UC-Berkeley, Michigan, and the New School as strongholds of materialist anthropology; Harvard as a pioneer in physical anthropology. But the relative weight departments give to the specialties can change rapidly in cultural anthropology, so you'll need to find out what specialties departments favor now.

The best cultural program for your needs will have several professors interested in working with you on a particular project. To rely on one professor is too risky: he or she could leave or your working relationship could change. Also, the reputation of the scholars you'll team up with and the prestige of the institution play a larger role than usual in the incredibly tight job market for cultural anthropologists. Since nearly every department is home to many cultural anthropologists, another objective is to match your interests to research projects which will still be active in five years. You should feel confident that the faculty will support your work and that the resources available to your department—particularly funds for travel—are adequate. Remember, cultural anthropologists often choose to study in far-flung places. Ask as well about the department's record of success in attracting outside funding from the NSF, government sources, and private support.

SPECIAL PROGRAMS

Some schools, like Case Western Reserve University and the University of Illinois at Urbana, offer special programs in medical anthropology or offer M.D./Ph.D.'s in conjunction with medical schools. The Medical Scholars Program at Illinois-Urbana publishes a registry of M.D./Ph.D. combination programs in medicine. For the anthropology of medicine without the M.D., you can stick to the American Medical Association's list of programs.

The program at the University of Southern Florida is the largest and most specialized for applied anthropology, with fifteen faculty teaching in applied fields. The program has a required full-time internship program—through which many graduates find their jobs. M.A. students in applied departments also regularly train in another discipline: for instance in a professional school for specialties such as public health or nursing.

Interest in visual anthropology is growing quickly, but training in the field is hard to find. NYU's program in culture and media, which incorporates theoretical and practical knowledge of film and video into generalist training in anthropology, is designed especially for visual anthropology Ph.D. students. Temple University has a graduate program of studies in the anthropology of visual communication, and the Center for Visual Anthropology at the University of Southern California offers an M.A. Although films are currently not taken as seriously as written ethnographies, many hope that as the field grows this will change.

Science and Technology Studies come in a variety of forms hard to describe in general terms. The welcome they give to students without a background in the sciences also varies. Cornell, MIT, UCLA, Rochester Institute of Technology, Virginia Polytechnic Institute, and the University of California at San Diego have leading STS programs, but you'll need to thoroughly investigate their readiness to sponsor anthropological work. If you are interested in writing about technology as a journalist, you might consider the Science and Environmental Reporting Program in NYU's School of Journalism.

THE JOB MARKET

As we've said, the academic job market is tightest for cultural anthropologists. Well-trained archaeologists and physical anthropologists, on the other hand, may find jobs in a range of departments and in areas outside the academy. Because job placement advising and professional training vary greatly from school to school, it's important to ask departments what they offer on these fronts and how their students have been doing on the market. According to the AAA *Guide*, in 1995 67 percent of Ph.D.'s rated their department's job-advice offerings as fair to poor. Some departments, however, work hard to help their students, offering instruction on everything from preparing a CV to publishing an article; others, apparently, are more laissez-faire.

The AAA literature repeatedly stresses that jobs outside of the academy often pay better, make people happier, and are easier to find than academic jobs. They are anxious to debunk a common bias that working outside the academy is a consolation prize. For instance, the AAA publication "Getting a Job Outside the Academy" remarks that "Anthropologists more than anyone should recognize that systems of reward and prestige are socially defined and hardly immutable." Still, the majority of graduate students continue to want academic jobs, and most programs train them almost exclusively to work in the academy. In 1995, 71 percent of Ph.D.'s got appointments of some kind in academic departments or research centers, but less than half of these appointments were tenure track.

A master's is theoretically still a sufficient qualification for many museum positions, but the market there is as tight as the academic market, with Ph.D.'s competing for the same jobs. There are, how-

RESOURCES

ASSOCIATIONS
American Anthropological
Association
(703) 528-1902

JOURNALS
American Ethnologist
Annual Review of Anthropology
Anthropology Newsletter
Yearbook of Physical Anthropology

NRC TOP TEN
Michigan
Chicago
UC-Berkeley
Harvard
Arizona-Tucson
Penn
Stanford
Yale
UCLA
UC-San Diego

BOOKS
American Anthropological Association,
Guide to Departments (AAA)

Clifford Geertz, *After the Fact: Two Countries, Four Decades, One Anthropologist* (Harvard)

Bruce Trigger, *A History of Archaeological Thought* (Cambridge)

WEB ADDRESSES
American Anthropological Association Web site
http://www.ameranthassn.org

ever, employment growth areas for anthropology M.A.'s: research jobs at corporations, advertising firms, government agencies and not-for-profits. Plus, because of their training in qualitative as well as quantitative analysis, anthropology M.A.'s may have an edge over their peers with political science or sociology degrees. M.A.'s in archeology will also find a healthy job market in the field of cultural resource management. (See Archaeology chapter for more details.)

LINGUISTIC ANTHROPOLOGY
Arizona-Tucson
Chicago
UCLA
UT-Austin

ARCHAEOLOGY
Arizona-Tucson
Penn
Vanderbilt

PHYSICAL ANTHROPOLOGY
Columbia
CUNY Graduate
  Center
Duke
Harvard
Northwestern
NYU
Penn State
SUNY Stony Brook
UC-Berkeley
UC-Davis

CULTURAL ANTHROPOLOGY
Chicago
Columbia
Harvard
Michigan
New School
Princeton
Rice
UC-Berkeley
UC-Santa Cruz
Virginia

APPLIED ANTHROPOLOGY
Southern Florida

SCIENCE AND TECHNOLOGY STUDIES
Cornell
MIT
Rochester Institute
  of Technology
UCLA

LINGUISTIC ANTHROPOLOGY
UCLA
UC-San Diego
Virginia Polytechnic
  Institute

VISUAL ANTHROPOLOGY
NYU
Temple
USC

CONSTELLATIONS

CHAPTER 20

ARCHAEOLOGY

"During several summers when I was an undergraduate, I worked on excavations in Greece and Italy," recalls Myles McCallum, "and that's when I got hooked on classical archaeology." McCallum, a fifth-year graduate student in the classics department at SUNY Buffalo, recently started to research his dissertation on Falerii Novi, an ancient hamlet fifty kilometers north of Rome. "I'm principally concerned with discerning ancient settlement patterns and their relationship to systems of communication, transportation, and land use." Besides having the opportunity to work outdoors in Italy during the summer, McCallum enjoys his research because "it's like doing a puzzle. You have some scraps of information from the written record and from excavations, and you use your imagination to fill in the gaps, to make from the pieces a picture of the ancient countryside."

Archaeology satisfies the need for historical continuity with a human past. For some people, a textual record is enough of a bridge to that past. But archaeologists seek a more material link in digs across the globe: a Chu dynasty village in eastern Jiangsu Province; an Iron Age fortress at En Hatzeva, Israel; the tomb of a Maya king at La Milpa in northwestern Belize; or an ancient hamlet near Rome.

WHY ARCHAEOLOGY?

The discipline of modern archaeology, which is grounded in anthropology and classics, endeavors to reconstruct and understand past human behavior by discovering, collecting, and interpreting the products of prehistoric and historic human societies and the traces of their impact on the environment. Drawing on laboratory science, social science, and the humanities, many archaeologists attempt to explain unrecorded or partially recorded human events, while those more inclined to theoretical questions hotly debate the field's goals and methods.

Before the nineteenth century, the past was more pillaged than pondered, because many archaeologists were amateurs. Ernest Hutton once described these amateurs as the "senile playboys of science rooting in the rubbish heaps of antiquity." The image of Thomas Howard, the earl of Arundel, furnishes a classic type: the adventuresome diplomat wielding pickax and spade, plundering Greece of sculpture and monuments, wishing for nothing less than to "transplant ancient Greece to England." Or consider Italy's King Charles III, who, to excavate the large, grassy mound that covered the ancient city of Herculaneum, employed the services of Rocque Joaquin de Alcubierre, a Spanish engineer who expedited his work by using gunpowder to tunnel through the sixty-foot layer of volcanic debris buried just beneath the grass.

Though the smuggling of artifacts continues, the days of plunder have given way to scientific rigor. Consider an excavation that recently took place in Foley Square in lower Manhattan. During the nineteenth century, Foley Square was known as Five Points, a tenement district famous as the home of thieves, thugs, and prostitutes. But the construction of a courthouse in Foley Square in the winter of 1996 supplanted this image of lawlessness. Acting in accordance with federal regulations requiring the excavation of historically valuable sites before construction, archaeologists unearthed some 850,000 artifacts, many of them testaments to the domestic lives of a law-abiding population of Irish immigrants. Among the finds were Staffordshire tea sets, high-quality bone toothbrushes, clay pipes decorated with Irish Home Rule slogans, and a monkey skeleton, suggesting that one of the residents was an organ grinder.

A team of archaeologists spent months in a lab underneath the U.S. Customs House near the World Trade Center assembling, photographing, X-raying, and dating artifacts. Instead of following the lead of Indiana Jones by blasting an underground passage to the Ark of the Covenant, the archaeologists were able to blast away inaccurate ideas about the past through their scientific analysis of seemingly mundane artifacts. As archaeologist Rebecca Yamin, the team's supervisor, remarked of the dig, "It's fascinating to have your preconceptions blown apart."

HOW ARCHAEOLOGY HAS TAKEN SHAPE

The discipline of archaeology traces its lineage to the antiquarian organizations of the eighteenth and early nineteenth centuries, such as the German Archaeological Society in Rome and the Imperial Odessa Society of History and Antiquity in Russia. The Society of Dilettante, founded in England in 1734, achieved great notoriety with its sponsorship and subsequent publication of James Stuart and Nicholas Revett's survey of ancient Greek monuments, *The Antiquities of Athens*. The success of such societies led to the formation of institutions like the British Museum and the Nationalmuseet of Copenhagen, both of which housed new-found archaeological treasures. Aided by the financial resources of European governments, each institution began to employ research departments with professional staffs.

These newfangled professional archaeologists turned to the comparative methods developed by German philologists Wilhelm von Humboldt and Franz Bopp. Empirical observations based on specific cases came to replace the search for universal rules about the past. C.J. Thomsen's elaboration of the Three Age System (Stone, Bronze, Iron) in the early nineteenth century at the Palace of Christiansborg is a well-known example. Although subsequently put into question, the division of artifacts into such a conceptual framework liberated archaeology from the narrow constraints of antiquarianism. Thomsen's derivation of a specific chronology from the observation of technological developments set the stage for future cultural taxonomies and the functionalist study of prehistory.

Thanks to an ever-increasing fervor about the ancient past—fueled to a large extent by Jean François Champollion's decipherment of the Rosetta Stone in 1822—archaeology made its predictable step into the academy. Champollion himself was elected to the first chair of Egyptology at the Collège de France in 1831. Across the English Channel, Oxford was gradually establishing a program in classical archaeology which developed into a full-fledged department by the 1880s. Overall, archaeology was established in European universities in the nineteenth century as a separate discipline rooted in the study of the remains of classical Egypt, Greece, and Rome.

In the United States, the establishment of the discipline followed a slightly different trajectory. The Peabody Museum of Archaeology and Ethnology was founded at Harvard University in 1866, and in that same year Daniel G. Brinton was appointed professor of archaeology at the University of Pennsylvania, the first such professor at an American university. In both cases the establishment of a doctoral program in archaeology was connected to the development of academic anthropology, a connection cemented at the turn of the century by Columbia University anthropologist Franz Boas. Boas specialized in the ethnographic study of Native Americans, and he realized that he could not accurately understand them without a thorough study of their present culture, their past culture, their biology, and their language. These topics became the basis of the four subdisciplines of anthropology: cultural anthropology, archaeology, physical anthropology, and linguistics.

> Before the nineteenth century, amateurs more often pillaged than systematically exhumed the past.

Ever since Boas's day, archaeology has been located mostly within anthropology departments in the United States. Archaeologists usually join the American Anthropological Association as well as an organization geared to their archaeological specialty, such as the Society for Historical Archaeology. Unlike anthropological archaeologists, however, classical archaeologists frequently draw on the resources of different disciplines: Specialists of the Mediterranean, North Africa, and the Middle East reside in classics and sometimes art history departments. Classical and anthropological archaeologists are distinct not only in their disciplinary affiliations, but also in their intellectual projects. For example, classical archaeologists have long done excavations primarily to fill in the gaps of the ancient written record, an approach not shared by anthropological archaeologists.

But the technological developments of this century, which have enabled anthropological and classical archaeologists to add sophisticated dating techniques to their toolbox, have brought the two camps closer together. In the late 1940s, Willard Libby of the University of Chicago developed a dating technique using a radioactive carbon isotope. The method's 70,000-year range enabled anthropological archaeologists to establish absolute dates for prehistoric sites, something they previously could do only through tree-ring dating. The range of absolute dating was increased greatly when archaeologists began to employ uranium and potassium isotopes, which decay at a much slower rate than carbon-14. It was a potassium-argon method, for example, that enabled scholars to date a hominid skull found in Tanganyika by the late Mary Leakey at between 1.5 million and 2 million years old. A recent development for classical archaeologists is neutron-activation analysis, which isolates the rare earth elements in ceramic artifacts. Knowing the elements in a pot, archaeologists can then pinpoint the physical location of the clay sources used in making the pot. This information aids in reconstructing trade routes, since archaeologists can trace a pot unearthed at one site back to its point of origin.

> Classical archaeologists now use neutron-activation analysis to isolate the rare earth elements in ceramic artifacts.

In terms of archaeological methodology, the greatest shakeup occurred in the 1960s with the emergence of what has come to be known as New Archaeology, which for the most part impinged upon anthropological archaeologists. Ground zero was Lewis Binford's 1964 manifesto, "A Consideration of Archaeological Research Design," published in *American Antiquity*. For some traditional archaeologists, "Binfordism" was nothing more than the flashy appropriation of techniques and methods stolen from the natural sciences and couched in annoyingly incomprehensible language. But the tide changed quickly, and by 1968, with the appearance of *New Perspectives in Archaeology*, authored by Binford and his wife, Sally, American New Archaeology was on its way to becoming the orthodoxy.

Binford set about training a formidable discipleship within the American university system. His most persuasive message was to denounce archaeology's hitherto untested reliance on subjective intuition: "Traditional methodology almost universally espouses simple induction as the appropriate procedure, and the archeological record is viewed as a body of phenomena from which one makes inductive inferences about the past." Deploring a lack of precision and rigor in terminology, Binford junked all *a priori* schemes of classification. In their stead he used a scientific methodology that allowed for the formulation and empirical testing of hypotheses about artifacts as a means of arriving at law-like generalizations about human behavior. Binford thought the rigors of scientific deduction would force archaeologists to see inductive methods as shoddy and to pay attention to the person behind the pot.

Though dissenters upbraided Binford for apparently assuming that the human past is absolutely knowable despite the trickiness of historical interpretation, it's undeniable that Binford enhanced the scientific prestige of archaeology. Just as importantly, he challenged archaeologists of all stripes to be more self-conscious about their data-collecting and data-analysis strategies.

WHAT'S NEXT

Although a student entering a graduate program in anthropological archaeology should have a good undergraduate grounding in anthropology, having some background in biology, botany, chemistry, and geology is also a good preparation for laboratory-oriented work. Students tend to bring laboratory experience to newer, less traditional subdisciplines in archaeology, such as paleoethnobotany, in which a site's botanical record is investigated to explain shifts in human cultural evolution. Background studies in statistics, computer science, and information science are becoming increasingly important too. If you need to bone up in those areas, you can probably do so with a year of introductory courses.

Because classical archaeologists work with artifacts to fill in the gaps of ancient written records, adequate preparation in Greek and Latin is indispensable. Douglas Welle, a graduate student in classics at SUNY Buffalo who works on ancient trade routes in the coastal regions of Tunisia, recommends that undergraduates interested in classical archaeology do as much work as possible on languages while in college. Graduate programs offer courses in ancient languages, but taking them means having less time to devote to coursework in archaeology. In addition to passing exams in Greek and Latin, students in many classical programs must also demonstrate proficiency in two modern languages: There's always the matter of speaking the language of the culture where one does fieldwork. For this reason anthropological archaeologists must be fluent in several languages, too.

Graduate students in both anthropological and classical archaeology stress that any serious student will enter graduate school already having done a substantial amount of fieldwork. Before going to graduate school, April Nowell worked on three different sites—in Ontario, Central America, and the Canadian High Arctic. Nowell, a graduate student in anthropological archaeology at the University of Pennsylvania, says these experiences taught her about different archaeological methods as well as the physical demands of fieldwork. In Ontario, she did historical archaeology in a reconstructed fort; in Central America, she did Mayan archaeology; and in the Canadian High Arctic, she did arctic archaeology among the Thule Inuit. "In graduate school you have to specialize almost immediately," explains Nowell, "and having been in the field and coming to know what kinds of archaeological methods I like and dislike, I felt confident choosing an area of specialization."

> Any serious student of archaeology will enter graduate school already having done a substantial amount of fieldwork.

In anthropology departments, archaeologists specialize according to geographic region (the Canadian High Arctic), artifact types (pottery, lithics), approach (bioarchaeology, geoarchaeology, cultural resources management), or dating techniques (radiocarbon, geographical information systems). Each specialization has its own set of requirements. Whatever the specialty, a graduate student should find a niche early on in a program to develop the necessary intellectual tools.

Apart from a good program at Penn, Ivy League schools do not have the leading archaeology departments. This is partly because for some time anthropology departments at newer schools have led the way in research. The archaeology of Native American cultures during many periods has traditionally been strongest at the state institutions of the Midwest and Southwest—the University of Michigan (one of the great overall powerhouses in most fields of archaeology), the University of Illinois at Urbana, the University of Illinois at Carbondale, the University of New Mexico, the University of Arizona at Tucson, and the University of Arizona at Tempe. But there are also strong programs at the University of California at Berkeley, the University of Minnesota at Twin Cities, the University of North Carolina at Chapel Hill, and Florida State University. For many fields there are concentrations of talent. In paleolithic archaeology, for instance, consider Penn, Rutgers University, Indiana University, and Arizona-Tempe. (To learn more about anthropology departments, read the Anthropology chapter in this guide.)

There are no definitive rankings of archaeology programs by the National Research Council or any other organization. The NRC does rank anthropology departments, but it does not rank departments according to their strengths in archaeology. As a rule, the large older programs that top the NRC rankings of anthropology departments are safe choices, but they are not necessarily the places to pursue particular subspecialties. Students interested in anthropological archaeology should consult the biennial *American Anthropological Association Guide to Departments*, which lists faculty interests in each department. To develop a list of the strongest programs in the areas you are considering, talk to professors and graduate students in archaeology. Check for specialization overlaps; urban archaeology, for example, can be done within the specialties of cultural resources management or historical archaeology. Also, look for a group of professors to work with and for strong ties between archaeology and other departments in other disciplines. Within any given subspecialty, faculty are in motion. You'll have to check around to make sure that scholars are still at the last institution listed in the *American Anthropological Association Guide to Departments*; the Web addresses listed at the end of this chapter can help you with that search. But at any given time a few hirings of top researchers in the archaeology of some subspecialties, for instance, the material remains of early states in the Middle East, can radically change the map.

> Funding is crucial for archaeologists because travel and fieldwork are nearly always expensive.

There are only two free-standing departments in classical archaeology in the United States: Boston University and Michigan. The Boston University program is closest to the traditional British model for archaeology. Like those at Cambridge, Sheffield, and others in the United Kingdom, it assumes that archaeologists have most in common with other archaeologists, rather than with scholars in any other discipline. So they bring together archaeologists in all periods, from early humankind to urban archaeologists, in one department.

But most classical archaeologists reside in classics departments—so make sure to read the Classics chapter in this guide as well. Notable departments in the United States are at SUNY Buffalo, the University of Texas at Austin, UNC-Chapel Hill, the University of Cincinnati, UC-Berkeley, the University of California at Santa Barbara, UCLA, Princeton University, and Florida State. UC-Berkeley has an interdisciplinary program in Ancient History and Mediterranean Archaeology. Penn has a similar arrangement, along with an important university museum collection for classical archaeology. In Canada, classics departments known for excellent work in archaeology are at the University of Alberta, the University of British Columbia, and McMaster University.

> Classical archaeologists often look to other disciplines—linguistics, history, anthropology—for resources.

Because their departments are not devoted wholly to archaeology, many classicists must look to other disciplines—linguistics, anthropology, European history, and art history—to assemble a toolkit for specializing. It's crucial to investigate what kinds of provisions a classics department has made for its students to do coursework in other departments.

Graduate study should include work in either a department's own collection of artifacts or an allied research museum, like the Hearst Museum of Anthropology at UC-Berkeley. Most programs require coursework in excavation and survey technique. This work depends, of course, on the availability of sites; check to see if faculty in a department are currently working on digs. Beyond the department, students interested in classical archaeology are encouraged to take advantage of the on-site programs offered by the American School of Classical Studies in Athens and the American Academy in Rome. (Because of their locations, competition for spots in these programs is fierce.) In anthropological archaeology, resources for finding out about digs include state historical and archaeological societies (many of which have field schools) and municipal museums. Major museums, like New York's Museum of Natural History, can inform you about summer digs for beginners.

Funding is more important for archaeologists than it is in most academic disciplines because travel and fieldwork are expensive. There are many funding sources. On the federal level, there is the National Endowment for the Humanities (NEH) and the Archaeology Program at the National Science Foundation (NSF). Senior archaeologists report that NSF funds are holding steady but not increasing, though competition for them intensifies. Since 1965, the NEH has awarded research grants for qualified archaeologists and Ph.D. candidates; applications are extensively reviewed and selected on merit. However, thanks to the 104th Congress, which drastically cut NEH funding, competition for these grants has become cutthroat.

Doctoral dissertation and senior research grants are available each year through the NSF, including grants for "Support of Systematic Anthropological Collections," or work in conserving, storing, or cataloging institutional collections. A panel of archaeologists convenes twice a year to evaluate applications, which are then submitted to outside professionals familiar with the student's field. The student's advisor should be able to assess which areas are suitable for funding and which are not. If, for example, a student is working with this country's urban archaeological record, he or she might consider seeking funds from a different source than the NSF, which is reluctant to approve grants for North American historical archaeology. Private foundations that fund dissertation research in archaeology include the National Geographic Society, the Leakey Foundation, and the Wenner-Gren Foundation for Anthropological Research.

The Fulbright Program awards grants to doctoral students carrying out dissertation research. Because the Fulbright pools grants by country and not by discipline, graduate students from different disciplines all compete for the grants allotted to any one country. Graduate students recommend that you think strategically about this arrangement: For instance, if you choose to do fieldwork in Tunisia instead of Italy—where archaeologists rub elbows with linguists, historians, and literary scholars—you could increase your chances of receiving a grant.

THE JOB MARKET

Competition for academic jobs which involve teaching, research, and curating is fierce. The consensus among faculty and graduate students is that although anthropological and classical archaeology have diversified tremendously over the last thirty years, branching into new research areas and new dating techniques, there has not been a corresponding increase in the number of available academic positions.

Classical archaeologists feel an added pressure. Due to the overall downsizing of humanities programs, classics departments are getting smaller, and faculty are being asked to wear many hats in the classroom. The trend is for new professors to be hired as "generalists" who teach courses in language and literature more often than courses in their area of specialization. "Being an expert in neutron-activation analysis won't get you a job at most schools," says Myles McCallum, "but being able to teach introductory and intermediate Greek and Latin will."

> The biggest growth area of employment for anthropological archaeologists is cultural resources management.

With their share of practical and technological training, archaeology M.A.'s and Ph.D.'s have more job opportunities outside the university than degree holders from other humanities disciplines. Positions in museums are highly sought, especially an attractive curatorship of a large research institution or a directorship of a state museum. A Ph.D. is required to hold a museum curatorship.

By far the biggest growth area of employment for anthropological archaeologists is cultural resource management (CRM). In the United States, more than half of all employed archaeologists are involved in CRM. They work for government agencies, like the U.S. Forest Service, National Park Service, Bureau of Land Management, and state historic preservation offices. They also work for university-based and private consulting firms. Most CRM projects are federally funded or licensed and take place on federal land. Most government positions involving CRM require an M.A., as do private sector positions with supervisory responsibilities.

CRM archaeologists now play major roles in planning and development because of the National Historic Preservation Act of 1966 and the Native American Graves and Repatriation Act of 1990, both of which place various legal restrictions on excavation and construction. Cultural resource management work has rural roots, having been put to use during the construction of the U.S. interstate and reservoir systems in the 1960s. In recent years, federal money for an increasing number of urban CRM projects has come from the U.S. Department of Housing and Urban Development. CRM archaeologists do everything from locating historic sites, excavating sites before they are obliterated by construction, and writing reports on excavations, to managing collections of excavated resources and managing protected sites. Archaeologists who work for oil companies and environmental organizations find that life tends to be nomadic during the first year in the field, since companies shuttle them around the country to explore new sites. But the advantage of living out of a suitcase is that you get to learn about different approaches to CRM.

RESOURCES

ASSOCIATIONS

American Anthropological Association
(703) 528-1902

Archaeological Institute of America
(617) 353-9361

Society for American Archaeology
(202) 789-8200

Society for Historical Archaeology
(520) 886-8006

Society of Professional Archaeologists
(919) 733-3141

JOURNALS

Archaeology
Current Archaeology
Federal Archaeology
Minerva
National Geographic
PIT Traveler

CONSTELLATIONS

ANTHROPOLOGICAL

Arizona-Tempe
Arizona-Tucson
Florida State
Illinois-Carbondale
Illinois-Urbana
Indiana
Michigan
Minnesota-Twin
  Cities
New Mexico
Penn
Rutgers
UC-Berkeley
UNC-Chapel Hill

CLASSICAL

Alberta (Canada)
Boston University
British Columbia
(Canada)
Cincinnati
Florida State
McMaster (Canada)
Michigan
Princeton
SUNY Buffalo
UC-Berkeley
UCLA
UC-Santa Barbara
UNC-Chapel Hill
UT-Austin

CRM is booming, but it is not without problems. Explains David Carlson, a professor at Texas A&M University, "Far more money is expended on surveys and excavations of endangered sites than on [continuing] projects funded by grants and focused on a particular research topic." For instance, CRM archaeologists often have to work in the shadow of bulldozers and backhoes, without the chance to return to a site and develop an on-going dig.

Archaeological Fieldwork Server
http://durendal.cit.cornell.edu/TestPit.html

Anthropological Resources on the Internet
http://www.nitehawk.com/alleycat/anth-faq.html

Anthropology on the Internet
http://dizzy.library.arizona.edu/users/jlcox/first.html

Frequently Asked Questions About a Career in Archaeology in the U.S.
http://www.museum.state.il.us/ismdepts/anthro/dlcfaq.html

Guide to Graduate Programs in Historical and Underwater Archaeology
http://www.azstarnet.com/~sha/sha col1.htm

National Trust for Historic Preservation
http://home.worldweb.net/trust/

World-Wide Web Virtual Library: Anthropology
http://www.usc.edu/deptv-lib/anthropology.html

World-Wide Web Virtual Library: Museums
http://comlab.ox.ac.uk/archive/other/museums.html

WEB ADDRESSES

CHAPTER 21

COMMUNICATION

Travis Dixon remembers taking an undergraduate course about racism and crime, and while the issues raised by the course fascinated him, the dearth of research on the subject left him perplexed. Today Dixon is doing his part to improve the situation for the next generation of undergraduates. A fifth-year graduate student at the University of California at Santa Barbara, Dixon is researching the relationship between race and crime on local and network television news broadcasts in Los Angeles. He is especially concerned with the impact of differences between the portrayal of black and white criminals on viewers' perceptions of blacks and whites generally. "If viewers see more black criminals than white ones, and if black criminals are portrayed as being more vicious than whites who have committed the same kind of crimes, do viewers become more fearful of blacks?" To test his hypothesis, Dixon is developing a code book to label the racist content of news broadcasts, which he will use to measure viewers' responses to the broadcasts.

Carolyn Brownstein is also interested in tracing media effects, but in a less quantitative manner. A sixth-year student at the University of Wisconsin at Madison, Brownstein is investigating coverage of the feminist anti-pornography movement of the 1970s and its impact on public perceptions of pornography. Past communication scholars have argued that media coverage corrupts social movements and dilutes their cultural impact by sensationalizing them. Brownstein's research has made her skeptical of this assertion. "If you look at how these women, who were not like Catharine MacKinnon or Andrea Dworkin but housewives and office workers, organized themselves, it's clear that they used the media to broadcast their message, without being captive to the media. And their message changed cultural attitudes about pornography."

WHY COMMUNICATION?

The media revolution is all the rage. Wherever you look, from *Wired* to the business pages of *The New York Times*, it draws attention. Some crow about using cyberspace to shuck off that most stubborn of physical entities, the body; some ponder the impact of interactive Internet communication on political life; and others editorialize about the economic implications of the Telecommunications Act of 1996. At the same time, it's becoming increasingly common for media to be studied throughout the university. Courses on film theory are taught in comparative literature departments, courses on television are taught in sociology, and courses on new media are cropping up in English.

Scholars in communication departments are flattered that media matters are attracting the attention of scholars beyond their precincts. But they are also wary of these other scholars, who may steal their thunder. What's more, communications scholars note that students from the humanities and social sciences still prefer to study media at the doctoral level in communication departments. Whereas English departments might have one, maybe two, professors teaching courses on media, communication departments house scholars who are all committed to the study of media—and from a variety of angles. It's this breadth, as well as depth, that has perennially attracted students to communication.

While breadth is one of the biggest draws to the field, it also makes it tough to get a handle on the field as a whole. David L. Swanson, a professor at the University of Illinois at Urbana, describes the field as being composed of a number of diverse subfields that are connected not so much intellectually as "politically by the organization of communication departments," and historically by the fact that most of them were established shortly after the end of World War II. The sub-fields he refers to range from radio to television to telecommunications to the Internet—and not everyone uses the same map, or search engine, to navigate it. And the range of subfields is as varied as the range of approaches. Michael Schudson, a professor at the University of California at San Diego, explains, "I think the truth is that though people have been trying to get an intellectual leverage point on the field from the early twentieth century on, no one's really quite done it, and the result is that the field is unusually eclectic, parasitic on other disciplines," such as sociology, anthropology, history, psychology, and literary study. In Schudson's department, roughly two-thirds of the professors have degrees in the traditional social sciences, while the other one-third have degrees in the humanities.

> The field's eclecticism is complicated by the fact that scholars are affiliated with various types of departments.

The field's eclecticism is further complicated by the fact that scholars are affiliated with various types of communication departments. They work in a Department of Communication at UC-Santa Barbara, UC-San Diego, Stanford University, and Ohio State University; in Speech Communication at Illinois-Urbana and the University of Georgia; in Communication Studies at the University of Kansas and the University of Iowa; in the School of Journalism and Mass Communication at the University of Colorado at Boulder, Wisconsin-Madison, and the University of Oregon; in the Annenberg School of Communication at the University of Pennsylvania and the University of Southern California; in Rhetoric and Communication at Temple University; in the College of Journalism at the University of Maryland at College Park; and in Radio-Television-Film at the University of Texas at Austin.

Moreover, some universities, especially big-ten type land-grant institutions, have several communication programs covering similar terrain. At Illinois-Urbana, for instance, there is a speech communication program as well as the Institute for Communication Research; at Indiana University, a telecommunications program alongside one in speech communication.

How, then, in light of all this intellectual and institutional eclecticism, can one ascertain what communication scholars actually do? A certain degree of clarity about the field's intellectual goings-on can be obtained if three things are kept in mind. First, although folks in com-

munication study interpersonal, group, and organizational communication as well as rhetoric, communication departments by and large
have consolidated around the study of mass media, and so this chapter
focuses only on mass media scholarship. Second, communication is less
a discipline than a hybrid field of the humanities and social sciences.
And third, research on mass media has followed three approaches: the
empirical study of media effects (social science), the qualitative study of
media audiences and cultures (cultural studies), and the critical study
of media institutions and economics (social critique).

Communication scholars, of course, blur the boundaries that exist
between research areas and methods. Nonetheless, it's best to consider
separately how each of these three approaches developed to highlight
the fundamental methods of each field, as well as what you might be
expected to do with them.

HOW COMMUNICATION HAS TAKEN SHAPE

MEDIA EFFECTS

Since the Greeks, critics in the West have thought of communication
in terms of rhetoric, the gentle art of persuasion. Democracy in
fourth-century B.C. Athens revolved around the discussion of political matters in a variety of public settings. To participate in public life,
a citizen needed to be an effective orator, which depended on knowing
how and when to use different styles of argument. The study of
rhetoric fulfilled a similar need in the American college of the eighteenth and nineteenth centuries. As members of the plutocracy, many
college students were destined for careers in law, politics, or the ministry, all of which placed a premium on skilled public oratory.

Communication departments were first established in the United
States in the late 1940s, and though they focused almost exclusively
on the persuasive power of communication, in part by teaching
courses in rhetoric and speech, they made their staple the study of the
behavioral effects of mass media—at that time newspapers, radio, and
film—on audiences.

Effects research grew out of an interest in media manipulation, the
roots of which stretch back before the late 1940s to Walter Lippmann,
a journalist and political philosopher who held that enlightened self-
reliance was the bedrock of democratic society. In a series of books

about news gathering on a nationwide scale, Lippmann systematically criticized both the press and the democratic public it created. In *Liberty and the News* (1920), Lippmann claimed that ideally media should transmit truths independent of power; in reality, however, because it trafficked in partisan coverage of events, the media communicated only half-truths. In *Public Opinion* (1922), he took his argument one step further, claiming the press can't better inform the public because the public was too fickle and ineducable. "Where all news comes at second-hand, where all the testimony is uncertain, men cease to respond to truths, and respond simply to opinions. The environment in which they act is not the realities themselves, but the pseudo-environment of reports, rumors, and guesses. Everything is on the plane of assertion and propaganda."

> The notion of media as information conduit has been the mainstay of effects research throughout the century.

What Lippmann was anticipating was the notion of media as information conduit, a model that has been the mainstay of effects research throughout this century. According to this model, a message travels one way, from sender to receiver, and the researcher's paramount task is to understand the message's effect on the receiver, rather than its production or interpretation by the sender. When in 1947 Wilbur Schramm founded the Institute of Communication Research at Illinois-Urbana, he designed a research program specifically around the model of media as information conduit. As Schramm explained in *The Process and Effects of Mass Communication* (1954), understanding the communication process involves analyzing "how attention is gained, how meaning is transferred from one subjective field to another, how opinions and attitudes are created and modified." A researcher, in other words, analyzes *who* says *what* to *whom* with what *effect*.

If effects researchers inherited a model of mass media from Lippmann, they got the tools for analyzing it from Paul Lazarsfeld. Born and educated in Austria, where he earned a doctorate in mathematics and taught psychology, Lazarsfeld came to the United States in 1933 as a Rockefeller Foundation traveling scholar and, through his interest in behavioral psychology, quickly established contacts with people in the fields of marketing, polling, and sociology. Lazarsfeld became the head of Columbia University's Bureau of Applied Social Research in 1939, and from there he drew on his academic and business contacts to put the Bureau at the forefront of empirical research about how audiences went about choosing radio programs. During World War II, along with Hadley Cantril of Princeton University and Wilbur Schramm of Illinois-Urbana, Lazarsfeld conducted propaganda research for the Office of War Information and the Army's Psychological Warfare Division. After the war, these scholars combined their wartime research experience with government funding of postwar communications research to nurture existing research centers—like Columbia's—and establish full-fledged communication departments—like Illinois-Urbana's.

> Lazarsfeld demonstrated that statistical and sampling methods could be used to evaluate and predict media effects.

Lazarsfeld established many precedents that still guide empirical research. For one, he demonstrated that statistical and sampling methods could be used to evaluate and predict media effects. For another, Lazarsfeld understood communication according to the template of marketing. In *The People's Choice* (1944), a study of voting behavior in Sandusky, Ohio, Lazarsfeld and co-authors Bernard Berelson and Hazel Gaudet saw the decision to vote for one candidate over another as akin to purchasing one brand instead of another, and campaigning as akin to brand-name advertising. Although Lazarsfeld and Gaudet concluded that the voting behavior of Sanduskyites was influenced more by community opinion leaders than campaign messages, their concern with understanding the influence of communication according to the logic of marketing remained unshaken.

Effects researchers have also inherited from Lazarsfeld a method for using industry needs for academic ends. For one thing, Lazarsfeld's administrative panache enabled him to fund Columbia's Bureau of Applied Social Research mostly through government and industry grants. (For years government money contributed up to 75 percent of the Bureau's annual budget.) When radio broadcasters, for instance, wanted to learn how better to cater their programming to audiences in order to increase the impact of advertising, Lazarsfeld was willing to tackle what he saw as basically a marketing question because it provided him with the opportunity to develop and test indexes, questionnaires, and laboratory setups, all of which yielded data that could be analyzed by communication scholars to explore the impact of media on human behavior.

Finally, whether surveying consumers to determine the impact of warning labels on products or observing children watching television to investigate the effect of violent programming on children's behavior, empirical researchers adhere to the fundamental premise of Lazarsfeld's method: Communication is information that has impacts upon the minds of individual readers, listeners, or viewers, and thereby causes a certain kind of behavior. And like Lazarsfeld, empirical researchers steer clear of investigating not only *why* such communication is produced in the first place, but also *how* it is interpreted.

Effects research is not without skeptics. Columbia professor Herbert J. Gans, for instance, has challenged researchers to develop a more supple understanding of the logic of effects. "Simulated violence has long been popular on entertainment television," Gans claims, "but America's high rates of violence have other causes"—such as poverty. "Violent television could even itself be an effect of other causes, even while concurrently acting in a cathartic fashion to help keep down actual violence." In addition to societal issues, Gans wants researchers to become more aware of how the media's effect on an audience is inseparable from how an audience chooses to use media, as catharsis, for instance. This is a tall order, for it means researchers can reasonably use the concept of effects only if they relinquish the notion of a passive audience. Until researchers understand the world in which people use media, Gans insists, "and provide a bedrock of interview and ethnographic findings, media researchers cannot judge the validity and reliability" of the statistical methods used to analyze effects.

> Skeptics want researchers to develop a more supple account of the logic of effects.

A current on-going study of television violence has risen to Gans's challenge. The National Television Violence Study (NTVS), funded by the cable television industry and administered and researched by communication professors at UC-Santa Barbara, Wisconsin-Madison, UT-Austin, and the University of North Carolina at Chapel Hill, aims to combat violence in society by studying how depictions of violence on television contribute to antisocial behavior. This has proven to be an extraordinarily complex task, not only because of the massive amounts of material that are being analyzed, but also because, as the 1994–95 research report readily admits, television violence does not have a uniform effect on viewers. "The outcome of media violence on viewers depends both on the nature of the depiction and the sociological and psychological makeup of the audience." The researchers are trying to understand effects by striking a balance between the analysis of violent content and the analysis of the context in which it is viewed.

For our purposes, the NTVS is notable in another respect—graduate training. Besides taking core courses in statistics and research methods, graduate students learn how to use the tools of effects research by working as research assistants on projects like the NTVS. According to Dale Kunkel, a UC–Santa Barbara professor who is a senior researcher on the project, most graduate students assist faculty on two or three research projects before researching their own dissertations. Of the seventeen graduate student research assistants involved in the NTVS, three are from UC–Santa Barbara, and Kunkel says they have been involved in the project from top to bottom. In the study's planning stages, they were involved in defining its fundamental concerns and methods, and in the working stages they have done everything from analyzing data and training undergraduate research assistants to writing sections of the reports.

"Research, research, and more research" is what graduate school is about, emphasizes Kunkel, and he strongly advises students who shy away from solitary work in the library or at a computer to think twice about entering the field. Communication programs tilted towards effects research, Kunkel adds, welcome students from a variety of educational backgrounds, though students familiar with the behavioral and empirical paradigms used in sociology or psychology will feel more at home than those educated in the humanities.

MEDIA AUDIENCES AND CULTURE

Effects researchers are unique in taking a strictly empirical approach to reception. For humanities-oriented scholars, communication is much more than the transmission of information from sender to receiver: It is a complex, two-way process whereby a culture is brought into existence, maintained over time, reinvented, and even challenged. Humanities-oriented scholars dispense with behavioral science and, in the words of Columbia professor James Carey, "examine the actual social process wherein significant social forms are created, apprehended, and used" by a group of people.

Carey is hardly alone in thinking the study of communication is indissolubly linked to the study of community. Earlier this century, while Walter Lippmann was railing against the shortcomings of public opinion, John Dewey was speculating about how people could use mass communication to cultivate a common ground of shared beliefs and thereby dispel the anomie of life in industrial America. Dewey wrote in *Democracy and Education* (1916), for instance, that people "live in a community in virtue of the things they have in common; and communication is the way in which they come to possess things in common." Carey claims Dewey is still indispensable for discussing communication as a form of culture. A glance at scholarship published in communication journals and books, however, suggests that today's researchers are indebted mostly to cultural studies. This interdisciplinary form of criticism gained a toehold in the American university in the late 1970s when North American scholars (influenced by the Birmingham Centre for Contemporary Cultural Studies, in England) started writing about the use of media in everyday life, often with a critical edge when discussing the relationship between culture and social liberation.

> Cultural studies replaces the sanitized notion of "information" with the grubbier idea of "interpretation."

Cultural studies established itself in communication by examining issues that effects research has systematically ignored—reception, taste, judgment, and interpretation. The model of media as information conduit, favored by effects research, casts audiences in the role of passive receivers of a signal. Cultural studies tries to complicate what is understood to happen on the reception end. Drawing on sociology, anthropology, and especially literary theory, it maintains that an audience is not a homogeneous group spellbound by a message but a mongrel mix of individuals who interpret texts with different values and tastes in mind. Communication, then, can't be analyzed apart from understanding a viewer's interpretation of it. In cultural studies, the emphasis on the sanitized term "information" is replaced by the emphasis on the grubbier term "interpretation." Finally, and perhaps most controversially, cultural studies critics like John Fiske of Wisconsin-Madison have pushed reception study to its limits with the claim that viewers, by constantly appropriating and subverting mass culture images, are capable of nothing less than a full-scale assault on the entire media industry. Punk meets the professoriate and becomes semiotic anarchy.

A landmark in reception studies was the publication of Janice Radway's book *Reading the Romance* (1984). Radway, a Duke University professor of literature, had a problem with how scholars have long dismissed popular-romance readers as philistines who uncritically lap up the genre's treacly prose and misogynist plots. She argued that mass culture scholars could arrive at such a perception only because, like effects researchers, they assigned a passive role to audience members. Moreover, Radway showed that scholars have judged romance readers without ever having spoken to them. In order to address this dearth of research, Radway logged sixty hours of interviews with forty-two Harlequin readers, each of whom she also asked to complete lengthy questionnaires. Combining this material with literary analysis of the novels, Radway concluded that Harlequin readers are hardly the dupes they have been made out to be. While they no doubt derive pleasure from reading the books, their pleasure stems as much from arguing with the books as from escaping into them.

> Ethnography has helped scholars demonstrate that viewers are active interpreters of texts.

Reading the Romance is a testament to the ways ethnography can fundamentally alter assumptions about the meaning and uses of mass communication. Indeed, as Sonia Livingstone of the London School of Economics explains, ethnography has been prominent in studies of film and television audiences and Internet users over the past ten years because it has helped scholars demonstrate "that viewers are active interpreters of texts and that viewing contexts vary widely in their impact on these interpretations."

But what ethnography has gained in prominence it has lost in consistency. For some scholars like Radway, who rely primarily on questionnaires and group and individual interviews for information, ethnography parallels the focus group studies made famous by marketing. For others, ethnography means the traditional anthropological method of going into the field as a participant observer, with one foot inside and one foot outside the group being studied. In the case of UC-San Diego professor Ellen Seiter, it involves using observations made while acting as an aide in a pre-school nursery to write her forthcoming book, a case study of how children from different social classes interact with each other via toys and cartoons.

Given this diversity of approaches, it is perhaps no wonder that ethnographers have come under fire for committing some serious methodological blunders. Typical are Radway's criticisms of her own methods for researching *Reading the Romance*. In the introduction to the book's second edition (1991), she faults herself for studying audiences from the top down instead of from the bottom up. Rather than observe a pre-existing community, as Seiter is doing, Radway observed a community that she herself had brought into existence through interviews and questionnaires. They were no more a natural community that would be a focus group interviewed about the appeal of a new laundry detergent. In the end, Radway claims that her self-criticisms are not a reason for abandoning ethnography but for doing it in a more modest manner—doing case studies of audiences without extrapolating from them to propose generalities about *the* audience.

POLITICAL ECONOMY/MEDIA INSTITUTIONS

Communication scholars who work in the tradition of political economy take a materialist, rather than a symbolic, approach to media production. They investigate connections between market structures and media meanings. If effects researchers and cultural studies scholars are interested in *what* is communicated and *to whom*, political economists are interested in *how*, *why*, and *with what means*.

Political economists are a contentious lot. Like Walter Lippmann, they are moralists who distrust mass media because it impoverishes the democratic process. Herbert Schiller, a professor at UC-San Diego and a guiding force among political economists of the media for nearly a half century, claims that "the ability to understand, much less overcome, increasingly critical national problems is thwarted, either by a growing flood of mind-numbing trivia and sensationalist material or by an absence of basic, contextualized social information." Unlike Lippmann, though, Schiller and other political economists employ various Marxist methods of analysis to explain how the principle of the free press is impoverished by corporate America's bottom-line mentality and its investment in maintaining itself as the status quo. Political economists write to stoke the flames of dissent, not only by analyzing the media scene but also by encouraging people to organize in the struggle against conglomeration, and to reclaim the media as a truly democratic forum.

> Political economists investigate connections between market structures and media meanings.

Research in this area has clustered primarily around two topics: the American media's infiltration of the Third World and the impact of corporate organization on the American broadcasting industry. Schiller caused quite a stir in the field with the publication of *Mass Communications and American Empire* in 1969, a well-documented study of how broadcasters colluded with the American government to establish American media monopolies in Latin America. Or take Michael Schudson's *Discovering the News* (1978), a study of how the late nineteenth-century transformation of the partisan press into a "neutral" press was governed more by the economic interests of U.S. newspaper combines than the ethical scruples of journalists. According to Schudson, it was cheaper for papers to run the skeletal stories picked up over the Associated Press wire, and the AP deemed these stories "objective" only after they met with wide acceptance.

> Many political economists chafe at effects research because it accepts media institutions at face value.

More recently, Robert McChesney, a professor at Wisconsin-Madison, has published *Telecommunications, Mass Media, and Democracy* (1993), a landmark history of the battle for control of radio broadcasting that occurred in the late 1920s. Like much work in political economy, McChesney's book is based on extensive research in public and corporate archives. It demonstrates how capitalists keen on radio broadcasting's advertising potential lobbied the FCC to commercialize a system that had been established by not-for-profit organizations interested in public service—and how these not-for-profits, bolstered by intense public dislike of commercialization, fought tooth-and-nail against the radio lobby. McChesney's is a cautionary tale with clear implications for today's netizens.

Because their mandate is not just analyzing the status quo but toppling it, political economists chafe at effects research, which they claim takes media institutions at their own estimation. Isolating the study of a message's effect from its context, they insist, makes the mistaken implication that the industry creating the message is benign. At the same time, many political economists eschew the polemical strain of cultural studies; they think it is deeply misguided to assume that a subversive interpretation of, say, a Madonna video amounts to rebellion against Time Warner. In fact, McChesney goes so far as to say that cultural studies scholars are nothing but apologists for corporate media empires, since by focusing on reception at the expense of production they "elevate individual consumption of commercial culture to the level of political activity." For political economists, discussing the political dimensions of culture is crucial, but only if such discussion begins in an analysis of culture's link to economic institutions, especially corporations.

JOURNALISM

Communication first became a viable research area when communication research units piggybacked on journalism departments after World War II. Schramm, for example, thought it logical to locate the Institute of Communication Research within Illinois-Urbana's journalism department. Although communication scholars were primarily social scientists, and journalists were primarily humanists, both groups focused on forms of mass communication. The journalism departments at the University of Minnesota at Twin Cities, Wisconsin-Madison, and Michigan State University quickly followed suit, setting up their own communication research units. As a result, journalism departments started to incorporate the social scientific approaches of communication scholarship into their curricula, as well as expanding the focus of study beyond newspapers and magazines to include radio, television, film, and advertising.

If communication gained a toehold in the university through journalism departments, journalism also gained something from the bargain: professional status. Fed by the government grants and contracts that followed World War II, schools like Illinois-Urbana and Wisconsin-Madison evolved from being predominantly teaching institutions into full-blown research universities. With this evolution toward research, the heads of journalism departments needed to have Ph.D.'s in order to upgrade their departments, so journalism departments began to offer doctorates in communication to give themselves academic legitimacy. As Schramm explained in 1987 while reflecting on the field's history, "As the doctorate became more necessary, more and more of the journalism schools began to offer doctorates, so that a prospective teacher or researcher in journalism could earn a doctorate in communication rather than political science, sociology, psychology, or history."

And with that doctorate, a gulf opened between vocational training and research. Says Stanford professor Steven Chaffee, "There's a general stress between those who teach professional skills and those who do research on the impact of mass communication." Though doctoral programs in communication owe much to journalism departments for their existence, they are not in the business of training journalists. If you want to be a journalist, you need to enroll in one of the M.A. programs offered by Northwestern University, Columbia, the University of Missouri, Stanford, New York University, and Wisconsin-Madison, among others, not a Ph.D. program.

WHAT'S NEXT

One can't turn to rankings to make sense of departmental differences because the National Research Council does not rank communication departments. But this is just as well, for if you've read other disciplinary chapters in this guide you've probably noticed a recurring issue: Faculty are rankled by the NRC rankings because they do not take into account departmental specialties.

If you are considering a Ph.D. in communication, you should begin by thinking about the kind of research you want to do. "Find the people who are leaders in the field you want to study," advises a graduating doctoral student in political communication at UC-San Diego. At a place like Stanford, suggests a recent graduate concerned with the psychology of human interactions with technology, it helps to be able to work in the same area of research as a faculty member: "You really have to do what someone else is doing." If you're not sure about whom on the faculty to work with or have yet to nail down a particular research topic, check with current graduate students in the departments you're considering in order to determine whether or not the lack of a strong faculty mentor will send you falling through the cracks.

It was the top reputation of the school, however, that drew Joe Borrell to Penn's Annenberg School of Communication, where he is studying radio. Borrell warns that because of its reputation, admission to Penn is tough. For programs generally considered the strongest in each of the three broad areas discussed above, consider the following list.

If you're interested in doing empirical research about media effects, well-known strong programs are UC-Santa Barbara (with Dale Kunkel and Edward Donnerstein), Indiana (with Walter Gantz), Michigan State, Minnesota-Twin Cities, Pennsylvania/Annenberg East (with Elihu Katz), Stanford (with Steven Chaffee and Byron

Reeves), UT-Austin, and Wisconsin-Madison (with Robert Hawkins, Jack McLeod, and Joanne Cantor).

Departments well-known for work on cultural studies are UC-San Diego (with Ellen Seiter), Columbia (with James Carey), Illinois-Urbana (with James Hay, David Desser, and Paula Treichler), Indiana (with Michael Curtin), Iowa, Maryland-College Park, Penn/Annenberg East (with Carolyn Marvin), UMass-Amherst, Northwestern, UT-Austin, University of Southern California/Annenberg West (with Marita Sturken), and Wisconsin-Madison (with John Fiske).

Institutions well-known for work on political economy and the history of media are UC-San Diego (with Dan Schiller and Michael Schudson), Illinois-Urbana (with John Nerone), Indiana (with Christopher Anderson), Iowa, UMass-Amherst (with Justin Lewis), Northwestern (with Susan Herbst), Oregon (with Janet Wasko), Penn/Annenberg East (with Oscar Gandy), UT-Austin, Stanford (with Ted Galasser), and Wisconsin-Madison (with Robert McChesney and Lewis Friedland).

THE JOB MARKET

Most people who earn doctorates in communication apply for academic teaching positions, and the academic job market in communication is not as promising as it was a decade ago. Like many humanities and social science departments, communication departments have suffered during the academy's recent economic downturn. Even top departments have been hit hard, primarily because they are at state institutions that have been forced by budget cuts to scale back on the hiring of full-time faculty. This downsizing coincided with the fact that, as Steven Chaffee of Stanford notes, the field itself is experiencing growth. Over the last decade, UC-Santa Barbara, the University of Alabama, Georgia Technical University, the University of Florida, Cornell University, and Oklahoma State University have all established Ph.D. programs in communication, with the result that there are now more Ph.D.'s than there were five years ago competing for roughly the same number of academic jobs. Faculty do note, though, that job-hunting isn't anywhere near as desperate as it is in English, where since 1989 the number of advertised job openings for Ph.D.'s has dropped nearly 50 percent, and the job placement rate for new Ph.D.'s is a measly 45 percent.

UC-San Diego professor Ellen Seiter recommends that job seekers go on the market well armed. Besides having solid scholarly credentials (the Ph.D. in hand, and one or two published articles), job seekers should also have developed the ability to teach a wide range of courses. Especially useful is experience in teaching a technical course, such as journalism, or introductory film—or video making. In a tough job market, Seiter says, breadth is a selling point to departments that, faced with a reduced budget, don't hesitate to ask faculty to wear several hats.

Whereas the grad student ranks in English and philosophy departments are almost exclusively filled with apprentice scholars, in communication departments apprentice scholars rub shoulders with aspiring entrepreneurs. Communication graduates who search for employment beyond academe's walls more often than not have M.A.'s, and they often land jobs in market research, political polling, public relations, or political consulting. (Those with a quantitative background have a leg up in the competition for these jobs.) Students are also landing jobs in telecommunications and new media. If you are interested in those fields, you might consider earning an M.A. at an

RESOURCES

NRC RANKINGS
Not Available

ASSOCIATIONS
International Communication Association
(512) 454-8299

Speech Communication Association
(703) 750-0533

FURTHER READING
Charles R. Berger and Steven H Chaffee, eds., *Handbook of Communication Science* (Sage)
"The Future of the Field," *The Journal of Communication* (Summer-Fall 1993)
Dan Schiller, *Theories of Communication* (Oxford)

WEB ADDRESSES
Communication Departments on the Web
http://cavern.uark.edu/comminfo/www/departments.html
Communication Resources on the Web
http://www2.soc.hawaii.edu/css/com/resources/com-resources.html
Cultural Studies and Critical Theory Server
http://www.eng.hss.cmu.edu/theory/

institution like the University of Baltimore or other programs with a strong practical bent.

Graduates of Penn, USC, and Stanford have traditionally been the most successful at landing jobs outside academe: USC/Annenberg West because of its proximity to Hollywood, and Stanford and Penn/Annenberg East because of connections with government research. Chaffee notes that over the last five years, the percentage of Stanford doctorates who land jobs in the nonacademic sphere has increased from roughly 10 to 30 percent, and that they land these jobs by design, not default, having never intended to become a professor. "That's where the action is, that's where the money is," says Youngme Moon, a recent Stanford graduate, pointing out that faculty themselves are delving into industry-related research in marketing and product development. A few years ago, she recalls "there was still a lingering lack of respect for applied research for industry, but by and large people don't even blink any more." That said, Moon herself turned down offers for high-paying jobs in Silicon Valley; instead, she'll be starting as an assistant professor at MIT.

CONSTELLATIONS

MEDIA EFFECTS	MEDIA AUDIENCES AND CULTURE	POLITICAL ECONOMY/MEDIA INSTITUTIONS
Indiana	Columbia	Illinois-Urbana
Michigan State	Illinois-Urbana	Indiana
Minnesota-Twin Cities	Indiana	Iowa
Penn/Annenberg East	Iowa	Northwestern
Stanford	Maryland-College Park	Oregon
UC-Santa Barbara	Northwestern	Penn/Annenberg East
USC/Annenberg West	NYU	Stanford
UT-Austin	Penn/Annenberg East	UC-San Diego
Wisconsin-Madison	UC-San Diego	UMass-Amherst
	UMass-Amherst	UT-Austin
	USC	Wisconsin-Madison
	UT-Austin	
	Wisconsin-Madison	

CHAPTER 22

ECONOMICS

If you're considering graduate study in economics, perhaps you've spent some time imagining yourself, fresh out of graduate school, joining the ranks of the 117,000 economists who grapple with the national, and increasingly global, economic forces that are the engines of daily life. Maybe you've pictured yourself forecasting the return on Pacific Rim investments from within a Wall Street citadel of steel and glass, pounding the pavement in a sweatshop district and educating workers about global markets, or explaining to a governor the growing inequality between income and wealth. Or maybe you've pictured yourself working inside the beltway for the Fed compiling statistics on income and poverty, or explaining the finer points of international banking to undergraduates. After all, of the nation's 117,000 economists, roughly 23,000 (or 20 percent) are academics who teach undergraduates, conduct research, write books and articles, and train graduate students to conduct research.

Joanna Wayland Woos has worked as an economist inside and outside the classroom. Woos is currently a private consultant for software companies, a career she embarked upon after having earned a Ph.D. in economics in 1991 and teaching at a liberal arts college for several years. Woos's interest in economics crystallized into a passion nearly two decades ago, when, after earning a B.A., she worked as an international economist for a major New York bank. Woos was enjoying her job, but sensed she needed more expertise in economic theory to face "the really interesting questions"—how, for instance, does widespread deregulation among nations impinge upon the international flow of financial services? She decided the only way she could learn how to approach such a question was by going to graduate school and acquiring more analytic tools.

Once Woos got to graduate school, she was shocked when her professors dismissed her work experience as an economist because, as she recalls, they didn't think it was relevant. While Woos eventually wrote a dissertation addressing the very question that prompted her to earn a Ph.D., during her stint in graduate school she was often taken aback by the lack of intellectual commerce between the university and the workaday world of the economics she loved.

WHY ECONOMICS?

Woos's experience doesn't imply that academic economists don't ponder markets or portfolios or international finance. A quick perusal of any academic economics journal will prove they do. And there are even a number of academic economists who have trained their formidable analytic skills on writing about economic issues for nonacademic publications. Paul Krugman of MIT has published articles in *Slate* and *The New York Times Magazine*; Gary Becker of the University of Chicago has written a column for *Business Week* for over a decade; Robert Heilbroner of the New School for Social Research has penned articles for *The New Yorker*, *The New York Review of Books*, and *Dissent* over the course of four decades. And all three regularly dispatch missives to the Op-Ed pages of the nation's most revered newspapers.

But the journalistic careers of Krugman, Becker, and Heilbroner are exceptions: The research and writing that most academic economists do is tailored to an academic audience, not an everyday one. In 1986 Herbert Stein explained that when he arrived in Washington in 1969 to serve on President Nixon's Council of Economic Advisors, "I could read and reasonably understand almost everything in the economic journals." But after having moved from the ivory tower to the nation's corridors of power, Stein could "read hardly any of it."

Together with Woos's reflection on her graduate school experience, Stein's observation hints at a fundamental truth about graduate study in economics: As a graduate student, you will be trained to become an *academic* economist, and the academic economics profession, by and large, favors mathematical theory building over and above any work redolent of philosophical speculation or political cage rattling. In all but a handful of programs, you will be challenged to master highly abstract mathematical models, among other things, and you will be asked to leave your dog-eared copies of Marx and Menger at the door.

HOW ECONOMICS HAS TAKEN SHAPE

Economists have often prescribed economic policies as an emollient of social ills, but without the guidance of a Hippocratic oath or the protection of malpractice insurance. If an economist's prescriptions are perceived to be right, people will rally around, as they did with Keynes. If proven wrong, people will think an economist a quack and, when truly incensed, even burn him in effigy, as they did with Paul Volcker, who was chairman of the Federal Reserve Board from 1979 to 1987. Economists, then, find themselves weighing the relative security of pure research against the dicey nature of public policy to balance the peculiar burdens of their professional role.

> Economists find themselves weighing the relative security of pure research against the dicey nature of public policy.

Indeed, as you ponder graduate school in economics and find yourself estimating the costs and rewards of this trade-off, you are reckoning with a tension that has shaped the academic economics profession from the outset. The American Economics Association was founded when academic economists splintered off from the American Social Science Association in 1885. At the AEA's inaugural convention in Saratoga Springs, conferees could not reach an accord about their association's official identity and became embroiled in debates about the political pitch of the association platform. The majority favored an apolitical platform that celebrated the research agenda of the modern university, while a minority hammered together a progressive platform that advocated the exposure of economic exploitation and the proposal of social reforms.

The majority eventually won the battle over the AEA platform, but they lost the larger war over the profession's role in the public sphere.

At a time when Gilded Age capitalists were crushing labor advocates, and some academic economists were advocating natural law theories of the economy that vindicated such tactics, progressive economists refused to repudiate their cause. The most caustic critic of capitalists and their academic apologists was Thorstein Veblen, the son of scrappy Norwegian farmers who had settled in Wisconsin. Schooled in philosophy, anthropology, and psychology, as well as economics, Veblen considered the organization of the economic system as extending beyond market interactions to include psychological needs, social institutions, and cultural values. Deeply influenced by Edward Bellamy's utopian novel *Looking Backward* (1888), Veblen lashed out against the unjust institutions and social mores that, in his view, corrupted the liberating force of technology and industry.

Should you follow in Veblen's footsteps, you will be practicing *heterodox* economics, and you will be rubbing elbows with the small number of academic economists who favor a philosophical, multidisciplinary inquiry into the goals of economies, and who refuse to accept capitalist markets at face value. Like Veblen, heterodox economists read widely and deeply in political and intellectual history. Moreover, they favor the empirical study and ethical appraisal of both the economic goals people set themselves and the social consequences of attempts to achieve those goals.

> Heterodox economists favor a philosophical, multidisciplinary inquiry into the goals of economies.

For instance, whereas natural law economists saw the individual as driven by the desire to maximize pleasure and minimize pain, Veblen, in *The Theory of the Leisure Class* (1899), scrutinized a certain class of individuals—conspicuous consumers—who emulated each other to gain social esteem. Taking issue with how this class sponged off the productive labor of others, he argued that wealth and virtue are not synonymous. And whereas natural law economists saw equilibrating tendencies in business cycles, he demonstrated in *The Theory of Business Enterprise* (1904) that business cycles in the United States were constantly rocked by instability due to excessive capitalization and a predatory price system. Moreover, Veblen proclaimed that capitalists are not the engineers of progress but its enemy, for they place industry in the service of business and profits, and not the needs of the greatest number of people. Veblen died in 1929, just as the stock market crash seemed to confirm one of his fundamental points: The pecuniary demands of business and government turn the productive resources of an economy into a shambles.

During and after the Great Depression, academic economics experienced a tremendous influx of European engineers, physicists, and mathematicians. Facing dim prospects in their original fields of research, and fleeing political strife at home, these scientists were lured to the field by money the Rockefeller Foundation poured into it to coax it into taking a scientific direction. Additionally, these converts were deeply influenced by Paul Samuelson's dissertation, *The Foundations of Economic Analysis* (a weighty tome circulated among the elect in 1937 and finally published in 1947), which earned economics a place in the temple of the natural sciences. Samuelson graced the title page of *Foundations* with the phrase "Mathematics is a language"—Yale University professor Willard Gibbs's rejoinder to his Yale colleagues as they debated whether students should be required to take courses in either languages or mathematics. In 1952, Samuelson admitted to having one regret about Gibbs's quote: "I wish he had made it 25 percent shorter—so as to read as follows: 'Mathematics *is* language.'"

> Orthodox economists use mathematics to define the types of goal-oriented activity undertaken by individuals.

Should you follow the "mathematics is language" principle, you will be joining the majority of academic economists, and you will be practicing *orthodox* economics, which sets itself the task of using mathematics to define the classes of goal-oriented activity undertaken by rational individuals and groups in a variety of markets. Orthodox economists work deductively from axioms about perfect competition, self-correcting markets, and rational individual choice. They use mathematics to create theoretical models of those axioms: If the mathematical demonstration of assumptions works out logically, then one has arrived at an economic law. Orthodox economists, moreover, prefer to think of themselves as doing pure science, and they believe that the Keynesian notion of fine tuning the economy is beyond their purview. Chicago professor Robert E. Lucas, for instance, thinks the primary forces driving society are economic, but holds that "economic policy is not a matter for a few economists to settle. There's too much else involved in it."

In fact, the work of Samuelson and Lucas represents everything antithetical to Veblen's brand of economics. Crucially, Samuelson shifted the tone of economics away from the discursive, sociological arguments favored by Veblen toward the terse style and formalist presentation of articles in physics journals. To take one example, Samuelson modeled an understanding of utility on the laws and equations of thermodynamics. He saw economic utility, the exchange between inputs and outputs, as a form of the conservation of energy. "Until the laws of thermodynamics are repealed," vowed Samuelson, "I shall continue to relate outputs to inputs—i.e., to believe in pro-

Samuelson's 1970 Nobel Prize signaled the triumph of mathematical theory in economics.

ductive functions." Indeed, to judge by the decisions of some librarians, Samuelson succeeded brilliantly at using mathematics to make economics a kind of physics. At Columbia University, copies of his equation-rich *Foundations* are housed in both the economics and engineering libraries.

In 1970, Samuelson became the first U.S. recipient of the Nobel Prize in Economic Science, and *The New York Times* dubbed the laureate "the Einstein of economics for developing a unified field theory of economic activity." The bestowal of the Nobel upon him symbolized the triumph of mathematical theory in economics. It was also in the early 1970s that Lucas (who would become a Nobel recipient himself) was publishing groundbreaking mathematical theory, and more and more economists were learning how to use computers to model data sets for theories. Today, articles versed in mathematical theory still dominate the pages of the profession's top journals: *American Economic Review, Econometrica, Economic Journal, Journal of Political Economy,* and *Quarterly Journal of Economics.*

Of course, the heterodox economists have plenty to say about the rise of orthodox economics. One of the most acerbic critics is the New School's Robert Heilbroner, who claims that as orthodox economics strives for mathematical rigor at the expense of social vision, it generates more heat than light. Orthodox economics, says Heilbroner, "comes more and more to resemble a game played with and against other economists, on whose outcome nothing much depends except academic prestige, rather than a serious undertaking that must be played out, for keeps, in the real word." Heilbroner takes issue with the major working assumption of orthodox economics: that ideas about how markets *ought* to work can be sealed off from ideas about how markets *actually* work. A junior heterodox economist concurs. Orthodox economics restricts economics to mathematical techniques, he says, "to get around the fuzzy moral problems that can't be modeled" and are inherent to economic decisions. Under the orthodox dispensation, contends the junior professor, economics is a discipline without a subject: "The profession's faith should be like Adam Smith's: It should value his *Theory of Moral Sentiments* alongside his *Wealth of Nations*."

According to Arjo Klamer and David Colander, though, students entering graduate school think that boning up on differential equations, rather than reading deeply in moral philosophy, is the best preparation for graduate study in mainstream economics. In *The Making of an Economist* (1990), their landmark study of graduate training in the field, Klamer, a George Washington University professor, and Colander, a Middlebury College professor, note that of the 212 students they surveyed, 43 percent believed that a knowledge of economic literature was unimportant for graduate school. Sixty-eight percent believed that a thorough knowledge of the economy was unimportant, while only three percent believed it was important. Fifty-seven percent believed that excellence in mathematics is very important, while two percent believed it was unimportant. There was a strong sense among the graduate students, Klamer and Colander report, "that economics was a game and that hard work in devising relevant models that demonstrated a deep understanding of institutions would have a lower payoff than devising models that were analytically neat."

> Boning up on differential equations is the best preparation for graduate study in economics.

Students from the United States seem less and less willing to play this game. In 1991, the Committee of College Faculty issued a stunning report which appeared in the *Journal of Economic Literature*, a journal published by the AEA. The Committee was composed of economics professors from Northeastern colleges (Oberlin, Amherst, Haverford, Middlebury, Smith, Swarthmore, Wellesley, Wesleyan, and Williams) whose graduates have traditionally excelled in graduate study in economics but have recently fared less well. It found that from 1966 to 1986 the number of Ph.D.'s in economics earned by students from the United States fell from 70 to 50 percent. Astonishingly, from 1983 to 1986 alone, enrollment of U.S. students dipped from 63 to 50 percent. The report surmises that U.S. students with a humanities background are turning away from graduate study in economics because of the discipline's disproportionate focus on mathematics: "The emphasis on technique, at the expense of attention to the analytical issues of economics, tends to depreciate the importance of the intuitive and creative talents of the liberal arts graduates."

The resulting decline in the enrollment of U.S. students shows no signs of reversing itself. In 1992 at Chicago, roughly 75 percent of the incoming graduate students were from abroad. In 1996 at Princeton University, roughly 70 percent were from abroad. Moreover, according to the National Research Council, of the 980 Ph.D.'s awarded in economics in 1995, nearly 42 percent were awarded to students from the United States, while roughly 55 percent were awarded to students from abroad studying in the United States on temporary or permanent visas. (The 1995 figures are virtually identical to those for 1994, 1993, and 1992.)

Many students from abroad report that they feel at home in U.S. economics departments because they hold advanced degrees in mathematics and engineering when they arrive. Departments, in turn, welcome these students because many are bankrolled by their national governments, sometimes with the stipulation that they will return home after their education and work for the government. Also, since the core of economic theory is mathematical, professors don't fret about having to surmount a language barrier with nonnative speakers, as might be the case in a literature or history program. What Samuelson announced forty years ago still rings true: Mathematics, not English, is the universal language of economics.

WHAT'S NEXT

As a consumer of economic programs, you face a homogeneous market, something akin to the phone system before it was deregulated. Colander estimates that 95 percent of all graduate programs in the United States teach an identical core curriculum. During the first year of study, students take the same set of courses: micro and macro theory, which draw heavily on matrix algebra and calculus, and econometrics, which is the application of statistics to economic data. Such graduate study, notes Klamer, does not complicate an undergraduate education in economics. Rather, it "builds vertically from undergraduate education.... It formalizes concepts the student met in undergraduate study—teaching new tools that can be used to analyze the same issues more carefully rather than teaching how to make better use of the undergraduate tools." You'll need these undergraduate basics to take the GRE subject test in economics, which graduate departments may require or recommend for admission. But a Princeton graduate student goes so far as to say that, unless you majored in mathematics or physics in college, graduate school will "destroy what you brought with you so it can build you up from scratch." A Chicago graduate student agrees: "It's not like studying economics. They have these tools that they want you to learn, and they throw them at you all at once. It's sink or swim." Graduate students liken the experience of learning how to use these tools to boot camp; it's grueling, boring, and dry.

> Ninety-five percent of all graduate programs in the United States teach an identical core curriculum.

Yet both the Chicago and Princeton students say that the second year promises a "reversal of fortune," since students can concentrate on mixing theoretical and applied work in field courses like labor, international trade, industrial organization, and public finance. At the end of the second year, students take their comprehensive examinations to demonstrate their knowledge of the core curriculum. During the third year they participate in workshops and seminars, essaying ideas to prepare for the dissertation, which most students then start writing during the fourth year.

There are several distinctions among orthodox programs. One is the saltwater/freshwater distinction. Programs on the East and West Coasts like Princeton, Harvard University, the University of California at Santa Cruz, and the University of California at Berkeley have traditionally been Keynesian and applied in orientation, whereas programs around the great lakes, like the University of Minnesota at Twin Cities, the University of Rochester, and Chicago, have been laissez-faire and austerely theoretical. The University of Wisconsin at Madison and the University of Michigan once stood apart from freshwater schools for their long-standing devotion to applied economics and public service, but recently they too have embraced the theoretical orientation.

There are also ideological distinctions. For instance, Chicago libertarians routinely scorn those Princeton liberals whose research supports a steady increase in the minimum wage. And in *The Making of an Economist*, Klamer and Colander demonstrated how this kind of ideological difference trickles down to graduate students by asking them to name which economist, dead or alive, they respect the most. At Chicago, the top five choices were, in descending order of popularity: Robert Lucas, Adam Smith, Milton Friedman, Gary Becker, and Paul Samuelson. The Harvard top five: J.M. Keynes, Karl Marx, Kenneth Arrow, James Tobin, and John Kenneth Galbraith. The MIT top five: Keynes, Samuelson, Marx, Robert Solow, and Joseph Schumpeter. The differences among these lists are striking, especially if you note that there is no overlap whatsoever between Chicago and Harvard. But the ideological differences that surface in the reading lists are not as deep-seated as they appear since graduate students at Chicago, Harvard, and MIT all learn the same orthodox curriculum.

> "Institutionalists" criticize the natural-law notion of *homo economicus*.

There are a handful of heterodox programs that reject the orthodox litmus test. Although their curricula will include econometrics and a heavy dose of mathematical theory, these programs are not exclusively mathematical in orientation, as they consider such issues as power, ideology, community values, irrational behavior, and social institutions. They cultivate interdisciplinary work in philosophy, political theory, institutional history, applied economics, and the history of economic thought. Heterodox programs are home to institutionalists, Marxists, experimentalists, Austrians, and feminists.

"Institutionalists" are the descendants of what was, through the early 1930s, the reigning school of economics in the United States. Predecessors include Veblen, who belittled the natural-law notion of *homo economicus* for being "a lightning calculator of pleasures and pains." Among contemporary institutionalists, Heilbroner is exemplary. Describing the social and political organization and control of the economic system is, for Heilbroner, the central focus of economic thought, and judging the power relations that govern economic outcomes is its central aim. Institutionalists have a professional society, the Association for Evolutionary Economics, and a journal, the *Journal of Economic Issues*. Departments with a strong institutionalist bent can be found at the University of Tennessee at Knoxville, Duke University, the University of Utah, the New School, the University of Notre Dame, Northeastern University, and Michigan State University.

Marxists, like institutionalists, argue that economic arrangements are social, not natural, in origin. What distinguishes Marxists from institutionalists is their radicalism and their belief in class struggle. Though Marxist economics commanded attention earlier in the century, and later, in the 1970s, the arguable but unavoidable association of Marxism with the former Soviet Union has hampered it from without, and fighting between different Marxist schools of thought has crippled it from within. As a result, the influence of Marxists is much diminished. And, as radicalism is anathema to most academic economists, Marxist analysis has been systematically barred from the profession's flagship journals, though it fills the pages of *Monthly Review* and *Rethinking Marxism*. There are Marxist camps at the New School, the University of California at Irvine, and the University of Massachusetts at Amherst.

> "Experimentalists" argue that people can act irrationally when making economic decisions.

"Experimentalists" argue that people sometimes act irrationally when making economic decisions. Contrary to Adam Smith's famous dictum, "it is not from the benevolence of the butcher, the brewer, or the baker that we expect our dinner, but from their regard to their own interest," experimentalists contend that the butcher's self-interest isn't so self-consistent, for it might just encompass something as unpredictable as benevolence. Though not allergic to mathematical modeling, experimentalists use it in an unorthodox way to factor psychological phenomena into an understanding of utility. The University of Arizona, California Institute of Technology, the University of Virginia, Texas A&M University, the University of Pittsburgh, New York University, and UMass-Amherst are home to experimentalists.

"Austrians" are the most liberal of economists, in the traditional sense of the term, in that they argue from a moral stance that values individual freedom and those markets that lead to its realization. (The name "Austrian" invokes the work of the early twentieth-century economists Carl Menger, Ludwig von Mise, and Joseph Schumpeter, all of whom hailed from Austria.) Because they put subjective individual judgments at the center of economic relationships, and because they scorn general equilibrium, comprehensive economic planning, and state intervention, Austrians favor microeconomic analysis. Rejecting mathematical approaches, they prefer to argue cases, drawing on a formidable knowledge of the history of economic thought for support. Austrians teach at NYU, George Mason University, and Auburn University.

It's only during the last few years that feminism has broken into the scholarly precincts of economics. In 1992, the International Association for Feminist Economics was organized, and the AEA's annual meeting included its first session on feminist economics. During the past five years, the Committee on the Status of Women in the Economics Profession has been assiduously lobbying for the inclusion of more women in the discipline.

Feminist economics does not advocate replacing economics about men with an economics by and about women. Rather, in order to correct and improve all economics, it exposes how perspectives rooted in gender inequality inform current economic theories. Why, for instance, should childcare be studied as an economic phenomenon when purchased from a business but not when done by someone in the home? No single graduate program is known as being feminist in orientation, although pockets of feminist economists can be found at UMass-Amherst, American University, the New School, and Notre Dame.

To locate specific professors or faculty with particular interests, look at the *American Economic Review*'s guide, *Survey of Members*. The Economics Institute publishes a more detailed and useful handbook: *Guide to Graduate Study in Economics and Agricultural Economics in the USA and Canada.*

Though a methodological and ideological consensus dominates the vast majority of graduate programs, there are substantial differences in perceived quality between them. Or so thinks the AEA, which has created a quality index to formalize these differences and standardize their evaluation. The index translates the NRC's ranking of graduate programs into a five-tier pecking order.

That being said, quality is itself an amorphous term, one that acquires meaning only in terms of the accomplishments deemed fit to be judged. In the index, quality depends on two such factors: faculty education and publication. Tier One programs are the acme of quality because their faculty have the highest concentration of degrees from the best graduate schools (Tier One schools), as well as the highest concentration of publications in the most prestigious professional journals (*American Economic Review*, *Econometrica*, *Economic Journal*, *Journal of Political Economy*, and *Quarterly Journal of Economics*).

What's most telling about the index itself is the fact that heterodox programs are at or near the bottom of the pecking order. This suggests that the rankings replicate the status quo. It's hardly surprising then that heterodox schools would appear at the bottom, for by pursuing research hostile to the orthodoxy, they fail to measure up to the index's standard of quality. Surveys of trends in article publishing, for instance, reveal that about two-thirds of the articles published in the *American Economic Review* contained mathematical models without any empirical data—an extremely orthodox approach heterodox economists reject.

> It's only during the last few years that feminism has broken into the scholarly precincts of economics.

Faculty from orthodox and heterodox programs alike stress that the index, as skewed as it appears to be, exerts tremendous influence over the unfolding of an academic career in economics. Faculty who hold positions at the few top universities wield a tremendous amount of power over hiring, publishing, and the granting of research funds, including federal government research funding through the National Science Foundation. Faculty from top programs edit the major academic journals; the journals publish articles written by economists from these selfsame programs; and the articles are invariably applications of the theory taught at the programs. Also, the hiring of new economists by the leading universities is in practice limited to those trained at only a few select graduate programs. For instance, in 1987–88 (the last years for which data are available), Tier One programs employed 64 percent of Tier One Ph.D.'s. Tier Two programs employed 28 percent of their own Ph.D.'s, and 64 percent from Tier One programs. Tier Three programs employed 15 percent of their own Ph.D.'s, with another 82 percent equally divided between Tier One and Tier Two programs. Tier Four programs hired 11 percent of their own Ph.D.'s, with another 80 percent equally divided among Tier One, Two, and Three programs. Tier Five programs hired 82 percent of their faculty from higher tier programs.

THE JOB MARKET

The word is that competition for jobs in economics departments has intensified, especially for jobs at Tier Two and Three schools, the majority of which are public universities. Decreases in federal and state funding for higher education have caused state universities to scale back their hiring. The academic job market in economics has not collapsed; according to the NRC, in 1994 nearly 60 percent of new economics Ph.D.'s had definite employment plans, and 26 percent were seeking employment. By way of contrast, among new English Ph.D.'s, 50 percent had definite employment plans, while nearly 37 percent were looking for work.

Along with the fact that competition for the top jobs at the top schools is always intense, economics professors and graduate students stress keeping in mind the discipline's two customary rules about the job market. If not quite ironclad, they are not whimsies either.

Rule One: When economists switch jobs, they tend not to experience upward mobility. That is, when hired away from one university or college to another, it's more likely that an economist

The AEA quality index exerts tremendous influence over the unfolding of an academic career in economics.

will go to an institution as prestigious, or less prestigious, than the former one. Rule Two: If, after earning a Ph.D., you work as an economist in government or business, all the while with an eye to becoming part of the professoriate, your chances of realizing your ambition are virtually nil. Call it the "Flummox Factor." As a Michigan graduate student explains: "Go straight to government or business, and you will have no chance to publish. You're writing, of course, but you're not writing academic material. So if you do go on the academic market, you just have your old dissertation to rely on, and you're competing with fresh Ph.D.'s who have not only published their dissertations, but two or three papers as well. It's research and publications that will land you an academic job, not industry experience." Of course, if you're among the select few who are appointed to the staff of the President's Council of Economic Advisors, the chances of your returning to academe are excellent.

Clearly, in light of these issues, if you have your sights set on a career in graduate level research and teaching, are mathematically savvy, or gravitate toward pure research, then your plan of action is simple. You should apply to a Tier One or Two graduate program. Once accepted, those who are studious and a little lucky can expect doors to open.

On the other hand, for those keen on heterodox economics, ambivalent about the rigid use of mathematics, or wavering between an academic and nonacademic career, devising a plan of action is more complicated. To hedge your bets, you could apply to top tier programs. If you are accepted to one, though, expect to pay your orthodox dues while taking the first year core. And once they are paid, you can try to bear down on your interests, or what's left of them, during the second year and the dissertation.

> For those students keen on pursuing heterodox economics, devising a plan of action is complicated.

Also, after the second year you can decide whether or not to continue working towards the Ph.D. or to take an M.S., which will provide you with a decided edge over undergraduate economics majors looking for jobs in business and industry. A master's degree in economics can net you jobs in government departments and agencies, accounting firms, and banks, particularly non-U.S. banks, which, according to Michigan professor George Johnson, tend to favor an M.S. in economics degrees more than an M.B.A. But as Notre Dame professor Philip Mirowski notes, few people pursue a master's degree as an end in itself, since the work consists mostly of the theoretical mathematical courses making up the "first hurdle" of a Ph.D. in economics.

A third option is to apply to heterodox programs—the best option for someone with an acute interest in philosophy, intellectual history, and policy analysis. Though you will not win many points on the quality index, at a heterodox program you will become well versed in dissenting traditions of thought, and you will have more liberty in honing your interests among thinkers whose ideals you share. Besides tolerating interdisciplinary coursework, heterodox programs are known for educating students who excel in public policy work or at undergraduate teaching because they are adept thinkers and communicators. They encourage applied research, they can clearly explain economic thought in nontechnical language, and they can argue about the justifications of research or policy because they are schooled in philosophy and the history of economic thought.

RESOURCES

ASSOCIATIONS

American Economic
  Association
(615) 322-2595

Association for
  Evolutionary
  Economics
(402) 472-3867

JOURNALS

American Economic Review
*Journal of Economic
  Behavior and
  Organization*
Journal of Economic Issues
*Journal of Economic
  Literature*
*Journal of Economic
  Perspectives*
Monthly Review
Rethinking Marxism

CONSTELLATIONS

NEOCLASSICAL

Chicago
Harvard
MIT
Princeton
Stanford
Yale

INSTITUTIONALIST

Duke
Michigan State
New School
Notre Dame
Northeastern
Tennessee-Knoxville
Utah

EXPERIMENTAL

Arizona
Cal Tech
Pittsburgh
Texas A&M
UMass-Amherst
Virginia

MARXIST

New School
UC-Riverside
UMass-Amherst

AUSTRIANS

Auburn
George Mason
NYU

FURTHER READING

David Colander and Reuven Brenner, eds., *Educating Economists* (Michigan)

The Economics Institute, *Guide to Graduate Study in Economics and Agricultural Economics in the USA and Canada* (Eon River Press)

"The Education and Training of Economics Doctorates," *Journal of Economic Literature* 29 (September 1991)

"The Education of Economists: From Undergraduate to Graduate Study," *Journal of Economic Literature* 29 (September 1991)

Arjo Klamer and David Colander, *The Making of an Economist* (Westview)

WEB ADDRESSES

AEA home page
http://www.vanderbilt.edu/AEA/

Resources for Economists on the Internet
http://csuchico.edu:80/econ/faq/faq4/EconFAQ/EconFAQ.html

AEA INDEX

TIER 1
Chicago
Harvard
MIT
Stanford
Princeton
Yale

TIER 2
UC-Berkeley
Penn
Northwestern
Minnesota-Twin
  Cities
UCLA
Columbia
Michigan
Rochester
Wisconsin-Madison

TIER 3
UC-San Diego
NYU
Cornell
Cal Tech
Maryland
Boston Univ.
Duke
Brown
Virginia
UNC-Chapel Hill
Washington-Seattle
Michigan State
Illinois-Urbana
Washington University
  in St. Louis
Iowa
UT-Austin

TIER 4
Johns Hopkins
Texas A&M
Pittsburgh
Ohio State
Arizona
Iowa State
UC-Davis
SUNY Stony Brook
USC
Florida
North Carolina State
Boston College
Indiana
Penn State
Rice
George Mason
Vanderbilt

TIER 5
UC-Santa Barbara
UMass-Amherst
Purdue
Rutgers
CUNY Grad Center
Colorado-Boulder
Georgetown
Syracuse
Houston
SUNY Buffalo
SMU
Claremont
Oregon
Florida State
Georgia
Kentucky
South Carolina
SUNY Binghamton
Arizona State
George Washington
Georgia State
UC-Riverside
Illinois-Chicago
American
Kansas
Auburn
Clemson
Southwestern Illinois
Wyoming
SUNY Albany
Knoxville
Tulane
Notre Dame
Louisiana State
  University and
  A&M College
Washington State
Connecticut
Hawaii-Manoa
Oklahoma

CHAPTER 23

GEOGRAPHY

As an undergraduate at the University of Texas at Austin, Sarah Washburn was as inclined toward English as toward engineering. Then after long indecision, she realized, "With geography, I could study the whole world." Washburn's master's thesis at the University of North Carolina at Chapel Hill was about malaria in 1920s North Carolina. Of the other fields she considered, "There aren't enough people in biology or ecology, and there isn't enough environment in sociology or history," she says. Washburn continues to focus on "identity and equity and how they play out in a specific location." Today she studies a host of issues—including race and class—raised by how diabetes patients are treated medically in a demographically mixed and changing North Carolina town.

Having many fields within their terrain makes it hard for geographers to explain themselves to others. "I'm not a misplaced anthropologist," insists Lorraine Dowler, a recent Syracuse University Ph.D. and new assistant professor of geography at Pennsylvania State University, "I'm a geographer." Initially, Dowler chucked her job at the advertising agency Saatchi & Saatchi for "something more creative" in landscape architecture. During her M.A. work, however, she discovered geography. Dowler's dissertation tackles everything from graffiti in public places to interview research with Irish women about the Troubles in Belfast. Geographers "cast a broad theoretical net while remaining place specific, and that's the beauty of geography."

WHY GEOGRAPHY?

Geography is the ultimate interdisciplinary discipline. You can, in the United States at least, take courses in such fields as political science, sociology, history, ecology, English, anthropology, geology, urban planning, economics, and women's studies en route to a graduate degree in geography. As one geographer, Strabo, wrote about 2000 years ago, "A work on geography also involves theory of no mean value, the theory of the arts...and of natural science, as well as the theory which lies in the fields of history and myth."

So what exactly is geography? In the broadest sense, it is about space (abstract, relational) and place (specific, grounded). The core of geography is the relationship between humans and their environment, a considerably dense subject. Putting aside the annoyingly persistent belief that geography involves nothing more than memorizing national capitals and the location of rivers, one may also say that geography is not just *where* is Nebraska, but *why* is Nebraska.

Why Nebraska, indeed, for it is Americans who find geography such a perplexing discipline. Compared with most other countries, including Canada, the number of American colleges and universities that offer geography is fairly small, and includes few of the most prestigious private institutions. A fair number of geography faculty in the United States hail from Britain and have degrees from British universities, and representatives from British and Canadian universities regularly attend the annual conference of the Association of American Geographers (AAG).

The United States may finally be giving geography its due, however. The National Academy of Sciences and the National Research Council have just published *Rediscovering Geography: New Relevance for Science and Society*, which reports that graduate enrollment in geography programs has increased at a rate twice that for all the social sciences. Catching the wave, the College Board is creating an Advanced Placement exam in geography, a step that may alert high schools that geography is actually a university-level (i.e., important) discipline. And geography is suddenly all the rage in publishing: Stylish academic presses like Routledge, Blackwell, and Minnesota have beefed up their geography lists, and bookstores are making room on their shelves for whole new geography sections.

People drawn to geography often confess an early love of travel as well as a fascination with the variations of life and landscape from place to place. And increasingly, folks migrate to geography through their concern for the health and degradation of the earth's natural environment. Oddly enough, a good sense of direction is not a prerequisite for becoming a geographer. Informal studies have shown that the more geographers in a vehicle, the more likely they are to get lost, particularly if they are following the directions of another geographer.

HOW GEOGRAPHY HAS TAKEN SHAPE

The most prominent traditions in geography—the science of space and the description of place (geography means "earth-writing")—go back for millennia. These approaches are hardly mutually exclusive, but at times, especially during the institutional skir-mishes of the first half of the twentieth century, the traditions have clashed. Today, they often divide into quantitative and qual-itative approaches.

Geography is perhaps best known as the discipline that maps space: measuring the earth's surface, delineating political bound-aries, and representing the spatial arrangements of natural and cul-tural phenomena. Those who define geography as a spatial science point to Ptolemy, who first plotted longitude and latitude, as an illustrious intellectual ancestor. And while geography's spatial sci-ence encompasses all the technologies that have been developed for the purposes of earth measurement—from Ptolemy's mathematics to satellite sensors—its intellectual core is the discernment of spatial patterns and the search for laws to predict and explain such patterns.

Geographers keen on the description of place point to Strabo, who collected and assessed travelers' tales from all over the known world to produce a geography of different places and the people who lived in them. This aspect of geography has long embraced the study of the interrelations of the physical environment and human culture within a region, as well as the study of how and why places differ from each other.

As geographers themselves have recently explained, geographical accounts of space and place have been integral to the momentous project of European exploration and empire building. David N. Livingstone, one of geography's leading historians, argues that the concept of scientific "discovery" itself is inseparable from fifteenth- and sixteenth-century European global conquests. Moreover, geographical societies, particularly in the eighteenth and nineteenth centuries, frequently took the lead in sponsoring such exploits, which often combined scientific aims and plunder.

Although European universities had chairs in geography from at least the eighteenth century (Kant taught physical geography), geography was slow to surface as a university discipline in the United States. Physical geography, specifically the mapping of the territory and analysis of its resources, appeared in the United States with the exploration of the frontier in the nineteenth century. Moreover, when geography was institutionalized in the United States in the late nineteenth century, geographers focused on separating the subject matter of geography from that of geology. They made it their mandate to investigate the shape and activities on the earth's surface, leaving to geologists everything below.

> Oddly enough, a good sense of direction is not a prerequisite for becoming a geographer.

William Morris Davis, a turn-of-the-century physical geographer, developed an evolutionary theory of geomorphology to explain what he called young, mature, and old landscapes. Intent on maintaining geography as a serious physical science, Davis resigned from the board of the National Geographic Society when the editor of the *National Geographic Magazine*, Gilbert H. Grosvenor, insisted on taking it in a popular direction. Davis promptly helped establish the AAG, for purely scientific and academic geographers; the AAG is the primary academic organization in geography today.

Academic human geography in the United States was largely imported in the early twentieth century from Europe, where geographers were busy contemplating socioenvironmental questions. Ellen Churchill Semple, who taught at several American universities, led the charge in introducing Friedrich Ratzel's German brand of anthropogeography to the United States. (Legend has it that Semple, when denied access to graduate classes because she was a woman, educated herself nonetheless by sitting just outside the classroom door.) Ratzel emphasized the power of environment in shaping people's lives. His concept of *Lebensraum* (living space), embedded in the idea of an organic state-society, was later misappropriated by the Nazis to explain that it was only "natural" for Germany to invade Poland and Czechoslovakia to accommodate the needs of the German population.

> Early geographers made it their mandate to investigate the earth's surface, leaving geologists everything below.

For several leading geographers in the early twentieth century, including Ellsworth Huntington of Yale University, environmental determinism was the ticket to combining both physical and human geography, thereby unifying the discipline. As the story goes, however, American geography's embrace of environmental determinism—the theory that people are physically and culturally shaped by their natural environment—was a theoretical wrong turn that forced causality where it didn't exist, and that ended up undermining the discipline's status among the social sciences. Never unidirectional, however, geography remained bigger than bad metatheory. Geomorphologist turned political-geographer Isaiah Bowman, for example, participated in the political remapping of the world following World War I and later advised President Roosevelt on the relocation of European refugees from World War II.

Carl Sauer turned the discipline from the drawing of territorial boundaries to the discernment of cultural landscapes. Geographers going into the field would "read" the landscape by carefully observing the types and varieties of material artifacts, such as agricultural cultivation, fences, houses, and burial grounds. Sauer's brand of cultural geography marked regions through meticulous archival or field research, which traced the diffusion of cultural innovations over time and space and interpreted landscapes as human cultural productions. Sauer's approach was influential enough to become known as the Berkeley School.

For much of the 1930s through the 1960s, the "region" was the central organizing concept in the discipline. But for an increasing number of geographers, the "scientific synthesis" orchestrated by Sauer in regional geography was not scientific enough. Reasserting geography's quantitative tradition over what they saw as ineffectual descriptions of place, these geographers followed their colleagues in the social sciences into positivism. Only the logical search for universal laws, they felt—not the assessment of regional particulars—could maintain geography's standing as a respectable science. The quantitative revolution of the 1950s and 1960s brought geography firmly into the world of statistical analysis and formal model-building, reorienting the way many geographers asked questions regarding human-environment relations and the organization of space.

Enter David Harvey, the British geographer whose books have tended to signal major shifts in geographical theory. *Explanation in Geography*, Harvey's 1969 philosophical treatise on positivism and its usefulness in describing and explaining spatial patterns, launched his reputation as a substantial geographical thinker. Like many in academia, however, Harvey was radicalized by the social upheavals of the late 1960s, even to the point of questioning the entire project of "objective" geographical science. In his landmark *Social Justice and the City* (1973), he began to develop a Marxist geography to explain the historical expansion of capitalism. Indeed, thanks to the work of Harvey and other Marxist geographers, the analysis of the spatial characteristics of capitalism—the mobility of capital and uneven development on many scales—is now pivotal to geographers' studies in Third World development, Western cities, and global change.

Whereas positivist geographers had worried about the place of the discipline within science, Marxist geographers concerned themselves with the place of the discipline in society. Moreover, much as anthropologists began to realize their discipline's entanglement with colonialism, Marxist geographers began to reassess geography's imperialist legacy. Marxists also established links between geography and social theory, smashing the barricades of geography's territorial isolationism to join the vanguard of social theorists from a range of backgrounds and disciplines. In addition to Harvey at Johns Hopkins University, geographers such as Neil Smith of Rutgers University, Ed Soja of UCLA (who is in the department of planning), Derek J. Gregory of the University of British Columbia, and Doreen Massey of the Open University, London, have been crucial in underscoring the importance of space in social theory and in developing sociospatial theories.

> In the 1950s, for many geographers the scientific synthesis was not scientific enough.

Marxists weren't the only ones who saw through the supposedly neutral language of numbers. While in the 1970s Marxists charged that "statistics don't bleed," humanist geographers of many stripes emphasized that positivist geography not only lacked important context and nuance, it lacked humanity: What law or equation could possibly describe or explain a "sense of place"? Behavioralist geographers delved into the realm of the cognitive, focusing, for example, on individuals' development of "mental maps."

At the same time, forms of feminist analysis began appearing in the 1980s. Whereas Marxist geographers criticized bourgeois ideas of "economic man" so prevalent in geographical theory and practice, feminist geographers began questioning the whereabouts of women in either picture. "Geographic perspectives on women" (the name of one of the AAG's forty-four specialty groups) assumes that because of their different social roles, including the division

> For David Harvey and Marxist geographers, slums next to high-rises were proof that statistics can't bleed.

of labor, women and men often inhabit different spaces. As with the social roles themselves, these spaces, patterns, and relationships vary from place to place and in different contexts of class, race, ethnicity, and culture. Seizing on gender as a category of social analysis, feminist geographers recast the real lives of men and women to highlight sociospatial constructions of masculinity and femininity.

The increasing presence of women in the field may be the biggest shift in geography in the last fifteen years. But there is still a long way to go, as the Geography Guerrilla Girls made clear at the 1996 AAG conference. The anonymous GGG's passed out "shame on you, geography" fliers listing all the departments at which there was no, or only one, female geographer in a tenure-track position.

Although there is a wide variety of approaches within the discipline, geography's relationship with postmodernism and poststructuralism can best be described as guarded. For many geographers—the vast majority, according to one technological hazards specialist—there's no need to fix what ain't broke; traditional, empirical positivist work gets results and gets grants, while postmodern transportation analysis (for example) will get you nowhere. The postmodern turn in the social sciences and humanities, however, has been taken quite seriously by geography's theoreticians, philosophers, and those concerned with the relationship between space and identity. Within geographic studies of identity, one of the most active foci has been sexual identities—in particular, gay and lesbian communities, exclusions, and spatial strategies.

The advent of cultural studies has reinvigorated cultural geography, although practitioners of the old Berkeley School may not agree. What has come to be called the "new" cultural geography differs from "traditional" cultural geography in its theories, orientation, and associations. Although the intellectual legacy of Sauer still looms large, Antonio Gramsci and Michel Foucault are the new luminaries of cultural geography. Paramount in this research are questions of power and hegemony, particularly in specific places.

Feminist geographers often assume that women and men inhabit different spaces.

Cultural studies and literary studies have had a significant impact on geography in the last decade or so, and those fields, it seems, would be lost without their geographical vocabulary, such as "space," "location," "borders," and "mapping." When they get over feeling territorial about the use of these terms, geographers are pleased that others are finally recognizing what they've been talking about all along: the importance of space in human social relations. "Geography offers analysis of how identity is always worked through space," says Susan M. Roberts, a gender theorist at the University of Kentucky. "A body is always somewhere."

Geographers are critical, however, of the extent to which geographic terms and concepts are flung about as metaphors and often see their role in cultural studies as keeping theory attached to the nitty gritty. "There's a yearning to ground postmodern theory," says Matthew Sparke of the University of Washington at Seattle. Geographers are concerned with "how to reconcile ideology and identity with materialism," says a feminist geographer at the University of Nebraska at Omaha. One of the most popular scholarly books by a geographer in recent years is Harvey's *The Condition of Postmodernity* (1989), which interprets postmodern culture within the context of the globally extensive restructuring of late capitalism.

Indeed, the phenomenon of global restructuring is one of the most important and popular areas of research in geography. Intertwining political, social, cultural, environmental and economic realms, geographers such as Michael Watts at the University of California at Berkeley, Dianne Rocheleau at Clark University, Cindi Katz at CUNY Graduate Center, Lakshman Yapa at Penn State, and John Pickles at Kentucky present different theories of a "local–global dialectic," in which local events and global structures influence each other. Some geographers are rolling up their sleeves and working on issues such as global warming, deforestation, and environmental change. For instance, the AAG, with the National Science Foundation, is funding workshops for the development of teaching modules in such areas as health, hazards, and urbanization, as well as an interdisciplinary project on Human Dimensions of Global Change. Both projects have pages on the Internet.

Alongside, although not always along with, critical evaluations of environmental change is the use of technology to map these changes. Geographic information systems (GIS), which include remotely sensed satellite pictures and global positioning systems, are the most recent versions of time-honored traditions of geographical measurement. Susan Cutter, chair of the geography department of the University of South Carolina, where "GIS is integrated into the curriculum like statistics used to be," defines GIS as an analytical and cartographic tool for managing and visualizing spatial information. The practical usefulness of GIS and related technologies in tracking and monitoring environmental change has not gone unnoticed by governments in such countries such as China and Kenya, which send scholars and departmental managers to North America to learn the new technologies. The computer technology of GIS allows for the processing of enormous quantities of data and multiple data sets, presenting a computer-enhanced version of so many maps—of population, of topography, of housing, of tree species—stacked one on top of the other.

> Michel Foucault and Antonio Gramsci are the new luminaries of cultural geography.

GIS is most often considered a research tool. Due to its rapid growth inside and outside the academy, however, GIS is making inroads as an area of research itself, with people studying its social impact as well as the cognitive psychology of spatial thinking. GIS "is getting more respectable as an intellectual subject," according to Helen Couclelis, a leading quantitative geographer at the University of California at Santa Barbara. She notes that the *International Journal of Geographic Information Systems* has just changed its name to the *International Journal of Geographic Information Science*.

While some geographers worry that the great expense of GIS technology further demarcates the split between those who have power over land decisions and those (often the residents) who do not, Couclelis argues that GIS has "democratized quantitative analysis," rendering data more accessible and their analysis easier and more visible. The centrality of the debate is evident in that the NSF-funded National Center for Geographic Information Analysis (NCGIA) Initiative has encouraged research and discussion not just on particular applications of GIS, but about social issues surrounding the new technology as well.

WHAT'S NEXT

Despite geography's many competing interests and methods, geographers maintain a civil discourse when debating issues. "I'm struck by the lack of rancor" in geography's debates, reports Derek Gregory of British Columbia. According to Donald Mitchell of Syracuse, it's not uncommon to have a spirited argument with someone in print and then to meet with your adversary for a "jovial pint or two." Perhaps the overall turn toward interdisciplinarity in academia is having an impact on geographers, who, feeling less defensive about the discipline, are more relaxed about the different directions within it.

Geography departments range wildly in the specialties they offer and in their degree requirements. Some expect proficiency in another language, some require a statistics course, and some require only an introductory seminar. While many departments stress fieldwork, others won't blink if you never leave your office. It is not unusual for Americans to enter geography programs as complete neophytes to the field. If you are new to geography, however, you may want to go to a department that can offer you a broad choice of geography classes, including a methodology course, for a master's degree. The interdisciplinary nature of geography can be great for someone who already has a focus, but can leave the undirected feeling lost.

As with any discipline, geography has its little niches and deep divisions—or, as one Ohio State graduate student says, little fiefdoms. In some departments, the physical geographers and the human geographers find little to say to each other, even socially. Social theorists tend to consider human geographers who do more traditional quantitative studies unsophisticated, unintellectual, and petty, while human geographers doing quantitative studies tend to consider the social theorists elitist, scientifically mushy, and petty. And while many geographers argue that GIS is good for geography, there is a significant contingent worried about geography's giddy embrace of technology.

In the United States, geography is a small discipline. At the graduate level, it exists mostly in state universities; the major exceptions are Clark, Johns Hopkins, Syracuse, and the University of Southern California. Historians of geography attribute this state of affairs to the discipline's malaise following the discrediting of environmental determinism. If the Ivy League is the measure of prestige, then geography is not very prestigious, with only Dartmouth College retaining its geography department. Columbia University disbanded its department in the mid-1980s. Even the University of Chicago, one of the premier institutions for geography at mid-century, has within the last few years downgraded its geography department into a geography "program."

What makes geography departments vulnerable to being cut? Part of the problem is American lack of understanding of what geography is as a discipline; since many institutions don't offer geography, their administrators have had no exposure to the subject in their own education. And while geographers consider geography's interdisciplinarity a strength, it also allows for easy dismemberment: Geography faculty have been relocated to stronger departments in economics, international relations, history, human ecology, urban/regional planning, anthropology, and sociology. New departments, such as urban studies, Southeast Asian studies, Latin American studies, and especially environmental studies, seem to have a cachet that dusty old geography—which could handily cover these areas—does not.

> While many departments stress fieldwork, others won't even blink if you never leave your office.

Lack of support from the administration can undermine even highly regarded geography departments. Not surprisingly, it helps to have a geographer in the administration, as strong and secure geography departments at Washington-Seattle and the University of Wisconsin at Madison will attest. And as one geography department chair noted, having moved from a small department to a larger one, "size makes a difference."

As does the existence of a GIS lab. Without doubt, GIS is geography's bread-and-butter. GIS technology is expensive, but the research is heavily funded by sources outside of the university; consequently, university administrations love it. Companies and government offices prefer people with GIS training, and so geography departments are eager to supply that demand. This, in turn, has created a high demand in geography departments for faculty who can teach and do research in GIS.

Geography departments known for GIS research include UC-Santa Barbara, SUNY Buffalo, Ohio State, Penn State, the University of Minnesota at Twin Cities, the University of Maryland, and Clark. Although its brand-new Ph.D. program emphasizes geographical education, Southwest Texas State University—the largest geography department in the country—has an M.A. program that provides GIS training. Given how quickly departments' strengths in GIS may increase in the next few years, check Web sites for the latest in GIS offerings.

In state universities, a larger faculty often makes for a stronger department and a stronger showing in the NRC rankings. Of the top five departments in the National Research Council rankings—Penn State, Wisconsin-Madison, Minnesota-Twin Cities, UC-Santa Barbara, and Ohio State, UC-Santa Barbara is the only small department. For highly ranked departments, the NRC report is good for bragging rights and bolstering administrative support. But, suggests University of Colorado at Boulder's John O'Laughlin, whereas a decade ago a high NRC ranking might have helped a geography department add resources, now the best it can do is keep a department from losing resources. In any case, professors note that the sample size of faculty interviewed for the rankings was small. And chances are a department may have changed, for better or worse, since the rankings came out. To ascertain department and faculty specialties and to find individual faculty, look at the AAG's *Directory of Geography Programs in the United States and Canada*.

> There is a significant contingent worried about geography's giddy embrace of technology.

One geographer at Florida State University characterizes geography departments as falling into one of three broad categories: the "good old warm seas," highly specialized smaller departments, and everywhere else. The "good old warm seas"—such as Minnesota-Twin Cities, UC-Berkeley, Penn State, UCLA, and Wisconsin-Madison—are large departments with long-standing, solid reputations in several fields of specialization. Their faculty have overlapping interests, to the extent that there may be "cliques and countercliques." Though cliquishness can spark bickering, an advantage is that if one professor leaves, you aren't stranded without someone else in your field of interest. (A "stranded" doctoral candidate at Penn State, however, suggests that those who benefit most from such "warm seas" departments are master's students seeking solid breadth in geography before heading into the depth of a Ph.D.) UC-Berkeley is now better known for the critical urban/industrial geographies of Allan Pred and Richard Walker, or Michael Watts's political economy of Third World development, than for the cultural geography of Sauer that put it on the map at mid-century. The Sauer legacy is probably strongest at Louisiana State University, although UT-Austin, the University of Tennessee, Penn State, Kansas, and Syracuse are also known for their historical-cultural geography.

> Companies and government agencies prefer geographers with GIS training.

Then there are the highly specialized smaller departments, such as the University of Southern California with its focus on urban economic social policy; Kansas State University—newly expanded into a Ph.D.-granting program—with its emphasis on rural geography; the University of Hawaii, with a strong regional focus on Asia and the Pacific; and Kentucky, with a strong social theory focus.

"Everywhere else" is the largest category of the three, and includes South Carolina, with its strengths in environmental geography and techniques and its concern for ties to the community; Michigan State University, which is large enough to be a warm sea, but not considered among the top departments; the University of Florida, with emphases on tropical agriculture and economic development and policy; San Diego State, a warm place not only because of its location, but also in terms of faculty-student interactions, where theoretical study of gender and of film is as possible and encouraged as is quantitative urban analysis; and West Virginia State University, representative of departments that have strong research commitments to their own surrounding landscape. For those who are particularly interested in the history and theory of cartography as well as in its current practice and developments, the University of Wisconsin at Milwaukee and Clark are well known for their cartographic specialties.

One could also distinguish between the "big-name nationals" at one end of the spectrum and what an assistant professor at Southwest Texas calls "compass point" universities, places such as Southwest Texas, UNC-Charlotte, the University of Cincinnati, and the University of Memphis that focus on training people for private- and public-sector employment in the region. Out of 1,490 Southwest Texas alumni, for example, around 1,200 work in the Austin–San Antonio corridor.

An economic development geographer at Indiana University suggests that you can also look at geography departments according to their quantitative specialties. There's the "Big Ten way," a midwestern approach to geography that is less oriented towards social theory than many of the schools on the East and West Coasts. Indiana, for example, emphasizes quantitative work in the various forms of economic geography taught in the department. The University of Iowa is known for its focus on locational analysis. Ohio State is a quantitative powerhouse, and even smaller places like Cincinnati tend to specialize in spatial science techniques. Quantitative methods prove useful outside of academia. Some master's graduates work as locational analysts for chain stores such as Wal-Mart, or as environmental-impact consultants for real estate development companies, while others find jobs in governmental agencies. A University of Illinois at Urbana Ph.D. student adds that the department's faculty tend not to attend conferences, which perhaps indicates a Big Ten disinclination toward both academic socializing and social theory, although at Illinois-Urbana, "graduate students are much more social than they once were," and "they like theory here."

> Chances are a department will have changed, for better or worse, before the NRC rankings come out.

Departments do vary widely in their social characteristics. In addition to seeking out departments that house particular scholars or nurture certain specialties, you may want to consider the feel of the place. If you're inclined toward a social place where students are involved in life outside the classroom, and where the faculty collaborate on projects with each other and with graduate students, you might check out Kentucky. Do you see yourself in an intense, hard-working mode throughout your graduate career? Try Clark, University of Southern California, or maybe Ohio State.

There are still some serious "old boys" departments in geography. There are happy bubbles for women geographers, however. Some of the women students at Wisconsin-Madison, a large department that developed a reputation among women geographers for having a revolving door for the female professor, started arranging their own social-academic events, such as organizing extra time with visiting female faculty. The University of Arizona has an unprecedented eleven women either in or affiliated with the geography department, and several in authoritative positions; one of geography's hardest-working and widest-known feminist geographers, Janice Monk, is head of the Southwest Institute for Research on Women there. Clark, Kentucky, Colorado-Boulder, Rutgers, Washington, Temple University, University of British Columbia, UCLA, and USC are some of the other places known for welcoming women graduate students as well as gender study.

Geography is an international field with an international scope, and graduate departments attract students from all over the world. Sad to say, however, there are still very few U.S. minorities in geography. No one place is better than another in that respect, except that some departments are located in major metropolitan areas with their own diversity.

If you're seriously considering graduate school in geography and can afford a round-trip airplane ticket, your best introduction to the current state of geography in the U.S. is the annual meeting of the AAG, held at the beginning of April (in Boston in 1998). You'll find plenty of graduate students to talk to at all stages of their graduate careers. Many will be presenting their work at the conference. Unlike conferences in other fields, the AAG encourages student participation by accepting all the paper abstracts submitted. The result is a maddeningly packed schedule of simultaneous panels that stretches for four full days, but allows time and space for every niche, from the archaic to the avant garde. And while plenty of schmoozing takes place, and there is a job-placement service, the conference is not the major site of job interviews in the way that, for example, the American Historical Association conference is for historians. This arrangement makes the general mood convivial rather than competitive: frantic, perhaps, but not uptight.

THE JOB MARKET

On the academic job front, since many institutions don't have geography departments, there are only a limited number of academic jobs available, and the majority are not in cosmopolitan places. As they do in most other disciplines at this point, academics in geography end up taking jobs in places not particularly appealing to them; there is an extra poignancy for geographers in these circumstances, however, because the discipline is all about the importance of place and location. At the same time, graduate degrees in geography prepare many people for jobs outside of academia—in environmental, transportation, and planning departments; in consulting, marketing, and communications firms; and in not-for-profit organizations.

A majority of the jobs advertised in academic geography call for applicants to do at least some GIS teaching, regardless of their other specialties. According to the 1995 *Professional Geographer*

RESOURCES

NRC TOP TEN
Penn State
Wisconsin-Madison
Minnesota-Twin Cities
UC-Santa Barbara
Ohio State
UC-Berkeley
Syracuse
UCLA
Clark
Washington-Seattle

ASSOCIATIONS
Association of American
  Geographers
(202) 234-4150

JOURNALS
Annals of the AAG
Economic Geography
Environment and Planning D: Society
  and Space
Gender, Place, & Culture
Political Geography
Professional Geographer
Urban Geography

BOOKS
William Cronon, *Nature's Metropolis* (Norton)

Susan Hanson, *Ten Geographic Ideas that Changed the World* (Rutgers)

David Harvey, *Justice, Nature, and the Geography of Difference* (Blackwell)

Doreen Massey, *Space, Place, and Gender* (Polity)

Laura Pulido, *Environmentalism and Economic Justice* (Arizona)

Joni Seager, *Earth Follies* (Routledge)

report, GIS is far and away the most popular specialty in the likely hiring searches in the next five years. A Rutgers graduate with a strong GIS background offers a caveat, however, for environmental activists intending to help save the environment: It's mostly the timber and oil companies who can afford to hire geographers and outfit them with state-of-the-art computer technology. Although you may not earn as much money, you will probably have more chances to do environmentally friendly research inside academia than outside it.

CONSTELLATIONS

GOOD OLD WARM SEAS
Minnesota–Twin
  Cities
Penn State
UC–Berkeley
UCLA
Wisconsin–Madison

GIS RESEARCH
Clark
Maryland
Minnesota–Twin
  Cities
Ohio State
SUNY Buffalo
UC–Santa Barbara

SPECIALIZED SMALLER DEPARTMENTS

Asia and the Pacific
Hawaii

rural geography
Kansas State

social theory
Kentucky

urban economic
 social policy
USC

COMPASS POINT
Cincinnati
Memphis
South West Texas
UNC–Charlotte

WOMEN-FRIENDLY
Arizona
British Columbia
Clark
Colorado–Boulder
Kentucky
Rutgers
Temple
UCLA
USC
Washington–Seattle

WEB ADDRESSES
AAG home page
http://www.aag.org

Virtual Geography Department
http://www.utexas.edu/depts/grg/virtdept/contents.html

includes links to geography department home pages in the U.S. and worldwide
http://www.utexas.edu/depts/grg/virtdept/resources/depts/depts.html

and to Internet Resources for Geographers
http://www.utexas.edu/depts/grg/virtdept/resources/contents.html

CHAPTER 24

LINGUISTICS

"I grew up in a multidialectical family," explains Charles Boberg, "and I studied several languages in high school and college. I wanted to study language in graduate school, but I didn't want to specialize in any one language, and I love the sounds of different languages and dialects. When I found out about linguistics, it was as if a new world had opened up." Now a sixth-year graduate student at the University of Pennsylvania, Boberg is still fascinated by language variation. In fact, he is writing a dissertation on it. Boberg's topic is the phonology of borrowing—when certain words are borrowed into English from foreign languages, how borrowings vary geographically among and within dialects, and how such variations can be explained theoretically.

For Norvin Richards, linguistics is a more formal endeavor. A fourth-year graduate student at MIT, Richards is dissertating about the interaction between syntactic dependencies, a subject that has fascinated him since his undergraduate days as a linguistics major. "I'm looking at syntactic dependencies across different languages to see if they can be reduced to a single theoretical principle." His dissertation doesn't involve fieldwork, but Richards nonetheless enjoyed the time he spent in the summer of 1996 compiling a dictionary of Lardil, a language spoken by ten people who live on a small island off the northern coast of Australia.

WHY LINGUISTICS?

One of the attractions of being a linguist is that you don't have to listen for long before finding something to work on. A curt phone message, a child gurgling its way toward a sentence, or a waiter barking out an order for fried eggs may seem quotidian, but it's all music to the ears of linguists. Linguists derive tremendous satisfaction from listening to speech, and even more from revealing the coherence and complexity implicit in the seemingly random minutiae of everyday language, both spoken and written. Whether studying diphthong merger in New Zealand English or verb tense choice in adverbial "when" clauses, linguists are obsessed with finding the kinks in the vernacular and demonstrating their underlying consistency.

Linguists, though, don't usually examine those kinks with the interpretive tools employed by literary critics or rhetoricians. Look up "Linguistics" in the most recent edition of any encyclopedia, and the description will begin with something like "Linguistics is the science of language," meaning that linguists—like biologists, chemists, or physicists—try to figure out the rules governing a class of naturally occurring phenomena. Consider the argument of MIT professor Steven Pinker's *The Language Instinct: How the Mind Creates Language* (1994). According to Pinker, it was when Noam Chomsky published *Syntactic Structures* exactly forty years ago that "a new science was born. Now called 'cognitive science,' it combines tools from psychology, computer science, linguistics, philosophy, and neurobiology to explain the workings of human intelligence." Like Chomsky, Pinker uses language as a window onto the mind's rich cognitive structure, and one could easily interpret the recent praise showered upon this approach in both the mainstream and academic press (from *The Economist* to *Etc.*) as a recognition that linguistics has come of age as a science.

If you visit a research university's library and peruse the current periodical holdings in linguistics, you'll discover that linguistics is more diverse than Pinker allows. Not all linguists consider themselves natural scientists, nor are all willing to accept that the black box of the mind can be unlocked. Pick up the journal *American Speech*, and after reading some articles about dialects, language change, and language atlases, you'll notice that linguistics still has roots in the comparative study of spoken languages. A survey of *Language and Communication*, which has published articles on orality and literacy, linguistic skepticism, and James Joyce's *Finnegans Wake*, would reveal a humanities orientation, especially toward aesthetics, national literatures, and the philosophy of language. Thumb through *Language and Society* or *Anthropological Linguistics*, which publish articles about heckling, the linguistic structures of kinship, and the speech codes of street gangs, and you'll discover that linguistics has earned a respected place in the social sciences through the analysis of language as a medium of communication, socialization, and acculturation. So linguists, it turns out, do research in propaganda as well as phonemes, pidgins as well as cognition.

Like linguistics journals, graduate linguistics departments crop up in diverse areas. Linguistics is one of the social sciences at the University of California at Berkeley but one of the humanities at Penn. Graduate students in linguistics, moreover, hail from a variety of undergraduate majors. Thirty-five years ago, this was not the case. The general rule was that students acquired a core of Indo-European languages in college and then did research in graduate school on national literatures, undocumented spoken languages, or endangered spoken languages.

Today, to be sure, linguistics still attracts polyglots as well as budding sociologists and anthropologists keen on the relationship between language and culture. But, due to the dominance of Chomskyan formalism (which neither requires a knowledge of many languages nor encourages the study of language as a social or cultural artifact), the discipline increasingly draws students with undergraduate degrees in mathematics, philosophy, and psychology who groove on solving intricate cognitive puzzles, and who prefer the theoretical bent of Chomsky and fellow grammarians to the empiricism of social scientists and the cultural bent of humanists.

HOW LINGUISTICS HAS TAKEN SHAPE

Though a linguist may be a theorist or an empiricist, all linguists endeavor to make explicit the structure implicit in language itself. A grammarian devises a grammar, or a system of rules that characterizes the properties of language that all humans intuitively know, and can produce something like Chomsky's *Syntactic Structures*. A dialectologist creates a taxonomy of the sound properties extractable from the language used in a specific speech community, which results in works like the famous French atlas of Jules Gilliéron and Edmond Edmont. A computational linguist renders natural languages into mathematical forms that can be absorbed and manipulated by an artificially intelligent entity, such as a voice-activated computer.

The desire to explain linguistic structure goes hand in hand with a defense of egalitarianism. Simply put, linguists think that languages or dialects cannot be compared to one another in terms of their relative structural complexity because all languages are equal in their capacity to make meaning. For linguists, if someone complains that rap is a plague on standard English and rappers are simple-minded, the complaint is based not on the failings of rap or rappers, but on that hearer's attitudes about rap and linguistic propriety.

Outside the academy, Noam Chomsky is undoubtedly more renowned for his anarchist criticism of the American state than for the political implications of his linguistic theory. In works such as *Deterring Democracy* (1991), Chomsky criticizes the state for being a coercive political institution that channels wealth, property, and privilege to a corporate elite cozy with state power even as it uses propaganda to recruit intellectuals into its service.

And although Chomsky doesn't correlate his political opinions with his linguistic theories, he does think there are political dimensions to his study of linguistics. As a linguist he maintains that the ability to use language is innate to all humans, and therefore that grammar is the bedrock of countless uses of language. For Chomsky, a linguist's task is to strip away the variations that occur in language usage. Variations are like noise in a message, wholly irrelevant, and the sooner they can be eliminated the better. Only then can a linguist identify the innate grammatical knowledge that is the common link between humans using language in different societies and cultures.

Chomsky's linguistics is anchored in the Enlightenment rationalism of the Port-Royal Grammar, first published in Paris in 1660. The Port-Royal Grammarians stipulated that the simple sentence is the central linguistic unit of discourse, and as such can be used as a doorway into the mind's capacity to reason. For Chomsky and these Grammarians, all humans are equal because they are endowed with the capacity to reason, and linguistic analysis allows one to reflect upon and defend it. As University of Washington at Seattle professor Frederick J. Newmeyer explains, Chomsky considers this notion of linguistics "in an entirely positive political light: Our genetic inheritance—our human nature—prevents us from being plastic, infinitely malleable beings completely subjugable to the whims of outside forces."

> Chomsky's linguistics is anchored in the Enlightenment rationalism of the Port-Royal Grammar.

One of Chomsky's premier critics is Penn professor William Labov, who, with the publication of two pioneering books, *Language in the Inner City: Studies in the Black English Vernacular* and *Sociolinguistic Patterns* in the late 1960s and early 1970s, gave theoretical muscle to the field generally known as sociolinguistics. ("Sociolinguistics" is, actually, a phrase used by publishers and other linguists to classify Labov's work, and he himself rejects it. "'Sociolinguistics,'" he explains, "implies that there can be a successful linguistic theory or practice which is not social.") Labov shrewdly noted that Chomsky reduced the social aspects of language to any one individual's innate knowledge of language. Labov countered such an approach by claiming that "linguistic theory can no more ignore the social behavior of speakers of a language than chemical theory can ignore the observed properties of the elements." (Labov was an industrial chemist for ten years before becoming a linguist.) And in *Language in the Inner City* and *Sociolinguistic Patterns*, Labov sought to prove this claim by drawing on extensive fieldwork in Harlem and Philadelphia to demonstrate the validity of several interrelated principles concerning the social use of language: namely, that linguistic variation can actually be observed and described, that variation follows a consistent pattern, and that variation reflects social factors like age, education, race, and gender. For Labov, then, a linguistics that forsakes variation to discover a universal grammar is empirically inaccurate and far from egalitarian, since it assumes, in Labov's words, that "the proper object of linguistic study is an abstract, homogeneous speech community in which everyone speaks alike and learns the language instantly."

But Labov had more in mind than elaborating upon a viable empirical alternative to Chomskyan linguistics. He was also waging his own battle against the racist jeremiads penned by critics of the War on Poverty. In 1969, Arthur Jensen published the notorious *Harvard Educational Review* article "How Much Can We Boost IQ and Scholastic Achievement?" Jensen surveyed studies that reported that black children were failing to benefit from the educational opportunities afforded them by the federally funded Operation Head Start, an education program for disadvantaged preschool children established under the Economic Opportunity Act of 1964. According to Jensen, the studies, which focused on language use among other factors, revealed that the middle-class white population is smarter than the working-class black population, the reason being not social class but genetics. In other words, Jensen's conclusion, defended in 1994 by Richard J. Herrnstein and Charles Murray in the opening pages of *The Bell Curve*, was that "black children are genetically deficient in the ability to form concepts and solve problems." For Jensen, the War on Poverty was lost before it even began. No amount of aid could improve the lot of black children, simply because they are "mentally retarded."

> Writing in the late 1960s, Labov was appalled by the use of standard English as a barometer of intellect.

Labov was appalled by Jensen's use of linguistic research—particularly the use of standard English as a barometer of intellect. As early as 1965, Labov had submitted a sixty-page report to the Department of Health, Education, and Welfare outlining how an understanding of nonstandard dialects, and especially of how social environments shape these dialects, could serve as a basis for teaching the speakers of those dialects to read. Children could benefit from Head Start, but only if teachers did not ignore or devalue the linguistic competence children had developed speaking nonstandard dialects. The cost of such ignorance had ended up revealing itself in Jensen's sneering racism.

In *Language in the Inner City*, Labov explained exactly why Jensen's remarks about nonstandard dialects were not only racist, but empirically dubious. Jensen assumed that nonstandard dialects are simply the accumulation of errors caused by the biological inability of black speakers to master standard English. Drawing on hundreds of hours of taped interviews and conversations, Labov demonstrated that nonstandard dialects like Black English Vernacular are highly structured, rule-governed systems, which express "the same logical content" in ways that are equivalent to other dialects.

420

Dealing with the languages people speak in the course of their everyday lives, Labov espoused an egalitarianism grounded in solid empirical research with actual speakers, and in so doing rejuvenated a pluralistic tradition in linguistics that stretches all the way back to Franz Boas in the early years of this century. Boas was an ethnologist, anthropologist, linguist, and a professor at Columbia University who trained an influential generation of anthropologists that included Ruth Benedict, Margaret Mead, Zora Neale Hurston, and Edward Sapir. In *The Handbook of American Indian Languages* (1911), Boas pitted himself against Old World linguists who devoted themselves to the comparative study of Indo-European languages, believing non-Western languages like Iroquoian and Algonquian to be "primitive" because they didn't fit into European grammatical categories. But instead of assuming the superiority of European language and imposing its regularities on American Indian languages, Boas attempted to extract regularities as they presented themselves within those languages. In so doing, he proved that variation between and within languages was not an impediment but a key to understanding a language's essential structure.

Boas's egalitarianism, in turn, underwrote the founding of the Linguistics Society of America in 1924. In the LSA's manifesto, "Why a linguistic society?" Leonard Bloomfield (then in the German department at Ohio State University) wrote that such a society could serve two interrelated purposes. First, it could create a community for the then largely dispersed group of linguists teaching at the university level. (Of the two hundred forty-six founding members of the LSA, two hundred forty-three members taught in language or literature or anthropology departments.) Second, Bloomfield hoped that under the auspices of the LSA, linguists could form a united front to counteract widespread objections to Boas's claim that the languages of "civilized" Europeans are on a par with those of "savages."

Today the LSA still finds itself blasting away bromides that tout prescriptive grammar as the means for rescuing America from intellectual primitivism. A few contrarian linguists, though, detect a whiff of hypocrisy in the LSA. The organization that condemned the "English Only" bills proposed in Congress in 1995, they point out, has also

> Boas pitted himself against Old World linguists who believed that Native American languages were "primitive."

recently issued "Guidelines for Nonsexist Usage." The LSA, these contrarians contend, has neglected a long-standing caveat for linguists: "describe, don't prescribe."

The LSA has grown substantially since its founding. It now boasts 6,000 members, and there are one hundred eighty undergraduate and graduate degree programs in linguistics in the United States and Canada. A sense of community has emerged and, while linguists like Labov and Chomsky continue to wield tremendous influence in it, faculty and graduate students report that a Pax Chomskyana prevails. Sociolinguists and dialectologists explain that though they are not under Chomsky's sway, they must be familiar with his latest work. And they are quick to note that an inverse obligation does not apply to grammarians, who can remain unschooled in cutting-edge research about dialects because Chomsky's work is their article of faith.

Actually, that's putting it lightly. The rock band Bad Religion, which in 1995 slapped a Chomsky lecture on the B-side of a single, is not the only group of Chomsky disciples. At one prominent northeastern university, no graduate classes in linguistics are scheduled on Thursday afternoons because no one would dare attend: It is *de rigueur* to be in attendance at Chomsky's Thursday afternoon class at MIT. And it's been said that one scholar, during sabbatical, trekked from Columbus, Ohio, to Cambridge, Massachusetts, every Thursday just to be in the master's presence.

> A long-standing caveat for linguists is: "describe, don't prescribe."

Some grammarians are disheartened that colleagues who dissent from Chomsky must keep to themselves in separatist communities rather than vying with the master, argument against argument. Those syntacticians who have broken off from Chomsky have splintered into three areas, all of which garner much attention: Head-Driven Phase Structure Grammar (Stanford University, Ohio State, and the University of Illinois at Urbana), Tree Adjoining Grammar (Penn), and Optimality Theory (MIT, Rutgers University, and Johns Hopkins University).

Relatedly, some graduate students are disconcerted by the way in which professionalism can hijack the research enterprise. Says one student, "In graduate school the intellectual stakes change. You realize that the knowledge of fundamentals like Bloomfield's *Language*, which you acquired as an undergraduate, is obsolete in the seminar room, which trains you to conduct original research. Sometimes this is intoxicating, and sometimes it leads to research that you really have to be devoted to if you're not to think it useless in the grand scheme of things." The research enterprise is about identifying an idea that can be used to blaze a trail through some unexplored corner of the field, but its professionalized logic is what disheartens the student. Sometimes an idea might not have much elegance, but it raises enough provocative questions about, say, floating quantifiers in English, and nods enough toward the right authorities to have shelf life as research. It should be noted that the student's anxiety is hardly unique to linguistics. The anxiety concerns the wages of academic professionalism, and any graduate student must inevitably balance a genuine interest in ideas with the academy's rituals of legitimation.

> Grammarians, syntacticians, and sociolinguists all report that linguistics has not made the postmodern turn.

Despite these failings, many linguists breathe a sigh of relief when they walk into their departments. Grammarians, syntacticians, and sociolinguists all report that, unlike English, comparative literature, or some branches of anthropology, linguistics has not made the postmodern turn. "To walk into a linguistics department," explains Geoffrey Pullum, a professor at the University of California at Santa Cruz, "is to leave postmodernism behind like a fugitive finding sanctuary or a traveler finding shelter. Derrida's absurd posturings and lunatic misunderstandings of philosophy are taken for just that and scarcely ever mentioned. The burblings of the there-is-no-truth brigade are not even a low murmur in the background. They are altogether absent." A graduate student who works on the phonology of borrowing concurs. He admitted, without a whit of embarrassment, that his coursework has not included Derrida, Foucault, or Althusser.

In the upper reaches of the academic community where postmodernism reigns, such an admission would be read as a sign of anti-intellectualism. Undismayed, linguists would simply remind postmodernists that they do theory too, but they do not suffer from intellectual whiplash when doing it because they have a clear object of study. Some linguists would love to see the field shaken up, but not at the risk of estranging one part of the discipline from another. Says Pullum: "If it is positivism to believe that a world with definite properties and empirical characteristics exists and can to some extent be extremely low student faculty ratios: nearly one to one at Rochester, two to one at Rutgers, and three to one at UMass–Amherst.

Those who turn to the National Research Council rankings to assess departments should be aware that they are skewed towards large departments. What's more, Sarah Thomason, a professor at the University of Pittsburgh, suggests that while the rankings are not "totally off base," they can be "years out of date by the time you see them." The NRC rankings don't take note of the specializations within linguistics, either. Your best bet to finding departmental strengths and individual faculty is to consult the LSA's *Directory of Programs in Linguistics in the United States and Canada.*

> Despite their various specialties, virtually all linguistic departments teach the same core curriculum.

The size of a department affects how much of the field it can cover. A small department isn't likely to be equally well staffed in formal linguistics, sociolinguistics, anthropological linguistics, cognitive science, computational linguistics, applied linguistics, phonetics, historical linguistics, and psycholinguistics. Although at first they may appear to be eclectic, departments actually specialize in one or two of these sub-disciplines, and you should be sure that there will be several faculty members available to work with you in your field of interest. And even when you have identified the one professor with whom you want to work closely, you need to have more than one on hand, not only to address the unexpected (your relationship goes sour with that professor, for instance) but also because you need to retain enough authorities to staff the committees that evaluate your work.

If you are keen on graduate study in linguistics but don't know whether you want to earn a Ph.D., bear in mind that many linguistics departments do not offer a terminal master's degree. But it's not unheard of for students to test the waters by earning a master's degree at one Ph.D. program and then transferring to another program to do the Ph.D.

Despite their various specialties and affiliated institutes, virtually all linguistic departments adhere to a standard formula regarding program requirements. During the first year, linguistics students take core courses in phonology, semantics, and syntax. Penn is one exception in that it requires students in sociolinguistics to take a course in fieldwork, which is a methodological course about studying speech communities. And at Ohio State, all students are required to do phonology and syntax their first year, along with two of the following four courses: sociolinguistics, historical linguistics, phonetics, and psycholinguistics. During the second year, after learning the fundamentals of sound, form, and meaning, students take specialized courses to lay the foundations for a research program.

While many humanities and social sciences programs require students to pass a qualifying exam before undertaking doctoral research, most linguistics departments require students to write two or three research papers in different areas to demonstrate that they are fully qualified to begin dissertation research. Students write the papers during the second and third years of study and defend them before a faculty committee or a faculty/student colloquium. All programs have language requirements. Students must demonstrate a proficiency in a language other than their native one, but the number of languages and the degree of proficiency required varies widely.

So in what areas do departments specialize? In terms of grammatical theory, it's generally agreed that the high rollers are the University of Chicago, MIT, Ohio State, Penn, Stanford, Rutgers, UC–San Diego, UC–Santa Cruz, UMass–Amherst, UCLA, and Washington–Seattle. UC–Berkeley, Penn, North Carolina State University, York University (Canada), and Georgetown University are top-flight sociolinguistics programs. UC–Santa Barbara, the University of Arizona, and UT–Austin teach anthropological linguistics. Check out Penn, Ohio State, Harvard, UCLA, and Cornell University for historical linguistics, and the University of Nevada at Las Vegas, the University of Georgia, and Michigan State University at Lansing for dialectology. Those interested in phonetics and phonological theory should consider Ohio State, UCLA, and UMass–Amherst. For computational linguistics, consider Stanford, Penn, Rochester, and Ohio State. SUNY Stony Brook stands out for its interest in the application of theory to practical problems in language learning, language teaching, and natural language processing. Actual training in language teaching seems to have migrated to education and language departments.

> During the second year, students take specialized courses to lay the foundations for a research program.

Many linguistics departments benefit from an affiliation with an institute or center that sponsors research, houses archives, and often successfully understood through systematic study and careful theory construction, then positivism reigns in linguistics. Linguists exploring a language take themselves to be investigating matters of plain external fact, even when they use their own intuitions of grammaticality as a guide to the structure of the sentences of their own native language."

Linguists cling to a clear sense of purpose in part because their departments are so regularly fingered as institutionally superfluous. To work in linguistics is not only to fight your own battle for distinction among your cohort but to rely on the survival of your department in these days of university downsizing. When deans must consider closing a department, they begin by monitoring undergraduate enrollments in the courses it offers. Courses with high enrollments earn high marks, and this is rarely the case for linguistics courses: Some linguistics departments regularly offer undergraduate courses but not an undergraduate major, and without a core group of undergraduates to fill their classrooms, enrollments are naturally low. What's more, the interdisciplinary strength of linguistics is also its vulnerability when it comes to departmental cutbacks. If a geology department is closed, the tenured faculty cannot be relocated within the university. But if a linguistics department is padlocked, tenured faculty can easily be relocated in a half dozen departments: English, comparative literature, philosophy, sociology, anthropology, and psychology. Given these restrictions, some departments have closed (Columbia), some have been threatened with cutbacks but still survive (Harvard University), and others have been reduced to interdepartmental "studies" (the University of Michigan).

> Linguistics departments cultivate a clear sense of purpose because deans sometimes target them for cutbacks.

WHAT'S NEXT

A few linguistics departments are large (UCLA, the University of Texas at Austin), but most are small. At Brown University and the University of Rochester, for instance, there are seven full-time faculty. There are eight at the University of California at Santa Barbara, nine at Rutgers and SUNY Stony Brook, ten at UC-Santa Cruz, thirteen at Ohio State, and fourteen at both Washington-Seattle and the University of Massachusetts at Amherst. Graduate student populations are small too. There are ten graduate students at Rochester, twenty at Rutgers, and thirty-five at UMass-Amherst. These numbers translate into catalyzes interdisciplinary projects. Here's a sampling to indicate the variety. UC-Berkeley has the Survey for California and Other Indian Languages, which manages an archive of field notes and a large collection of audio tapes, and also provides funding for fieldwork. UC-San Diego houses the Center for Research in Language, which specializes in research on neural networks, while UC-Santa Barbara houses the Linguistic Minority Research Institute. At SUNY Stony Brook, a Semantics Lab produces software tools for linguistic research and education. And Stanford is home to the godfather of all linguistics institutes, the Center for the Study of Language and Information. Founded in 1983 with the then unheard-of sum of $20 million from the System Development Fund, CSLI is a lab devoted to research in the science of information, computing and cognition, and is supported by corporate affiliates like Microsoft, NEC, and IBM, who send it researchers to participate in projects onsite.

Cognitive science has become the big growth industry among linguistics departments. UC-Berkeley, Brown, MIT, Ohio State, Penn, Rutgers, Stanford, Johns Hopkins, and UC-San Diego, among others, either offer programs in cognitive science or boast a faculty contingent who specialize in the field. Even if the notion of neurological research conjures up visions of *Frankenstein* or *Shock Corridor*, you should consider applying to a department with a cognitive science program. These programs funnel tens of thousands of dollars in research money from the defense, medical, and information industries into linguistics, which makes it easier for a department to support all of its graduate students, regardless of their predilections. On the score of funding, Stanford is well-known for only admitting as many students as it can fully fund, while Ohio State offers students five years of funding, a package based on the assumption that it takes students between five and six years to do a Ph.D.

Students are attracted to cognitive science because there is ample room for discovery and innovation. Says a Rutgers graduate student: "None of the faculty training us have degrees in cognitive science. They're linguists, philosophers, biologists, psychologists. We're the first generation of graduate students, which means in a way that we're pioneers." At Rutgers, for instance, the cognitive science faculty includes the linguists Alan Prince and Jane Grimshaw, philosophers Jerry Fodor and Stephen Stich, and

> Many linguistics departments benefit from an affiliation with a research institute.

psychologists Alan Leslie and Zenon Pylyshyn. Another plus is the common purpose that attracts scholars from different fields to cognitive science. "Intellectually, psychology departments in most universities are in disarray. Social psychologists and clinical psychologists pretty much don't talk to each other. These factions form a department only on paper, as a political union for getting funding. This is not the case in cognitive science, where people from different fields apply various research methods to the problem of mind."

THE JOB MARKET

Faculty report that 1995 was the first year that even the best students from the top departments had trouble finding academic jobs. Graduate students expect to compete with linguists who earned their degrees four or five years ago and have been teaching part-time or holding down post-docs while applying for full-time jobs. And those who have the hardest time getting jobs are the students who do research in the more humanistic fields of linguistic research, like dialectology or historical linguistics.

A contracted market has created the demand for job flexibility and adaptability among job seekers. Given the small size of most linguistics departments, and the fact that departments are perennially at the top of a dean's hit list, no linguist should go on the market with qualifications in just one field. Most linguistics Ph.D.'s should be prepared to teach within a foreign language, comparative literature, sociology, anthropology or English department.

Should you follow this strategy, be advised that it is no guarantee of intellectual rewards. When linguistics is taught within a literature or language department, those of your colleagues who are mainly interested in literary interpretation sometimes regard your field as cold and sterile, a way of manipulating language that belittles its social or aesthetic meaning. A language department can be an uncomprehending environment for a linguist, despite the fact that a linguist's knowledge of a language's sociology and history can complement a literary perspective. Continuing research on purely linguistic questions may rarely be possible and it won't necessarily win institutional approval even when it is.

What about the nonacademic market? According to many observers, silicon valleys and alleys are teeming with lucrative job opportunities for linguists. Due to the amazing array of languages used on the Web, machine translation is a burgeoning industry, and companies that write translation programs need linguists to do the morphological and phonological work necessary for building lexicons. Elsewhere, companies developing speech-recognition software need dialectologists and computational linguists to build pronunciation dictionaries that incorporate dialect variations and to check their accuracy against real speech.

> According to many observers, silicon valleys and alleys are teeming with lucrative job opportunities for linguists.

Fear becoming a microserf? Then consider working in forensic linguistics. Linguists are sometimes hired as expert consultants. Linguists have been asked to testify in trademark disputes about the status of a noun, in inheritance disputes about the authenticity of a page inserted into a will, and in bribery cases about the authenticity of a voice print entered as evidence.

And for those who want to enforce the civil laws instead of just describing linguistic ones, the FBI beckons from the ad it periodically runs in the back of the LSA *Bulletin*. If you survive Quantico, you could find yourself examining forgeries, using Native American languages to develop coded communication, or logging hundreds of hours at a computer to nab hackers on the Web.

Who knows? There could even be a screenwriting career awaiting you when you retire to Florida on your pension. What with the post–Cold War paranoia profitably packaged by the *X-Files*, you could sell to the highest bidder the rights to your memoirs (authored under a pseudonym, of course): *I was a Linguist for the FBI.*

Better yet, maybe an academic linguist will read it and explain the kinks in it.

RESOURCES

NRC TOP TEN
MIT
Stanford
UCLA
UMass–Amherst
Penn
Chicago
UC–Berkeley
Ohio State
Cornell
UC–Santa Cruz

ASSOCIATION
Linguistics Society of
America
(202) 835-1714

JOURNALS
American Speech
Anthropological Linguistics
Language
Language and
Communication

CONSTELLATIONS

GRAMMATICAL THEORY
Chicago
MIT
Ohio State
Penn
Rutgers
Stanford
UCLA
UC–Santa Cruz
UC–San Diego
UMass–Amherst
Washington–Seattle

SOCIOLINGUISTICS
Georgetown
North Carolina State
Penn
UC–Berkeley
York (Canada)

HISTORICAL LINGUISTICS
Cornell
Harvard
Ohio State
Penn
UCLA

DIALECTOLOGY
Georgia
Michigan State University
University of Nevada at Las
Vegas

ANTHROPOLOGICAL LINGUISTICS
Arizona
UC–Santa Barbara
UT–Austin

PHONETICS AND PHONOLOGICAL THEORY
Ohio State
UCLA
UMass–Amherst

COMPUTATIONAL LINGUISTICS
Ohio State
Penn
Rochester
Stanford

COGNITIVE SCIENCE
Brown
Carnegie Mellon
Johns Hopkins
MIT
Ohio State
Penn
Rutgers
Stanford
UC–Berkeley
UC–San Diego

DEPARTMENTS ASSOCIATED WITH INSTITUTES
Stanford
SUNY Stony Brook
UC–Berkeley
UC–San Diego

FURTHER READING
Randy Allen Harris, *The Linguistics Wars* (Oxford)
Frederick Newmeyer, *The Politics of Linguistics* (Chicago)

WEB ADDRESSES
Linguistics page of the Virtual Library
http://www.cog.brown.edu/pointers/linguistics.html

Linguistics Institute
http://www.lsade.org

LINGUIST job list
http://www.emich.edu/~linguist/jobs.html

CHAPTER 25

POLITICAL SCIENCE

Rob D'Onifrio came to graduate school in political science after having been an MIT undergraduate bent on studying nuclear physics. But working on a political campaign was one of the factors that shifted his interest from the hard sciences to political behavior. "I'm not a fan of the two-party system, and statistics show that about 80 percent of the public is with me now. When my generation—people now in their twenties—become more active in politics, we'll have the chance to reconnect all the theories now in the air to actual policy decisions." While as an undergraduate D'Onifrio was impressed by less systematic accounts of Congressional votes, in graduate school he has mastered rational choice and game theory in order to study voting behavior more scientifically. "The mathematical models are good, useful as simplifying assumptions. But of course on their own they don't necessarily tell you much about the public."

At Stanford University, where D'Onifrio is now a second-year graduate student, there are plentiful opportunities to develop a more sophisticated view of voting behavior than mathematical modeling allows. One can do interdisciplinary research in sociology, psychology, and comparative politics. D'Onifrio plans to teach after finishing the program and perhaps also to work in a policy-oriented think tank—at the moment an educational think tank tops the list.

WHY POLITICAL SCIENCE?

Imagine the entering graduate class at a premier political science department in the fall of 1998. The group might include a Chicano from a major state university who had been heavily involved in campus politics, an Ivy League graduate with a master's degree in English, a magazine writer, a lesbian activist, a Peace Corps volunteer fresh from two years in the Philippines, and a Russian economist with an advanced degree in applied math from a British university. Students much like these have entered political science departments around the country recently. What holds the clan together? As Yale University professor Steven Skowronek puts it, they "join a passion for politics— for the study of power—to an academic sensibility for abstraction, generalization, and theory building."

This passion for politics—and the desire to effect political change— most distinguishes political scientists from their colleagues in kindred disciplines like history and economics. Some 90 percent of those who earn Ph.D.'s in political science pursue careers in academia, but over the years a steady stream of political science professors have traded the classroom for the caucus room. A short list of those who have made the leap to the public arena would include President Woodrow Wilson, Vice President Hubert Humphrey, Secretary of State Henry Kissinger, National Security Advisor Zbigniew Brzezinski, United Nations Ambassador Jeane Kirkpatrick, Illinois Senator Paul Douglas, Minnesota Senator Paul Wellstone, and New York Senator Daniel Patrick Moynihan.

For those who remain in academia, the options for research and involvement are many. Political science has long been divided into four major subfields—political theory, American politics, comparative politics, and international relations—and, within reason, in each the range of subjects and approaches is vast. But multiculturalism, environmentalism, and the women's movement (including the well known credo that "the personal is political") have all expanded political science research even more. Today the directory of the American Political Science Association (APSA) lists eight possible fields of interest and thirty-three organized sections ranging from "Computers and Multimedia" to "Law and Courts." There's even a section devoted to "Ecological and

Transformational Politics," which seeks ways to "better integrate the personal, professional, political and sacred aspects of our lives."

If a passion for politics is one distinguishing feature of the discipline, methodological diversity is another. Born as a branch of history, political science has always drawn heavily on the premises and practices of its humanistic cousins, history and philosophy. Since World War II, political scientists have found new inspiration in the methodologies of sociology, social psychology, and most recently, economics. In the 1980s, three presidents of the APSA—sociologist Seymour Martin Lipset, of George Mason University, economist Charles E. Lindbloom, then of Yale, and social psychologist Philip Converse, then of the University of Michigan—held Ph.D.'s from fields outside of political science. Today, prominent sociologist Theda Skocpol holds forth in Harvard University's government department, while renowned philosopher John Rawls casts a long shadow from just beyond the doorway.

> Scholars weaned on discussions of sovereignty are now confronted by others more interested in the thinning ozone layer.

This topical and methodological diffusion gives political science meetings the air of intellectual bazaars, where text-scrutinizing political philosophers rub shoulders with number crunchers and game theorists. In recent years, the proliferation of approaches has sparked debate about whether political science has a core. While all the social sciences debate this question, political science's centrifugal forces have intensified in the 1990s, as conceptions of politics have continued to broaden and methodologies diverge. Scholars weaned on discussions of representation, sovereignty, and the operation of interest groups now find themselves confronting colleagues who are more interested in the thinning ozone layer or the biological bases of aggression. The ascendance of mathematical modeling in some quarters and the proliferation of poststructuralist terminology in others has ushered out the era when each member of the APSA could understand every article published in the *American Political Science Review*. Lipset, who recently left Stanford University's political science department to join George Mason's Institute of Public Policy, says that many political science departments now operate as "coterie[s] of subfields." And one young political theorist, a self-described feminist and poststructuralist, has gone so far as to say she has less in common with attendees at political science meetings than with the people she would see "on any random street in America."

All this means that your choice of a graduate program is more important than ever. Because of the continuing expansion and fragmentation of political science, graduate programs vary vastly in the topics they cover and the methodologies they stress. Do you want a program built around a core curriculum, or one that operates cafeteria style? Do you want a program that propels you immediately toward a dissertation, or one that gives you more time and space to explore? How quantitative do you want your training to be, and where will you place the balance of theoretical focus and empirical grounding? How important is prestige, and what are the trade-offs between a well-rounded program and one that is tops in your particular area of interest? Finally, should you be applying to political science programs at all, or would you be better off in one of the schools of public affairs and international relations that are springing up at universities around the country? To answer these questions, you will need to think hard about your academic interests, your background and strengths, and your career goals.

> "Political science is the most distinctively American social science," says John Gunnell.

HOW POLITICAL SCIENCE HAS TAKEN SHAPE

"Political science," writes John Gunnell, a SUNY Albany political theorist and a leading historian of the discipline, "is the most distinctively American social science," in that it originated in the United States. Although the study of politics can be traced back to Aristotle, political science as an academic discipline and profession first emerged in the United States in the mid-nineteenth century. It was then that Francis Lieber, a German émigré scholar, adapted the German historical and comparative study of the state, or *Staatslehre*, to an American context, namely America's indigenous tradition of moral philosophy, which had long aimed to instill civic virtue in American citizens and public leaders. Following the Civil War, this version of political science became a standard part of university curricula. In 1880, Columbia University and Johns Hopkins University established two of the first graduate programs in political science.

Nevertheless, political science remained a stepchild of history until 1903, when the APSA became a separate organization formed by members of the American Historical Association. Initially, political science's split with history was more ideological than methodological.

434

Historians, a generally conservative lot, were content to wield their pens for the edification of present and future generations. Political scientists, by contrast, were infused with the politics of Progressive reform and yearned for a more immediate impact. Led by Frank Goodnow, the first president of the APSA, they aimed not only to advance the scientific study of politics but gain practical authority over it. Progressive Era political scientists, says Gunnell, believed that if they explained the "facts of politics" to the American people, "a democratic public would rise up and take control."

In advocating the scientific study of politics, these early political scientists dealt with a tension that has shaped all the social sciences to the present day: the desire to bridge the gap between academia and public life. Only a "scientific" understanding of political processes, they've argued, can win public regard and catalyze progressive social change. And certainly there have been those researchers who have hoped to borrow the prestige of laboratory sciences and technology to win the respect of leaders and the general public.

But in advocating the scientific study of politics, these political scientists have had to deal with a tension that has shaped all of the social sciences, from their own field to sociology to anthropology to history. They've been opposed by those who argue that by striving to emulate the natural sciences, political scientists obscure the role of values in their work, shore up the status quo, and abdicate their role as leaders of the quest for a fairer society. And these attacks have been bolstered by the fact that they tap into the populist mistrust of science, technology, and large powerful organizations. The irony is that too often the common goal—social change—and common optimism of both groups are obscured by antagonistic attitudes about research methods.

> Early political scientists dealt with a tension that has shaped all the social sciences: the gap between academia and public life.

Despite the hopes of the Progressive Era political scientists that they could make awareness of the scientific laws of politics common, by the 1920s their optimism had largely faded. World War I had led to a sharp rejection of German influences in political science—particularly the emphasis on the state—and focused growing attention on democratic pluralism and interest-group politics. In this context, Charles Merriam, a professor at the University of Chicago, called for a "truly scientific" political science that would command the attention of political and social elites. If the American public as a whole wouldn't listen to experts, he argued, then the experts should "speak truth to power."

Merriam's appeal for an even more rigorously scientific study of politics was drowned out by the gathering din of the 1930s. Faced with totalitarianism abroad and Depression at home, few political scientists had time for detailed observation or quantification. But in the wake of World War II, a new group of scholars—many trained by Merriam himself—answered his call. Borrowing heavily from sociology and social psychology, behavioralists like Paul Lazarsfeld, Robert Dahl, Philip Converse, Herbert Simon, Gabriel Almond, and Karl Deutsch attempted to create a new science of politics modeled closely on the natural sciences. The behavioralists used empirical methods and quantitative techniques—questionnaires, interviews, sampling, and regression analysis, among other things—to study aggregate political behavior and to develop overarching theories about the behavior of groups.

With its stress on scientific objectivity, behavioralism appealed to political scientists' long-held belief that scientific authority was the route to public influence. What's more, it put political science in line for the ample postwar funding that flowed to sciences of all sorts from government agencies and foundations. Behavioralism also represented the quintessential intellectual response to an era of prosperity, Cold War, and McCarthyism. By describing existing political behaviors rather than exploring or prescribing alternatives, behavioralism promoted complacency and diverted attention from social reform. David Easton, of the University of California at Irvine, notes that "objective, neutral, or value-free research represented a protective posture" for scholars fearful of Sen. Joseph McCarthy's "reign of psychological and legal terror." Behavioralism reflected an overall diminution in critical social thought during the late 1940s and 1950s, and "offered [scholars] intellectually legitimate and useful grounds for fleeing from the dangers of open political controversy."

> Behavioralism appealed to political scientists' belief that scientific authority was the route to public influence.

For all their claims to value neutrality, however, most behavioralists—like most political scientists before them—embraced the normative account of pluralist democracy in which liberal institutions, values, and political processes produced consensus out of conflict. They saw the story of politics as the story of the progress of liberal ideas and institutions. During the 1950s and 1960s, however, both of these assumptions came under increasingly sharp attack from political theorists of both the right and left. Haunted by the specter of Nazism, European émigrés like Leo Strauss and Herbert Marcuse repudiated the notion of triumphant liberalism. Instead, they blamed liberalism and scientism for what they saw as the degeneration of modern politics into totalitarianism. What's more, *The American Voter* (1960) by Angus Campbell et al., showed that the public's awareness and understanding of political issues fell far short of what political scientists had previously thought. "Knowing little of the [government's] particular policies and what has led to them," the study's authors concluded, "the mass electorate is not able either to appraise its goals or the appropriateness of the means chosen to secure these goals." By the mid-1960s, a diverse group of left-wing theorists—including reform-minded types, Marxists, political theorists, and followers of the civil rights movement—had joined the assault, attacking mainstream political science for its preoccupation with empirical methods and its failure to predict or speak to contemporary political issues like civil rights, the urban crisis, or the Vietnam War.

> Despite claims to neutrality, most behavioralists saw the story of politics as the story of the progress of liberal institutions.

For nearly two decades, the face-off between behavioralists and their critics gave political science its defining debate. In the 1970s, that debate finally wound down as political scientists retreated from behavioralism and focused instead on policy analysis. While many political theorists, traumatized by the experience of the previous decades—and increasingly influenced by intellectual trends in philosophy, linguistics, and literary studies—turned their back on the rest of the discipline, the departure of political theory from center stage has profoundly shaken political science as a whole. For decades, political theory—particularly the development of political thought, from Aristotle to Harvard's John Rawls—gave the field much of its sense of cohesion and self-awareness. Although only a minority of political scientists have ever considered themselves theorists, even the most statistics-bound behavioralist had to imbibe Plato, Marx, and Nietzsche for qualifying exams.

This is no longer the case. The unending debate over whether the field, in its latest incarnation, has a core has much to do with the loss of political theory and the unifying effect it once had. Now, although it remains housed in political science departments, much of its intellectual content is far removed from the concerns of the discipline as a whole. "Most political scientists don't really understand political theory. And most political theorists don't know much about political science," says a prominent historian of the profession. "I can't think of any other discipline" where parts of the discipline are "so alienated that they don't even fight with each other anymore."

In a much-discussed article published in 1988, Stanford's Gabriel Almond, one of the discipline's grand old men, and now a professor emeritus, described his fellow practitioners as sitting at "separate tables," communicating with each other only about departmental billets and budgets. While many political scientists share Almond's concerns about the field's fragmentation, not all mourn this development. "It's not [that] the discipline has split apart. It's [that] the discipline is offering you more choices," says one former staffer at the APSA. Benjamin Barber, a political theorist who heads the Walt Whitman Center of Political Science at Rutgers University, calls this the "big tent" theory of political science.

One burgeoning group of scholars, rational choice theorists, believe that political science does have a core, and they have found it. Like the behavioralists, rational choice theorists draw conclusions about collective political action by extrapolating from the behavior of individuals. But there the similarity between the two ends. While behavioralism encompasses a variety of scientific approaches that rely on inductive method—practitioners develop theories from reams of empirical data—rational choice is fundamentally deductive. And while behavioralists often rely on psychological explanations of human behavior, rational choice theorists adopt many of the assumptions of classical economics. The political arena is simply another marketplace, they argue, where individuals competing for scarce resources make rational choices designed to maximize their own interests. Alongside *homo economicus*, rational choice theorists place *homo politicus*.

> For decades, political theory gave the field much of its sense of cohesion.

Rational choice's present form, which incorporates mathematical modeling and game theory, first emerged in economics departments in the early 1950s. (Nobel Prize-winning economist Kenneth Arrow is sometimes credited with launching the field in his 1951 book, *Social Choice and Individual Values*.) In the 1960s and 1970s, it was championed by a few political scientists, most notably the late William Riker at the University of Rochester. But only since the mid-1980s has this insurgent methodology made a bid for the discipline's core. Over the last decade, rational choice, also known as formal theory or public choice, has spread from the Americanist subfield into political theory, international relations, and comparative government. Today, differential equations fill the pages of leading political science journals; political science departments vie to hire the hottest young prospects in the field; and rational choice theorists, many with undergraduate backgrounds in applied math, economics, or engineering, model everything from the behavior of Congressional subcommittees to the conditions under which nations go to war.

For rational choice theorists, the political arena is simply a marketplace where individuals maximize their own interests.

Proponents of rational choice display an almost messianic zeal in promoting their approach, which they see as bringing the virtues of rigor and deduction to political science. Two leading rational choice theorists, James E. Alt and Kenneth A. Shepsle of Harvard, have argued in *Perspectives on Positive Political Economy* that rational choice may make possible the development of a "coherent and unified theoretical view of politics and economics," a goal that has long eluded political scientists. Such a unified theory, some proponents of the methodology argue, could give political scientists the kind of influence in public debate that economists and sociologists have long had.

Indeed, even some doubters concede that rational choice theory has "recast much of the intellectual landscape" of political science. In *Pathologies of Rational Choice* (1994), Yale professors Donald P. Green and Ian Shapiro note that rational choice models have "generated a series of theorems about the logic of majority rule" that raise the possibility "that democratic institutions might be profoundly dysfunctional in ways that had not hitherto been appreciated." Rational choice models have been used to explain erratic patterns of policy making, systemic inflation, deficit spending, and a continuously expanding public sector, Green and Shapiro note. Such models have also called into question "the normative foundations of democracy."

If apparent majorities are often chimerical, if minorities can manipulate democratic decision rules toward the results they desire, and if there is no way to amalgamate individual desires into a "general will," as Rousseau had claimed in *The Social Contract*, then the nature and desirability of democracy require reevaluation.

439

Such conclusions alarm some critics of various political persuasions, who assail what they see as the ideological implications of rational choice. Others attack the methodology's assumptions about human psychology and rationality; they are unconvinced that people vote or contribute time and money to political campaigns because they expect to receive a concrete benefit. *Homo politicus*, these critics say, exists primarily in the imaginations of rational choice theorists.

Even some who applaud the theoretical sophistication of the new modeling techniques worry that most rational choice theories have yet to be empirically tested. One rational choice theorist quips that highlighting the methodology's empirical achievements would be "a bit like dwelling on the modesty of Dennis Rodman." Green and Shapiro argue that few rational choice models have been tested in the real world and those that have been examined either proved faulty or in the end supported "banal" propositions. As a result, they conclude, these models have as yet added "exceedingly little" to our understanding of politics.

Finally, many political scientists—particularly the less mathematically inclined—feel alienated by a method that has given political science journals the look of calculus texts. Developing the technical virtuosity needed to understand rational choice theorems requires years of coursework, time that some political scientists say would be better spent studying subjects more clearly related to politics. The ascendance of rational choice leaves many other traditional political scientists feeling "very much betwixt and between," says Yale's Steven Skowronek. "They don't know where their discipline went." This sense of estrangement is compounded by what is seen as the self-righteousness of rational choice theorists: In a discipline that has thrived largely by fostering methodological pluralism, some complain that rational choice theorists feel "it's their way or the highway."

Luckily for those who aren't attracted by theories of rational choice, there are many alternatives. Classic political theory has attracted a steady stream of students over the years, despite the fact that professors admit that one must study it as a labor of love. (Its continuing popularity, together with the lack of obvious employment possibilities outside of academia, makes it the most difficult subfield from which to land a job.) Political theory has never been confined to political science departments, and in recent years this subfield has been enriched by interdisciplinary crosscurrents. New approaches emanating from philosophy and literature departments—among them hermeneutics, poststructuralism, and postmodernism—have called into question traditional assumptions about the nature of historical "truth." At the same time, the rise of feminism and ethnic identity movements, the proliferation of multinational corporations, the identification of global environmental problems, and the revitalization of transnational institutions like the European Community have challenged political theory's traditional focus on the public institutions of the nation-state.

Understanding rational choice theorems requires years of study, time some say would be better spent studying politics.

Political theorists can generally be divided into two broad groups: those who take the historical "great books" approach to political thought and those who instead analyze political concepts like democracy, utilitarianism, or liberalism. The former group includes scholars of diverse persuasions, but in recent decades it has been dominated by disciples of Leo Strauss. Straussians believe that every great political work contains a secret text, which can be deciphered only through close textual analysis. Straussians tend to be erudite and politically conservative. The most famous Straussian of the last decade was the late Allan Bloom, author of the 1987 best-seller *The Closing of the American Mind* and formerly a professor at Chicago.

If Straussians have dominated the historical approach to political theory of late, the hottest debates among analytical political theorists in recent years concern the viability of the liberal tradition. The champions of liberalism are led by John Rawls, the Harvard philosopher whose 1971 classic, *A Theory of Justice*, reinvigorated discussions of liberalism and political theory more generally. Drawing on game theory, economic modeling, and the assumptions of rational choice theorists, Rawls tried to develop a set of valid and demonstrable criteria for justice. Other scholars have since followed his lead, developing moral theories about equality, freedom, international justice, and legitimacy, all based on assumptions of human rationality.

In recent years, liberalism has come under attack from several quarters. Communitarians, inspired by Hegel, assail liberalism for being, among other things, hyperindividualistic and blind to the virtues of community. Michael Sandel, of Harvard, and Michael Walzer, of The Center for Advanced Studies in Princeton, New Jersey, are proponents of this critique. Meanwhile, a diverse group of post-modern critics attack liberalism at its Enlightenment roots. Taking their cue from Nietzsche and Michel Foucault, these scholars challenge traditional understandings of truth and modernity and believe societies are structured through power-laden discourses.

American politics has always been the largest subfield in political science, and together with international relations it has been the most strongly affected by rational choice theory. But formal theorists do not have the field to themselves. Experts in urban politics and public-law scholars, many with joint appointments in law schools, have been only marginally influenced by rational choice. What's more, Americanists are heavily represented in the emerging intellectual movement known as new institutionalism. A reaction to behavioralism, which focused on the individual citizen, new institutionalism attempts to revive political science's traditional interest in the political institutions of the state. While some new institutionalists employ rational choice theory, many others adopt a temporal approach, studying institutions like the presidency, political parties, or even the post office in a historical context.

> The hottest debates among analytical political theorists in recent years concern the viability of the liberal tradition and its institutions.

For long-standing historical reasons, comparative politics encompasses the study of all countries other than the United States. It remains the most traditional of political science's subfields, although it too is beginning to be affected by rational choice theory. Not surprisingly, it has also been the most strongly influenced by the collapse of communism and the emergence of the post–Cold War order. These developments have forced some scholars, particularly those studying the former Soviet Union, to retool completely. In an era where Russia's archives are open, its elections are competitive, and its public officials give interviews on CNN, scholars can no longer build their careers by scrutinizing newspapers for clues to what is happening in the Kremlin.

The cascade of political changes in Eastern Europe and in so many other parts of the world in the last decade has had an energizing effect on comparative politics, attracting new students and opening new lines of inquiry. While political scientists were notoriously unsuccessful at predicting the fall of communism, this very failure has helped spur a wave of interest in democratization. Ada Finifter, a professor at Michigan State University, went to Moscow in 1989 to help conduct the first joint American-Soviet national public opinion survey of the Soviet Union; her hotel was packed with U.S. political scientists. The collapse of communism, together with the growing influence of economics on political science as a whole, has also reinvigorated the field of political economy. "Not only did democracy spread to other nations, but so too did market reforms," notes Harvard professor Robert Bates. "The construction of capitalist systems highlighted the political foundations of the private economy."

The end of the Cold War and growing trends towards globalization and internationalization have also breathed new life into an ongoing debate about the proper approach to comparative politics. For decades, comparative politics has effectively meant area studies, a region-by-region approach to studying the world beyond U.S. borders. Departments wishing to hire typically advertise for an expert on Europe, Africa, or the Middle East rather than a specialist on international migration or comparative judicial systems.

> The cascade of political changes in Eastern Europe in the last decade has had an energizing effect on comparative politics.

But recently a growing number of scholars—together with important grant-making agencies like the Ford, MacArthur, and Mellon foundations—have challenged this approach. They see the region-by-region strategy as anachronistic, an artifact of the Cold War when analysts divided the world into potential battlegrounds for superpower politics. These scholars suggest that regions like Africa and the Middle East are not nearly as unified as area studies advocates would suggest. Global issues are the order of the day. Moreover, they argue that area studies is theoretically impoverished. More can be learned from truly comparative work and studies focused on global issues like international migration or peace and security.

Cutting across all these subfields, but representing an emerging field in its own right, is the study of women and politics. For decades, political science largely ignored the role of gender in public affairs: In the first two-thirds of the century, only eleven political science dissertations focused on women. With the rise of the women's movement and the birth of women's studies programs in the 1970s, this situation changed dramatically. Scores of gender-related papers are now presented at the annual APSA meeting or published in the journal *Women and Politics*. Some feminist scholars critique the traditional exclusion of women from political theory and research, while others gradually add women back into the political equation. A third group tries to reconceptualize political science's existing frameworks and assumptions to make more room for women as political actors.

WHAT'S NEXT

In 1995, the National Research Council released a survey of political scientists that ranked sixty Ph.D. programs according to the scholarly quality of their faculty and their effectiveness in educating research scholars. If you are interested in an academic career at a major research university, you would do well to consider schools in the top tier of the NRC list, bearing in mind, of course, that all such rankings should be taken with a grain of salt. Professional reputation, as one political theorist notes, is a "subtle and difficult thing to get at," and schools occasionally rise or fall in the rankings dramatically: The University of California at San Diego, which was rated twenty-ninth in terms of the scholarly quality of its faculty in 1982, surged to ninth place in the latest survey. More importantly, schools that are ranked slightly lower overall may be tops in a particular subfield. Johns Hopkins, for instance, is particularly strong in political theory, while Rutgers is noted for its feminist scholarship. Cal Tech, a powerhouse in rational choice theory, does not have a separate political science department—it awards Ph.D.'s in social science—and is not included in the NRC rankings at all.

So rankings like those put out by the NRC should be only one factor you consider as you select a graduate program. Programs vary vastly in their research strengths and pedagogical approaches. As departments beef up their formal theory and quantitative methods, you can expect more schools with mathematically-minded requirements. Students with mathematics or economics backgrounds tend to accept this tendency with glee, but it can prove a roadblock for those unprepared for such an emphasis. Still, many students appreciate a strong methodological grounding; Julie Conrad, a second-year Ph.D. student at Rochester, calls the department's quantitative requirements "a learning experience, but not an unwelcome one." Johns Hopkins, on the other hand, "gives you incredible amounts of freedom; you can do interdisciplinary work at the drop of a hat," says Deborah Candreva, a third-year doctoral student. She warns, though, that students entering such an arena without a background in political science can be at a real disadvantage, forever feeling groundless and underschooled in the field.

It is not out of the ordinary in political science for someone to get a master's at one school and get a Ph.D. at another. If you are a new-comer to the discipline, however, be sure to enroll in an M.A. pro-gram that will provide you with broad training so you'll be well prepared for further study. It is, however, harder for master's stu-dents as such to get funding, and many departments no longer actively offer a terminal M.A., so make further inquiries if you are considering this path. It's equally important to keep in mind that students in Ph.D. programs are under growing pressure to choose a dissertation project early, and with spe-cialization the order of the day, most students have less time to explore the field's many nooks and crannies. Thus, finding a department that fits your particular interests is now more important than ever, professors say.

> As departments beef up offerings in formal theory, expect more schools with mathematically-minded requirements.

A good first step in your research is to consult the APSA's *Graduate Faculty and Programs in Political Science*, published every three years: The 1997 edition will be the standard-bearer until the end of the century. The 1993 edition of *Political Science: The State of the Dis-cipline*, edited by Michigan State's Ada Finifter and published by the APSA, does not discuss graduate programs per se, but it does provide an excellent overview of political science theories and methodologies, as well as the state of research in various subfields. In addition, you would do well to consult political science journals, including those mentioned above, and the APSA's monthly publication *PS*. Again, think about which programs fit your interests and academic strengths.

If you are interested in mathematical modeling and rational choice theory, you might consider Harvard, Stanford, Princeton University, Rochester, Michigan, or Cal Tech, all programs where that approach is particularly strong. If statistics and quantitative methods are not your strong point, you might think twice about applying to Michigan.

A behavioralist approach to American politics still reigns in some quarters, particularly Michigan, where it never went out of style. Michigan's world-renowned Institute of Social Research makes the university a center for electoral studies and public opinion research. New institutionalists publish a semiannual volume, *Studies in American*

Political Development, and are particularly strong at Yale, UCLA, and the University of Virginia.

Professors cite the University of Minnesota at Twin Cities, Princeton, Harvard, Yale, Chicago, SUNY Albany, and Johns Hopkins as among the strongest overall departments in political theory. Straussians continue to reside at Chicago, as well as at Harvard, the Claremont Graduate School, and the University of Toronto. Although liberals can be found in most major political science departments, they are particularly thick on the ground at Princeton. William Connolly, at Johns Hopkins, is perhaps the most prominent postmodernist, but strong contingents can also be found at Northwestern University and Arizona State University.

Many comparativists are associated with area studies research institutes like the Russian Research Center at Harvard, the Russian Institute at Columbia University, or the Asia/Pacific Research Center at Stanford. Area studies proponents argue that a detailed knowledge of the language and culture of a particular region is vital to understanding its politics, so it's best to have significant knowledge under your belt before you consider any leading program. Most political science departments remain divided on these issues, although some, like Harvard, Michigan, and UCLA, have particularly strong area studies programs.

In 1986 Rutgers, known also for political theory, became the first university to offer women and politics as both a major and minor field of study toward the Ph.D. While no other program yet offers an equivalent program, the University of Washington at Seattle, the University of Wisconsin at Madison, and Minnesota-Twin Cities each house more than one feminist theorist, and places such as Cornell University offer an interdisciplinary option that allows for concentration on women and politics. Most major departments now have at least one faculty member specializing in such issues.

THE JOB MARKET

In the academic arena, the job market in political theory and international relations is very tight, largely due to the overproduction of Ph.D.'s. Peter Stone, studying political philosophy at Rochester, notes that the job market is "always lousy for philosophers." A third-year political theory student at Johns Hopkins uses "ugly" and "grim" to describe the job market in her field. On the other hand, "the market doesn't seem to be too bad for Americanists," according to Roger Moiles, an advanced graduate student in American politics at Michigan State. An American legal-system specialist finishing up at Ohio State University notes that the traditional pattern of completing one's dissertation while moving into a tenure-track assistant professor position has been replaced by a new routine of Ph.D.'s heading off to one- and two-year positions.

Because the field is currently so tight, you should consider whether your goal is to be an academic researcher at a large university or a professor at a small liberal arts college. While you should stick to the top-ranked schools for the best shot at the former, your options are broader if teaching is your primary goal. In both cases, it's a good idea to ask to see the placement record of a department in which you are interested. If you want primarily to teach, see if the program you're considering offers graduate students teaching experience; departments may pride themselves on restricting the teaching of undergraduate courses to faculty, but that won't give you the teaching experience you need.

In the nonacademic realm, political science Ph.D.'s run polling operations for CBS and *The New York Times*; work as political consultants, fundraisers, and campaign managers; and hold numerous posts in both the executive branch and on Capitol Hill. Many with training in comparative government or international relations join the foreign service or perform risk analysis for corporations that are considering expanding abroad. A growing number of foreign students with political science Ph.D.'s return to key posts in their countries' governments. Faculty, though, do stress that there is no clear path from the Ph.D. to nonacademic employment. Landing a job takes a little luck and a lot of initiative.

Those with master's degrees from separate programs in such areas as public policy and international affairs can head straight into a career in policy analysis, whether for corporations, consulting firms, or in the public sector. Students preparing for careers in government and business at Rochester's M.A.-level public policy program, for example, are optimistic about their job prospects, and suggest that things look best for people with training in quantitative methods of analysis.

RESOURCES

NRC TOP TEN
Harvard
UC–Berkeley
Yale
Michigan
Stanford
Chicago
Princeton
UCLA
UC–San Diego
Wisconsin–Madison

ASSOCIATIONS
American Political
Science Association
(202) 483-2512

JOURNALS
*American Political
Science Review*
*Journal of American
Political Science*
*Studies in American
Political Development*
Women and Politics

CONSTELLATIONS

POLITICAL THEORY
Harvard
Chicago
Claremont
Graduate School
Johns Hopkins
Minnesota–Twin
Cities
Princeton
SUNY Albany
Toronto
Yale

BEHAVIORALISM
Michigan

RATIONAL CHOICE
Cal Tech
Harvard
Princeton
Rochester
Stanford

STRAUSSIAN
Chicago
Claremont Graduate
School
Harvard
Toronto

NEW INSTITUTIONALISM
UCLA
Virginia
Yale

POSTMODERNISM
Arizona State
Johns Hopkins
Northwestern

AREA STUDIES
Columbia
Harvard
Michigan
Stanford
UCLA

WOMEN AND POLITICS
Cornell
Minnesota–Twin
Cities
Rutgers
Washington–
Seattle
Wisconsin–
Madison

FURTHER READING
Ada Finifter, ed., *Political Science:
The State of the Discipline* (APSA)

APSA, *Graduate Faculty and Programs in Political Science*

WEB ADDRESSES
Political Science Virtual Library
http://www.lib.uconn.edu/PoliSci

Political Science Internet Resources
http://www.wcsu.ctstateu.edu/socialsci/polscies.html

CHAPTER 26

PSYCHOLOGY

Serena Chen is putting the last touches on her social psychology dissertation at New York University. Her work explores the effect of intimate relationships on cognition. In particular, she is studying the mental narratives people develop based on their previous relationships, and she compares how these narratives affect her subjects' current perceptions of significant others, acquaintances, and group stereotypes.

Much previous social-cognitive research has focused on how the perception of static traits, like honesty or generosity, affects our understanding of others. Chen takes this work further, positing that the knowledge we have of significant others is more dynamic than previously assumed. In intimate relationships, Chen says, we can often predict how a significant someone might behave in certain contexts at certain times—and why this might be so. Using interviews and questionnaires combined with measuring the time it takes a subject to recall information about various people—with whom they are and are not intimate—her data suggests that the degree of intimacy affects cognition.

Chen's research lies within traditional areas of social psychology, like person-perception, relationships, and emotions. But it also has clear clinical implications. For instance, it might help therapists to consider when and how their clients' past relationships come into play in their current relationships.

WHY PSYCHOLOGY?

To people with little knowledge of the field, "psychology" connotes psychotherapy, not scientific research. This is natural, since the public gleans most of what it knows about the discipline from popular culture. Woody Allen films, true crime novels, and sitcoms like *Frasier* are what most people associate with this profession. However, there are many possible permutations and interpretations of what it means to be a psychologist. Psychologists perform scientific research, teach, and diagnose and treat patients. Some work in schools, some in prisons. Some counsel professors who are existentially unsatisfied, and others counsel heroin addicts. It is a demanding, often taxing line of work. Yet the intellectual excitement of learning psychological theory and doing research—and the inspiration which comes from connecting with and helping to heal others—gives this kind of work a rare intensity and integrity.

While most students know that psychology proper is divided into two camps—clinical and experimental—few realize that the structure of the discipline has further subdivisions and nuances. The one that's most important for you to know about before you start researching graduate programs concerns training. There are three routes to a career in psychology: the scientist-practitioner, the scholar-practitioner, and the research-scientist.

The scientist-practitioner paradigm, considered the most prestigious, was graduate psychology's first model. This kind of training is often referred to as the "Boulder Model" because its principles were outlined in 1949 at a famous conference in Boulder, Colorado. Although graduate schools following this model purportedly train students equally in research, teaching, and practice, this is not always the case, as some institutions favor one sphere over another. Regardless of their specialties, programs must adhere to most of the principles of the Boulder model to earn the accreditation of the American Psychological Association (APA).

The scholar-practitioner model trains students whose main focus is clinical work. This model, called the Vail Model, was created to accommodate those whom the Boulder Model did not. The Vail Model offers doctoral level clinical training, but, unlike the Boulder Model, it does not train students to become researchers. The degree scholar-practitioners receive—a Psy.D., or Doctorate of Psychology, rather than a Ph.D.—reflects this emphasis. Although there are only twenty APA-accredited Psy.D. programs in the U.S., their class sizes are large enough that they produce nearly as many clinicians as the 140 APA-accredited Ph.D. programs combined. Some Psy.D. programs are affiliated with major universities, while others, like the Massachusetts School of Professional Psychology, exist as freestanding professional schools. There are a handful of schools (like the California School of Professional Psychology) that award a Ph.D. which is actually more like a Psy.D., emphasizing clinical training over research.

Finally, the research-scientist model trains psychologists to do research in experimental, social, and developmental psychology. It does not train students to administer psychological testing or to conduct therapy.

HOW PSYCHOLOGY HAS TAKEN SHAPE

EXPERIMENTAL PSYCHOLOGY: FROM ITS FOUNDING TO THE PRESENT

Experimental psychology today seeks quantifiable evidence for theories about the mind. In the nineteenth century, Ernst Weber, Gustav Fechner, and Herman von Helmholtz, among others, paved the way for such work with their experimental investigations of the relationship between psychological and physical experience. Wilhelm Wundt refined and expanded these scientists' methods, creating a socially recognized and independent science of psychology. At the time of psychology's founding—usually marked by Wundt's establishment of the first official laboratory exclusively for psychological research in Leipzig in 1879—the field combined psychological, physiological, and philosophical elements.

Wundt was interested in the study of consciousness, a subject that William James, a Harvard University professor of philosophy, also explored. James began a movement called pragmatism, which, among other things, decreed that psychology should have practical applications. Wundt and James believed that the mind's internal processes could and should be studied.

This "mentalistic" approach declined sharply around 1912, with the flowering of behaviorism. The behaviorist school objected to the notion of studying the "mind." That entity could not be seen or even empirically proven to exist, and was therefore deemed unsuitable for scientific research. John Watson and B.F. Skinner were two of the most influential members of this movement, which sought to study and define all of human and animal experience in terms of stimulus and response.

> The pragmatist William James decreed that psychology should have practical applications.

The behaviorist mission ultimately proved unsuccessful. In the 1960s, partly because of Noam Chomsky's attack on Skinner's stimulus-response account of language, the concept of mind—which had lain dormant since Wundt and the study of consciousness—was once again considered legitimate fodder for psychological study. Allen Newell and Herbert Simon's success in programming computers to play chess, which hinted at the potential intricate "internal" processes of machines, inspired interest in the intermediate stages between stimulus and response. With the appearance of more and more research which seriously weakened the behaviorists' doctrine, the "cognitive revolution" was born. Behaviorism sought refuge in behavioral neuroscience and in certain kinds of clinical research—for example, in experiments with schizophrenics and autistic children which incorporated certain Skinnerian principles.

Cognitive psychologists now study, among other things, memory mechanisms, language comprehension, logic, and genetic inheritance of cognitive abilities like intelligence. They also deal with tricky research issues. What influences the accuracy of eyewitness' testimony? Can a computer be created which could simulate all human mental functions? Can dolphins be trained to use symbols in a system comparable to human language?

Some programs have individual cognitive psychology departments. Other programs combine cognitive psychology with several other subdisciplines under the umbrella of "experimental psychology." We will now turn to the other subdisciplines which warrant individual description.

Physiological Psychology

Biopsychological research is one component of physiological psychology. It examines the endocrine system, hormonal changes, and metabolic systems. Another branch of physiological psychology, neurophysiology, studies people who have suffered head injuries, strokes, or damage from epileptic seizures. Psychophysiologists, working more often on animals than on people, also record and study physiological responses using EKGs or EEGs.

Up until the 1920s, neurologists and neurophysiologists mostly studied the brain. One of the first of such researchers was Karl Lashley, who tried to determine the localized areas of the brain which stored and dictated behavior by first teaching rats a particular behavior and then destroying selected portions of their brains. He had little success.

As technology improved, physiological psychology's methods became more sophisticated. Walter Hess implanted electrodes in cats, stimulating a region in their hypothalamuses which induced them to attack or flee. For this work, Hess was awarded the Nobel Prize in 1949. Using electrodes to observe and record mental functions, D.H. David Hubel and Torsten N. Wiesel discovered that some visual cortical cells in the brain respond to complex features of visual perception, such as a line with a particular spatial orientation or one which moves in a certain direction. Hubel and Wiesel's work inspired further research investigating whether or not particular brain functions could be localized to small clusters of neurons, or even to individual neurons. Today, with optical imaging, physiological psychologists can observe neural activity on the brain's surface by monitoring changes in the refraction of ultraviolet light from the exposed cortex.

> Using optical imaging, physiological psychologists observe neural activity on the brain's surface.

New programs in neural science or neuroscience combine relevant methods from biology, chemistry, mathematics, and computer science with psychological methods to study the nervous system. Behavioral neuroscience conducts much of the animal research which once came under the heading of physiological psychology. Psychologists who do cognitive neuroscience, a combination of neuroscience and cognitive psychology, often examine patients with noninvasive techniques, including the magnetoencephalogram (based on neuromagnetism), the PET scan (radioactive tracers

453

showing the amount of metabolic activity), and the functional MRI (based on nuclear resonance.)

With such tools, researchers can determine which areas of the brain are active during specific cognitive processes and they may also provide empirical grounding for assumptions that were formerly purely theoretical. Technological tools are also advancing neuropsychological research in its ability to determine how damage to specific areas of the brain affects cognition and behavior. Neuropsychology has developed applications for clinical areas as well; there are now psychology tests which assess deficits in brain functioning from trauma or disease and help to treat these problems.

> Classifying research as "hard neuroscience" keeps experimental psychology in the funding stream.

Partly for financial reasons, the term "cognitive neuroscience" now covers more and more areas of experimental psychology. As federal funding for research keeps decreasing, more money has been cut from "soft" social research than from "hard" natural sciences. Classifying psychological research as "hard" neuroscience is one way to keep experimental psychology in the funding stream. Although cognitive neuroscience's progress is impressive, there is tension in the wider field: psychologists from other branches believe neuroscience is prospering at the expense of their own research areas. Social psychologists are among those who feel that their research on the consequences of mental illness is just as important, and deserves the same funding, as neuroscience.

For an overview of contemporary physiological research, look to *Behavioral Neuroscience and Psychobiology*. For cognitive psychology, see the flagship *Journal of Experimental Psychology* (*JEP*) or its spin-off, *JEP: Learning, Memory, Cognition. Memory and Cognition* and *Cognitive Psychology* are also useful. If you are interested in behaviorism and physiological research, see the *Journal of Applied Behavior* and *JEP: Animal Behavior Processes*.

Developmental Psychology

Developmental psychology deals with people's cognitive, social, and moral development from infancy through old age. Developmentalists observe and evaluate changes in subjects, rather than trying to alter the behavior of subjects. Developmental psychology stems from the child psychology of the early twentieth century, which sought to determine at what ages children mastered behavioral and cognitive abilities. Jean Piaget stands out in this tradition, positing particular, sequential stages of cognitive and behavioral development. Freud, Erik Erickson, and Lawrence Kohlberg also saw development as occurring in major stages. Piaget's work was published in English in 1926. It did not become popular in the U.S., however, until the earlier-mentioned cognitive revolution of the 1960s.

In the late 1950s, New York University's Jerome Bruner added another dimension to developmental psychology. Looking for an alternative to stimulus-response theory's reductive treatment of behavior, Bruner studied people's ways of constructing meaning. Bruner also broke with the branch of the cognitive revolution that favored a computer model of the mind. He believed that this mechanistic model of cognition could not fully explain a child's understanding of people's actions and motivations in a particular culture. Bruner's approach led to the "constructivist" movement, which examines the cognitive developmental processes underpinning one's self-perception.

Developmentalists often specialize in researching certain age groups, but many are currently studying cognitive development over the whole lifespan, asking: How does intelligence change as one ages? How does language acquisition and use change over time? The leading journals in this area are the *Journal of Applied Psychology* and *Life-Span, Development, and Behavior.*

Social Psychology

Social psychology studies the relationships both among individuals and between individuals and groups. This field began in the nineteenth century, when Wilhelm Wundt, the pioneering experimentalist previously discussed, posited two branches of psychology: physiological and social (*Volkerpsychologie*). It was the second type which examined folk beliefs and psychological differences between people of various social classes. By the early twentieth century, *Volkerpsychologie* had evolved into social psychology, which now includes the study of the psychological and behavioral effects of alienation or inclusion in groups.

Kurt Lewin's work at MIT's Research Center for Group Dynamics in the late 1940s turned the field's attention to social climates and the personal dynamics within small groups. Lewin not only established the field that became known as group dynamics but also founded sensitivity training, the precursor to contemporary programs which promote the acceptance of cultural diversity. All the research areas Lewin first cultivated (emotion, motivation, personality, and group dynamics) later became major fields of study. Possibly Lewin's greatest contribution, however, was proving that personality and other complex, slow-to-develop phenomena could be empirically studied—a view not widely accepted before his work.

Stanley Milgram's experiments about obedience and authority intrigued, and shocked, the public.

Partly due to the cognitive revolution and also because of the socio-cultural politics of the time, social psychology was especially prominent in the early 1960s. In 1964, a student of Lewin's, Leon Festinger, published *Conflict, Decision, and Dissonance.* This work argued that when presented with a pair of contradictory ideas or beliefs, people tend to dismiss one of them. Other researchers investigated topics from the workings of social activism to factors affecting helping behavior during an emergency. During this period social psychology and sociology cross-pollinated, and sociologists like Erving Goffman and Herbert Blumer contributed influential ideas to the psychology of everyday interaction.

But perhaps nothing had more impact on the public's conception of social psychology than Stanley Milgram's infamous experiments about obedience and authority. Conducted in the early 1960s at Yale, Milgram's studies showed that many subjects willingly administered electric shocks to others when so "ordered" by an authority (the experimenter). Because of its implications about the dark side of human nature, Milgram's work still fascinates the public. Milgram's manipulative techniques prompted other researchers to endeavor to investigate the seamier side of human thought and behavior without exploiting experimental subjects. Professional associations established protocols, and universities set up committees to monitor the ethical standards of psychological research.

Today, social psychology is an interdisciplinary field which combines cross-cultural psychology, sociobiology, and evolutionary biology. Some researchers are focusing on love and long-term relationships, particularly romantic attachments and their potentially stress-reducing effects. Many social psychologists study social cognition, particularly the development of social attitudes, the use and effects of persuasion, affect and social judgment, and the psychological features of prejudice.

Personality psychology is sometimes included in social psychology programs. However, there are some programs devoted solely to personality psychology which attempt to measure the social manifestations of stable individual traits, like introversion and extroversion. Personality research also examines emotional development, childhood friendships, and the transition from adolescence to adulthood. Because personality factors are both complicated and interwoven, the field has had to develop sophisticated research techniques called "psychometrics"—a large field of research on its own. (Willingly or not, anyone who takes standardized tests like the GRE is a guinea pig for psychometrics.) To learn about the variety of research both in social and personality psychology, see the journals *Social Psychology* or *Social Psychology Bulletin*.

> I/O psychologists study how workplace factors cause burnout, stress, and turnover.

Industrial/Organizational Psychology

Harvard's Hugo Munsterberg was one of the first founders of this field. At first a cordial colleague of William James, he later rejected James's interests in psychoanalysis and mysticism, and instead concentrated on applied psychology. His *Vocation and Learning* (1912) and *Psychology and Industrial Efficiency* (1913) were milestones in I/O research. His earlier best-selling *On The Witness Stand* (1908) showed the inaccuracy of eye-witness' testimony, and he is often credited with founding forensic psychology.

In the early twentieth century, I/O psychologists concentrated on assessing aptitude. They refined tests which compared general intelligence, personality traits, vocational interests, and specific mental abilities. By the 1920s, tests focused heavily on the questions of employee hiring, motivation, satisfaction, and teamwork. People still do research on similar issues: refining personnel selection, evaluating performance, determining influences on motivation and productivity, and improving the effectiveness of training in the workplace. I/O psychologists also study the effects of race, gender, and sexual attraction on employee hiring and appraisal, and the factors that affect employee burnout, stress, and turnover.

Lewin's social psychological research on the behavior of small groups influences contemporary industrial psychology. At present, there is strong interest in studying leadership, the dynamics and effectiveness of work groups, and the formation of and adjustment to organizational cultures. Industrial psychologists study everyone from space shuttle and flight crews to computer programmers and on-line communities. *The Journal of Applied Psychology* and the *Personnel Journal* are useful sources for further information.

Community Psychology/Health Psychology

The first community psychology programs were established after a 1965 conference in Swampscott, Massachusetts, which formalized some of the field's goals. Many of the psychologists present at Swampscott were unhappy with the low quality of mental health care available to the poor and sought to improve it. Within the ranks of psychologists, community psychologists still tend to be the most politically active.

Community psychologists insist that mental health research occur in natural settings, not just in labs and clinics. They attempt to prevent mental illness through effective psychotherapy or counseling, and through education, sports, and recovery programs. Community psychologists also search for ways to empower marginalized people within their communities. Two important issues which

> Industrial psychologists study everyone from space shuttle crews to on-line communities.

currently concern community psychologists are finding the best ways to deal with welfare reform and reducing school dropout rates.

Health psychologists, social psychologists, and groups of sociologists and social workers have recently sponsored projects formerly conducted by community psychologists. Community psychologists fear this intrusion because they believe that such projects tend to focus too much on the psychology of the individual, overshadowing research on communities and groups. As you can see, the relationship between the various branches of community and health psychology can be tense. For further information on community psychology, see *The American Journal of Community Psychology*, which is a forum for both research and activism.

CLINICAL PSYCHOLOGY: ROOTS TO CURRENT RESEARCH

Clinical psychology, the other main branch of the discipline besides experimental psychology, is committed both to determining the causes of mental illness—from relatively mild neuroses to severe psychoses—and to developing treatments for them.

Lightner Witmer founded the first U.S. program with formal training in clinical psychology at the University of Pennsylvania in 1896. In 1906 Morton Prince, a neurologist, founded *The Journal of Abnormal Psychology*, which fast became the leading journal in the field. The early clinical psychologists primarily did psychological testing, which sparked interest in providing therapy to test subjects. M.D.'s opposed psychologists conducting psychotherapy, and blocked them from doing this kind of work and from prescribing medication.

World War II, however, created an enormous demand for psychological testing of soldiers and for psychotherapy and counseling for veterans, and there were too few qualified M.D.'s to provide these services. Over the objection of M.D.'s, state legislatures began to pass licensing laws which allowed psychologists to practice psychotherapy. The Boulder conference of 1949, mentioned earlier, established the standards for training clinical psychologists.

People are sometimes still confused about the differences between psychiatrists and psychologists. Psychiatrists go to medical school, earn an M.D., and prescribe medications. Furthermore, they generally follow a medical model of mental illness. Psychologists, on the other hand, go to graduate school, get a Ph.D., practice psychotherapy, follow cognitive-behavioral or psychoanalytic models, and cannot prescribe medication. Over the last decade, psychologists have lobbied for the right to prescribe medication, which has added fuel to the ever-present tension between Ph.D.'s and M.D.'s.

> World War II created an enormous demand for psychological testing and for psychotherapy.

Undeterred in their desire to heal people, clinical psychologists created a variety of alternative treatments by the 1950s. Various psychoanalysts become prominent around this time, including Harry Stack Sullivan, Melanie Klein, Karen Horney, and Heinz Kohut. Their approaches continue to influence certain kinds of psychotherapy. Psychologists were especially successful in using learning and conditioning principles to treat phobias and neurotic symp-

459

toms. These techniques became known as "behavior therapy," drawing from Joseph Wolpe's process of systematic desensitization (based on Pavlovian or classical conditioning) and from Watson and Skinner's principles of operant conditioning. Behavioral and cognitive therapy merged, becoming "cognitive-behavioral therapy," which is a form of treatment many U.S. psychologists use.

> Clinical research has never been as vibrant as it is now.

Clinical research has never been as vibrant as it is now. One area focuses on short-term psychotherapy outcomes and investigates appropriate treatments for specific disorders, like phobias or alcoholism. Short-term psychotherapy usually consists of twenty or fewer sessions, often taking a "solution focus" designed to help patients with concrete and immediate problems. With HMOs on the rise, short-term therapy is increasingly popular, since it is significantly cheaper than long-term therapy.

The predominant research today explores the potential effects of genetic and psychological factors on mental illness. There is also growing interest in perceptual and cognitive characteristics within a diagnostic category—such as anorexic patients who develop distorted body images or the apparent differences in brain laterality in bipolar patients. The latest psychiatric research includes testing new psychoactive drugs such as Prozac, and scanning patients' brains. *The Journal of Abnormal Psychology* and *The Journal of Consulting and Clinical Psychology* are leading venues for clinical research.

Counseling Psychology

The clinical research mentioned above mostly centers around diagnosing and treating serious mental illnesses. Counseling and school psychology seek ways to improve ordinary people's relationships to their goals and to society.

Counseling psychology got its start in 1907, when the psychologist Jesse B. Davis incorporated the first occupational guidance courses into a public school curriculum. In Boston, one year later, Frank Parsons—civil engineer, lawyer, and political activist—established the first bureau for "vocational guidance," a term he coined. Parsons wanted to improve career advice for the average worker.

As it did with clinical psychology, World War II created new demands for counseling psychology. Soldiers needed vocational testing to obtain appropriate jobs, and wounded veterans needed vocational rehabilitation.

Counseling research still focuses largely on career development and group counseling, but recently the field has taken a self-reflexive turn. Hoping to improve the counseling process, psychologists are proposing theories designed to focus on the therapist-patient relationship. They do not believe that one style of therapy fits all. These researchers devote much attention to the efficacy of different counseling techniques for ethnic minorities, gays, lesbians, and other groups which older therapeutic models did not sufficiently understand or address.

Psychologist Carl Rogers laid the groundwork for explorations of therapist-patient relationships. His brand of psychotherapy surfaced in the 1950s and is still at the heart of many psychologists' techniques. Rogerian therapy respects clients' autonomy and encourages therapists to offer only minimal advice. It is often called "client-centered" or "non-directive therapy."

Counseling programs must follow the Boulder model to maintain APA-accreditation. From counseling to social psychology, there are new and lively debates concerning some basic assumptions of experimental science, such as evaluation and comparison of data—the bedrock upholding the Boulder model standards. *The Journal of Counseling Psychology*, *The Counseling Psychologist*, and *The Journal of Counseling and Development* are good places to get an overview of such debates as well as other issues in the field.

School Psychology

School psychology is, in a sense, the oldest clinical field; the first full-fledged psychology clinics of the 1890s studied potential treatments for children having trouble in school. By the 1920s, fledgling clinics specializing in child behavior trained school guidance counselors as well as psychologists. By the 1940s, school psychologists focused on assessing children with special educational and emotional needs, leaving guidance counselors to focus on students' vocational choices.

Testing and assessment are still central to school psychology, but the field's methods and approaches have expanded. They now include classroom observation, one-on-one interviews, curriculum-based assessment, evaluation of academic and social skills, and personal and emotional assessment. School psychologists also consult with parents, teachers, and school personnel, develop home/school collaboration programs, work with families, provide individual and group counseling, and develop programs for crisis intervention and for identifying children at risk.

School psychologists are researchers as well as practitioners. One crucial area of research involves evaluating specific interventions, such as techniques for classroom-management or substance abuse prevention. School psychologists also strive to improve methods for assessing various learning difficulties, such as Attention Deficit Disorder. The field addresses issues outside of the school as well, assessing the impact of divorce and of parenting style on school performance, and identifying child neglect. *The Journal of School Psychology* and *School Psychology Quarterly* are two among many periodicals you may find helpful.

> School psychologists strive to improve methods for assessing learning difficulties.

Whatever specialty they pursue, clinical psychologists have different concerns from research psychologists. The two branches are so distinct that it has been hard to bridge the divide; this is clear from the formation and evolution of psychological organizations. From its inception in 1892 until shortly after World War II, the American Psychological Association catered to research-scientists who wished to have a forum for experimental discussions. By the 1960s, however, the number of scholar-practitioners had increased so much that they dominated the APA. Research-scientists tried to counteract their own loss of power by forming several research-specific societies. But they also wanted an organization which would encompass all areas of research. This wish led to the founding of the American Psychological Society (APS) in 1988.

The APA is the more prominent of the two organizations, with a 1996 membership of 151,000, as opposed to the APS's 16,000 members. It is also the more powerful. The APA accredits various psychology programs, and a psychologist must have a degree from such a program to obtain a license to practice psychotherapy. The APA publishes research journals and guidebooks, including *Graduate Study in Psychology*, a comprehensive list of faculty and their research specialties across the country. It also publishes guides to careers in psychology, to admission to psychology programs, and to many of psychology's sub-specialties. (Check out the APA Web site at http://www.apa.org.)

WHAT'S NEXT?

The general prerequisite for admission into a doctoral program is a B.A. or B.S., preferably with a psychology major. People who did not major in psychology should complete a set of basic psychology courses, including general psychology, statistics, research design (experimental), and at least three of the following: cognitive, physiological, sensation/perception, learning, social, and developmental. Prospective clinical applicants should also take courses in abnormal and personality psychology. However, doctoral programs can vary on the undergraduate courses they specify as prerequisites. Usually the only courses which are absolutely required are general psychology (or several basic courses), statistics, and research/experimental. Most doctoral and master's programs require the general GRE test, while some ask also for the GRE psychology subject test.

To be considered an appealing and compelling candidate to psychology graduate programs, you will need to have research experience. Classroom laboratory work is not enough. If you did not do undergraduate research with a professor, you should consider volunteering at a college or university with a solid research program before applying to graduate school. Apart from acquiring research experience for its own sake, you may earn a valuable letter of recommendation outlining your excellent research abilities.

A word to those whose primary interest is research: Ask professors and students about which research areas are the best-funded to help you determine a particular program's research priorities and emphases.

You do not need a master's degree to be admitted into most doctoral programs. The first two years of study often serve as a built-in master's program which all students must complete—even those who have an M.A. or M.S. from another program. (The number of transfer credits from a master's to a doctoral program varies, but the typical limit is twelve to fifteen credits.) In counseling psychology, however, students are encouraged to get a master's degree before applying to a doctoral program, as this provides the practical experience Ph.D. programs favor. Be advised, though, that few Ph.D. programs will admit a student who intends to leave the program after earning an M.A.

If you are certain you will not later wish to get a Ph.D., a "terminal" master's program may be your best choice. These programs often combine practical training with academic courses, and you can complete the degree in one or two years. Usually there are evening classes so students can work full-time while studying part-time. Some programs require a research thesis, some a comprehensive exam, some neither. (An M.A., but not an M.S., requires a thesis.) A caveat: Master's programs in counseling tend to be the longest in terms of required classroom hours and practical training.

> Having considerable undergraduate research experience will prepare you well for a Ph.D. program.

Doctoral programs are the most grueling, requiring between sixty and ninety semester hours, or 120 to 200 hours on the quarter system. This makes it more difficult than in many other Ph.D. programs to work while going to school. Ph.D. students take courses, attend colloquia and symposia, grade exams or lead discussion sections for undergraduate courses, do research for at least four years, and then defend their dissertations.

Besides doing all of the above, clinical Ph.D. students start their therapeutic training in their first or second year. Counseling and school psychology students do not start this kind of work until the third year. In addition to the minimal four years of coursework and research which other Ph.D. programs require, clinical, counseling, and school psychology students must do a one-year, paid, APA-approved internship. Clinical psychology Ph.D. programs take at least five years to complete and can easily take six or seven.

In research-oriented programs, students begin supervised research with a mentor in their first year. Most students also work ten to twenty hours a week as research or teaching assistants, as part of their financial aid package.

The Psy.D. is somewhat less demanding than the Ph.D. It can usually be completed within five years, including a one-year internship. Psy.D. students begin learning to do assessments and psychotherapy earlier in their program than Ph.D. students. The standards for the Psy.D. dissertation call for "scholarly value" while dissertations for the Ph.D. are expected to "make an original contribution to research," as their respective catchphrases go.

Psy.D. and master's programs offer little financial aid, and are considered less prestigious than the Ph.D; therefore they are less competitive. They are also not as likely as the Ph.D. programs to require prior research experience. However, having clinical experience—volunteering at a clinic or hotline, for example—is important when applying to these programs.

Practitioners who want to be psychoanalysts attend an accredited institute at which they take seminars, do supervised work with patients, and usually undergo psychoanalysis themselves. The most competitive psychoanalytic institutes (like New York's William Alanson White Institute and the Psychoanalytic Institute in Los Angeles) will only take applicants who already have an M.D. or Ph.D, but most other places will take people with any licensed degree, including a Master's of Social Work. Some institutes specialize in behavioral, cognitive, family, child, or group therapy. Most, however, are psychoanalytically oriented, adopting particular approaches, including Freudian, Jungian, and Lacanian.

THE JOB MARKET

Most students who plan to go to graduate school in psychology have clinical rather than experimental interests. Of the more than 3,200 recipients of psychology doctorates in 1995, over half listed their primary activity as clinical practice, as opposed to teaching or research. The intended specialty of just under one-third of all students, in fact, was providing psychotherapy.

Scientist-practitioners can teach, do research, and practice psychotherapy. Research-scientists have the option of doing either academic or experimental work; the former involves teaching, the latter entails doing original research. Because people with Psy.D.'s are, first and foremost, practitioners, it is much easier to find a university teaching position with a Ph.D. than with a Psy.D. Another obstacle for Psy.D.'s on the academic job market is the profession's bias towards researchers. Plus there is already a superfluity of Ph.D.'s, all of whom have the research experience which the Psy.D. lacks—another impediment to the Psy.D.'s academic job opportunities.

Having obtained a Ph.D., Psy.D., M.A., or M.S.W., the next hurdle is getting licensed to practice psychotherapy. In forty-two states, applicants must pass a standardized written exam, along with other requirements. (Students should get in touch with the licensing board of the state in which they intend to practice for these requirements.) In twenty-three states and in the District of Columbia, potential therapists need an APA-accredited doctorate to sit for the exam; in these states, master's degree holders cannot be licensed. In the other nineteen states, there is a second-tier level of licensing for master's. The eight states without licensing laws have certification laws or title acts.

To an extent, there is a negligible difference between licensure and certification. Both licensed and certified psychologists are called "licensed." However, licensing laws bar unlicensed people from practicing clinical psychology, while certification laws only prohibit such practitioners from calling themselves "psychologists." The APA considers practicing psychotherapy without a license unethical, and does not allow unlicensed psychotherapists to join the organization.

As in many other fields, it has become more difficult in recent years to get teaching positions in psychology. Even one-year positions, which entail burdensome teaching loads, are tremendously competitive. On the experimental front, it is possible to obtain a job as a researcher working on grants administered by a university, hospital, or research institute. Permanent research positions at these places, however, are rare. In fact, these days many Ph.D.'s go through at least two years of postdoctoral training before finding a faculty position or other permanent work.

> More and more Ph.D.'s work in private industry, most likely earning more than they would in academia.

More and more Ph.D.'s work in private industry, most likely earning more than they would in academia. Some physiological psychologists and behavioral neuroscientists work for pharmaceutical companies. Information-technology companies like Lucent Technologies, which eagerly seeks to make its products as "consumer friendly" as possible, hire cognitive psychologists. Developmental and educational psychologists are hired by companies like the Children's Television Workshop. Social psychologists often work for survey and research organizations, such as the Harris Poll. Industrial and orga-

466

nizational psychologists work in corporate human resources departments or for management consulting firms.

Clinical Ph.D. graduates have the most career options. They can teach at the high school or college level, they can do research, and they can provide psychotherapy in a variety of settings. Psy.D. graduates can get the same hospital jobs and have the same access to private practice as Ph.D.'s, but they are less likely to do research or to teach, for reasons already discussed.

Counseling psychologists have similar career options to clinical psychologists, except that instead of working in mental hospitals, they tend to have jobs in schools and colleges, career placement offices, rehabilitation clinics, and hospices. Some set up their own businesses or work for corporations. They can have private psychotherapy practices if they go to training institutes, usually treating relatively normal people who are undergoing crises. School psychologists who are bilingual or who plan to work in urban areas are highly marketable.

Clinical Ph.D. graduates have the most career options.

M.A.'s work in the same circles as Ph.D.'s, but at less prestigious jobs. They can teach, but rarely at the graduate level. They are often hired to do research, but generally work under a Ph.D. who designs, interprets, and publishes the study.

In industry, M.A. job opportunities are similar to those for people with Ph.D.'s. M.A.'s can play important roles in human resources departments, and can rise to the top of management consulting firms. M.A.'s in counseling have a good chance—twice that of M.A.'s in general psychology, according to the APA—of being hired by a corporation's employee-assistance program.

There are many master's-level psychologists in the clinical arena throughout the country, working in community mental health centers, psychiatric hospitals, halfway houses, and residential treatment centers. They work with different kinds of patients, including the developmentally disabled, the chemically addicted, and the chronically schizophrenic. In most states, people with master's degrees commonly have private psychotherapy practices, usually supervised. In a few states with less stringent licensing laws, these psychologists are not required to be supervised. In many states M.A. counselors can be certified in drug and alcohol rehabilitation, in marriage and family counseling, and in other specialties. Surveys have shown that the bulk of master's-level counselors do some kind of psychotherapy or vocational assessment.

Aspiring practitioners must consider the effects of managed care, or HMOs, on psychology. HMOs favor short-term over long-term psychotherapy because it is less expensive. But since health care benefits have rarely ever covered all of long-term therapy, this trend may not have as large an impact on the field as some believe. After all, there will always be people who want and can afford lengthy psychotherapy. However, it is better to be versed in, and willing to do, both kinds of work.

The potentially detrimental effects of HMOs are not the only difficulties psychologists must face. Different types of therapists and mental health workers—psychiatrists, psychologists, social workers, psychiatric nurses, and M.A.-level psychological associates or counselors—compete with each other for clients and patients. Social workers can legally practice psychotherapy in any state. And, as the

RESOURCES

NRC TOP TEN
Stanford
Michigan
Yale
UCLA
Illinois-Urbana
Harvard
Minnesota-Twin Cities
Penn
UC-Berkeley
UC-San Diego

ASSOCIATIONS
American Psychological Association
(202) 336-5500

American Psychological Society
(202) 783-2077

FURTHER READING
Patricia Keith-Spiegal, *The Complete Guide to Graduate School Admission, Psychology and Related Fields* (Lawrence Erlbaum)

Tracy J. Mayne, John C. Norcross, and Michael A. Sayette, *Insider's Guide to Graduate Programs in Clinical Psychology* (Guilford)

WEB ADDRESSES
American Psychological Association
http://www.apa.org

American Psychological Society
http://psych.hanover.edu/APS/

move toward HMOs continues, M.A.-level therapists, willing to work for less pay and with more constraints than Ph.D.-level psychologists, will be in greater demand. There is moreover the ongoing debate between psychiatrists and psychologists concerning the former's monopoly on prescribing medication.

Going into psychology is not an easy or smooth ride, both in terms of getting into a program and what comes after it. If you are determined and persistent, however, you will be able to have a career in the field.

We have listed below the names of institutes and faculty members recommended by the professors we interviewed, but there are many more departments and faculty members of note in every subfield than it's possible to mention. You will need to check with individual departments about their emphases and offerings, and about how faculty collaborate within and between subfields.

ANIMAL LEARNING AND COGNITION

Duke *John Staddon*
Penn *Robert Rescorla*
SUNY Binghamton
Ralph R. Miller

CLINICAL

Boston University
David Barlow

CUNY Graduate
Center
Paul Wachtel

Northwestern
Susan Mineka

Penn *Martin Seligman*
Rutgers *Cyril Franks*
UCLA *John Weiss*
Washington-Seattle
John Gottman

COGNITIVE COUNSELING

Colorado State
Kathlene McNamara

Florida
Gregory Neimeyer

Kansas *James
Leichtenberg*

Maryland *Mary Anne
Hoffman, Ruth Fassinger*

South Illinois
University
Howard Tinsley

UT-Austin
Lucia Gilbert

DEVELOPMENTAL

Arizona State
Nancy Eisenberg

Duke *John Coie*
Michigan
Jacqulynee Eccles
UCLA
Rochel Gelman

HEALTH

Pittsburgh
Karen Matthews

UC-Riverside
M. Robin DiMatteo

UC-San Francisco
*Nancy Adler,
Susan Folkman*

UCLA *Christine
Dunkel-Shetter,
Shelley Taylor*

CONSTELLATIONS

CONSTELLATIONS

INDUSTRIAL/ORGANIZATIONAL

NYU
Madeline Heilman

UC-Berkeley
Tom Tyler

UT-Austin
Robert Helmreich

PERSONALITY

Columbia *Walter Mischel, E. Tory Higgins*

UC-Berkeley *Oliver John, Richard Lazarus*

Wisconsin-Madison
Avshalom Caspi

PHYSIOLOGICAL

Minnesota-
Twin Cities
William Iacono

NYU *Joseph LeDoux*

Princeton
Bartley Hoebel

Radford
Karl H. Pribram

UC-San Diego
Larry Squire

USC *Richard Thompson*

PSYCHOLOGY OF WOMEN

Indiana State
Michele Boyer

Kentucky *Pamela Reimer, Judith Worell*

SCHOOL

Maryland
Sylvia Rosenfield

Minnesota-
Twin Cities
Sandra Christenson

NYU *Judith Alpert*
Yeshiva University
Louise Silverstein

SOCIAL

Carnegie-Mellon
Margaret Clark

Connecticut
Dave Kenny

Harvard
Daniel Gilbert

Maryland
Chuck Stangor

Michigan
Norbert Schwarz

Northwestern
Alice Eagly

NYU *Jim Uleman, Shelly Chaiken, John Bargh, Yaacov Trope*

Ohio State
Richard Petty

Rochester
Harry Reis

Stanford
Hazel Markus

UC-Santa Barbara
Dave Hamilton

UMass-Amherst
Icek Aizen

QUANTITATIVE

Chicago
Larry Hedges

Ohio State
Michael Browne

UCLA *Peter Bentler*

Virginia
Jack McArdle

CHAPTER 27

SOCIOLOGY

Denise Baird credits her mother's criticisms of gender roles, marriage, and family life with sparking her sociological imagination early on, "even though much of what she said appears at a glance to be ordinary advice to give a daughter." Baird began to refine her mom's knowledge with theory at the University of Akron, where she majored in sociology. She concentrated mostly on theories of social psychology, but her interests took an empirical turn when, as an assistant to a professor conducting research into the quality of health care for the elderly, she discovered that she also enjoyed conducting interviews and analyzing data sets. Then, after a course about the sociology of women and family violence, Baird set her sights on graduate school, with the intention of studying the family and the life-cycle from a feminist perspective.

Baird is now at Purdue University, at work on a dissertation about the adjustments that bedevil divorced families—and particularly women who must suddenly make the transition from homemaker to head of household. Her research will combine interviews and case histories with data on women's salaries, divorce rates, employment, levels of education, and shifts in income.

When Karen McKinney started the M.A. program in sociology at the University of Tennessee, she worried that her lack of background in the discipline would be a disadvantage: McKinney earned a B.A. in political science from the University of Tennessee but decided to switch to sociology for graduate school. Her fears were laid to rest by necessity, however: Awarded a teaching assistantship almost immediately, she quickly widened and deepened her knowledge of the field.

Now a Ph.D. student at the University of Florida at Gainesville, McKinney studies race relations through the prism of everyday interactions. She's grown fascinated with postmodern theories of identity, visual sociology, and documentary film, and she plans to write a dissertation about the formation of self-perception in children—partly because she thinks children are too often studied as passive subjects rather than active agents.

Baird and McKinney occupy what have traditionally been considered opposite ends of the sociological continuum: quantitative research into small groups (Baird on the family) as opposed to qualitative theory applied to large groups (McKinney on social identity). But like many students we interviewed, both of them caution prospective graduate students against becoming preoccupied with this longstanding dichotomy. Your time is better spent scrutinizing the culture of particular departments: How much attention does a department pay to ensuring that M.A. and Ph.D. students are trained in *both* applied and theoretical work? Must students assist professors in grant-supported research in order to receive full attention and generous funding? What are the chances of building a solid résumé of publications before one graduates? The challenge of graduate study in sociology lies in investigating bread-and-butter questions without losing sight of this protean discipline's ever-widening theoretical and research possibilities.

WHY SOCIOLOGY?

Sociology, the youngest of the social sciences, inquires into virtually anything created, transformed, or destroyed by humankind: organizations, social movements, family and life-stage transitions, intellectual advances, social policy, intimate interactions, and much more. A humanistic concern for social and political reform is one motivating force behind sociological inquiry; another is theoretical speculation about society. Reform-minded sociologists may seem to belong to a different discipline than social theorists who spend their time in the library and the lecture hall, but sociology welcomes both.

Through the 1960s sociologists were often defined by their research methods. Depending on whether they lived among the groups they studied, used survey and polling research, or surveyed large-scale social issues as they developed over time, sociologists were labeled with hyphens: field-ethnographers, survey-researchers, economic-historians. And hyphenated sociologists, in turn, were traditionally classified by the scale on which they conducted their inquiries. Scholars who mapped broad social perspectives or asked large theoretical questions were dubbed macrosociologists, while those who focused on interpersonal relations, small groups, or closely defined theories supported by empirical evidence were called microsociologists.

Sociologists study virtually anything created, transformed, or destroyed by humankind.

These distinctions are not that useful today. For one thing, sociologists no longer have a monopoly on doing research that draws on both statistics gathered in surveys and information culled from interviews; anthropologists and economists have long employed those methods. Also, the American Sociological Association, the professional organization for sociologists, now divides itself into sections that recognize not only broad research methods but also on subfields of sociological study. Among the ASA's subdivisions are alcohol and drugs; crime, law, and deviance; medical sociology; social psychology; collective behavior and social movements; political economy of world systems; sociology and computers; race, class, and gender; rural sociology; and urban sociology.

Because sociologists have such a variety of specialties, sociology may seem sprawling and chaotic to outsiders. Yet most incoming graduate students gravitate to the field precisely because they can study nearly anything, and few sociologists expect a grand theoretical synthesis to emerge from their more specialized pursuits. There are, however, key over-arching issues in the field, and these are worth spotlighting because they still affect how departments define themselves and how they allocate resources.

HOW SOCIOLOGY HAS TAKEN SHAPE

Sociology began to stand apart from other disciplines in the nineteenth century, when Karl Marx, Emile Durkheim, and Max Weber penned their systematic analyses of society. These founding European thinkers developed sweeping theories on topics ranging from the origins of religion and capitalism to the nature of social customs. Marx excepted, these sociologists presented their research as speculative, not as guides to policy-making or political action.

Sociology in the U.S. focused instead on problem-solving and on developing an empirical science of society. The first, and for decades the largest, department of sociology in the world was established in the late 1890s at the University of Chicago. Known as the Chicago School, this department founded sociology's first academic journal, *American Journal of Sociology,* as well as its first professional organization. And two Chicago faculty, Robert Park and Ernest Burgess, wrote the first textbook for college-level sociological study, *Introduction to the Science of Society* (1921)—often called the "Green Bible" because it so authoritatively codified sociological missions and methods between its green covers.

Chicago became a disciplinary powerhouse by addressing many urban issues that are still studied today: immigrants and their cultures, the working class and neighborhood life, race and ethnicity, crime and deviance. W.I. Thomas and Park established comprehensive guidelines for gathering qualitative data in those areas. Park, a skillful interviewer who came to sociology after a long career as a newspaper reporter and editor, insisted that empirical studies of race, class, and city life had to be combined with subjective accounts— life histories told to researchers by their subjects. Thomas and Park also popularized ethnography and field study, methods by which sociologists intensively investigated group and community histories.

Other notable Chicago School theorists were Charles Horton Cooley, Herbert Blumer, and the philosophers George Herbert Mead and John Dewey. This group sometimes collaborated and sometimes quarreled but nevertheless managed to establish the field of social psychology and the theory of symbolic interactionism (SI). Social psychology emphasizes the role of groups and institutions in molding an individual's thoughts, feelings, and behavior. Symbolic interactionism postulates that individuals come to understand the world at least partially through the various roles they must occupy in their interactions with friends and family members.

By the 1930s, sociologists had turned away from the urban and problem-solving preoccupations of the Chicago School and sought instead to provide the discipline with a unifying formal theory. After the publication of *The Structure of Social Action* (1937), Talcott Parsons of Harvard University gradually became the best-known sociological theorist—to such an extent that even Parsons's many critics tended to frame their objections to his thought in Parsonian terms. The first important translator of the German polymath Max Weber, Parsons drew extensively on the European tradition of sociological thought. He ranged widely over economics, psychology, anthropology, history, and law, attempting to make sociology a unifying science of society that incorporated insights across disciplines. Parsons's work was particularly important to medical sociology, the sociology of education, social psychology, and the sociology of the professions.

The pendulum of the discipline swings between the reform impulse and the empirical tradition.

Parsonian theory, now known as structural-functionalism, asserts that society is maintained by the consistent and stable functioning of all of its elements, from the family and educational system to social-class positioning and the marketplace. Functionalists held that even warring societal elements contributed to the stability of the whole. Partly because functionalism was highly abstract, and partly because it suggested very complex interconnections, the theory was virtually impossible to apply to specific social forces or events, and thus could be neither refuted nor validated. Furthermore, functionalism's critics charged that its focus on static structures gave short shrift to conflict and change.

Robert Merton of Columbia University, a former student of Parsons, addressed all of these problems. In *Social Theory and Social Structure* (1949), he developed models of functionalism more amenable to empirical assessment, and thereby more open to change and refinement. Because Merton was well versed in Marx's theories of conflict and social change (albeit evacuated of their political overtones), he paid special attention to the consequences of dysfunctional social interactions and institutions.

Recognizing that functionalism was applicable not only to society as a whole but also to smaller institutions and group dynamics, Merton called for theories of the "middle range": broad enough to explain complex phenomena but limited enough to be verified by applied research. Among the issues that middle-range theory handled best were anomie, education, the history of science, and the culture of scientific inquiry.

Merton was not only a theorist but also a practical researcher. One of his most famous projects examined a housing development to reveal the social psychology underlying its organization. Using in-depth interviews and observation, Merton studied a suburban community of seven hundred families to determine how the predominantly working-class residents related to each other in both formal groups and informal settings. Merton's later work, *The Focused Interview* (1956), offered a blueprint for focus-group research, the polling technique that today allows advertisers and talking heads to evaluate everything from consumer products to governmental policies. If the question for the Chicago School was how to study urban life and poverty, the question for Parsons, and later Merton, was how best to study the problems of class mobility and conflict in the mushrooming suburbs and expanding institutions of postwar America.

Merton's work was complemented by dramatic improvements in statistical research in the 1940s and 1950s, thanks to Paul Lazarsfeld at Columbia's Bureau for Applied Social Research. (Lazarsfeld established the Bureau in 1939, and Merton joined him shortly thereafter.) Lazarsfeld developed mathematical modeling techniques that drew on the latest research in economics, psychology, and physics. He revolutionized large-scale survey methods in *The People's Choice* (1944), a study of voting behavior in the presidential election, and he conducted groundbreaking research on the effects of media, propaganda, and advertising on public opinion. The statistical techniques he developed are still in use today.

Although structural-functionalism dominated sociological theory from the late 1930s through the 1950s, there were also influential alternatives. The New School for Social Research, home to refugees from Nazi Germany, introduced U.S. scholars to the Frankfurt School, whose sociological theory conjoined Marxism and psychoanalysis. The New School's Alfred Schutz ignited interest in sociological phenomenology—the study of the meanings that people ascribe to social situations and how these meanings affect their actions. A number of black scholars, such as E. Franklin Frazier and W.E.B. Du Bois, studied the impact of culture, politics, and cities on racial identity. The New School became—and remains—a locus of radical political theory.

In the 1950s Harvard was home not only to Parsons but also to social psychologist George Homans, a pioneer in behaviorism. Homans is best known for his contributions to exchange theory, which holds that most social interaction is a reciprocal exchange between parties seeking to maximize their rewards and minimize their costs. Exchange theorists (like rational choice theorists, their better-known cousins in political science and economics) view people as calculating actors who principally seek to realize predetermined self-interested goals.

Even Parsons's many opponents often came to frame their objections to him in the terms he set for debate.

At the University of California at Berkeley, the seeds of another enduring methodology were planted when Erving Goffman adapted the symbolic interactionist model of Chicago-trained theorist Herbert Blumer. Most of Goffman's publications in the 1950s and 1960s centered on dramaturgical theory, his own variant of SI. In *The Presentation of Self in Everyday Life* (1959), Goffman explored how people manipulated their public images to suit their audiences' agreed-upon conventions of public performance. Mustering observations about how individuals use dress, language, symbols, signs, and social codes, Goffman hypothesized that private self-conception was also a product of social interaction. Critics of Goffman's methods objected not only to his focus on the literal meanings of words and actions, but also to his relative lack of interest in large social issues—the staple concerns of U.S. sociology since its early days.

Harold Garfinkel's writings on ethnomethodology, or the study of commonsense interpretations of societal structures, met with similar complaints. Garfinkel's most famous work involved "breach experiments" in which researchers intruded into courthouses, police stations, medical clinics, country clubs, and even ordinary homes to record people's reactions when everyday social interaction was disrupted. Garfinkel's critics, like Goffman's, charged that his experiments probed only the surface of social interaction and rested on shaky empirical foundations. Despite these objections, Goffman's and Garfinkel's theories intrigued anthropologists, psychologists, and even literary critics.

The most famous critic of the functionalist mainstream, however, was neither Goffman nor Garfinkel but Columbia professor C. Wright Mills. Although Mills won popular acclaim as a journalist and author, many academic sociologists considered him an enemy from within. Drawing on his own political activism, as well as Marxism, phenomenology, and liberal intellectualism, Mills argued in *The Sociological Imagination* (1959) that sociologists were so preoccupied with legitimizing the science of their profession that they ignored real-world issues of social justice. Mills's criticism of the military-industrial complex and his analyses of the precariousness of white-collar privilege became articles of faith for a small cohort within sociology. Even so, most sociology departments continued to channel their energy into refining the empirical techniques they favored.

But perhaps it was Mills's influence that inspired a spate of reform-minded research in the mid-1960s. The late James Coleman, a rigorous experimentalist in the tradition of Lazarsfeld, argued that educational inequality was due more to economic disparities than to racial discrimination. Senator Daniel Patrick Moynihan, a political scientist trained in urban sociology, published the famous report *The Negro Family: The Case for National Action* in 1965. This study applied to black urban life a dysfunction and pathology model, directly challenging sociologists who did not see poverty as a disease.

> Goffman was widely criticized, but his work intrigued anthropologists, psychologists, and even literary critics.

Christopher Jencks of Harvard, among others, took up the call and wrote about poverty from a reform-minded perspective. Richard A. Cloward of the Columbia School of Social Work and Frances Fox Piven of CUNY Graduate Center analyzed the impact of welfare policy on the quality of life of the poor. Robert Staples of the University of California at San Francisco initiated a new chapter in the unending sociological debate about race- and class-based differentiation and discrimination in American culture. This resurgence of the reform impulse culminated with *The Coming Crisis of Western Sociology*, by Columbia's Alvin Gouldner. Like Mills, Gouldner advocated that sociologists strive not to create a neutral "science" so much as to undertake a moral—and radical—enterprise.

Concurrent with the revival of the reform impulse in the late 1960s and early 1970s was the rise of the study of world social systems. Randall Collins of the University of California at Riverside rediscovered and refined the dormant field of conflict theory in *Conflict Sociology* (1975). Arguing that conflicts on the micro and macro scales were actually similar in form, Collins demonstrated that the same analytical techniques could be applied to both. He was particularly interested in stratification, or the competition between social groups over power, autonomy, and scarce resources. Whereas Collins was especially perceptive about small-scale conflicts in everyday life, Immanuel Wallerstein of SUNY Binghamton operated on the largest macro scale. In *The Modern World System* (1974), Wallerstein used Marxian theory to outline relationships of domination and dependency between rich and poor nations.

C. Wright Mills, acclaimed as a journalist, was seen by many sociologists as an enemy from within.

Emboldened more by the feminist movement of the 1960s than by the rejuvenation of conflict theory, feminist theory began to take root in sociology departments in the 1970s and early 1980s. Some feminists revamped sociological theory to account for questions about sex and sexuality previously ignored in the discipline, while others devised new theories sensitive to the role of gender in daily life. Kristin Luker of UC-Berkeley, for instance, used rational choice theory to study women's use of contraceptives, while Luker's colleague Dorothy Smith laid the foundations of what has come to be known as standpoint theory, which accounts for the gender-bound aspects of women's perspectives on social relationships. Feminist sociologists also rolled up their sleeves and built, from the ground up, institutions that would make their work more visible in the profession. They founded and contributed to journals like *Gender and Society*, *Feminist Studies*, and *Signs*, and organized the Society of Women Sociologists and the feminist-friendly Marxist section of the ASA.

Race, like gender, captured the sociological imagination by the end of the decade, when William Julius Wilson—then at Chicago, now at Harvard—and Harvard professor Charles V. Willie hotly debated the relative significance of race and class in the U.S. Wilson's subsequent books, *The Declining Significance of Race* (1978), *The Truly Disadvantaged* (1987), and *Poverty, Inequality, and the Future of Social Policy* (1995) added fuel to that fire and made him perhaps the best known sociologist today.

The late 1970s were a fertile time for still more new impulses in sociology. Comparative political sociology, which focused on economic and state theory models as well as policy analysis, emerged through the work of Theda Skocpol of Harvard's Kennedy Center, David Apter and Juan Linz at Yale, and Johns Hopkins's Alejandro Portes. At the same time, sociologists elsewhere began to assess the legacies of 1960s social movements—how some movements dismantled the status quo, and how others were co-opted by it. Charles Tilly's *From Mobilization to Revolution*, and NYU professor Todd Gitlin's many studies of media and politics, continue to influence sociologists in this direction.

Thanks in part to the influence of scholars such as Luker, Wilson, Skocpol, and Gitlin, by the 1980s the varied and diffuse state of sociology began to be accepted rather than lamented. For the last ten years, there have been few efforts to create a single unifying theory, and few books declaring a "crisis" in sociology—two trends in the discipline that once seemed intractable. Cultural studies, postmodernist theory, standpoint theory, queer theory, black feminist theory, and other movements that have swept through the humanities and social sciences have found their place in sociology as well. But because sociology has always been a multiperspectival discipline, long familiar with the idea that a congeries of conflicting groups and ideas all contribute to a society, postmodern theories have been met with more calm in sociology than in older disciplines, which often seek to protect established canons and traditional methods.

> By the 1980s most sociologists began to accept, rather than lament, the varied nature of the field.

A few sociologists, like Jeffrey Alexander of UCLA and Anthony Giddens of Cambridge University and the University of California at Santa Barbara, grapple with the sociology of sociology and the legacy of the discipline's grand theoretical schemes. But Alexander has recently remarked that "the divisions in post-Parsonian sociology—between conflict and order theories, micro and macro approaches, structural and cultural views—were not fruitful." There is little nostalgia for the days when much effort went to charting the meaning and nature of the divisions between subfields and to constructing grand unifying theories. The consensus is that certain sub-specialties are thriving, that the emphasis on quantitative research is still in force, and that, at the moment, no overarching theory is compelling enough to unite sociologists throughout the discipline.

Despite the absence of an all-embracing theoretical framework that might serve as its mandate, the reform impulse within sociology continues. The New School's Terry Williams, Penn's Elijah Anderson, Patricia Hill Collins of the University of Cincinnati, William Kornblum of NYU, Herbert Gans of Columbia, and Kathryn Edin of Rutgers have all revived the practical investigation of social issues such as racism, sexism, urban life, youth and violence, drug use, and welfare. Urban sociology, criminology and criminal justice, medical sociology, political sociology, and other specialties are thriving.

WHAT'S NEXT

Though enrollments in graduate sociology programs, after a sharp decline in the 1970s and 1980s, are now rising, the discipline is nonetheless experiencing end-of-the-century growing pains. A few universities, most notably Washington University in St. Louis, eliminated their sociology programs in the late 1980s and early 1990s, while others, such as Yale, publicly questioned whether sociology was even distinct enough from other social sciences to merit its own department. Compounding the perceived ills of the discipline's diffuseness is the fact that since the 1980s the federal government has rolled back its funding for social sciences overall, especially those, like sociology, with a reputation for challenging the status quo.

Given these changes, it's especially important that you research the specialties and funding policies of particular departments. Besides visiting departments, a good way to conduct "field research" is by attending the regional or national conventions of the ASA, which draw faculty from all over the U.S. When buttonholed, most faculty will be glad to talk about the state of the discipline and of particular departments. Those students who have been inducted into Alpha Kappa Delta, the sociology honors society, can learn much about the field at society-sponsored events.

Sociology welcomes undergraduate majors from every university discipline and from around the world. SUNY Binghamton professor Immanuel Wallerstein points out, "We have a student from

Turkey this year. What he studies—business demographics—is often done in economics departments there. Here it is usually done in sociology." Boston College professor William Gamson, whose research interests center on politics and the media, says simply, "I couldn't care less about someone's disciplinary loyalties." Most programs, in fact, do seek students with a well-defined set of research interests, but if those cut across disciplines—as would the study of the psychological roots of conflict, the formation of political factions, or the symbolic depiction of disputes on television—so much the better.

Sociology welcomes undergraduate majors from every discipline— and from around the world.

Given such different paths and interests in the discipline, what constitutes adequate preparation for graduate study? Undergraduate sociology majors might have an advantage, but faculty agree that a statistics course and some lab research in either sociology or psychology will stand non-majors in good stead. Cultural theorists in sociology add that becoming expert in using the two main social science software packages, SPSS and SAS, is adequate training in quantification to do a wide range of research.

The majority of graduate programs require applicants to take the general exam section of the GRE, but not the subject exam in sociology. (Exceptions are Chicago, Duke University, Emory University, Florida-Gainesville, and the University of Massachusetts at Amherst.) Most departments discourage applicants from taking the subject test for a simple, practical reason: With students coming from such varied backgrounds, the exam cannot accurately measure a student's aptitude in all of the sociological subspecialties.

Some sociology programs, such as CUNY Graduate Center, require graduate students to do core coursework in theory, research methods, and statistics in order to equip themselves with skills that will qualify them for a variety of jobs. Other programs have no required courses. At programs with a core, expect to take theory and general methods in your first year, and perhaps a generalist seminar that covers a range of methodologies and is often team-taught by faculty from different subfields or disciplines. But rather than asking about curricula, talk to professors in programs you are considering about what resources you'll need in order to undertake particular projects, like the study of the family or race relations. Will a particular department have the faculty and the funding to support your work?

Graduate programs in sociology come in many shapes and sizes. Some specialize in research methods, some in theory; others are linked to professional schools or research centers, and still others are geared more toward training master's students in an array of applied fields. The ASA's *Guide to Graduate Departments* lists 246 sociology programs, including all the major research programs in the U.S., Canada, the U.K., and several other countries. The *Guide* lists the faculty (educational history, specialties, and joint affiliations), admissions requirements, and specialties of each department as their institutions reported them to the ASA.

Some state schools offer only a master's degree in sociology because they do not have all of the resources for a fully developed Ph.D. program. Even so, M.A. programs at such institutions often offer courses on both the theory and the history of the field. But in most cases, institutions that emphasize the M.A. do so because it is useful as a practical credential for applied work in criminology, health, education, and social work. If you wish to study penology and the law, public health issues in social policy, or juvenile delinquency, a master's program may offer the right combination of classroom instruction and applied experience.

> An M.A. in sociology is a useful credential for applied work in criminology, health, and education.

Leading master's programs in criminology include the University of Delaware, the University of Texas at Austin, CUNY Hunter College, CUNY Queens College, and the University of Colorado at Boulder. For education, check out Emory and Harvard, keeping in mind that though the Harvard program is housed in the School of Education, many of its faculty are trained sociologists. The University of Massachusetts at Boston and Rutgers University are among the strongest programs in health and medical sociology, while programs known for applied methods include CUNY Hunter College, UMass-Amherst, the University of Illinois at Chicago, and Northeastern University.

A Ph.D. program is the way to go if you want to produce original research, teach at a college or university, or do research for the government or private industry. Some Ph.D. programs are affiliated with research centers, which allow students (often with the aid of assistantships and fellowships) to develop contacts with faculty from related disciplines, other universities, and the private sector. Such institutes include the Center for the Social Sciences (formerly the Bureau of Applied Social Research) at Columbia, the Center for the Study of Race and Ethnicity at Brown University, The AIDS Institute at Harvard, and the Center for AIDS Prevention Studies at the University of California at San Francisco. Yale boasts the Institute for Social Policy Studies, while the University of Memphis has a renowned Center on Women. Private institutes that hire sociologists, such as the Russell Sage Foundation or the Hudson River Institute, are scattered around the country, with their highest concentration, predictably, in Washington, D.C. and the Boston-to-Baltimore corridor.

Our overview of the discipline has concentrated on large, old, financially prosperous programs—Chicago, Columbia, Harvard. These programs have been best at attracting empirical research funding from various government, military, and medical institutions. They also have strong ties to large corporations and research institutes. But the status of the older departments in the profession has often been matched by state universities. For example, thanks to its effectiveness in training students in empirical methods, the University of Wisconsin at Madison has vied with Chicago for the top slot in the National Research Council's rankings of graduate sociology programs. For the same reason, the University of Michigan, UCLA, Washington–Seattle, and Indiana have also ranked high in the NRC top twenty.

It's wise not to judge a department on the basis of the NRC rankings alone since they tend to present a skewed portrait of departmental strengths and reputation. *Footnotes*, the newsletter of the ASA, recently pointed out that if departments are ranked by the number of publications by faculty, not by the reputation of the department, lower-ranked institutions can suddenly rise by ten places or more. And many professors we interviewed, at top-ranked and lesser-ranked departments alike, point to the "horizontal" organization of the discipline. Schools outside the top twenty have their own network of hiring, connections to institutions outside the academy, and regional if not national reputations.

Given sociology's fragmentation, few departments actually specialize in more than a handful of methodological areas. Some maintain a strong allegiance to particular methods or are recognized as being more politically oriented. Michigan, Wisconsin-Madison, Chicago, the University of Pittsburgh, and UMass-Amherst offer comprehensive training in quantitative methods. Qualitative methods, fieldwork, and ethnography are taught at Boston College, the University of Georgia, and Penn.

What about theory? According to CUNY Graduate Center social theorist Stanley Aronowitz, the short list of programs "where you can genuinely do theory" is SUNY Binghamton, SUNY Buffalo, NYU, UC-Berkeley, CUNY Graduate Center, the University of North Carolina at Chapel Hill, and Boston College. All of these institutions stand out because they have cultivated relationships with research centers and corporations.

> Investigate which grants professors are working on, and whether that research matches your own interests.

As far as research areas and the departments that specialize in them are concerned, we have compiled a list that is far from exhaustive. It highlights areas that tend to attract a lot of graduate students as well as those departments at the center of disciplinary debates. For collective behavior/social movements, check out the University of Arizona, UC-San Diego, CUNY Graduate Center, the New School, and Yale. For criminal justice and criminology, Colorado-Boulder and the University of Delaware are strong, while for cultural sociology, Arizona, UC-San Diego, UC-Santa Barbara, CUNY Graduate Center, the New School, NYU, and Princeton are all top-notch. Brown, Princeton, and Stanford stand out in demography; Boston University and UCLA in ethnomethodology. For medical sociology, add Brown, UC-San Francisco, and the University of Massachusetts at Boston to your list. For politics, explore UCLA, Columbia, the New School, SUNY Albany, and Yale. Arizona, CUNY Graduate Center, Florida, Harvard, SUNY Albany, and Temple University are well known for work on race and ethnicity, and the University of Connecticut, Michigan State, and Rutgers earn high marks for research on sex and gender. Outstanding work in stratification is done at Brown, UC-Riverside, UCLA, and Chicago. And for urban sociology, look into UCLA, CUNY Graduate Center, Howard University, the New School, and Penn.

Regardless of your interests, an important consideration is the availability of faculty in any one department. The rule of thumb is to pick a department with two or three faculty in a given area—to avoid being stranded if your interests or working relationship with one professor changes. As in other fields, eminent scholars sometimes do little teaching and move around from university to university. Faculty with joint appointments may offer an added bonus because they are likely to be flexible in terms of interdisciplinary studies. Traditionally, sociology faculty can maintain joint appointments in political science, psychology, ethnic studies, American studies, and medical and law schools.

THE JOB MARKET

The bulk of sociology Ph.D.'s seek academic jobs, but the market is extremely tight. In 1993, 539 Ph.D.'s were awarded in sociology, and although professors at even the most elite institutions can tell stories about how hard it was to place their best students, no one has hard data on how many academic jobs were available that year. (Mind you, these are quantitative sociologists!) According to Dean Savage, a Queens College sociologist who studies the employment patterns of U.S. Ph.D.'s, the academic job market in sociology is mysterious by nature. "Many of the jobs advertised in *Notes* (the job list published by the ASA) are phantoms," Savage says. "They vaporize when you get close to them." This is partly because departments frequently advertise positions without first securing administrative funding. Moreover, many departments are required by law to advertise positions, even when they already have an oversupply of excellent local candidates. The best job information can be culled from the 1993 National Study of Post-Secondary Faculty, a huge poll of professors conducted by the National Science Foundation for the Department of Education (a Web summary is at www.nap.edu./readingroom/books/grad). The NSF will send you a CD-ROM of its data-set at no charge, but interpreting that mass of data is something of a research project in its own right.

As in other academic fields, candid professors will advise you to think twice about going into sociology unless you are offered solid funding at one of the twenty top-ranked departments. But the good news is that lucrative and attractive nonacademic jobs have existed for sociologists from all types of universities ever since the Chicago School made sociology integral to urban reform projects. Think tanks, research centers, government agencies, advertising firms, telecommunications companies and private consulting firms all employ sociologists, especially those with solid empirical training. Polling companies and other survey and research agencies draw liberally from the pool of sociology Ph.D.'s, while corporations hire sociologists trained in social psychology to help them manage their organizational and developmental programs.

> Talk to students at M.A. and at Ph.D. programs as well as faculty about the mix of applied and theoretical training you'll need.

At a recent ASA convention, representatives of the advertising giant Young and Rubicam, the business information company Standard and Poor's, and Equitable Insurance led a panel on sociologists crossing over from academia to the business world. Another panel on nonacademic employment included a senior administrator for the University of Michigan's health plan, the director of the Peace Corps's Inspector General's office, the head of institutional research at the Fashion Institute of Technology, and an executive at WESTAT, which does statistical contracting work for the federal government. All of the participants held advanced degrees in sociology.

Criminology and medical sociology have always had strong job markets. Be advised, however, that for many jobs in these fields, the M.A. is the highest credential necessary. If you are very committed to working in criminology or medical sociology, enrolling in a Ph.D. program might be the most expensive and laborious route to take. But keep in mind that setting out for a Ph.D. will help you keep your options open, since switching to a Ph.D. program from one that awards only the M.A. is sometimes difficult. Ask both kinds of programs to put you in touch with students who have made the jump from one level of training to the other.

RESOURCES

NRC TOP TEN
Chicago
Wisconsin–Madison
UC–Berkeley
Michigan
UCLA
UNC–Chapel Hill
Harvard
Stanford
Northwestern
Washington–Seattle

ASSOCIATIONS
American Sociological Association
(202) 833-3410

JOURNALS
American Sociological Review
Contemporary Sociology
Gender & Society
Journal of Health and Social Behavior
Social Psychology Quarterly
Sociology of Education
Teaching Sociology
Theory and Society

CONSTELLATIONS

M.A. PROGRAMS

CRIMINOLOGY
Colorado–Boulder
Delaware
Hunter College
Queens College
UT–Austin

EDUCATION
Emory
Harvard

HEALTH AND MEDICAL SOCIOLOGY
Rutgers
UMass–Boston

APPLIED METHODS
Hunter College
Illinois–Chicago
Northeastern
UMass–Amherst

FURTHER READING
American Sociological Association Guide to Graduate Departments (ASA)
Charles M. Lemert, *Sociology After the Crisis* (Westview)
Donald N. Levine, *Visions of the Sociological Tradition* (Chicago)
Edward Shils, *The Calling of Sociology* (Chicago)
Neil J. Smelser, *Problematics of Sociology* (California)

WEB ADDRESSES
ASA Web site:
http://www.asanet.org/

PH.D. PROGRAMS

CONSTELLATIONS

THEORY
CUNY Graduate
 Center
NYU
SUNY Binghamton
SUNY Buffalo
UC-Berkeley

QUANTITATIVE METHODS
Chicago
Michigan
Pittsburgh
Wisconsin-Madison
UMass-Amherst

COLLECTIVE BEHAVIOR/SOCIAL MOVEMENTS
Arizona
CUNY Graduate
 Center
New School
UC-San Diego
Yale

CRIMINAL JUSTICE AND CRIMINOLOGY
Colorado-Boulder
Delaware

CULTURAL SOCIOLOGY
Arizona
CUNY Graduate
 Center
New School
NYU
Princeton
UC-San Diego
UC-Santa Barbara

DEMOGRAPHY
Brown
Princeton
Stanford

ETHNOMETHODOLOGY
Boston University
UCLA

MEDICAL SOCIOLOGY
Brown
Rutgers
UC-San Francisco
UMass-Boston

POLITICS
Columbia
New School
SUNY Albany
UCLA
Yale

RACE AND ETHNICITY
Arizona
CUNY Graduate
 Center
Florida State
Harvard
SUNY Albany
Temple

SEX AND GENDER
Connecticut
Michigan State
Rutgers

STRATIFICATION
Brown
Chicago
UC-Riverside
UCLA

URBAN SOCIOLOGY
CUNY Graduate
 Center
Howard
New School
Penn
UCLA

APPENDIX: JOBTRACKS

WHO GOT HIRED WHERE

Every year, *Lingua Franca* magazine compiles and publishes Job-Tracks, a list of the names of those who have been newly hired to full-time junior positions, be they tenure-track or non-tenure-track. *Lingua Franca* gathers this information by conducting an annual survey of junior hirings at all four-year colleges and universities in the United States and Canada.

Because it lists names, JobTracks allows those in the profession to catch up with old friends who have been hired. But because it sorts the information according to where new junior faculty did their most advanced graduate training, readers can also see at a glance some of the graduate programs that are doing a good job in placing their newly-minted Ph.D.'s. For this reason, we are including in this guide the JobTracks list of the junior hirings in the humanities and social sciences that took effect as of the fall 1996 term. (As this book goes to press, data for 1997 has not yet been received.)

JobTracks is the most complete list available of its kind, and while it is based on a careful survey, it is incomplete. Here are its important limitations:

(I) Our major source of information is the hiring institutions, and out of 1,200 questionnaires sent to four-year colleges and universities, 600 responded, including most of the larger institutions. Yield: 3,700 names. We then sent a draft of these lists to the graduate deans of the nation's 250 Ph.D.-granting institutions, inviting them to add any missing placements of their students. Yield: another 700 names. Total: 4,400 names, accounting, we figure, for roughly half of all placements, and so enough to give a general idea of the shape of things, but certainly *incomplete in terms of the new Ph.D.'s from any one school.*

(2) This is an account of the hirings in just one year. A department varies year-by-year in how many people it puts out on the job market. And of that number, it might well have a lean year (placing zero, one or two candidates) followed by a fat year (eight or nine). Furthermore, these are lists of only those students who got hired in 1996, but many of those hired may have gotten their degree a few years ago, or many years ago. So, the names are not necessarily representative of the annual 'crop'. To smooth out the idiosyncrasies of a single year, we are planning to consolidate more than one year's worth of JobTracks in future editions of this guide. For now, bear in mind that *no one year's hiring is representative of any single department's yearly output of new scholars.*

(3) There is nothing to indicate that large schools are able to place a larger proportion of their students in jobs than small schools. Simply by virtue of having a larger number of students on the market, some of whom find jobs in a given year, *large departments tend to look better in lists like this one.* You cannot, however, assume that your chances on the job market are necessarily better at a large department.

(4) *These are not necessarily tenure-track jobs.* For one thing, there are several colleges that do not grant tenure. For another, currently colleges are seeking to fill their faculty needs with an increasing number of one-year positions. What we ask of our respondents is that they tell us who has just been hired to a full-time job (so, part-time and adjunct positions are not on these lists), but that position may be non-tenure-track or "visiting." Most new faculty get this straight before they apply for the job.

Despite its limitations, how can this list serve you? It can be a starting point as you talk to professors about their department's job placement record. But more importantly, it can give you a sense of the real connection between where you might go to grad school and where you might get an academic job.

TRAINED BY	NAME	HIRED BY
AFRO-AM/ETHNIC/WOMEN'S STUDIES		
Brigham Young U	Walk, Richard	Brighm Yng, HI
Colorado, U of	Kempadoo, Kamala	Colorado, Bldr
Cornell U	Lal, Jayati	New York U
Denver, U of	Lazzari, Marceline	S Colorado, U of
Duke U	Darling, Marcia J.	Georgetown U
Emory U	Browne, Joy	Louisville, U of
Emory U	Umoja, A.K.	Georgia S U
Florida, U of	Griggens, Camilla	Carlow C
Georgia, U of	Williams, Michelle	Connecticut, U of
Harvard U	Blair, Cynthia	Illinois, Chicago
Kentucky, U of	Jones, Ricky	Louisville, U of
Maryland, U of	Cooke, Michael	W Illinois U
Mass, Amherst	Prou, Marc E.	Mass, Boston
Michigan, U of	Collins, Chiquita	Illinois, Chicago
Michigan, U of	Ransby, Barbara	Illinois, Chicago
Minnesota, U of	Ginsberg, Ruth	Beloit C
Minnesota, U of	Hase, Michiko	Colorado, Bldr
N Illinois U	Smallwood, Andrew	Nebraska, Oma
New School	Wangari, Esther	Towson S U
New York U	Oboler, Suzanne	New School
Ohio S U	Fonow, Mary Margaret	Ohio S U
Ohio S U	Ross, Charles	Mississippi, U of
SUNY, Bngmtn	Mack, Kibibi	Maryland, BaltCnty
SUNY, Bngmtn	Washington, Patricia	San Diego S
Temple U	Gray, Cecil	Gettysburg C
Temple U	Livingston, Samuel	San Diego S
UC, Los Angeles	Woods, Clyde	Penn S U
UC, Santa Cruz	Campbell, Nancy	Ohio S U
UC, St Barbara	Jackson, Shirley	Bowling Green S
CAN-York	Gotell, Lise	Alberta-CAN
SWT-Geneva	Fasrer, Cary	Penn S U
ANTHROPOLOGY/ARCHEOLOGY/FOLKLORE		
Arizona S U	Curet, Luis	Colorado, Denv
Arizona, U of	Mamadou, Baro	Arizona, Tucson
Arizona, U of	Norcini, Marilyn	New Mexico S U
Arizona, U of	Walker, William	New Mexico S U
Boston U	De Wolfe, Elizabeth	Westbrook C
Chicago, U of	Anderson, Jeffrey	Colby C
Chicago, U of	Moore, Robert	New York U
Chicago, U of	Schattschneider, Ellen	Emory U
Chicago, U of	Watts, David	Yale U
Chicago, U of	Wright, Lori	Texas A&M U
Colorado, U of	Thomas, Jan	Kenyon C
Columbia U	Owens, Bruce	Wheaton C (MA)
CUNY	Davila, Arlene M.	Syracuse U
CUNY	Hammar, Lawrence	Lewis & Clark C
Harvard U	Arnold, Bettina	Wiscnsn, Milw
Harvard U	Doi, Mary M.	Bryn Mawr C
Harvard U	Hendon, Julia	Gettysburg C
Harvard U	Hiebert, Fredrik	Penn, U of
Harvard U	Yan, Yunxiang	UC, Los Angeles
Illinois, U of	King, C. Richard	Drake U
Illinois, U of	Wesson, Cameron	Oklahoma, U of
Illinois, Urbana	Torres, Arlene	Illinois, Urbana
Indiana U	Argyrou, Vassos	Colgate U
Indiana U	Farnell, Brenda	Illinois, Urbana
Indiana U	Hardin, Kris	Beloit C
Indiana U	Hardy, Bruce	Kenyon C
Indiana U	Jaffe, Alexandrta	S Mississippi, U of
Iowa, U of	Semendeferi, Ekatarini	UC, San Diego
Iowa, U of	Sexton, Rocky	Augustana C (IL)
Johns Hopkins	Ali, Kamaran	Rochester, U of
Mass, Amherst	Hyatt, Susan	Temple U
Mass, Amherst	Kingsolver, Ann	S Carolina, Clm
Mass, U of	Markowitz, Lisa	Louisville, U of
Michigan S U	Morsy, Soheir	Tufts U
Michigan, U of	Blum, Susan	Colorado, Denv
Michigan, U of	Kozaitis, Kathryn	Georgia S U

TRAINED BY	NAME	HIRED BY
Michigan, U of	Leonard, William	Florida, Gnsvl
Michigan, U of	Manson, Joseph	UC, Los Angeles
Michigan, U of	Perry, Susan E.	UC, Los Angeles
N Carolina, ChpH	Lassiter, Luke E.	Ball S U
New Mexico, U of	Alexander, Rani	New Mexico S U
New York U	Thomas-Houston, M.	S Carolina, Clm
Northwestern U	Williams, Sloan	Illinois, Chicago
Ohio S U	White, Vibert	Illinois, Sprngf
Pomona C	Neuman, Lisa	St Norbert C
Rutgers U	Cruz Torres, Maria	UC, Riverside
S Illinois U	Oetkaar, Gerald	Calgary-CAN
S Methodist U	Browne, Katherine	Colorado S U
S Methodist U	Hill, Christopher L.	Montana S U
S Methodist U	LoMonaco, Barbara	Transylvania U
S Methodist U	Masucci, Maria	Drew U
S Methodist U	Tung, Wuan-chao	Nat'l Taiwan-TAIW
S Methodist U	Walker, Debra	Florida Int'l U
S Methodist U	Zedeno, Maria	Arizona, Tucson
Stanford U	Gaudio, Rudolf	Arizona, Tucson
Stanford U	Lugo, Alejandro	Illinois, Urbana
Stanford U	Maurer, William	UC, Irvine
SUNY, Albany	Mertz, Brent	Grinnell C
SUNY, Bngmtn	Pike, Iny	James Madison
SUNY, Bngmtn	Thomas, Brian	St Mary's C
SUNY, Stny Brk	Waddle, Diane	Colorado S U
Tennessee, U of	Falsetti, Anthony	Florida, Gnsvl
Texas, Austin	Giuffre, Patti	Grand Valley S
Texas, Austin	Lefkowitz, Dan	Kansas, U of
Texas, Austin	Masson, Marilyn	SUNY, Albany
Texas, Austin	Meintjes, Louise	Arizona, U of
Texas, Austin	Morter, Jonathan	Charleston, C of
Texas, Austin	Sammons, Kay	Arizona, U of
Texas Woman's U	Childers, Cheryl	Washburn U
Tulane U	Fischer, Edward F.	Vanderbilt U
UC, Berkeley	Hall, Kira	Yale U
UC, Berkeley	Jacquemet, Marco	Barnard C
UC, Berkeley	Nabokov, Isabelle	Princeton U
UC, Berkeley	Nunley, Michael	Oklahoma, U of
UC, Berkeley	Tomaskova, Silvia	Texas, Austin
UC, Davis	Clarke, Margaret R.	Tulane U
UC, Los Angeles	Lucero, Lisa	New Mexico S U
UC, Los Angeles	Pang, Keng-Fong	Mt Holyoke C
UC, St Barbara	Lambert, Patricia M.	Utah S U
Utah, U of	Bennion, Janet	Maine, Fort Kent
Vanderbilt U	Foias, Antonia E.	Williams C
Virginia, U of	Adams, Abigail	Cntrl Connecticut
Virginia, U of	Bamford, Sandra	Lethbridge-CAN
Virginia, U of	Gable, Edward E.	Mary Washngtn C
Virginia, U of	Piot, Charles	Colorado, Bldr
W Michigan U	Rynbrandt, Linda	Grand Valley S
Washington U	Hofling, Charles	S Illinois, Crbndl
Washington, U of	Goolsby, Rebecca	Alaska Pacific U
Wiscnsn, U of	Thornburg, John	Illinois Benedctn
Yale U	Everett, Margaret	Portland S U
CAN-Br Columbia	Orie, Olanike Ola	Tulane U
CAN-Br Columbia	Underhill, Anne P.	Yale U
CAN-McGill	Rethman, Petra	McMaster-CAN
CAN-Montreal	Sicotte, Pascale	Calgary-CAN
CAN-Toronto	Routledge, Bruce	Penn, U of
CAN-Toronto	Whitehead, Judith	Lethbridge-CAN
CAN-York	Menzies, Charles	Br Columbia-CAN
GER-Freie U Berlin	Bernbeck, Reinhard W.	Bryn Mawr C
AREA STUDIES		
Chicago, U of	Prashad, Vijay	Trinity C (CT)
Harvard U	Lowry, Kathryn	UC, St Barbara
UC, Riverside	Githinji, Mwangi	Gettysburg C
UC, San Diego	Dong, Yue	Washington, U of

THESE TABLES reflect first-time hirings to full-time junior positions effective as of the '96-'97 academic year in the humanities and social sciences at 600 four-year colleges and universities in the United States and Canada. • **THEY** should be read as follows: the institution in the third column hired for the first time the individual in the second column to a full-time junior position. (It may not be the first junior position the individual has gotten.) The individual received graduate training at the institution in the first column. • **THOUGH** most of these hirings are to multi-year, tenure-track contracts, many are for one-year positions only. • **INFORMATION** about graduate training was in most cases obtained either from the hiring institution or from the individual. This information has not been double-checked in all cases with each training institution. "N/A" means this information was not available at press time. • **WHERE** we have a campus name (e.g. "Illinois, Urbana"), we use it. But someone trained there might just as well be listed under the general university name (e.g., "Illinois, U of"). • **LINGUA FRANCA** goes to great effort to insure that our data is accurate and as complete as possible. However, we know that **JOBTRACKS** is, as we go to press, incomplete and still not free from all errors. Consequently, we cannot be responsible for errors and omissions, and readers are advised not to act on any of this information without verifying it.

ART/ART HISTORY/ ARCHITECTURE

TRAINED BY	NAME	HIRED BY
Academy of Art C	Crane, Ferris	Maryland, BaltCnty
American U	Cebulash, Glen	Wright S U
Arizona, U of	Chism, Sandra L.	Tulane U
Art Inst Chicago	Bock, Monica	Connecticut, U of
Art Inst Chicago	Jeck, Douglas	Washington, U of
Art Inst Chicago	LeBergott, Karen	Lake Forest C
Art Inst Chicago	Ledgerwood, Judy	Northwestern U
Art Inst Chicago	Lee, Jin	Illinois S U
Art Inst Chicago	O'Toole, Helen	Washington, U of
Art Inst Chicago	Tamblyn, Christine	UC, Irvine
ArtCntrCollDesign	Shields, Charles	Cal S, Fresno
Cal Inst Arts	Floyd, Nancy	Georgia S U
Cal Inst Arts	Schreiber, Rachek	IndianaPurdu,Ind
Cal S, Fresno	McQuone, Richard	Cal S, Fresno
Carnegie Mellon	Siefert, Christopher	LSU, BatnRoug
Chicago, U of	Kaminishi, Ikumi	Tufts U
Chicago, U of	Kita, Sandy	Maryland, CollPk
Chicago, U of	Mathews, Karen	Colorado, Denv
Chicago, U of	Reimer, Karen	Bethel C (MN)
Cincinnati, U of	Hodge, Challis	Wiscnsn, Stout
Cincinnati, U of	Lindsay, Michael	Georgia S U
Claremont Grad	Singerman, Howard	Virginia, U of
Columbia U	D'Alleva, Anne	St Thomas, U of
Columbia U	Fairbanks, Karen	Barnard C
Columbia U	Long, Jane	Roanoke C
Columbia U	Sanders, Joel	New School
Cranbrook Acad	Moren, Lisa	S Oregon S C
Cranbrook Acad	Schorn, Brian	E Michigan U
CUNY	Feeser, Andrea Van Laer	Hawaii, U of
CUNY	Luftschein, Susan Elise	Parsons
CUNY	Roth, Nancy Ann	Folmouth C of Arts
Duke U	Weitz, Ankeney	Denison U
E Carolina U	Maune, Dietrich	Frostburg S U
E Texas S U	Waters, Laura	Muskingum C
Florida S U	Causey, Carley	Mississippi C
Florida S U	Floyd, Minuette	S Carolina, U of
Florida S U	Pope, Robert	Alabama, U of
Georgia, U of	Zarur, Elizabethy	New Mexico S U
Grad Theol Union	Lucas, Thomas	SanFrancisco, U of
Harvard U	Anez-Spangler, Martha	Wesleyan U
Harvard U	Cadogan, Jean	Trinity C (CT)
Harvard U	Mansfield, Elizabeth	South,U of the
Illinois, Chicago	Weisson, Barbara	Barat C
Illinois, U of	Ciganko, Richard	Indiana U of PA
Indiana U	Barrow, Jane	S Illinois, Edwrds
Indiana U	Brogmann, Cindy	IndianaPurdu,Ind
Indiana U	Brueggenjohann, J.	Missouri, Clmb
Indiana U	Rakic, Svetlana	Franklin C
Indiana U	Zurbrigg, Susan	Grinnell C
Iowa S U	Bartlett, Robert	Drake U
Iowa, U of	Hanna-Vargas, Emily	Georgia S U
Iowa, U of	Younger, Dan	Missouri, St L
James Madison	Meredith, Richard	Valley City S
Kansas, U of	Janzen, Reinhild	Washburn U
Kansas, U of	Wetzel, S. Jean	Cal Polytech
Kent S U	Balistreri, John	Bowling Green S
Kent S U	Shidler, Dale	Loyola, Chicago
Kentucky, U of	Tomasek, Aimee	Valparaiso U
Maryland, U of	Libby, Susan H.	Washington C
Mass, Amherst	Fay, Patricia	LebanonValley
Memphis C of Art	Redmond, Jerry	MissippiValley
Michigan S U	Nash, Gary	MissippiValley
Michigan, U of	Balck, Charlene M.	Michigan S U
Minneapolis Art/Des	Baugnet, Julie	Wiscnsn, RiverF
Minnesota, U of	Jost, Scott	E Mennonite C
Minnesota, U of	Lois-Borzi, Anna	St Cloud S U
Missouri, U of	Black, Bonnie	Arkansas, LtlRk
Moore C of Art	Saraullo, Carol	Beaver C
N Carolina, ChpH	Rhodes, Robin	Notre Dame, U of
N Carolina, Grns	Boone, Harry W.	Indianapolis, U of
N Carolina Sch Arts	Swanson, John	Cal S, Bakersfld
N Florida, U of	Hill, William	W Virginia Wslyn
N Texas, U of	Fairlie, Carol	Sul Ross S U
Nebraska, U of	Palmeri, Nancy	Texas, Arlington
Nevada, U of	Callister, Jane	UC, St Barbara
New Mexico, U of	Bernstein, Barbara	Cal S, Fresno
New Mexico,U of	Klages, Ricki	Wyoming, U of
New Mexico, U of	Parke Harrison, Robert	Holy Cross C of
New York U	Cernuschi, Claude	Boston C
New York U	Ryor, Kathleen	Carleton C
New York U	Vergara, Alexander	Columbia U
Ohio S U	DeVriese, Todd	Ohio S, Marion
Oregon, U of	Aguilera, Frederick	SUNY, Oswego
Penn, U of	Dempsey, Anna	Grinnell C
Penn, U of	Engman, Bevin	Colby C
Penn, U of	Lupkin, Paula	Denison U
Penn, U of	Muldrow, Ralph C.	Charleston, C of
Penn, U of	Robertson, Jean	IndianaPurdu,Ind
Pittsburgh, U of	Schroeder, Ivy	S Illinois, Edwrds
Pratt Institute	Sayre, Roger	Pace, WhitePl
Princeton U	Escobar, Jesus	Fairfield U
Princeton U	Steinhoff, Judith	Houston, U of
Purdue U	Green, Rebecca	Bowling Green S
R I Design	Catlin, Jane S.	Utah S U
R I Design	Smith, Joseph	Mt Holyoke C
R I Design	Taylor, Judith	Beaver C
Rensselaer Poly	McCoy, Kevin	CUNY, City C
Rutgers U	Belic, Zoran	Denver, U of
Rutgers U	Brown, Pamela	Kenyon C
Rutgers U	Earenfight, Philip	Juniata C
Rutgers U	Guttzeit, Carol	Oregon S U
Rutgers U	Montgomery, Scott	Oregon S U
Rutgers U	Raverty, Dennis	Pittsburg S U
S Carolina, U of	Keown, Gary	SE Louisiana U
S Illinois U	Bromley, Kimble	N Dakota S U
SUNY, Bngmtn	Hamme, Nancy	W Georgia, S U of
SUNY, Bngmtn	Perera, Nihal	Ball S U
SUNY, Bngmtn	Socki, James	Beloit C
SUNY, Buffalo	Hoover, Brian	S Utah U
SUNY, Stny Brk	Vacanti, M. Monica	Canisius C
Syracuse U	Larson, Stephan	Mississippi, U of
Tennessee, Knox	Benson, Aaron	Union U
Texas, Austin	Grant, Kim	Longwood C
Texas, Austin	Headrick, Annabeth	Western S C
Texas, Austin	Newsome, Elizabeth	UC, San Diego
Texas, Austin	String, Tania	Bristol-UK
Texas Tech	Prater, Michael E.	Ball S U
Texas Woman's U	Hall, Kathryn	Texas Weslyn
Tulsa, U of	Wong-Ligda, Ed	Grand Valley S
UC	Linebarger, David	Northeastern S U
UC, Berkeley	Doherty, Brigid	Johns Hopkins
UC, Berkeley	Eyerman, Charlotte	Union C
UC, Berkeley	Fraser, Sarah	Northwestern U
UC, Berkeley	Meyer, Richard	S California, U of
UC, Berkeley	Stewart, Carol	Rhodes C
UC, Los Angeles	Klein, Jeanette	Berea C
UC, San Diego	Nohe, Timothy	Mass, Boston
UC, Santa Cruz	Bork, Robert	South, U of the
UC, St Barbara	Bergman, Sky	Cal Polytech
UC, St Barbara	Everman, Charlette	UnionC (NY)
Utah S U	Harris, Susan	S Utah U
Utah S U	Sessions, Wilona	Cal S, SnBrndno
Virginia Cmnwlth	Petrillo, Jane	Colby-Sawyer C
Virginia Cmnwlth	Rowe, Peyton	S Carolina, Clm
Virginia, U of	Mauzerall, Hope	Grinnell C
Washington & Lee U	Marshall, Donald	SE Louisiana U
Washington U	Gondek, Jessica	Loyola, Chicago
Washington, U of	Liddy, Timothy	Fontbonne C
Washington, U of	Ascheim, Deborah	Drew U
Washington, U of	Mayra, Roland	W Carolina U
Wesleyan U	Wright, William	Cntrl Connecticut
Wichita S U	Milbrandt, Melody	W Georgia, SUof
Wiscnsn, Madsn	Germany, Robin	Texas Tech
Wiscnsn, Milw	Richards, Jacqueline	Illinois S U
Wiscnsn, U of	Simpson, Judith	Boston U
Yale U	Armstrong, Frank	Connecticut, U of
Yale U	Brody, David	Washington, U of
Yale U	Delano, Pablo	Trinity C (CT)
Yale U	Dillon, Diane	Northwestern U
Yale U	Reed, Christopher	Lake Forest C
BULG-AcadFineArts	Natchev, Alexi	Connecticut, U of
CAN-Victoria	Cadge, Catie	S Oregon S C
GER-Hamburg	Heinrichs, Jurgen	Swarthmore C
UK-Courtland Inst	Barber, Charles	Notre Dame, U of
UK-London, U of	Harney, Elizabeth	New York U
UK-St Andrews	Delancey, Julia	Truman S U

ASIAN LANG & LIT

TRAINED BY	NAME	HIRED BY
Columbia U	Ericson, Joan	Colorado C
Columbia U	Laughlin, Charles	Yale U
Columbia U	Lee, Ann Jung-Hi	Washington,U of
Columbia U	Lippit, Seiji Mizuta	UC, Los Angeles
Cornell U	Bourdaghs, Michael K.	UC, Los Angeles
Cornell U	Yamada, Reiko	Williams C
Georgetown U	Wilkerson, Kyoko T.	Wake Forest U
Harvard U	DeBlasi, Anthony	SUNY, Albany
Harvard U	Goldin, Paul	Penn, U of
Harvard U	Schaberg, David C.	UC, Los Angeles
Illinois, Urbana	Mori, Yoshiko	Georgetown U
Iowa, U of	Cai, Jie	Harvard U
Iowa, U of	Chiba, Toru	Michigan, U of
Michigan S U	Zhou, Minglang	Colorado, Bldr
Michigan, U of	Cook, Scott	Grinnell C
Michigan, U of	Cui, Shuquin	S Methodist U
Ohio S U	Yotsakura, Linsay	Maryland, CollPk
Penn, U of	Iino, Masakazu	Cal S, LosAngls
Purdue U	Adachi, Yumi	Weber S C
Rochester, U of	Pan, Da'an	Muhlenberg C
S Indiana, U of	Inokawa, Mutsumi	S Indiana, U of
Stanford U	Cho, Young-mee Y.	Rutgers,NBruns
Stanford U	Sargent, Stuart	Colorado S U
Stanford U	Yoda, Tomiko	Duke U
SUNY, Buffalo	Choi, Hyaeweol	Smith C
Texas, Austin	Helm, Anthony	Guilford C
Texas, U of	Omura, Yoshihiro	Shippensburg
UC, Berkeley	Holman, J. Martin	Gettysburg C
UC, Berkeley	Myhre, Karin	Swarthmore C
UC, Berkeley	Su, Karen	New York U
UC, Berkeley	Zakim, Eric	Duke U
UC, Los Angeles	Hum, Tarry	New York U
UC, Los Angeles	Shirai, Yashuiro	Cornell U
Washington, U of	Manring, Rebecca	Indiana U
Washington, U of	Slaymaker, Douglas	Kentucky,U of
Washington, U of	Yu, Zhiqiang	CUNY, Baruch
Wiscnsn, Madsn	Mori, Junko	Iowa, U of
CAN-Br Columbia	Hagiwara, Takao	Case Western Res
CAN-Toronto	Oketani-Lobbezoo, H.	E MichiganU
PRC-Hunan Normal	Hsuan-Chin, Xsiong	Wiscnsn, RiverF

CLASSICS

TRAINED BY	NAME	HIRED BY
Brown U	Graver, Margaret	Dartmouth C
Brown U	Lindheim, Sara	UC, St Barbara
Brown U	Rutledge, Steven	Maryland, CollPk
Bryn Mawr C	Ajootian, Aileen	Mississippi, U of
Bryn Mawr C	Glowacki, Kevin T.	Indiana, Blmngtn
Bryn Mawr C	Houghtalin, Liane	Mary Washngtn C
Columbia U	Gregory, Andrew Pearce	Yale U
Cornell U	Barrett, James	Mississippi, U of
Cornell U	Hope, Louise	San Diego S U
Duke U	Phillips, Darryl	Vanderbilt U
Harvard U	MacKay, Christopher	Alberta-CAN
Harvard U	Nagel, Rebecca	Alberta-CAN
Harvard U	O'Neill, Jeanne	Davidson C
Harvard U	Williams, Demetrius K.	Tulane U
Illinois, Urbana	Churchill, J. Bradford	Colorado, Bldr
Iowa, U of	McCauley, Barbara	Concordia, Mrhd
Johns Hopkins	Afsaruddin, Asma	Notre Dame, U of
Loyola, Chicago	Cueva, Edmund	Xavier U
Michigan, U of	Dix, T. Keith	Georgia, U of
Michigan, U of	Guinee, David	DePauw U
Michigan, U of	Kraus, Matthew A.	Williams C
Michigan, U of	McNellen, Bard E.	Vanderbilt U
Michigan, U of	Sumi, Geoffrey	Mt Holyoke C
N Carolina, ChpH	Mueller, Hans-Friedrich	Florida S U
Penn, U of	Bregstein, Linda	Penn S U
Penn, U of	Marsilio, Maria	St Joseph's (PA)
Princeton U	DeFilippo, Joseph	N Dakota, U of
Princeton U	Worman, Nancy	Barnard C
Stanford U	Vasunia, Phiroze	S California, U of
Texas, Austin	Francese, Christopher	Dickinson C
UC, Berkeley	Gunderson, Erik	Ohio S U
UC, Berkeley	Orlin, Eric	Bard C
UC, Berkeley	Peek, Cecilia	Brighm Yng U
UC, Los Angeles	Laskaris, Julie	Richmond, U of
UC, Los Angeles	Schlegel, Catherine	Notre Dame, U of
Washington, U of	Haynes, Holly	New York U
Yale U	Mattern, Susan	Bucknell U
Yale U	Meltzer, Gary	Eckerd C
CAN-Toronto	Allen, Michael	Chicago, U of
UK-Oxford	Brittain, Charles	Cornell U
UK-Oxford	Colvin, Stephen	Yale U

COMMUNICATIONS/JOURNALISM

TRAINED BY	NAME	HIRED BY
Alabama, U of	Stoker, Kevin	Georgia Southern
Arizona, U of	Reichert, Tom	N Texas, U of
Arkansas S U	Malala, John	BethuneCookmn
Austin Peay S U	Moseley, John	Austin Peay S
Boston U	Napoli, Philip	Boston U
Boston U	Paterson, Chris	Georgia S U
Boston U	Tierney, Regina	New York Tech, Wstbry
Bowling Green S	Johnson, Scott	Richmond, U of
Bowling Green S	Schimmel, Kathryn M.	Pfeiffer U
Brigham Young U	Kelly, Martin	Valley City S
Cal Inst Arts	Seat, Josh	Master's C & Sem
Carnegie Mellon	Werner, Mark	Colorado, Denv
Cincinnati, U of	Constantindou, Fofi	Miami U, Oxford
Cincinnati, U of	Sivadas, Eugene	Emerson C
Columbia U	Papper, Robert A.	Ball S U
CUNY	Oates, Margaret	Yeshiva-Einstein Med
Delaware, U of	Holderman, Lisa	Beaver C
Emerson C	Beechner, Sara	Nebraska, Kearney
Emerson C	Robinson, Kelly	Emerson C

TRAINED BY	NAME	HIRED BY
Florida S U	Gaddis, Susanne	Houston, ClrLk
Florida S U	Turner, Leslie Jackson	Nebraska, Oma
Florida S U	Woods, Steven	William Jewell C
Florida, U of	Cassidy, W. Keith	Gardner-Webb C
Florida, U of	Davis, Charles	S Methodist U
Florida, U of	Leonhirth, William	Florida Tech
Georgia, U of	Elam, Angela	Missouri, KansC
Georgia, U of	Robins, Melinda	Emerson C
Georgia, U of	Shome, Raka	Washington, U of
Houston, ClrLk	Wier, Patrick	Houston, ClrLk
Howard U	Jackson, Ronald	Shippensburg
Howard U	Osunde, Samuel	MissippiValley
Illinois S U	Wilson, Elighie	Millikin U
Illinois, U of	Kosloski, David	Hastings C
Illinois, Urbana	Deem, Melissa	Iowa, U of
Indiana U	Seel, Peter	Colorado S U
Iowa, U of	Barnes, Melane	DePauw U
Iowa, U of	Boxman, Dieter	Tennessee, Chat
Iowa, U of	Cheshier, David	Georgia S U
Iowa, U of	Clark, Norman	Appalachian S U
Iowa, U of	Cousineau, Marie	Concordia-CAN
Iowa, U of	Delicath, John	Pittsburgh, U of
Iowa, U of	DeLuca, Kevin	Penn S U
Iowa, U of	Erbert, Larry	CUNY, Baruch
Iowa, U of	Feng, Peter	Delaware, U of
Iowa, U of	Friedline, Julie	St Thomas, U of
Iowa, U of	Fuglsang, Ross	Morningside C
Iowa, U of	Hamilton, Heidi	Augustana C (IL)
Iowa, U of	Hurst, Anthony	Buena Vista C
Iowa, U of	McConnell, Jane	Oklahoma, U of
Iowa, U of	McDaniel, James	Drake U
Iowa, U of	Serone, James	Midwestern S
Iowa, U of	Simonson, Peter	Allegheny C
Iowa, U of	Stein, Sarah	N Carolina S
Iowa, U of	Tjardes, Susan	Puget Sound
Iowa, U of	Wurtzler, Steve	Bowdoin C
Kansas S U	Landholm, Bambi	Washburn U
Kansas, U of	Gribas, John	Idaho S U
Kansas, U of	Shaner, Jaye	Georgia S U
Kansas, U of	Voss, Cary	Liberty U
Kent S U	Cos, Grant	Texas A&M, CrpsC
Kent S U	Horvath, Cary W.	Westminster (PA)
Kent S U	Zhong, Mei	Doane C
Kentucky, U of	Beavers, Lynnda	Liberty U
Lesley C	Mazur, Gail	Emerson C
Louisiana S U	Taylor, Kelly	N Texas, U of
Marshall U	Simmons, Elizabeth	Marshall U
Mass, Amherst	Patton, Cynthia	Emory U
Miami U, Oxford	Wittenbaum, Gwen M.	Michigan SU
Michigan S U	Bahk, Chang Mo	Cincinnati, U of
Michigan S U	Hasbach, Corinna	Albion C
Michigan S U	Meyer, Marcy E.	Ball S U
Michigan S U	Na, Louisa	Oklahoma, U of
Michigan S U	Rao, Nagesh	Maryland, CollPk
Michigan, U of	Blakeley, Stewart	Brenau U
Michigan, U of	Tewksbury, David	Illinois, Urbana
Minnesota, U of	Berg, Patricia	Wiscnsn, RiverF
Minnesota, U of	Dow, Bonnie	Georgia, U of
Minnesota, U of	Johnson, Katharine	Wiscnsn, RiverF
Minnesota, U of	Lucas, Suvellana	Wiscnsn, RiverF
Minnesota, U of	Torrens, Kathy	St Thomas, U of
Minnesota, U of	Voight, Philip	Gustavus Adolph
Minnesota, U of	Wilson, Sherrie	Nebraska, Oma
Missouri, Clmb	Dorries, Bruce	Winona S U
Missouri, Clmb	Speckman, Karon	Truman S U
Missouri, U of	Allen, Chris	Nebraska, Oma
Missouri, U of	Cox, Stephen A.	Denison U
Missouri, U of	Lee, Byung	Elon C

TRAINED BY	NAME	HIRED BY
Missouri, U of	Shires, Jeff	Campbellsville U
Missouri, U of	Whitehouse, Virginia	Whitworth C
MIT	Sheldon, James	Emerson C
Morehead S U	Corea, Brian	Salem-Teikyo U
N Arizona U	Jacobs, Ellen	Nebraska, Oma
N Dakota S U	Venette, Theresa	Winona S U
N Dakota S U	Dahlberg, Margaret	Valley City S
N Texas, U of	Gary, Tracey	N Texas, U of
Nevada, LasVegas	Robinson, Thomas E.	Ball S U
New York U	Barnes, Susan	Fordham U
New York U	Douglas, Jane	Florida, Gnsvl
New York U	Jew, Kimberly	Pittsburgh, Bradford
New York U	Mindich, David	St Michael's C
Northwestern U	Althaus, Scott	Illinois, Urbana
Northwestern U	Ceccarelli, Leah	Washington, U of
Northwestern U	DeWerth-Pallmeyer, D.	Cal Polytech
Northwestern U	Laffoon, E. Anne	Colorado, Bldr
Northwestern U	Payson, David	Keene S C
Northwestern U	Suchy, Patricia	LSU, BatnRoug
Northwestern U	Watts, Eric K.	Wake Forest U
Ohio S U	Borden, Sandra	W Michigan U
Ohio S U	Clowers, Marsha	Fordham U
Ohio S U	Gonzalez, Martin	San Francisco S
Ohio S U	Lawrence, David	Alma C
Ohio S U	McGee, Deborah	Texas Tech
Ohio S U	Messman, Susan	Penn S U
Ohio U	Emmers, Tara	Oklahoma, U of
Ohio U	Reynolds, Mary	Marshall U
Ohio U	Sweeney, Michael S.	Utah S U
Ohio U	Winokur, Dena	New York Tech, Wstbry
Oklahoma S U	Wanjohi, Elsie	BethuneCookmn
Oklahoma, U of	du Pre, Athena	SE Louisiana U
Oklahoma, U of	Shaver, Lynda	Bowling Green S
Oregon, U of	Masse, Mark H.	Ball S U
Oregon, U of	Wynn, Monica	Valparaiso U
Penn S U	Brooks, Kathy	Shippensburg
Penn S U	Olsen, Stephen	Wiscnsn, RiverF
Penn S U	Troup, Calvin	Duquesne U
Pittsburgh, U of	Biesecker-Mast, Gerald	Bluffton C
Pittsburgh, U of	McBride, Sheila A.	Westminster (PA)
Purdue U	Cornwell, Nancy	W Michigan U
Purdue U	Gruber, Diane	Arizona S West
Purdue U	Hearit, Keith	W Michigan U
Purdue U	Marshall, Alicia	Texas A&M U
Purdue U	Pokora, Rachel M.	Nebraska Wslyn
Rochester Tech	Evans, Margaret	Shippensburg
Rutgers U	Edley, Paige	Bowling Green S
Rutgers U	Guttman, Nurit	Tel Aviv U-ISRL
S California, U of	Dickinson, Greg	La Sierra U
S California, U of	Flanagin, Andrew	UC, St Barbara
S California, U of	Hoyes, Kevin M.	Denison U
S California, U of	Margerum, Eric	Carthage C
S Carolina, U of	Lowe, Evelyn	Shaw U
S Carolina, U of	Spell, Leigh Ann	Columbia U
S Carolina, U of	Steppling, Mary	Columbia U
S Dakota S U	Binsfeld, Douglas	Hastings C
S Illinois U	Marlow, Eric	Weber S C
S Illinois U	Rich, Anita	E Michigan U
S Illinois U	Roark, Virginia	S Illinois, Edwrds
S Illinois U	Worley, David	Indiana S U
S Methodist U	Broyles, Sheri	N Texas, U of
S Mississippi, U of	Bridges, Jack	W Georgia, S U of
S Mississippi U	Herold, Kelly	Winona S U
Southern U	Buisson, Gerald	S Mississippi, U of
Stanford U	Kassabian, Anahid	Fordham U
SUNY, Buffalo	Dahlberg, John S.	Canisius C
SUNY, Buffalo	Rosenfeld, Heather	Washburn U

TRAINED BY	NAME	HIRED BY
Syracuse U	Downes, Edward	Boston U
Syracuse U	Souza, Pamela	Washington, U of
Syracuse U	Yu, Yanmin	Bridgeport, U of
Temple U	Bresnahan, Rosalind	Cal S, SnBrndno
Temple U	Gunzerath, David	Old Dominion U
Temple U	Singer, Kevin	Emerson C
Tennessee, U of	Boone, Jeff	Texas, Permian
Tennessee, U of	Evans, Lea Helen	Mississippi, U of
Tennessee, U of	Macon, Tommy	Idaho S U
Texas, Arlington	Lambiase, Jacques	N Texas, U of
Texas, Austin	Depysler, Bruce	Incarnate Word
Texas, Austin	Garcia-Buckalew, Walter R.	Texas, Austin
Texas, Austin	Grady, Dennis	E Michigan U
Texas, Austin	LeBaron, Curtis	Colorado, Bldr
Texas, Austin	Smith, Edward B.	Georgetown C
Texas, Austin	Sumpter, Randall	Texas A&M U
UC, San Fran	Chambers, Tricia	Pacific, U of the
Utah, U of	Gomez, Jaime	San Francisco S
Utah, U of	Gribble, Joanne	UC, Davis
Utah, U of	Hammond, Scott	Brigham Young U
Utah, U of	Kuen, Ahn Dong	N/A-KOR
Utah, U of	Palmer, Allen	Brigham Young U
Vanderbilt U	Neal, John	Webster U
Vanderbilt U	Windley, Susan	St Thomas, U of
Vermont C, Norwich	Weis, John	Winona S U
W Kentucky, U of	Corbett, Kevin	S Indiana, U of
W Virginia, U of	Frazier, C. Hood	Maine, Preseq
W Virginia, U of	Wanzer, Melissa	Canisius C
Washington S U	Dong, Qingwen	Pacific, U of the
Washington, U of	Borden, Diane L.	George Mason U
Washington, U of	Bullock, Jeffrey	Dubuque, U of
Washington, U of	Johnson, Michelle	Westfield S C
Washington, U of	Li, Fengru	Montana, U of
Wayne S U	Dillon, Shayne	Pacific, U of the
Wayne S U	Henoch, Miriam	N Texas, U of
Wayne S U	Williams, Susannne	N Dakota S U
Wiscnsn, Madsn	Glueck, Lisa	Winona S U
Wiscnsn, Madsn	Hallahan, Kirk	Colorado S U
Wiscnsn, Madsn	Oravec, Jo Ann R.	Ball S U
Wiscnsn, Madsn	Sedey, Allison	Colorado, Bldr
Wiscnsn, Milw	Metzler, Bruce	Carthage C
Wiscnsn, U of	Kersten, Kevin	Boston U
Yale U	Manuel, Sharon	Emerson C
UK-York	Livesey, Margot	Emerson C

COMPARATIVE LITERATURE

TRAINED BY	NAME	HIRED BY
Columbia U	Fischer, Sibylle	Duke U
Harvard U	Calotychos, Evangelos	New York U
Illinois S U	Leen, Mary	W New Mexico
Iowa, U of	Fox, Claire	Stanford U
Iowa, U of	Stahl, Aletha	Earlham C
Rutgers U	Honaker, Lisa	Stockton S C
Stanford U	Schocket, Eric	Hampshire C
SUNY, Bngmtn	Dassback, Elma	Southwest S U
SUNY, Bngmtn	Jagne, Signa	Spelman C
SUNY, Bngmtn	Rader, Gary	Texas Lutheran
SUNY, Buffalo	Rashidian, Ziba	American U
UC, Berkeley	Pao, Angela C.	Indiana, Blmngtn
UC, Santa Cruz	MacKinnon, Patricia	Golden Gate U
UC, Santa Cruz	Swensen, Cole	Denver, U of
SWT-Geneva	Dykman, Aminadav	Penn S U

DRAMA/DANCE/FILM/VIDEO

TRAINED BY	NAME	HIRED BY
Adelphi U	Rowen, Jacqueline	Boston U
Art Inst Chicago	Bacon, Karen	Trinity C (CT)
Bank Street C	Trompetter, Amy	Barnard C
Buglisi Foreman Dance	Foreman, Donlin	Barnard C
Butler U	McMahon, Alice	Illinois S U
Cal C Arts /Crafts	Plays, Dana	Occidental C
Cal S, Fullerton	Taulli, James	Pacific, U of the
Cal S, Stnslaus	Robinson, Richard	Palm Beach Atlantic
Carnegie Mellon	Deer, Joseph	N Texas, U of
Carnegie Mellon	Shaffer, Henry	Bridgewater S
Catholic U Amer	Berman, Karen	Georgetown U
Catholic U Amer	Dox, Donnalee	Arizona S U
Catholic U Amer	Heckler, Mark	Colorado, Denver
Catholic U Amer	Kline, Joseph	Allentown C
Catholic U Amer	Ouellette, Thomas	Rollins C
Connecticut, U of	Fulton, Jim	Rollins C
CUNY	Kahan, Sylvia	CUNY, StatIsl
Denver, U of	Prescott, James	Rollins C
Florida S U	Sawyer-Dailley, Mark	Bellarmine C
Georgia, U of	Smith, David	Arkansas, LtlRk
Harvard U	Warburton, Edward	S Methodist U
Idaho, U of	Bouchard, Kimberley	SUNY, Potsdm
Illinois, Chicago	Dai, Dansi	Webster U
Illinois S U	Cavin, Scott	Chadron S C
Indiana U	Hodge, Julie A.	Mary Washngtn C
Indiana U	Smith, Gretchen	S Methodist U
Iowa, U of	Cooper, Thea	Iowa, U of
Iowa, U of	Henderson, Rachel	Iowa, U of
Iowa, U of	Larche, Doug	Grandview C
Iowa, U of	Taylor, Robert	Arizona S West
Kansas S U	Malone, Travis	Bethel C (MN)
Kent S U	Douns, Kathleen	Tennessee Wesleyan
Mankato S U	Wickelgren, Bruce	St Olaf C
Mass, Amherst	Hamilton, Sabrina	Williams C
Mass, Amherst	Moore, Kym	Hampshire C
Mass, U of	Langton, Paula	Boston U
Miami U, Oxford	Olson, Marcus	Wright S U
Michigan S U	Lenhoff, Bentley	Westminster (PA)
Michigan, U of	Lanier, Nancy	Stockton S C
Mills C	Mezur, Katherine	Cal S, LosAngls
Minnesota, U of	Bell, Gregory	Otterbein C
Minnesota, U of	Draheim, Steven	Alma C
Minnesota, U of	Ruebhausen, David	N Alabama, U of
MIT	Pena, Richard	Columbia U
N Carolina, ChpH	Fike, Raymond	N Texas, U of
N Carolina, ChpH	Lester, Carle	BethuneCookmn
New York U	Barlow, Melinda	Colorado, Bldr
New York U	Harmon, Richard	Transylvania U
New York U	McEniry, Deborah	Palm Beach Atlantic
New York U	Turner, Laura	Charleston, C of
New York U	Vactor, Vanita	Illinois S U
Northwestern U	Wolford, Lisa	Bowling Green S
Ohio S U	Craig-Quijada, Balinda	Kenyon C
Ohio S U	Weiss, Steven	St Olaf C
Ohio U	Arnold, Dawn	Roosevelt U
Oklahoma, U of	Levin, Melinda	N Texas, U of
Oregon, U of	Davenport, Dennis	Rockford C
Oregon, U of	Gupton, Janet	Bowling Green S
Oregon, U of	Smith, Dana	Doane C
Pratt Institute	Goldstein, Abby	Fordham U
S California, U of	Everett, Anna	Colorado, Bldr
S California, U of	Provenzano, Thomas	Cal S, SnBrndno
S California, U of	Vandervort-Cobb, Joy	Charleston, C of
S Carolina, U of	Leoffler-Bell, Chester	N Carolina, Wlm
S Dakota, U of	Hynick, Harold	Drake U
S Dakota, U of	LaGrange, Paul	Winona S U
S Illinois U	Elwell, Jeffrey	Marshall U
S Illinois U	Haas, Christopher	Lenoir-Rhyne C
S Illinois U	Parrot, Mark	NW Missouri S
S Illinois U	Sloan, Leslie	Indiana S U
S Methodist U	Fitch, Thomas	Alabama, U of
Stanford U	Orenstein, Claudia	Barnard C
Stanford U	Rogers, Wendy	UC, Riverside
Stanford U	Saltz, David	Georgia, U of
SUNY, Brockport	Pulvino, Lori	Alabama, Brmng
SW Texas S U	Crew, Scott	SW Oklahoma S
Tennessee, Knox	Harris, Gary	Lyon C
Texas, Austin	Fluker, Laurie Hayes	SW Texas S U
Texas, Austin	Hong, Junhao	SUNY, Buffalo
Texas, Austin	LaFeber, Scott	S Indiana, U of
Texas, Austin	Meadows, Jennifer Anne	Cal S, Chico
Texas, Austin	Metz, WalterCarl	Texas, Austin
Texas, Austin	Mullen, Megan	New Hmpshire, U of
Texas, Austin	Negra, Diane	N Texas, U of
Texas, Austin	Turnbull-Langley, Cynthia	Denison U
Texas, Austin	Wilkinson, Kenton	Texas, San Antonio
Texas, Austin	Zuberi, Nabeel	Auckland-NZEAL
Texas, U of	Hunter, Jeffrey	Cal S, Fresno
Texas Woman's U	Santos, Eluza Maria	N Carolina, U of
Texas Woman's U	Strauss, Marc	SE Missouri S
Texas Woman's U	Williams , Valerie	Ohio S U
Texas Woman's U	Yagerline, Joyce	Kansas S U
Trinity U	Montgomery, Reginald	Trinity C(CT)
UC, Irvine	Baker, Annaliese	SUNY, Oswego
UC, Los Angeles	Lucas, Nina M.	Wake Forest U
Utah, U of	Byrd, Neeya	James Madison
Utah, U of	Lives, Amy	Brigham Young
Utah, U of	Moulton, Lisa	Ohio U
Virginia, U of	Hunter, James	S Carolina, Clm
Washington, U of	Anderson, Lisa	Purdue U
Washington, U of	Ernst, Amy	Arizona, U of
Washington, U of	Jones, Jennifer	Denver, U of
Washington, U of	Malcolm, Rebecca	Kent S U
Washington, U of	Redd, Tina	Arkansas, U of
Washington, U of	Simpson, Maria	Washington, U of
Washington, U of	Wilcox, Dean	Texas Tech
Wiscnsn, LaCro	Nofsinger, Kim	Winona S U
Wiscnsn, Madsn	Bodroghkozy, Aniko	Alberta-CAN
Wiscnsn, Madsn	Gilliam, Leah	Bard C
Wiscnsn, U of	Blackinton, Carolyn	Georgia, U of
Yale U	Cummings, Scott	Boston C
Yale U	Margio, Elizabeth	Fordham U
Yale U	Saternow, Timothy	Connecticut,U of
Yale U	Schwentker, Fritz	Texas, Austin
CAN-Grand Theatre	Tomlinson, Charlie	Alberta-CAN
CAN-Nat'l Ballet	Brown, David Allean	UC, Irvine
CZECH-N/A	Faflak, Marcella	Northern S U

ECONOMICS

TRAINED BY	NAME	HIRED BY
Arizona, U of	Kruse, Jamie	Texas Tech
Auburn U	Adams, Frank	Gustavus Adolph
Boston U	Adsera, Alicia	Autonoma-SPN
Boston U	Chen, Yongmin	Colorado, Bldr
Boston U	Chen, Zhixiang	Southwest S U
Boston U	Hodgkin, Dominic	Brandeis U
Boston U	Johri, Alok	McMaster-CAN
Boston U	Park, Kihong	Purdue U
Boston U	Pitarakis, Jean-Yves	Reading-UK
Boston U	Sonuanathan, Rohini	Emory C
Boston U	Tamura, Akiko	Hosei-JAPAN
Carnegie Mellon	Sieg, Holger	Duke U
Carnegie Mellon	Thornton, Saranna	Hampden-Sydny
Chicago, U of	Ireland, Peter N.	Rutgers, NBruns

TRAINED BY	NAME	HIRED BY	TRAINED BY	NAME	HIRED BY	TRAINED BY	NAME	HIRED BY
Chicago, U of	Miller, James	Smith C	Michigan, U of	Mazumdar, Joy	Emory U	UC, Davis	Olmstead, Jennifer	American U
Chicago, U of	Todd, Petra	Penn, U of	Michigan, U of	Secondi, Giorgio	American U	UC, Davis	Siegler, Mark	Bates C
Chicago, U of	Topa, Giorgio	New York U	Minnesota, U of	Alvarez, Fernando	Chicago, U of	UC, Los Angeles	Beesaw, John	Chapman U
Cincinnati, U of	Das, Jayoti	Elon C	Minnesota, U of	Doss, Cheryl R.	Williams C	UC, Riverside	Alarcon, Diana	American U
Colorado S U	Brooks, Stacey	Clarkson U	Minnesota, U of	Gollin, Douglas	Williams C	UC, San Diego	Robles, Jack	Colorado, Bldr
Colorado S U	Carroll, Michael	W Virginia S C	Minnesota, U of	Lagunoff, Roger D.	Georgetown U	UC, St Barbara	Chiaramonte, Peters	Chapman U
Colorado S U	Casstello, Sergio	Mobile, U of	Mississippi, U of	Brown, Curressia	MissippiValley	UC, St Barbara	Jewell, Robert	N Texas, U of
Colorado S U	Jasek-Rysdahl, Kelvin	Cal S, Stnslaus	MIT	Moscarini, Giuseppe	Yale U	UC, St Barbara	Karr, Timothy	Chicago, U of
Colorado, U of	Van Stowe, Jill	Holy Cross, C of	MIT	Reiley, David	Vanderbilt U	UC, St Barbara	Rowland, Patrick	Fordham U
Cornell U	Bayazitoglu, Berna	Bogazici-ITL	N Carolina, ChpH	Chase, Jennie	N Texas, U of	Union Institute	Daris, Norman	Albertus Magnus C
Cornell U	Bhattacharya, Joydeep	S California, U of	N Carolina, ChpH	Rous, Jeffrey	N Texas, U of	Utah, U of	Greiner, Daniel	UC, Riverside
Cornell U	Chun, Rodney	Hong Kong-HNGKNG	N Carolina, U of	Schwabe, Kurt	Ohio U	Utah, U of	Henage, Richard	Claremnt McKenna
Cornell U	Clark, Jeremy	Br Columbia-CAN	N Carolina, U of	Quispe-Agnoli, Myriam	Tulane U	Utah, U of	Kliman, Andrew	Pace, WhitePl
Cornell U	Kulshreshtha, Praveen	Virginia Tech	New School	Dickens, Edwin	Drew U	Valparaiso U	Burnette, Joyce	Wabash C
CUNY	Dasgupta, S.	Fairleigh Dickerson U	New York U	Michalik, Geraldine	St Peter's C	Virginia Tech	Dobkins, Linda	Emory & Henry C
CUNY	Durnin, Ellen D.	S Connecticut S U	Northwestern U	Canjels, Eugene	New School	Virginia, U of	Burrus, Robert	Kenyon C
CUNY	Klein, Esther	CUNY, StatIsl	Northwestern U	Coppejans, Mark	Duke U	Washington U	Hansen, Bradley A.	Mary Washngtn C
CUNY	Lin, Jang-Shee	Husson C	Northwestern U	El-Gamal, Mahmoud	Wiscnsn, Madsn	Washington U	Kinghorn, Janice	New School
CUNY	Long, Mary Margaret	Drexel U	Northwestern U	Lizzeri, Alessandro	Princeton U	Washington U	Nesslein, Thomas	Wiscnsn, GrnB
CUNY	McSweeney-Feld, M.	St Joseph's C (NY)	Northwestern U	Persico, Nicola	UC, Los Angeles	Washington, U of	Tangen, Kenneth	Chapman U
CUNY	Pantzalis, Christos E.	Manitoba-CAN	Northwestern U	Tournas, Ioannis	Rutgers, Newark	Wiscnsn, Madsn	Peterson, Elaine	Cal S, Stnslaus
CUNY, Baruch	Cohen, Gorden	CUNY, Brooklyn	Northwestern U	Wegge, Simone	Lake Forest C	Wiscnsn, Milw	Bahr, Kevin M.	Lakeland C
Duke U	Pineres, Sheila	Texas, Dallas	Oregon, U of	Caplan, Arthur	Weber S C	Wiscnsn, U of	Earnhart, Dietrich	Fairfield U
Duke U	Taylor, Robert	San Diego S	Penn S U	Morgan, John	Princeton U	Wiscnsn, U of	Lee, Byung-Joo	Notre Dame, U of
Florida S U	Abuhasan, F.	Kolej Terengganu-MALAY	Penn S U	Yerger, David	Lycoming C	Wiscnsn, U of	Pepper, John	Virginia, U of
Florida S U	Compton, William	W Illinois U	Penn, U of	Ali, Salman Syed	Islamic U-PAK	Worcester Poly	Ahearne, Michael J.	Indiana, U of
Florida S U	Friday, Swint	S Alabama, U of	Penn, U of	Brown, J.	Stockholm Schl of Eco-SWED	Yale U	Ackerberg, Daniel	Boston U
Florida S U	Higgins, Eric	Drexel U	Penn, U of	Goh, Aiting	Singapore, U of-SNGP	Yale U	Conning, Jonathan H.	Williams C
Florida S U	Lawson, Robert	Capital U	Penn, U of	Hendricks, Lutz	Arizona S U	Yale U	Dimand, Mary Ann	Albion C
Florida S U	May, David	Oklahoma City	Penn, U of	Katz, Kimberly	Mt Holyoke C	Yale U	Pendleton, Linwood	California, U of
Florida S U	Narayanan, Rajesh	Concordia U	Penn, U of	Kilian, Lutz	Michigan, U of			
Florida S U	Nichols, Mark W.	Nevada, Reno	Penn, U of	McLennan, Michele	Lafayette C	CAN-Toronto	Hollis, Aidan	Calgary-CAN
Florida S U	Sellen, Patsy	Georgia, U of	Penn, U of	Olivier, Jacques	HEC-FRN	CAN-Toronto	Lo, Kin Chung	Alberta-CAN
Florida S U	Tyler, Floyd	Memphis, U of	Penn, U of	Quadrini, Vincenzo	Pompeu Fabra-SPN	NETH-Amsterdam	Goeree, Jacob	Virginia, U of
Florida, U of	Thompson, Peter	Houston, U of	Penn, U of	Sandroni, Alvaro	Northwestern U	S.AFR-Capetown	Malherbe, Paul	American U
Fordham U	Samanta, Prodyot	Manhattan C	Penn, U of	Scott, Elizabeth	Penn S U	UK-Cambridge	Huynh, Hsueh-Liing	Boston U
Fordham U	Winczewski, Greg	Manhattan C	Penn, U of	Solnick, Sara	Miami, U of	UK-London Sch Eco	Spector, David	MIT
Harvard U	Brainerd, Elizabeth	Williams C	Rochester, U of	Yorukoglu, Mehmet	Chicago, U of			
Harvard U	Chatak, Maitreesh	Chicago, U of	S California, U of	Liberty, James	Chapman U			
Harvard U	Dennis, Benjamin	Pacific, U of the	S Carolina, U of	Nape, Steven	Gordon C			
Harvard U	Haughton, Jonathan	Wellesley C	S Illinois U	Dresdow, Sally	Northern S U			
Houston, U of	Brandl, Michael	W Texas A&M	S Illinois U	Holiemun, Cynthia	Iowa Wesleyan C			
Illinois, U of	Stimpert, Larry	Colorado C	S Methodist U	Razzolini, Laura	Mississippi, U of			
Illinois, Urbana	Martin, Richard	Agnes Scott C	S Methodist U	Ross, Leola	E Carolina U			
Illinois, Urbana	Segura, Gary	Claremont Grad	S Methodist U	Walker, Gaston Craig	Delta S U			
Indiana U	West, Clifford	Virginia Military	St Louis U	Helbing, Hans	Fontbonne C			
Iowa S U	Rahnama, Masha	Texas Tech	Stanford U	Che, Jiahua	Notre Dame, U of			
Iowa, U of	Gorgens, Tue	Australia, U of-ASL	Stanford U	Ito, Harumi	Brown U			
Iowa, U of	Wen, Yi	Science & Tech, U of	Stanford U	Mazzoleni, Roberto	Vermont, U of			
Iowa, U of	Wurtz, Allan	NewSouthWales-UK	SUNY, Bngmtn	Belay, Halefom	Whitman C			
Iowa, U of	Ziliak, Steve	Bowling Green S U	SUNY, Bngmtn	Dogan, Ergun	N/A-TRKY			
Kentucky, U of	Jones, John Travis	Georgetown C	SUNY, Bngmtn	Graham, Glenn	SUNY, Oswego			
Louisiana S U	Mitias, Peter	Hampden-Sydney	SUNY, Bngmtn	O'Neil, James	Concordia -CAN			
Louisiana Tech	Totten, Jeffrey	St Norbert C	SUNY, Bngmtn	Trost, Alice	Mass, Boston			
Maine, U of	Maxey, Joel	E Oregon S C	SUNY, Buffalo	Geide-Stevenson, Doris	Weber S C			
Marquette U	Suri, Rajneesh	Northern S U	Swarthmore C	Shaffer, Eric	Indiana, Blmngtn	**ENGLISH/AMERICAN LANG & LIT**		
Maryland, CollPk	Bandyopadhyay, Usree	W Michigan U	Tennessee, Chat	Hayes, Travis	Tennessee Wesleyan	Alabama, Hntsvl	Hinton, Rita	Alabama A & M
Maryland, CollPk	Wilson, Brian	W Michigan U	UC, Berkeley	Ely, Jeffrey C.	Northwestern U	Alabama, U of	Holmes, Thomas	E Tennessee S
Maryland, U of	Akindahunsi, Oluwole	Missipi Valley	UC, Berkeley	Friedman, Eric J.	Rutgers, NBruns	Alaska, U of	Knott, Kip	Muskingum C
Maryland, U of	Heckelman, Jac C.	Wake Forest U	UC, Berkeley	Furuya, Kaku	UC, Irvine	Alaska, U of	Pennington, Debra A.	Alaska, Anchrg
Mass, Amherst	Danby, Colin	Dickinson C	UC, Berkeley	Geohegan, Jacqueline	Clark U	American U	Corredor, Mary	Sul Ross S U
Mass, Amherst	Skrabis, Kristin	Dickinson C	UC, Berkeley	Golan, Amos	American U	American U	Smith, Davina	American U
Mass, U of	Garnett, Jr., Robert	Texas Christian	UC, Berkeley	Weiler, Stephen	Colorado S U	Arizona, U of	Hindman, Jane	San Diego S
Michigan S U	DeLoach, Stephen	Elon C	UC, Berkeley	Wells, Robin	MIT	Arizona, U of	Moneyhun, Clyde	Youngstown S
Michigan, U of	Brown, Annette	W Michigan U	UC, Berkeley	Wydick, Bruce	SanFrancisco, Uof	Arizona, U of	Thomas, John	SUNY, Oswego
						Arkansas, U of	Perabo, Susan	Dickinson C
						Ball S U	Peterson, Raileen L.	Ball S U
						Kentucky, U of	Hawkins, Ann	Austin Peay S
						Boston U	Armstrong, James	Northwestern U
						Boston U	Burgess, Miranda	New Brunswick CAN
						Boston U	Eaton, Mark	Oklahoma S U
						Boston U	Hartley, Andrew	W Georgia, S U of
						Boston U	Kodat, Catherine	Hamilton C
						Bowling Green S	Anderson, Antje	Dickinson C
						Bowling Green S	Auten, Janet	American U
						Bowling Green S	Campbell, Richard	Winona S U
						Bowling Green S	Krause, Steven	S Oregon S U
						Bowling Green S	Thursby, Jacqueline	Brigham Yng U
						Bowling Green S	Young-Minor, Ethel	Mississippi, Uof
						Brandeis U	Daileader, Celia	Alabama, Brmng
						Brandeis U	Goldner, Ellen	CUNY, StatIsl
						Brandeis U	Halliday, Mark	Ohio U

TRAINED BY	NAME	HIRED BY	TRAINED BY	NAME	HIRED BY	TRAINED BY	NAME	HIRED BY
Brandeis U	Quay, Sara	Kenyon C	Duke U	McLaughlin, Joseph	Ohio U	Indiana U of PA	Thomas, Dorothy	Hampton U
Brandeis U	Travis, Jennifer	Illinois S U	Duke U	Nolan, Maura	Notre Dame, U of	Iowa, U of	Anderson, Kathleen	Palm Beach Atlantic
Brown U	Kilgore, Dewitt	Indiana, Blmngtn	Duke U	Talbot, Robert	Coker C	Iowa, U of	Basaninyenzi, Gatsinzi	Oakwood C
Brown U	Lowney, John	St John's U	Duke U	Waldrep, Shelton	Georgia S U	Iowa, U of	Chaffee, Mary Jane	Campbellsville U
Brown U	Matusukawa, Yuko	SUNY, Brckprt	Duke U	Walker, Julia A.	William & Mary	Iowa, U of	Gutjahr, Paul Charles	Indiana, Blmngtn
Brown U	Scott, Helen C.	Wilkes C	Duquesne U	Boyle, Louis	Carlow C	Iowa, U of	Johnson, Kerry	Merrimack C
Brown U	Young, Kevin	Georgia, U of	Duquesne U	Dimarco, Diane	Slippery Rock U	Iowa, U of	McCauley, Lawrence	New Jersey, Cof
Carnegie Mellon	Blakeslee, Ann	E Michigan U	E Tennessee S	Clark, Linda	Maryville (TN)	Iowa, U of	Spaulding, Carol	Drake U
Carnegie Mellon	Fleming, David	New Mexico S U	Emory U	Boswell, Marshall	Rhodes C	Iowa, U of	Swenson, Kristine	Augustana C (IL)
Catholic U Amer	Peterson, Zina	Brigham Yng U	Emory U	Brown, Amy	W Georgia, S U of	Iowa, U of	VanSluijs, Sharon	SUNY, Oswego
Chicago, U of	Henze, Catherine	Wiscnsn, GrnB	Emory U	Ingram, Randall	Davidson C	Johns Hopkins	Canuel, Mark	Illinois, Chicago
Chicago, U of	Morrisson, Mark	Penn S U	Emory U	Jackson, Gerri-Kai	New School	Johns Hopkins	Glimp, David	Miami, U of
Chicago, U of	Ramey, Lauri Lee	Illinois Benedctn	Emory U	Kilpatrick, Kathy	Rowan C	Johns Hopkins	Hewitt, Elizabeth	Grinnell C
Chicago, U of	Shannon, Laurie J.	Duke U	Evansville, U of	Smith, Martha K.	S Indiana, U of	Johns Hopkins	MacPherson, Sandra	Ohio S U
Chicago, U of	Tolliver, Jr., Willie	Agnes Scott C	Florida S U	Applegate, Nancy	Floyd C	Johns Hopkins	McGill, Meredith	Rutgers, NBruns
Clark U	Bowen, Angela	Cal S U, Long Beach	Florida S U	Crossley, Gay Lynn	Marian C	Kansas, U of	Marshall, Tod	Rhodes C
Columbia U	Anderson, Mignon	Maryland EShore	Florida S U	Lewis, Simon	Charleston, C of	Kansas, U of	Reiff, Mary Jo	Youngstown S
Columbia U	Castiglia, Christopher	Loyola, Chicago	Florida S U	Meekins, Beth	W Carolina U	Kent S U	Patterson, Daniel	Cal S, SnBrndno
Columbia U	Crain, Patricia	Princeton U	Florida S U	O'Donnell, Thomas	Loyola, Chicago	Kentucky, U of	Kessler, Valerie	Campbellsville U
Columbia U	Cummins, June	San Diego S U	Florida S U	Snyder, Jr., William	Concordia, Mrhd	Lehigh U	Glanz, Elaine Marie	Immaculata C
Columbia U	Dawson, Ashley	Iowa, U of	Florida S U	Viera, Joseph	Nazareth C	Louisiana S U	Kristensen, Randi	St Lawrence U
Columbia U	Henderson, Diana	MIT	Florida S U	Woodberry, Bonnie	Glasgow–UK	Louisiana S U	Mazel, David	Livingston U
Columbia U	Herman, Peter C.	San Diego S	Florida, U of	Brenner, Wendy	SUNY, Brckprt	Louisiana S U	Peeples, Scott	Charleston, C of
Columbia U	Holsinger, Bruce	Colorado, Bldr	Florida, U of	Holland, Flournoy	Mass, Amherst	Louisiana S U	Russell, Henry M.	Franciscan Steuben
Columbia U	Joshi, Priya	UC, Berkeley	Florida, U of	Michel, Steven	Florida, Gnsvl	Louisville, U of	Shiffman, Betty	Spalding U
Columbia U	Kelen, Sarah	Allegheny C	Florida, U of	Ruth, Katrina	Liberty U	Loyola, Chicago	Gusick, Barbara	Troy S, Dothan
Columbia U	Lye, Collen	UC, Berkeley	Florida, U of	Soud, Stephen	Maryville (TN)	Loyola Mrymnt	Guttman, Naomi	Hamilton C
Columbia U	Morrissey, Lee	Clemson U	Fordham U	Carubia, Josephine Gloria	Penn SU	Maine, U of	Carlson, Clifford	Springfield C
Columbia U	Mufti, Aamir	Michigan, U of	Fordham U	De Angelis, Rose	Marist C	Maryland, BaltCnty	Kamdibe, Muata	Maryland EShore
Columbia U	Rankine, Claudia	Barnard C	Fordham U	Jones, John	Jackson S U	Maryland, Coll Pk	Harrington, Susan	Maryland EShore
Columbia U	Rohrbach, Augusta	Oberlin C	Fordham U	Murphy, Brian	Monroe C	Maryland, CollPk	Birge, Amy	Temple U
Columbia U	Schoenberger, Nancy	William & Mary	Fordham U	Ruth, Todd	Mercy C	Maryland, U of	Pedreira, Mark	Boston U
Cornell U	Aravamudan, Srinivas	Washington, U of	George Mason U	Thiers, Naomi	American U	Mass, Amherst	Conway, Katherine	Wheaton C (MA)
Cornell U	Goodman, Beverly	E Michigan U	Georgetown U	Rudnytzky, Kateryna	Marshall U	Mass, Amherst	Isaacs, Emily	Montclair S C
Cornell U	Greene, Laura	Augustana C (IL)	Georgia S U	McCaffrey, Kelly	Palm Beach Atlantic	Mass, U of	Bromley, Anne	Rhodes C
Cornell U	Haynes, Rosetta	Indiana S U	Georgia, U of	Harrison, W. Dale	Youngstown S	Mass, U of	Higgins, Andrew	American U
Cornell U	Orr, Bridget	Iowa, U of	Hampton U	Peoples-McDonald, M.	Maryland EShr	Mass, U of	Madigan, Mark	Nazareth C
Cornell U	Shafer, Yvonne	St John's U	Harvard U	Korobkin, Laura	Boston U	Mass, U of	Smith, Robert	Knox C
Cornell U	Sharpe, Christina E.	Hobart/WmSmth	Harvard U	Oliver, Elisabeth	LSU, BatnRoug	Miami U, Oxford	Black, Laurel	Indiana U of PA
Cornell U	Sicari, Stephen	St John's U	Harvard U	Schware, Kathryn	Vanderbilt U	Miami U, Oxford	Fair, Stephen J.	Malone C
CUNY	Collins, Jane M.	Pace U	Hawaii, U of	Winskowski-Jackson, Christine	Lewis U	Michigan S U	Barbier, Stuart I.	IndianaPurdu,FW
CUNY	Corradetti, Arthur R.	Long Island U	Houston, U of	Williams, Thomas	Wiscnsn, GrnB	Michigan S U	Gourdine, Angeletta	LSU, BatnRoug
CUNY	Jacquette, Kathleen M.	SUNY	Illinois S U	Pullen, Terri	W Georgia, S U of	Michigan S U	Jooma, Minaz	St John's U
CUNY	Nelson, Deborah	Chicago, U of	Illinois S U	Ruzicka, Dennis	Winona S U	Michigan S U	Peters, Jason	Augustana C (IL)
CUNY	Rudden, Patricia Spence	CUNY	Illinois, U of	Gruber, Sibylle	N Arizona U	Michigan S U	Rempe, Robert	Charlstn, U of
CUNY	Samuels, Peggy	Drew U	Illinois, U of	Hancin-Bhatt, Barbara	S Carolina, Clm	Michigan S U	Winters, Carol	Grand Valley S
CUNY	Weisberg, David	Wesleyan U	Illinois, U of	Mourao, Manuela	Old Dominion U	Michigan Tech	Latterell, Catherine	Texas Tech
CUNY	Williams, Lisa	Ramapo C	Illinois, Urbana	Canning, Rick	Armstrong S C	Michigan Tech	Selber, Stuart	Texas Tech
Delaware, U of	Nisly, Lamar	Bluffton C	Illinois, Urbana	Chen, Ieann	Prescott C	Michigan, U of	Barnes, Natasha	Emory U
Delaware, U of	Stable, Susan	Texas A&M U	Illinois, Urbana	Fonteneau, D. Yvonne	Illinois, Edwrds	Michigan, U of	DeStigter, Todd	Illinois, Chicago
Denver, U of	Haslem, Lori	Knox C	Illinois, Urbana	Powers, Richard	Illinois, Urbana	Michigan, U of	Fox, Maria	Georgia Southern
Denver, U of	Iverson, Kristen	Metropolitan S C	Illinois, Urbana	Pratt, Susan	Concordia, StPl	Michigan, U of	Gidal, Eric	Iowa, U of
Denver, U of	Joplin, David	Black Hills S	Illinois, Urbana	Rachels, David	Virginia Military	Michigan, U of	North, Marcy	Florida S U
Denver, U of	Meek, Sandra	Berry C	Indiana U	Bizup, Joseph	Yale U	Michigan, U of	Warner, Mary	W Carolina U
Denver, U of	Stein, Elizabeth	James Madison	Indiana U	Heithaus, Joseph	DePauw U	Michigan, U of	Won, Joseph	Vermont, U of
Denver, U of	Tabakow, Philip	Bridgewater S	Indiana U	Livingston-Weber, Joan	W Illinois U	Minnesota, U of	Landman, James	N Texas, U of
Duke U	Amos, Mark	Wilkes C	Indiana U	Rudy, Jill	Brighm Yng U	Minnesota, U of	Lewis, Charles	Westminster C
Duke U	Brewster, Glen	Westfield S C	Indiana U	Scrimgeour, J.D.	Salem S C	Missouri, Clmb	O'Conner, Michael	Millikin U
Duke U	Chism, Christine	Rutgers, NBruns	Indiana U	Smith, M. Rick	Kent S C	N Arizona U	Basena, David	Bowie S U
Duke U	Desai, Gaurav	Tulane U	Indiana U of PA	Chitrapu, Devi	Cntrl Missouri S	N Arizona U	Conrad, Susan	Iowa S U
Duke U	Flatley, Jonathan	Virginia, U of	Indiana U of PA	Haskell, Kathy	Arkansas, Mntcl	N Arizona U	Rowley, Kelley	SUNY, Oswego
Duke U	Hedges, Warren	S Oregon S C	Indiana U of PA	Mackall, Joseph	Ashland C	N Carolina, ChpH	Floyd-Wilson, Mary	Yale U
Duke U	Hicks, Heather	Villanova U	Indiana U of PA	Purnell, David	Muskingham C	N Carolina, ChpH	Groover, Kristina	Appalachian S
						N Carolina, ChpH	Hood, James	Mars Hill C
						N Carolina, ChpH	Ivory, James	Appalachian S

TRAINED BY	NAME	HIRED BY	TRAINED BY	NAME	HIRED BY	TRAINED BY	NAME	HIRED BY
N Carolina, ChpH	Lloyd, Theresa	E Tennessee S	Rollins C	Groth, Suzanne	Rollins C	UC, Berkeley	Brown, Kate	S Carolina, Clm
N Carolina, Wlm	Cornell, Meredith	Marshall U	Rutgers U	Breen, Margaret	Connecticut, U of	UC, Berkeley	Camfield, Gregg	Pacific, U of the
N Texas, U of	Favor, Leslie	Sul Ross S U	Rutgers U	Cobb, John	Wofford C	UC, Berkeley	Chiang, Mark	Penn, U of
N Texas, U of	Williamson, Richard	Muskingum C	Rutgers U	Franks, Jill	Austin Peay S	UC, Berkeley	Ciccone, Nancy	Colorado, Denv
Nebraska, Lncn	Bracks, Lean'tin	Fisk U	Rutgers U	Miracky, James	Holy Cross, C of	UC, Berkeley	Davis, Simone	New York U
Nebraska, Lncn	Coleman-Hull, Philip	Luther C	Rutgers U	Perkins, Priscilla	Roosevelt U	UC, Berkeley	Del Rio, Elena	N Colorado, U of
Nebraska, Lncn	Kruse, Martha	Nebraska, Kearney	Rutgers U	Reynolds, Jonathan	Livingstone C	UC, Berkeley	Green, Laura Morgan	Yale U
Nebraska, Lncn	Martin, Lee	N Texas, U of	Rutgers U	Roliston, Lou Ethel	St Peter's C	UC, Berkeley	Hamilton, Carol	Carnegie Mellon
Nebraska, Lncn	Radelich, Michael	Drake U	Rutgers U	Williamson, Michael	Indiana U of PA	UC, Berkeley	McGee, Timothy	New Jersey, C of
Nevada, Reno	Ghyman, Esther	Nevada, Reno	S California, U of	Ferrario, Larry S.	Cal S, Domngz	UC, Berkeley	Targoff, Ramie	Yale U
New Mexico, U of	Burkhalter, Nancy	Colorado, Denv	S California, U of	Hammond, Lynn	Golden Gate U	UC, Berkeley	Traister, Bryce	W Ontario-CAN
New Mexico, U of	Villa, Judith	Indiana U of PA	S Carolina, U of	Haughey, James	Cntrl Wesleyan	UC, Berkeley	van Court, Elisa Narin	Colby C
New School	Wagner, Constance	St Peter's C	S Carolina, U of	Hufnagel, Jill	Edinboro U	UC, Davis	Hoyer, Mark	S Dakota, U of
New York U	Abdoo, Sherlyn	St Peter's C	S Carolina, U of	Hynes, Jennifer	W Virginia U	UC, Irvine	Daigre, Victorine	Georgia Southern
New York U	Gregor, Roselyne	St Peter's C	S Carolina, U of	Martyniuk, Irene	Fitchburg S U	UC, Irvine	Pickitt, Todd	Biola U
New York U	Hesfird, Wendy Sue	Indiana, Blmngtn	S Carolina, U of	Smith, Ramdall	Nyack C	UC, Los Angeles	Bamberg, Betty	Cal S, LosAngls
New York U	White, Katheryn	St Peter's C	S Carolina, U of	Wilson, Carol	Wofford C	UC, Los Angeles	Blaine, Diana	N Texas, U of
New York U	Wondrich, F. David	St John's U	S Florida, U of	Brown, Stephen	Rollins C	UC, Los Angeles	Bower, Stephanie	Claremnt McKenna
Northeastern U	Semrow, Susan	Northeastern S U	S Florida, U of	Bunting, Ann	Henderson S U	UC, Los Angeles	Dodge, Georgina	Ohio S U
Northwestern U	Willey, Ann Elizabeth	Louisville, U of	S Florida, U of	Phillabaum, Sheri	Texas, Permian	UC, Los Angeles	Frost, Elisabeth	Fordham U
Notre Dame, U of	Archambeau, Robert	Lake Forest C	S Illinois U	Jones, Donald	Tri-State U	UC, Los Angeles	Martin, Jack	William & Mary
Ohio S U	Barnett, Timothy	Wittenberg U	S Missouri, U of	Zheng, Jianqing	MissippiValley	UC, Los Angeles	Ortiz, Richard	Dartmouth C
Ohio S U	Bowman, Rebecca	Otterbein C	San Diego S U	Karalis, Harriet Lee	American U	UC, San Diego	Boyd, Richard	San Diego S
Ohio S U	Chambers, Diane M.	Malone C	Stanford U	Alfano, Christine	Colorado, Denv	UC, San Diego	Cutler, Edward	Brighm Yng U
Ohio S U	Eisenstein, Paul	Otterbein C	Stanford U	Horvath, Richard P.	Fordham U	UC, San Diego	Dillon, Kimberley	Miami U, Oxford
Ohio S U	Greer, Jane	Missouri, KansC	Stanford U	Light, George E.	Mississippi S	UC, San Diego	Haywood, Chanta	Florida S U
Ohio S U	Hanstedt, Paul	Roanoke C	Stanford U	Mays, Kelly	New Mexico S U	UC, Santa Cruz	Whitson, Carolyn	Metropolitan S U
Ohio S U	Hogsette, D.	New York Tech, Wstbry	Stanford U	Teutsch-Dwyer, Marya	St Cloud S U	UC, St Barbara	Alvarez, Alma	S Oregon S C
Ohio S U	Mountford, Roxanne	Arizona, Tucson	Stanford U	Vanderborg, Susan	S Carolina,Clm	Utah, U of	Fitzgerald, Kathryn	Utah S U
Ohio U	Allen, Edward	S Dakota, U of	SUNY, Albany	Hewett, Greg	Wiscnsn, RiverF	Utah, U of	Gadeken, Sara	Texas Tech
Ohio U	Elliot, Rennae	Oakwood C	SUNY, Bngmtn	Covi, Giovanna	Trento-ITL	Vanderbilt U	Fesmire, Julia	Mdl Tennessee
Ohio U	Mayo, Wendall	Bowling Green S	SUNY, Bngmtn	Drake, Jennifer	Indiana S U	Vanderbilt U	Knadler, Stephen	Spelman C
Oklahoma, U of	Johnson, Frances	Rowan C	SUNY, Bngmtn	Howlett, Jeffrey	Nebraska, Kearney	Vermont C, Norwich	Connor, Joan	Ohio U
Oregon, U of	Piper, Karen	Missouri, Clmb	SUNY, Bngmtn	Sands, Peter	Maine, U of	Vermont C, Norwich	Kenna, Gail	American U
Oregon, U of	Wallerstein, Nicholas	Rockford C	SUNY, Bngmtn	Schaefer, Charles	Liberty U	Vermont C, Norwich	Sandlin, Lisa	Wayne S C
Oregon, U of	Yukman, Lidia	Pacific U	SUNY, Buffalo	Smith, Amy	Hilbert C	Virginia Tech	Moore, John	Purdue U
Penn S U	Bernstein, Susan	Shippensburg	SUNY, Buffalo	Valbuena, Olga L.	Wake Forest U	Virginia, U of	Beltwood, Scott	Emory & Henry C
Penn S U	Charles, Asselin	SE Louisiana U	SUNY, Buffalo	Zimmer, Joseph	Grand Valley S	Virginia, U of	Coldiron, Anne	Towson S U
Penn, U of	Eide, Marian	Texas A&M U	SUNY, Stny Brk	Rhodes, Winthrop	Colorado S U	Virginia, U of	Gustafson, Kevin	Texas Christian
Penn, U of	Noyes, Dorothy	Ohio S U	SW Louisiana	Bernard, Ernest	Louisiana C	Virginia, U of	Novak, Phillip	Colgate U
Penn, U of	Rudy, Mary	Chadron S C	SW Louisiana	Fallon, April	Lousiana, Btn Rge	Virginia, U of	Rody, Caroline	Virginia, U of
Penn, U of	Saeger, Jamey	Vassar C	SW Louisiana	Fleming, John	N Carolina,Wlmngtn	Virginia, U of	Sherer, Susan	Indiana U East
Penn, U of	Vrettos, Athena	Case Western Res	SW Louisiana	Larson, Leah Jean	Lady of the Lake U	W Virginia, U of	Dalporto, Jeanne	Charlstn, U of
Penn, U of	Waples, Tim	Davidson C	Syracuse U	Griner, Paul	Louisville, U of	Wake Forest U	Lee, Andrew	Lee C
Pittsburgh, U of	Galin, Jeffrey	Cal S, SnBrndno	Syracuse U	Zenowich, Christopher	Denison U	Washington S U	Gil-Gomez, Ellen	Russell Sage C
Pittsburgh, U of	Ross, Christine	UC, Irvine	Tennessee, Knox	Papa, Lee	Ball S U	Washington S U	Haswell, Janis	Texas A&M,CrpsC
Pittsburgh, U of	Tinkcom, Matthew	Georgetown U	Tennessee, Knox	Parkinson, Tracy	Lee C	Washington U	Esteve, Mary	Texas Christian
Princeton U	Barash, Carol	Seton Hall U	Tennessee, U of	Adkins, Jennifer	Marshall U	Washington U	Walter, Brian	U of the Ozarks
Princeton U	Brown, Sylvia	Alberta-CAN	Tennessee, U of	Ball, Melissa	Emory & Henry C	Washington, U of	Anger, Suzy	Maryland, BaltCnty
Princeton U	Churchill, Suzanne	Davidson C	Tennessee, U of	Curtis, David	Belmont U	Washington, U of	Brande, David	Illinois State
Princeton U	Conner, Marc	Washington&Lee	Texas A&M	Gaither, Kevin	Jarvis Christian C	Washington, U of	Bube, June	Seattle U
Princeton U	Fossett, Judith	S California, U of	Texas, Austin	Dobranski, Stephen	Georgia S U	Washington, U of	Christmas, Bill	San Francisco S U
Princeton U	Park, Hyungji	Union C (NY)	Texas, Austin	Kolko, Beth	Texas, Arlington	Washington, U of	Chuh, Kandice	Maryland, CollPk
Princeton U	Thomson, David	Texas, Arlington	Texas, Austin	Lenard, Mary	Alma C	Washington, U of	Hasseler, Terri	Bryant C
Purdue U	DeJoy, Nancy	Millikin U	Texas, Austin	Rothermel, Beth	Westfield S C	Washington, U of	Kendrick, Michelle	Washington S U
Purdue U	Hovde, Marjorie	IndianaPurdu,Ind	Texas, Austin	Rouzie, Albert	Ohio U	Washington, U of	Shiller, Dana	Evansville, U of
Purdue U	Langstraat, Lisa	Idaho S U	Texas, Austin	Steele, Karen	Texas Christian	Washington, U of	Shimakawa, Karen	Vanderbilt U
Purdue U	Parvin, Kathleen	Juniata C	Texas, Austin	Weeks, Denise	Weber S C	Washington, U of	Taylor, Marcy	Cntrl Michigan U
Purdue U	Sirabian, Robert	MissippiValley	Texas Tech	Morgan, Trevor	Howard Payne U	Washington, U of	Turely, Hans	Texas Tech
Purdue U	Toner, Lisa	Wheeling Jesuit	Texas Tech	Orbell, Branda	Arkansas, LtlRk	William & Mary	Ashe, Bertram	Holy Cross, C of
Rhode Island, U of	Mayberry, Bob	Grand Valley S	Trinity U	Chavez, Denise	New Mexico S U	William & Mary	Raney, David	W Georgia, S U of
Rhode Island, U of	Williamson, Judith	American U	Tufts U	Jones, Jill	Rollins C	Wiscnsn, Madsn	Harris, Ronald	SE Louisiana U
Rice U	Mintz, Susannah	Wittenberg U	Tufts U	Shankar, Lavina	Bates C	Wiscnsn, Madsn	McCabe, Tracy	Emerson C
Rice U	Sullivan, M. Nell	Houston, Dntn	Tulane U	Steward, Julie	Samford U	Wiscnsn, Madsn	Steinke, Jocelyn	W Michigan U
Rice U	Toombs, Veronica	Wittenberg U	Tulsa, U of	Meyers, Cherie	Oral Roberts U	Wiscnsn, Madsn	Strand, Sharon	Black Hills S
Rochester, U of	Anderson, Mark	Hobart/WmSmth	UC	MacComb, Debra	W Georgia, S U of	Wiscnsn, Milw	Belmont, Cynthia	Northland C
Rochester, U of	Stevens, Scott	Cal S, Fresno	UC, Berkeley	Berliner, Todd	N Carolina, Wlm	Wiscnsn, Milw	Callaway, Susan	St Thomas, U of
						Yale U	Anderson, Jennifer	Cal S, SnBrndno

TRAINED BY	NAME	HIRED BY
Yale U	Anderson, Randall	Lawrence U
Yale U	Goldsby, Jacqueline	Swarthmore C
Yale U	Hai, Ambreen	Smith C
Yale U	Hamilton, Ross	Barnard C
Yale U	Harries, Martin	Princeton U
Yale U	Oser, Lee	Millikin U
Yale U	Russell, Thomas	Tennessee Wesleyan
CAN-Alberta	Charles, May	Wheeling Jesuit
CAN-Br Columbia	Mellow, J. Dean	N Arizona U
CAN-Dalhousie	McAdam, R. Ian	Lethbridge-CAN
CAN-McGill	Barsky, Robert	W Ontario-CAN
CAN-McMaster	Zackodnik, Teresa	Alberta-CAN
CAN-Queen's	McNeilly, Kevin	Br Columbia-CAN
CAN-Queen's	Stewart, Anthony	Dalhousie-CAN
CAN-Toronto	Caldwell, Tanya	Georgia S U
CAN-Toronto	Powell, Stephen	Texas Christian
CAN-W Ontario	Lingard, John	Cape Breton-CAN
FRN-Paris, U of	Christophe, Michel	Maryland EShore
FRN-Paris, U of	Tall, Sonia	Roosevelt U
IND-Punjabi	Gulshan, Rima	Maryland EShore
NIG-Ibadan	Laoye, G. Oty	Gettysburg C
SPN-Toledo	Filetti, Jean	ChrstphrNewport
UK-Birmingham	Vince-Howard, Alycia	Berea C
UK-Cambridge	Harrison, Carey	CUNY, Brooklyn
UK-Cambridge	Li, Hao	Alberta-CAN
UK-East Anglia	Freidin, Deborah	Marshall U
UK-Kent	Gregg, Veronica	Colgate U
UK-Oxford	Eltis, Sos	Boston U
UK-Oxford	Higgins, Geraldine	Emory U
UK-York	Khanna, Ranjana	Washington, U of

FRENCH/ITALIAN LANG & LIT

TRAINED BY	NAME	HIRED BY
Brown U	Strazzeri, Guiseppe	Seton Hall U
Chicago, U of	Maggi, Armando	Penn, U of
Cincinnati, U of	Pfenninger, Ariane	New Jersey, C of
Columbia U	Etienne, Isabelle	Barnard C
Columbia U	Schulman, Peter	Old Dominion U
Connecticut, U of	Galluci, Carole	William & Mary
Cornell U	Malena, Anne	Alberta-CAN
CUNY	Hayes, Jarrod L.	Michigan, U of
Duke U	Levy, Gayle	Missouri, KansC
Duke U	Spires, Margaret	Millikin U
Emory U	Hinds, Leonard D.	Indiana, Blmngtn
Florida S U	Brown, Carol	Penn S U
Florida, U of	Ayoun, Dalila	Arizona, Tucson
Harvard U	Frank, Claudine	Barnard C
Harvard U	Mormando, Franco	Boston C
Indiana U	Murchison, Nancy	Dallas, U of
Kansas, U of	Imhoff, Guy	Hampden-Sydny
Kansas, U of	Tonen, Frederick	Ohio U
Kentucky, U of	Harrison, Lucia	SE Louisiana U
Louisiana S U	Loichot, Valerie	Washington C
Louisiana S U	Pallez, Frederic	SE Louisiana U
Maryland, U of	Crosley, Bernadette	Distrct Columbia
Michigan, U of	Bordean, Catherine	Lyon C
Michigan, U of	Von Flotow, Luise	Ottawa-CAN
Minnesota, U of	Frindethie, K. Martial	Maryland, CollPk
N Carolina, ChpH	De Pree, Julia	Agnes Scott C
N Carolina, ChpH	Fregnac-Clave, F.	Washington&Lee
New York U	Baehler, Aline	Vanderbilt U
New York U	Curran, Andrew	Union C (NY)
New York U	Gosnell, Jonathan	Smith C
New York U	Ingram, Mark	Goucher C
Northwestern U	Holmes, Olivia	Yale U
Ohio S U	Spoiden, Stephane	Michigan, Drbrn

TRAINED BY	NAME	HIRED BY
Oregon, U of	Fleshman, Sherrie	N Dakota, U of
Oregon, U of	Hess, Erika	Rust C
Oregon, U of	Lifongo, Vetinde	Lawrence U
Oregon, U of	Pactat, Michel	Miami U, Oxford
Penn S U	Burnett, Joanne E.	S Mississippi,U of
Penn, U of	Allen, Anthony	Ohio S U
Penn, U of	Carden, Sally Tartline	Missouri,U of
Penn, U of	Descas, Marie-Jo	Monmouth C
Penn, U of	Paige, Nicholas	UC, Berkeley
Penn, U of	Palacio, Eric	S Florida, U of
Penn, U of	Solomon, Julie	Texas Christian
Princeton U	Bamps, Yvan	Emory U
Princeton U	Santoro, Milena	Georgetown U
Princeton U	Sanyal, Debarati	Yale U
Purdue U	Allen, Linda	Missouri, St L
Rutgers U	Picarazzi, Teresa	Arizona, Tucson
Stanford U	Paoli, David	Dickinson C
Stanford U	Rhyue, Robert	SW Louisiana
Stanford U	Stampnino, Maria	Miami, U of
Texas, Austin	Ghillebaert, François	Texas, Austin
Texas, Austin	Khorrami, M.	Monterey Inst Int'l
Texas, Austin	Porcello, Valerie	Susquehanna U
Texas, Austin	Whittaker, Odile	Southwestern U
Tulane U	Silver, Susan	Smith C
UC, Berkeley	Frisch, Andrea	Colorado, Bldr
UC, Berkeley	Riley, Patrick	Oklahoma, U of
UC, Davis	Alalou, Ali	Columbia U
UC, Los Angeles	Baldi, Andrea	Rutgers, NBruns
Vanderbilt U	Brooks, Amanda	Miami, U of
Washington, U of	Mazzola, Claudio	Holy Cross, C of
Wiscnsn, Madsn	Krause, Virginia	Brown U
Wiscnsn, U of	Olson, Linda	S Connecticut
Yale U	Lehmann, Anna	Barnard C
Yale U	Ricciardi, Alessia	Colorado, Bldr
Yale U	Thomas, Dominic	Notre Dame,U of
CAN-Montreal	Gural-Migdal, Anna	Alberta-CAN
CAN-Montreal	Mopoho, Raymond	Dalhousie-CAN
CAN-Montreal	Nzabatsinda, Anthere	Vanderbilt U
CAN-Toronto	Heap, David	W Ontario-CAN
CAN-Toronto	Nadasdi, Terry	Alberta-CAN
FRN-Nantes	Kabia, Mahamed	Distrct Columbia
FRN-Paris, U of	Le Calvez, Eric	Georgia S U
SWT-Geneva	Elslande, Jean-Pierre	Washington, U of
UK-Kings	Siebelman, Simon	Shippensburg

GEOGRAPHY

TRAINED BY	NAME	HIRED BY
Arizona S U	Blake, Kevin	Wyoming, U of
Arizona S U	Lines, Lee	Rollins C
Boston U	Azary, Irisita G.	UC
Boston U	Schaaf, Crystal	Boston U
Carleton C	Moorman, Brian	Calgary-CAN
Clark U	Dow, Kristin	S Carolina, Clm
Clark U	Gilbert, Melissa	Temple U
Clark U	Hartwick, Elaine	Cntrl Connecticut S U
Clark U	Kyem, Peter	Florida, U of
Clark U	Mattingly, Doreen	San Diego S
Clark U	Mitchell, Jeffrey	Clark U
Clark U	Robbins, Paul	Iowa, U of
Clark U	Roth, Linda	Kentucky, U of
Clark U	Savage, Lydia	S Maine, U of
Clark U	Steinberg, Philip	Bucknell U
Clark U	Theyel, Gregory	New Hmpshire, U of
Clark U	Young, Stephen	Salem S U
Cornell U	Smith, Laurence	UC, Los Angeles
Denver, U of	Marr, Paul	Shippensburg
Emporia S U	Fraser, Rolland	W Michigan U

TRAINED BY	NAME	HIRED BY
Georgia, U of	Gong, Hongmian	Fort Hays S U
Georgia, U of	Luo, Yu	Indiana S U
Idaho, U of	Couch, Samuel	Dickinson S
Idaho, U of	Haddock, Gregory	NW Missouri S
Illinois, Urbana	Montagu, A. Simon	Miami U, Oxford
Indiana U	Lorah, Paul	St Thomas, U of
Kent S U	Edgell, Dennis	N Carolina, Pembroke
Louisiana S U	Qiu, Hong-Lie	Cal S, LosAngls
Mass, U of	Kotval, Zenia Z.	Michigan S U
Michigan S U	Bierly, Gregory	Indiana S U
Michigan S U	Fischer, Julie	W Michigan U
Minnesota, U of	Kinman, Edward	Missouri, Clmb
Minnesota, U of	Lockwood, Catherine	Chadron S C
Minnesota, U of	Wyly, Elvin	Rutgers, NBruns
N Carolina, U of	Allen, Thomas	Old Dominion U
N Carolina, U of	Patrick, Kevin	Indiana U of PA
Nevada, Reno	Burbey, Thomas	Virginia Tech
NW Missouri S	Bradley, Jeffrey	NW Missouri S
Ohio S U	Wang, Fahui	N Illinois U
Oklahoma, U of	Stradford, Todd	Wiscnsn, Platv
Purdue U	Andresen, Jeffrey A.	Michigan S U
Purdue U	Lehman, Jeffrey	Otterbein C
Rutgers U	Johns, Rebecca	S Florida, U of
Rutgers U	Millar, Susan	Cntrl Connecticut
Rutgers U	Tuason, Julie	SW Texas U
S Carolina, U of	Hodgson, Michael	S Carolina, Clm
S Carolina, U of	Nelson, Elisabeth	San Diego S
SUNY, Buffalo	Li, Gang (Gary)	Cal S U, Hayward
Tennessee, U of	Benhart, John	Indiana U of PA
Texas A&M	Anderson, Timothy	Ohio U
Texas A&M	Ridenour, Gregory	Austin Peay S
Texas, Austin	Pittman, Jeffrey	Colorado, Denv
Texas, Austin	Reese, Joseph	NW Missouri S
UC	Dezzani, Raymond	Boston U
UC, Berkeley	Aoyama, Yuko	Georgia, U of
UC, Berkeley	Hsing, You-Tien	Br Columbia-CAN
UC, Berkeley	Mutersbaugh, Tad	Iowa, U of
UC, Berkeley	Suryanata, Krisnawati	Colorado, Denv
UC, Davis	Lescinsky, Halard	Otterbein C
Utah, U of	Lupo, Karen	N Texas, U of
Virginia Tech	Munn, Barbara	Shippensburg
Washington, U of	Delaney, Edward	N Michigan U
Washington, U of	Harvey, Francis	Ecole Poly Federal-SWT
Washington, U of	Krishnasamy, R.	Singapore Nat'l-SNGP
Washington, U of	Oakes, Timothy	Colorado, Bldr
Washington, U of	Zaslavsky, Ilya	W Michigan U
Wiscnsn, Madsn	Anderton, John	N Dakota, U of
Wiscnsn, Madsn	Hoelscher, Steven	LSU, BatnRoug
Wiscnsn, Madsn	Till, Karen	LSU, BatnRoug
Wyoming, U of	Leite, Michael	Chadron S C
CAN-Br Columbia	Hole, John	Virginia Tech
CAN-Calgary	Townshend, Ivan	Lethbridge-CAN
CAN-McGill	Dupigny-Giroux,Lesley	Illinois, Edwrds
CAN-McMaster	Woudsma, Clarence	Calgary-CAN
CAN-Saskatchewan	Saku, James	Frostburg S U
CAN-Sherbrooke	Hall-Beyer, Mrya	Calgary-CAN
CAN-Toronto	Boone, Christopher	Cal S, LosAngls
CAN-Waterloo	Dallen, Timothy	Connecticut S U
CAN-Waterloo	Peddle, Derek	Lethbridge-CAN
CAN-Waterloo	Timothy, Dallen	Cntrl Connecticut
CIS-HydrologicalInst	Lapenis, Andrei	SUNY, Albany
CIS-Tbilisi	Knjazihhin, Juri	Boston U

TRAINED BY	NAME	HIRED BY	TRAINED BY	NAME	HIRED BY	TRAINED BY	NAME	HIRED BY
UK-Edinburgh	Xu, Hui	Frostburg S U	Carnegie Mellon	Miller, Montserrat	Marshall U	Harvard U	Tsang, Carol	Illinois, Chicago
UK-Leeds	Gahbauer, Mary	Otterbein C	Carnegie Mellon	Szylvian, Kristin	W Michigan U	Hawaii, U of	Jin, Qiu	Old Dominion U
UK-London Sch Eco	Lee, Michael	Cal S U, Hayward	Chicago, U of	Andrews, James	Connecticut, U of	Illinois, Chicago	Bucur-Deckard, Maria	Indiana, Blmngtn
			Chicago, U of	Armstrong, Charles	Columbia U	Illinois, Urbana	Coleman, David	Minnsota, Dlth
GERMAN LANG & LIT			Chicago, U of	Aso, Noriko	Portland S U	Illinois, Urbana	Guelcher, Gregory	Morningside C
Cincinnati, U of	Coury, David	Wiscnsn, GrnB	Chicago, U of	Bliss, Katherine	Mass, Amherst	Illinois, Urbana	Wigginton, Russell	Rhodes C
Cincinnati, U of	De Vries, Jr., H.	Connecticut, U of	Chicago, U of	Calder, Lendol	Augustana C (IL)	Indiana U	Black, Thomas C.	Washington C
Cincinnati, U of	Weirick, Allen	Georgia, U of	Chicago, U of	Ebersale, Gary	Missouri, KansC	Indiana U	Chapell, John	Webster U
Illinois, Urbana	Boniger, Marianne	Kenyon C	Chicago, U of	Eghigian, Greg	Texas, Arlington	Indiana U	Green, Kathryn	Cal S, SnBrndno
Johns Hopkins	Breithaupt, Fritz	Indiana, Blmngtn	Chicago, U of	Martin, Terry	Calgary-CAN	Indiana U	Hanson, Randy	Colby-Sawyer C
Mass, Amherst	McLary, Laura	Mississippi, U of	Chicago, U of	Schultz, Mark	Lewis U	Indiana U	Hudson, Lynn	Cal Polytech
Mass, U of	Herrman, Mareike	RandlphMacon	Claremont Grad	Garcia, Matthew	Illinois, Urbana	Indiana U	Jacobs, Nancy	Brown U
Mass, U of	von Held, Kristina	Smith C	Colorado, U of	Thoma, Pamela	Colby C	Indiana U	Sunderland, Willard	Cincinnati, U of
Michigan, U of	Blickle, Peter	W Michigan U	Columbia U	Ben-Atar, Doron	Fordham U	Iowa, U of	Arrow, David	Dayton, U of
Michigan, U of	Brueggeman, Aminia	Old Dominion U	Columbia U	Dallek, Robert	Boston U	Iowa, U of	Bonakdarian, Mansour	Arizona S West
Minnesota, U of	Goblirsch, Kurt	S Carolina, Clm	Columbia U	Dobson, Sean	Portland S U	Iowa, U of	Bucklin, Steven	S Dakota, U of
Minnesota, U of	Thorson, Helga	Arkansas, LtlRk	Columbia U	Henry, Sarah	Union C (NY)	Iowa, U of	Child, Brenda	Minnsota, TwnC
Minnesota, U of	Zinn, Gesa	Louisville, U of	Columbia U	Holquist, Peter	Cornell U	Iowa, U of	Darrow, David	Dayton, U of
Oregon, U of	Witthoeft, Heide	Virginia Tech	Columbia U	King, Jeremy	Mt Holyoke C	Iowa, U of	Deslippe, Dennis	Shippensburg
Penn, U of	Appl, Cynthia	Baker C	Columbia U	Simoncini, Gabriele	Pace, WhitePl	Iowa, U of	Despille, Dennis	Australian Nat'l-ASL
Penn, U of	Bryant, Keri	Murray S U	Columbia U	Thompson, Elizabeth	Virginia, U of	Iowa, U of	Groch, John	Pittsburgh, U of
Penn, U of	Miller, Vincent	N Mexico S U	Columbia U	Wiese, Andrew	San Diego S	Iowa, U of	Gutjahr, Paul	Indiana U
Penn, U of	Spreizer, Christine	Queens C	Cornell U	Amoroso, Donna	Wright S U	Iowa, U of	Halverson, James	Judson C
Penn, U of	Wagner, Lori	Lehigh U	Cornell U	Campt, Tina	UC, St Cruz	Iowa, U of	Handy-Marcello, B.	N Dakota, U of
Princeton U	Richter, Gerhard	Wiscnsn, Madsn	Cornell U	Crowston, Clare	Illinois, Urbana	Iowa, U of	Kilroy, David	Wheeling Jesuit
Texas, Austin	Bokel, Franz	Centre C	Cornell U	Doyle, Michael W.	Ball S U	Iowa, U of	Moten, Derryn	Alabama S U
Texas, Austin	Ehrstine, Glenn	Iowa, U of	Cornell U	Geibel, Christoph	Mississippi S U	Iowa, U of	Neilson, Kim	Macalester C
Texas, Austin	Moyer, Alene	Georgetown U	Cornell U	Gidlow, Liette	Hobart/WmSmth	Iowa, U of	Otterness, Philip	Warren Sillson C
Texas, Austin	Schwink, Frederick	Illinois, Urbana	Cornell U	Giebel, Christoph J.F.	Mississippi S	Iowa, U of	Porter, Kimberly	N Dakota, U of
UC, Berkeley	Nenno, Nancy	Wellesley C	Cornell U	Lanza, Janine	Appalachian S	Iowa, U of	Quiroz, Anthony	TexasA&M, CrpsC
UC, Berkeley	Tobias, Rochelle	Johns Hopkins	Cornell U	Lu, Yan	New Hmpshre, U of	Iowa, U of	Roberton, Natalie	Prairie View U
UC, Los Angeles	Burt, Raymond	N Carolina, Wlm	Cornell U	Matt, Susan	Clark U	Iowa, U of	Strayer-Jones, Jennifer	S E Missouri S
UC, Los Angeles	Eidecker, Martina	Georgia S U	Cornell U	Montgomery, Charles	Florida, Gnsvl	Iowa, U of	Tumn, Nancy	Wiscnsn, U of
UC, Los Angeles	Lashgari, Mahafarid	Haverford C	Cornell U	Oropeza, Lorena	UC, Davis	Iowa, U of	Turner, Nancy	Wiscnsn, Plattv
UC, Los Angeles	Sazaki, Kristina	Holy Cross, C of	Cornell U	Robinson, Geoffrey	UC, Los Angeles	Johns Hopkins	Giles-Vernick, Tamara	Virginia, U of
UC, San Diego	Fischer, Barbara	Samford U	Cornell U	Sims, Amy	Golden Gate U	Johns Hopkins	Graham, Lisa	Haverford C
Utah, U of	Yang, Peter	Case Western Res	Cornell U	Zinoman, Peter	UC, Berkeley	Johns Hopkins	Marion, Rene S.	Ball S U
Washington U	Baer, Gregory	Carthage C	CUNY	McCrie, Robert Delbert	CUNY	Johns Hopkins	Parker, Alison	Texas, Arlington
Washington U	Grair, Charles	Texas Tech	CUNY	Sample, Dana Lynn	Hampton U	Johns Hopkins	Rabuzzi, Daniel	Luther C
Washington U	Nathenson, Cary	Grinnell C	Delaware, U of	Specht, Neva	Appalachian S	Johns Hopkins	Roorda, Eric	Bellarmine C
Wiscnsn, U of	Kagel, Martin	Georgia, U of	Duke U	Celenza, Christophe	Michigan S U	Johns Hopkins	Zelizer, Julian	SUNY, Albany
Yale U	Olson, Laura	Colorado, Bldr	Duke U	Higham, Carol	Texas A&M U	Kansas S U	Rook, Robert	Fort Hays S U
			Duke U	Price, Wendy L.	Mary Washngtn C	Kansas, U of	Rome, Adam	Penn S U
CAN-Br Columbia	Hirata, Hosea	Tufts U	Emory U	Crawford, Vicki	W Georgia, S U of	Kentucky, U of	Glover, Loori	Otterbein C
GER-Munich	Gobig, Michaela	NW Missouri S	Emory U	Rodrigue, John	LSU, BatnRoug	Louisiana S U	Nicassio, Susan	SW Louisiana
			Emory U	Sandlund, Vivien	Hiram C	Loyola, Chicago	Candy, Catherine	Gonzaga U
HISTORY/AMERICAN STUDIES			Florida S U	Alvarez, Jose	Houston, Dntn	Mass. Amherst	Field, Gregory	Michigan, Drbrn
Arizona S U	Bales, Rebecca	SUNY, Oswego	Florida S U	Cain, Alana	Morehead S U	Miami, U of	Fernandez, Elisa	Louisville, U of
Arizona, U of	Smith, Phyllis	Mars Hill C	Florida S U	Dunn, John	Valdosta S U	Miami, U of	Metallo, Thomas	Oral Roberts U
Auburn U	Rieff, Lynne	N Alabama, U of	Florida S U	Fai-Podlipnik, Judith	SE Louisiana U	Miami, U of	Penry, Sarah	New Mexico S U
Boston C	Norris, Janice	St Norbert C	Florida S U	O'Neill, Mark	Auburn U	Miami U, Oxford	Calvert, Kenneth	Hillsdale C
Boston U	McGrath, John	Boston U	Florida S U	Riordan, Patrick	Middlesex U-UK	Miami U, Oxford	Eaker, Susan A.	Morehouse U
Boston U	McIntyre, Sheila	Boston U	Florida S U	Smith, Douglas	Naval War C	Miami U, Oxford	Wineland, John	Roanoke Bible C
Boston U	Mitchel, Maria	Franklin & Marshall	Florida, U of	Bushnell, Amy	Charleston, C of	Michigan S U	Cheeseboro, A.	S Illinois, Edwrds
Boston U	Wolde Mariam, T.	Addis Abba-ETHIO	Florida, U of	Cole, Stephanie	Texas, Arlington	Michigan S U	Griffin, Junius	Emory & Henry C
Bowling Green S	Allison, William	Bowling Green S U	Florida, U of	Horn, Randolph	Samford U	Michigan S U	Pierce, Richard	Notre Dame, U of
Bowling Green S	Saddington, James	Taylor U	Fordham U	Bellitto, Christopher	St Joseph's Sem	Michigan, U of	Bachin, Robin	Miami, U of
Brandeis U	Connolly, James J.	Ball S U	Georgetown U	Phillips, Steven	Gettysburg C	Michigan, U of	Balaghi, Shiva	Vermont, U of
Brandeis U	Hametz, Maura	Old Dominion U	Georgetown U	Smith, Michael	Purdue U	Michigan, U of	Ener, Mine	Villanova C
Brandeis U	Pleck, Elizabeth	Illinois, Urbana	Georgia, U of	Bryant, Jonathan	Georgia Southern	Michigan, U of	Frazier, Lessie Jo	S Carolina, Clm
Brandeis U	Schen, Claire S.	Wake Forest U	Harvard U	Brennan, James	UC, Riverside	Michigan, U of	Hickey, Georgina	Georgia Southern
Brown U	Douglas, Raymond	Colgate U	Harvard U	Brown, Thomas	S Carolina, Clm	Michigan, U of	Kwass, Michael	Georgia, U of
Brown U	Drell, Joanna	Colgate U	Harvard U	Heretz, Leonid	Bridgewater S	Michigan, U of	Kwass, Michael Alan	Yale U
Brown U	McCleary, Ann	W Georgia, S U of	Harvard U	Kaplan, Benjamin	Iowa, U of	Michigan, U of	Samantrai, Ranu	Claremont Grad
Carnegie Mellon	Cole, Lori	Drake U	Harvard U	Martin, Russell E.	Westminster (PA)			
			Harvard U	Schechter, Ronald	William & Mary			
			Harvard U	Schmidt, Benjamin	Washington, U of			

TRAINED BY	NAME	HIRED BY	TRAINED BY	NAME	HIRED BY	TRAINED BY	NAME	HIRED BY
Michigan, U of	Schafer, Daniel	Belmont U	Stanford U	McKittrick, Meredith	Georgetown U	CAN-Toronto	Beattie, Blake	Louisville, U of
Michigan, U of	Walker, Barbara	Nevada, Reno	Stanford U	Millward, James A.	Georgetown U	CAN-Toronto	Jurkowitz, Edward	Illinois, Chicago
Minnesota, U of	Buff, Rachel	Bowling Green S	Stanford U	Romano, Renee	Wesleyan U	CAN-Toronto	Kolbaba, Tia	Princeton U
Minnesota, U of	Diaz, Arlene	Indiana, Blmngtn	SUNY	Mendez, Cecilia	UC, St Barbara	CAN-Toronto	Traver, Andrew	SE Louisiana U
Minnesota, U of	Wimmer, Linda	Bridgewater S	SUNY, Bngmtn	Babbitt, Kathleen	St Lawrence U	CAN-York	Holman, Andrew	Bridgewater S
MIT	Mindell, David	MIT	SUNY, Bngmtn	Bates, Anna	Loras C	FRN-Paris, U of	Bernault, Florence	Wiscnsn, Madsn
MIT	Wang, Jessica	UC, Los Angeles	SUNY, Bngmtn	Boisseau, Tracey	Mass Col Art	FRN-Paris, U of	Reeves, Caroline	Williams C
N Carolina, ChpH	Dollard, Catherine L.	Denison U	Temple U	Ott, Katherine	American U	GER-Munich	Palmie, Stephan	Maryland, CollPk
N Carolina, ChpH	Goda, Norman	Ohio U	Tennessee, U of	Morrow, Diane	Georgia, U of	UK-Cambridge	Botelho, Lynn	Indiana U of PA
N Carolina, ChpH	Philyaw, Scott	W Carolina U	Texas A&M	Duffy, Stephen	TexasA&M,CrpsC	UK-Cambridge	Hall, Jonathan	Chicago, U of
N Carolina, ChpH	Thurber, Timothy	SUNY, Oswego	Texas A&M	Huckemer, Curt	S Dakota, U of	UK-Cambridge	Weiland, David J.	Utah S U
N Carolina, Grns	Pennell, Myra	Appalachian S	Texas A&M	Johnston, Janice	W Texas A&M	UK-London, U of	Devereux, David R.	Canisius C
N Carolina, U of	Bergen, Doris	Notre Dame, U of	Texas, Austin	Hiltpold, Paul	Cal Polytech	UK-London, U of	MacKinnon, Aran	W Georgia, S U of
N Carolina, U of	Hayse, Michael	Stockton S C	Texas, Austin	Hosmer, Brian	Wyoming, U of	UK-Warwick	Rozario, Kevin	Wellesley C
New Mexico, U of	Hunner, Jon	New Mexico S U	Texas, Austin	LaWare, David	Houston, ClrLk			
New Mexico, U of	Pasztor, Suzanne	Pacific, U of the	Texas Christian	Stroud, Jackie	Winona S U	**LANGS & LITS, OTHER**		
New York U	Tang, Edward	Colgate U	Tulane U	Pattridge, Blake	Babson C	Cal S, Nrthrdg	Cagle, Keith	Gardner-Webb C
New York U	Thompson, Christopher S.	Ball S U	Tulane U	Stricklin, David	Lyon C	Florida, U of	McGarry, Richard	Appalachian S
Northwestern U	Shannon, Timothy	Gettysburg C	UC, Berkeley	Benson, Carlton	PacificLutheran	Harvard U	Gruendler, Beatrice	Yale U
Notre Dame, U of	Rinderle, Walter	S Indiana, U of	UC, Berkeley	Cody, Lisa	ClaremntMcKenna	Illinois, U of	del Carmen Faccini, Maria	Utah S U
Notre Dame, U of	Wigger, John	Missouri, Clmb	UC, Berkeley	Geraci, Robert	Virginia, U of	Mass, Amherst	Fidalgo, Reyes	Mass, Boston
Ohio S U	Anderson, Carol	Missouri, Clmb	UC, Berkeley	Grayzel, Susan	Mississippi, U of	Ohio S U	Bosnakis, Panayiotis	Missouri, St L
Ohio S U	Damms, Richard V.	Mississippi S	UC, Berkeley	Julian, Catherine	W Michigan U	UC, Berkeley	Kleeman, Faye	William & Mary
Ohio S U	Feis, William	Buena Vista U	UC, Berkeley	Steinberg, Mark	Illinois, Urbana	UC, Berkeley	Kleeman, Terry	William & Mary
Oklahoma, U of	Kneeland, Timothy	Greenville C	UC, Berkeley	Weston, Timothy	Colorado, Bldr	UC, San Diego	Martinez-Gutierrez, Maria	Cal S, Fresno
Oregon, U of	Birsch, Douglas	Shippensburg	UC, Los Angeles	Feczor-Stewart, B.	Arizona S West	Washington, U of	Sands, Tracey	Augustana C (IL)
Oregon, U of	Hertzel, David	SW Oklahoma S	UC, Los Angeles	Johansen, Shawn	Frostburg S U	Wiscnsn, Madsn	Hintz, Ernest	Fort Hays S U
Penn S U	Domino, Brian	E Michigan U	UC, Los Angeles	Kim, Mi Gyung	N Carolina S U	Yale U	Erasmo, Mario	Wellesley C
Penn, U of	Adderly, L. Roseanne	Tulane U	UC, Los Angeles	Latham, Michael	Fordham U			
Penn, U of	Joshi, Sanjay	N Arizona U	UC, Los Angeles	Winer, Rebecca	Villanova U	**LINGUISTICS**		
Penn, U of	Lawrence, David	Arizona S West	UC, Riverside	Laing, Annette	Georgia Southern	Cornell U	Rubin, Edward	Utah, U of
Penn, U of	Lockenour, Jay	Temple U	UC, San Diego	Barrera, Catherine	Gustavus Adolph	Cornell U	Takahashi, Chioko	Yale U
Penn, U of	Page, Max	Georgia S U	UC, St Barbara	Huneycutt, Lois	Missouri, Clmb	CUNY	Utakis, Sharon L.	North Adams S
Penn, U of	Schenk, Ingrid	Georgia S U	Utah, U of	Mills, David	Marshall U	Florida S U	Maurice, Keith	Colorado, Bldr
Penn, U of	Schrader, Abby	Franklin & Marshall	Utah, U of	Ore, Janet	Colorado S U	Florida S U	Sims, James M.	Tunghai-TAIW
Penn, U of	Schulten, Susan	Denver, U of	Vanderbilt U	Lay, Shawn	Coker C	Harvard U	Jonas, Diane	Yale U
Princeton U	Akarli, Engin	Brown U	Vanderbilt U	Williams, James	Mdl Tennessee	Maryland, U of	Thompson, Ellen	Puerto Rico, U of
Princeton U	Baun, Jane	New York U	Virginia, U of	Guest, Karen	Georgetown C	Mass, Amherst	Benua, Laura	Maryland, CollPk
Princeton U	Bell, David	Johns Hopkins	Virginia, U of	Mutongi, Kenda	Williams C	MIT	Noyer, Rolf	Penn, U of
Princeton U	Dain, Bruce	Wyoming, U of	W Virginia, U of	Drobney, Jeffery	Youngstown S	MIT	Schutze, Carson	UC, Los Angeles
Princeton U	Forsyth, Douglas	Bowling Green S	Washington U	Madison, Julian	Youngstown S	MIT	Truckenbrodt, Hubert	Rutgers, NBruns
Princeton U	Gregg, Robert	Stockton S C	William & Mary	Boulton, Alek	Villa Julie C	Ohio S U	Lasersohn, Peter	Illinois, Urbana
Princeton U	Hamdani, Sumaiya A.	George Mason U	William & Mary	Hagedorn, Nancy	St John's U	Penn, U of	DeGraff, Michael	MIT
Princeton U	LeGall, Dina	Rutgers, NBruns	William & Mary	Johansen, Mary Carroll	Appalachian S	Rutgers U	Burton, Strang	Br Columbia
Princeton U	Porter, Susie	Utah, U of	Wiscnsn, Madsn	Cruikshank, Bruce	Hastings C	Rutgers U	Samek-Ludovici, Vieri	Konstanz-GER
Princeton U	Robinson, David	Colgate U	Wiscnsn, Madsn	Figueroa, Luis	Trinity C (CT)	Rutgers U	Sharvit, Yael	Pennsylvania, U of
Rice U	Frost, Ginger	Samford U	Wiscnsn, Madsn	Grant, Jonathan	Florida S U	S California, U of	Sanchez, Lilliana	Carnegie Mellon
Rice U	Klein, Joanne	Salem C	Wiscnsn, Madsn	Lindsay, James	Colorado S U	Stanford U	Blake, Renee	New York U
Rutgers U	Frederickson, Kair	Central Fl, U of	Wiscnsn, Madsn	Shariff, Ayesha	Smith C	Texas, Austin	Aceto, Michael	P Rico, U of
Rutgers U	Helstosky, Carol	Penn, U of	Wiscnsn, Madsn	Thomson, Sinclair	New York U	Texas, Austin	Carleton, Troi	San Francisco S U
Rutgers U	Hoffman, Beatrice	N Illinois U	Wiscnsn, U of	Brown, Kathleen	Penn, U of	Texas, Austin	Elorrieta, Jabier	Texas, Austin
Rutgers U	Kaufman, Suzanne	Miami U	Yale U	Biddle, Tami D.	Duke U	Texas, Austin	Queen, Robin	Kent S U
Rutgers U	McCarthy, Maureen	St Anselm's U	Yale U	Gedge, Karin	E Michigan U	Texas, U of	Gess, Randall	Utah, U of
Rutgers U	Reeder, Linda	Missouri, Clmb	Yale U	Hitchcock, William I.	Yale U	UC, Berkeley	Childs, George	Portland S U
Rutgers U	Sandage, Scott	Carnegie Mellon	Yale U	Johnson, Susan	Colorado, Bldr	UC, Berkeley	Cotter, Colleen M.	Georgetown U
Rutgers U	Whitney, Susan	Carleton-CAN	Yale U	Klubock, Thomas	Ohio S U	UC, Berkeley	Macaulay, Monica Ann	Wiscnsn, Madsn
S California, U of	Koos, Cheryl	La Sierra U	Yale U	Lepore, Jill	Boston U	UC, Berkeley	Zoll, Cheryl	MIT
S California, U of	Mahar, Karen	TexasA&M,CrpsC	Yale U	Lipton, Sara	William & Mary	UC, Los Angeles	Dart, Sarah	Macalester C
S Carolina, U of	Smith, Mark	S Carolina, Clm	Yale U	Lyons, Clare	Maryland, CollPk	UC, Los Angeles	Golston, Chris	Cal S, Fresno
S Indiana, U of	Alonzo, Armando	Texas A&M U	Yale U	McFadden, Margarert	Colby C	CAN-Carleton	Taylor, Shelley	Utah, U of
S Indiana, U of	Wood, William	Pt Loma Nazrn	Yale U	Phillips, Kimberly	William & Mary	CAN-Toronto	So, Sufumi	Carnegie Mellon
St John's, U of	Cadigan, Sean	Dalhousie-CAN	Yale U	Ramos, Raul	Utah, U of			
St Louis U	Chapman, Grant	Webster U	Yale U	Rubin, Rachel	Mass, Boston	**MUSIC**		
St Mary's U Law	Arrick-Kruger, Theressa	Winona S U	Yale U	Stoll, Steven B.	Yale U	Abilene Christian	Tolosa, Gustavo	Eastman Sch Music
Stanford U	Bronstein, Jamie	New Mexico S U	Yale U	Waldstreicher, David	Yale U	Alabama, U of	Douglas-Brown, D.	N Alabama, U of
Stanford U	Eskildsen, Robert	Smith C	Yale U	Wickberg, Daniel	Texas, Dallas			
Stanford U	Mayhall, Laura M.	Catholic U Amer						

TRAINED BY	NAME	HIRED BY
Alabama, U of	Orman, Evelyn K.	George Mason U
Alabama, U of	Scheib, Joy	Wiscnsn, RiverF
Arizona S U	Hansen, Deborah	Whitworth C
Arizona, U of	Boers, P. Geoffrey	Washington, U of
Arizona, U of	Burns, Kimberly J.	Ball S U
Arizona, U of	Clauter, Nancy	Luther C
Arizona, U of	Hughes, Thomas	Texas Tech
Austin S U	Brumfield, Susan	Texas Tech
Ball S U	Clarke, Steven	Bethany Bible C-
Ball S U	Creasap, Susan	Moorehead S U
Ball S U	Harris, Kristine	Ozarks, C of
Ball S U	Hendericks, Steven	Bemidji S U
Ball S U	Innis, Joy	Banff Cntr for Arts-CAN
Ball S U	Locke, Scott	Murray S U
Ball S U	Rediger, JoAnn	Taylor U
Ball S U	Sadler, Judy	Northwest Nazarene
Ball S U	Shannon, A.	Banff Cntr for Arts-CAN
Brigham Young U	Belnap, Michael Keith	Indiana, Blmngtn
Catholic U Amer	Griggs, Patricia	Shenandoah U
Catholic U Amer	Hawkins, Scott	Shenandoah U
Catholic U Amer	Holt, Joseph	American U
Catholic U Amer	Litzelman, James	Catholic U Amer
Catholic U Amer	Norcross, Brian	Franklin & Marshall
Catholic U Amer	Pesses, Michael	Pacific U
Catholic U Amer	Rooney, Patrick	James Madison
Catholic U Amer	Ruhling, Michael	Goshen C
Catholic U Amer	Teske, Casey	Clarion S U
Chicago, U of	Fritts, Lawrence	Iowa, U of
Cincinnati, U of	Barefield, Robert	S Methodist U
Cincinnati, U of	Lynch, John	Emory U
Cincinnati, U of	Randall, Annie	Bucknell U
Cincinnati, U of	You, Yali	Hamline U
Columbia U	Graulty, John P.	Indianapolis, U of
Cornell U	Taylor, Stephanie	Illinois S U
CUNY	Clemmons, William	Pt Loma Nazrn
CUNY	Goldstein, Thomas	Maryland, BaltCnty
CUNY	Hisama, Ellie Michiko	Ohio S U
E Illinois U	Sparks, Marvin	Missouri, St L
E Tennessee S	Tottle, Jack	E Tennessee S
Eastman Sch Music	Waterbury, Susan	Memphis, U of
Eastman Sch Music	Alexander, Kathryn Jane	Yale U
Eastman Sch Music	Bugbee, Fred	New Mexico S U
Eastman Sch Music	Evans, Charles	Coastal Carolina
Eastman Sch Music	Hensel, Larry	Wyoming, U of
Eastman Sch Music	Meville, Nicola	Heidelberg C
Florida S U	Barton, Karl	Thomas C
Florida S U	Bergeest, Lothar	Mississippi, U of
Florida S U	Chambers, Heather	Centre C
Florida S U	Chambers, Mark	E Kentucky U
Florida S U	Connors, Thomas	Kent S U
Florida S U	Daugherty, James	Radford U
Florida S U	Donich, Desiree M.	Utah S U
Florida S U	Forrester, Sheila	Florida S U
Florida S U	Frego, David	Ohio S U
Florida S U	Hannah, Melissa	St Cloud S U
Florida S U	Jetter, Katherine	Ft Lewis C
Florida S U	Martin, Roger	Tennessee Tech
Florida S U	McClung, Alan	NE Louisiana U
Florida S U	Misenhelter, Dale	Alabama, U of
Florida S U	Oby, Jason	Texas Southern U
Florida S U	Scott, Allen	Luther C
Florida S U	Tyler, Philip	McNeese S U
Florida S U	Walter, Steve	Furman U
Florida S U	Williams, Moffatt	Stetson U
Florida S U	Zielke, Steven	Arizona, U of
Florida, U of	Eaton, Renee	S Illinois, Edwrds
Florida, U of	Hudson, Mark	Limestone C
Georgia, U of	Bender, Rhett	S Oregon S C
Harvard U	Krims, Adam	Alberta-CAN
Holy Names C	Xiques, David	Holy Names C
Illinois, Chicago	Perkins, Caroline	DePauw U
Illinois, Chicago	Zielinski, Richard	Indiana S U
Illinois, U of	Lemons, Mary	LebanonValley
Illinois, U of	Russell, Melinda	Carleton C
Illinois, Urbana	Coan, Darryl	S Illinois, Edwrds
Illinois, Urbana	Krueger, Michael	Morningside C
Indiana U	Harb, Charlene	Mdl Tennessee
Indiana U	Liotta, Vincent J.	Indiana, Blmngtn
Indiana U	McCarrey, Scott	Brighm Yng, HI
Indiana U	Neely-Chandler, Thomasina	Spelman C
Indiana U	Reed, Teresa	Tulsa, U of
Indiana U	Scott, Michael	Concordia, StPl
Indiana U	van der Beck, Ralph H.	Utah S U
Iowa, U of	Belser, Robert	Wyoming, U of
Iowa, U of	King, Terry	Texas Tech
Iowa, U of	Macomber, Jeffrey	Bemidji S U
Iowa, U of	McReynolds, Myron	Albion C
Iowa, U of	Ruiter-Feenstra, Pamela	E Michigan U
Iowa, U of	Sharpe, Paul	Texas Tech
Iowa, U of	Suderman, Mark	Georgetown C
Iowa, U of	Taddie, Ann	Maryville (TN)
Iowa, U of	Weber, Paul	Lenoir-Rhyne C
Johns Hopkins	Dolezal, Darry	Missouri, Clmb
Juilliard Schl	Kim, Michael	Lawrence U
Juilliard Schl	Littlefield, Cameron	Idaho, U of
Kansas, U of	Auffarth, Mark	SE Louisiana U
Kent S U	McAllister, Peter A.	Ball S U
Kentucky, U of	Harrold, Robert	Fort Hays S U
Louisiana S U	Davis, Hope	Baldwin-Wallace
Mannes C of Music	Diamond, Douglas	Grinnell C
Maryland, U of	Wulfhorst, Dieter	Indiana U of PA
Memphis, U of	Carroll, Kevin	Fisk U
Miami, U of	Grant, Darrell	Portland S U
Michigan S U	Cole, Kimberley	E Michigan U
Michigan S U	Wilcott, Ronald	S Carolina, Aiken
Michigan S U	D'Addio, Daniel	Cntrl Connecticut
Michigan, U of	Gaunt, Kyra	Virginia, U of
Michigan, U of	Koga, Midori	Michigan S U
Michigan, U of	Lysloff, Rene	UC, Riverside
Michigan, U of	McMullen, Diane	Union C (NY)
Michigan, U of	Mordue, Mark L.	Ball S U
Michigan, U of	Taylor, Timothy	Columbia U
Michigan, U of	Vance, Paul	Winona S U
Michigan, U of	Wong, Deborah	UC, Riverside
Minnesota, U of	Adamek, Mary	Iowa, U of
Minnesota, U of	Hamessley, Lydia	Hamilton C
Missouri, U of	Dunham, Robert	Cal S, SnBrndno
Missouri, U of	Jagon, Shelley	Wright S U
Missouri, U of	Kennedy, John	Cal S, LosAngls
Missouri, U of	Nolker, Brett	Augustana C (IL)
Morgan S U	Mallory, Lloyd	Oakwood C
N Carolina, U of	Bennett, Alan Lee	Indiana, Blmngtn
N Colorado, U of	Bell, Sondra	Gustavus Adolph
N Colorado, U of	Fraser, Teresa	Northeastern U
N Colorado, U of	Landry, Dana	Mdl Tennessee
N Colorado, U of	MacDonald, R. Richard	Winona S U
N Colorado, U of	Stamer, Rick A.	Utah S U
N Texas, U of	Spence, Marcia	Missouri, Clmb
New England Cnsrv	Todd, JoElla	Missouri, Clmb
New Orleans, U of	Watters, Harry	SE Louisiana U
New York U	Kisliuk, Michelle	Virginia, U of
Norfolk S U	Wells, Donovan	BethuneCookmn
Northwestern U	Bussert, Victoria	Baldwin-Wallace
Northwestern U	Cain, Bruce	Southwestern U
Northwestern U	Sullivan, Todd	Indiana S U
Northwestern U	Twomey, Michael	Dickinson C
Ohio S U	Griffing, Joan	E Mennonite U
Ohio S U	Hollenbeck, Eric	Alabama, Brmng
Oklahoma, U of	DeSeguirant, David	U of the Ozarks
Oral Roberts U	Sutliff, Richard	Oral Roberts U
Oregon, U of	Farrell, Tim	Valley City S
Oregon, U of	March, Wendy	Cal S, Fresno
Penn, U of	Blechner, Andrew	Westchester C
Penn, U of	Crumb, David	Duke U
Penn, U of	Hoyt , Peter	Wesleyan U
Penn, U of	Jalbert, Pierre	Rice U
Penn, U of	Korstvedt, Benjamin	Iowa, U of
Penn, U of	Olsen, Morten	N/A-AUSTRIA
PrairieViewAM	O'Neal, Ronald	Jarvis Christian C
Princeton U	Sheppard, W. Anthony	Williams C
Rochester, U of	Heardon, Kathryn	Shippensburg
Rutgers U	Lindeman, Stephan	Brigham Young U
Rutgers U	Ross, Julian	Baldwin-Wallace
Rutgers U	Shinehouse, Patricia	Drake U
S Baptist Theol Sem	Dennis, Pam	Union U
S Carolina, U of	Bankston, David	Coastal Carolina
S Carolina, U of	Hamilton, Vivian	Furman U
S Carolina, U of	Kirkland , Norma	Anderson C
S Carolina, U of	Shotts, Ouida	Pfeiffer U
S Dakota, U of	Arroe, Catherine	Campbellsville U
San Francisco S	Reniger, Marc	Charleston, C of
Stanford U	Dirst, Matthew	Houston, U of
Stanford U	King, Richard	Maryland, CollPk
SUNY	Rose, Douglas	Albion C
SUNY, Buffalo	Trawick, Eleanor F.	Ball S U
SUNY, Stny Brk	Fredrikson, Brandt	Lawrence U
SW Baptist Sem	Heape, Mary	Bluefield S C
Temple U	Cosenza, Glenda	Vermont, U of
Tennessee, Knox	Deaton, Anthony	Lee C
Tennessee, Knox	Wyatt, Alan	Lee C
Texas, Austin	Carnochan, Robert	Northeastern SU
Texas, Austin	Redfield, Stephen	S Mississippi, U of
Texas Tech	Reigles, Barbara	Houghton C
UC, Berkeley	Tenzer, Michael	Br Columbia-CAN
UC, Los Angeles	Makubuya, James	MIT
UC, San Diego	Dobrian, Christopher	UC, Irvine
UC, San Diego	Lucia, Margaret	Shippensburg
UC, St Barbara	Heard, Richard E.	Wake Forest U
W Illinois U	Meier-Sims, Kimberly	Memphis, U of
Washington U	Bauer, Glen	Webster U
Washington, U of	Averill, Ron	Int'l C of Music-MALAY
Washington, U of	Bamman, Richard	E Connecticut S U
Washington, U of	Hoffman, Elizabeth	Washington, U of
Washington, U of	Lang, Barbara Rose	Houston, U of
Webster U	Herman, Sara	Missouri, St L
Wesleyan U	Perlman, Marc	Brown U
Wiscnsn, Madsn	Armstrong, James	William & Mary
Wiscnsn, Madsn	Pearsall, Edward	Texas Tech
Wiscnsn, Madsn	Springer, Mark	St Cloud S U
Wiscnsn, Milw	Ledvina, Brigetta	Lawrence U
Yale U	Galand, Joel	Rochester, U of
Yale U	Jowers, Florence	Lenoir-Rhyne C
Yale U	Moreno, Jairo	Duke U
Yale U	Thomas, Stephen	Cal S, Stnslaus
Yale U	Trester, Francine	Austin C
Yale U	Woldu, Gail	Trinity C (CT)

PHILOSOPHY

American U	Shosky, John	American U
Bowling Green S	Aulisio, Mark	Pittsburgh, U of (Medicn)

TRAINED BY	NAME	HIRED BY
Bowling Green S	Cust, Kenn	Central Missouri S U
Bowling Green S	Daly, Barbara	Case Western Res(Medicn)
Bowling Green S	May, Thomas	S Illinois U (Medicn)
Bowling Green S	Walkiewicz, Lynn	Cazenovia C
Bryn Mawr C	Beck, Martha	Lyon C
Catholic U Amer	Tomarchio, John	Boston U
Chicago, U of	Bassler, Bradley	Georgia, U of
Colorado, U of	Linsenbard, Gail	North Adams S
Columbia U	Hahn, Susan	Johns Hopkins
Connecticut, U of	O'Roake, Shannon	Houghton C
Cornell U	Adams, Don	Hobart/WmSmth
Cornell U	Denis, Lara	UC, Irvine
Cornell U	Hause, Jeff	St John'S Sem
Cornell U	Kristinsson, Sugurdur	Missouri, St L
Cornell U	Metz, Thaddeus	Nebraska, U of
Cornell U	Pasnau, Robert	St Joseph's U
Cornell U	Robb, David	Davidson C
Cornell U	Sullivan, Stephen J.	S Indiana, U of
Cornell U	Torrago, Loretta	Utah, U of
Cornell U	Vogel, Jeffrey	Iowa S U
Cornell U	Wilson, Robert	Illinois, Urbana
CUNY	Arkway, Angela J.	Cincinnati, U of
CUNY	Clark, Chalmers	CUNY, StatIsl
CUNY	Dolling, Lisa M.	St John's U
CUNY	Linker, Maureen	Michigan, Drbrn
CUNY	Vinueza, Adam	Colorado, Bldr
DePaul U	Powell, Marilyn	Marshall U
Duke U	Burkett, Delbert	LSU, BatnRoug
Duke U	Carson, Scott	Ohio U
Duke U	Wilson, Jack	Washington&Lee
Duquesne U	Aarons, Leslie Kinsman	Cal S, Bakersfld
Duquesne U	Ophardt, Michael J.	Malone C
Duquesne U	Scott, Gary Allan	Skidmore C
Emory U	Barlow, Brian	Brenau U
Emory U	Bertland, Amexander	Scranton, U of
Emory U	Grenberg, Jeanine	St Olaf C
Florida S U	Sneed, Richard	Spring Hill C
Fordham U	Berman, Sophie	St Peter's C
Fordham U	Cameron, Scott	Loyola-Marymount
Fordham U	Pagan, Peter	Wheeling Jesuit C
Georgetown U	Stempsey, William	Holy Cross, C of
Harvard U	Herman, Jonathan	Georgia S U
Harvard U	Laden, Anthony	Illinois, Chicago
Harvard U	Lee, Mi-Kyoung	Illinois, Chicago
Harvard U	Miller, Dana	Fordham U
Harvard U	Shelton, Mark	Old Dominion U
Indiana U	Iseminger, Karen A.	Indianapolis, U of
Iowa, U of	Elliot, Terri	Cal S U, Chico
Iowa, U of	Kelley, Andrew	Texas Woman's U
Iowa, U of	Knight, Gordon	Central C
Iowa, U of	Richards, Randy	St Ambrose U
Johns Hopkins	Brender, Natalie	Wesleyan U
Johns Hopkins	Manion, Jennifer	Carleton U
Johns Hopkins	Snyder, Laura	St John's U
Kentucky, U of	Farr, Arnold	St Joseph's (PA)
Loyola, Chicago	Altman-Moore, Lloyd	Waynesburg C
Loyola, NewOrl	Dolinko, Ann	Shimer C
Loyola, NewOrl	Werlin, Steven	Shimer C
Marquette U	Moore, Rebecca	N Dakota, U of
Mass, Amherst	Adkins, Karen	Regis U
Mass, Amherst	Curran, Angela	Bucknell U
Mass, Amherst	Reid, Heather	Morningside C
Mass, U of	Litch, Mary	Alabama, Brmng
Mass, U of	Lombardo, Jerry	Springfield C
Michigan S U	Katherine, Amber	St Mary's (IN)
Michigan, U of	Gensler, Harry	Scranton, U of
Michigan, U of	Huddlestun, John	Charleston, C of
Michigan, U of	Jacobson, Daniel	Charleston, C of
Michigan, U of	Sobel, David	Bowling Green S
Minnesota, U of	Green, Judith	Fordham U
MIT	Stoljar, Daniel	Colorado, Bldr
N Carolina, U of	Downard, Jeffrey	N Arizona U
N Carolina, U of	Durland, Karann	Austin C
N Carolina, U of	Rubenstein, Eric	Colgate U
Nebraska, U of	Lubling, Yoram	Elon C
New School	Allison, Henry	Boston U
New School	Duarte, Eduardo	Hofstra U
New School	Goodin, Patrick	Howard U
New School	Lee, Richard	Penn S U
New School	Mendieta, Eduardo	San Francisco, U of
Northwestern U	Allen, Amy	Grinnell C
Northwestern U	Cronin, Ciaran	Illinois, Chicago
Notre Dame, U of	Grcic, Joseph	Indiana S U
Notre Dame, U of	Sperry-White, Elizabeth	William Jewell C
Notre Dame, U of	Vessey, David	Beloit C
Notre Dame, U of	Williams, Thomas	Iowa, U of
Ohio S U	Korcz, Kevin	Winona S U
Oklahoma, U of	Edwards, Ann	Austin Peay S
Penn S U	Desmond, William	Boston U
Penn S U	Ward, Roger	Georgetown C
Penn S U	Willett, Cynthia	Emory U
Penn, U of	Batitsky, Vadim	St John's U
Pittsburgh, U of	Parsons, Keith	Houston, ClrLk
Princeton U	Ismael, Jenann	Arizona, Tucson
Princeton U	McGowan, Mary	Maryland, BaltCnty
Princeton U	O'Rourke, Michael	Idaho, U of
Princeton U	Thau, Michael	UC, Los Angeles
Purdue-Calumet	Imbo, Samuel O.	Hamline U
Rice U	Goad, Candace	Colorado, Denv
Rochester, U of	Butler, Barbara	Wiscnsn, StevPt
Rochester, U of	Sencerz, Stefan	Texas A&M, CrpsC
Rutgers U	Callendar, Craig	London Sch Eco-UK
Rutgers U	Gillett, Carl	Illinois Wesleyan
Rutgers U	Huggett, Nicholas	Illinois, Chicago
Rutgers U	Laurence, Stephen	Hampshire C
Rutgers U	Sisko, John	William & Mary
Rutgers U	Strevens, Michael	Iowa S U
Rutgers U	Taylor, Paul	Kentucky, U of
St Louis U	Morris, John	Rockhurst C
Stanford U	Burke, Thomas	S Carolina, Clm
Stanford U	Smit, A. Houston	Arizona, Tucson
Stanford U	Washington, Corey	Maryland, CollPk
SUNY, Bngmtn	Bushwick, Nathaniel	Penn S U
SUNY, Bngmtn	Mamary, Anne	St Lawrence U
SUNY, Bngmtn	Mullen, D.	Christopher Newport C
SUNY, Bngmtn	Tyler, Alexandra	Grand Valley S U
SUNY, Buffalo	Blessing, Kimberly	Canisius C
SUNY, Stny Brk	Andrew, Barbara	Montana, U of
SUNY, Stny Brk	Feder, Ellen	Vassar C
SUNY, Stny Brk	Keller, Jean	St Benedict C
SUNY, Stny Brk	Kemp, Catherine	Colorado, Denv
SUNY, Stny Brk	Michelman, Stephen	Wofford C
SUNY, Stny Brk	Seitz, Brian	Babson C
Syracuse U	Francescotti, Robert	San Diego S
Syracuse U	Halwani, Raja	Rollins C
Texas, Austin	Bayer, Greg	William & Mary, C of
Texas, Austin	Bradshaw, David	Indiana U NW
Texas, Austin	Farrell, Anne	S Methodist U
Texas, Austin	Myers, Bill	Birmingham Southern
Texas, Austin	Newman, Davud	W Michigan U
Texas, Austin	Powers, Tom	Cntrl Michigan S U
Texas, Austin	Smith, Anne Collins	Susquehanna U
Texas, Austin	Westacott, Emrys	Alfred U
UC, Berkeley	Anderson, Carl	Reed C
UC, Berkeley	Avigad, Jeremy	Carnegie Mellon
UC, Berkeley	Hough, Sheridan	Charleston, C of
UC, Los Angeles	Evnine, Simon	Cal Polytech
UC, Los Angeles	Rickless, Samuel	Florida S U
UC, Riverside	Arisaka, Yoko	SanFrancisco, Uof
UC, Riverside	Light, Andrew	Montana, U of
UC, San Diego	Wittrup, Eleanor	Pacific, U of the
UC, St Barbara	Waxman, Wayne	Colorado, Bldr
Vanderbilt U	Piker, Andrew	TexasA&M, CrpsC
Vanderbilt U	Shade, Patrick	Rhodes C
Virginia, U of	Ashcraft, William	Truman S U
Wiscnsn, Madsn	Bauder, Mark	Our Lady Lake
Wiscnsn, Madsn	Kinnaman, Theodore J.	George Mason U
Yale U	O'Donovan-Anderson, M.	St John's C(MD)
BLG-Catholic Louvain	Zola, Charles	Scranton, U of
CAN-Alberta	Berkeley, Istvan	SW Louisiana
CAN-Queen's	Koggel, Christine M.	Bryn Mawr C
CAN-W Ontario	Lu, Zhaolu	Hampshire C
GER-Saarland	Pozzo, Ricardo	Catholic U Amer
ITL-Pontifical	Masalo, Dismas	Louisville, U of
POL-Warsaw	Boltuc, Piotr	St Olaf C
UK-Oxford	Abela, Paul	Loyola, Chicago

POLITICAL SCIENCE

TRAINED BY	NAME	HIRED BY
American U	Gill, Jefferson	Cal Polytech
American U	Smith, Ginger	Colegio Univ de Este-PR
American U	Snow, Nancy	New England C
Arizona, U of	Gerlak, Andrea	Guilford C
Boston C	Bartlett, Robert	Rhodes C
Boston U	Borer, Douglas	Virginia Tech
Brandeis U	Siplon, Patricia	Wilkes C
Carnegie Mellon	Lowenthal, Diane	Bucknell U
Carnegie Mellon	McCarty, Nolan	Columbia U
Chicago, U of	Behnegar, Nassrt	Boston C
Chicago, U of	Carpenter, Daniel	Princeton U
Chicago, U of	Fernandes, Leela	Rutgers, NBruns
Chicago, U of	Goemans, Henk E.	Duke U
Chicago, U of	Kydd, Andrew	UC, Riverside
Chicago, U of	Roselius, Becky	Duke U
Chicago, U of	Sullivan, Vickie	Tufts U
Chicago, U of	Wang, Vincent	Richmond, U of
Chicago, U of	Wolpert, Robin	S Carolina, Clm
Claremont Grad	Freyss, Siegrun	Cal S, LosAngls
Claremont Grad	Switzy, Robert	SUNY, Brckprt
Colorado S U	Jones, Lilias	S Dakota S U
Colorado, U of	Pickett, Brent	Chadron S C
Columbia U	Adler, E. Scott	Colorado, Bldr
Columbia U	Alexander, Gerard	Virginia, U of
Columbia U	Chambers, Michael	St Olaf C
Columbia U	Francis, Corrina-Barbara	Missouri, Cbm
Columbia U	MacLachlan, Patricia	Calgary-CAN
Columbia U	Mercer, Jonathan	Washington, U of
Columbia U	Paris, Michael	Rutgers, NBruns
Columbia U	Reinhart, Eric	Emory U
Columbia U	Walker, Brian D.	UC, Los Angeles
Connecticut, U of	Walsh, Julie	St Joseph's C (NY)
Cornell U	Abinales, Jo Jo	Ohio U
Cornell U	Apostolidis, Paul	Cornell U
Cornell U	Bush, Kenneth	Carleton U-CAN
Cornell U	Cook, Alexandra	Chicago, U of

TRAINED BY	NAME	HIRED BY	TRAINED BY	NAME	HIRED BY	TRAINED BY	NAME	HIRED BY
Cornell U	Gaddie, Ronald	Oklahoma, U of	Michigan S U	Janiskee, Brian	Cntrl Connecticut	Smith C	Henderson, Christine	Marshall U
Cornell U	Gatch, Loren	C Oklahoma, U of	Michigan, U of	Borquez, Julio	Michigan, Drbrn	Stanford U	Boylan, Delia	MIT
Cornell U	Hedman, Lotta	Nottingham-UK	Michigan, U of	Freer, Regina	Occidental C	Stanford U	Busza, Eva	William & Mary
Cornell U	Leaman, David	NEastern Illinois	Michigan, U of	Guidry, John	Augustana C (IL)	Stanford U	Drezner, Daniel	Colorado, Bldr
Cornell U	McGovern, Steve	Penn, U of	Michigan, U of	McKissick, Gary	Emory U	Stanford U	Kim, Sunhyuk	S California, U of
Cornell U	Mood, Michelle	Providence C	Michigan, U of	Stam, Allan	Yale U	SUNY, Bngmtn	Blasi, Gerald	SUNY, Brockprt
Cornell U	Remick, Elizabeth	Oregon, U of	Michigan, U of	Wang, Jianwei	Wiscnsn, StevPt	SUNY, Bngmtn	Camobreco, John	New Hmpshire, U of
Cornell U	Reynolds, David	Wayne S U	Minnesota, U of	Kellestedt, Paul M.	Brown U	SUNY, Bngmtn	Cohen, Frank	SUNY, Bngmtn
Cornell U	Szymanski, Ann-Marie	Oklahoma, U of	Minnesota, U of	Schultz, David	Wiscnsn, RiverF	SUNY, Bngmtn	Davenport, Christian	Colorado, Bldr
Cornell U	Thomas, Daniel	Illinois, Chicago	Mississippi S U	Herron, Sharron	Cal S, Fresno	SUNY, Bngmtn	Goldman, Frances	SUNY, Bngmtn
Cornell U	Wallace, Sherri	SUNY, Buffalo	Missouri, Clmb	Roper, Steven	Pace, WhitePl	SUNY, Bngmtn	Quainoo, Samuel	E Strassburg-GER
Cornell U	Wawro, Gregory	Columbia U	Missouri, St L	Clark, Michael	St Xavier U	SUNY, Bngmtn	Senese, Paul	Vanderbilt U
Cornell U	Wilson, Scott	South, U of	MIT	Aho, C. Michael	Columbia U	SUNY, Bngmtn	Shi, Yuhang	E Carolina U
CUNY	Strom, Elizabeth A.	Rutgers U	MIT	Alter, Karen	Smith C	SUNY, Buffalo	Barreto, Amilcar	Northeastern U
CUNY	Waddell, Brian	Connecticut, U of	N Arizona U	Boylan, Timothy	Winthrop U	SUNY, Stny Brk	Serra, George	Bridgewater S
Drake U	Dicker, Todd	W Michigan U	N Arizona U	Ridgeway, Sharon	SW Louisiana	SUNY, Stny Brk	Stenner, Karen	Duke U
Duke U	Constantelos, John	Grand Valley S	N Carolina, ChpH	Rivers, Patrick	Bates C	Tennessee, Knox	Stefanovic, Dragan	Appalachian S
Duke U	Davidson, Elisa	Shimer C	N Carolina, Grns	Morgan, Betty	Elon C	Texas A&M	Andrade, Pydia	N Texas, U of
Duke U	Lubert, Howard	Alma C	N Carolina, U of	Bratton, Kathleen	SUNY, Bngmtn	Texas, Austin	Bailey, Michael	SW Texas S U
Duke U	Sloat, James	Dickinson C	N Carolina, U of	Ferguson, Margaret	Indiana Purdu, Ind	Texas, Austin	Dorussen, H.	Trondheim-NORW
Duke U	Smyth, Regina	Penn S U	N Carolina, U of	Haynie, Kerry	Rutgers, NBruns	Texas, Austin	Frensley, Nathalie	Wichita S U
Emory U	Davis, Sue	Grand Valley S	N Carolina, U of	Sparks, Cheryl	Ohio S, Mnsfld	Texas, Austin	Morris, John	Connecticut, U (of
Emory U	Fox, Richard	Union C (NY)	New School	Allegro, Linda	Boricua C	Texas Tech	Farmer, Brian	Lubbock Chrstn
Florida S U	Fording, Richard	Kentucky, U of	New School	Faist, Thomas	Bremen-GER	Trinity C (CT)	Reddy, Movindri	Occidental C
Fordham U	Badger, Jonathan	St Johns (MD)	New School	Fakhari, Mohammed	CUNY	Tulane U	Turner, Brian	Randolph-Macon
Fordham U	Schaeffer, Denise	Holy Cross, C of	New School	Gallagher, Susan	Mass, U of	UC, Berkeley	Cohen, Shari	Wellesley C
Georgetown U	Ciliotta-Rubery, Andrea	SUNY, Brckprt	New School	Grossman, Andrew	Albion C	UC, Berkeley	Csajko, Karen	Winona S U
Georgetown U	Farnsworth, Stephen	Mary Washngtn C	New School	Holland, Catherine	Missouri, U of	UC, Berkeley	Darst, Robert	Oregon, U of
Georgetown U	LeBauvre, Laura	Northwestern U	New School	Klausen, Jytte	Brandeis U	UC, Berkeley	Dawson, Jane	Oregon, U of
Georgetown U	Mayer, Jeremy D.	Kalamazoo C	New School	Kryder, David	MIT	UC, Berkeley	Diamant, Neil	Tel Aviv U-ISRL
Georgetown U	McAteer, John	Wheeling Jesuit	New School	Marien, Daniel	York-CAN	UC, Berkeley	Doherty, Eileen	Case Western Res
Georgetown U	Siavelia, Peter	Wake Forest U	New School	Marien, Margarita	Illinois, U of	UC, Berkeley	Hauptmann, Emily	W Michigan U
Harvard U	Crystal, Jonathan	Georgia S U	New School	Mele, Christopher	SUNY, Albany	UC, Berkeley	Martel, James	Wellesley C
Harvard U	Gordon, Mark	Columbia U	New York U	Tpgman, Jeffrey	Seton Hall U	UC, Berkeley	McEnnerney, Dennis	New School
Harvard U	Philpott, Daniel	UC, St Barbara	Notre Dame, U of	Schorn, Timothy	S Dakota, U of	UC, Berkeley	Oliver, Eric	Princeton U
Harvard U	Schuessler, Alex	New York U	Ohio S U	Bruce, John	Mississippi, U of	UC, Berkeley	Patashnik, Eric M.	Yale U
Harvard U	Stone, Randall	Rochester, U of	Ohio S U	Healy, Sally	Grinnell C	UC, Berkeley	Sil, Rudra	Penn, U of
Harvard U	Treisman, Daniel S.	UC, Los Angeles	Ohio S U	Hislope, Robert	Antioch C	UC, Berkeley	Teske, Nathan	Miami, U of
Hawaii, U of	Hua, Shiping	Eckerd C	Ohio S U	Klein, David	Wittenberg U	UC, Berkeley	Verges, Francoise	Sussex-UK
Houston, U of	Orth, Deborah	Grand Valley S	Ohio S U	Kuzman, Lynn	N Dakota S U	UC, Berkeley	Wedeen, Lisa	Wesleyan U
Illinois, U of	Leitch, Richard	Gustavus Adolph	Ohio S U	Van Winkle, Steve	New Orleans, U of	UC, Berkeley	Wright, Teresa	Cal S U
Illinois, Urbana	Dalager, Jon	Georgetown C	Oklahoma, U of	Gagnere, Nathalie	Ohio U	UC, Los Angeles	Quinn, John	Truman S U
Illinois, Urbana	Kozhemiakin, Alexander	Georgia S U	Oklahoma, U of	Kean, Steve	Loras C	UC, Los Angeles	Topper, Keith	S Carolina, Clm
Indiana U	Layman, Geoffrey	Vanderbilt U	Oklahoma, U of	LaPlant, James	Valdosta S U	UC, San Diego	Sposito, Frank	Chicago, U of
Iowa, U of	Adams, Gregory	Carnegie Mellon	Oklahoma, U of	Mason, Dale	New Mexico, U of	Union Institute	Paitakes, John	Seton Hall U
Iowa, U of	Krassas, Nicole	E Connecticut S U	Oregon, U of	Everest, Marcy	Weber S C	Virginia, U of	Dougherty, Beth	Beloit C
Iowa, U of	Levy, Dana	Texas Tech U	Oregon, U of	Schlosberg, David	N Arizona U	W Michigan U	Liggett, Barbara	W Michigan U
Iowa, U of	Steger, Wayne	DePaul U	Pittsburgh, U of	Egan, Michelle	American U	W Virginia, U of	Patten, Joseph	Buena Vista U
Johns Hopkins	Engelmann, Stephen	Illinois, Chicago	Pittsburgh, U of	Nagengast, Emil	Juniata C	Washington & Lee U	Rugeley, Edward	Wheeling Jesuit
Johns Hopkins	Evans, Tina	BethuneCookmn	Princeton U	Clements, Paul	W Michigan U	Washington S U	Maule, Linda	Indiana S U
Johns Hopkins	Harris, Douglas	Colgate U	Princeton U	Fordham, Benjamin	SUNY, Albany	Washington, U of	Banerjee, Sikata	Lethbridge-CAN
Kansas, U of	Bath, Michael	Concordia, Mrhd	Princeton U	Johnson, Juliet	Loyola, Chicago	Washington, U of	Nixon, David	Georgia S U
Kansas, U of	Schmiedeler, Tom	Washburn U	Princeton U	Londregan, John B.	UC, Los Angeles	Washington, U of	Singleton, Sara Gail	Tulane U
Louisiana S U	Bond, Edward	Alabama A & M	Princeton U	Pickus, Noah M.J.	Duke U	Wayne S U	Guerrieri, Mark	Michigan, Drbrn
Maryland, CollPk	Occhipinti, John	Canisius C	Princeton U	Wang, Hongying	San Diego S	Wiscnsn, Madsn	Beck, Linda J.	Barnard C
Maryland, U of	Burack, Cynthia	Florida, Gnsvl	Princeton U	White, Stuart	MIT	Wiscnsn, Madsn	Cohen, Edward	Westminster (PA)
Maryland, U of	Cochran, David	Loras C	Rutgers U	Filkohazi, Christine Kelly	Mt Holyoke C	Wiscnsn, Madsn	Conanat, James K.	George Mason U
Maryland, U of	Kaminski, Marek	New York U	Rutgers U	Larsen, Carlton	Drake U	Wiscnsn, Madsn	Giaimo, Susan	MIT
Maryland, U of	Melchoir, Alan	Towson S U	S Carolina, U of	Blanton, Robert	Georgia C	Wiscnsn, Madsn	Murphy, Patrick	San Francisco, Uof
Maryland, U of	Yoder, Jennifer	Colby C	S Carolina, U of	Blanton, Shannon	Georgia C	Wiscnsn, Milw	Keiser, Lael	Missouri, Clmb
Mass, Amherst	Petterson, Paul	Cntrl Connecticut	S Carolina, U of	Kitts, Ken	Francis Marion U	Wyoming, U of	Heo, Uk	Wiscnsn, Milw
Miami, Oxford	Armstron, Dlynn	Slippery Rock U	S Carolina, U of	Lindquist, Stefanie	Georgia, U of	Yale U	Ely, Robin	Columbia U
Miami, Oxford	Penksa, Susan	Westmont C	S Carolina, U of	Morton, Jeff	Florida Atlantic	Yale U	Smith, R. Drew	Butler U
Miami, Oxford	Powell, David	E Illinois U	S Carolina, U of	Sharpe, Barry	Georgia Southern U	Yale U	Suarez-Lasa, Sandra	Temple U
			S Carolina, U of	Sulfaro, Valerie	James Madison	CAN-Dalhousie	Malaquias, Assis	St Lawrence U
			S Carolina, U of	Twing, Steven	Virginia Tech	CAN-Toronto	Frost, Bryan-Paul	SW Louisiana
			S Illinois U	McBride, Allan	S Mississippi, U of			

TRAINED BY	NAME	HIRED BY	TRAINED BY	NAME	HIRED BY	TRAINED BY	NAME	HIRED BY
CAN-York	Carbert, Louise	Dalhousie-CAN	Fuller Theol Sem	Anguiano, Susan	Chapman U	Michigan, U of	Fleeson, William	Wake Forest U
ITL-European	Urbinati, Nadia	Columbia U	Fuller Theol Sem	Strawn, Brad	Pt Loma Nazrn	Michigan, U of	Kessler, Jane A.	Detroit Mercy
UK-Cambridge	DeSousa, Norberto	Dartmouth C	Georgia, U of	Laygo, Ranilo	NW Missouri S	Michigan, U of	Landman, Janet	Babson C
UK-Oxford	King, Charles	Georgetown U	Georgia, U of	Wright, Lester	W Michigan U	Michigan, U of	Leach, Coflin	Swarthmore C
UK-Oxford	Muirhead, J. Russell	Williams C	Harvard U	Hart, Allen	Amherst C	Michigan, U of	Price, Paul	Cal S, Fresno
UK-University C	Arneil, Barbara	Br Columbia-CAN	Harvard U	Kirschner, Suzanne	Holy Cross, C of	Minnesota, U of	Jewett, David	Barat C
			Harvard U	Lamb, Sharon	St Michael's C	Minnesota, U of	Regan, Pamela	Cal S, LosAngls
PSYCHOLOGY			Harvard U	Marsolek, Chad	Minnsota, TwnC	Minnesota, U of	Scott, Britain	St Thomas, U of
Arizona S U	Curran, Patrick J.	Duke U	Hawaii, U of	Wilson, William G.	Duke U	Mississippi, U of	Grieve, Frederick	Austin Peay S
Arizona S U	Green, Beth	Portland S U	Hofstra U	Hynes, Robert	Limestone C	Mississippi, U of	Gustafson, Scott	S Dakota, U of
Arizona S U	Lecci, Len	N Carolina, Wlm	Howard U	Levermore, M.	Palm Beach Atlantic	Mississippi, U of	McGrath, Melanie L.	Tulane U
Arizona S U	Lengua, Liliana	Washington, U of	Illinois, Chicago	Hopmeyer, Andrea	Occidental C	Missouri, Clmb	Anderson, Kathryn	Our Lady Lake
Arizona S U	Schaller, Mark	Br Columbia-CAN	Illinois, U of	Ahn, Woo-Kyoung	Yale U	Missouri, StL	Highhouse, Scott	Bowling Green S
Arkansas, U of	Galupo, Marlene	Towson S U	Illinois, U of	Barton, Richard	W Georgia, S U of	Missouri, StL	Hendricks, Frederica	Austin Peay S
Ball S U	Broderick, Dan	Ball S U	Illinois, U of	Scott, Walter	Miami, U of	MIT	Chun, Marvin Myungwoo	Yale U
Ball S U	Wickes, Kevin	Taylor U	Illinois, Urbana	Davis, Anita	Rhodes C	MIT	Xu, Fei	Northeastern U
Ball S U	Winsted, Donald	LeTourneau U	Illinois, Urbana	Fabiani, Monica	Missouri, Clmb	Montana, U of	Karkowski, Andrea M.	Denison U
Biola U	Entwistle, David N.	Malone C	Illinois, Urbana	Gratton, Gabriele	Missouri, Clmb	N Carolina, ChpH	Arriaga, Ximena	Claremont Grad
Boston U	Galli, Rachel	Kenyon C	Illinois, Urbana	Parker, Jeffrey	Penn S U	N Carolina, ChpH	Burwell, Rebecca W.	Brown U
Cal Sch Prof Psych	Fernando, April	Holy Names C	Illinois, Urbana	Zickar, Michael	Bowling Green S	N Carolina, ChpH	Gonzales-Vallego, Claudia	Ohio U
Carnegie Mellon	Blessing, Stephen	Florida, Gnsvl	Indiana U	Levine, Gary	Albright C	N Carolina, Grns	Bondurant, Barrie	Lyon C
Carnegie Mellon	Munakata, Yuki	Denver, U of	Indiana U	McDonald, Hugh	Bates C	N Carolina, Grns	McCandies, Terry	Wheaton C (MA)
Carnegie Mellon	Zemel, Rich	Arizona, Tucson	Indiana U	Vincent, Mark	Augustana C (IL)	N Carolina, U of	Burwell, Rebecca	Boston U
Case Western Res	Luo, Dasen	Indiana U of PA	Iowa S U	Smith, Gabie	Frostburg S U	N Carolina, U of	Eby, Lillian T.	Georgia, U of
Case Western Res	Meliska, Charles	S Indiana, U of	Iowa S U	Swiater, Mary Ann	Lafayette C	N Dakota, U of	Jensen, Heidi	Thomas More C
Catholic U Amer	Nestor, Paul	Mass, Boston	Iowa, U of	McDowell, Bradley	Augustana C (IL)	Nebraska, Lncn	Penn, David	LSU, BatnRoug
Chicago, U of	Mix, Kelly Sue	Indiana, Blmngtn	Iowa, U of	Ones, Deniz	Minnsota, TwnC	Nebraska, U of	Thorn, George	Boston U
Cincinnati, U of	Basso, Michael	Tulsa, U of	Iowa, U of	Prieto, Loreto	Oklahoma, U of	New Hmpshire, U of	Hakala, Christopher	Lycoming C
Clark U	Dillon, James	Holy Cross, C of	Johns Hopkins	Johnson, Douglas	Colgate U	New Hmpshire, U of	Hammond, Billy	Arizona S West
Clark U	Herrenkohl, Leslie	Washington, U of	Johns Hopkins	Mordkoff, J. Toby	Penn S U	New Hmpshire, U of	Rizzella, Michelle	Hobart/WmSmth
Clark U	Kanner, Bonnie G.	Merrimac C	Kansas, U of	Burris, Christopher	Christian Bros	New York U	Lu, Zhong-Lin	S California, U of
Colorado S U	Harvey, Mark	N Carolina, U of	Kent S U	Chambers, Karen	Gettysburg C	Northeastern U	Schirillo, James A.	Wake Forest U
Colorado, U of	Bartsch, Robert	Texas, Permian	Kent S U	Neuhoff, John	Lafayette C	Notre Dame, U of	Hudson, Bryan A.	Indianapolis, U of
Colorado, U of	Vik, Peter	Idaho S U	Kent S U	Tryon, Georgiana	CUNY, GradCntr	Notre Dame, U of	Nath, Pamela	Bluffton C
Columbia U	Amsel, Eric	Weber S C	Kent S U	VanMeter, Rhonda	NW Missouri S	Ohio S U	Brannun, Laura	Oklahoma, U of
Columbia U	Esgalhado, Barbara	Duquesne U	Kentucky, U of	Crawford, Cynthia	Cal S, SnBrndno	Ohio S U	Eberly, Mary B.	Oakland U
Columbia U	Shoda, Yuichi	Washington, U of	Kentucky, U of	Dose, John	St Norbert C	Ohio S U	Gardner, Wendi	Northwestern U
Connecticut, U of	Chu, Ling-Chuan	SUNY, Oswego	Kentucky, U of	McKenzie, Karyn	Georgetown U	Ohio S U	Meyer, Dinah	Ohio S, Marion
Cornell U	Beale, James	Grand Valley S	Liberty U	Sale, Gene	Liberty U	Ohio S U	Tigner, Robert	Truman S U
Cornell U	Hayes, Andrew	New England, U of	Louisville, U of	Druen, Perri	York C of PA	Ohio U	Harasty, Amy	Connecticut, U of
Cornell U	Johnson, Scott	Gettysburg C	Loyola, Chicago	Abell, Steven	Detroit, U of	Ohio U	Kvaal, Steven	Roosevelt U
Cornell U	Zeifman, Debra	Vassar C	Loyola, Chicago	Browning, Kimberly	Detroit Mercy	Oklahoma, U of	Lackey, James	SW Oklahoma S
CUNY	Addelston, Judi	Rollins C	Loyola, Chicago	Dell'Angela, Kim	Loyola, Chicago	Oklahoma, U of	Swickert, Rhonda J.	Charleston, C of
CUNY	Beach, III, King D.	Michigan S U	Loyola, Chicago	Frazier, Julie	Purdue U	Oregon S U	Ponzetti, James	W Illinois U
CUNY	Drucker, Philip Martin	St John's U	Loyola, Chicago	Helford, Michael	DePaul U	Oregon, U of	Dehle, Crystal	Idaho S U
CUNY	Gooler, Laura Ellen	Claremont Grad	Loyola, Chicago	Meyer, Greg	Alaska, U of	Oregon, U of	Jennings, Peggy	Wyoming, U of
CUNY	Seitz, Jay A.	CUNY	Loyola, Chicago	Nestor, Thomas	St. John's Sem	Penn S U	Conte, Jeffrey	LSU, BatnRoug
CUNY	Ticke, Lynne Arlene	Rutgers U	Loyola, Chicago	Njus, David	Winona S U	Penn S U	Elliott, Teresa	American U
Delaware, U of	Abe, JoAnn	S Connecticut	Maryland, CollPk	Bell, Martha Ann	Virginia Tech	Penn S U	Goodwin, Paige	W Illinois U
Denver, U of	Weimgreslague, Ella	Mary, U of	Maryland, U of	Fyock, Jr., John	Dickinson C	Penn S U	Roemer, Lisabeth	Mass, Boston
Drew U	Peters, Ralph	Concordia C (NY)	Maryland, U of	Wade, Jade	Fordham U	Penn S U	Tesluk, Paul E.	Tulane U
Duke U	Covey, Ellen	Washington, U of	Maryland, U of	Witt, Diane	SUNY, Bngmtn	Penn, U of	Chapman, Gretchen	Rutgers, NBruns
Duke U	Dunsmore, Julie	Hamilton C	Mass, Amherst	Stevens, Laura	Bates C	Penn, U of	Robbins, Steven	Beaver C
Duke U	Grant, Robert	Indiana S U	Mass, U of	Kennison, Sheila	Oklahoma, U of	Pittsburgh, U of	Marsh, David	Pittsburgh, Bradford
Duke U	Newman, Elana	Tulsa, U of	McGill U	Ruggiero, Karen	Harvard U	Princeton U	Multhaup, Kristi	Davidson C
Duquesne U	Dodson, Eric	W Virginia U	Memphis, U of	Townsend, Bill	Rhodes C	Purdue U	Adams, Paul	Fort Hays S U
Emory U	Carton, John	Beloit C	Miami, U of	Daugherty, Timothy	Valparaiso U	Purdue U	Burgy, Lean	Cornell College
Emory U	Cunningham, Michael	Tulane U	Michigan S U	Campbell, Rebecca	Illinois, Chicago	Purdue U	Edmondson, Christine	Cal S, Fresno
Florida Atlantic U	Eastman, Kathleen	N Arizona U	Michigan S U	Cortina, Jose Manuel	George Mason U	Rochester, U of	Knee, Clifford	Houston, U of
Florida Intl U	Franco, Nathalie	Rollins C	Michigan S U	Eberhard, Kathleen	Notre Dame, U of	Rochester, U of	Murphy, Walter	Lenoir-Rhyne C
Florida, U of	Calvert, Patricia	Rhodes C	Michigan S U	Fastenau, Philip	Indiana Purdu, Ind	Rochester, U of	Spivey-Knowlton, Michael	Cornell U
Florida, U of	Holmes, Heather	SE Louisiana U	Michigan S U	Gully, Stanely M.	George Mason U	Rochester, U of	Straub, Kathleen	Villa Julie C
Florida, U of	Pitts, Raymond	N Carolina, Wlm	Michigan S U	Hill, Nancy E.	Duke U	Rutgers U	Kalbaugh, Patricia	S Connecticut
Florida, U of	Welch-Ross, Melissa	Georgia U	Michigan S U	Landis, Ronald S.	Tulane U	S California, U of	Brennan, Patricia	Emory U
Fordham U	Dunsmore, Beryl	Concordia U	Michigan S U	Meyers, Steven	Roosevelt U	S California, U of	Long, Jeffrey	St John's U
Fordham U	O'Kane, Jeannine	Immaculata C	Michigan S U	Sheppard, Lori	Appalachian S	S California, U of	Scarpa, Angela	Georgia, U of
Fort Hays S U	Shepherd-Adams, Cheryl	Fort Hays S U	Michigan, U of	Acker, Michele	Wittenberg U	S California, U of	Weisman, Amy	Mass, Boston

TRAINED BY	NAME	HIRED BY	TRAINED BY	NAME	HIRED BY	TRAINED BY	NAME	HIRED BY
S Carolina, U of	Barakat, Lamia	Drexel U	Vermont, U of	Brooks, Douglas	Cal S, Fresno	Duquesne U	Mueller, Joan	Creighton U
S Carolina, U of	Bell-Hundemer, N.	Citadel, Military C	Virginia Cmnwlth	Bowers, Bonita	S Indiana, U of	Duquesne U	Tkacik, Michael	Flagler U
S Carolina, U of	Conway, Andrew	Illinois, Chicago	Virginia Tech	Curtin, Lisa	Appalachian S	Emory U	Gathje, Peter	Christian Bros
S Carolina, U of	Fancett Pagels, Carrie	Valdosta S C	Virginia, U of	Boker, Steven	Notre Dame, U of	Emory U	Hill, Harvey	Berry C
S Carolina, U of	LaPointe, Linda B.	Winthrop C	Virginia, U of	Britner, Preston	Smith C	Emory U	Linafelt, Tod A.	Georgetown U
S Illinois U	Byravan, Anupama	Fordham U	Virginia, U of	LaFleur, Suzanne	Smith C	Emory U	Morrill, Bruce	Boston C
S Methodist U	Dickens, Charles	Biola U	W Virginia, U of	Breitenstein, Joseph	Luther C	Emory U	Wiggins, Daphne	Texas Christian
St Louis U	Nicks, Sandra	Christian Bros	Washington S U	Gargano, Gary	St Joseph's (PA)	Fordham U	Hoffman, Coleen	St Peter's C
Stanford U	Engle, Stephen A.	UC, Los Angeles	Washington U	Goldstein, Miriam	Gustavus Adolph	Grad Theol Union	Batstone, Davic	SanFrancisco,Uof
Stanford U	Kelley, Colleen	Florida S U	Washington, U of	Cordova, James	Illinois, Urbana	Grad Theol Union	Grimsrud, Theodore	E Mennonite C
Stanford U	Lillard, Angeline	Virginia, U of	Wayne S U	Owens, Chiarina	Michigan, Drbrn	Harvard U	McNally, Michael	Texas Christian
Stanford U	Locke, Kenneth	Idaho, U of	Wiscnsn, Madsn	Friedman, Elliot M.	Williams C	Harvard U	Nguyen, Cuong Tu	George Mason U
SUNY	Dusek, Jeffrey	Boston U	Wiscnsn, Madsn	Heidenreich, Susan	SanFrancisco, U of	Harvard U	Shapiro, Marc	Scranton, U of
SUNY, Albany	Hosoda, Megumi	Pace, WhitePl	Wiscnsn, Madsn	McKinley, Nita	Bates C	Harvard U	Stoltzfus, Philip	Bethel C (MN)
SUNY, Albany	McCall, Maureen	Louisville, U of	Wiscnsn, Madsn	Spiegel, David	Boston U	Harvard U	Vanderhooft, David	Boston C
SUNY, Albany	Mistretta, Jennifer	Youngstown S	Wiscnsn, U of	Deppe, Roberta	Oglethorpe U	Harvard U	Walsh, Carey	Rhodes C
SUNY, Bngmtn	Anastasi, Jeffrey	Francis Marion U	Wiscnsn, U of	O'Donnell, Sean	Washington, U of	Illinois, Urbana	Lekan, Todd	Muskingum C
SUNY, Bngmtn	Bohemier, Gregory	Culver-Stockton C				Iowa, U of	Johnson, Christopher	Buena Vista U
SUNY, Bngmtn	Briihl, Deborah	Valdosta S C	CAN-Br Colombia	Wood , Emma	Boston U	Loyola, Chicago	Clark, Peter	St Joseph's (PA)
SUNY, Bngmtn	Hall, Michael	Washington, U of	CAN-Br Colombia	Fouladi, Rachel T.	Texas, Austin	Marquette U	Shippee, Steven	St Thomas, U of
SUNY, Bngmtn	Stewart, Paul	SUNY, Oswego	CAN-Carleton	Foster, Mindi	N Dakota, U of	Marquette U	Wennemann, Daryl	Fontbonne C
SUNY, Buffalo	Emer, Denise	St Bonaventure	CAN-Concordia	Graham, Susan	Calgary-CAN	Marquette U	White, Richard	Benedictine C
SUNY, Buffalo	Reed, Sheila	N Texas, U of	CAN-McGill	Aube, Jennifer	Rochester, U of	Master's Seminary	Bolen, Todd	Master's C & Sem
SUNY, Buffalo	Zebb, Barbara	Texas Tech	CAN-Toronto	Hamann, Stephen	Emory U	Michigan, U of	Cole, Alan	Lewis & Clark C
SUNY, Stny Brk	Burns, Lawrence	Grand Valley S	CAN-Toronto	Shaw, Raymond	Merrimack C	Notre Dame, U of	Schlabach, Gerald	Bluffton C
SUNY, Stny Brk	Eshun, Sussie	E Stroudsburg PA	CAN-Toronto	Vinden, Penelope	Clark U	Penn S U	Rock, John	Wheeling Jesuit
SUNY, Stny Brk	Newman, Michelle	Penn S U	CAN-W Ontario	Galea, Lisa	Br Columbia-CAN	Penn, U of	Boucher, Daniel	Franklin Marshall
SUNY, Stny Brk	Pridal, Cathryn	Westminster C	CAN-W Ontario	Tett, Robert	Wright S U	Penn, U of	Pinzine, Jane Marie	Grinnell C
SUNY, Stny Brk	Zevenbergen, Andrea	N Dakota, U of	CAN-Waterloo	Barrett, Lisa	Boston C	Princeton Theol Sem	Lambert, Lake	Wartburg C
Syracuse U	Johnson, Jean	Utica C (Syracuse)	CAN-Waterloo	Davidson, Karina	Alabama, U of	SW Baptist Sem	Keown, Gerald	Gardner-Webb C
Temple U	Rabin, Beth E.	Immaculata C	CAN-Waterloo	MacDonald, Tara	Lethbridge-CAN	SW Baptist Sem	Lyle, Kenneth	Bluefield S C
Tennessee, Knox	Thomas, Julie	Youngstown S	NETH-Leiden	Li, Ping	Richmond, U of	S Methodist U	Ilesanmi, Simeon	Wake Forest U
Tennessee, U of	Couch, Laurie	Fort Hays S U	UK-Leicester	Mate-Kole, C.	Cntrl Connecticut	S Methodist U	Thompson, Richard P.	Olivet C
Texas A&M	Gonzalez, Cynthia	Our Lady Lake	UK-Sussex	Kelley, Micahel	Liberty U	Stanford U	Adamek, Wendi	Iowa, U of
Texas A&M	Olivares, Orlando	Bridgewater S				Stanford U	Csikentmihalyi, Mark	Davidson C
Texas, Austin	Dempsey, Margaret T.	Tulane U	**RELIGION**			Stanford U	Unno, Mark	Carleton U
Texas, Austin	Jones, Theresa	Washington, U of	Boston C	Schutz, Cornelia	St Michael's C	Syracuse U	Glass, N. Robert	St Olaf C
Texas, Austin	Morris, Kathryn	Butler U	Boston U	Scirghi, Thomas	Fordham U	Temple U	Lusthaus, Dan	Florida S U
Texas Christian	Schneider, Laura	Texas Weslyn	Boston U	Staley, Ronald	Boston U	Temple U	Varner, William	Master's C & Sem
Texas, U of	Hahn, Lance	Penn S U	Brandeis U	Zank, Michael	Boston U	UC, Berkeley	Burgaleta, Claudio	St Peter's C
Tulane U	Overstreet, Stacy	Tulane U	Brite Divinity Schl	Cartwright, David	Jarvis Christian C	UC, Berkeley	Hayes, Christine	Yale U
UC, Berkeley	Joseph, Julian	Nevada, Reno	Brown U	Clausing, Kimberly	Reed C	UC, Berkeley	Kitts, Margo	Merrimack C
UC, Berkeley	Nigg, Joel T.	Michigan S U	Brown U	Foat, Michael	Reed C	Union Theol Sem	Grangaard, Blake	Heidelberg C
UC, Davis	Schultz, Todd	Pacific U	Catholic U Amer	McDonald, Margaret S.	Immaculata C	Vanderbilt U	Appolis, Keith	Fisk U
UC, Los Angeles	Chun, Kevin	SanFrancisco,Uof	Catholic U Amer	Regan, Jane	Boston C	Vanderbilt U	Fehribach, Adeline	Spalding U
UC, Los Angeles	Dana, Edward	Chapman U	Catholic U Amer	Shelley, Thomas	Fordham U	Vanderbilt U	Griffin, Horace	Missouri, Clmb
UC, Los Angeles	Gould, Elizabeth	Princeton U	Catholic U Amer	Soule, W. Beckey	Oxford-UK	Vanderbilt U	Pacwa, Mitchell	Dallas, U of
UC, Los Angeles	Kim, Jeansok John	Yale U	Chicago, U of	Britt, Brian	Virginia Tech	Virginia, U of	Johnson, Maria	Scranton, U of
UC, Los Angeles	Rorty-Greenfield, M.	Claremnt McKenna	Chicago, U of	Patton, Laurie	Emory U	Virginia, U of	Jones, Charles B.	Catholic U Amer
UC, Los Angeles	Ullman, Jodie	Cal S, SnBrndno	Chicago, U of	Prentiss, Karen	Drew U	Virginia, U of	Layton, Richard	Illinois, Urbana
UC, Los Angeles	Wayment, Heidi	N Arizona U	Chicago, U of	Raj, Selva	Albion C	Virginia, U of	Mongoven, Ann M.	Indiana, Blmngtn
UC, Riverside	Colwell, Catherine	Alaska Pacific U	Chicago, U of	Simonaitis, Susan	Fordham U	Virginia, U of	Randels, George	Pacific, U of the
UC, Riverside	Costello, Michael	Grand Valley S	Chicago, U of	Sweek, Joel	Georgetown U	Western Theol Sem	Deffenbaugh, Daniel	Maryville (TN)
UC, Riverside	Johnson, James	Florida S U	Columbia U	Todd, Jesse	Colgate U	Wiscnsn, Madsn	Pryds, Darlene	Virginia Tech
UC, Riverside	Martin, Leslie	La Sierra U	Cornell U	Johnson, Paul	Missouri, Clmb	Yale U	Bashir, Shahzad	Holy Cross, C of
UC, San Diego	Moore, Cathleen	Penn S U	Cornell U	Noegel, Scott	Rice U	Yale U	Gordon, Lewis R.	Brown U
UC, San Diego	Preston, Ray A.	Charleston, C of	Dallas, U of	Frank, Therese	Dallas, U of	Yale U	Patton, Connine	St Thomas, U of
UC, San Diego	Ryan, Lee	Arizona, Tucson	Denver, U of	Brooks, James	BethuneCookmn	Yale U	Thompson, Jennifer	Swarthmore C
Union Institute	Bewley, Anne	Colby-Sawyer C	Drew U	Kaltner, John	Rhodes C			
US Internationl U	Moriarty, Anna	Springfield C	Duke U	Cartwright, Michael	Indianapolis, U of	CAN-McGill	Ressor, Rachel	Bluffton C
Utah, U of	Williams, Paula	Loyola, Chicago	Duke U	Gravett, Sandra	Appalachian S	ITL-Augustinianum	Doyle, Daniel	Villanova U
Vanderbilt U	Anderson, Timothy	Ohio U	Duke U	Powery, Emerson	Lee C	ITL-Gregorian	Kopfensteiner, Thomas	Fordham U
Vanderbilt U	Halpern, Leslie	SUNY, Albany	Duke U	Udoh, Fabian	Hobart/WmSmth	ITL-Gregorian	Pastizzo, Michael R.	Canisius C
Vanderbilt U	Kurtz, John E.	Villanova U	Duquesne U	Detisch, Scott	Gannon U	ITL-Italian Ministry	Rambelli, Fabio	Williams C
Vanderbilt U	Shirley, Mariela	N Carolina, Wlm	Duquesne U	Magnusen, Carmina	Allentown C	ITL-Pontifical	Putti, Joseph	Westminster (PA)
Vanderbilt U	Yu, Karen	South, U of the	Duquesne U	McCormaick, John	Kansas Newman C	UK-London, U of	Haq, Syed Nomanul	Rutgers, NBruns
						UK-London, U of	Takim, Liyakat	Vanderbilt U
						UK-Oxford	Daley, Brian	Notre Dame, U of
						UK-University C	Holland, Francis	St John's C

RUSSIAN/SLAVIC LANG & LIT

TRAINED BY	NAME	HIRED BY
Brown U	Danaher, David	Denver, U of
Chicago, U of	Sternstein, Malynne	Chicago, U of
Columbia U	Fink, Hilary	Yale U
Columbia U	Wanner, Adrian	Penn S U
Cornell U	Waite, Sarah T.	Rochester, U of
Harvard U	Buckler, Julie	Harvard U
Harvard U	Tolczyk, Dariusz	Virginia, U of
Michigan, U of	Evans-Romaine, Karen	Ohio U
Michigan, U of	Milman, Nyusya	Indiana, Blmngtn
Penn, U of	Chernetsky, Vitaly	Columbia U
Wiscnsn, U of	Matveyev, Rebecca	Lawrence U
Yale U	Shrayer, Maxim	Boston C
CIS-Acad of Science	Pichugin, Valentina	Florida S U

SOCIOLOGY/CRIMINAL JUSTICE

TRAINED BY	NAME	HIRED BY
Addams Schl Soc Wk	Swanson, Lara	W Illinois U
Alabama, Brmng	Cheurpakobkit, Sutham	Texas, Permian
Alabama, Tsclsa	Woodruff, Linda	SE Louisiana U
Alabama, U of	Bryant, Carolyn	Mississippi S
Alabama, U of	Ross, Mary	MissippiValley
American U	Kalof, Linda	George Mason U
American U	Pryor, Douglas	Towson S U
Arizona S U	Cameron, Kathleen	Arizona S West
Arizona S U	Goldschmidt, Jona	Loyola, Chicago
Arizona, U of	Hope, Trina	Oklahoma, U of
Arizona, U of	Markowitz, Linda	S Illinois, Edwrds
Boston U	Swartz, David	Boston U
Bowling Green S	Backer, Paul	Morehead S U
Bowling Green S	Fuentes, Angel	Texas Christian
Bowling Green S	Swinford, Steven	Montana S U
Bowling Green S	Yang, Renxin	N Michigan U
Brandeis U	Wegar, Katarina	Old Dominion U
Brandeis U	Williams, Johnny	Trinity C (CT)
Brown U	Hunter, Lori M.	Utah S U
Brown U	Pingle, Vibha	Rutgers, Newark
Brown U	Sassler, Sharon	Wellesley C
C Michigan U	Goering, Marilyn	Madonna C
Chicago, U of	Aponte, Robert	IndianaPurdu,Ind
Chicago, U of	Chambler, Meale	W Michigan U
Chicago, U of	Hao, Lingxin	Johns Hopkins
Chicago, U of	Kao, Grace	Penn, U of
Chicago, U of	May, Reuben	Georgia, U of
Chicago, U of	Sohrabi, Nader	Iowa, U of
Cincinnati, U of	Haas, Frank	Cal S, Bakersfld
Cincinnati, U of	Moon, Melissa	E Tennessee S
Colorado, U of	Deflem, Mathieu	Kenyon C
Colorado, U of	Koester, Stephen	Missouri, KansC
Cornell U	Lee, Marlene	LSU, BatnRoug
Cornell U	Smith, Deborah	Missouri, KansC
Cornell U	Togunde, Dimeji	Albion C
Cornell U	van Beek, Martijn	Aarhus-DENM
Cornell U	Ver Beek, Kurt	Calvin C
Cornell U	Wolfer, Loreen	Scranton, U of
CUNY	Adams, Jeanne Ann	SUNY
CUNY	Blake-Steele, Tina	Georgia Southern
CUNY	Dalmadge, Heather	Roosevelt U
CUNY	Duncombe, Stephen Ross	SUNY
CUNY	Haynes, Bruce Daniel	Yale U
CUNY	Lubrano, Annteresa Fiore	CUNY
CUNY	McLaughlin, Neil	McMaster-CAN
Delaware, U of	Linn, John	Gustavus Adolph
Duke U	Pieratt, Carey	Wittenberg U
Emory U	Hewitt, Cynthia	Georgia, U of
Emory U	LaFountain, Sheila	W Georgia, S U of
Emory U	Stone, Sandra	W Georgia, S U of
Florida S U	Breedlove, William	Charleston, C of
Florida S U	Bufkin, Jana	NE Louisiana U
Florida S U	Ho, Taiping	Ball S U
Florida S U	Hogue, Mark	N Alabama, U of
Florida S U	Knapp, Stan	Brigham Young U
Florida S U	Powell, Marlene	N Carolina, Pmbrk
Florida S U	Robinson, Debbie	Valdosta S U
Florida S U	Schafer, Edward	Mercer U
Florida S U	Sittig, Jeralynn	Miami U, Oxford
Florida S U	Stombler, Mindy	Texas Tech
Florida, U of	Hodge, Michael	Georgia, U of
Harvard U	Macy, Michael	Cornell U
Harvard U	Tilly, Charles	Columbia U
Harvard U	Warren, Mark	Fordham U
Hawaii, U of	Chang, Deanna	Indiana U of PA
Illinois, U of	McCammon, Lucy	Moravian C
Illinois, U of	O'Brien, Gerald	W Illinois U
Illinois, Urbana	Woodrow-Lafield, Karen	Mississippi S
Indiana U	Buchmann, Claudia	Duke U
Indiana U	Buddenbaum, Katherine	Butler U
Indiana U	Croyle, Connie	Manchester C
Indiana U	Gunkel, Steven	Doane C
Indiana U	Hecht, Laura	Cal S, Bakersfld
Indiana U of PA	King , Tammy	Youngstown S U
Indiana U of PA	McSkimming, Michael	Monmoth C
Indiana U of PA	Okereafoezeke, Nonso	W Carolina U
Indiana U of PA	Payne, Brian	Old Dominion U
Iowa S U	Larsen, Naomi	Union U
Iowa, U of	Evans, Wayne	S Illinois U
Iowa, U of	Ko, Jongwook	Joongbu U-KOR
Johns Hopkins	Elliott, Marta	Nevada, Reno
Johns Hopkins	Itzigshon, Jose	Brown U
Kansas S U	Said, Ishmail	Luther C
Louisiana S U	Crudden, Adele	Mississippi S
Maryland, CollPk	Piquero, Alexis	Temple U
Maryland, CollPk	Sweet, Stephanie	Roger Williams U
Maryland, U of	Capowich, George	Idaho, U of
Maryland, U of	Tibbetts, Stephen	E Tennessee S
Mass, Amherst	Brush, Paula	W Michigan U
Mass, U of	Brenton, Barrett	St John's U
Mdl Tennessee	Sandifer, Jacquelyn	Lee C
Michigan S U	Cox, Stephen	Cntrl Connecticut
Michigan S U	Dohoney, JoMarie	Samford U
Michigan S U	Juska, Arunas	Nebraska, Oma
Michigan S U	Theado, Deborah	Beloit C
Michigan, U of	Delgado, Hector	UC, Irvine
Michigan, U of	Froehle, Mary	American U
Michigan, U of	Gezon, Lisa	W Georgia, S U of
Michigan, U of	Kane, Emily	Bates C
Michigan, U of	Spencer, Elizabeth	Madonna C
Michigan, U of	Wang, Feng	UC, Irvine
Minnesota, U of	Sandifer, Margaret	St Thomas,U of
Mississippi, U of	Mallory, Stephen	S Mississippi,U of
Missouri, U of	Sun, Yongmin	Ohio S, Mnsfld
N Carolina, ChpH	Boyd, Robert	Mississippi S
N Carolina, ChpH	Curran, Sara	Princeton U
N Carolina, ChpH	Huang, Hui	Rowan C
N Carolina S U	Danaher, William F.	Charleston, C of
N Carolina S U	Parker, Karen	Florida, Gnsvl
N Carolina, U of	Giuffre, Katherine	Colorado C
N Carolina, U of	Owens, Chequita	Oklahoma, U of
N Texas, U of	Wang, Guan-Zhen	Russell Sage C
Nebraska, Lncn	Riedmann, Agnes	Cal S, Stnslaus
Nevada, LasVegas	Miller, William	Ohio U
New Hmpshire, U of	Carmody, Dianne	Old Dominion U
New School	Alario, Margarita	Illinois, Urbana
New School	Shey, Thomas	Chapman U
Northeastern U	Hadjicostandi, Joanna	Texas, Permian
Northwestern U	Avalos-Bock, Lisa	Grinnell C
Northwestern U	Miller, Laura	UC, Los Angeles
Notre Dame, U of	Kiekbusch, Richard	Texas, Permian
Notre Dame, U of	Nyce, Lynda	Bluffton C
Ohio S U	Karpov, Vyacheslav	W Michigan U
Ohio S U	Keil, Jacqueline	Roanoke C
Ohio S U	Miller, Jody	Missouri, St L
Ohio S U	Obligacion, Freddie	W New England
Ohio S U	Schock, Kurt	Rutgers, Newark
Oklahoma S U	Guan, Jan	Phillips U
Penn S U	Meyer, Bernard	Pittsburgh, Bradford
Penn, U of	Campbell, Cameron	UC, Los Angeles
Pittsburgh, U of	Korol, Darla	Wiscnsn, StevPt
Pittsburgh, U of	Shalin, Tracey	Wright S U
Pittsburgh, U of	Tomlinson, Virginia M.	Westminster(PA)
Princeton U	Boychuk, Terry	Macalester C
Princeton U	Clydesdale, Timothy	New Jersey, C of
Princeton U	Strickler, Jennifer	Vermont, U of
Purdue U	Boguinil, David	Wright S U
Rutgers U	Kersting, Robert	Westfield S C
Rutgers U	Pisano-Robertiello, Gina	Seton Hall U
S California, U of	Mills, Terry	Florida, Gnsvl
S Carolina, U of	Garrison, Jean	Boston U
S Dakota S U	Norman, J. Mark	Winona S U
S Mississippi, U of	Payne, Thomas E.	S Mississippi, U of
Sam Houston S	Alarid, Leanne	Missouri, KansC
Sam Houston S	Gay, Bruce	Texas, Arlington
Sam Houston S	Long, Lydia	Indiana S U
St Thomas, U of	Dachelet, Helen	Winona S U
Stanford U	Boyle, Elizbeth Heger	Minnsota, TwnC
Stanford U	Chang, Patricia	Notre Dame, U of
SUNY, Albany	Dorne, Clifford	SW Louisiana
SUNY, Albany	McNulty, Thomas	Georgia, U of
SUNY, Albany	Robert, Pamela	Roosevelt U
SUNY, Bngmtn	Derlugiuan, Georgi M.	Northwestern U
SUNY, Stny Brk	Phelan, Jo	S California, U of
Syracuse U	Fuller, Abigail	Manchester C
Syracuse U	Park, Byeong-Chul	Texas, Arlington
Temple U	Ozeyegin, Gul	William & Mary
Tennessee, U of	Gibson, Amy	Maryville (TN)
Tennessee, U of	Hubbard, Ronald	Benedictine C
Tennessee, U of	Smith, Dani	Fisk U
Texas A&M	Hartman, Mark	Arkansas, LtlRk
Texas, Austin	Gill, Elizabeth	RandlphMacon
Texas, Austin	Motter, Jon	Charleston, C of
Texas, Austin	Phillips, Cynthia	Our Lady Lake
Texas, Austin	Pittman-Munke, M.	E Louisiana U
Texas, Austin	Sharp, Susan	Oklahoma, U of
Texas, U of	Steele, Tracey	Wright S U
Tulane U	Dalton, Terrilee A.	Utah S U
UC, Berkeley	Arum, Richard	Arizona, Tucson
UC, Berkeley	Carroll, Leah	St Lawrence U
UC, Berkeley	Massolo, Maria	Allegheny C
UC, Berkeley	Torpey, John	UC, Irvine
UC, Davis	Lewis, Tammy L.	Denison U
UC, Irvine	Grant, Diana	Cal S, Stnslaus
UC, Irvine	Parson, Deborah	Cal S, SnBrndno
UC, Irvine	Vogel, Brenda	Cal S, Bakersfld
UC, Irvine	Young, Karen	Chapman U
UC, Los Angeles	Apodaca, Paul	Chapman U
UC, Los Angeles	Bienenstock, Elsia J.	Stanford U
UC, Los Angeles	Budros, Art	McMaster-CAN
UC, Los Angeles	Chen, Sheying	CUNY, StatIsl
UC, Los Angeles	Townsley, Eleanor	Mt Holyoke C
UC, Los Angeles	Zamudio, Margaret	Colorado, Bldr
UC, Riverside	Lee, Cheoleon	New Jersey, C of
UC, Riverside	Li, Jie-Li	Ohio U
UC, Riverside	Priest, Ronda	S Indiana, U of

TRAINED BY	NAME	HIRED BY
UC, Santa Cruz	Hartigan, John	Knox C
UC, Santa Cruz	Rosga, AnnJanette	Knox C
UC, St Barbara	King, Neal	Belmont U
Vanderbilt U	Madriz, Esther	SanFrancisco,Uof
Virginia, U of	Baunach, Dawn	Georgia S U
Virginia, U of	Griffin, Monica	William & Mary
Virginia, U of	Mullis, Jeffrey S.	Wake Forest U
Virginia, U of	Nolan, James L.	Williams C
Washington S U	LaRose, Anthony	W Oregon S C
Washington S U	Mertig, Angela G.	Michigan S U
Washington S U	Reiseig, Michael D.	Michigan S U
Washington U	Torstrick, Rebecca	Indiana, S Bend
Washington, U of	Jones, Teresa C.	Michigan S U
Washington, U of	King, Valerie	Penn S U
Wayne S U	Lucido, Samuel	Madonna C
Wayne S U	Mosby, Lynnette M.	Oakland U
Wiscnsn, Madsn	Bashi, Vilna	Northwestern U
Wiscnsn, Madsn	Bauman, Kurt	American U
Wiscnsn, Madsn	Hattery, Angela J.	Ball S U
Wiscnsn, Madsn	Pitts , Melinda	Boston U
Wiscnsn, Milw	Hagedorn, John	Illinois, Chicago
Wiscnsn, U of	Keyes, Grace	Our Lady Lake
Yale U	Ammarell, Eugene	Ohio U
Yale U	Hudd, Suzanne	William & Mary
Yale U	White, Renee	Cntrl Connecticut
CAN-Alberta	Krull, Catherine	Nebraska, Oma
CAN-Carleton	Perry, Barbara	N Arizona U
CAN-Guelph	Dupuis, Sherry	McMaster-CAN
CAN-Manitoba	Larsen, Nick	Chapman U
CAN-McGill	Zhao, Dingxin	Chicago, U of
CAN-New Brunswick	Beaman-Hall, Lori	Lethbridge CAN
CAN-Quebec	Martel, Joane	Alberta-CAN
CAN-York	Ramp, William	Lethbridge-CAN

SPANISH/PORTUGUESE LANG & LIT

TRAINED BY	NAME	HIRED BY
Alabama, Tsclsa	Vance, Claudia	N Alabama, U of
Alabama, U of	Luna, Alberto	Samford U
Arizona, U of	Cortina, Guadalupe	Texas A&M U
Arizona, U of	Migliaccio-Dussias, Paolo	Illinois,Urbana
Arizona, U of	Yang, Mimi	Carthage C
Brown U	Dunn, Christopher	Tulane U
Brown U	Langle de Paz, Teresa	Lawrence U
Brown U	Lopez-Sanchez, Ana	Smith C
Brown U	Rodriguez, Victor	Pacific U
Colorado, U of	Clark, Stephen	Indiana S U
Colorado, U of	Garabano, Sandra	Gettysburg C
Columbia U	Boggs, Bruce	Oklahoma, U of
Columbia U	Campis, Adora	Marshall U
Columbia U	Sanchez, Hernan	Maryland, CollPk
Cornell U	Den Tandt, Catherine	Alberta-CAN
Cornell U	Lopez-Carretero, Luis	Missouri,Clmb
Cornell U	Macias-Fernandez, Paz	Georgia S U
Cornell U	Perez-Sanchez, Gema	Fordham U
CUNY	Ahumada, Alfredo	E Stroudsburg PA
CUNY	Ayalamacedo, Duilo Ovidio	MIT
CUNY	Castillo, Jenny M.	CUNY, Baruch
CUNY	Lago, Eduardo	Sarah Lawrence C
CUNY	Lozano-Renieblas, Isabel	Dartmouth C
Delaware, U of	Matthews, Thomas	Weber S C
Duke U	Avelar, Idelber	Illinois, Urbana
Duke U	Hoff, Ruth	Wittenberg U
Duke U	Valiela, Isabel	Gettysburg U
Emerson C	Ramos, Carlos	Wellesley C
Florida Intl U	Abella, Julie	Rollins C
Florida S U	Isen, Antonio	W Michigan U
Florida, U of	Clemons, Gregory	Mars Hill C

TRAINED BY	NAME	HIRED BY
Florida, U of	Loisel, Clary	Muskingum C
Florida, U of	Sotelo, Clara	BethuneCookmn
George Mason U	Ata, Jorge	American U
Georgetown U	Castro, Obdulia	Colorado, Bldr
Georgetown U	Cloutier, Carole	Frostburg S U
Georgetown U	Medina, Pablo	New School
Georgetown U	Shepherd, Gregory	St Joseph's (PA)
Georgia, U of	Mantero, Jose Maria	Xavier U
Harvard U	Gonzalez-Arias, Francisca	Merrimack C
Harvard U	Pilar-Rodriguez, Maria	Columbia U
Harvard U	Rios-Font, Wadda	Brown U
Illinois, U of	Mandell, Paul	Wyoming, U of
Illinois, Urbana	Solares-Larrave, Francisco	Indiana, Kokm
Illinois, Urbana	Vann, Robert	W Michigan U
Indiana U	Brignoni, Gladys	Old Dominion U
Indiana U	Leonard, Candyce	Wake Forest U
Indiana U	Richey, Scott	S Utah U
Iowa, U of	Bustamante, Cecilia	Luther C
Iowa, U of	Linares, Luis	Charleston, C of
Iowa, U of	Maier, Nicole	C Florida, U of
Iowa, U of	Milano, Benjamin	Virginia Tech
Iowa, U of	Reyes, Israel	Dartmouth C
Iowa, U of	Rosell, Sara	St Lawrence U
Iowa, U of	Schweizer, Dawn	Luther C
Iowa, U of	Skattebo, Steven	Northeastern S U
Johns Hopkins	Zavales, Viki	Dickinson C
Kansas, U of	Carbon Gorell, Lynn	Arizona,Tucson
Kentucky, U of	Andrews, Robert	S Carolina, Aiken
Kentucky, U of	Barr, Lois	Lake Forest C
Kentucky, U of	Garcia, Mara	Brighm Yng U
Maryland, CollPk	Traverso-Rueda, Soledad	Penn S, Erie
Mdl Tennessee	Jordan, Angela	South, U of the
Memphis, U of	Glosson, Julie	Union U
Michigan, U of	Fossa, Lydia	Arizona, Tucson
Michigan, U of	Hill, Ruth	Virginia, U of
Michigan, U of	Saenz, Rudolph	Madonna C
Michigan, U of	Sanhueza, Maria T.	Wake Forest U
Michigan, U of	Valezio, Salvador	Lewis & Clark C
Michigan, U of	Wyszynski, Matthew	Texas, Arlington
Middlebury C	Hitchcock, David	Wesleyan C
Minnesota, U of	Chen, Zhiyuan	Appalachian S
Minnesota, U of	Vague, Stephanie	Winona S U
MIT	Montalbetti, Mario	Arizona, Tucson
N Carolina, ChpH	Bianco, Paola	Wilkes U
Nebraska, Lncn	Ruiz-Aviles, Miguel	Austin Peay S
New Mexico, U of	Olivier, Louis	W New Mexico
New Mexico, U of	Watts, Keith	Grand Valley S
New York U	Dainotto, Roberto M.	Duke U
Ohio S U	Burgueno, Maria	Marshall U
Ohio S U	deLourenco, Cileine	Allegheny C
Oregon, U of	Gavilan, Yolanda Molina	Eckerd C
Penn S U	Anderson, Cathleen	Dickinson C
Penn S U	Weatherford, Douglas	Brighm Yng U
Penn, U of	Barrau, Oscar	SW Louisiana
Penn, U of	Espejo-Saaveeora, Ramon	Dartmouth C
Penn, U of	Guardiola, Maria Luisa	Swarthmore C
Penn, U of	Ryan, R. Cecilia	McNeese S U
Penn, U of	Schuhl, Mark	Fort Hays S U
Penn, U of	Selimov, Alexander	Delaware, U of
Penn, U of	Sellers, Vanisa	Ohio U
Penn, U of	Tissen, Graciela	S Carolina, Clm
Penn, U of	Varela-Garcia, Fabiola	Loyola, Chicago
Pittsburgh, U of	Lopez-Cabrales, Maria	Colorado S U
Princeton U	Campos, Victoria	New Jersey, C of

TRAINED BY	NAME	HIRED BY
Princeton U	Garcia-Bryce, Ariadna	Columbia U
Princeton U	Madero, Roberto	Stockton S C
Princeton U	Rosman-Askot, Adriana	New Jersey, C of
Purdue U	Soto-Crespo, Ramon	Wiscnsn, GrnB
Rutgers U	Baques, Angela	Shippensburg
Rutgers U	Yepes, Enrique	Bowdoin C
S Mississippi, U of	Gilkeson, Evelin	La Sierra U
Stanford U	Corona, Ignacio	Ohio S U
Stanford U	Fox, Patricia D.	Indiana, Blmngtn
Stanford U	Lopez, Miguel	S Methodist U
Stanford U	Mendoza-Denton, Norma	Ohio S U
SUNY	de Mateo, Soledad	Miami, U of
SUNY, Albany	Mosher, Mark	Wayne S C
SUNY, Buffalo	Toletti-Gong, Gabriela	Old Dominion U
SUNY, Stny Brrk	McGiboney, Donna	Wright S U
Syracuse U	Sanjines, Jose	Coastal Carolina
Syracuse U	Villagra, Andreas	Pace, WhitePl
Temple U	Otero, Agustin	New Jersey, C of
Texas A&M	Valdez-Benavides, B.	TexasA&M, CrpsC
Texas, Austin	Bedford, David	Texas Christian
Texas, Austin	Buckwalter, Peggy	N Colorado, U of
Texas, Austin	Gier, Richard Daniel	Wiscnsn, Oshkosh
Texas, Austin	Hobbs, Dianne	N Carolina, Wlm
Texas, Austin	Ledgard, Melvin	Pace, WhitePl
Texas, U of	Hassig, Debora	Oklahoma, U of
Tulane U	Browning, Richard	Doane C
UC, Berkeley	Galindo, Martivon	Holy Names C
UC, Berkeley	McCormick, Anne	Miami U, Oxford
UC, Davis	Moreiras-Menor, Cristina	Yale U
UC, Irvine	Falce, Juliet	Chapman U
UC, Irvine	Marrero, Teresa	N Texas, U of
UC, Los Angeles	Carter-Cram, Kimberly	Idaho S U
UC, Los Angeles	Mitchell, Jacque	Pt Loma Nazrn
UC, Los Angeles	Nanfito, Jacqueline	Case Western Res
UC, San Diego	Conway, Christopher	Texas, Arlington
UC, San Diego	Velazquez-Castillo, Maura	Wiscnsn,GrnB
UC, St Barbara	Jimenez, Enrique	Goucher C
UC, St Barbara	Vaquera-Vasquez, S.	Texas A&M U
UC, St Barbara	Waldemer, Thomas	St Olaf C
Vanderbilt U	Godo-Solo, Hossiri	Fisk U
Virginia, U of	Graf, Eric	Smith C
Washington U	Tuninetti, Angel	Lebanon Valley
Washington, U of	Diaz, Cesar	New Zealand-NZEAL
Washington, U of	Pinot-Ojeda, W.	New Zealand-NZEAL
Wiscnsn, Madsn	Arias Stevens, Santa	Florida S U
Wiscnsn, Madsn	Armacangui-Tipacti, Elia	Lawrence U
Wiscnsn, Madsn	Bertsche, Allen	Augustana C (IL)
Wiscnsn, Madsn	Gago-Jover, Francisco	Holy Cross, C of
Wiscnsn, Madsn	Osorio, Myriam	Heidelberg C
Wiscnsn, Madsn	Tuten, Donald	Emory U
ARG-Inst Biblico	Navarro, Benjamin	Grace C
BRZ-Sao Paulo	Santos, Lidia	Yale U
CAN-Montreal	Jonassaint, Jean	Duke U
SPN-Complutense	Mendoza, Esperanza	George Mason U
SPN-del Pais Vasco	Izaguirre, Pedro	Rockford C
SPN-Escuela Normal	Flores-Ocampo, Audias	Gettysburg C
SPN-Sevilla	Marks, Emilia	Ohio U
UK-Cambridge	Jagoe, Catherine	Wiscnsn, Madsn

About *Lingua Franca*, The Review of Academic Life

Lingua Franca has been covering the academic landscape since 1990 with frank, provocative writing on the latest disciplinary debates, professorial scandals, and unlikely scholarly pursuits. Publishing nine issues a year, the magazine casts an affectionate but skeptical eye over the intellectual scene, tackling everything from anthropology's obsession with cannibalism to feminism's defense of pornography. In addition, every issue features updates on significant new books and the most recent academic hirings in every discipline.

Called "independent-minded, idiosyncratic and brainy" by *The Boston Globe*; a "smart, lively mix" by *The Washington Post*; "an insider's guide to the groves of academe" by *The New York Times*; and also chosen as winner of the National Magazine Award for General Excellence, *Lingua Franca* ventures into books for the first time with *The Real Guide to Grad School*.

Lingua Franca
22 West 38th Street
New York, NY 10018
www.linguafranca.com